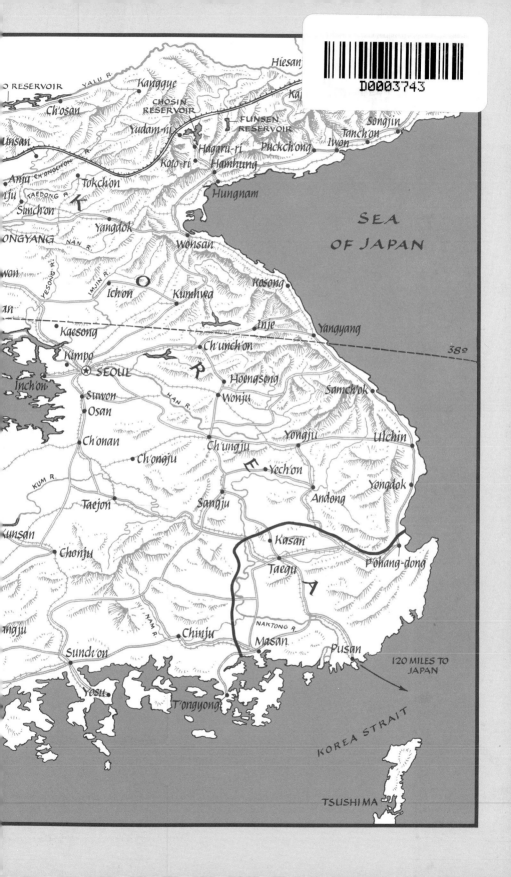

THE KOREAN WAR

Pusan to Chosin

AN ORAL HISTORY

Donald Knox

THE
KOREAN
WAR

Pusan to Chosin

AN ORAL
HISTORY

HARCOURT BRACE JOVANOVICH, PUBLISHERS

San Diego   New York   London

Library of Congress Cataloging-in-Publication Data
Knox, Donald, 1936–
The Korean War: Pusan to Chosin.
Includes index.
1. Korean War, 1950–1953. I. Title.
DS918.K53   1985   951.9'043   85-8567
ISBN 0-15-147288-2

Designed by Joy Chu
Maps by Rafael D. Palacios
Printed in the United States of America
First edition
A B C D E

TO NEIL AND ALEC

"And everybody praised the Duke
 Who this great fight did win."
"But what good came of it at last?"
 Quoth little Peterkin.
"Why that I cannot tell," said he,
"But 'twas a famous victory."

Robert Southey

Contents

Photographs follow pages 208 and 368.

List of Maps

Acknowledgments

I should like to thank some of the people who have given so much help and encouragement over the past three years. A book of this kind could not have been written without the contributions of many historians who have minutely studied the large numbers of campaigns and battles involved and through their writings pointed the way for me. Special acknowledgment is extended to Roy E. Appleman and his United States Army in the Korean War volume *South to the Naktong, North to the Yalu* and to Lynn Montross and Capt. Nicholas A. Canzona, USMC, who together wrote *U.S. Marine Operations in Korea, 1950–1953*.

Excerpts from *General Dean's Story* by Maj. Gen. William F. Dean and William L. Worden, copyright 1954 by William F. Dean, renewed © 1982 by Mildred D. Dean, reprinted by permission of Viking Penguin Inc. Excerpts from *War in Korea* by Marguerite Higgins, copyright © 1951 by Marguerite Higgins, reprinted by permission of Doubleday & Company, Inc. Excerpts from Harold H. Martin's "The Epic of Bloody Hill," reprinted from *The Saturday Evening Post* © 1950, The Curtis Publishing Company. Excerpts from Capt. R. C. McCarthy's "Fox Hill" and 1st Lt. Joseph R. Owen's "Chosin Reservoir Remembered" are reprinted by permission of the *Marine Corps Gazette*.

Individuals and various government agencies have lent their aid whenever they were asked for it, and a few must be mentioned as having been particularly kind and helpful: Hanna M. Zeidlik, Chief,

Historical Records Branch, U.S. Army Center of Military History; William Lewis, Modern Military Field Branch, Washington National Records Center; Leroy Jackson, Military Archives Division, National Archives and Records Center; D. C. Allard, Head, Operational Archives Branch, Naval Historical Center, and archivist Martha Crawley and historians Jeanette Koontz and George (Wes) Pryce; Paul Stillwell, Director of Oral History, United States Naval Institute; Benis M. Frank, Head, Oral History Section, Marine Corps Historical Center, and his assistant Sandy Chaker; Joyce E. Bonnett, Head, Archives Section, Marine Corps Historical Center, and her assistant Joyce Conyers; L. G. Tennison, Head, Fleet Support Branch, Department of Navy. Their assistance has been invaluable.

Dr. Stanley Falk, Naomi Grady, and Eric Hammel commented on sections of the preliminary manuscript, and I thank them for making valuable suggestions.

I am indebted more than I can ever tell to those officers and men who, having participated in the actions described, willingly and helpfully gave of their store of knowledge for the sake of allowing an accurate narrative to be written. In all cases, their assistance has been invaluable and in all cases it was cheerfully given. I am particularly indebted to Lt. Col. Luther F. Weaver, USA (Ret), and Col. N. F. J. Allen, USA (Ret), who spent much time answering what must have been, for them, elementary questions, and to Victor Fox, who has labored longer than I in tracking down veterans. I claim the traditional author's privilege of absolving them of all responsibility for the book's defects and shortcomings.

I should also like to thank that peerless type-writer, Diane Koppy, who again superbly transcribed hundreds of difficult tapes.

Lastly, I owe so much to Kathleen Rucker for the encouragement to write, and for so many other things.

DEFEAT

25 June-2 August 1950

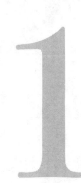

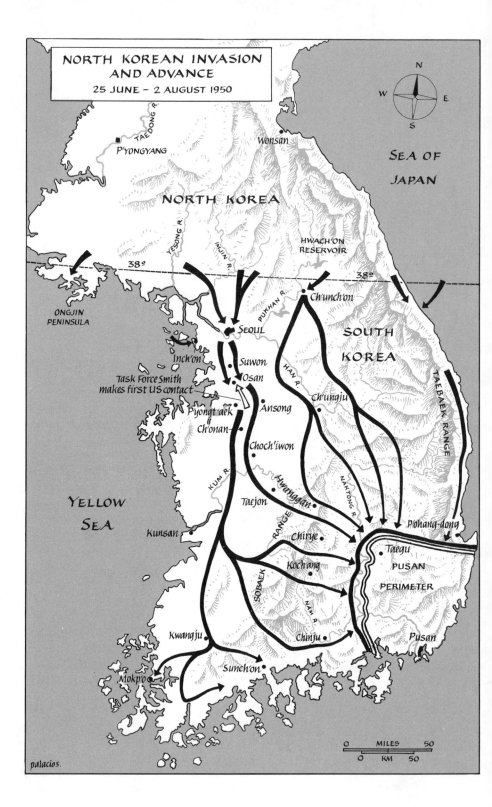

NORTH KOREAN INVASION
AND ADVANCE
25 JUNE – 2 AUGUST 1950

N
W   E
S

TAEDONG R.
P'YONGYANG
Wonsan

NORTH KOREA

SEA OF
JAPAN

YESONG R.
IMJIN R.
HWACH'ON
RESERVOIR

38°   38°
Ch'unch'on
ONGJIN
PENINSULA
PUKHAN R.
SEOUL   SOUTH
Inch'on   KOREA
Suwon
Osan   HAN R.
Task Force Smith
makes first US contact   Ch'ungju
Pyongt'aek   Ansong
Ch'onan

TAEBAEK RANGE

Choch'iwon

KUM R.

Hwanggan
Taejon
NAKTONG R.
YELLOW
SEA   Chirye   P'ohang-dong
Kunsan
Koch'ang   Taegu
SOBAEK RANGE   PUSAN
NAM R.   PERIMETER

Kwangju   Chinju
Sunch'on   Pusan
Mokp'o

palacios.

0   MILES   50
0   KM   50

Following World War II the Korean nation began a new historical era. It had struggled for forty years as a Japanese colony; now it would begin to struggle as a pawn in the newly created Cold War. Representatives of the Soviet Union and the United States meeting in Potsdam during the summer of 1945 decided they could best handle the surrender of Japanese forces in Korea by dividing the country at the 38th Parallel. In August Russian officers accepted the Japanese surrender north of the Parallel; in September American officers did the same south of the Parallel.

Shortly after the Japanese capitulation, the Soviet Union abruptly stopped movement across the Parallel, and Korea, without international agreement or treaty, found itself divided into a Communist north and a democratic south. Unexpectedly, the 38th Parallel had become the political frontier between two nations. Above the border the Soviet Union prepared North Korea to become one of its satellite states; below this border the United States prepared Korea to become a free nation.

Between 1945 and 1950 the North Korea People's Army (NKPA or In Min Gun) was trained and equipped by the USSR; the Republic of Korea's (ROK) Army was trained and equipped by the USA. Soon North Korea had a large, rigorously trained, aggressive military force well supplied with Russian small arms, artillery, armor, and propeller-driven fighter aircraft. Moreover, nearly all of its commissioned and noncommissioned officers were combat veterans of the Chinese civil war or *Manchurian guerrilla operations. Below the Parallel, South Korea faced this menace with a smaller and more poorly equipped armed force. By 1950 the balance of power had dramatically shifted to the north. In late spring of that year, the North Koreans had 150 Russian-built T34 tanks, the South Koreans had no tanks; the North Koreans had three types of artillery, the South Koreans one, and in actual numbers of divisional artillery pieces, the NKPA exceeded the ROK Army three to one; the North Koreans had a small tactical air force, the South Koreans had none; the North Koreans had seven full-strength combat divisions, the South Koreans four; the North Koreans had 89,000 assault troops, the South Koreans 65,000.*

The North Koreans, emboldened by their military might and Soviet support, resolved to confront their neighbor in a decisive struggle for national supremacy. Gambling that the United States would have too much to lose if it interfered, the North Korean People's Republic determined to unify Korea by direct military action. During the period 15–24 June, North Korea secretly moved to the area of the 38th Parallel seven infantry divisions, one armored brigade, one separate infantry regiment, one motorcycle regiment, and one border constabulary brigade. By the 25th, a rainy, blustery Sunday in Korea, the Communists had 90,000 combat troops poised within striking distance of South Korea.

Geography has condemned Korea, as it has Poland, to chaos and conflict. Like all buffer states, Korea has suffered the disastrous consequences of many invasions. Seen from China or Russia, the country is the gateway to the Asian heartland. For Japan, Korea is a bridge that directly leads to the home islands. From Korea, any one of these historically imperialistic powers can threaten the other two.

The Korean peninsula, which from space looks somewhat like Florida, is roughly equivalent in size to Great Britain. A great north-south wall of mountains reaches down its eastern coast from the Yalu River in the north to the port of Pusan in the south; smaller ranges and hills extend inland. The west coast consists of broad, flat, muddy river plains. Movement through much of the country entails walking up or down hill. The view from one treeless hill is that of another treeless hill, and then of another, for as far as the eye can see. This monotony is broken only when the hills grow steeper and become jagged, granite-faced mountains.

Although Korea is at the same latitude as San Francisco and Philadelphia, the weather is harsh, especially during the bleak winters, when bitter, biting Siberian winds blow down from the Asian interior. Summers are hot and moist with a monsoon season that turns Korea's many unpaved roads into quagmires. Temperature extremes range from 105° F to minus 40° F. Not without reason, Korea is known as the Hermit Kingdom.

The large population is poor. Most Koreans live off the land, growing rice, barley, and soybeans. They follow a variety of religious beliefs including nature-spirit worship, Buddhism, Confucianism, and Christianity.

In 1950 the Americans who arrived in the hundreds of thousands found Korea to be a country of high, rough-hewn mountains; steep, narrow valleys; wide, deep rivers; endless hills; threadlike paths; bad roads; heavy rain and deep snow; rice paddies and mud-plastered villages. And it smelled foul. Korea lacked charm or natural beauty and was neither quaint nor rustic. It should have been the last place on earth where anyone would want to fight a war.

June 24, 1950

North Korean forces, consisting of seven divisions and five brigades, with an air force of 100–150 Soviet-made planes crossed the 38th Parallel at 4 A.M. Korean time, June 25. The main attack was down the Pochon-Uijongbu-Seoul corridor. Other attacks were launched in the Ongjin Peninsula in the west, against Ch'unch'on in the eastern mountains, and down the east coast road. The ROK forces initially available for defense numbered only five divisions with no air force or armor. Ambassador [John J.] Muccio's report of the attack was received by the State Department at 9:20 P.M. (EDT).

DEPARTMENT OF STATE CHRONOLOGY OF PRINCIPAL EVENTS
RELATING TO THE KOREAN CONFLICT

Sgt. C. W. "BILL" MENNINGER
3d Battalion/34th Infantry*

When the invasion of the south came, of course everyone was interested, but it never occurred to us that we Americans serving in Japan in the Army of Occupation would ever get involved. For me, it was a typical Sunday night in Japan. I was at home with my family. It had rained all day. My wife was giving the kids a bath prior to putting them to bed, and I was reading a book and nursing a drink when the call came for me to report at once to headquarters! The wife wanted to know what the call was about. "Something must be wrong with next week's training schedule," I answered. "I'll be back as soon as I can." (Which happened to be eleven months later.)

Cpl. LACY BARNETT
Medical Company/34th Infantry

When word reached us in Japan on that rainy Sunday, the first reaction by many members of my unit was, "Where is Korea?" The next reaction, "Let the gooks kill each other off." Among the majority of men there was absolutely no fear or thought that the United States would become involved in the war. During the next few days it was business conducted as usual.

Cpl. NORTON GOLDSTEIN
Headquarters Company/21st Infantry

I was playing on the regimental softball team, but really just goofing off. The weekend the war in Korea began saw so much rain in Ku-

---

*The rank given is that held by the man at the time of the experience he relates and, unless otherwise specified, the unit denotes his company and regiment.

mamoto that our doubleheader with the 19th Infantry was called off. Rumors started flying but nobody really knew what was going to happen. I was so unconcerned on the morning following the North Korean invasion of the south I wrote home telling my parents how much I looked forward to the next weekend when we'd be playing division artillery. That next weekend, it turned out, I wasn't playing ball. I wasn't even in Japan.

June 25

At 3:00 A.M. (EDT) the U.S. requested an immediate meeting of the Security Council. The UN Commission on Korea (UN-COK) reported that the situation was serious and assuming the character of full-scale war threatening world peace and security. At 2:00 P.M., the Security Council met and adopted a resolution determining that the attack constituted a breach of the peace and calling for a cease fire and the withdrawal of North Korean forces to the 38th Parallel. All members supported the resolution except Yugoslavia, which abstained. The USSR representative did not attend.

President [Harry S.] Truman called the situation serious but not alarming. After a conference attended by the President, the Secretaries of State and Defense, and the Joint Chiefs of Staff, Gen. Douglas MacArthur, the Commander in Chief, Far East (CINCFE), was authorized to furnish military supplies to the ROK.

June 27

At noon (EDT) President Truman announced that he had ordered U.S. air and sea forces to give ROK troops cover and support in accordance with the Security Council resolution of June 25.

UNCOK reported that the North Koreans would not heed the Security Council resolution or accept the good offices of the Commission. The Security Council met at 3:00 P.M. (EDT) and adopted a resolution recommending that UN members furnish all necessary assistance to the ROK to repel the attack.

June 28
North Koreans took Seoul and the ROK capital was reportedly
moved to Taejon. UN Forces were placed under the command
of General MacArthur.

DEPARTMENT OF STATE CHRONOLOGY

*[This UN force comprised four understrength, ill-equipped American
Divisions that had been stationed in Japan at the end of World War
II. These units, the 7th, 24th, and 25th Infantry Divisions and the
1st Cavalry Division (infantry) were under the direct command of Lt.
Gen. Walton H. Walker's Eighth Army.* This little army of occupation averaged about 70 percent of its full war strength, with each regiment less one battalion. Its World War II equipment was old and
worn. The men who served in it, although enlistees, enjoyed the good
life provided by a rapidly recovering Japanese economy. World War II
had been quickly forgotten; no one joined the American Army after
1945 to fight a war.]*

Pfc. LEONARD KORGIE †
L Company/34th Infantry

Occupation duty was heaven. I was the troop information and education NCO [noncommissioned officer] at Sugamo Prison, where
Japanese war criminals were held. My unit did very little military
training. Life away from the prison consisted mostly of athletics, clubs,
nightly dances, theater, and Japanese girls. Although in those days

---

* The 7th Division was composed of the 17th, 31st, and 32d Infantry Regiments; the 24th Division of the 19th, 21st, and 34th Infantry Regiments; the 25th Division of the 14th, 27th, and
35th Infantry Regiments; the 1st Cavalry Division of the 5th, 7th, and 8th Cavalry Regiments.
(See Appendix, pp. 682–85, for a table of organization and equipment.)
† Len Korgie was born in 1924 in a rural Nebraska town. After high school he attended a Catholic seminary, but discovered it wasn't for him and he enlisted in the Army for three years. At
the time of the Korean War, Korgie had just turned twenty-seven.

alcohol made me sick, there was always plenty to drink. GI money and cigarettes went a long way on the black market.

1st Lt. PHILIP DAY, JR.
C Company/21st Infantry
The enlisted men left something to be desired. Enlistees, I learned, were not a very bright bunch of guys. The two smartest men in my outfit, a company clerk and a supply clerk, were draftees, and when their tour ended a month before Korea began, they were shipped home. With most of the enlistees, we really did have disciplinary problems, everything from VD to fighting, disobeying orders to showing up late, going AWOL to drinking too much.

Just before Korea started one of my jobs as the company exec [executive officer] was to try to get rid of the troublemakers. This wasn't easy because to bust out of the Army required five court-martials. I finally got rid of five guys, all real bad customers. When they left Camp Wood,* they left in handcuffs. When they reached the Yokohama stockade, they were to be sent back to the States. The war began just as they arrived in Yokohama. You know what happened? Someone up there decided C Company could not do without these five thugs and they were shipped back to us.

Cpl. LACY BARNETT
Medical Company/34th Infantry
The troops always talked about booze or broads. Even the lowest-ranking private was able to afford a steady "shack gal" and all the beer he could drink. VD was quite prevalent and although there were exceptions, many of the GIs were unlucky or ignorant enough to get a good case of gonorrhea.

In Sasebo † I was assigned as a clerk. Within a couple of months, I became company clerk. The first sergeants I worked for were good men and had all served during World War II. As time passed I gained

---

*The 21st Infantry Regiment, 24th Division, was stationed here near Kumamoto, Kyushu, Japan.
† The 34th Infantry Regiment, 24th Division, was stationed in Sasebo, Kyushu, Japan.

additional responsibilities which should never have been performed by a corporal. For example, the Regimental Combat Effectiveness Report was due every three months. Regiment would hold a quarterly conference on how to complete the report. I was detailed to attend these conferences. Afterward I would report to my CO and try to explain the report to him. His instructions to me were always the same: "Make sure the medical company looks combat effective." I would then prepare the lengthy report and the CO would sign without reading it.

1st Lt. PHILIP DAY, JR.
C Company/21st Infantry
We used World War II leftovers and we apparently had a lot left over. We had, for example, the 2.36-inch rocket launcher [bazooka]. I learned later it hadn't worked in the Second World War and it sure as heck didn't work on Russian T34 tanks* in Korea. No question about it, much of our gear and equipment was shabby. Being on the southernmost island in Japan, the 21st Infantry Regiment was literally at the end of the supply line.

June 29
President Truman said U.S. action in Korea was a police action, not a war.

June 30
It was reported that ROK forces still held Inch'on. The fate of Suwon was uncertain.
President Truman authorized General MacArthur to use ground troops in Korea. . . .
                                    DEPARTMENT OF STATE CHRONOLOGY

---

*The Russian T34, the Soviets' main battle tank of World War II, had a low silhouette, weighed thirty-two tons and was capable of thirty-four miles per hour. It mounted an 85-mm gun and carried two 7.62-mm machine guns.

[Unable to slow down, let alone stop the onrushing North Korean divisions, with Seoul and Inch'on in enemy hands, with Suwon and Taejon threatened, the young Republic of Korea faced extinction.

Time and North Korea would be MacArthur's enemies in July 1950, and, if he was to win this new war, he would have to battle and defeat both. Unless he could stem the enemy torrent, there would not be enough time to land the reinforcements and matériel needed to drive the enemy out of the south. Accordingly, he was forced by circumstances to commit his forces piecemeal. On 30 June he ordered Eighth Army to send the 24th Division's 19th, 21st, and 34th Infantry Regiments to Korea immediately.* General Walker then instructed the division's commanding general, William F. Dean, to move his command as soon as possible to the front.]

Pfc. LEONARD KORGIE
L Company/34th Infantry

I saw my name on a list of men scheduled to go to Korea. I would go as part of an escort company bringing North Korean POWs back to Japan.

The camp got real quiet. Guys were scared. I was thrilled! How in hell could you get shot escorting prisoners? The chaplain went around giving us encouragement. Those whose names were not on the list consoled those whose names were. I felt the whole situation was being blown out of proportion.

Our officers told us to take our dress summer uniforms—we'd need them in a few weeks for the victory parade in Seoul. I loaded everything in my duffel bag and along with my group from Sugamo was taken to the Replacement Depot in Yokohama—150 men and two officers. There, the officer in charge knew nothing about a POW escort unit, had never even heard of us. After General MacArthur had been called about this confusing situation, we were told that the good general had said, "Hell, we're not taking any prisoners in Ko-

---

* The 24th Division was selected for immediate commitment because it was stationed on Kyushu, the Japanese island closest to Korea.

rea, we're being taken prisoner. Put them all in the infantry!" "Wow!"
I shouted to my buddy, "We're going to fight!"

Cpl. LACY BARNETT
Medical Company/34th Infantry
By 11:00 P.M. curfew on June 30, most of the men from the company had returned to the barracks after the usual Friday-night good
time of hitting the bars and the "shacks." Whether they had to be put
to bed or could make it on their own, all were soon in a deep, intoxicated sleep.

Two hours later key NCOs were awakened and ordered to report
to our CO's office immediately. We learned there the regiment had
been alerted for movement. The CO stated that our destination was
unknown and that we should not speculate about where we were going
with the men. The 1st Battalion would prepare to be airlifted that
afternoon. The 3d Battalion would fly out a day later.

We woke the men up and, although a majority of them had had
only two hours' sleep and were hung over, everything proceeded
smoothly.

Just about everyone still believed we were not destined to go to
Korea. There was general agreement that we were going to Taiwan
to act as a deterrent if Red China planned to invade the island.

It rained heavily all Saturday morning. By noon the 1st Battalion aid station was ready to move. A little later word arrived that because of the weather, we would not fly but move instead by ship. For
the remainder of that day we received conflicting information about
deployment times and methods. Saturday night we were still in Japan
and our CO continued to claim truthfully that he did not know our
destination.

Around midnight final orders were received. A short while later
Medical Company personnel boarded an old Japanese hospital ship.
As we pulled out of Sasebo, the company learned its voyage would
be a short one. Our destination was Pusan,* Korea.

---

*All Korean place names are spelled in accordance with the Army Map Service transliteration
system.

Advance at once upon landing with delaying force in accordance with the situation, to the north by all possible means, contact the enemy now advancing south from Seoul towards Suwon and delay his advance.

EIGHTH ARMY OPNS ORD 2: 010315K JULY 1950

Maj. Gen. WILLIAM F. DEAN
Commanding General, 24th Division

My orders specified that a task force of two reinforced rifle companies, with a battery of field artillery, was to be flown to Korea immediately and would report to Brig. Gen. John H. Church,* who had flown from Tokyo to Taejon. Taejon was well south of the battle line and an obvious choice for a defensive headquarters. The entire 24th Infantry Division was to move to Korea by surface transportation as rapidly as possible.

Lt. Col. Charles B. [Brad] Smith was picked to command the task force. † No commander likes to commit troops piecemeal, and I'm no exception, but Smith was definitely the man for the job if it had to be done. He had a fine World War II record in the South Pacific and was a natural leader. So he and his 406 riflemen, plus a few artillerymen, were on their way to a landing field outside Pusan on July 1. From there they could move by train to the front lines, then somewhere between Seoul and Suwon—the exact location depending on which Republic of Korea Army intelligence report you believed. ‡

[General Dean met Lieutenant Colonel Smith early in the morning of 1 July in Japan at Itazuke Air Base. It had been raining heavily for many hours. There wasn't much Dean could tell Smith about the situation in Korea. Colonel Smith, who would soon lead the first Amer-

---

*General Church had flown to Korea on 24 June as the head of GHQ Advance Command and Liaison Group (ADCOM). This small survey group was ordered to assess the situation for CINCFE and to lend to the ROK Army all possible assistance.

† This force, which became known as Task Force Smith when it arrived in Korea, was composed of units of the 1st Battalion, 21st Infantry Regiment, about 440 men in all.

‡ Maj. Gen. William F. Dean and William L. Worden, *General Dean's Story* (New York: Viking, 1954), 17–18. Hereafter, *Dean's Story.*

ican ground troops to meet the enemy in the Korean War, did all of the listening.]

Maj. Gen. WILLIAM F. DEAN
Commanding General, 24th Division
"When you get to Pusan, head for Taejon. We want to stop the North Koreans as far from Pusan as we can. Block the main road as far north as possible. Contact General Church. If you can't locate him, go to Taejon and beyond if you can. Sorry I can't give you more information. That's all I've got. Good luck to you, and God bless you and your men." *

1st Lt. WILLIAM WYRICK
C Company/21st Infantry

The phone rang in my quarters; it was one of the first sergeants. "Lieutenant, you'd better get down here in a hell of a hurry." I thought there had been a Saturday-night fight in the barracks. I explained the situation to my wife and the couple we were playing bridge with and left for the company area.

I was met by the company commander [Capt. Richard Dashner]. "Where's your bag?" "What bag?" I asked. He answered, "We're going to Korea. You have fifteen minutes to go home, pack a bag, and get back here." Undoubtedly I took more than fifteen minutes, but I had very little time to say good-bye to my family and arrange for their safekeeping while I was gone.

When I returned to the company, ammunition and C rations were being issued to the men. Someone asked, "How should we leave the barracks?" The answer came back, "Leave it just like for inspec-

---

* Roy E. Appleman, *South to the Naktong, North to the Yalu (June–November 1950)*, United States Army in the Korean War, vol. 2 (Washington, D.C.: Office of the Chief of Military History, 1961), 60.

tion." So, before flying to Korea, we actually cleaned the barracks and left them immaculate.

The 1st Battalion loaded on all types of transportation—school buses to dump trucks—and were taken [1 July] to Itazuke Air Force Base in northern Kyushu.

1st Lt. PHILIP DAY, JR.
C Company/21st Infantry

When we arrived at Itazuke it was raining hard. Lt. Col. Charles Smith, the battalion commander, with two other officers had already gone on ahead. We started loading some C-54s with gear and equipment. It's sort of funny, you take all those courses on how to load airplanes with jeeps and cannons and so forth; then when you actually do it, you just sit and hold the jeep in place with your feet and hope it doesn't roll out of the airplane.

No one believed we were going anywhere to fight. I sort of had the impression we were going to protect and help Americans leaving the country. Because of the bad weather, we stayed at Itazuke most of the day. Finally we took off. No one then called us Task Force Smith. I didn't learn that's what we were until 1951. On the way to Korea, we were just 1st Battalion, 21st Infantry.

1st Lt. WILLIAM WYRICK
C Company/21st Infantry

I noticed we were flying about fifty feet off the water. I asked the pilot, "Why so low?" He replied, "There's YAKs [Russian-built fighter] in the air and we have no air cover. We're flying low to evade the enemy fighters." Later, wanting to show my knowledge about air transportability, I said to the pilot, "Well now, to help get you back in the air as quick as possible, it's my understanding we are supposed to start untying our equipment when your wheels touch down." (In training we'd been instructed to do this.) "No," he said, "my God, no. Don't touch anything. Don't touch. You all stay strapped in." What I didn't know was one of the C-54s ahead of us had blown a tire and been taxied to the end of the short runway and our aircraft would have to stop before it ran into that one. When we landed on the dirt strip in

Korea, the pilot applied his brakes, on, off, on, off; a dozen times the aircraft's nose dipped, then rose, dipped, then rose. We eventually stopped just short of the parked C-54.

The strip in Korea was without taxiways or loading ramps. It was, therefore, a very slow process and it took the better part of two days to get the unit (minus the artillery) to Pusan.*

1st Lt. PHILIP DAY, JR.
Task Force Smith
We were taken in trucks to the railroad station in Pusan. The city wasn't very big in those days. We got all our gear and climbed onto flatcars. As we waited to pull out, a train from up north came in. It was covered with human beings—troops, officers, old men, women, children, and, most important, at least to me, wounded. My God, I thought, maybe there was a real war going on! Hysteria and panic traveled with this train. I heard a gunshot. Someone learned that a South Korean Army officer sitting in the train had committed suicide. We were told his family had been captured in Seoul. We didn't have time to think much about that because it was then that our train moved out of the station.

1st Lt. WILLIAM WYRICK
Task Force Smith
During our trip north I saw wounded in boxcars coming back from the fighting. Many of them were badly hurt. Our train would stop in a station and on the next track would be these cars of wounded South Koreans who as far as I could see were not receiving adequate medical attention. It was a very heartrending sight. It affected me when I realized what I was going into.

After we arrived in Taejon at 8:00 A.M. [2 July], the train was divided into two sections. Company C continued to Ansong while

---

*Dense fog in the Pusan area, which closed the airstrip for a time, also contributed to the delay.

the others went to P'yongt'aek. Early the next morning [3 July] we arrived in Ansong. There was a tremendous crowd of people at the railroad station to meet us. Everyone cheered when we rolled in. I've told people they cheered our arrival, but what I really think is they cheered the arrival of the train, because after we climbed off, a lot of South Koreans climbed on and the train left for the south.

Maj. Floyd Martin, the battalion's executive officer, was in command, and he held a conference with the mayor and some other people. Charlie Company then went north of the town and set up a regular defensive position.

July 2
The North Koreans took Suwon. General MacArthur appointed Maj. Gen. William Dean Commander United States Army Forces in Korea (USAFIK).

July 3
Enemy forces reached Yongin and Kumyangjang. The NK 2d Division moved thirty miles east of Suwon. The enemy claimed the capture of Tachwa.

DEPARTMENT OF STATE CHRONOLOGY

[As part of the 24th Division, the 34th Infantry Regiment, which at the time consisted of only two understrength battalions, was the second unit rushed to Korea from Japan to help halt the North Korean invasion. The regiment sailed from Sasebo on 2 July and arrived in Pusan that evening.]

Cpl. LACY BARNETT
Medical Company/34th Infantry
We had no breakfast or lunch on Monday, July 3. The ship carrying our rations had not yet arrived at Pusan. What rations we had were all opened and put in thirty two-gallon GI cans. These were heated and at dinnertime everyone passed through the chow line. As we had missed the two earlier meals, this meal tasted particularly good.

Many of the men believed once the North Koreans discovered

American troops had entered the war they would begin to pull back. No one yet had briefed us on the military situation or on anything else about Korea and its people and culture.

On Tuesday [4 July] we piled on a train in Pusan and headed north. Surely, we continued to believe, there would be no way a rag-tag North Korean force would dare take on the superior military might of the United States.

Our train stopped at Taejon and Colonel [Jay B.] Lovless, who commanded the 34th Infantry Regiment, went to General Dean's headquarters. Because the military situation north of Taejon was un-known, the 34th Infantry was ordered to proceed as far as it could go.* Then it was to spread out in a defensive position and wait for the situation to develop. The rain was still quite heavy and all roads in the area were muddy and slippery.

Before we pulled out of Taejon, we were surprised to learn that another American unit, one from the 21st Infantry, was somewhere on the road ahead of us.

1st Lt. WILLIAM WYRICK
Task Force Smith
The night had been awful. Without repellent, the mosquitoes ate us alive. On the 4th we held several conferences in the city. We had no maps and I had only a general idea of where in Korea Ansong was.

There were some prisoners kneeling on the ground, their hands behind their backs and tied to their ankles. They were beaten across the thighs with a bamboo stick. I was told these people were accused of being Communists. I heard later they'd been executed but I don't know that to be true.

1st Lt. PHILIP DAY, JR.
Task Force Smith
We celebrated the 4th of July with a bottle of cold beer someone found. Later that day we got back in our trucks and rejoined B Company at

---

*On 4 July the 34th Infantry had a strength of 1,981 men. At the end of August there would be 184 men left—the rest would be killed, wounded, or missing in action.

P'yongt'aek. Many of us took this opportunity to get rid of the gas masks and blankets that had begun to weigh us down.

At P'yongt'aek Captain Dashner told us we were going north a few miles and, above Osan, take a position astride the main road. We moved at night, arriving around 3:00 A.M. Everyone was tired. Then it began to drizzle—a cold, wet, penetrating drizzle. The men began digging foxholes on the hill east of the highway. Guys went down to bring up ammunition and because of conditions, the hill became muddy and slippery. Time went by. It was raining now. Everyone was tired, wet, cold, and a little bit pissed off. The feeling was, why not wait for daylight to do all this climbing and digging?

1st Lt. WILLIAM WYRICK
Task Force Smith
It was a slow rain, not hard, but more than a drizzle. Digging in with a poncho on is always a hassle and many of the men couldn't make up their minds whether to keep them on or take them off. It was easy digging in my platoon area. There were a few trees and low vegetation, so clearing fields of fire was accomplished with little difficulty. My platoon was on the company's right flank and covered the railroad tracks. To my left front I could see the main highway and at first light I noticed some movement on it.

1st Lt. PHILIP DAY, JR.
Task Force Smith
In the early gray dawn of July 5, Sgt. Loren Chambers yelled, "Hey, look over there, Lieutenant. Can you believe?!" Looking down the road toward Suwon, I made out a column of tanks. Seems like there were eight of them. I couldn't believe my eyes. "What are those?" I asked. Chambers answered, "Those are T34 tanks, sir, and I don't think they're going to be friendly toward us." The company commander was called. Everybody got real excited about them. The day was beginning in earnest.

Really in earnest. Dashner said, "Let's get some artillery on them." Behind us the 105-mm howitzers [of the 58th Field Artillery Battalion] fired several rounds but without effect. The tanks kept coming.

Behind the first group came another, then another. They passed through B Company, which was spread out on either side of the road. Lt. Ollie Connor had a bazooka in a ditch beside the road. He hit several tanks, but they continued to roll through our position. At any one time seems like there'd be four tanks behind us curling up the hill, five going through B Company and two coming down the road toward me. Several of them swiveled their turrets and began shooting. I was with a 75-mm recoilless-rifle team. "Let's see," I shouted, "if we can get one of those tanks." We picked up the gun and moved it to where we could get a clean shot. I don't know if we were poorly trained, weren't thinking, or if it slipped our minds, but we set the gun on the forward slope of the hill. When we fired, the recoilless blast blew a hole in the hill which instantly covered us in mud and dirt. The effect wasn't nearly as bad on us as it was on the gun. It jammed and wouldn't fire until we'd cleaned the whole damn thing.

When we were ready again, we moved the gun to a better position and began banging away. I swear we had some hits, but the tanks never slowed down. One we hit in the tracks and it slewed sideways off the road. More of the tanks began shooting at us. I saw their explosions walking up the hill. I don't know what happened to the other two guys with me, but one blast knocked me and the gun over backward. I began bleeding from my ears. I wasn't unconscious, just stunned by the damn concussion.

In a little less than two hours, thirty North Korean tanks rolled through the position we were supposed to block as if we hadn't been there. That was our first two hours in combat.

1st Lt. WILLIAM WYRICK
Task Force Smith
My assistant platoon sergeant, Loren Chambers, called back on the sound-powered telephone for some 60-mm mortar fire on the enemy tanks. The answer was, "They won't reach that far."

"Well, how about the 81-mm mortars?"

"They didn't come over with us."

"How about the 4.2s [mortars]?"

"The 4.2s can't fire."

"How about the artillery?"

"No communications."

"What about the Air Force?"

"They don't know where we are."

"Call the Navy."

"They can't reach this far."

"Well, then, send me a camera. I want to take a picture of this."

About an hour after the tanks went through our position, a long convoy of trucks, bumper to bumper and as far as I could see, rolled down the road from the direction the tanks had come. They were packed with North Korean troops.

1st Lt. PHILIP DAY, JR.
Task Force Smith

When the trucks arrived near our line, troops jumped out of them. Sergeant Chambers said, "That's their infantry. This is not going to be good, you know." "Why?" I asked. "They're going to come in behind us," he answered. "We're sitting here guarding about 400 yards and they'll simply walk around us. You know, do an end run." By now the road ahead was bumper to bumper with trucks. I waited for our artillery to open on them. Later I learned the wire back to the howitzers had broken and the radios weren't functioning properly. In any event, the artillery never fired a shot.

Rain continued to fall.

1st Lt. WILLIAM WYRICK
Task Force Smith

Colonel Smith decided to form a perimeter on the main hill east of the road. C Company moved to the south side of the hill. My new position there looked directly south and I could see a disabled enemy tank (but one that could still fire) on the side of the road near the base of the hill. We dug foxholes, but it was more difficult to do than at our original position. Our company's 60-mm mortars, which were located directly behind my position, were firing in support of B Company. The enemy tank once in a while fired its machine gun in our direction. Some people were trying to knock the tank out but they never did. Some North Korean artillery and/or mortars landed in my platoon area. I felt a sense of frustration—shells were falling, I could see the tank firing and I could hear our mortar section chief giving his tubes fire-adjustment commands, but there wasn't anything I could direct my platoon against. I wanted desperately to fire my weapon, but there just wasn't anything within range.

1st Lt. PHILIP DAY, JR.
Task Force Smith

Enemy infantry units, now out of sight, moved somewhere along our flanks. When the enemy appeared on our left, the platoon from B Company, which was over on that side, was withdrawn to the east side of the road. This was my first day of combat, but I knew from just looking around that the enemy had a lot more men than we had. About then we started receiving small-arms fire on our flanks. An attack was made on our front but was broken up. Enemy mortar fire began to fall on our line. I could hear bullets snapping around me. We fired back. Still raining.

1st Lt. WILLIAM WYRICK
Task Force Smith

In midafternoon—it was hot now—Lieutenant [Harold] Dill [another platoon leader in C Company] and I were called to the company CP [command post]. Colonel Smith was there and he instructed us to take our platoons to a ridgeline east-southeast of our present position and there cover the withdrawal of the rest of the battalion. Dill would be on the left and I'd be on the right.

I called together my platoon sergeants and gave them a fragmentary defensive order, pointing out the flanks of our new position. I instructed my platoon sergeant, "I'm going to reconnoiter. Get the platoon up, Sergeant, get their weapons and equipment and move them to that point," and I pointed to an identifiable position in our new location, "and I will join you there."

1st Lt. PHILIP DAY, JR.
Task Force Smith

Enemy fire got worse, especially on the flanks. Sergeant Chambers yelled, "Hey, look! There they are on the knoll behind us!" I looked around and, Christ, there were North Korean troops behind us! Dashner ordered us back off the hill. "Fall back to the next ridge-line!" We were to go by platoons, leapfrogging each other.

When we moved out we began taking more and more casualties. [2d] Lt. Carl Bernard ran up. His glasses were wet. "Get your platoon on back there, we'll cover you from here!" Bernard was having a ball.

Guys fell around me. Mortar rounds hit here and there. One of my young guys got it in the middle. My platoon sergeant, Harvey Vann, ran over to him. I followed. "No way he's gonna live, Lieu-tenant." Oh, Jesus, the guy was moaning and groaning. There wasn't much I could do but pat him on the head and say, "Hang in there." Another of the platoon sergeants got it in the throat. He began spit-ting blood. I thought sure . . . For the rest of the day he held his throat together with his hand. He survived, too.

On the other side of the hill we crossed into a rice paddy. In combat boots you don't go very fast in mud and water. Although we were young, we became exhausted just trying to run. This was a ter-rible time. All around I saw enemy fire kicking up spurts of water. Guys stopped and removed their boots, threw their helmets away, stripped themselves of everything that slowed them down. A hundred yards farther, Sergeant Vann called to me, "Hey, Lieutenant, sir, I'm not gonna go running across this damn field like a water bug. Look, we got six or eight guys down here. I'm gonna stay with them. Let me stay. Somebody's got to take care of them. They're in bad shape. They can't walk. We can't carry them. It's too far."

"Jesus, Sergeant," I said, "we gotta go. We got our orders. I or-der you to come on." My assistant platoon sergeant, Bailey, a younger feller, Texan, ran over to me. "Sir, I'm gonna stay with Harvey." I yelled, "Now wait a minute! What's going on here? I got a platoon and we got a company—" Bailey interrupted, "Harvey's old and he can't take care of himself. If I don't stay with him, who's to know what's gonna happen?" They said, "We're gonna stay with the wounded." And they did.*

1st Lt. WILLIAM WYRICK
Task Force Smith

I made my reconnaissance and moved to the designated area on the new hill but my platoon never joined me. (I found out later it had gone south with the main body and had not followed me east.) I looked around and found some men. By this time the battalion had withdrawn off the main hill and I could see enemy soldiers moving south. The small group I was with started east toward the railroad. Between us and the tracks were rice paddies. (These were actually small, irregular ponds surrounded by narrow dirt dikes. Because of their irregularity there was never a direct route across a rice paddy.) When it was my turn to cross, a machine gun behind me on my left opened fire. It was a terrifying experience. The dikes were narrow and slippery; if I'd fallen off, I would have been waist-deep in mud and water. Bullets hit around me. I became separated from the men I'd been with. I made the tracks and on the other side met 1st Lt. Bodie Adams. We climbed a hill and were fired on all the way to the top. Bodie and I actually took turns assisting each other up the hill.

Eventually we joined a group of men with whom I moved east. About a quarter of them still had their weapons. We moved slowly because we carried some wounded with us. We reached a valley and turned south.

1st Lt. PHILIP DAY, JR.
Task Force Smith

It was raining still, and it was lousy. No one set up another defensive position. We moved as fast as we could. Everything had broken down

---

* Sgt. Harvey Vann died while a POW. Sergeant Bailey survived his forty-month imprisonment.

and it was every man for himself. I was in a small column. We kept
to the rice paddies and away from the road where we knew the NK
[North Korean] tanks were. If we heard something, we went the other
way. All day we wandered around over the landscape.

1st Lt. WILLIAM WYRICK
Task Force Smith

I do not have any idea of the time of day when we rested, but it had
to be late afternoon. (We still had several hours of daylight, as it didn't
get dark until 9:00 or 9:30 P.M.) I did not have a map, but I have a
good sense of direction and I knew that the town where C Company
had been dug in the night of July 3 [Ansong] was located several valleys to the east and then several miles to the south. We moved east
slowly as we had some wounded with us. I would say that about 25
percent of the men had weapons at that point. I organized the column so that some of the men who had weapons were on point and
the remainder were following up as rear guard. The wounded were
in the center of the column to be assisted by the men who had lost,
or whatever, their weapons.

As we moved to the east, we caught up with a U.S. Army Engineer captain and one or two sergeants. They had been advisers to a
Korean Army Engineer unit and were visiting our battalion headquarters when the enemy attacked. Since he outranked me, I requested that the captain, as senior line officer, take charge. He refused to do so, indicating he was not an infantry officer.

As we reached the valley where I had decided to turn south, we
met some South Korean soldiers moving down the valley from north
to south. It was touch and go for a few minutes before we decided (at
a distance) that each other was friendly. Soon afterward I had a dis-
agreement with the engineer officer concerning the direction we would
take and he departed to the east with his group. The South Koreans
either went with him or departed on their own within a short time.

We had crossed the mountains by following trails, but now we
moved south on the dirt road running down the middle of the valley.
It must have been 7:00 or 8:00 P.M., although it was still good daylight. I don't remember any rain after crossing the first ridge east of
the railroad. We had little or nothing to eat as all rations had been

consumed or thrown away earlier during the day. Some men would run out into the fields on either side of the road to dig vegetables to eat. We were not able to physically stop them, and once they left the road they didn't respond to our orders to return. I know some of them did return to the column after finding some food. (We never had a list of the group and there was never a roll call afterward, so there isn't any method to determine if all of those who ran off looking for food ever made it back to friendly lines or not.) We continued to move, stopping only for breaks every thirty to forty minutes. We were exhausted and it was very difficult to get everyone up and moving again as most were falling asleep during the short ten-to-fifteen-minute breaks. It is awfully hot in Korea in July. We were out of treated water and were drinking out of the rice paddies. By the time it grew dark (9:00 to 10:00 P.M.), we were completely exhausted and were stopping for breaks more frequently. It became more and more difficult to get everyone up and moving again.

All of a sudden I woke up. I was flat on my back and it was raining. I was alone. Very quickly I rolled off to the side of the road and concealed myself from the view of anyone walking on the road. The last thing I remembered doing with the group was going up a hill. It was around 2:00 A.M. I was now fully alert. The rain was just a sprinkle and it was very clear. I could see the high ridgelines of mountains on either side of the road, but I could not detect signs of life or lights. I realized I had slept through the end of a break and the group had moved off without me. I decided I would travel south (by compass) on the low ground by night and hole up on a ridgeline during the daytime. While moving I would avoid habitations and during the day I would be able to observe any enemy movement in the area.

Keeping my carbine at the ready, I moved south for about an hour and a half without incident. About 3:30 A.M. I came to a road junction. There was a village off to the left, while the main road continued to the south. It was a dirt road and in the mud I could see many tracks turning to the left toward the village. I decided that my group had gone to the village, but I had no idea what sort of a reception they had gotten. I knew from several years' experience in Japan that it would be practically impossible to walk around the edge of a village at night—rice paddies, dogs, "honey" pits, and so forth. I decided to approach the village using the road and was ready to beat a hasty retreat if I met an unfriendly reception. Just before I reached the edge of the village, I heard a challenge in Korean. (I knew three Korean words at that time. On the way north someone had told us that "me-gook" meant "American," that "ee-da-wa" meant "come here," and "ka-da" meant "get away.") I responded "me-gook" and the guy, a Korean policeman, didn't shoot at me. He let me approach and use his telephone to call the police station in the center of town. I discovered that my group, plus a group led by my company commander, Captain Dashner, were already at the police station. Someone then took me there.

It was about 4:00 A.M. when I arrived at the station. In addition to those previously named, Lieutenant [Philip] Day and First Sergeant Godbey were there. The group now numbered thirty or forty individuals, including some from battalion headquarters. Captain Dashner told me he had been in contact with a unit of the 34th Infantry Regiment in the next town to the south and that they would send trucks for us at first light. I had a hot cup of coffee and something (probably rice) to eat. Then I made a mistake; I took off my wet boots and went to sleep. About an hour later, around 6:00 A.M., someone shouted that the North Koreans were approaching the north edge of town. I had a very difficult time getting my boots on; in fact, I thought for a while I was going to go barefoot. We took off on foot and arrived at the next town about an hour later without incident. There was a battalion of the 34th there and we rested alongside the road while we waited for transportation. I remember that some women brought us balls of rice to eat; in fact, that was all we had to eat that day. It tasted very, very good.

[*Twenty-four hours earlier, almost at the same time Task Force Smith engaged the column of T34 tanks near Osan, the 34th Infantry's 1st Battalion began to dig in farther south on the same road, at P'yongt'aek.*]

1st Lt. CHARLES PAYNE
1st Battalion/34th Infantry

After setting up the battalion CP in a schoolhouse [5 July], the old fog of war set in—no one knew a thing about what was out front. Panic-stricken refugees screaming "Tanks" poured south. I waited for something to happen. In a while along came several war correspondents—Marguerite Higgins, Carl Mydans, Keyes Beech, and Roy McCartney.

MARGUERITE HIGGINS
New York Herald Tribune

At P'yongt'aek that morning there was only gloom in the air and in the mind. We were all cold and tired by the time we found the battalion command post hidden in a tiny thatched hut surrounded by a sea of mud. Col. Harold "Red" Ayres, commander of the 1st Battalion of the 34th Infantry, shared his command post with a filthy assortment of chickens, pigs, and ducks.

We had barely had time to enjoy a cup of hot coffee when Brig. Gen. George B. Barth* strode into the hut. "Enemy tanks are heading south," he said. "Get me some bazooka teams pronto."

Then, apparently aware of our startled reaction, he added, "Those Communist tanks are going to meet Americans for the first time— Colonel Smith's battalion is up forward. We can depend on him to hold on, but if any tanks do get by those batteries they'll head straight for here." †

---

* Acting commanding general of the 24th Division artillery.
† Marguerite Higgins, *War in Korea* (Garden City, New York: Doubleday, 1951), 58–59. Hereafter, Higgins.

1st Lt. CHARLES PAYNE
1st Battalion/34th Infantry

I volunteered to take the bazooka teams north to see what we could. During the Second World War a buddy and I helped destroy a German Tiger Tank and its crew. My buddy, Clarence Harmon, posthumously received the Medal of Honor for this action. That was July 1944, and the 2.36-inch bazooka was a new weapon.

In Korea when that experience was called for I was cocky enough to volunteer to go tank hunting. The youngsters who went with me trusted me enough to volunteer as well. We took nine 2.36-inch launchers and three rounds each—all we had. Everyone loaded onto jeeps and in the rain we drove north toward the village of Sojong.

MARGUERITE HIGGINS
New York Herald Tribune

I was filled with a very uncomfortable mixture of apprehension and excitement as we followed the bazooka teams to the unknown front. Wrapped in rain-soaked blankets, we traveled swiftly behind the small convoy of trucks and command cars carrying the bazooka and rifle teams. Then, on the crest of a hill, the convoy suddenly halted. We could see soldiers jumping out of the trucks and spreading out on a ridge parallel to the road. The road was clogged with South Korean soldiers in what seemed an endless procession southward. One South Korean soldier on horseback, his helmet camouflaged with bits of branches sticking up at absurd angles, came cantering toward us, shouting, "Tanks! Tanks! Tanks! Go back!"

A little farther on we found Lt. Charles Payne—a dapper, fast-talking young veteran of World War II. He had been examining the marks of huge tank treads on the road and told us that the tank had sighted us, turned around, and backed into a nearby village. "We're going to dig in here," he added, "and send out patrols to hunt him down." *

---

* Higgins, 59–60.

1st Lt. CHARLES PAYNE
1st Battalion/34th Infantry
The tanks found us first. I really thought we could stop them by penetrating their armor or setting fire to their treads. I had a lot to learn.

1st Lt. WILLIAM CALDWELL III
A Company/34th Infantry
One tank, in maneuvering to fire at us, had become lodged on some railroad tracks and lost its mobility. It did, however, still have full use of its coaxial machine gun as well as its main gun. The 2.36 rocket-launcher teams attempted to knock the tank out. Every piece of ammunition we fired was a dud. I then sent back to the company and got two more rocket-launcher teams and ammo. I positioned these teams around the tank and hid them behind mounds in a Korean graveyard. By using a system of signaling, we managed to decoy the tank to swing its guns in one direction while we fired from another. Again the rockets were either duds or bounced harmlessly off the tank's armored sides.

MARGUERITE HIGGINS
New York Herald Tribune
When orders to attack first went out to the fifty-odd youngsters in our bazooka team, they gazed at the tanks as if they were watching a newsreel. It took prodding from their officers to make them realize that this was it—that it was up to them to attack. Slowly, small groups of them left their foxholes, creeping low enough through the wheat field toward the tank. The first swoosh from a bazooka flared out when they were nearly 500 yards away from the tanks. But the aim was good and it looked like a direct hit.

But apparently it didn't look good to Lieutenant Payne. "Damn," he said, "those kids are scared. They've got to get close to the tanks to do any damage." *

1st Lt. CHARLES PAYNE
1st Battalion/34th Infantry
Hitting the T34 head-on merely produced a bounce-off. We soon ran out of ammo and had one man killed in action [Pvt. Kenneth Shadrick]. I pulled everyone back while our 4.2-inch mortar engaged their tanks. I saw one tread on fire and we made their infantry scramble. There were many more North Korean trucks on the road immediately to our north. Having run out of ammo, the bazooka teams and the 4.2s dropped back.

MARGUERITE HIGGINS
New York Herald Tribune
Time passed, and suddenly, after an hour, we saw the bazooka boys coming back toward us across the fields.
"What's going on?" I asked a sergeant.
"We ran out of ammo," he answered bitterly. "And the enemy infantry moving up way outnumbers us. Besides, these damn bazookas don't do any good against those heavy tanks—they bounce right off." †

Cpl. LACY BARNETT
Medical Company/34th Infantry
It was still raining on the morning of July 6. One of our company cooks, Corporal Laxamana, who had combat experience in the Philippines during World War II, borrowed a pair of binoculars and began scanning the road north of where we were dug in. In a few minutes he reported seeing a column of trucks moving in our direction.

---

* Higgins, 61–62.
† Ibid., 62–63.

At first this news was played down. Some thought it was South Korean troops, others figured it was probably men from that American unit we knew was north of us. Corporal Laxamana would have none of this. He insisted the column he saw was North Korean. His persistence finally persuaded our CO. We loaded up and moved out smartly. You could sense the troops beginning to feel a little apprehensive about the situation. Some fear began developing that all was not under control.

Medical Company had moved a short distance when suddenly one of our vehicles slid into a ditch and became hopelessly stuck in the mud. Our CO was determined to get that vehicle back on the road. No way was he going to catch hell from Colonel Lovless for abandoning a vehicle.

Much time elapsed, but the vehicle was still in the ditch. Corporal Laxamana again spied the column of unidentified trucks rapidly moving down the road in our direction. After destroying the vehicle the company moved south about ten miles, stopping finally near our regimental headquarters.

South Korean soldiers heading south passed our camp. We felt they were too cowardly to stay and, with no enemy in sight, were merely bugging out.

The first time we realized we were in a nasty situation was when the first survivors of Task Force Smith straggled into our lines and we began to process their sick and wounded.* Even though some of these guys were wounded and had real war stories to tell, some of our men still persisted in the belief the North Koreans would turn tail once they found American troops on the ground. This fantasy was utterly destroyed when the body of Private [Kenneth] Shadrick was brought to the collecting station for processing by Graves Registration. He had been killed the morning before south of Osan when his unit came upon a North Korean tank. Shadrick had been raked across the chest by a machine gun.

---

*A count of Task Force Smith survivors taken on 6 July showed about 150 men killed, wounded, or missing. The North Koreans lost approximately 42 killed and 85 wounded at Osan on 5 July.

July 6

Attempting to localize the war, U.S. air and sea units had instructions not to violate Soviet or Chinese Communist territorial waters.

Enemy attacks continued along the Suwon-Singal-Kumyangjang line. Enemy 1st, 2d and 4th Divisions pressed toward Osan and P'yongt'aek. U.S. troops retreated.

DEPARTMENT OF STATE CHRONOLOGY

[It was now obvious that North Korea had no intention of pulling back because they faced a few Americans in battle. More than a small force of GIs was going to be needed to accomplish that task. A strong natural defense position capable of holding the enemy would also have to be found. The most likely position was the Kum River. If that failed, there was the Naktong River. Beyond the Naktong, there was only the sea.

During the first days of the war, additional units of the 34th and 21st Infantry Regiments continued to arrive at the port of Pusan. As soon as they unloaded, they were rushed northward. A desperate race against time began. The question was whether General MacArthur could get enough troops and firepower into the war before the Communists overran the entire Korean peninsula. The question would remain unanswered for several more terrible weeks.]

Pfc. LEONARD KORGIE
L Company/34th Infantry
Just before we sailed from Japan, about sixty men marched on board our ship. What made this interesting was that these men were under guard. I learned later they were prisoners from the Eighth Army's stockade who had been given a chance to clear their records in combat. Some of our guys were given ammunition and told to guard these men until we got to Pusan. I thought, How hard up can the 24th Division be?

Cpl. THERMAN COSSAIRT, JR.
B Battery/11th Field Artillery Battalion
I landed in Pusan off an LST [landing ship, tank] on July 7 as a replacement for a 155-mm howitzer battery. It was all very different to me because my last unit had been a heavy mortar company. I figured I was only going to be in Korea for two weeks or so, so what the hell!

There were railroad flatcars waiting to take us north to Taejon. On the way, as we passed through tunnels, cinders from a coal-burning engine flew into our eyes. There were young Korean boys standing guard at all the bridges and stations. Someone pointed out they were only armed with wooden rifles. Right then, most of us began to wonder what we were getting into.

We arrived in Taejon and unloaded in a drenching rainstorm. Everyone was soaked. Wounded South Koreans lay all over the platform and station. Eventually we moved to the Taejon airstrip and from there to the Kum River, where B Battery finally set up for the night. We began firing early the next morning.

Sgt. C. W. ''BILL'' MENNINGER
3d Battalion/34th Infantry
We loaded our equipment on a train and headed north. We were the only ones going north; the South Korean Army was heading south. One train passed us during the trip. The last car in that train was a flatcar that carried land mines. We observed Korean soldiers dropping the mines off between the tracks and idly wondered what in the world they expected to blow up.

We finally detrained and moved into a defensive position near the town of P'yongt'aek. We were completely unaware of any other American troops ahead of us. We found out there were, when some survivors of Task Force Smith straggled into our lines. Sometime during the night we received orders to withdraw and set up a defensive position north of Ch'onan.

[For these Americans thrown unit by unit into the front lines, it was a time of confusion, retreat, sacrifice, and death. The 24th Division lacked the numbers and weapons to defeat the well-trained, well-led, and well-armed North Korean Army. It had little choice but to trade

space for time. A series of short, sharp, and, for the Americans, bloody delaying actions marked the enemy's advance along the railroad line that ran south from Osan. Americans died in towns few had ever heard of, places like P'yongt'aek, Choch'iwon, and Ch'onan. The 21st and 34th Infantry Regiments fought as well as could be expected but, alone, they could not hold the North Koreans.]

1st Lt. WILLIAM CALDWELL III
A Company/34th Infantry

Colonel Ayres arrived at our company early so he could view the situation to see what was happening. Shortly after he arrived I saw through my field glasses what I took to be a unit of the 21st Infantry withdrawing over a hill toward our lines. Colonel Ayres instantly scanned these men with his glasses. He shouted, "That's the whole damn North Korean Army." We immediately fired on the North Koreans, who continued to deploy. It became apparent to Colonel Ayres that we would soon be outflanked and cut off. After checking with the regimental commander [Colonel Lovless] and receiving his permission, we withdrew to a town called Ch'onan. We reached Ch'onan while it was still light and began preparing positions for the next enemy onslaught, which we knew would come that night.

1st Lt. PHILIP DAY, JR.
C Company/21st Infantry

While we were in Taejon recovering and receiving replacements, our sister regiment, the 34th, moved up and attempted to stop the North Korean juggernaut. Their 3d Battalion established a blocking position at Ch'onan, which is between Osan and Taejon. The enemy arrived.

Capt. FRANK THOMPSON, JR.
Medical Company/34th Infantry

The 34th Infantry patrols made contact with the advancing Reds north of Ch'onan. Artillery had joined us, as had a platoon of light tanks. By early afternoon one of the most savage battles of the campaign developed as the regiment fought to defend Ch'onan. During the afternoon and for hours after nightfall, our litter jeeps roared back and forth between the aid stations and the collecting station. We used all our weapons carriers and borrowed two more to move patients to the railhead. The railcar shuttled to and from Taejon at top speed. Our jeeps continued to go in and bring wounded out of Ch'onan after the town was virtually surrounded and all roads were under enemy fire. Even so, many wounded were overrun and killed. Jeeps running between collecting and the aid stations were fired upon. Finally, the 3d Battalion was ordered to retreat and began to fight its way out of the town. The 1st Battalion, on the left, and the artillery also began to fall back.

Maj. Gen. WILLIAM F. DEAN
Commanding General, 24th Division
Then I received astonishing information: the 34th had pulled back south of Ch'onan—more than fifteen miles from the [Kum] river defense line with its flank on the sea. I jumped in my jeep and rushed up toward Ch'onan to find out what was wrong, why they had not held on the river. But by the time I got there the whole regiment was south of Ch'onan, most of the men having ridden back on the trucks. I should have said, "Turn around and get going now," but rather than add to the confusion, and risk night ambushes, I told them, "All right, hold tight here until I give you further orders."

When I reached my own headquarters once more I issued such orders: to advance until they made contact with the enemy, then fight a delaying action.

I have always believed that when there is confusion in orders, the person issuing those orders is at fault for not making himself entirely clear; so the fault in this affair was mine. But whatever the fault, the results were tragic.

On the afternoon of July 7, after relieving Colonel Lovless, I gave command of the 34th Regiment to Col. Robert B. Martin. *

* *Dean's Story*, 23–24.

Cpl. LACY BARNETT
Medical Company/34th Infantry

When General Dean arrived at regimental headquarters, he was highly perturbed that we were not set up north of Ch'onan. Colonel Lovless explained to General Dean why he had pulled back. The general did not accept his explanation and relieved him of command.

The 34th Infantry soon discovered that hidden among the fleeing refugees who constantly flowed through our lines were North Korean soldiers. Our defensive lines were always established north of a town. After a battle, when we withdrew through that town, our rear and flanks would be clobbered by these enemy infiltrators. It is my belief that Colonel Lovless set up his defensive line south of Ch'onan to avoid this kind of ambush.

Col. Robert Martin assumed command of the 34th.* In a matter of hours he was dead.†

Pfc. ROBERT HARPER
Headquarters Company/34th Infantry

We heard all kinds of fighting going on up north but didn't really know what was happening. Soon our platoon sergeant came around [7 July], took every available man not essential to regimental headquarters, loaded us in trucks and jeeps and told us we were going up to Ch'onan. We would try to hold the position there as long as possible.

Ch'onan was a pretty good-size town with a large railroad depot, and we set up near it. I was behind some railroad tracks, very close to a long, deep sewage ditch full of nothing but stinking filth. It stunk all day. A line battalion [the 3d Battalion] pulled in and got organized along the length of the railroad tracks. We all waited to see what would happen and put in a long, hot, sweaty day.

---

*This change in command took place at 6:00 P.M. on 7 July.
†Colonel Martin was killed in Ch'onan around 8:00 A.M. on 8 July.

During the day I talked to some of the officers and men who'd been fighting farther north. One officer told me the biggest problem was in not being able to stop the Russian T34 tanks. Our bazookas were too small and firing one of them at a tank was the same as throwing a rock at it; the shells just bounced off the armor. He said we had to somehow try to stop the tanks because that would also slow down their infantry. Some soldiers came down the railroad tracks and passed out hand grenades. I tucked three into my pockets. It just was a real nervous time, not knowing what would happen next.

I heard sporadic small-arms fire and figured it was the North Koreans trying to find where we were positioned. South Korean civilians spent the day evacuating the town. They carried everything they could on their backs or in ox-drawn carts. ROK soldiers questioned the refugees coming down from Ansong, trying to get an estimate of the enemy's strength. The estimates were anywhere from 1,000 to 5,000 enemy soldiers. Two things the refugees agreed on: there were many North Koreans and they had tanks. By evening the town was nearly empty of civilians. A few old men and women too crippled or old to be taken on the road stayed behind. Also left behind were a few mangy, scared dogs.

The sun went down. It was a long, long night; quiet, no firing. If you had to move, you moved in the dark real slow and tried to make no noise. As daylight broke [8 July], we heard this loud clanking noise off the the left. We understood now what was happening— their tanks were coming. Eventually I could see them dimly, moving through the morning mist. I counted them. When I got to nine, an order was given to pull back off the railroad tracks and set up in the first row of houses behind the sewage ditch. From there I saw the North Korean infantry moving to my right across the field in front of the railroad depot. I could hear occasional small-arms and machine-gun fire. Mortar rounds began falling nearby. The tanks continued to roll down the road toward us. We had no way of stopping them. They came to the end of the road and I could hear them firing. I did not know which of our companies were down there but knew they were catching hell. We were ordered back to a narrow street, where we waited to see what would happen next. I heard the new CO, Colonel Martin, tried to take on one of the tanks with a bazooka. The tank scored a direct hit on the colonel and he was killed on the spot.

We began receiving real heavy mortar and tank fire. We ran down to the depot to reinforce a company which was being heavily attacked. Down in the depot one of our rifle companies was cutting loose across the road. The North Koreans were knocking hell out of the roof of the depot and shooting the windows out with machine-gun fire. All around me wood and steel fell. The din made by both sides was unbelievable.

I heard a rumor that the Communists had managed to hide two tanks in Ch'onan the night before. A patrol was sent out to see if it could locate these tanks. We did not want them sneaking up behind us. The patrol never returned and I do not know whether they found the two tanks.

We were then ordered a little farther back down the road. The North Koreans fired at us the entire time. I climbed up to the second story of a building so I could see better. Two GIs I'd never seen before joined me there. I was in the front room, the other two were in the back. We tried to spot where the small-arms fire was coming from. I saw movement off the street in a building. I knew there were no more civilians in the town and I knew how the ROKs were dressed. The two guys I saw wore brown uniforms—North Koreans. I know from personal experience that two enemy soldiers did not go south that day. The two guys in the back ran up wanting to know what I had fired at. We figured we'd better get out of our building because there were probably more North Koreans around us. We waited a few minutes, then went down the stairs. From inside the doorway we carefully looked around. I didn't particularly want to cross the street and see the two North Koreans I'd shot. I wanted to leave them alone.

We ran down through some alleys and met some more GIs who said orders had been issued to evacuate the town. I could hear a lot of small-arms and mortar fire behind me. We went to the east edge of town, worked our way through rice paddies and got to the road. There were quite a few civilians still on the road. We joined them in heading south. We drew heavy artillery fire and began to lose a lot of people.

Maj. Gen. WILLIAM F. DEAN
Commanding General, 24th Division
A sweating officer coming from Ch'onan told us that North Korean tanks were in the town, although we could not see them. He said Colonel Martin had grabbed a bazooka and was leading his men with it, actually forcing the tanks to turn and run, when one tank came around the corner unexpectedly and fired from less than twenty-five feet. The shot blew Colonel Martin in half. Thereafter, resistance had disintegrated and now our troops were bugging out.*

Sgt. C. W. "BILL" MENNINGER
3d Battalion/34th Infantry
On the withdrawal I ran into a dear friend, Sgt. Hank Leerkamp. When we arrived at a road junction south of Ch'onan and could not decide which branch was the safest to take, we separated and went off in different directions.†

Alone on the road, I walked until I found myself in a small farmyard. Surprisingly, a 4.2 mortar with a few shells sat unattended in the middle of this yard. In the hope of finding its crew, I yelled as loud as I could. No one answered. Having once been a mortar instructor, I decided to fire the gun. I dropped in a shell and ran like hell to the corner of the farm building to see where it hit; then I ran back, made a correction, dropped in another shell and ran to see where that one hit. I did this till I used up all the ammunition. I have no idea whether I did any damage, but it sure felt good knowing I was scaring the hell out of someone.

Maj. Gen. WILLIAM F. DEAN
Commanding General, 24th Division
Now a new decision faced me. The highway below Ch'onan divides. Both routes had to be defended. I ordered the 34th to back down the

---

* *Dean's Story,* 25.
† Sergeant Menninger arrived back safely at his battalion CP. Sergeant Leerkamp was captured and spent the war in a North Korean prison camp.

Kongju road and the newly arrived 21st Regiment to fight a delaying action on the route to Choch'iwon.*

1st Lt. PHILIP DAY, JR.
C Company/21st Infantry

As soon as we were able, we took up a position behind Ch'onan, at a town called Choch'iwon. By sunrise on July 11 we were in position along the highway just north of the town. Stragglers from the 3d Battalion trickled back.

Cpl. NORTON GOLDSTEIN
Headquarters Company/21st Infantry

Outside of Choch'iwon the wire communication between 3d Battalion and 1st Battalion was not working. Lieutenant Mitchell, our CO, decided he was going to take a crew up to find out where the break was. Unfortunately for me, I became a part of the crew. A fellow named Jack Colbert and I carried a roll of wire and along with Lieutenant Mitchell we got a ride on a tank going north. Somewhere along the road the tank decided it wasn't going any farther and turned around and went back to town. Colbert, Lieutenant Mitchell, and I continued north. We could hear a battle going on somewhere ahead of us. About then I saw my first napalm. It was being dropped by two of our planes on a ridgeline some distance off. Knowing it was being dropped on people who were trying to kill me made me feel pretty good. It's hard to explain that feeling to people who weren't in the situation.

That night I learned from another wire team who had also been out that day what happened to the line between 1st and 3d Battalions. A guy from Oklahoma, name of Billy Wells, was following the line by hand when he came around a bend in the road. He yelled back to his buddies, "I see what's the matter. There's a T34 tank on the damn wire!" At that, its turret began to swing toward him, but

---

Dean's Story, 25–26.

before the cannon fired, Wells and his team were on their way back
to Choch'iwon.

1st Lt. PHILIP DAY, JR.
C Company/21st Infantry
It was soon 1st Battalion's turn again. We put out two companies on
the hills overlooking the road and tried to protect the main north-
south highway. The same old crap happened. We began to receive
an infantry attack, and enemy artillery and mortar rounds landed along
our hill front. We were clobbered. The left flank took a beating.
Casualties mounted up. Soon we began backing off the hill. The
withdrawal was orderly. On the road we met some trucks that were
waiting for us. We didn't have to walk this time.

Capt. FRANK THOMPSON, JR.
Medical Company/34th Infantry
The fight near the highway intersection north of Choch'iwon devel-
oped with the Reds using their now familiar tactics. The battalions
were hit with a massive frontal attack by numerically superior forces.
Then, after all American elements were engaged, large numbers of
North Koreans moved around both flanks.

No particular difficulties with regard to evacuation were experienced here. The roadnet was favorable and during the first phase of
the engagement we were able to send ambulances all the way into
the forward aid stations. Railcars were brought into the Choch'iwon
station only a short distance from the collecting station, which operated in a girls' school. A large number of casualties came through
during this battle and we were also receiving wounded from elements
of the 21st Infantry Regiment, which were in contact with the enemy
east of the town.

A few hours before dawn on the second day [11 July], the battered battalions began to withdraw and break contact with the Reds.
Convoys began to pass our position moving to the rear, and when the
men we posted on the road reported that HQ and HQ Company were
passing by, we loaded up and fell in at the end of the column. The

railcar had left a short time before and for the first time it was necessary for us to carry patients with us.

There was the long withdrawal to Kongju to the south and west of Choch'iwon and the beginning of the establishment of the Kum River line. The 34th Infantry's sector was the city of Kongju and an area extending along the riverbank in both directions. The 21st and 19th Regiments fell back to positions along the river line to the east. For the first time since the beginning of hostilities we were to fight as a division.*

[By the first week of the war, Republic of Korea losses had reached 44,000 men killed, captured, or missing in action. The south was in shambles. Homes were destroyed or abandoned; hundreds of thousands of fleeing civilians clogged the roads; wrecked or abandoned vehicles and equipment littered the countryside.

Two weeks into July three main enemy columns led by tanks continued to blaze their way down the Korean peninsula. Although the North Koreans had yet to be held, let alone defeated, American forces had begun to slow their advance. Every hour of delay meant more American troops and firepower could arrive at Pusan. The 25th Division was already in the country and moving north. The 1st Cavalry was about to arrive. Help was also on the way from the continental United States. A provisional Marine brigade, complete with Marine air from Camp Pendleton, California, and the 2d Infantry Division from Camp Lewis, Washington, were under orders to proceed to the Far East.

Tragically, the dispirited men of the 24th Division who faced the enemy onslaught had no way of knowing that their sacrifices were slowly, imperceptibly, turning the war in their direction. For them, Korea in July was a hell that had to be endured. Summer was at its height. Torrents of rain fell three or four times a day. Bone-tired infantrymen went to sleep wet and woke up wet. Asleep or awake, they were tormented by flies, fleas, and lice. Clothes rotted, equipment rusted. To escape roads covered by enemy roadblocks, men slithered through stinking rice paddies fertilized with human excrement. Trudging along slip-

---

*The 24th Division's strength just before the battle for Taejon was 11,440 men. Two weeks before it had numbered 12,197 men.

pery, mud-thickened trails, waiting in filthy huts for food that often never arrived, climbing endless hills and mountains, some shoeless, some bruised or bloody, all sweat-soaked and miserable, the men of the 24th Infantry Division, individually or in scattered units, continued to stop and fight whenever and wherever they were ordered.]

Sgt. C. W. "BILL" MENNINGER
3d Battalion/34th Infantry
Communication was practically nil. Most of the radios didn't work, and the fact that the enemy was often between our headquarters and the rifle companies made it extremely hazardous to lay phone wires. Almost all communication, therefore, was by runners, and they often simply disappeared.

By the time we would plot the locations of our companies on a situation map, in most cases they'd no longer be there. There was no front line.

The enemy was often mistaken for friendly ROK troops and vice versa. Fleeing civilians blocked the roads. They cut up our phone wire to tie bundles of belongings. Many of these civilians were actually enemy soldiers. Once they got behind us, weapons would appear and we'd have another roadblock to fight our way through.

Cpl. THERMAN COSSAIRT, JR.
B Battery/11th Field Artillery Battalion
Because of the intense heat, water was always a problem. To make matters worse, the North Koreans dumped dead bodies into any wells they came to. That spoiled a lot of water.

Cpl. LACY BARNETT
Medical Company/34th Infantry
We evacuated a lot of nonbattle casualties during the first two weeks we were in Korea. These were primarily men who had gastrointestinal problems caused by drinking bad water. Many of them, without immediate access to clean water, would drink rice-paddy water. Others would find a well of cool water, and rather than put it in their canteens along with purification tablets, would drink it right away.

Heat-related casualties were another problem. Many men simply were not in good enough physical condition to do what they were
expected to do in the intense heat and humidity of a Korean summer. No one had told them how to manage and conserve their energy. I found that soldiers who had prior military training were the
ones who survived. Having been in similar situations during World
War II paid off for them.

Many of our company aidmen instantly became battle casualties. They were nice guys and had good intentions, but in a combat
situation these men were losers. Many aidmen were killed or wounded
as soon as their platoon became engaged in a firefight. A rifleman on
his left would be hit and he would crawl to the man and render first
aid. Before he was finished another man would go down, then another. They'd begin to yell, "Medic!" Instead of crawling to these men,
the excited aidman would jump up and attempt to run to the next
wounded man. It was then that he, too, would be hit by rifle fire or
a shell burst. The man's desire to act quickly must be admired from
a humanitarian standpoint, but from a military point of view, the
aidman was now either dead or wounded. Three down instead of two,
and no one to treat anyone else. It was a tragic situation which occurred with depressing frequency.

Sgt. C. W. ''BILL'' MENNINGER
3d Battalion/34th Infantry
The local people in Sasebo, Japan, had planned to help us celebrate
our 4th of July there. Across a railroad overpass they had strung a
huge banner which announced in bold letters, AERIAL DISPLAYS, FIRE-
WORKS, AND FOOTRACES. During those first days in Korea, someone
remarked we should have brought the banner with us as an example
of Oriental prophecy.

Cpl. LACY BARNETT
Medical Company/34th Infantry
On the night of July 14, the entire 34th was withdrawing by motor
convoy. Somewhere on the road the convoy stopped. As usual no one
except those in the lead serial knew why it had stopped. The Medical

Company motor sergeant was a loud and plainspoken individual. He dismounted from his vehicle and, being in the middle of the convoy, wondered along with the rest of us why we had stopped. Soon a tall man walked up to this sergeant and asked why the convoy wasn't moving. Without looking around, the motor sergeant replied, "I don't know, but whoever is running this show sure is all fucked up!" Almost before the words were out of his mouth, he turned around and saw a helmet with two stars on it. General Dean did not reply. He walked on toward the head of the convoy. The motor sergeant was ready to rip his stripes off.

[*In mid-July nothing stood in the way of the North Korean thunderbolt but Walker's depleted Eighth Army. And it was Dean's 24th Division that would bear the real brunt. The Americans still had no reserves to call upon and faced an enemy three times their strength and vastly superior in armor. In a desperate effort to check the North Korean offensive, General Dean decided to make his stand at Taejon. He chose the city because of its location: a highway and double-tracked railroad ran south from it to Pusan, and the broad Kum River enclosed it in a horseshoe-shaped loop. To the north the 24th Division stopped and dug in behind the river. The 34th Infantry was placed on the left, the 19th Infantry on the right. The 21st Infantry, which had lost half its strength in its first week of combat, was ordered to take up a blocking position south of the town. There were no surprises here. The obvious key to holding Taejon was in preventing the North Koreans from crossing the natural moat formed by the Kum. On 13 July the battered and reeling American units were in place for what would be the first large-scale encounter battle of the war.*]

Capt. FRANK THOMPSON, JR.
Medical Company/34th Infantry
At first, defensive positions were taken up several thousand yards north of the river. A second line of positions was prepared along the north bank and the huge bridge spanning the Kum was loaded with explosives. The aid station set up along roads that converged at the bridge. Behind these lines was the town of Kongju.

The broad river seemed to provide a sense of security, but study of the situation map was not reassuring. The 1st Battalion was alone on line. What men and officers remained of the badly mauled 3d Battalion were assembled in Kongju. A major asked for volunteers to form a provisional company. To the last man these ragged, exhausted, magnificent GIs shouted their readiness to continue to fight. There were just enough left of the original five companies of the battalion to form one small composite unit. The 3d Battalion aid station set up with these people when they took a position in front of the city on the south bank of the river.

Cause for dissatisfaction with our position came when the Medical Company learned that many elements of the artillery were placed to our rear. As the firefight began it became apparent that the enemy was in great strength. Reports of infiltration across the river by small boats began to come in. By nightfall the 1st Battalion was heavily engaged and the distance between the thin line of resistance and the river began to shrink. At dawn the map indicated our position could be reached by enemy artillery from many areas and by heavy mortar fire. We asked and received permission to move to a new position on the south edge of Kongju. Although this was still not a good spot, the artillery being behind us, we had no other alternative.

As the situation continued to disintegrate, the battalion held the north bank of the river as long as possible and backed into Kongju. When all troops were across the Kum, the bridge was blown [4:00 A.M., 13 July]. Our situation was approaching desperation. The 1st Battalion was far understrength and throughout the regiment key officers had been killed or wounded. Of the original regimental staff, only the executive officer and the S-4 [supply officer] remained. The Medical Company had lost many men. All available men, including cooks and assistant drivers, were with the forward stations and line companies replacing men killed and wounded. Vehicles were breaking down. Litter racks on jeeps, of too light construction to begin with, had become contraptions of wire and wood.

Enemy infiltration continued, more artillery was lost, and enemy patrols were sighted along the river to our rear and left.

Maj. WADE HERITAGE, M.D.
Headquarters/24th Division

The day after we learned that all the bridges across the Kum River had been destroyed, it was reported that enemy patrols were fording the river in several spots [14 July]. At that time, after consulting with the G-4 [CO, divisional logistical section] and speaking to General Dean, we decided to evacuate all the patients from the clearing platoon in Taejon. At the same time the medical battalion, minus the clearing platoon and the ambulance company, was sent by infiltration to a position south of that taken by the 21st Infantry. With the transportation officer we set up a train at the Taejon station which would take all the casualties back to the port of Pusan.

After giving the clearing platoon commander some time to load his patients and get down to the RTO [Rail Transportation Office], I went down to the railroad station myself to observe what was going on. While we were engaged in putting the wounded aboard, gunfire broke out to the north. The Korean engineer immediately jumped aboard his locomotive and started to pull out of the station. The clearing platoon sergeant and I both shouted at the engineer to stop. He continued to go. Both of us then swung our carbines and fired shots through the roof of his cab. He immediately pulled on the brakes. I ordered the sergeant aboard the cab of the locomotive with instructions to shoot the engineer if he made another effort to escape. The loading then continued with no further mishaps. As the sounds of gunfire increased, I got on the phone and called headquarters to find out what the situation was. I was advised to form a perimeter around the station and to defend it if necessary until help reached us. There were about a dozen assorted troops in the RTO and I ordered them out onto the street to take up positions around the station. This they did, and we lay in our positions, listening to gunfire in the town, for perhaps fifteen or twenty minutes. At the end of that time, the shooting died down. There being no apparent activity, I called again and was told it would be all right to return to the RTO since a patrol was coming down into our area to give assistance.

[The North Koreans crossed the Kum River on their first attempt. Under the sheer weight of the enemy attack, the 34th Infantry collapsed

and fell back, leaving the 19th Infantry's left flank vulnerable. Unable to hold its line, the 19th—the old "Rock of Chickamauga" unit of Civil War fame—was ordered to fall back to a position closer to Taejon. Before the withdrawal could be managed, the enemy established a strong roadblock to the regiment's rear. A bitter, bloody night battle was fought on 16 July. The "Chicks" eventually fought their way through the trap but not before the regiment lost 19 percent of its effective combat strength. Less than one-half of its 1st Battalion managed to escape to Taejon.]

Cpl. LACY BARNETT
Medical Company/34th Infantry
After the Kum River defenses crumbled, the Medical Company moved about fifteen miles south and set up in a schoolhouse several hundred yards from the main road. This position was nowhere near the regimental CP (forward), the unit which normally provided security for us.

About 3:00 P.M. [17 July] the CO ordered me to get a jeep, go to regiment, and ask the 34th Infantry's commander, Colonel [Charles E.] Beauchamp, whether we were too far back, and if so, where did he want us to go? I knew the regimental CO should not be bothered with details like this, but orders are orders!

When I arrived at the regimental CP, the adjutant wanted to know why a corporal from the Medical Company wanted to see the colonel. I told him my reason, and the staff officers in the area had a good laugh. I was informed that Colonel Beauchamp was with one of the forward rifle companies. Having my orders, I drove forward and tried to locate this company. When I did, the company's commander told me the colonel was at one of the outposts and he highly recommended or, should I say, ordered me not to proceed any farther. This lieutenant further advised and recommended I return to my company and tell my CO to do his job properly and not waste regiment's time with such matters.

Around dusk I returned to my unit. The routes I had traveled were dangerous because enemy infiltrators were everywhere. My CO became visibly shaken when I reported the results of my afternoon's journey to him. He also became highly perturbed at my inability to fulfill the mission I'd been assigned. The Medical Company, at least for the moment, stayed where it was.

That night we heard vehicles on the nearby road moving south. At first we thought they belonged to the South Korean Army. After a couple of hours of this, say around 10:00 P.M., two of our men walked out to the road. They returned in a few minutes with the news that the entire regiment was engaged in a withdrawal. If we had not accidentally learned this information, in a half hour at most, the 34th Infantry's Medical Company would have been the regiment's forwardmost unit. Needless to say, we loaded up and in a matter of minutes were moving south.

Sgt. ROBERT DEWS
Headquarters Company/34th Infantry
We were taken at once to Taejon. The American high command was so desperate for replacements that almost as soon as I arrived in Japan I was placed with a group going to Korea. We were put on a Japanese fishing boat that smelled to high heaven of dead fish. When we arrived in Pusan, everyone was quite sick. Still smelling of fish, we were immediately sent north. The road south was clogged with refugees, walking wounded, and trucks carrying the dead and severely wounded. Everything in Taejon was in turmoil. We replacements were picked up like stray cattle by hungry units looking for bodies.

[Lacking the necessary reserves to defend its flanks, the bulk of the 24th Division was ordered to withdraw before it was surrounded. Two hardened North Korean divisions supported by armor, now across the Kum River, began pouring into the vicinity of Taejon. The enemy's plan of attack was one they had successfully used more than once, and more than twice—pin the Americans down by hitting them head-on, then outflank them and send infiltrators to their rear to cut off any retreat.

Against this powerful enemy General Dean could only bring into the line the remains of his three shattered regiments. In addition to their numerical inferiority, the GIs were tired, their morale poor. General Dean braced himself for the coming disaster.

A fierce, chaotic rearguard battle was fought in and around Tae-

jon on 19–20 July. Not everyone who escaped remembers what others remember. Times and locations differ. One thing is certain—the battle was as grim and desperate as any the Americans in Korea had fought up to this time.]

Cpl. LACY BARNETT
Medical Company/34th Infantry
General Dean had to be both mentally and physically exhausted on July 19. He'd arrived in Korea on or about July 1 and there had been critical military situations around the clock since his arrival. Every day we saw him going to the front or coming back. He knew more than anyone how critical the situation was and the danger of the entire 24th Division being wiped out before help could arrive.

Maj. Gen. WILLIAM F. DEAN
Commanding General, 24th Division
Various officers of the 25th Division already had been up to look over the front, and I knew that division would come to help us just as soon as they secured a vital airfield on the east coast.* The 1st Cavalry also was on the way. So I moved my own divisional command post east to Yongdong but stayed behind in Taejon myself. . . . On the night of July 19 I went to sleep to the sound of gunfire. †

Pfc. ROBERT HARPER
Headquarters Company/34th Infantry
I sat in the dark with some other soldiers and tried to figure what the hell we were going to do next. Nobody had any idea what was going on, but we knew the situation around Taejon wasn't looking good. After eating something we were told to find a place to lie down and see if we could get some sleep. Most of us picked up our gear, went inside a nearby building, and lay down on the floor. I hadn't slept in

---

*The 25th Infantry Division was the second U.S. division committed in the war and began arriving in Korea on 10 July.
† *Dean's Story,* 28–29.

two days and was totally exhausted, but being so excited and not knowing what would happen the next day, there was no way I could go to sleep. I just lay there in the dark and listened to the activity outside.

1st Lt. CHARLES PAYNE
1st Battalion/34th Infantry
I knew in my heart that by daylight of the 20th we would again be overrun, only this time on a large scale. I felt my time had come. My orders were to stay where I was. Two or three other men and I stayed on a forward knoll watching and listening, going through the hell of sweating each second. Earlier in the day I had directed artillery fire north of Taejon till it became too dark to do so.* Before the sun set I could see through my glasses large enemy movements of men, trucks, and tanks about 3,500 to 5,000 yards away massing in front of our lines.

About 3:00 in the morning NK scouts and patrols arrived with their noises, whistles, and grenades, to feel out our position. Shortly afterward, the main force came in like a slow tornado and engulfed everything and everyone. I knew then what the Oriental tactic of mass attack was all about.

Maj. Gen. WILLIAM F. DEAN
Commanding General, 24th Division
In the morning more gunfire knit a ragged and shrinking border around the city. I awoke very early, although I had been short of sleep for almost a month. I heard the sound of the sporadic firing and inhaled the odors, which no one ever escapes in Korea, of rice-paddy muck and mud walls, fertilizer and filth, and, mixed with them now, the acrid after-odor of cordite from the artillery, indefinable odors of thatch-roofed houses slowly burning. †

---

* Lieutenant Payne's 1st Battalion, 34th Infantry, was four miles northwest of Taejon across the highway to Kongju.
† *Dean's Story*, 29.

1st Lt. CHARLES PAYNE
1st Battalion/34th Infantry
By first daylight my little knoll was covered with dead, dying, and wounded. My men were dead and I was alone. The battalion area to my rear was quiet. I figured they, too, had been overrun. I knew, though, that our battalion position was not at the point of the enemy wedge and that just possibly, if I could stay alive, I might be able to sideslip through the left flank and make my way out of the trap.

With the sun up full I sat on the hill, half-dressed, foaming at the mouth. By pretending insanity, I felt I might escape. Many, many North Koreans looked at me as they hurried past, most shying away, none taking the time to kill me. One tore off my dog tag and several others spat on me.

When I felt the main body had passed, I staggered back through what had been our battalion's lines and its CP. I saw many dead friends, some of whom had been killed while they lay on stretchers. With the help of a one-over-one-million map and a compass, I could see how to possibly make my way to a mountainous area south of Taejon.

Maj. Gen. WILLIAM F. DEAN
Commanding General, 24th Division
I remember especially the hour of 6:30. It was then Lieutenant Clarke relayed a report that North Korean tanks had been seen in Taejon itself, although the battle line was still presumed to be well north and west.

This was the sort of report with which the whole division was thoroughly familiar by this time—and of which every man in it was deathly sick.*

Sgt. F/C HERSHEL ANDERSON
Medical Company/34th Infantry
At dawn an enemy tank pulled up about 100 yards in front of the collecting station. I alerted everyone of its presence. Captain Thomp-

---

* *Dean's Story*, 30.

son saw it and said, "It's one of ours." About that time they raked the building we were set up in with machine-gun fire. I said, "Must be some crazy Americans in that tank." Then the tank fired several cannon rounds that smashed the collecting station. Captain Thompson was wounded and a man lying on a stretcher was killed.

Maj. WADE HERITAGE, M.D.
Headquarters/24th Division
In Yongdong communication with the front was bad. Having no idea of the medical situation a few miles north in Taejon, I received permission to go there and inspect the clearing platoon. After picking up my jeep driver and Capt. Isador Yeager, a new medical officer who was trying to reach his unit, sometime after first light on July 20 I set off for Taejon.

There were no problems on the road that morning until we arrived on the outskirts of the town. Near the viaduct, where the road turned left, we suddenly heard a tremendous explosion. A large billowy black cloud rose from the area of the railroad station. We watched it for a while, then, when nothing more happened, moved on.

Crossing under the viaduct we took the road into Taejon. Glancing up at a two-story building in the town, we saw a civilian aiming a rifle at us. Before he had a chance to shoot, Captain Yeager and I fired at him with our carbines and my driver with his .45 automatic. The man fell back out of sight. As the way appeared to be clear again, we continued through the streets of Taejon, and soon arrived at the division CP. Although there was the sound of distant gunfire north of the town and the column of smoke continued to rise from the direction of the station, the town seemed quiet. Most of the headquarters personnel were gathered outside the building and appeared to have set up a defensive perimeter around the CP. When I attempted to call the clearing platoon, I found the line dead. At this point Captain Yeager went off to find his unit.

Back in our jeep my driver and I headed for the school building, about a mile distant, where I expected to locate the platoon. As we turned onto one street, we almost ran up the back of a T34 tank. Fortunately, he didn't see us. Quickly backing out of the street, I decided this was not the time to visit the clearing platoon.

Cpl. THERMAN COSSAIRT, JR.
B Battery/11th Field Artillery Battalion
We set up on street corners, fired our 155s point-blank at the North
Korean tanks. The day was very hot and dusty. We would receive
mission and march orders at the same time. We'd fire into some tanks,
then move and set up again two or three blocks away. We did this
most of the day.

Maj. Gen. WILLIAM F. DEAN
Commanding General, 24th Division
I do remember that after a time we went tank hunting once more,
and this time located both a weapon and two more enemy tanks. The
weapon was a bazooka, for which the soldier carrying it had just one
remaining round of ammunition. The two tanks were on the same
street as the two dead tanks [destroyed earlier in the day], and behind
the ammunition carrier, which still was burning. Our first attempt to
get close to them ended abruptly when we began to receive machine-
gun fire just over our heads, apparently coming from the turrets. We
scuttled out of the line of fire and came up again from behind the
buildings along the side of the street. This time smoke from the burning trailer and the protection of ruined buildings enabled us to get
within ten or fifteen yards of the street, well behind the tanks. Just as
we did, one of the live tanks managed to turn around in the narrow
street and started back the way it had come into the town, and the
other followed.

This was our day for bad shooting. The bazooka man too was
nervous. His one round was fired at a range of a hundred yards but
fell far short. The last tank rumbled right up to us and on past, within
twenty yards.

There was nothing we could do to stop it. Some people who escaped from Taejon that day reported they last had seen me firing a
pistol at a tank. Well, they did, but I'm not proud of it. As that last
tank passed I banged away at it with a .45, but even then I wasn't
silly enough to think I could do anything with a pistol. It was plain
rage and frustration—just Dean losing his temper.*

* *Dean's Story*, 31–32.

Maj. WADE HERITAGE, M.D.
Headquarters/24th Division
Sometime after noon headquarters advised me to return to Yongdong. I proceeded back down the main street until I found a small
convoy of parked jeeps and three-quarter-ton trucks under the command of Colonel Beauchamp, the 34th Infantry's commander. He
told me I was welcome to join their convoy, which was going to move
back to a new position south of the town.

Driving out of town, after Colonel Beauchamp's vehicle and another had passed under the viaduct, the convoy came under small-
arms fire. We jumped out of our vehicles and scurried behind a row
of houses. From there we determined that a North Korean machine
gun was in one of the buildings across the road from us. Two GIs
ran across the road and crept up to the house that held the enemy
gun. They heaved a couple of grenades through a window and the
enemy gun stopped firing. We mounted up again and the convoy sped
off.

1st Lt. CHARLES PAYNE
1st Battalion/34th Infantry
By late afternoon, before darkness, anyway, I had managed to get beyond Taejon. Soon I came upon Colonel [Harold B.] Ayres, my battalion CO, and General Dean. We were on a small hill, a little south
of the town. From there I could watch the final destruction of our
troops in Taejon. It was like a huge, terrible movie. Medical-aid vehicles just moved from place to place. They couldn't stop and set up,
and with the main highway now under heavy fire, they were unable
to leave the town.

General Dean told us he was going back to Taejon. Colonel Ayres
and I volunteered to go with him. He allowed Ayres to go with him.
The colonel then told me to take the thirty or forty walking wounded
who had collected in the area and with them try to make my way
south. Colonel Ayres thought we just might make it back to the 1st
Cav's lines, which were supposed to be somewhere behind us. Then
we shook hands and Colonel Ayres, General Dean, and a small group
of staff officers headed for the road.

Sgt. F/C HERSHEL ANDERSON
Medical Company/34th Infantry

During all the fighting no one could find anyone in charge. General Dean had taken some men and the large bazooka [3.5-inch rocket launcher] and was out chasing tanks and no one could find Colonel Beauchamp. The town was on fire. In all directions I could see enemy troops moving in columns on the hills around the town. The captain wanted me to take a jeep and find the regimental CP and get some orders, but no one knew where the CP was or if there still was one.

Maj. Gen. WILLIAM F. DEAN
Commanding General, 24th Division

This was a day in which I had no sense of time. Time got lost. Although I hardly had been conscious of any lapse of hours since early morning, it was almost evening when we came back to the command post for the last time.*

[*Hundreds of North Korean soldiers dressed in the traditional white clothing worn by Korean civilians infiltrated the city. Snipers began appearing everywhere. Black smoke blown by a hot wind drifted through the town. Around five o'clock in the afternoon, obviously surrounded, General Dean ordered Taejon evacuated.*]

Pfc. ROBERT HARPER
Headquarters Company/34th Infantry

Some officers asked for volunteers to find a way out of town. David R. Young (whom we called D. R.), Joe C. Young (known as J. C.), Bob Hardy, and I volunteered. We were given a jeep and told if we found a way out of town that was not under fire we should return to the CP and tell the others. The idea was to go down to the main

---

* *Dean's Story,* 35–36.

intersection, then go either east or west and see which route out of town was best.

When we arrived at the crossroads, we decided to turn left (which was west). We traveled down a narrow road flanked on either side by two-story buildings. We went about half a mile, made a few turns, and did not draw any small-arms fire—didn't see anyone, either. We turned another corner. Half a block away, sitting in the middle of the road, was an enemy tank! J. C., who was driving, hit the brake and all hell broke loose. We all jumped from the jeep. I dashed to the side of a building. The tank was evidently disabled because it didn't move in our direction, but underneath it the North Koreans had set up a machine gun. This gun opened fire on us. We also began drawing rifle fire from some of the two-story buildings around us. I looked for a door to dive through. Back on the street D. R. and J. C. were standing by the jeep shooting at some second-story windows. Where Hardy was, I have no idea. I'd run to the right side of the road so perhaps Hardy had run to the left side. I screamed to the two Youngs to get away from the jeep. I couldn't move. When I tried to, I drew heavy fire. The Youngs remained in the road by the jeep. Sitting here in 1985 I can close my eyes and visualize perfectly what happened that day in Taejon. I can feel my heart beginning to pound. Hard to explain my feelings. Unless you were in Taejon and saw what was happening it would be difficult to understand the emotions.

I finally moved behind some buildings. I left D. R. and J. C. by the jeep and to this day have never seen them again and don't know if they made it off the road. Same with Hardy. I knew I couldn't get back to regimental headquarters; it was too far away now. There was still a lot of shooting coming from the road where I'd left the Youngs. I hoped I'd run into some other GIs and with them find a way out of town. I moved down a road and went through some buildings. I saw a small group of about eight Americans down near a schoolhouse. I hollered and they stopped and waited for me. I told them what had happened and asked if they'd return with me and help the Youngs. They said most likely if we went back we'd be trapped and wouldn't get out of town. There was an officer in the group. They also had with them a man who'd been wounded in the leg. The lieutenant said the best thing for us was to get out of town and make for the mountains. Since he said he had a general idea of the way to go, we decided to follow him.

The plan we followed was to move slowly along side streets until we got to the outskirts of Taejon. We took turns carrying the wounded man. Once through the town, we worked our way up the slope of a hill that led to some high ground. Behind me I could still hear a lot of firing. Up on the hill I looked back down at Taejon and saw it was on fire.

Capt. FRANK THOMPSON, JR.
Medical Company/34th Infantry
Large sections of the city were burning as we moved through. Wires were down and the streets covered with debris, but the convoy smashed its way through. One street was strewn with hand grenades, which were cleared with no casualties. The battalions had begun withdrawing through and around the city. We moved out with three ambulances loaded with wounded.

Once clear of Taejon, the convoy began to receive automatic-weapons fire from the hillsides. It was a matter of running a gauntlet of fire for about three miles. That any vehicles came through seemed unbelievable. The entire valley was under a pall of dust and smoke from burning trucks. Gasoline blazed, ammunition blasted, and tracers laced through the convoy, but the road was cleared again and again and the line continued to move.

Cpl. LACY BARNETT
Medical Company/34th Infantry
The day was hot and the roads were dry. The first vehicles created so much dust that the drivers of the other vehicles had virtually zero visibility. Once the convoy was under way, many vehicles were hit and wrecked. Disabled vehicles had to be pushed off the road so those behind could pass. Some of the wounded and injured on the wrecked vehicles were picked up and placed on other vehicles, but pretty arbitrarily. By this time the attitude of "every man for himself" prevailed.

My best friend, Cpl. Russell Talley, was riding in a three-quarter-ton truck in this "suicide" run. After the convoy left Taejon, the driver of Talley's truck was hit by rifle fire and wrecked the vehicle. The truck overturned, pinning three men, including Russell Talley, beneath it. The gasoline tank ruptured and Corporal Talley, who was lying directly under it, was soaked with raw gas. His entire body acted as a sponge. Although everyone knew there were three men trapped under the truck, some unknown authority decided, since it was too dangerous then to rescue the men, that they be left and, if possible, brought out at night.*

Sgt. DANIEL CAVANAUGH
Medical Company/34th Infantry
We were outmanned, outgunned, outtanked, and outflanked. They had roadblocks set up on all the roads leading out of Taejon. Myself and a few others were lucky enough to run the roadblocks in a vehicle. We shot our way out! The first vehicle I was in was a jeep, but it ran off the road and I ended up in a ditch. Next I managed to get on a three-quarter-ton truck which carried plenty of M1s, carbines, and ammo. There were eight men on it when we started out. Before we drove out of Taejon, it carried about fifteen. On our way down the road, we kept shooting in all directions, at buildings, small houses, abandoned vehicles. The whole town was on fire. But the smoke made it more difficult for the North Koreans to see, and I believe that helped us a lot. The whole time I could hear bullets hitting and snapping around me.

Outside Taejon there were two North Koreans by the side of the road operating a machine gun. It looked like they were having trouble with it; it was probably jammed. I let go with a couple of rounds from my M1 [rifle]. I'm not sure I hit either one.

We raced south for about twelve miles. Then, pulling off the side of the road, we waited to see if anyone else had been as lucky as we'd been. Shortly after dark some vehicles with their lights on came down the road. No one was sure if they were our people or North

---

* After dark a group of GIs returned to the overturned truck and rescued the three men. Corporal Talley was later evacuated to Fukuoka, Japan, where he died on 27 July 1950.

Koreans. When they got close enough I called out to them to halt. They yelled back for me not to shoot. Approximately five vehicles drove up. There were plenty of wounded on the jeeps and in the trucks. We didn't stay long in that area but took off at once for Pusan.

Maj. Gen. WILLIAM F. DEAN
Commanding General, 24th Division
Just about dusk, light tanks from the 1st Cavalry Division, on temporary assignment to us, came up from the rear and we organized a column of vehicles—the first of the regimental headquarters—to start out under their protection. But only moments after they left the schoolhouse, we heard them in a firefight near the center of town.

Shortly afterward Pappy Wadlington* suggested that it was time for us to go too. He showed me a last message he proposed to send to division headquarters, but I rewrote it because I thought it sounded, in his version, too much like asking rescue for me personally. As a substitute I wrote, "Enemy roadblock eastern exit Taejon. Send armor immediately. Dean."

In Europe I had ordered a lot of stations closed, without minding. This time I minded. If I had realized that this was the last formal order I was to issue for three years, perhaps I might have phrased it better—one of those ringing things that somebody would remember. But I didn't know then, and now I can't think of anything better to have said.

We organized the remaining miscellaneous headquarters vehicles into a rough column and started out toward the east, the way the previous column had gone with the tanks. As we pulled through the city we ran into the tail of this column, which had been ambushed. Some trucks were on fire, others slewed across a narrow street where buildings on both sides were flaming for a block or more. Our own infantry, on one side of the street, was in a vicious firefight with enemy units in higher positions on the other side.

We drove through, careening between the stalled trucks. It was a solid line of fire, an inferno that seared us in spite of our speed. A

---

* Lt. Col. Robert L. Wadlington was the 34th Infantry Regiment's executive officer.

block farther on my jeep and an escort jeep roared straight past an intersection, and almost immediately Clarke, riding with me, said we had missed a turn. But rifle fire still poured from buildings on both sides, and turning around was out of the question. I looked at a map and decided we should go on ahead, south and east, on another road that might let us make more speed than the truck-jammed main escape route. I had been away from my headquarters too long, and had to get back very soon. So we bored down the road in the general direction of Kumsan, while snipers still chewed at us from both sides of the road.

We were all by ourselves.*

July 20

U.S. Forces withdrew from Taejon at midnight and retreated to a position four miles southeast of the city. General MacArthur said that the loss of Taejon would have no psychological repercussions for the Koreans, and that the city had no special significance.

DEPARTMENT OF STATE CHRONOLOGY

[Seventeen days of sustained, bitter combat had cost the 24th Division nearly 30 percent of its personnel, of which an unusually high portion had been officers. More than 2,400 of its men had been reported missing in action. Relentless North Korean pressure had driven it back 100 miles from where Task Force Smith first faced the enemy north of Osan. Charged with the mission of delaying the Communists, the division had held the enemy on its front to an average gain of about six miles a day. They hadn't covered themselves in glory, but in the two battles being fought in Korea, one for ground and one for time, the men of the 24th Division had come out with no worse than a draw.

As serious a loss as Taejon was for General Walker's Eighth Army, the war now began to take a new turn. No longer would the 24th

---

*Dean's Story, 38–39. General Dean was captured by the North Koreans on 25 August 1950, and spent three years as a POW. He was repatriated to American officials at Panmunjom on 4 September 1953. For his part in the battle of Taejon General Dean was awarded the Medal of Honor.

Division have to stand alone. Two new divisions had arrived in Korea and were already on line. The 25th moved into the mountains of central Korea east of Taejon. There, they were to bolster ROK forces already in the area and prevent a major enemy column from advancing into the valley of the upper Naktong.

The 1st Cavalry Division had also arrived, and by 22 July was in a blocking position across the main Taejon-Taegu corridor. A week earlier the division had been rushed aboard a convoy hastily made up of British and American ships. A possible amphibious landing in the enemy's rear had been considered, but the crisis around Taejon forced General Walker's hand and he had to commit the division sooner than he wished.]

12 July 1950

The regiment loaded on trucks at 0830 and was driven to Yo-kosuka Naval Base. As Heavy Mortar Company was the last to load on the USS *Cavalier* some men were forced to sleep on deck [14 July]. As the ventilation system on the *Cavalier* was very poor this proved to be a pleasure instead of a hardship. Everyone expected information to be passed out. A short briefing was held, but generally the information as to troop strength, disposition, weapons, and enemy fighting tactics was very vague.

After an uneventful . . . boat ride, a landing was made at Pohang-dong [18 July]. Afterward the regiment assembled and was moved by motor into an assembly area.

5TH CAVALRY REGIMENT JOURNAL

1st Lt. HENRY GOGUN
Pioneer & Ammunition Platoon
1st Battalion/5th Cavalry

The first night we bivouacked in some fields. Before nightfall many curious Korean civilians were mingling in our lines. This could have compromised our security if some North Koreans had been among them but, thankfully, none were.

That night some young trooper got jittery and fired his rifle. The nervousness spread and in no time a terrific one-sided battle was in progress. Having been in the Philippines in World War II, I recognized the problem—early combat jitters. There was an interesting by-product from this event; the next day the Korean civilian population stayed a safe distance from us.

We boarded a train and were sent to reinforce the 24th Division, which was having a bad time at Taejon. As we went forward, we passed many men of that division going in the opposite direction in what appeared to be a disorganized withdrawal. The 5th Cav traveled as far as Yongdong. Here the regiment got into its first firefight. The most common remark from the rifle company casualties was, "We stacked them up like cordwood, but they still kept coming."

We held the enemy for a day or so before moving [25 July] to a new line east of Yongdong. Then we made another strategic withdrawal, this time to Hwanggan. There things became a little bit more exciting. One morning, when the unit ahead of us moved back and somebody didn't get the word to us to display our air identification panels, we were attacked by a flight of twin-Mustangs that thought we were the enemy. I can tell you, being on the receiving end of multiple .50-caliber machine-gun fire wakes you up real fast. Luckily no one was hit, although I suspect that many underdrawers had to be changed.

This unfortunate event had an interesting result. The North Koreans, seeing our planes strafing the position, concluded that, like the outfit ahead of us, we, too, had pulled out. Without any preparation, therefore, they started up the hill, walking out in the open and in groups. We gave *them* a surprise! A North Korean lieutenant we captured told us how surprised he had been to find the hill still occupied.

When the pressure got to be too much, our regiment again pulled back. We thought we'd let the North Koreans know we weren't "bugging out." Before we left the position, we emptied all the sandbags and took them with us to use another time.

Sgt. ED HENDRICKS
F Company/5th Cavalry
The company was full of raw replacements, young kids, same as I'd
been in World War II.

Fox Company walked south. I lost a lot of kids—snipers, mortars, artillery. By the time we got to Taegu, everybody was either
withdrawing, in the hands of the medics, or dead.

Taegu had been bombed and shelled and was on fire. There was
no transportation for us. Trucks were full up bringing back the dead.

*[The 1st Cavalry Division and the 25th Infantry Division, harassed
by infiltrators, outflanked and outmanned, went on withdrawing, retreating, or realigning their lines. Whatever it was called, the results
were the same, and Eighth Army's defensive perimeter continued to be
whittled down; its lines slowly, inexorably moved toward the small corner
in southeast Korea that held the UN's only major port, Pusan. Taejon, Yongdong, Hwanggan, Chirye, Kumch'on, and Sangju fell to the
enemy. Town by town, hill by hill, each day the front moved a little
farther south and east. Eight North Korean divisions rolled forward;
four more crossed the 38th Parallel and moved south.*

*As July drew to a close, the monsoon rains suddenly ended and
were replaced with daylong scorching heat and countrywide drought.*

Two days after the shattered 24th Division was driven from
Taejon, it had been relieved by the 1st Cavalry Division. But war,
like death, isn't always as tidy as a neatly typed order, as the men in
the division's battle-stunned units would soon learn. After Taejon, a
North Korean division had audaciously swung wide in the west and
was threatening Eighth Army's left flank and rear. General Walker
reacted immediately to this desperate situation. With no other reserve
to draw upon, he again called for the 24th Division. After only one
day in Army reserve, with no time to regroup or refit, the division (minus the 21st Infantry) was hastily sent southward and ordered to stop
the enemy from completing its planned envelopment. The 19th Infantry moved to Chinju, the 34th to Koch'ang. By 27 July they were dug*

---

* Now commanded by General Church.

in a few miles in front of the country's last natural barrier before the sea, the Naktong River. As it had throughout all of July, the division waited one more time for the North Koreans to attack.]

Pfc. LEONARD KORGIE
L Company/34th Infantry
I don't think the 34th Infantry had too many officers left after Taejon. Guys like me just moved with a bunch. I recall only three officers around during this time; the rest were lost at Taejon. The rifle company I joined as a replacement had lost most of its men in the battle.*

My group of replacements was assigned to the 34th Infantry. In Pusan we were put on a train and carried toward the fighting.† We'd go five miles forward, then five miles backward. In the morning a hospital train going south stopped alongside. There were wounded GIs lying in bunks one on top of the other. Some faces were covered with blankets. The ambulatory guys were thin and terror-stricken. Seats of their pants were soiled. "Casualties from Taejon," we were told.

Somewhere else along this endless trip to the front we slowly passed a train with flatcars which carried some battered unit back toward Pusan. These GIs, too, were dirty, worn out. They looked like hell. Didn't talk much. When they found we weren't carrying any ammo, they gave us some clips.

Eventually our train stopped somewhere north of Taegu and, as the sun had gone down, we loaded on trucks in the dark. An hour later we pulled up alongside a hill. Quiet as a tomb. We climbed out. No one knew this was the front line. No orientation, no news, one clip of ammo—what a screwed-up mess.

A young second lieutenant carrying a light came out of somewhere. He told us he was the CO of L Company, 34th Infantry Regiment, and, God, was he happy to see us! He was so humble, beat

---

*L Company, 34th Infantry, the regiment's rear guard, reported 107 casualties out of 153 men after Taejon.

†The 34th Infantry defended the Koch'ang approach to the Naktong and was in position on 27 July. The 3d Battalion, on line with approximately 350 men, occupied high ground across the Anui road two miles west of the town.

down, pathetic-looking. I thought he'd kiss each of us. On the hill
he showed us where to dig our holes. We dug like hell. I still carried
the duffel bag that held my dress summer khakis. A victory parade in
Seoul seemed a long way away that night.

An L Company regular by the name of Sergeant Parsons came
up and gave us the lowdown on Taejon, then what we might face in
the morning. He was a kid about nineteen but looked older. He'd
made it out of Taejon driving a jeep. The gooks, he told us, were
probably going to hit us in the morning. I liked Parsons. He was kind
of excitable but, if it hadn't been for him, we replacements wouldn't
have known anything. I would feel bad in early September when I
heard he'd taken a direct artillery hit at P'ohang.

What Parsons told us wasn't much, but it was something. We
knew now there was nothing on our left, nothing on our right, we
were dug in in a semicircle on a hill and there was a road down below on which, at that very moment, he advised, the North Koreans
were probably advancing toward us.

No one slept much. Throughout the long night a .50-caliber
machine gun firing tracers sporadically raked the hill opposite. At
daybreak the second lieutenant and two other guys went out on patrol. They never came back. All that day I never saw another officer.
A few old grizzly sergeants went around yelling at us. The morning
was clear and cool. I ate a ration of beans and hot dogs.

Looking around in the sunlight I saw we were right out in the
open. We didn't know any better. Nobody corrected our position and
nobody seemed to care. We had about 100 men who were dug in on
the forward slope of this hill. I looked across the valley and, God,
there on the opposite slope, just like in *Macbeth*, hundreds of small
trees were moving! This was no optical illusion. Our guys opened fire.
Then the NKs began firing back. It was like being in a deadly hailstorm. The gooks were trying to close in on us, to get in under our
artillery, which hadn't fired yet, and our planes, which never showed
at all that day.

Some gooks behind us opened fire. Four or five GIs went back
and knocked that position out. The firefight went on hard and heavy
all day. Some kid ran up showing me a hole he had in his hand. He
carried that hand in the air like a trophy—it was a million-dollar baby.

The afternoon heat was terrible. The NKs came up the slope.

Their fire was heavy. A lot of guys didn't know what to do. Some started taking off to God knows where. Some came back. A hut out on one of the flanks seemed to move toward us. A bazooka team laid a round into it and everything blew to pieces.

Just before the NKs got into position on the slope to rush us, our artillery finally opened up. The artillery fire, in order to hit the downward slope to our front, just barely cleared the ridgeline. Some rounds fell nearby. White phosphorus exploded around me. I ducked into my hole and didn't get any. I don't know about others.

Our guys began getting disorganized and panicky—were we going to stay here and hold, or leave? Some guys took it upon themselves to give the word to go—and some left. The old sergeants ran around yelling and giving orders. It got real confusing. With Taejon in mind, nobody wanted to be left behind. Who was in command? What was an official command? This was not war the way I'd read about it or been trained in it. Certainly this wasn't maneuvers. I didn't know what would happen to our wounded or dead if we left. The feeling was that no one was accountable to anyone. It looked like it was going to be every man for himself, and when the time came, make sure you got your ass out in one piece.

Sometime during the afternoon [29 July] the whole unit pulled out and headed for the road. Everyone fired as he moved. A bazooka team tried to knock out a small bridge to our front. The projectile bounced off the structure like it was a rubber ball. Strangely, the enemy lifted their fire when we hit the road. I wondered if this was the Asian thing of letting a beaten enemy "save face"?

A couple of hours later, a few miles away, we climbed another hill and dug in again for another night.* I saw one officer and remembered him later only because he became our company commander. We dug in closer together, but still on the forward slope of the hill. Why couldn't they have had us dig in on the ridge or behind it so we would have had some cover? We were too tired to care then. When you're thrown to the slaughter, when you figure out you're only

---

*The 34th Infantry withdrew eastward fifteen miles to hill positions near Sanje-ri on the road to Hyopch'on.

there to slow the enemy down until another unit gets into a better position, who really gives a shit!

About 11:00 P.M. we were dug in. Nobody had given us anything to eat or drink all day. Thirst consumed us. Nevertheless, as soon as our holes were dug, we crawled into them and fell fast asleep. Some time later I was awakened by screams! Next to me, three North Koreans were jabbing their bayonets into a foxhole. The guy with me and I fired into them. They scattered or dropped, I can't remember which any longer. One of the GIs in the hole died, the other had his shoulder torn up. Everyone tried to stay awake then. I had a helluva time trying to keep my eyes open. I began to see figures floating toward me. I opened fire. They went away. I saw them again. I held my fire. Sure as hell, they disappeared again. To this day I swear they were real. I was too beat to know for sure.

At daylight [30 July] we began taking small-arms fire. People dressed in white—civilians being driven in front of the enemy or North Koreans dressed as civilians—appeared on the opposite hill, hundreds of them. They came down the hill and into the valley heading straight for us. Our officers didn't know what to tell us. The incoming fire picked up and was by now very heavy. No one waited for instructions. We opened fire and poured it back. The white-clad figures kept coming.

Zoooom! Three P-51 Mustangs flew close over our heads and opened fire with machine guns and rockets. Before one returned for another strafing run, he dropped his auxiliary fuel tank on our lines. I didn't know what he was doing, thought he was bombing us. I swore at him.

As soon as the planes flew away to put out another fire somewhere else, the NKs hit us again. We fought on and off all day. The enemy used knee mortars. They dropped those shells on us like raindrops. They weren't big, sounded like six-inch firecrackers, but if they hit in a hole they'd do a job. I saw one kid who had his stomach laid open as if a surgeon had done the job. Nothing inside was torn up. The medics flopped the skin back over the hole and sent him out on a stretcher.

The front-line medics were superb. When someone got hit, even if he was probably finished, the medics would go down to him. God,

they were brave! Legends are made of this kind of stuff. Every medic
that day should have received a medal for valor. Unfortunately, only
in nice, tidy actions does anyone have time to write someone up for
a medal. That day the action was chaotic and I'm sure no one remembered who did what for whom when. Many medics went down
that day and were never recognized for their extraordinary bravery.
What a shame, especially when afterward I saw people get medals
who didn't do one-tenth of what these medics had done. I remember
one in particular, a heavyset kid, don't even know what unit he belonged to. A guy got hit on the slope below me. The fire was very
heavy. This GI kept yelling for help. The medic jumped out of his
hole. We yelled to him to get back, that he'd never make it. We tried
to cover him. He died on the way down the hill. Damn!

On this day the heat was unbearable. It just steamed in on us.
No wind, humid, exposed to the sun, very little water, no salt pills,
guys began collapsing. I took my helmet off. The rim of the liner had
trapped my sweat, the water poured down my face. Someone located
a creek across the road. Without orders, guys ran down to get water.
No one cared if the North Koreans had a machine gun zeroed in on
the road we had to cross. We ran the gauntlet. Anything for water.
Anything to relieve the heat of the open oven we were in.

When the fire on our flanks got real bad, we pulled out again.
Only our rear was open. One big kid—he'd been a cook with us in
Japan—very overweight and out of shape, but a nice guy, collapsed.
We were told to leave him behind and all the others who couldn't
make it out by themselves. Someone felt we couldn't get them and
us out at the same time. Two months later, in September, we marched
back past this position. What a funny feeling. We were heading north,
chewing the North Koreans up. We stopped for a few minutes below
this hill. Why, I don't know. Graves Registration people were collecting the bodies we'd left behind in July. What I could see made it
look as if these bodies were made of coal. They were just pitch-black.

On the road in July, pulling back again from another blocking
position, it was exactly like the day before, except now I was more
tired and miserable than I'd been twenty-four hours earlier. I don't
know what the official Army history says about us at this time, but
I'm sure those who later recorded these events weren't around to witness the mess. We dragged along to the next position a few miles far-

ther south. Guys, sweat soaked, shitting in their pants, not even dropping them, moved like zombies. You can't think when you're as fatigued as we were. I just sensed we were going to find another hill and be attacked, then find another hill and so forth, endlessly, forever. Where was it going to end? Weren't there any other GIs in this Army?

On the new hill an officer I'd never seen before ate a box of C rations. Then all hell broke loose. The North Koreans hit us with self-propelled guns. I fantasized an air strike, not on the enemy, but on me. I was about done. As soon as the barrage lifted, the word went around, "We're pulling out!" I can't remember much after that. I imagine we were close to the Naktong. I faintly remember 1st Cavalry guys waiting by the road as we crossed the river; maybe by then we were in trucks. *

[Eighth Army units began an orderly withdrawal across the Naktong on 2 August. It proceeded smoothly and by the next day General Walker's forces were redeployed to the main defensive positions of the Pusan Perimeter.]

Sgt. ROBERT DEWS
Headquarters Company/34th Infantry
When the retreating Americans burst over the last hill and looked down on the muddy, swirling, wide, shallow river, an amazing sight met their eyes. Thousands of refugees were being led out of the mountains and hills to a bridge that was still standing and guarded by a semicircle of Patton tanks and dug-in half-tracks. The 24th Division MPs were herding the refugees across—this was the last bridge in our sector left on the Naktong. For days the South Korean police, the interpreters, Psychological Warfare boys with their loudspeakers on jeeps, planes, and tanks had been advising the South Koreans to leave their hiding places and go across the river with the Americans. They came in droves.

I crossed with the paratroopers. The last of the refugees were being

---

* The 34th Infantry crossed the Naktong in the area of Yongsan on the morning of 2 August.

pushed across. Some engineer boats would remain a little while for
stragglers, the old, the sick, and the lame, and would bring them across
to safety. The tanks and half-tracks would pull across the bridge and
take their places in the great line to the south that was still forming
and digging in for the mighty assault of the Red Army that was bound
to come.

At 10:00 P.M. came the mighty roar and the geysers of smoke,
water, cement blocks, and steel. The 24th Division engineers had
blown the bridge [2 August].

[As July 1950 passed into history, the North Koreans could look back
on a month of spectacular gains and dramatic victories. August promised to be better. With a stranglehold on the peninsula's southeastern
extremity, the Communists were, in places, no more than thirty miles
from Pusan and were in position to drive directly on it.

East of the Naktong, determination ran high along the thinly held
rim of the Eighth Army's defensive perimeter. Up and down the line
there was a feeling that the Americans had not withdrawn this time
to withdraw again. Round one of the Korean War was over. Round
two was about to begin.]

Lt. Gen. WALTON H. WALKER
Commanding General, Eighth Army
General MacArthur was over here two days ago; he is thoroughly
conversant with the situation. He knows where we are and what we
have to fight with. He knows our needs and where the enemy is hitting the hardest. General MacArthur is doing everything possible to
send reinforcements. A Marine unit and two regiments are expected
in the next few days to reinforce us. Additional units are being sent
over as quickly as possible. We are fighting a battle against time. There
will be no retreating, withdrawal, or readjustment of the lines or any
other term you choose. There is no line behind us to which we can
retreat. Every unit must counterattack to keep the enemy in a state
of confusion and off balance. There will be no Dunkirk, there will
be no Bataan, a retreat to Pusan would be one of the greatest butch-
eries in history. We must fight until the end. Capture by these people
is worse than death itself. We will fight as a team. If some of us must

die, we will die fighting together. Any man who gives ground may be personally responsible for the death of thousands of his comrades.

I want you to put this out to all the men in the division. I want everybody to understand that we are going to hold this line. We are going to win.*

Sgt. C. W. ''BILL'' MENNINGER
3d Battalion/34th Infantry
When the order came down from General Walker, "We will not retreat another foot; we will fight to the death," an old sergeant rolled his eyes and said, "Fight to the death? What does he think we've been doing for a month!"

---

* Address to 25th Division Staff, 29 July 1950.

PUSAN

---

3 August-15 August 1950

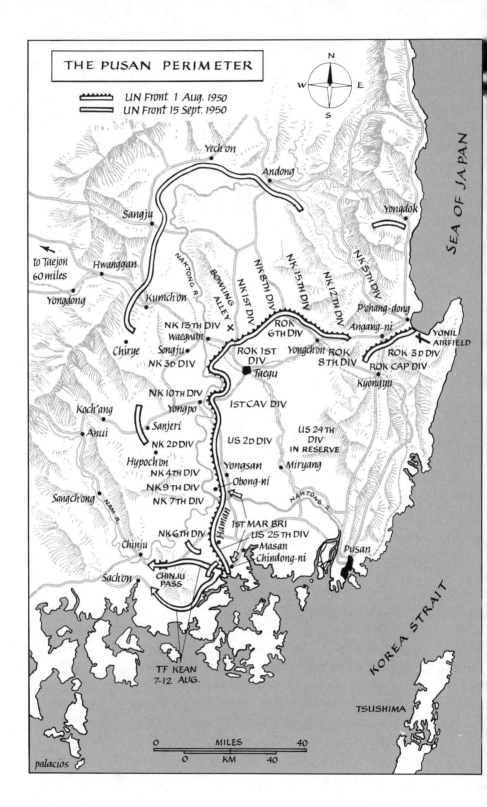

THE PUSAN PERIMETER

UN Front 1 Aug. 1950
UN Front 15 Sept. 1950

SEA OF JAPAN

Yech'on
Andong
Sangju
Yongdok
to Taejon 60 miles
Hwanggan
Yongdong
Kumch'on
NAKTONG R.
BOWLING ALLEY
NK 1ST DIV
NK 8TH DIV
NK 15TH DIV
NK 12TH DIV
NK 5TH DIV
P'ohang-dong
NK 13TH DIV
Waegwan
ROK 6TH DIV
Angang-ni
YONIL AIRFIELD
Chirye
Songju
NK 3D DIV
ROK 1ST DIV
Yongch'on
ROK 8TH DIV
ROK 3D DIV
ROK CAP DIV
Taegu
Kyongju
Koch'ang
NK 10TH DIV
Yongpo
1ST CAV DIV
Anui
Sanjeri
NK 2D DIV
US 2D DIV
US 24TH DIV IN RESERVE
Hypoch'on
NK 4TH DIV
Yongsan
Miryang
Sangch'ong
NK 9TH DIV
NK 7TH DIV
Obong-ni
NAKTONG R.
NAM R.
Haman
1ST MAR BRI
US 25TH DIV
Chinju
NK 6TH DIV
Masan
Chindong-ni
Pusan
Sach'on
CHINJU PASS
TF KEAN 7-12 AUG.
KOREA STRAIT
TSUSHIMA
palacios

0 MILES 40
0 KM 40

Pfc. LEONARD KORGIE
L Company/34th Infantry

When we drove into the Pusan Perimeter, you never in your life saw a more beat-up bunch of soldiers. God, were we tired. We had had no rest or letup anywhere on the road. The gooks had kept on our tails. The heat was atrocious. All I wanted to do now was drink water, any kind, anywhere I could find it. Rice-paddy water caused searing and bloody dysentery.

Inside the Perimeter the company stopped by an apple orchard and dropped in place. No one unhooked his gear. I collapsed with head resting inside my helmet. I don't remember moving until the next day.

About noon we received some rations and six cans of hot Pabst beer. I took a deep swig but couldn't drink more. The guys were very quiet. They realized what they'd been through and that much more was coming. Many faces that I'd known were missing. I thought of the days to come. The gooks had hellish numbers and equipment. We were very, very thin in both.

[By 4 August General Walker's Eighth Army and the ROK divisions had successfully withdrawn to a small toehold in South Korea that became known as the Pusan Perimeter. It might not have been everything General MacArthur wanted, but now, at least, his paper-thin *defenses were behind natural barriers, were in a continuous line, and had flanks that were firmly anchored on the sea.*

The Pusan Perimeter was about 50 by 90 miles and enclosed a rectangular area of 200 miles. The Sea of Japan formed the eastern boundary, the Korea Strait the southern boundary. The wide, deep Naktong River, which flows south, marked the Perimeter's western barrier; high, rugged mountains that run above Waegwan to Yongdok defined the northern line. ROK divisions held the northern, mountainous half of the Perimeter; Eighth Army held the front along the Naktong River.

A prolonged struggle for control of the Perimeter would last through mid-September. It developed as a series of bitter clashes, which, at one time or another, would be fought along the entire front. For General Walker, these battles could only be hand-to-mouth affairs as an inferiority in manpower once again forced him into a scheme of patchwork defensive tactics. But August would not be a replay of July. The Perimeter offered definite advantages that Walker would use wisely and effectively. Because Eighth Army enjoyed interior lines of communication, superior mobility, and control of the air, its units could be moved quickly. The craft would come in pulling a unit out of a quiet sector and efficiently plugging it into a threatened one; the art would be in knowing when to make the switch and with what size force. In this game of robbing Peter to pay Paul, there could be no errors; if Walker moved one unit too soon or too late, the Perimeter could be breached and the war quickly lost.

On the other side of the Perimeter, the North Korean People's Army in early August probed, then paused and aligned nine combat-disciplined divisions. Undefeated in six weeks of cruel, punishing combat, it was eager to end the war.]

Comrades, the enemy is demoralized. The task given to us is the liberation of Masan and Chinju and the annihilation of the remnants of the enemy. We have liberated Mokpu, Kwingju, and Yosu and have thereby accelerated the liberation of all Korea. However, the liberation of Chinju and Masan means the final battle to cut off the windpipe of the enemy. Comrades, this glo-

rious task has fallen to our division! Men of the 6th Division, let
us annihilate the enemy and distinguish ourselves.

                                   NORTH KOREAN 6TH INFANTRY DIVISION

*[After the disasters of July, General Walker's troops were used up, dis-
couraged, and resentful. The strength of the American units had been
sharply reduced by sickness and casualties, and replacements, when
they did arrive, were often young and inexperienced.]*

2d Lt. RALPH HOCKLEY
C Battery/37th Field Artillery Battalion
I spent my first night in the Pusan Perimeter in an area known as the
Bowling Alley.* Two other FOs [forward observers] and I, having just
arrived in Korea with ROTC commissions, were assigned three hills.
Our battery and an infantry unit lay below in the valley. The night
did not go well.

   With me on the hill were my radio operator, an old sergeant
and his four seventeen-year-old infantrymen. They were there to guard
the hill. Connecting the FOs to each other and the battery were a
radio and a wire telephone known as a "hot loop."

   Obviously, I was not an experienced combat officer. Nevertheless, my heart was in it. I was convinced President Truman had done
the right thing and we belonged in Korea. Now here I was on the
front line. In front of me was the enemy.

   The weather was miserable; it was raining—hard.

   The night did not begin well. I spoke to my radio operator, a
very quiet American Indian Pfc. "Have you checked the radio?"

   "Sir, it's not working."

   "What do you mean, it's not working?"

   "It's not working. My radio is not working."

   "Why do you have it? I mean, why didn't you check it before
we got up here?"

---

* A stretch of the Taegu-Sangju road that runs in a straight line through a narrow river valley
in the northern sector of the Perimeter.

No answer. The rain fell in sheets. "Well, if the damn thing isn't working, you know, you're not going to be much help here. We gotta get you in a hole so you can defend this position if we're attacked. Why don't you dig yourself a foxhole?"

"Go fuck yourself, Lieutenant!" Quote, unquote.

In a matter of seconds, all my military education flashed through my mind. What does a lieutenant do when a private tells him to "go fuck himself"? I don't remember being taught that answer. The man's radio wasn't working, he was insubordinate, and he wasn't going to be much help if we were attacked. I sent him off the hill. "Tell the battery commander I'll talk to him about this later if he wants to know why I sent you back."

The sergeant with me was OK. He was fairly old, probably forty. He'd been a boxer but now was kind of boxed out and he drank quite a bit. The four infantrymen I'd met that day. They were very young. I don't believe I ever knew their names.

I peered through the night. The rain made everything darker. In front there were no targets that I could see. I only knew that to my front was a valley, then another hill and the enemy. It was a hell of a way to fight a war, but it was a beginning. Those early days on the Pusan Perimeter we were fighting just to survive.

In the middle of the night I realized the four infantrymen were sleeping. They must have needed their beauty rest. I gave the sergeant a mission. "Sergeant, if you don't do anything else this night, you'll keep those men awake. We can't defend the world by ourselves."

The rain fell steadily. I huddled in my field jacket, my .45 under my arm, my carbine somewhere. Suddenly, the phone rang. Riiiiiiing! This infuriated the hell out of me. If the North Koreans didn't know where I was before, they knew now. On the other end was a first lieutenant who had harassed us ROTC lieutenants from the day he'd met us. Speaking for the other two FOs, whose phones had also rung, I felt compelled to say, "Look, Lieutenant, you don't have to ring. You're giving our positions away. We're wearing the phones, just whistle or start talking." I received the following answer. "What's the matter, gentlemen? Don't tell me you're afraid! This is your career. You're Army officers. Combat is what you're in the Army for." To say the least, this individual was very obnoxious.

The rest of the night was strictly an infantry affair. About four o'clock, the bugles blew and the North Koreans came at us. I yelled to the kids, "Hey, they're charging. You guys better be there. We're gonna fight!" I leaned over the hill and looked down its forward slope. A few feet in front of me a North Korean appeared. He had a long rifle with a thin bayonet attached to it. I grabbed my carbine. Of course, as carbines go, this one acted normally. It didn't fire. It was soaking wet. It's nice to be told to keep it dry, but spend a night in the pouring rain and you tell me how to keep it dry. The North Korean did something with his rifle. I pulled my .45 from its shoulder holster. BANG! I shot and killed the guy. The infantrymen—the kids—and their old sergeant opened fire and stopped the enemy cold. Shortly afterward more American troops from the other side of the hill came up and drove the enemy off. Right then I learned something. I learned I didn't want to be in the infantry and have to fight for a living.

Cpl. LACY BARNETT
Medical Company/34th Infantry

The men of the 34th were weary, but those from the original group that had come over in the first days of July were not particularly bitter. General Walker issued an order that there would be no further withdrawals from the Naktong River line. This had no special meaning to us. We were convinced that by September the U.S. would be pushed out of Korea. In the meantime, however, everyone seemed determined to do the best he could. Then we began to hear rumors that substantial help was on the way.

[This time it was more than a rumor. In fact, powerful reinforcements reached Korea in late July and early August. Only by an eyelash had General MacArthur won the race for ground and time. From Hawaii came the 5th Regimental Combat Team, fourteen M26 Pershing tanks, and the 555th ("Triple Nickel") Field Artillery Battalion. From Ta-

coma came the 2d Infantry Division, the first ground troops to reach
Korea from the United States.*

The third unit to arrive had been requested by General Mac-
Arthur at the beginning of hostilities. On Sunday, 2 July, while Task
Force Smith was moving toward Osan, CINCFE sent a cable to
Washington urgently requesting the immediate dispatch to Korea of a
Marine regimental combat team and its supporting air group. That
very day Adm. Forrest Sherman, chief of naval operations, with the
approval of the Joint Chiefs of Staff and the president, ordered the
Marines to the Far East.]

Brig. Gen. EDWARD CRAIG †
Assistant Division Commander,
1st Marine Division

Each summer in Camp Pendleton the Marines held an annual carnival and rodeo. It was quite a big affair. We'd build a big rodeo area
and various organizations would supply the booths and rides. One of
these events was scheduled for July 1950. I had made all the arrangements. The night before the carnival was to begin, I received a call
from Headquarters, Marine Corps, informing me that due to the situation in Korea all liberty should be stopped. Shortly afterward in
another call the assistant commandant, Gen. O. P. Smith, ordered
me to organize the 1st Provisional Marine Brigade and have it ready
to mount out at the earliest possible date. The carnival ran one night;
the rodeo was canceled. A day or so later, the 1st Marine Division
had scheduled a full-scale combat review to which many distinguished visitors had been invited. In view of the fact that all the
equipment was already assembled and on the field and the troops were

---

*The 2d Division was made up of the 9th, 23d, and 38th Infantry Regiments.
†General Craig had entered the Marine Corps as a second lieutenant in 1917 at the age of
twenty-one. In World War II he led the 9th Marine Regiment at Bougainville and Guam and
was awarded the Bronze Star and Navy Cross for gallantry. As operations officer for V Amphibious Corps, Craig helped plan the Iwo Jima operation. He became the 1st Marine Division's ADC in 1949.

set to go, I decided to proceed with the review. It proved to be the last review the 1st Marine Division would hold for some time.

The next day [7 July] we organized the 1st Provisional Marine Brigade. To do so I practically had to strip the division. With General [Graves B.] Erskine* away and being in command of the base and the division, I had the choice of taking anybody I wanted. Naturally, I took the best I could find.†

[General Craig's 1st Provisional Marine Brigade was a heavily armed advance component of the 1st Marine Division ‡ and was composed of a headquarters group and Lt. Col. Raymond Murray's § 5th Marine Regiment.‖

After World War II the Marine Corps, like the other military branches, had been forced to take cuts in appropriations and the results would now be felt. When the Marine brigade sailed from San Diego for Korea, its main battle component was understrength; the 5th Marine Regiment's three battalions had two rifle companies each instead of the usual three.# This meant there would be no reserves; when a Marine rifle battalion went on line it would have to stay until the job was done. What the brigade lacked in numbers, however, it

---

* Maj. Gen. Graves B. Erskine was the 1st Marine Division's commanding general in 1950.
† Gen. Edward A. Craig interview, Oral History Collection, Marine Corps Historical Center, Washington, D.C. Hereafter, Craig interview, MCHC.
‡ The 1st Marine Division comprised the 1st, 5th, and 7th Marine Regiments. The 11th Marines was the division's artillery regiment.
§ Lieutenant Colonel Murray graduated from Texas A&M in 1935 and entered the Marines as a second lieutenant. During the Second World War, he fought with distinction at Guadalcanal, Tarawa, and Saipan. Awarded the Navy Cross, two Silver Stars, and the Purple Heart, Murray, as the Marine Corps official history of the Korean War points out, "made a name for heroism that was noteworthy even in Marine circles." At thirty-seven years old he would command the 5th Marine Regiment in Korea.
‖ The 1st Provisional Marine Brigade also included a company each from the division's Signal, Motor Transport, Medical, Shore Party, Engineer, Ordnance, and Tank Battalions, as well as detachments from the Service Battalion, Combat Service Group, Reconnaissance, and Military Police Companies, and the 1st Amphibian Tractor Company and Amphibian Truck Platoon. The 1st Battalion, 11th Marines, with three firing batteries was also attached. In all, the Marine brigade ground forces numbered 266 officers and 4,503 men. The brigade's air component from the 1st Marine Air Wing of three fighter squadrons and an observation squadron amounted to 192 officers and 1,358 men.
On its arrival in Korea, the 5th Marine Regiment numbered 132 officers and 2,452 enlisted men. Its battalions were made up of: 1st Battalion—Companies A and B, Weapons Company, H & S Company; 2d Battalion—Companies D and E, Weapons Company, H & S Company; 3d Battalion—Companies G and H, Weapons Company, H & S Company.

made up in experience. Most of its officers and two out of three NCOs were veterans of the tough island fighting of the Second World War; company commanders and platoon and squad leaders had been bloodied at places like Peleliu, Guam, Bougainville, Iwo Jima, and Okinawa. In Korea these men would be able to apply the lessons of speed, mobility, and firepower that had been learned on those distant Pacific beaches. The fluid situation the brigade would encounter in the Pusan Perimeter would demand the very elements the Marines had in abundance—courage, initiative, élan. Their ability to operate under the most adverse conditions was made possible by the trust they had in each other. It was simply taken for granted that everyone would exercise initiative to get the mission accomplished. As a result morale in the rifle companies was extremely high. In spite of what they'd heard, the Marines knew the North Koreans could be beaten. The Marine Corps was sending to Korea the best it had.]

2 August 1950

The 5th Marines arrived at Pusan, Korea. A conference of the Commanding Officer, Regimental Staff, and Battalion Commanders with the Brigade Commander was held on board the USS *George Clymer* at 2100. At this time Brigade Operation Plan 3-50 was issued and ordered executed. Units were embarked expeditiously, with no unusual or unforeseen event taking place.

SPECIAL ACTION REPORT, 5TH MARINES

2d Lt. TOM GIBSON
*Mortar Company/5 **

The word was spread aboard ship: "Before you go down the gangplank, load and lock!" Now, that's an incredible order to receive. We marched down the gangplank, loaded and locked.

---

*To help distinguish Marine units from Army units, the former will be shortened. Marine companies will be designated by a letter only, battalions by a number; numbers following the slash indicate regiments, thus D/5 is D Company, 5th Marine Regiment, and 1/7 is 1st Battalion, 7th Marine Regiment. All other Marine units will be spelled out, e.g., Weapons Company, H & S Company. A Marine company may also be referred to in the text by its phonetic name—Able 5 is A Company, 5th Marine Regiment; Baker 7 is B Company, 7th Marines; Charlie 1 is C Company, 1st Marines, and so forth.

In Pusan there was a tension and excitement that was palpable. It was like being in a college town on homecoming Saturday. There was also another emotion you could sense, almost feel—fear. The people were scared to death. The North Koreans were very close. In the distance you could hear the artillery.

The kids were terrific. We had a number of seventeen-year-olds in the company. They didn't walk off the dock, they swaggered off. Their attitude said, "Don't worry about it. The Marines are here!"

Pfc. DOUG KOCH *
D/5

It dawned on me suddenly: by God, the Marines have landed! On board the Greasy George [USS *George Clymer*], Korea seemed a long way away. Guys had talked about strange ideas, about having premonitions. One night in the middle of the Pacific a good buddy, Henry Thomas David LeBlanc, told me he had this dream that he wouldn't come back. LeBlanc wasn't alone in having this dream. But in Pusan this was behind us. There would be no time for premonitions. I'm sure LeBlanc forgot his.

Capt. FRANCIS "IKE" FENTON, JR.
B/5

We started debarking two to three hours after arriving in Pusan. The first thing we did was run the troops ashore. Then we started general

---

* Pfc. Koch grew up in a small South Dakota farm town where he played some football, ran track, and marched in the local Legion Drum and Bugle Corps. Looking for adventure and an opportunity to see the world, he joined the Marines right out of high school.

unloading. We worked throughout the night. Since the ship was not combat-loaded, we had a great problem trying to segregate gear after it got on the deck. By 6:00 A.M., August 3, ammunition and rations were ashore and issued to the men.

Pfc. FRED DAVIDSON *
G/5

We went down the gangway and fell into a loose formation on the dock. There each Marine was issued two hand grenades, and the ammo carriers for the rocket launchers and mortars were given their loads.

Capt. JOSEPH FEGAN
H/5

On the dock at Pusan, when the *Pickaway* landed, we were met by a band and Korean schoolgirls carrying flowers. What made the greatest impression on me, however, was talking to a reporter whose name or publication I no longer remember. The first thing he said was, "The Army's being kicked off the peninsula, what are you going to do about it?" I had no idea nor did I believe the situation was really that bad. But doom and gloom were afoot.

---

*Born in Oklahoma, but raised in California, "Fred" Davidson dropped out of high school after the tenth grade and at fifteen enlisted in the Army. He was sent to Korea and served with the 7th Division. At the end of a two-year hitch, Davidson left the Army a staff sergeant and joined the Marines as a private. He was eighteen when the war in Korea began.

1st Lt. ROBERT BOHN
G/5

The thing I remember most about arriving in Korea is being briefed by some Army people who, in retrospect, had obviously never been out of Pusan. These fat lieutenants told us all these horror stories. Although they didn't know what the hell they were talking about, they were very successful in scaring us. Aboard *Pickaway* we'd received very limited information about the enemy; in Pusan we were deluged with information from these rear-area types who were really only repeating rumors. We all began to think the North Koreans were about ten feet tall.

Pfc. FRED DAVIDSON
G/5

A little after midnight the company left the dock area and marched out on a road that led toward the center of Pusan. Shortly afterward we stopped and by the side of the road most of us relaxed. Several hours later, when the commotion of men moving around and talking died down, I swore I could hear the thump-thump of distant artillery fire. I'm convinced now I didn't hear it, the front being too far away, but that night I was sure I had.

3 August 1950

The 1st Battalion departed for Ch'angwon via motor at 0630 and arrived at 1000. The 3d Battalion and H & S Company departed at 0700 by train and arrived Ch'angwon at 1230. The 2d Battalion departed at 0900 and arrived Ch'angwon at 1500. CPs established.

SPECIAL ACTION REPORT, 1/5

Pfc. FRED DAVIDSON
G/5

The sun was up by the time the troops arrived at the Pusan rail yards [3 August]. We boarded a train and for the next few hours traveled toward the front. The trip took a long time because every mile or so the train would stop. During these stops South Korean civilians crowded round our cars selling, or at least trying to sell, food. We had been told not to eat any fruit since it was unsafe for ingesting. None of this seemed too strange to me. A few years earlier, while serving in the Army, I had been stationed in Korea. During that tour I'd taken advantage of a twelve-week evening course on spoken Korean offered by the University of Seoul. When my enlistment ended I returned to the States and was discharged from the Army as a sergeant. In July 1949 I enlisted in the Marine Corps as a private.

While the train carrying the brigade to the front made its frequent stops, I found that I was really quite rusty at speaking the language. I was only capable of carrying on a fairly decent conversation with a four- or five-year-old Korean child. Nevertheless, because I was the only Korean speaker he had, in the weeks ahead my company commander, Lieutenant "Dewey" Bohn, used me as an unofficial interpreter.

When the little train eventually completed its mission and chugged into a station where the brigade unloaded, I managed to ask a Korean where we were. He answered, "Ch'angwon." As the front was still some miles away, George Company walked until it came to a single railroad track that crossed the road we were on. Turning left, the company moved for about two miles along this track. From there we began climbing a high, steep hill, the first of many high, steep hills I was to climb in Korea.

Pfc. DOUG KOCH
D/5

It took us most of the afternoon to get to Ch'angwon. One of the first sights we had in Korea was all the refugees coming down the road. They pushed what they could, carried the rest. After seeing this, most of us agreed we'd rather fight the war in Korea than back in the United States. No one wanted his family to go through the ordeal these Koreans were going through. The look on their faces was something I'll never forget.

Pfc. HERBERT LUSTER
A/5

The road was crowded with people who were loaded down with children and personal belongings. Fear and uncertainty were on their faces. Where were they coming from? Where were they going? They all looked so very tired—they must have walked a long way. Most of the people were going the opposite way the Marines were going. The road wasn't wide enough for two-way traffic, so the whole scene was a dusty mess.

"Let's go, men," came the order, "it'll be dark soon." And the troops pushed ahead once more.

Capt. FRANCIS "IKE" FENTON, JR.
B/5

Right from the very first day in Korea we began having a water problem. Although we had had water hours aboard ship the water tanks on the *Henrico* had practically run dry. Consequently, a lot of the men left for Ch'angwon with little water in their canteens. It wasn't until late in the afternoon that they were able to refill their canteens.

The 1st Battalion had preceded the brigade to the village of Ch'angwon, where, to the rear of the 25th Division, on the high ground above the Masan-Pusan highway, it set up a bivouac area and a general defense line. The men were told to prepare two-man or buddy foxholes. We were told that the enemy was infiltrating through the 25th Division and was coming back into our rear areas.

We were quite nervous the first two nights. Our first exposure to the combat area was very much like a kid's first days in boot camp; not knowing what to expect, he imagines a lot of things. The first two nights at Ch'angwon we certainly imagined a lot of things.

Pfc. FRED DAVIDSON
G/5

On top of the hill, the men settled down and began digging their foxholes. I decided to dig mine on the slope of a gully and take advantage of some small scrub bushes growing there. When I'd finished I
climbed topside where Sergeant Potter, our company's first sergeant,
handed me a walkie-talkie and asked me to tell him what was being
said on it. The voice I heard was speaking Korean so fast I couldn't
tell Potter whether I was listening to a military broadcast or a com-
mercial radio station.

Next, a fire team from higher up on the hill brought down a
Korean civilian who spoke more slowly. I figured out he was a farmer
who lived at the bottom of the hill. His day had begun as all the
other days of his life had begun: that morning he had said good-bye
to his family, climbed the hill above his home, and, on the other
side, worked his fields. That evening, to return home, he left his fields,
recrossed the hill, and met George Company. We let him pass through
our lines. When he got to his hut, he must have told some story.

I spent the rest of the twilight hours working on my foxhole. When
I finished I really had a good hole. Moments after last light, M/Sgt.
Astle Ryder came to the edge of my gully and informed me that I
wasn't in too safe a position and that I should climb up to where he
was standing and dig another foxhole there.

I started digging the second hole in the preferred location, but
as it had gotten inky dark and I was making so much noise I decided
to stop digging before someone shot me. It was as dark a night as I'd
ever seen. You couldn't see two feet in front of you.

Lieutenant Bohn yelled, "Everyone put a round in his chamber!" Oh, God, I thought, the gooks are going to attack and I don't
even have a decent hole to hide in. It got real quiet. Everyone held
his breath. I lay motionless on the ground. I strained to see through
the darkness, my carbine at the ready. That night the password was
"Mutton," the countersign, "Tallow." Over to my left Sergeant Ryder yelled, "Mutton!" No answer. He yelled again, "Mutton! Mutton, Goddamn you!" This was followed by the sound of a rifle stock
hitting flesh and bone. Someone let out a long, loud moan, like he
was really hurt. Silence, again. Damn, I thought, the gooks are all
around us and Ryder just got himself one. I was scared.

Moments later I heard a helmet hit the ground and roll down into the gulley where I had dug my first hole. Somewhere in the dark, across the gulley, was a rocket team in a two-man foxhole. They'd dug their hole the same time I'd dug mine so I knew they were there. I knew for sure the gooks were now between me and that 3.5 rocket team. "Andy, are you in your hole?" He hollered back, "Yeah!" I yelled, "Mutton!" Nothing. Silence. I raised my carbine and squeezed the trigger. The muzzle flash blinded me. For the next few seconds I saw lights and stars. Andy shouted, "Hey, you almost hit me!" Oh, God, I didn't know I was aiming in that direction. It was so dark I couldn't see my front sight. I said to myself, You better take it easy, ol' buddy, before you kill some Marine. Over to my rear someone else pulled off a round. Next it was someone to my front. Then the firing pinballed from place to place all over the hill and back down toward the railroad track. It kept up for some while. Finally Lieutenant Counselman yelled, "Hey, cut out the shooting!" On the hill all firing ceased. At the bottom of the hill, the one-sided firefight continued hot and heavy for a little while longer.

The rest of the night I lay awake, scared, my finger on the trigger. In the morning I learned the following: the "gook helmet" I'd heard fall belonged to another Marine; Lieutenant Counselman ordered the shooting to cease when the stock on his carbine was shattered by a wild round; with his rifle stock Sergeant Ryder had taken out a young Marine who had wandered by and failed to remember the countersign. I found out later the guy was really hurt bad—Ryder's blow had crushed his chin and jawbone, and torn his nose almost completely off his face.

5 August 1950

Routine security patrols continued. No enemy contact. A warning order was received from brigade at 2130 directing 5th Marines to be prepared to move by motor to vicinity Chindong-ni and be prepared for offensive operations against the enemy.

SPECIAL ACTION REPORT, 5TH MARINES

Pfc. HERBERT LUSTER
A/5

Corporal Evans brought me my mail. I had a letter from Peggy! It
didn't take but a few moments to read: "Dear Herbert, I have a boy
friend now and feel I must ask you not to write me again. You will
be pleased to know he is a Marine, too." It was the old Dear John
letter so often talked about by sad Marines too far away to compete.
I had named my BAR* "Peggy" and decided not to change it. I still
liked her anyway.

*[While the Marines became reacquainted with the vicissitudes of life
in a combat zone, General Walker's thinly spread divisions spent the
early days of August trying to blunt the enemy's Naktong River cross-
ings. Along the entire length of the river, the North Koreans probed
for weaknesses and gaps in Eighth Army's defenses.*

*The Naktong formed a long, twisting moat along the Perimeter's
western flank. Hills cut by rice-paddy valleys dominated both its banks.
A third of the way up the Perimeter, a few miles north of where the
Nam enters the big river, the Naktong curls into a large loop. This
loop became known as the Naktong Bulge, and it was here the Communists determined to break through Eighth Army. The crossing of the
Naktong would be made by one of the North Koreans' premier units,
the 4th "Seoul" Division. The honorary title "Seoul" referred to the
division's vital role in capturing that city on 28 June. And one week
later, on that rainy morning outside Osan, it had been the 4th Division that Task Force Smith met. At Taejon, the division had played
a role in destroying General Dean's Kum River line. In the first week
of August, it was again ready to take center stage.*

*At midnight, 5 August, above the Naktong Bulge, red and yel-
low flames pinwheeled through the night sky and the 4th "Seoul" Division began to force the river. Across from the North Korean unit, in
the heights, lay its old sparring partner, the U.S. 24th Division.]*

---

*The Browning automatic rifle, or BAR, weighs sixteen pounds, may be fired from the hip,
shoulder, or from a bipod and can fire 500 rounds per minute. It is the rifle company's principal automatic weapon, with one or more issued to each squad or fire team.

Enemy are across river in force in center of my sector. It's pretty dark and situation is obscure. I am committing my reserve [1st Battalion] at daylight to clear up the situation.

COL. CHARLES BEAUCHAMP TO CG 24TH DIVISION

1st Lt. CHARLES PAYNE
1st Battalion/34th Infantry

My worst day in two wars was August 6. The CO of one of the units was down and I was ordered to go and help out. This was on the Naktong; masses of gooks poured over the hills and through the gaps like a flood. Our people were fighting like seasoned troops but were just being overpowered. The company that I was expected to help out was caught in a hopeless crossfire. Nearly all the troops were dead or wounded. I found myself in the middle of a terrible situation, no way out, not even able to move. The gooks were on the high ground, the company was below them. Lieutenant Martin and I crawled into a culvert and returned the fire. Our men were being destroyed. The survivors of this attack were pinned down or moved in circles. The trap had been sprung and there was no way out.

Martin and I decided we'd try to make it to a nearby gristmill and there try to hold on until help arrived. If we made it, his plan was to dig a hole in the dirt floor, cover himself with dirt, breathe through a straw, and pray the North Koreans missed him when they overran the position. I could not do this. I would never stop fighting until I somehow managed to rejoin the regiment. We made our move. Martin was hit. I didn't see where he fell.

In the building I discovered ten GIs, another twenty or more dead or wounded lay on the ground. The building was made of tin and by now was riddled with holes. Quickly looking around I realized I knew most of the men by name. I shouted at them to conserve their ammunition and to collect all the ammo, water, and first-aid packets they could find from the dead and wounded.

Hour after hour we held the North Koreans off. At first we let them get within eight or ten feet of the mill. Then we'd fire a volley and the enemy would fall back. Heavy fighting for hours. We used all our grenades. Time and time again the gooks rushed us. Each time we'd lose a man, the gooks would lose many. In front of the mill, the ground was covered with their dead. We stacked our dead around us for protection. The battle seemed to go on forever.

There was a young soldier who held his dying buddy in his arms. He wouldn't, or couldn't, put him down, just kept adding bandages to his wounds. I told him we needed his rifle, his buddy was dead, and he had to get into the fight. This went on for some time. Finally, I made him join us. He cursed me badly and said he'd settle with me later. He would not believe his friend was dead. It was so obvious the man was dead; his brains bulged out of a hole in his head.

Then, without warning, about three football fields away, one little old American tank poked its nose around the curve. The five or six of us who were still on our feet yelled with joy. We were saved. A sergeant, I believe his name was Cartwright, had been scrapping great all day, inspiring each of us with his guts. That damned tank fired a round. It crashed into the mill and hit Cartwright in the waist. The explosion was the last thing in the mill I remember.

I awoke and found myself on a truck carrying dead men. I wondered whether I too was dead. A firefight broke out around the truck. The driver was hit, the truck ended up in a ditch. I crawled to the other side of the truck to get away from the firing. I checked myself and found blood coming from my mouth and nose. I had been nicked all over by fragments of stone and metal. A short time later the gooks moved off. *

[General Walker rushed units from one crucial sector to another, and field commanders desperately tried to contain the Communist penetrations. The North Koreans poured fresh troops into the holes they had ripped in the Perimeter's fragile defenses.]

---

* For his actions that day, Lieutenant Payne was awarded the Silver Star.

Pfc. FLOYD AKINS
B Company/5th Cavalry
The North Koreans came at us with everything they had. We had a
new lieutenant. He spent one day with us on the line. Then he took
his .45 automatic and shot himself in the foot. I think he did it on
purpose. That first day he said he wouldn't be in Korea long.

I had not had a bath in ten days. We lived like cavemen. I thought
of my mother, who had not wanted me to join the Army. The 1st
Cav didn't know the word "rest." My friend told me, "I know we're
all going to heaven because now we are spending our time in hell."

Sgt. ED HENDRICKS
F Company/5th Cavalry
I walked my men to Hill 303.* On the way to the hill, I lost half my
kids—snipers, mortars, artillery. Trucks brought the dead back. The
wounded were brought back on jeeps, others limped into aid stations.
This is very hard for me to talk about. We went up the hill called
303, a beautiful hill—nothing on it but foxholes. From the hill you
could look down on the Naktong. When the sun set the river turned
red.

I think we took that hill ten or fifteen times. Got run off it just
as often. On that hill we had plenty of entertainment. Every morning, every night, we had company. North Koreans came up blowing
whistles and bugles. A real fright program. "Banzai! GI die!"

At night they sneaked around, tried to infiltrate our positions.
Whatever we done, we done in our foxholes. Two men to a hole:
one slept, one kept watch. We strung communication wire around
the perimeter and tied our C-ration cans on it so we could hear our
little friends at night when they came visiting. When we heard them,

* All hill numbers in Korea refer to height in meters above sea level.

we never got out of our holes. We'd pull the pin of a grenade and roll the grenade down the hill.

We'd take the hill one day, give it back the next. The heat was the worst you ever felt. It would sometimes rain. Walking in the mud was almost impossible. Many times we were surrounded. Got low on ammunition, nothing to eat. Our air force made air drops, but on those hills it was hard to hit the target. Ammo and food often drifted over to the enemy. Fighting was so bad medics couldn't get in to carry the dead out. The wounded were lucky sometimes. If they got off, they didn't have to come back to Hill 303.

1st Lt. HENRY GOGUN
1st Battalion/5th Cavalry

I took a group of men up to the battalion CP. Halfway there we heard a shot. After looking around and seeing nothing unusual we continued on our way.

One of the men called out to me, "Look, Lieutenant, there's no need to go forward; our troops are pulling out." Sure enough, there behind us was a long single file of men, rifles slung over their shoulders, moving roughly from our forward position to our rear. "They can't be moving out," I called out to my men, "we're expecting an attack this morning. You guys stay here." Picking a man named Henry Ross, I ordered, "Come with me. Let's find out what's going on."

We walked rapidly across a rice paddy toward the file of men. Nearing them I called, "Hey, where'n the hell are you going?" They yelled back, but I couldn't hear what had been said. Closer to them I saw that something was wrong. At first I thought they were ROK troops, but then remembered there were none assigned to our outfit. Closer now I recognized my mistake. These men were not withdrawing 5th Cav troopers; they were advancing North Koreans.

One of the Communists fired. The round hit the ground near my foot. A North Korean, apparently an English-speaking officer, shouted, "Hands up. Surrender!" I thought, If I do, they'll torture

me. I whipped my carbine down and from the hip fired a clip. *Brrrrt!*
It stopped. Christ, it's jammed, I thought. I yanked off the magazine
and checked the receiver. It was empty. On full automatic I had fired
fifteen rounds in less time than it takes to sneeze.

Glancing up I saw several Koreans grab their stomachs; the others fired at me. Ross and I ran toward our group. I took no more than
five strides when a bullet grazed my jaw, cutting off the tops of seven
lower front teeth. I called to Ross, "I'm hit." "Me, too," he cried
back. Twenty more steps. I dropped to the mud and aimed a burst
that skimmed the ground. I reloaded and ran again for my men. Mud
kicked up around me. A round went through my buttock and exited
my right leg. Right then I remembered I had nothing to worry about.
A day earlier I had applied for $10,000 of free life insurance. I man-
aged to continue running until I reached the men. My platoon sergeant asked, "Where's the man who went with you?" "Oh, gosh," I
said, "I've got to go back for him." Just then Ross staggered in. He,
too, had been shot in the leg. In the process of getting away, he'd
lost his rifle.

One of the men asked, "Why's everybody shooting? We're all
Americans." "Those aren't Americans," I answered, "they're North
Koreans." Until then no one had known the enemy was behind our
lines. The North Koreans did not continue their attack. I spread the
men out in a defensive position, then moved them back to the main
road.

On the road we stopped a jeep coming from the front and learned
that everything was quiet in that direction. Ross and I climbed into
the jeep for a ride to the aid station. (The rest of the men in the group
returned to the forward command post.) My injuries looked worse than
they were. I was covered with mud and blood.

News sure traveled fast. When the jeep pulled into the battalion
command post (rear), nobody was there.

Pfc. FLOYD AKINS
B Company/5th Cavalry
We began checking the Korean refugees who were on the road. North
Koreans were believed to be hiding in their columns. I found a man
hiding a hand grenade. My sergeant told me to take him down the

side of the road and kill him. I marched the Korean away from the others. When I found a spot out of sight of the road, I pointed my carbine at him. He began to cry. I could not shoot him. When I returned to the road with the man, the sergeant said the MPs would take him to a prisoner compound. I was glad I had not been able to shoot this Korean.

Several days later, out on patrol, my squad found twenty-six American GIs. They were lying in a ditch and they had their hands tied behind their backs. They'd all been shot in the back of the head. What made it so bad for me was finding my old company commander from back at Camp Drake, Japan. Right then and there my heart made a change. I told a lieutenant standing next to me I was now ready to fight the North Koreans to the death if that's what it took. Lieutenant Barr, that was his name, said, "OK, you blood-thirsty GI, we're going to give them hell if we capture them now. We'll give them some of their own medicine." Since that day I don't think I've ever been the same.

Pfc. ROBERT HARPER
Headquarters Company/3d Battalion/
19th Infantry *

We began to receive more air support and I saw we had more tanks. There also seemed to be more people around to help us. But the North Koreans kept coming. At times the fighting got so bad we would have to pull off the line and let the enemy have a hill or ridge. Artillery and fighter planes would be called in and they'd paste the Reds. Next day we would counterattack and drive the North Koreans back across the river. That's the way it went: seesaw, back and forth. I've heard at times there were so many enemy bodies in the river the water was actually red. Well, I saw a lot of bodies but I never did see the water turn red.

* In the Pusan Perimeter Pfc. Harper had been reassigned to the 19th Infantry.

[While GIs fought the enemy to a standstill in the hills above the Naktong, another battle, miles to the south, was beginning to take shape. A potentially dangerous Communist thrust toward Pusan had forced General Walker to concentrate his newly arrived reinforcements on the Perimeter's southern flank.]

Brig. Gen. EDWARD CRAIG
Commanding General, 1st Provisional Marine Brigade
I proceeded to the 25th's headquarters [5 August] and there met with General Kean* and General Walker. The Eighth Army's commander told me he was going to launch an offensive against the Communists. He informed everyone present that no one was to fall back again to the rear, that we were going to stop the enemy where he was, and, if necessary, we would fight to the death. General Walker made these points very strongly. †

[The time had come to abandon the strategy of trading time for space. Task Force Kean, named for the 25th Division's commanding general, would have the honor of launching the Americans' first counteroffensive. The task force was composed of the 25th Division, the newly arrived 5th Regimental Combat Team [RCT], and the 1st Provisional Marine Brigade. The advance, it was hoped, would both clear the enemy from the Perimeter's southern flank and ease the pressure on the Naktong Bulge and other enemy bridgeheads by forcing the Communists to send reinforcements to the south.

The three-pronged offensive would proceed west along the Masan-Chinju corridor. A regiment of the 25th Division would be on the right, the 5th RCT in the middle, the Marine brigade on the left. The two Army units were to capture Chinju; the Marines, Sach'on.

On 7 August, Task Force Kean moved west.]

---

* Maj. Gen. William B. Kean commanded the U.S. 25th Infantry Division.
† Craig interview, MCHC.

Pfc. DOUG KOCH
D/5
When we drove through Masan it was dark and very eerie. I was twenty years old. Except for the officers and staff NCOs, most of us were kids—eighteen-, nineteen-, twenty-year-olds. No doubt we were gung ho. We thought we were pretty tough, too. Underneath, though, we were pretty scared. Anyone who says he wasn't is lying.

West of Masan, in the distance, I could hear artillery. Then, not more than 100 yards away, an enemy shell exploded! Right then and there we kids were ready to bail out of the truck and hit the ditch. Old Gunny Reeves stood up and growled, "Shit, set your ass down. By God, when you see me getting nervous and excited, that's the time to really get nervous and excited." We sat back down. The gunnery sergeant settled us kids right down. The truck went up the road a little farther and about daylight we unloaded.

7 August 1950
At 0135 a directive was received from CO 27th Infantry Regiment who passed on an order from Commanding General 25th Infantry Division to detach one rifle platoon plus 1 LMG [light machine gun] section for commitment in high ridgeline and directed to occupy and hold high ground until relieved. First Platoon of George Company, with one section of light machine guns under Lt. Cahill, was detached and directed to report to Regt. Comdr. 27th Inf. Regt. for assignment.

SPECIAL ACTION REPORT, 3/5

2d Lt. JOHN CAHILL
G/5
When I checked in at the Army CP, Colonel [John] Michaelis told me to go up there [Hill 342] and relieve one of his companies that was being eaten up by the North Koreans. He told me, "You're ex-

pected to hold this hill at all costs!" You know, what was I supposed to say? I figured, though, I better not tell this to my platoon.

1st Lt. ROBERT BOHN
G/5

Blackie Cahill's platoon was detached from the company. An Army unit was in trouble and brigade had been told to send Cahill's platoon in to get the soldiers out. I really bitched about it. Unity of command is something that's very important. Secondly, I knew that Cahill could no longer count on me to take care of him. I strenuously objected to the battalion commander. [Lt. Col. Robert] Taplett told me to mind my own business. Later I learned Taplett had strongly protested the move to Murray and Murray had done the same with Craig. Because the brigade was temporarily attached to the 25th Division, Craig, of course, had no choice but to do what he was ordered to do.

2d Lt. JOHN CAHILL
G/5

I was given an Army guide, who took me to the CP of the 2d Battalion, 5th RCT. There I was again told to relieve an Army company and with my platoon hold the position. "Where's the front line?" I didn't know, so I thought I'd ask. The answer surprised me: "A thousand meters ahead." "A thousand?" I said. I was astounded. We didn't operate that way. A Marine CP would have been no more than fifty meters behind the line. Eventually, I was given another guide, who became lost trying to find the trail that led to the summit of Hill 342.

> At approximately 0500 the first platoon of G Company arrived at a position to the rear of the objective. Three artillery shells fell in the vicinity. Earlier an army unit on the Marines' left flank fired on the platoon. Apparently the Army did not know friendly forces were in the area. After daylight the platoon leader, Lieutenant Cahill, moved his men up a high hill where the Army had an observation post for its artillery forward observers. During

the climb eight men collapsed from the severe heat. At 0800 the
platoon was hit by enemy automatic weapons fire.

SPECIAL ACTION REPORT, 3/5

2d Lt. JOHN CAHILL
G/5
What really hurt was that on the trail we got hit with NK machine-
gun fire and a couple of the first people to go down were BAR men.
There went some of my firepower. If you lost your BAR, you were
in a little bit of trouble.

We finally reached the top of the hill and moved in with the
soldiers. To help steady them we put Marines in among them. The
heat was terrific. I now saw we were situated on the front slope of the
hill, sitting there like ducks in a shooting gallery. Once we climbed
into the holes, we couldn't get out of them. The North Koreans really
had us zeroed in.

I tried to call in artillery. Told them my position and asked them
to throw out a registration round. I'll be a sonovabitch, they dropped
it right behind me! Forget it, I thought. I'll do without.

The heat just baked us. Then the water ran out. At one point
some people went down with canteens and came back with rice-paddy
water. As a result we all ended up with worms. Hell, in that oven we
were so thirsty we'd have drunk anything.

I called in an air drop of water and ammo. Here comes this R4D
[transport plane]. Great, dropped the entire load on the enemy. Jeez,
I thought, we're in trouble now. Sergeant Macy then went down to
a nearby village [Taepyong-ni] with a small carrying party and returned with fresh water.

> Late in the afternoon, Lt. Cahill, an Army lieutenant, and a
> Marine sergeant, Jack Macy, contacted Dog Company, 2d Bat-
> talion, 5th Marines, which had moved into position 1,700 yards
> behind the one occupied by Cahill's platoon and the Army unit.
> Cahill was informed that relief or reinforcements for the men on
> the hill could not be obtained until ordered. Lieutenant Cahill's
> party returned to the hill around dusk when a night defense was
> organized. Men who during the day had suffered from heat ex-

haustion were placed in foxholes with men who were in better physical condition. Although no enemy fire was received during the night, at dawn the Americans were hit with heavy small-arms and machine-gun fire. Mortar rounds and grenades also landed inside the perimeter. Several men were hit. As the sun slowly rose enemy attacks continued.

SPECIAL ACTION REPORT, 3/5

2d Lt. JOHN CAHILL
G/5
Next morning we were hit early by several enemy bayonet attacks. We managed to hold on until relieved by Dog Company. I'd gone down earlier to talk to Captain John Finn about what his company was going to face. Here was a whole company coming to relieve a platoon. They came up and we went down.

I lost some good guys on Hill 342. I hated to see them go. When I saw Dewey Bohn I was pretty spent.

1st Lt. ROBERT BOHN
G/5
It took a hell of a long time to get Cahill out of there. He finally walked out. When he rejoined the company, it was a very dramatic time. Jesus, he cried and I cried. He'd lost a lot of people.

1st Lt. ED JAWORSKI
G/5
We had a kid in the company named Willy Tome. When he learned we were going to Korea, he said he didn't want to go. Said he'd desert first. He had a brother in World War II who'd been killed. "No doubt," he said, "if I go to Korea, I'm gonna get killed just like my brother." Our gunnery sergeant, Ace Ryder, brought him to see me. Ace and I spent a lot of time talking to Willy. We finally reached him. He didn't go over the hill. He went to Korea.

Willy Tome was in Blackie Cahill's platoon. He was one of the first men killed on that damned hill.

[Before Hill 342 would be secured, more Marines than Pfc. William Tome would die on its slopes. D Company was next in line to see if it could take and hold the crest of the objective. Strong North Korean positions still ringed the northern half of the hill.

D Company's ordeal on Hill 342 had actually begun the day before. On the afternoon of 7 August, while Cahill was desperately holding his portion of the hill and looking for a source of fresh water, Captain Finn's Dog Company had been ordered to relieve Cahill's platoon and the Army company, and then seize the remainder of Hill 342.]

Pfc. DOUG KOCH
D/5
It was getting toward late afternoon [7 August], and as we climbed farther up, we began losing more guys to the heat. This was on the backside of Hill 342. The word was that we were to relieve an Army unit and some Marines that were holding the top of the hill. By late afternoon we were only two-thirds of the way up. Word filtered up that we were going to hold for the night where we were. While we set up a defense perimeter, our stragglers caught up with us. At this time each platoon was given two jerricans of water to distribute. Even though it was getting dark, Lieutenant [Wallace] Reid made sure each man in his 2d Platoon received a fair share of water. The company then settled in for the night.

I'd served under Lieutenant Reid for over a year. In World War II he'd been an enlisted man. Afterward he'd gone through officer candidate school. When we were getting ready to leave Camp Pendleton, Mr. Reid's wife and two little boys would drive to the parking lot just to the south of the barracks. Whenever he could, he would go out and sit in this old '41 four-door Ford and be with his family. I liked Lieutenant Reid.

In the morning [8 August] we received word we were going to relieve the hill. As we climbed close to the crest, the company received a lot of fire on both flanks. The survivors of the Army unit and the Marine platoon from George Company [Cahill's] came back over the crest. On the top of the hill, we were kind of in single file. The 1st Platoon went around to the left side and Mr. Reid's 2d Platoon went around to the right. There was a lot of incoming fire flying around. Lieutenant Reid pointed out a small depression where someone had begun to scratch out a foxhole. "Jump in there, Doug. As soon as you can, return that fire." Then with the rest of the platoon he went out of sight around the hill. I jumped into the little dent in the ground and pulled out the legs on the bipod of my BAR. Looking carefully over the side of the hill, I couldn't see an awful lot to shoot at. The company continued to take a lot of fire. Whenever something below me moved, I cut loose with a burst. I was only in place a few minutes when back along the line word came that Lieutenant Reid had been hit. I felt pretty bad. This was a very hectic time. There'd been a lot of climbing, we were under fire, I kept looking for targets. A few more minutes went by. From around the side of the hill, someone hollered that the lieutenant was dead. I was so busy it took some time before the news hit me.

About this time Captain Finn, our company CO, crawled by my position. The map pouch kept getting in his way. He told me he was going to see if he could help Lieutenant Reid. Firing was hot and heavy. Guys fell around me. All of a sudden I received word that Captain Finn was down.

A few minutes went by. I looked up and here came the captain slowly crawling in my direction. He'd been grazed in the forehead. Blood flowed into his eyes and he was having a hard time seeing where he was going. He passed close by. I saw his pale color and dazed expression. "Good luck, Cap'n."

For the next hour or so, the North Koreans tried to push us off the hill. A little to my left they came almost to our line. The firefight grew fiercer. Word kept passing between holes. Lieutenant Oakley from the 1st Platoon was dead. Sometime after this Lieutenant Emmelman's wounding was reported. Someone then shouted that Lieutenant [Robert] Hanifin was our new CO. A little bit later I learned he too was down. The heat had gotten to him and he had collapsed. We were, I won't say shook up by all this bad news, but we were really concerned. Word passed from hole to hole that Gunny Reeves would now be our company commander. Those of us who'd served with him took heart at this turn of events. Master Sergeant [Harold] Reeves had somewhere over twenty-nine years in the Corps. When he chewed you out, he had the blackest eyes. You could see the sparks flying from them when he really got worked up. Word was he was part Cherokee.

As the battle continued Sergeant Reeves crawled around our perimeter telling us to conserve our ammo, to shoot only when we had targets. We were cut off and he didn't know when we'd be resupplied. We hung on and late in the afternoon we were still there, hanging on. I learned later Hill 342 overlooked a crossroads the North Koreans wanted. As long as we held the hill, they couldn't cut the road.

As the sun began to set, the firing let up and we kind of took stock of our situation. Guys looked for buddies and found out how many of their friends were gone. We discovered our losses had been heavy. But we were still on the hill. Gunny Reeves kept our morale up. We figured, by God, we really did hang on. No matter what the enemy threw at us, we were still there.

The next morning [9 August] the company was told it would be relieved that afternoon. Shortly after first light Gunny Reeves and our platoon sergeant, who became platoon leader when Mr. Reid was killed, volunteered me and two other guys to go around and pick up the bodies that littered the perimeter. We were to bring the bodies down to the CP so the Graves Registration people could process them. We also needed their water, C rations, and ammo. I'd never handled a body before nor had the other two Marines with me. It didn't make much sense putting the job off, so we got right to it. I learned that day about the smell of death. A dead person smells different than a dead animal and the smell is something you never forget. It's something that can't be put on television or in newsreels. They can capture the sound and some of the confusion of battle, but the smell of death is something they can't record.

During the morning we came under some enemy small-arms fire. I remember one body. Although rigor mortis had set in and he was hard and stiff, when we ran with him his stomach and intestines still sloshed. Down by the CP, Gunny Reeves hollered, "Don't you drop that sonovabitch. You get him here."

About this time, with all the shooting, the running, and the heat, the three of us were pooped out. "You better not pick up too many more," Gunny Reeves said. "The gooks are going to start zeroing in on you guys and we're gonna have to carry you off next."

I lay alongside the row of bodies we'd carried down from the top of the hill. It was panting hot. I had only one canteen. I leaned over a body, didn't know him, but knew he'd been a Marine in our platoon, and from his cartridge belt I took his canteen. Now I would have two. Then Gunny walked by and told me to pour the water that was left into a jerrican that would be used by everyone. Then he changed his mind, "Naw, you've worked hard for it. Keep it." There wasn't much, and it was hot, but it sure tasted good.

Late in the afternoon what was left of the company kind of reassembled at the bottom. Our new company CO, Captain Andrew Zimmer, relieved Sergeant Reeves. Some of the other platoons got new leaders. Sergeant Dickerson continued as our leader.

That evening we received some mail and had plenty of water to drink and C rations to eat. I sat by a little pond, drank all the water I wanted, and ate some cold beans and a can of fruit. Sometime after dark I filled my two canteens and with the rest of the company marched down the road.

[At first, Task Force Kean's advance on Chinju and Sach'on had run into difficulty, and during the first forty-eight hours covered little ground. However, on the 9th, while D/5 mopped up Hill 342, enemy activity in front of the brigade lessened and the Marines were able to resume their advance. It was at this time they encountered a new enemy.]

Capt. JOSEPH FEGAN
H/5
The heat was vicious. Trying to move along the ridgelines was godawful. We were constantly wet with sweat. The company had the lead one day and I became particularly concerned because so many men were dropping from heat prostration. I reached the point of not knowing whether the company could keep going. It was a long hike and the men began feeling sorry for themselves. I had to do something. One man told me, "Cap'n, I can't go any further." I told him, "Well, the only thing I can tell you to do is put your bayonet on your rifle, stick

it in the ground upside down, put your helmet on it, and lie down alongside it. If the enemy doesn't get you first, we'll pick you up on the way back." At that, the lad miraculously revived and moved out right smartly.

Pfc. JACK WRIGHT
G/5

Guys almost went mad for water. I never felt the kind of heat I felt in Korea. I just burned up. My hands went numb. I couldn't help myself; I began crying like a baby. I was ashamed. I felt I could crawl into a mousehole and die, but I couldn't help what was happening to me.

Corporal [Raymond] Giaquinto, my fire-team leader, pulled me off the line and sent another Marine to relieve me. Giaquinto laid me down and poured water over my head and on my dungaree jacket. It was some time before I could look anyone in the eye again.

[A normal Korean summer drenched the countryside with monsoon rain. But August 1950 was an exception; it was a time of drought. With little rain, temperatures soared into the 100s. During the first two days, the newly arrived leathernecks lost more men on the road to the heat than to the enemy.]

Capt. FRANCIS "IKE" FENTON, JR.
B/5

We moved through the rice paddy single file. There was no talking. Everyone sweated it out going across. The whole battalion made it to the high ground without a shot being fired. We reached the high ground and went into position at approximately 4:00 A.M. [9 August]. A half hour later the battalion received an order to attack and seize the high ground to our immediate front, which had been designated Regimental 0-1. This order was hard to take. You expect hardship in war, but the men had been up since 6:00 A.M. the previous morning and 50 percent of them had been up half the night of August 7–8. The men were tired after having crossed the rice paddy. Worst of all, our water was practically out. There was no water available on the hill, and it was quite a problem to get water up to us, especially since we had no civilian laborers.

However, we jumped off at 6:00 A.M. and moved along the ridgeline to more dominating terrain. There we established defense positions. At this time B Company received orders to proceed to the ridgeline on our left front and check it to see if there were any enemy troops in the area. The heat was terrible. Most of the men were out of water. We were all tired, but we moved off. After about three hours of terrific effort, we reached our assigned ridgeline. And then another order arrived! Move off the high ground, go down to the road, and continue the advance toward Paedun-ni.

We had encountered no enemy opposition going over to this ridgeline, but the heat-prostration cases in the company grew to an alarming number. The men were dropping like flies. We requested that water be sent to us by air drop or carried to us by civilian laborers. The company was "shot," and we didn't believe we could get them off the ridge without first having water. Two of our heat-prostration cases were so bad that we requested a helicopter to come in and take them off. They were completely out of their heads. The battalion commander [Lt. Col. George Newton] had issued the order for us to follow A Company off the ridge to the road, but we had only thirty men and two officers who were in good enough shape to get down off the hill without collapsing. The rest of the men just couldn't make it. They were out cold, lying on the ground. When they were able, they crawled under bushes to get a little shade. The battalion commander ordered as many of the company as possible off the hill. He said that at the earliest opportunity he would try to get water to the remainder of the men.

Captain [John] Tobin, the company commander, was in fairly bad shape. While another officer and I led thirty men down to the road, he stayed with the rest of the men on the hill. The troops that had passed out had to be left where they had fallen since no one had the strength to move them. The men who had heat prostration, but weren't out, tried to place themselves along the ridge where they could cover their fallen buddies in case of an enemy attack. The heat reached 114 degrees, and I personally don't believe that our men on the hill could have repulsed ten enemy troops.

On reaching the road with my group, I passed out. The descent down the ridgeline had been very steep and sapped us of all our remaining energy. After being revived, watered down, and given an hour's rest in the shade, we were again ready to move out. We fell in on the tail end of the column as the battalion started moving along the road toward Paedun-ni. By five o'clock that evening, having encountered heavy sniper fire, we had moved only a mile and a half. At this time we received the order to hold up and defend for the night. The irony of this situation was that B Company was given the mission of protecting the battalion's left flank, which placed it on the same high ground it had just come off. Fortunately, about 85 percent of the company was still on top of the hill. By this time we had some civilian laborers, and with them I was able to take water loads up to the rest of the company. Then I used the civilians to carry down the remainder of the heat-prostration cases. They brought down about fifteen men, who then had to be treated at the battalion aid station.

[Despite the torrid weather, there was nonstop activity along the coastal road where the 1st Provisional Marine Brigade marched. Battalions shuttled back and forth along the column. Rifle companies replaced each other on the point, along the flanks, and in the rear. On either side of the road, there were hills to climb, and to the front, whenever they materialized, enemy roadblocks to be overcome. The brigade rolled forward, mile by mile, hour by hour, from before sunrise to after sunset—through Taedabok Pass, then south to Kosong, west to Ch'angch'on, northwest to Sach'on. In danger at the head of the long, dusty column or relatively safe, but dirtier, at the rear, the Marines witnessed all around them the toll the war was taking.]

Pfc. FRED DAVIDSON
G/5

The call, "Interpreter up front!" had me running toward the head of the column. The battalion was somewhere between Chindong-ni and

Kosong. The day was scorching hot. White clouds looking like mounds of shaving cream hung in the distance. By a bridge over a dried-up riverbed, I saw a young Korean woman holding a baby. A Navy corpsman was bandaging a deep gash on the baby's leg. The woman had a fragment wound in her upper arm. I was told to explain to her that a doctor was coming up from the rear. The baby had diarrhea, and while its leg was being wrapped, it defecated on the corpsman. To the left of the road, a young boy lay on his back. I walked over to him. He had a stomach wound. I told him he'd be treated soon. Although the pain must have been awful, the boy did not make a sound.

The day had grown hotter. How this could be I don't know. The woman asked me about her daughter. I hadn't seen anyone but the boy and the woman and her baby. I climbed down the bank and looked under the bridge. A young girl of around ten lay in the dust. She was dead.

It seems that when the point reached this spot someone had thrown a grenade under the bridge to smoke out any North Koreans hiding there. The grenade had exploded among a family that was using the bridge as a refuge.

The woman did not know about her daughter and continued to ask about her. With my limited knowledge of the language, how in the hell was I supposed to tell her that her daughter had been accidentally killed? I found some words that told her what had happened and how sorry we were. She looked at me with a blank stare. When I was sure I had done everything I could, I rejoined my unit. A few moments later a few of us climbed on some passing tanks and the brigade continued its march toward Sach'on.

2d Lt. FRANK MUETZEL *
A/5

Beyond Masan, alongside a river, a fumigation and bath platoon had set up operation. Equipped with pumps, boilers, washing machines, and portable showers, the platoon supported combat troops by supplying them with hot showers and a laundry service.

A unit would simply discard their old clothes, and when bathed would pick up the clothes of another unit whose uniforms had already been cleaned. This unit's dirty discarded clothes would then be washed and given to the next unit waiting for the showers. The system always made for interesting size searches.

I had ordered my platoon to stack arms, had posted a guard over them, and we'd gone on and showered. Clean clothes had been issued, our weapons picked up, and the platoon began loading on a truck. A pile of unguarded weapons lay nearby on the ground. I asked a laundry NCO who it belonged to. He informed me it was the property of the Army unit that was then showering. With that I selected an M1919AG light machine gun, threw it into the back of the truck, mounted up, and ordered the truck to move out. The gun proved to have some minor deficiencies, but who was I to question a gift?

10 August 1950

At 0055 CO 5th Marines directed a regimental attack on Kosong and continuous attacks and capture of Sach'on. 3d Battalion was directed to follow 2d Battalion in trace.

SPECIAL ACTION REPORT, 3/5

---

* Frank Muetzel was born in Redwood Falls, Minnesota, of working-class parents. He had three older brothers and a younger sister. Impressed by an older brother's dress-blue Marine uniform, he enlisted in the Marine Corps after high school. His career was typical: Recruit Depot, Parris Island; Infantry Training Regiment, Camp Lejeune; Sea School, San Diego; Marine Detachment, USS *Boxer*; 2d Marine Division, Camp Lejeune; 1st Marine Division, Camp Pendleton. He was a platoon sergeant when selected for officer candidate school. In 1950 Muetzel was twenty-four years old. He describes himself at that time as being young, in good physical condition, impressionable, and patriotic.

Pfc. FRED DAVIDSON
G/5
The road was rough and dusty. Everyone covered his mouth with his hand to avoid breathing too much of the dirt. We passed through one of the other battalions.

About 5:00 in the afternoon two American fighters zoomed down the road around 150 feet above our heads.

2d Lt. JOHN COUNSELMAN
G/5
They came in with machine guns blazing—*chung*—*chung*—*chung*—*chung*. You could see where the bullets hit the ground. The kids flew in every direction and tried to bury themselves behind rocks, pebbles, anything they could find.

Pfc. FRED DAVIDSON
G/5
No matter where I ran, I couldn't seem to find an escape. Their .50-caliber bullets hit that hard, dry road and it sounded as if each was exploding. There was just nowhere to go to get out of the line of fire. Someone screamed, "Break out the air panels! Get the air panels!" The fighters left as suddenly as they had arrived.

After this terrible experience I always loved attacking the enemy when they were being strafed. I just knew the Communists would have their heads down and at that moment not be worrying about me. There's no way a sane man is going to lift his head when he's being strafed.

10 August 1950
CO 3d Battalion issued verbal orders for G Company to pass through elements of 2d Battalion at 1830 and continue attack toward Kosong. G jumped off at 1830 against sniper and auto-

matic weapons fire. At 1950 G was held up along road by two enemy machine guns.

SPECIAL ACTION REPORT, 3/5

Pfc. FRED DAVIDSON
G/5

A North Korean machine gun opened fire from a concealed position on a hill to the company's right. Most of the Marines made it safely to the cut in the road at the base of the hill. The platoon leaders immediately got us up and moving toward the concealed enemy position. Many small scrub pines and bushes offered some concealment if not protection.

Lieutenant Westerman sent a 3.5 rocket squad down the road to a point where it could cut in on the right, climb the hill, and drive down on the enemy's flank. "Big Jack," which was the lieutenant's nickname, ordered me to go with these men. The rocket squad had already run down the ditch to the right of the road and had come to the point where they were going to begin to climb the hill. I was about twenty-five yards behind, crouched over, running hard, when small-arms fire hit around me. I dropped into the ditch. Each time I tried to move forward and join the bazooka team, the sniper put a round close enough for me to change my mind.

The ditch was shallow, so I had no problem sneaking peeks down the road. The rocket team kept waving to me to join them. It was then that I noticed an empty American jeep in the middle of the road up ahead. I couldn't figure out what it was doing there. Best that I knew the company was the battalion's point. There should have been no Americans in front of us. The sun was going down right into my eyes. Suddenly, two figures whose silhouettes I could see came around the jeep and headed toward the rocket team. The Marines hadn't seen them. I yelled, "Watch it!" Then I fired at the two figures. I let go six rounds. They hit in front of them. My carbine jammed. The two men ran back toward the jeep and disappeared behind it.

A fire team sent by Lieutenant Westerman ran up to me. The sniper opened up on them. They made it to the ditch without getting hit. But with five Marines now huddled in a shallow ditch, it was just a matter of time before the North Korean sniper got lucky. I said,

"Let's cross the road and get into that rice paddy." The bank from the road to the paddy was at least four feet high. Together we jumped up and raced across the road.

As we moved through the paddy, Big Jack showed up and wanted to know what the holdup was. I explained about the two figures I'd seen near the jeep and how they had dodged back behind the vehicle when I fired at them. I had no more than finished my report when we heard someone from the direction of the jeep calling, "Corpsman. Corpsman." Westerman took charge. "When I throw a grenade you all open fire on the hill. I'm gonna get that man." He threw the grenade. As soon as it exploded, he jumped up and ran for the jeep. The fire team and I poured our fire into the hillside. I never saw anyone, but I continued to fire until Big Jack returned. He had a man slung over his shoulder. Behind the bank we helped get the wounded man off the lieutenant's shoulder. "Damn," Westerman raged, "I've hurt my back. Damn!" I suggested he return to the platoon and the rest of us would bring the wounded man in. Lieutenant Westerman limped back to the platoon. I noticed then the wounded man was a Marine major. I didn't recognize him. He'd been hit three times: once in the shoulder, once in the right upper arm, and once in the chest. He was hurt bad and in a great deal of pain. His eyes were closed. All he wanted was water from my canteen. I gave him some. Then it was time to carry him back to our lines. Four of us picked him up, the fifth gave cover. It was just terrible. Every time we took a step, we sank to our knees in muck and dropped the wounded man. He moaned in agony. "Goddamn it," I cursed, "let's get him up on the road where we can carry him back without killing him." Despite the sniper, this was the only chance we had of getting the man back alive. On the road we stumbled into a corpsman and a stretcher-bearer whom Lieutenant Westerman was sending down to us. The corpsman took over, placed the major on the stretcher, and organized the carrying party.

Back with the platoon I suddenly remembered the 3.5 rocket team. Picking up my carbine I retraced my earlier route; this time there was no sniper to delay me. When I arrived at the point in the ditch where I'd last seen them, the rocket team was no longer there. I stopped and yelled. No answer. I yelled again. No answer. I returned to the platoon.

It had begun to get dark. I was pooped. I reached for my canteen. It wasn't in its cover. When I had given the major a drink, I must have laid it on the ground. "Oh . . . !" I found a Marine tank and had one of the tankers give me a cupful of their water. Then I climbed a few yards up the hill and settled in for the night. I removed my wet shoes and socks. That night I didn't dig a hole.

Sometime during the night the Marine major we had carried back died of his wounds. I learned later that his name was Morgan McNeely.*

11 August 1950

The night passed quietly with only sporadic rifle fire in defense position. At 0700 3d Battalion was directed to insure that battalion area was clear of enemy troops. No enemy were found and at 0808, G Company led the attack toward Kosong.

SPECIAL ACTION REPORT, 3/5

Pfc. DOUG KOCH
D/5

We just kited along in this jeep. I sat in the back. Up ahead the road made a little elbow. Next to me one of the guys said, "By God, it sure is quiet, isn't it?" About then the shit hit the fan. The North Koreans opened up. Over to the side of the road walked a little old Korean man. He sure was in the wrong place at the wrong time. A lot of guys fired at him; the poor old guy just disintegrated.

The gooks cut up the first couple of jeeps pretty bad. My group tumbled and ran for the ditch. I landed calf-deep in warm water. I heard machine guns chattering around me. Dirt kicked up along the road that was now lined with abandoned jeeps.

Sergeant Dickerson shouted over the noise, "Those hills, the little low ones, over to the right, we gotta get over there. Gotta return fire from there." I picked up my BAR and, crouched over, ran down the ditch. I went about ten yards before I found Gunny Reeves. He

---

*Major McNeely, 2/5's S-3 (operations and training officer), had been on a patrol in front of the brigade when he was ambushed by the enemy.

lay in the ditch. A corpsman was patching him up. I stopped. "How you doing, Gunny?" "Well," he said, "the sons of bitches finally got me." I looked down. He'd been hit through both legs just below the knees. Someone behind hollered to keep moving and I ran on. That's how I said good-bye to Gunny Reeves.

Cpl. LOGAN PARNELL *
1st Provisional Marine Brigade
Near sunset on August 11 I stood by the side of the road watching and listening to an old Korean man being questioned by an ROK second lieutenant and a Marine lieutenant colonel. One of the guys nearby who'd been watching longer than I had said, "We've got one now."

A little earlier the old Korean had been caught under a bridge with a case of North Korean belted machine-gun ammunition. The man wore the traditional white Korean costume, although now it was dirty and wrinkled. He knelt on the ground. The ROK officer asked the old man what he was doing carrying ammo. Was he a spy? Was he a Communist? The man kept his head bowed and did not answer. He was ordered to empty his pockets and remove his shirt. He laid a crumpled pack of Korean cigarettes and a box of matches on the ground. Then without getting up he took off his shirt. A red mark around his shoulders clearly showed where he had carried the ammo case with its rope sling. The lieutenant placed the muzzle of his carbine against the back of the old man's head and threatened to kill him if he didn't answer the questions. Still the old man refused to say anything. In disgust, the lieutenant jabbed the old man's head with his carbine and cursed him. The man said nothing. The ROK officer turned to the Marine lieutenant colonel. "Sir, if you turn him loose, he'll go right back to the enemy and help them again." The lieutenant colonel turned and caught my eye. "Take him back to the Korean police," he ordered, "and have him shot!" Everybody then just drifted away, leaving me alone with the old man.

I motioned for him to get up and put on his shirt. He gestured he would like his cigarettes. I nodded. After he lit one I marched him

* Pseudonym.

to the rear where I met the South Korean police detachment that was assigned to the brigade. To a police sergeant I explained I had orders to have the old man shot and that I needed someone to do the job. The sergeant selected a young man not much older than I who spoke English.

The young policeman, the old man, and I walked along the road; I was looking for a suitable place to hold the execution. I noticed the policeman was unarmed. I figured I'd let him use my carbine.

I found a spot down by a shallow river that afforded the privacy I was looking for. We moved down off the road and walked to the near-dry riverbed. The old man asked if he could wash his hands. The policeman translated. I nodded. By now I was confused and scared. I was about to have a civilian killed. Suddenly it seemed ludicrous that I was allowing the old man to wash his hands when in a few minutes he would be dead. I hollered. The old man stood up. He shook his wet hands to dry them. He still didn't know he was going to be shot. I motioned for him to walk on. About twenty-five feet away he stopped and turned. Why weren't we behind him? Was he free to go? I offered my carbine to the policeman. He pushed the weapon away and backed off. In broken English he told me he didn't know how to use it. His voice was shrill. I yelled at him to take it. At this, the old man realized what was going to happen. "No! No!" he pleaded in Korean. The policeman backed away. I shouted some more. The old man began to cry. Falling to his knees he clasped his hands as if he was praying. Between sobs he continued to plead for his life. Something had to be done. I ordered the old man to stand up. The policeman yelled to him to stand up. He did. I shot him twice. He fell like a stone.

I ran to the road. I didn't check to see if the old man was dead— he had to be. I walked until I came to the battalion HQ area. I told the lieutenant colonel what I'd done. He made no comment. I decided not to rejoin the company but to spend the night where I was. After I settled down, I couldn't sleep. Nearby two officers quietly spoke to each other. I heard one say, "That Marine had to shoot the old man." The other said, "I don't think I could do that."

By the shallow river everything had happened so fast. Everyone was screaming at once. No one but the policeman and I would have known if I'd let the old man go. It had all happened so fast.

In the morning, when I rejoined my company, one of the sergeants told me, "Don't worry about it. Think of Tome and Smythe." They'd been killed a few days before. I never learned how the sergeant knew what I'd done.

On the road that day I tried to swagger. We passed hundreds of Korean civilians. They all seemed to look at me.

12 August 1950

At 0630 the 1st Battalion passed through the 3d Battalion and continued the advance as far as Ch'angch'on.

Fifty enemy-abandoned motorcycles with sidecars, twenty Russian-built Ford jeeps, and numerous quantities of small arms were passed, burned or camouflaged beside the road, all having been abandoned by the enemy as a result of the rapid movement of the brigade and air strikes.

SPECIAL ACTION REPORT, 5TH MARINES

Capt. FRANCIS ''IKE'' FENTON, JR.
B/5
We moved out at a very rapid pace, knowing that we were getting close to Sach'on. Everyone was anxious to get there. We had received reports that the Army was moving right along. Everyone wanted to take Sach'on before the Army occupied Chinju. Morale was very high. There was the normal amount of grumbling, but nothing worth listening to.

There was evidence of considerable enemy disorganization; equipment lying along the road, vehicles burned, dead bodies. We had them on the run and wanted to finish them off. Marine air continued to hit the enemy hard.

Brig. Gen. EDWARD CRAIG
Commanding General, 1st Provisional Marine Brigade
When I returned to brigade headquarters, which was then at Kosong, General Kean ordered me to proceed to his headquarters for a conference. . . . Kean informed me that two Communist divisions had broken through the Naktong area and it would be necessary for the

brigade to pull out from the drive and move to the Naktong, where
it was to restore that position to its original status.*

[In the week that followed their crossing of the Naktong River, the North
Korean 4th "Seoul" Division had not only overrun the Naktong Bulge
but had begun to push eastward out of the bridgehead. In a series of
bitterly fought engagements, the Army units in the area had not been
able to stop the Communists' advance. General Walker called upon
the Marines to plug the hole. Before the brigade could be shipped
northward, it would first have to break contact with the enemy—
something the Marines would find difficult to do.

The 1st Battalion, 5th Marines, had beaten off several North Korean attacks near Ch'angch'on on 12 August and darkness fell before
B Company, which had been fighting all day, could set up a proper
defensive perimeter. Their objective, Sach'on, was only four miles away,
and the leathernecks anticipated they would reach it the next day.]

Capt. FRANCIS ''IKE'' FENTON, JR.
B/5
Darkness caught us before we had had time to complete our perimeter defenses. This was our first chance to really reorganize and find
out what we had lost during the day. Our casualties had been three
dead, thirteen wounded, and two missing in action. It was close to
midnight before we were completely set up.

About 4:50 A.M. [13 August] we received a report from the 2d
Platoon that there was activity to its immediate front and that someone was feeling out a gap between the 1st and 2d Platoons. About
this time a flare burst above our immediate front, and on our left
flank all hell broke loose. Under cover of darkness the enemy had
evidently moved into position right under the noses of a few of our
men who were supposed to be awake but who had fallen asleep. Our
entire left flank was overrun and the machine-gun section was completely wiped out. Ten men in the section were killed and the elev-
enth was severely wounded. The enemy then took over the two ma-

_____
*Craig interview, MCHC.

chine guns and turned them on the rest of the company. A runner was sent to the 3d Platoon with orders to fall back into a company perimeter. The enemy had managed to cut our wire to the 3d Platoon and runners were the only means left of communication.

The enemy had a small mortar, and we were taking a lot of mortar rounds in our company command post. We asked the battalion commander to give us all the 81, 4.2, and artillery fire that he could, and not to hesitate in bringing it close to the company. We had reached the point where in order to hit the enemy, the fire had to come right in on top of us. The ridgeline sloped off to the right and the enemy occupied the high point. At first the artillery forward observer was able to call down artillery fire with his own radio, but he took a machine-gun burst in his radio set. Thereafter, we had to call for all our artillery through the battalion tactical net.

At this point, around midnight, we received word from the battalion commander that at dawn we were to pull off the hill and return to the battalion area. The battalion had received orders to move to a new area. We didn't know exactly what the score was; all we had then was this warning order.

After the 3d Platoon pulled down, we spotted the enemy machine guns. We took one of our 3.5 rocket launchers and fired a round into the machine-gun emplacement, knocking it out and killing its crew. The rocket launcher proved so effective that we employed all three of our 3.5s on the enemy positions. We eventually succeeded in knocking out another machine gun.

With daylight rapidly approaching we could see that from their positions on the high ground of the ridge the enemy had the upper hand. We decided the best thing we could do was pull back to the 2d Platoon's position on the right portion of the ridge, and there reorganize for a counterattack.

In the meantime the artillery was doing a wonderful job. We had called them in to somewhere between fifty and seventy-five yards. We took a round or two ourselves, but their fire was very effective. The 81s were also doing a magnificent job; they were putting them right in our lap. Just before first light we were all back with the 2d Platoon. During this withdrawal the supporting fire accompanied us down the ridge and prevented the enemy from following us.

About 0700 we were reorganized. The battalion had landed

enough artillery and mortars on the enemy's position that we thought we could jump off and retake the ridge. When we requested permission to do so, we received a negative. We were ordered to come down off the ridge at once and return to the battalion. We immediately notified battalion that we had left some dead on the ridge. We thought we could go back up without too much difficulty, seize the ground, and, at least, take out our dead. The battalion commander stated we must pull off immediately! This was very demoralizing to us. We felt terrible about having to go off and leave our dead.

It was decided that I would take part of the 1st Platoon and carry all the wounded out. While we proceeded across the rice paddy, Captain Tobin would remain with the other two platoons and cover our withdrawal. At this time our air showed up and struck the ridgeline. Our artillery fired continually and with only sporadic small-arms enemy fire shooting at us we managed to get off the ridge and across the rice paddy.

When we returned to battalion, the company was told it was going back to Chindong-ni; the enemy had broken through up north and the brigade was going to have to retake the ground. Our advance on Sach'on, which was just a few miles ahead, had been canceled. The men couldn't believe it. I couldn't believe it. It didn't seem possible, with all the lives we'd lost taking this ground, that we'd now just walk off and leave it. Baker Company's casualties for that morning's counterattack alone were twelve dead, sixteen wounded, and nine missing in action. And I'm certain those last nine were dead, too.

We were told that a battalion from the 5th RCT was coming up and would try to hold what we'd taken. If headquarters was only going to send a battalion, we felt it was just giving that ground back to the enemy. As soon as the North Koreans probed and found only a battalion blocking their way, they'd break through and come right back down to Chindong-ni.

I found it difficult to see men, veterans of the last war, older guys, sitting by the side of the road crying. They just didn't give a hoot. They were tired, disgusted. People just couldn't understand this part of the war.

Brig. Gen. EDWARD CRAIG
Commanding General, 1st Provisional Marine Brigade
At Chindong-ni I received orders from Eighth Army to detach the
brigade from the 25th Division and to report to the commanding
general of the 24th Division, General Church. The brigade commenced moving our heaviest equipment that night, and in the morning sent the troops by truck and rail to our rendezvous area, a place
called Miryang.

At Miryang the brigade camped in a grove of trees that lay near
a stream which ran behind the position. The field kitchens set up and
gave the troops their first hot meals since they had landed almost two
weeks before. The men were also able to get into that stream and
wash up. We stayed at Miryang for about twenty-four hours.*

Pfc. FRED DAVIDSON
G/5
We camped in a grove of pine trees near the main road. The bridge
across the river was close by. That evening, mail caught up with us
and I received several letters from my girlfriend and my sister. A short
time later a nearby shot rang out. I jerked and saw a Marine a little
way off whose right hand was still on the trigger of his M1. His left,
bleeding profusely, was held in the air. A couple of his buddies grabbed
him and wrapped his hand. Then all three left the area looking for a
corpsman.

Capt. FRANCIS ''IKE'' FENTON, JR.
B/5
B Company went into a bivouac area located in a grove of trees by a
fast-flowing river. While we were bathing we received word that there
was a woman reporter in the area. We were to tell the men they were
not to run around naked or expose themselves. You can imagine what
the troops had to say about what that woman could do if she didn't

---

* Craig interview, MCHC.

like seeing Marines without their uniforms on. Of course they continued to swim as they had before.

Pfc. FRED DAVIDSON
G/5
Of course we swam in the nude. The bridge made a great diving board. I lay on the riverbank and watched the diving, enjoying life. All of a sudden, like falling dominoes, Marines on the bridge dove into the river. A jeep crossed the bridge. There was no mistaking the blond next to the driver—Maggie Higgins!

Capt. JOSEPH FEGAN
H/5
I believe H Company was the last unit to close Miryang. I hadn't changed my clothes for ten days. My baggage, along with the packs of the mortar section, had been swiped earlier by an Army unit. This left me without any change of clothing. Not only did I smell to high heaven, I also had dried blood all over my jacket. At Miryang I paid a Korean woman a little something and she washed my clothes as well as she could. When they dried they were as stiff as cardboard. The rule was that if your uniform had an arm or leg ripped off, you could get a new one. I didn't qualify because mine was just smelly. Apparently, my Korean laundress didn't use strong enough soap. On the road the next day, my gunnery sergeant, Ray Morgan, said to me, "Skipper, I hate to tell you this, but you still stink!" And I did.

Pfc. DOUG KOCH
D/5
Late in the afternoon we went down to the mess area, where we were served fried chicken, mashed potatoes, hot vegetables, ice cream, and steaming coffee. No Christmas dinner ever tasted so good. Guys from the rifle companies lucked out; no one drew mess duty. We sat on the ground eating and shooting the breeze. After dinner everyone re-

ceived two cans of beer. We drank one and cooled the other in the river. That night was pretty quiet. We didn't even pull exterior guard duty and got to sleep all night. I tell you, I really thought I was living on top of the world.

BATTLE

16 August-6 September 1950

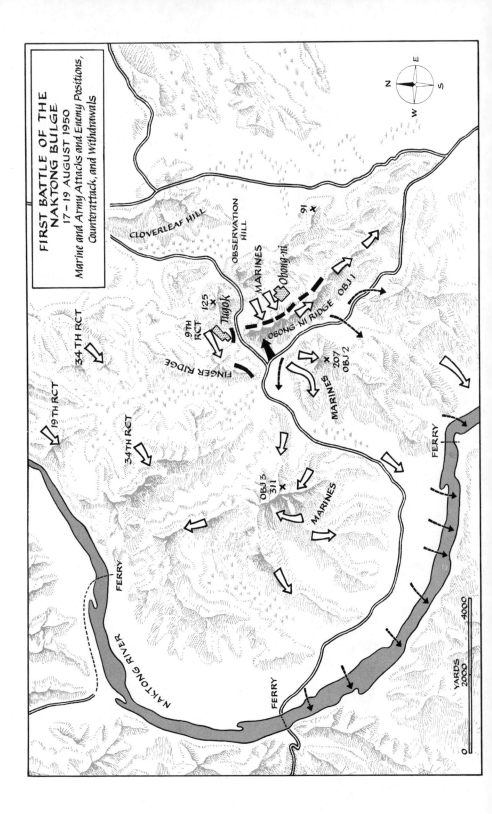

FIRST BATTLE OF THE
NAKTONG BULGE
17-19 AUGUST 1950
*Marine and Army Attacks and Enemy Positions,
Counterattack, and Withdrawals*

CLOVERLEAF HILL

OBSERVATION HILL

91

MARINES

Obong-ni

125

Tugok

9TH RCT

OBONG NI RIDGE   OBJ 1

FINGER RIDGE

207
OBJ 2

MARINES

34 TH RCT

19TH RCT

34TH RCT

OBJ 3
311

MARINES

MARINES

FERRY

FERRY

FERRY

FERRY

NAKTONG RIVER

YARDS

0   2000   4000

Brig. Gen. EDWARD CRAIG
Commanding General, 1st Provisional Marine Brigade

I reported to the CG of the 24th Division, General Church [15 August]. His division had been pretty hard hit. He was a fine officer and promised every assistance. We were to go into the line and retake an area around what was then being called the "Naktong Bulge."*

Pfc. DOUG KOCH
D/5

About noon we received orders that we were going to pull out. We heard a new name, someplace called the Naktong River. The next day we loaded aboard trucks and headed for this river. We thought we were old hands at this fighting business. But I think anytime a guy gets off the line for a rest and then heads back toward the front, he gets a tight feeling in his gut.

---

* Craig interview, MCHC.

[The Naktong Bulge was the brigade's first large-scale engagement in the Korean War. In the history books, the battle's climax on the slopes of Obong-ni Ridge (aka No-Name Ridge, Bloody Ridge) reads like a classic. In August 1950, however, to the men on the ground who fought it, the first battle of the Naktong seemed anything but classic.

By the time the Marine brigade reached the killing ground, the battle had been going on for ten bloody days.

In conjunction with the U.S. 24th Division, reinforced, which would operate on their right,* the Marines were given the mission of capturing three ridgelines, designated brigade Objective One, Two, and Three. The plan was simple enough: the 5th Marines would attack in a column of battalions, that is, one in front of the other, with the 2d Battalion in assault followed by the 1st and 3d. Each would go as hard as it could, then be replaced by the one behind, until all objectives were taken. Once Objective Three, which was the highest and overlooked the Naktong, was occupied, the enemy would be forced to recross the river.

It was well known that the objectives were heavily defended. The meager intelligence then available suggested that Objectives Two and Three would present the greater difficulty; Objective One was thought to be more lightly defended and therefore easier to seize. The events of 17–18 August would prove the reverse to be true. The attack was scheduled to be launched at 8:00 A.M. on 17 August, at which time the 2d Battalion would jump off and seize Objective One—Obong-ni Ridge.†]

2d Lt. TOM GIBSON
Mortar Company/5

The night before the first battle of the Naktong I sat in SACC [Supporting Arm Coordination Center] monitoring the regimental tactical net. I heard one of the battalion commanders speaking with Colonel Murray. In a very dispassionate voice, Lieutenant Colonel Newton [1/5] told the regimental CO, "We're in such and such a position

---

* The 19th Infantry and 34th Infantry would attack the North Korean bridgehead from the northeast; in the center, the 9th RCT would attack frontally and cover the Marines' right flank.
† Hill 207 was Objective Two; Hill 311 was Objective Three.

doing this and this." Murray said to him, "You *must* take that ground tomorrow! You have to get on that ridge and take it. Understood?" The last word was a question, you know, "Do you understand what I've said?" George Newton came back, "Understood! Understood! This battalion goes only one way—straight ahead! Out." I cheered. I really did.

16 August 1950
The 3d Battalion relieved elements of the 34th Regiment prior to daylight 17 August.

SPECIAL ACTION REPORT, 3/5

Pfc. FRED DAVIDSON
G/5

We boarded trucks in the dark. The road was rough and it was nearly impossible to sleep. Sometime later we off-loaded and began walking in the black of night toward the front.

Around 4:00 A.M., after a force march of six or seven miles, the company left the road and started climbing a hill. It was really dark. Everyone was tired from the long walk. Trying to climb this hill and not being able to see where we were going had everyone cussing and complaining. Finally, our NCOs ordered everyone to quit bitching and shut up. They were as frustrated as the rest of us.

Sometime before first light we stopped and waited for further orders. I tried to sleep. Everyone was quiet. When the sun finally rose, I saw we were on a ridge. I later learned it was part of Cloverleaf Hill. I thought, Just what the hell am I doing on this hill, thousands of miles away from home and American women?

Pfc. LEONARD KORGIE
L Company/34th Infantry

While we rested by the side of the road, a Marine unit on trucks rode by. You could see they were ready. They yelled to us, "Where in hell are the gooks?" That's the way to go into combat, full of piss and vinegar.

17 August 1950
The 2d Battalion completed its movement into the assembly area at 0130. . . .

SPECIAL ACTION REPORT, 2/5

Pfc. DOUG KOCH
D/5

Captain Zimmer gave us our orders. D and E Companies would take a ridge. It was thought not to be heavily defended. The ridge was simply called Objective One [O-1]. D Company would be on the right, E Company on the left. My platoon would climb a nearby hill [125] and lay down a base of fire on the objective. I thought this was pretty straightforward.

17 August 1950
Thirty-five minutes preparation by artillery and air on Obong-ni Ridge (Objective 1) had been planned by regiment. No artillery preparation was received on Objective 1 and only one air strike was received prior to H-Hour.

SPECIAL ACTION REPORT, 2/5

17 August 1950
0740: Eighteen F4Us [Corsairs] conducted prebriefed strike against Objectives 1 and 2, Napalm and 1,000 lb. GP.

1ST MARINE AIR WING

HAROLD MARTIN *
The Saturday Evening Post

Finally they had done all that they could do and the infantry moved out. They went in long, thinly spaced files across the emerald rice paddies, walking upright despite the sniper fire, for in war men sometimes grow so weary they do not give a damn whether they live or die, and these men were going into battle tired. They reached the terraced lower slopes where patches of peas and red peppers and scraggly cotton lay, and then they were moving upward into the scrubby pines. †

Pfc. DOUG KOCH
D/5

The guys from the 1st and 3d Platoons moved toward the ridge. Farther away, I could see E Company moving out. The "gunny" began picking targets he wanted us to shoot at. I fired my BAR at the top of the ridge, although I didn't see any specific targets. The guys from the two platoons were across the road and now were moving through rice paddies. They were in good shape and the formation was textbook. About two-thirds across some guys began to fall. On our hill we started taking long-range machine-gun fire. When I again looked down at the attacking platoons, quite a few men were lying out in the sun.

Sometime later Sergeant Dickerson hollered we were going down to support the 1st Platoon. As soon as we crossed the road, we too began taking casualties. All around guys started dropping. I looked at the top of the ridge but couldn't see anything. How had they zeroed in on us so quickly? We fired as we moved. I ran to the bottom of the ridge, then began climbing. I got some way up, crawled over a wall, moved another ten feet, and hit the deck. I looked around. Except for two dead Marines nearby, I was alone.

I fired a couple of magazines toward the top of the ridge, then

---

*Martin watched the battle with General Craig and the brigade staff from a ridge on Observation Hill, which overlooked the battlefield as a balcony overlooks a stage.
†Harold Martin, "The Epic of Bloody Hill," *The Saturday Evening Post,* 14 October 1950. Hereafter, Martin, *Post.*

moved back down and crouched behind the wall. There I met two other guys, one of them my buddy Dick Fletcher. Every time we raised up to shoot we took heavy fire. If we couldn't see the enemy, how could they see us? We were really puzzled. Later I learned the casualties 1st and 2d Platoons took that morning were caused by enemy fire coming from our right flank, a flank that was supposed to be secured by an Army unit [9th RCT]. Instead of the Army protecting this flank, it was wide open and the North Koreans were firing right into our positions. *

More and more guys reached the wall. After a while quite a few had collected there. Artillery and mortars opened up on the top of the ridge. We didn't know where Sergeant Dickerson was; maybe he'd been hit. We hung on where we were with what we had. Some of the guys risked their necks and brought in wounded Marines who lay in the area.

As elements of D Company reached the ridge, the enemy made extensive use of hand grenades. Mortar fire was received throughout the advance up the slope.

SPECIAL ACTION REPORT, 2/5

Pfc. DOUG KOCH
D/5
One time on a little trail that ran around the side of the hill we saw a Marine walking toward us. "My God," I said in disbelief, "here comes Sergeant Jones from over'n 1st Platoon." Right up to the corner of the wall he came. When he saw the men huddled against it, he shouted, "What'n hell are you guys lying here for?" No sooner had he said these words than a North Korean slug caught him in the stomach. He folded like an accordion. Another man and I reached out and, grabbing his boots, dragged him behind the wall. His dungaree top was cut away. He was bleeding a little. The bullet had gone right on through him. He was still alive, kind of surprised and in shock.

---

* The 9th RCT had not kept up with the advance of the 2d Battalion, 5th Marines, and the North Koreans were consequently free to pound the battalion's open right flank.

I couldn't help myself, and said, "Well, Sergeant, now you know why in hell we're lying here. We can't get over it and we can't get around it." Someone bandaged the wounds as best he could.

Our small group continued to lie behind the wall. The sun was hot, hot. Artillery continued to pound the top of the ridge. Anytime anyone exposed himself the wall received heavy fire.

In half an hour the shock of the bullet wound wore off. Sergeant Jones moaned, "God, is that ever burning." He was in a lot of pain. He told us he felt as if a hot poker had been run through his gut.

Our platoon guide, who'd been shot earlier in the morning, lay about twenty-five yards away. He'd been hit in the legs. Two guys ran out to him. When they tried to drag him behind the wall, his legs caught in some high weeds. He screamed and hollered. With nothing else to do, they laid him between two burial mounds that afforded him some cover.

A man named McLaren had been shot in the head and was now completely out of his skull. His helmet was gone and his head was bathed in blood. He'd been with the company for quite a while. We shouted at him to come over to the wall. He stumbled around and talked out of his head. I'm sure he didn't know we were there. During the morning the gooks occasionally shot at him but they didn't hit him again.

Toward noon our artillery really pounded the ridgeline. The big shells going over sounded like freight trains.

The ridge was gained three times but was untenable each time due to intense enemy automatic weapons fire.

SPECIAL ACTION REPORT, 2/5

HAROLD MARTIN
The Saturday Evening Post
Twice in the long morning small handfuls reached the top, and each time it was an eye-tingling thrill to see those tiny figures valiant against the sky. But the first time they were driven back, and the second time they were pulled back so that an air strike could be laid on.

When the air strike ended, the thin green line on the slopes rose and charged again. And again the grenades came down on them, and you could see men fall and roll, for a wounded man could not cling to the steep slopes where the earth lay loose underfoot. Watching through field glasses, General Craig saw the fighting in all its minute detail.

"You can see the puffs of dirt kick up around a Marine where a machine gun is firing on him," he reported. "He'll drop and lie there a minute, and then he'll stand up and suddenly fire, and go down again. I don't believe our kids can see the guns that are hitting them." *

2d Lt. MICHAEL SHINKA
D/5

Fire from Hill 143 was gaining in intensity, and they had observation over our position. † Fire was also coming from the hill to our front [Hill 207]. ‡ I reported the situation to Captain Zimmer [D Company CO]. A short time later phosphorus shells exploded on Hill 143. This slowed the fire but it never did stop.

My resupply of ammo did not arrive. Running short of ammo and taking casualties, with the shallow enemy slit trenches for cover, I decided to fall back until some of the fire on my left flank could be silenced. I gave the word to withdraw and take all wounded and weapons. About three-quarters of the way down, I had the men set up where cover was available. I had six men who were able to fight.

I decided to go forward to find out if we left any of our wounded. As I crawled along our former position (on the crest of Hill 109), I came across a wounded Marine between two dead. As I grabbed him under the arms and pulled him from the foxhole, a bullet shattered my chin. Blood ran into my throat and I couldn't breathe. I tossed a grenade at a gook crawling up the slope, didn't wait for it to explode, turned and reached under the Marine's arms, and dragged him as far as the military crest.

Another bullet hit my right arm, and the force spun me around.

---

* Martin, Post.
† Obong-ni Ridge's narrow spine was dominated by a series of peaks that overlooked the slope leading to its summit. Hill 143 was one of these peaks and was held in strength by the North Koreans.
‡ Hill 207, Brigade Objective Two, was a dominating hill mass that rose above and looked down on Obong-ni Ridge from the west.

I rolled down the hill for a considerable distance before I could stop myself.

I walked into my lines and had a battle dressing tied on my face and arm. I learned the ammo was up and that a relief was contemplated; and then I walked back to 2/5's aid station where they placed me on a jeep and took me to regimental aid. *

Pfc. DOUG KOCH
D/5
From where I lay I watched a lot of things going on around me. The Navy corpsmen had a lot of guts. Along with native stretcher-bearers, they braved the fire storm and went through the rice paddy picking up wounded men.

After midday loudspeakers on the hill where 2d Platoon had begun the battle announced that survivors of D and E Companies should pull back with as many wounded and dead as they could carry.

At about 1500 both companies [D & E] held the ground approximately halfway up the objective when the 1st Battalion was ordered to pass through the 2d Battalion and continue the assault.

SPECIAL ACTION REPORT, 2/5

[Earlier in the day, about the time Pfc. Koch found refuge behind the low wall, the 1st Battalion, 5th Marines, the next unit in line to assault Obong-ni Ridge, was moving into position.]

---

* Lynn Montross and Capt. Nicholas A. Canzona, USMC, *The Pusan Perimeter,* vol. 1 of *U.S. Marine Operations in Korea, 1950–1953* (Washington, D.C.: Historical Branch, G-3, Headquarters, U.S. Marine Corps, 1954), 183.

2d Lt. FRANK MUETZEL
A/5

By the time the 1st Battalion detrucked near the brigade CP, the 2d Battalion was already in action. To the west artillery and small-arms fire could be heard. As A Company passed through, I had an opportunity to chat with Lt. Col. Joe Stewart, the brigade G-3 [operations and training section], and Col. Ed Snedeker, the chief of staff. Although it was mostly small talk between friends, they advised that the 2d Battalion effort was moving slowly.

The 1st Battalion moved up the road in a column. We halted alongside a burned-out T34 the Army had killed the preceding night. The battalion aid station was a short distance down the road. From the steady stream of jeep ambulances I observed coming and going, it was apparent the attack was not going well.

Pfc. HERBERT LUSTER
A/5

Up ahead was an enemy T34 tank that had been burned by napalm. To the right was a small hill, and the left side of the road dropped off into a swampy flat. The column stayed to the right, against the hill. A battle raged over the hill.

Off the road to the high ground, the company was ordered to wait. I pulled out my food and decided to try to eat a can of fruit. One bite was enough. My stomach protested and I passed the peaches to my new assistant BAR man, Pfc. Baxter. "I'm going for a head call down in that ditch."

"OK, Luster, don't take too long."

It was no use, the hot chow of the day before had constipated me.

2d Lt. FRANK MUETZEL
A/5

After a short halt Captain [John] Stevens [A Company CO] called the officers forward and issued a tactical order. A Company would pass through the 2d Battalion on the left. 1st Lt. Bob Sebilian's 1st Platoon would be on the company's right; 2d Lt. Tom Johnston's 2d Platoon would be on the left. George Fox's 3d Platoon would be battalion reserve. The machine-gun section was to be attached to the rifle platoons.

At this, Bob Sebilian, who had won a Silver Star on Peleliu, erupted. He was in a rage at what he considered a foolhardy frontal assault on a well-placed enemy position that had already chewed up one battalion. We were to be a spearhead that hammered straight ahead. Most of us listening to this felt Sebilian was correct but that orders were orders.

Pfc. HERBERT LUSTER
A/5

The company again hit the road. The T34 sat where the road turned to the right, and the column halted again. Baxter and I took positions up the hill from the tank beside a bean patch.

The pole beans offered some shade from the high sun. I placed my rifle near Baxter, lay on my back, and through the leaves of the bean plants looked up into the blue sky. I began to feel better. Above my face something hit the top of the bean vines. I couldn't see a bird or grasshopper. It happened again and this time it was no mistake. Someone was shooting at the hill and hitting the beans above me. Again the call came to saddle up.

Waiting on the side of the dusty road, I began looking above a little village to the hill. A soldier trying to cross an open space near a clump of pines was hit. I watched him work his way down to the road. By the time my fire team reached the cut in the road, I had seen many wounded men carried out of the valley.

A Pershing [M26] tank sat just past the cut where the road turned to the right around the hill. It served as a shield. Nearby a dead soldier lay faceup on a slab of rock. As we took a path leaving the road, we walked past a grass hut with three dead soldiers lying beside it. One had his eyes open; they were blue and seemed to say, "It's not my time to get up for guard duty."

The valley of rice paddies was divided by a small creek lined with cool, shady willow trees. Beyond the creek stood a large beautiful tree with enough shade for all of A Company. From where I stood it looked like a big Arkansas oak. For a second I wondered if I'd see Arkansas again.

Ahead, the sun, as it finally dropped toward the west, cast shadows on the ridges. We stopped at the creek for final orders. The gunny sergeant gave it to us straight. He wanted my fire team to flank a saddle that was about 400 yards away. He pointed to the machine-gun position and said they would be ready to give fire support when called for. I asked about the high ground that was at our backs. I didn't want to get shot in the back like some had earlier on the Kosong and Sach'on roads. "Don't worry about that hill," the sergeant reassured. "Good luck, men."

[By noon the 2d Battalion assault had hopelessly stalled. In four hours of fighting it had lost 23 dead and 119 wounded. At 1:00 P.M. the 1st Battalion was ordered to pass through the 2d and continue the attack on Obong-ni Ridge.]

Pfc. HERBERT LUSTER
A/5

Off we went, passing the .30-caliber air-cooled Browning machine gun. As we started up through the dry fields above the valley floor, the gunner wished us well.

The men spread out five yards apart to present a poor target. The scrubby pine trees were thick and a whole platoon of enemy could be concealed there. As the hill got steeper, I slipped the rifle sling over my head so both hands would be free to climb. The BAR hung in front of me so I could fire quickly if needed. Suddenly, a recoilless 75-mm rifle opened up on the objective. The whole team stopped. "Move out!" came a shout from the valley. I moved ahead faster.

Capt. FRANCIS "IKE" FENTON, JR.
B/5

Captain [John] Tobin [B Company's CO] went forward to the ridge-line that ran parallel to Obong-ni Ridge. This ridgeline was 400 yards to the southwest of Obong-ni Ridge, and where D Company's commander was located. While Captain Tobin was obtaining information from Capt. Andy Zimmer [D Company CO], Zimmer and his radio operator were wounded and had to be evacuated. Captain Tobin immediately ordered me and the platoon leaders to come forward to where the road passed through a saddle of the ridgeline. Captain Tobin met us there. We hugged the right side of the road. John Tobin was on my left, the radio operator on my right. An enemy machine gun opened up and stitched John six or seven times. It also hit the radio operator. I wasn't scratched. When he was hit John did what an actor in a Western does when he gets shot in a barroom fight—staggers across the room, hits a wall, and slowly collapses. John was knocked backward, hit the side of a cliff, and slowly slid to the ground. He was covered with blood and obviously badly hurt. All of a sudden it dawned on me that he had the only map in the company that showed our objectives. I immediately knew I had to get this map before poor John bled all over it. I also hoped the gooks hadn't shot any holes in it. It goes to show how you think in combat. Here was a good friend of mine badly wounded and I thought about a map.

Fortunately, the 2d Battalion's aid station, which we had just passed, was only 200 yards or so down the road. Only because it was so close did he survive the shooting. Had he been up forward and been nailed it would have taken an hour to get him down to the aid station. On the way he would have bled to death.

I immediately notified the battalion commander and assumed

command of B Company. With Tobin's map in hand, B Company jumped off in the attack.

2d Lt. FRANK MUETZEL
A/5

As my machine guns had been attached to the rifle companies, I moved onto the reverse slope of Observation Hill. From there I could see the leading platoons of A and B Companies moving up the ridge. When it became apparent that they too were running into trouble on Obong-ni, the company executive officer, 1st Lt. Fred Eubanks, a rifleman from the 3d Platoon, and I moved to an abandoned machine-gun emplacement on the forward slope. From there we lay down fire on the crest of Obong-ni. I was armed with an M1903 sniper rifle and although it was too far for me to identify specific targets, the extreme accuracy of the weapon allowed me to hit areas where I strongly suspected the enemy lay. Eubanks was a team shot and I used my field glasses to spot for him.

The use of the abandoned machine-gun emplacement proved to be a mistake. Enemy mortars and artillery had already registered on it. I had fired the better part of a bandolier when, without registration of any kind, four rounds of enemy 82-mm mortar fire landed around it. The blasts lifted me off the ground, my helmet flew off. A human body to my left disintegrated. Being rather shook up and unable to hear, I crawled back to the CP and told Captain Stevens that Eubanks was dead. About the time my hearing and stability returned, Fred Eubanks stumbled over the ridge. I thought of the 3d Platoon rifleman. Fred and I returned to look for him. One of the mortar rounds must have landed in the small of his back. Only a pelvis and legs were left. The stretcher-bearers gathered up the remains with a shovel.

About this time Captain Stevens advised that the rifle platoons were nearing Obong-ni and we should move forward.

Pfc. HERBERT LUSTER
A/5

It was useless to be cautious. Because the young pines were thick I couldn't see ten feet ahead of myself. Suddenly, I broke through on the top of the ridge. Although I couldn't see the other side, I could see everything on this side. There was the saddle. Gunny didn't say what to do when we got to the top. Everything was quiet except my heart. Had the enemy gone from the hill while I was climbing? No, men began to crawl quickly from the crest to the saddle and uncover their guns.

"Evans, do we have anyone in that direction?" I asked quickly. "No," was the reply. "Send some machine-gun fire up that draw," I ordered. I could see a fire team of four men in A Company walking right toward the enemy position I had spotted. Someone asked, "Do you still see them?" It was evident no one saw the enemy but me. I started to throw a grenade, but remembered the sarge said to save them for night. I pulled back the bolt to cock the action of the BAR, pushed off the safety, settled back on my right foot, and opened fire. The flying dirt and tracers told me where my rounds were going. I emptied the rifle. I pulled the sling back over my head, pushed the magazine release—the magazine didn't fall out. I pushed the release with my right thumb and pulled the empty magazine out, stuck it in my jacket pocket, loaded, and raised the BAR to my shoulder. Before I got it all the way up, red dirt kicked up in my face. A big jerk at my right arm told me I'd been hit. I looked down and saw blood squirting onto the broken BAR stock.

Remembering my first aid, I lay back in the shallow ditch and tried to relax my body. "I'm hit—pretty bad," I called to the team. "Where?" came the reply. "In the arm," I returned. Then the whole ridge erupted with gunfire.

A Corsair swooped down to fire on the saddle area. I put my left arm over my face to protect it from falling empty shells. Soon Corporal Evans appeared and tore open my right shirt sleeve. He then disappeared as quickly as he had come. "Corpsman! Corpsman!" Then there was silence.

Evans had spoken to me and I was sure it had been Evans who called for the corpsman. I got in position to roll to the brink of the ridge. My right arm flopped loosely. I began to scoot down the hill until the wounded arm got caught on a scrub pine. I was stuck!

All I could do was wait. Because of the loss of blood, my eyesight was failing. I could, however, still identify the valley below and the place where the dead soldiers lay. A breeze came up from the valley floor; I couldn't tell if it was hot or cool.

Capt. FRANCIS ''IKE'' FENTON, JR.
B/5
Under heavy enemy fire the 2d Platoon moved up to what we called "Red Slash".* This slash or wash was the boundary between A and B Companies. The 1st Platoon had moved to the base of the right side of Obong-ni, but due to heavy fire from a village on their right flank, which was in the 9th RCT's sector, they were unable to advance without suffering heavy casualties. Because of the hilly terrain between the 1st Platoon and my position, I was unable to observe that village and Lt. Nick Schryver, who commanded the 1st Platoon, had to observe and adjust the mortar artillery fire by relaying it over his SCR536. We fired continuously for about twenty minutes into this village before the 1st Platoon was able to move out and seize their portion of the ridge. Upon reaching the top they were able to relieve the pressure of the 2d Platoon's front, and the 2d Platoon moved up and seized its portion of the ridge. B Company seized Obong-ni Ridge at approximately 5:00 P.M.

In the meantime, on our left flank A Company was having a very tough time. Company B's seizure of the right portion of the ridge did relieve a little pressure on them, but their casualties were quite heavy and they were experiencing great difficulty securing the high points on the ridge.

About 1900 there was a great lull in the fighting and B and A Companies tied in and prepared for a night of defense.

---

* This was the name given the gully between Hills 109 and 117 that ran down from the summit of Obong-ni Ridge to the rice paddy far below. At the top of the gully, red clay had been exposed through erosion and gave the area its colorful sobriquet. Some war correspondents also nicknamed it No-Name Ridge.

Pfc. HERBERT LUSTER
A/5

The journey continued back toward the aid station. We came to a deep gully. One corpsman got on the other side and the other pushed from below. Soon we were in another deep gully. It was shady, but I couldn't feel the cool.

"You stay with him," panted one man. "I'll go get a litter."

Some time passed before the corpsman again peered into the gully. "Give me his good hand," said the corpsman on top.

"I can't reach that high," replied the other.

Then they both lifted me. While one held me against the bank, the other pulled from above. After a struggle the one on top said, "Come on, Luster, just a little farther!" I heaved myself, and fell face first over the edge. Both men congratulated me for my great effort.

"Don't worry now, Marine," they assured me. "We can get you back now." They lifted me onto a litter.

I could see the beautiful tree again, and I knew I was only about 300 yards from the road. One corpsman asked to stop and rest. The other told him that they could not stop. Their victim was in bad shape, and they had to hurry.

"Just stop for a minute," the man pleaded, "then I promise not to ask again."

The other consented, and stood to shade my face from the sun. After a moment we continued on. As we neared the road, a tanker said, "Put him up here," motioning to his big machine. "I'll take him back."

"That's OK." The corpsman shook his head no. "We can make it." Shortly, a tall black man lifted me off the stretcher and into a small ambulance jeep.

"You're gonna be all right, Marine," someone inside calmly said.

The next thing I knew, I was inside a large tent.

"Luster, do you have anything in your pockets you want to keep?" I was being readied for treatment.

"I have some postcards in this pocket," I replied.

"How about this note pad?" Someone was feeling in my pockets.

"No, thanks anyway," I said.

As a man began to cut away clothing I said, "Charge these things to the Navy." They checked my dog tags for my blood type, and then to double-check asked me if "O" was the correct type.

I felt terrible, but could see figures moving around. One man came and stood beside me and started a process known to Catholics as last rites. "You don't have to do that," I said calmly, "I'm a Christian." The chaplain paid no attention, and continued with his business. Shortly afterward the Protestant chaplain appeared and talked to me for a few minutes. He reminded me of the services I had helped with and commented that they were good services.

Someone interrupted. "Luster, can you make a fist for me?" I doubled up my left hand and the doctor tried to find a vein for blood plasma. Another doctor tried; they seemed to take turns. My veins had collapsed. The doctors were finally able to enter a vein, and soon I felt a cooling in my arm, chest, legs, and feet.

With some other wounded men, I was quickly loaded into a field ambulance. The driver and guard continually talked as they drove down the rough road. Each time the ambulance hit a bump, all the men in the back groaned. By the number of voices I guessed about six or eight were taking the ride.

Someone shouted, "Slow down, you're killing these guys!"

"I can't," the driver returned, "or we won't make it in time!"

Once the ambulance was fired on, and the guard returned the fire with his dinky little carbine. It was a long ride before we jerked to a stop. Relaxed and confident voices appeared at the back door, and strong arms lifted us out. Soon we were loaded onto the "Purple Heart Special."

I now lost all track of time, but recognized the dimly lighted rail yard at Miryang—the friendly town with lots of water, cool and peaceful. When the train bumped into motion, many voices groaned and moaned with pain. I recognized my own voice among them—I called for water. Soon the call was echoed all around: "Water, water."

"Are you wounded in the stomach?" The standard question was asked over and over. "Here is your water; don't choke."

The water didn't seem to quench my thirst at all. I was stuck to my litter with dried blood. I kept trying to pour enough water down my parched throat. I strained to lift myself up.

[While Pfc. Luster—as well as many, many other wounded Marines—was making the painful journey back to a naval hospital, the brigade was preparing for its first night on the battlefield. The 1st Battalion's two rifle companies had not been able to dislodge the North Koreans from all the hills that dominate Obong-ni Ridge. When the sun went down, the battalion ceased its attack and dug in for the night.]

Capt. FRANCIS "IKE" FENTON, JR.
B/5
One of my men called my attention to two enemy tanks to our immediate rear. Just about this time, Air Force P-51s spotted them and made runs on them. Their runs were ineffective and they did not score any hits or stop them. I then spotted a third tank that followed the other two at a distance of about 1,000 yards. I immediately gave the "flash" and to battalion reported "enemy tanks in the area."

HAROLD MARTIN
The Saturday Evening Post
The telephone tinkled. Lt. Col. Joe Stewart answered, grunted, and hung up. He told the general [Craig], "Regiment says three gook tanks are coming up the road toward the 1st Battalion CP. The observation plane spotted them. They are already behind our position on the hill."

Naval Capt. Eugene Hering, brigade surgeon, jumped to his feet. "God Almighty!" he said. "The aid station's just a quarter of a mile from there! [Lt. (j.g.) Bentley] Nelson [one of the battalion's medical officers] won't leave his wounded! If those tanks break through—"

"They won't," the general said. "Newton [1st Battalion CO] will know what to do." *

The tank platoon was still in the process of replenishing ammunition at 2000 when three enemy tanks were reported approaching the lines. In a matter of seconds the platoon was on

---

* Martin, *Post.*

the road moving forward. About 300 yards from the enemy our advance was held up by trucks parked in the middle of the road and abandoned by their drivers. Tank crewmen drove these trucks from the road enabling the tanks to continue the advance. Upon order from the platoon leader the first section loaded 90-mm APC [armored personnel carrier]. Immediately upon rounding the bend in the road at a range of 100 yards the lead tank came face to face with an enemy tank.

> SPECIAL ACTION REPORT, 1ST PROVISIONAL MARINE BRIGADE
> (1ST TANK BATTALION)

HAROLD MARTIN
The Saturday Evening Post
It must have been like the slaughter of great beasts wallowing up out of some prehistoric fen. At the aid station, when the word came that the tanks were coming, Don Kennedy, rifleman, with a shell fragment in his shoulder, got up, got his rifle, and walked up the narrow road and over the hill to the forward slope. He lay down there to watch.

"It was after sundown," Kennedy said later, "but there was plenty of light. I watched the bend in the road where it came around the nose of the hill. You could see the dust rising, and then this long bulb-nosed gun sort of poked around the corner and wavered back and forth, and then the tank came on. It came on slow and nothing happened, and then all of a sudden the bazooka men waiting on the slope started thowing those big rockets into its flanks, *whoosh-bam*, *whoosh-bam*, and the rockets went into the sides and into the treads and the bogey wheels. It stopped and began to swing right and left, like an elephant swinging its head, but not moving forward, and it was firing all its guns, but it was firing wild.

"But it didn't fire long, for as soon as the rockets hit and the tank stopped, the 75s cut loose, head-on, and where the 75s hit they tore right through." *

---

* Martin, *Post*.

2d Lt. FRANK MUETZEL
A/5

A second T34 moved around the first one just in time to come under fire from one of our Pershings that had moved forward into the cut in the road. The idea was to protect the aid station and CP by physically blocking the road. The second shot from the Pershing blew straight through the T34's turret and put it immediately out of action. A third enemy tank now turned the curve. It came under fire from everyone in sight—M26s, 3.5s, 75-mm recoillesses. In a few minutes it was all over. Everyone jumped into the air and cheered as if he was at a football game.

The lead T34 had been burning ever since it had been hit. We all waited to see if the crew would try to escape through the belly hatch or come out the top. When the top hatch opened and someone tried to escape, everyone and his brother opened up on him. It was worth your life to be in the area. A half hour later, as we were climbing the reverse slope of Obong-ni, an internal explosion blew the tank lid right off.

HAROLD MARTIN
The Saturday Evening Post

Back at brigade CP, when the word finally came through that the tanks had been killed, everybody felt a little better. To the left and right, as darkness fell, [Lt. Col. Ransom] Wood's * guns were slamming their shells toward the hill ahead and walking along the banks of the far-off river. Occasionally, there was a responding whine overhead, and off toward Wood's gun positions there would come the dull roar of an explosion, and once an air burst puffed blackly in the sky.

"Incoming mail," the general [Craig] said. "We'll probably have some shelling here tonight. But whatever we get will be nothing compared to what the kids on the hill will go through. The other people are bound to attack. I only hope our men can hold." †

---

* This officer commanded the 1st Battalion, 11th Marines.
† Martin, *Post*.

2d Lt. FRANK MUETZEL
A/5

On the reverse slope of Obong-ni, we began to organize a defense. We tied into B [Company] on the right, but did not hold the high ground on the left. I stayed busy making sure all the guns had fields of fire and were in action. I couldn't locate either Lieutenants Sebilian or Johnston. (Later I would learn Sebilian had a shattered thigh and had been evacuated, and Johnston had been killed.)

I dug a foxhole and was opening some C rations when a number of rounds of WP [white phosphorus] fell amid the mortar section to my rear. We had a miserable time mixing mud to put on the damned stuff and getting the wounded evacuated. For the rest of the night the 60s [mortar] were out of commission.

It was now quite late and pitch-dark. I was totally exhausted. I finished digging a shallow foxhole, covered the excavated soil with my poncho, and went to sleep. It was a serious error. No one knew better than I that in a fighting foxhole you should never be alone.

Capt. FRANCIS ''IKE'' FENTON, JR.
B/5

We were quite worried about getting another night counterattack and cautioned all the men that this time we would have a 25 percent listening watch. We settled down to wait the night out.

18 August 1950
Coming down Obong-ni Ridge from the south, the enemy counterattacked at 0230.

SPECIAL ACTION REPORT, 1/5

Capt. FRANCIS ''IKE'' FENTON, JR.
B/5

About 2:30 A.M. my 2d Platoon reported enemy activity to the immediate front. A few minutes later a flare went off and the enemy hit us with great force right where the two companies were tied in.

The enemy method of attack was to have one squad rise up and throw grenades and then advance a short distance, firing to their front and flanks with automatic weapons. They would then hit the deck and another squad would repeat the same movements.

SPECIAL ACTION REPORT, 1/5

Capt. FRANCIS "IKE" FENTON, JR.
B/5

Aided by the darkness, their ferocious attack managed to break through our lines. A Company received counterattacks along their entire front.

2d Lt. FRANK MUETZEL
A/5

I awoke to explosions and machine-gun fire—at close range. Whenever a 51-mm illumination shell burst overhead all activity would cease. When the flare fizzled out, the battle would begin anew. We were being attacked and, it seemed, overrun. A crouched-over figure carrying a burp gun appeared. I threw my only grenade. BLAM! I fired a single round from my .45, which promptly jammed. My single-shot sniper rifle, superb as it was, wasn't much use to me now. A grenade landed near my poncho. I crammed myself inside the hole. The explosion went upward. My helmet flew off and small bits of iron and gravel bit into my forehead. I was knocked cold.

Capt. FRANCIS "IKE" FENTON, JR.
B/5

Upon receiving news that the enemy had broken through, I immediately ordered my 2d Platoon to pull back toward the company and form company perimeter defense with my other platoons. The enemy took full advantage of their breakthrough, and a great number of them managed to overrun my 2d Platoon. Some of them pushed into my company CP, where it was actually a case of hand-to-hand fighting. About then the battalion commander notified me that it was of utmost importance that I hold at all costs. A Company had three breakthroughs on their company front, and if B Company was pushed off the ridge, we'd have to take it all over again in the morning. The situation was confused. It was very dark, there was considerable firing going on, and it was impossible to see the enemy except at very close hand. It turned into a real donnybrook. During the battle the truly salty Pfcs, corporals, and sergeants really stood out. Although I was not to find out until morning, except for me, the company had lost all its officers. Pfcs took over fire teams and squads; corporals and sergeants took over platoons. Displaying outstanding gallantry, they reformed the survivors and led them in a counterattack. They finally pushed the enemy from our perimeter.

> After the initial penetration B Company was able to drive out or kill all the enemy in their position. . . . A Company was in such a position that the enemy was on the high ground immediately above them and was able to throw and roll grenades down into their positions.
>
> SPECIAL ACTION REPORT, 1/5

2d Lt. FRANK MUETZEL
A/5

When I came to, I knew instantly I was in trouble. I smelled the heavy odor of the garlic the North Koreans carried with them. There was movement around me but I couldn't see anyone. Ridiculous as it sounds, I wondered whether it would be considered yellow if I lit out and looked for help.

During a break between flares, I crawled to the area where the CP had been. It was deserted. I knew for certain now the company had been overrun. I was afraid to move. I didn't know in which direction I'd find friendlies, and was only too aware of the proximity of the hostiles. Gathering up my helmet, rifle, pistol, and ammunition, I waited for the next blackout. Then, running as hard as I could, I launched myself downhill. Finding a steep ravine I dove headfirst into it. I rolled and ended up on my feet in the company CP. Too surprised to react, the guys there didn't shoot me. Having assumed my body would be recovered when the attack resumed the next morning, everyone was glad to see me alive.

Stevens had just ordered Eubanks to take a squad and see if he could outflank the enemy. I went along. Having no information, we did not accomplish anything and soon returned to our lines. For the rest of the night, we stayed put and waited for sunrise.

The intensity of the attack on A Company diminished toward daylight, leaving the enemy in position on Hill 117.

SPECIAL ACTION REPORT, 1/5

Capt. FRANCIS ''IKE'' FENTON, JR.
B/5

About an hour after our counterattack, the 9th RCT received an attack that folded their left flank and drove them back about 250 yards. They reorganized, launched a counterattack, and retook their position.

When daylight arrived I discovered I was the only officer left in the company. The previous afternoon the company counted 190 men and 5 officers. In the morning 88 men were left on the line. The 2d Platoon, which had borne the brunt of the night attack, had but 11 men left.

First Lieutenant Nick Schryver from the 1st Platoon was reported to have been killed. My gunnery sergeant, Ed Wright, said he'd been hit by a grenade burst. I thought it would be demoralizing to the men to have a dead lieutenant lying around, so even though we were only evacuating the wounded, I told Ed, "Put Schryver on the first available stretcher and take him off the ridge." A short time later I looked up and, gee whiz, I thought I was looking at a ghost! There stook Nick. With all the bandages wrapped around his head he looked like a mummy. "My God," I said, "what are you doing here? They told me you were dead." He told me, "Skipper, back in the aid station I got to thinking. The last couple of days we've seen a lot of action. I thought your number would be up. You know, Skip, very seldom does a young lieutenant get to command a company. Since you're long overdue, I just figured if I could get back here, I'd get myself a company."

2d Lt. FRANK MUETZEL
A/5
With full light I saw the company had occupied the slope of Obong-
ni in the area the 2d Platoon had assaulted the day before. In other
words, we were halfway up. The North Koreans fired at us from the
high ground. Without my entrenching tool, which I'd left in my hole,
I went to work using my helmet as a shovel. I tried to kick more dirt
out with my feet. WHACK! I caught a slug on a flat trajectory. It
punched a hole in my foot. Blood spurted from the wound. I was in
so much shock I couldn't tell how badly I'd been hit.

Capt. FRANCIS ''IKE'' FENTON, JR.
B/5
During the night a few stragglers from A Company had joined me.
Reorganizing fifteen of them into a patrol, we had them move down
the ridge toward the enemy, while the rest of A Company moved up
toward the ridgeline in a coordinated attack.

2d Lt. FRANK MUETZEL
A/5
Close as we were to the crest, we walked (I limped) bolt upright the
rest of the way. From the top we threw a few hasty shots down a very
steep reverse slope at the departing North Koreans.

The entire company came up. We tied in on the right with B
Company and hastily organized a defensive perimeter. The top of the
hill was a mess. The dead from both A and E Companies lay around
us. The wounded were taken down; we were stuck with the rest. Dead
North Koreans lay where they had fallen. Since some had been there
since the previous day, they had begun to get a little ripe.

Stevens told me they had just recovered Tom Johnston's body.
He also informed me that he, Eubanks, Fox, and I were the only
officers in the company left alive. I wasn't much to look at, though,
with my bloody boot and god-awful limp, a helmet that resembled a
colander, and blood all over my jacket from the minor head cuts I
had sustained the night before.

Stevens told me to take what was left of Johnston's 2d Platoon and set up a defense on the crest of the high ground. Up there we had plenty of dead North Koreans for company. We threw them out of their holes and used them as sandbags on the firing side. While digging in, I counted noses and found I had only eighteen men. Johnston's platoon sergeant had been wounded and evacuated. Mine was dead.

In an effort to calm the men after all they'd been through, I told them to break out rations and eat while they had a chance. I sat on the side of a hole and dangled my feet. On the other side of the hole lay a dead North Korean. He had caught one through the top of the head and looked pretty ugly. I was twenty-three years old and to reassure the men I tried to pull off a John Wayne stunt. When I was halfway through my can of meat and beans, decomposing gases caused the cadaver to belch. Black blood foamed out of its mouth and nose. I promptly lost my entire lunch. By the time the platoon got through laughing, the tension was broken and they were ready to go back to work.

Later, after it had become reasonably quiet, I told Captain Stevens I was going down to the aid station to have my wounded foot attended to. On the road below Obong-ni I again ran into Lieutenant Colonel Stewart and Colonel Snedeker. As Tom Johnston and I had shared an apartment in Oceanside, I took it upon myself to inform Colonel Snedeker, whose daughter Mary had been engaged to Tom, that he had lost his future son-in-law.

About then the 3d Battalion passed by to continue the attack. I spotted some friends and wished them well. As the next two objectives were even higher than Obong-ni, I figured they were in for it.

Capt. FRANCIS ''IKE'' FENTON, JR.
B/5
We received orders to sweep down the ridge to the left and secure all the high ground on the ridge. The 3d Battalion was going to pass through us and take Objective Two, which was the high ground to our immediate front.

[The 1st Battalion, 5th Marines, resumed its advance down the high, narrow spine of Obong-ni, and by midmorning of 18 August had cleared

all the summits on Objective One. Artillery, mortars, and air strikes hammered the North Koreans, whose orderly withdrawal suddenly turned into a rout. The 3d Battalion was then directed to pass through 1st Battalion and begin its assault of Hill 207, the enormous hill mass west of Obong-ni known as Objective Two. Lieutenant Bohn's George Company and Lieutenant Fegan's How Company jumped off at 11:30 A.M., and an hour later, after advancing against moderate enemy resistance, pushed over the western half of the objective.]

1st Lt. ROBERT BOHN
G/5

Objective Two was not much of a fight. Thanks to the efforts of the other two battalions, by the time we got there, the enemy had already been broken. When we climbed to the top of Two, the whole area opened up before us. Below, a road snaked around the low ground before it reached the towering hill [311] that was Objective Three. The hill lay right next to the Naktong, and from where I was it looked massive and very, very steep. It should have been a regimental objective and at any other time would have been. But in this case George and How Companies had been ordered to take it.

We came off Objective Two, back down to the saddle, crossed the road, and started up one of the two spurs that led to the summit of Objective Three. George Company took the spur closest to the Naktong. Joe Fegan's H Company took the one to the right. As we climbed, we stayed in contact on the radio. I began taking some fire, which I believe came from above How Company. We used our air support very effectively and continued to climb.

Pfc. FRED DAVIDSON
G/5

On the climb I went up to a North Korean soldier who had been wounded in the leg. A Marine stood nearby and guarded him. Someone had given him an American cigarette and he grinned like

a monkey. I asked him if he was in much pain and he replied, "Yes."
I explained to him that a corpsman would be by soon to take care of
his wound. I climbed on up the hill.

1st Lt. ED JAWORSKI
G/5

The wounded North Korean couldn't have been more than sixteen.
He couldn't walk, couldn't move. The company was strung out on
the trail. It was important that we get in and set up before dark. No
one knew what lay above us. I yelled up ahead, "We've got a prisoner
here. What do you wanna do with him?" Someone shouted back,
"We can't take him with." I couldn't shoot him. One of the platoon
sergeants said, "I'll take care of it, Lieutenant." Fine. Walked away
fifteen steps. I just didn't do it myself.

At 1655 air, artillery, and 4.2 mortars delivered preparatory fire
on Objective 3.

SPECIAL ACTION REPORT, 3/5

HAROLD MARTIN
The Saturday Evening Post

To the rear of where we stood, the 155s began to roar and the snub-
nosed 105s, and to one side the mortars were barking, and in front
the squat tanks were slamming away with the 90-mm guns whose
muzzle blast can knock a man down at thirty feet, and above the hill,
swooping low, the planes were diving in. You would see the smoke
and the fire flash of the rockets leaving the wings, and then would
come the great tearing sound the rocket made in flight and then the
roar of its bursting against the hill. And after the rockets had gone
you would see the little round dots of smoke in the sky as the wing
guns fired, and all the crest of the hill in front of How Company was
a roaring jumping hell of smoke and flame and dust and noise.

"Ah, that Taplett [3d Battalion CO]," Joe Stewart kept saying.
"He's a sweetheart. He knows how to call down the fire." *

* Martin, *Post.*

18 August 1950
At 1825 H Company was pinned down by fire on top of Objective 3 and was unable to advance against enemy. . . .

SPECIAL ACTION REPORT, 3/5

Pfc. FRED DAVIDSON
G/5

When George Company secured their portion of Objective Three, there was still an area of the hill to our right that was higher. I knew How Company was somewhere in that direction and assumed this was their objective.

We were told we would not go any farther and because it was turning dark we should dig in. On my right I made out the distant sound of a firefight. About twenty minutes later I was surprised to see three walking wounded Marines coming from the direction of the firefight. They told me that How Company had run into a buzz saw.

Capt. JOSEPH FEGAN
H/5

We were ordered to attack, companies abreast. George Company went up one spur, How Company went up the other. The two spurs separated by a gully converged at the summit. We made good progress until about 200 yards from the objective, where my men were stopped. This was another case of literally fighting uphill. The problem was compounded by the sun that was setting directly behind the enemy's position and right into our eyes. We couldn't see.

The enemy lay across the summit. I tried to flank him on the right. I tried to flank him on the left. I tried a frontal attack. The sun continued to blind me. I'd tried everything the book said to do— right, left, up the middle. Nothing had worked. We weren't doing our job, we were stalled, and I was growing impatient. The enemy was shooting and hitting my people. I called in some mortar fire but couldn't see where it fell. I was frustrated. To get a better view, I stood up. No surprise; as I should have been, I was hit.

My first sergeant announced to the company that I had had my testicles shot off. Inasmuch as it wasn't accurate, I didn't think it was quite as hilarious as he did.

1st Lt. ROBERT BOHN
G/5
After George Company reached its objective we began taking heavy fire from the knob that lay above How Company. I heard Joe Fegan had been hit. To take the heat off H Company, I tried to establish a base of fire. It was terrible. I could not get the machine-gun section into action. I kept losing people. The enemy poured fire down upon us.

I decided then to envelop the North Korean position. I sent Cahill's platoon around on the left. It was now growing quite dark. A heavy firefight broke out where Cahill's platoon should have been.

2d Lt. JOHN CAHILL
G/5
As soon as I got behind the North Koreans, they turned their attention away from How Company and concentrated on my platoon. It was getting dark. All of a sudden stuff started coming out of the ground. I hadn't realized it until then, but the enemy was dug in underground. During a nasty firefight I was shot in the shoulder. I asked my sergeant to get Dewey [Bohn] on the radio and find out what he wanted me to do.

1st Lt. ROBERT BOHN
G/5

Cahill's platoon sergeant explained that the platoon had engaged the enemy but could not dislodge them. Blackie had been hit and wanted instructions. I told 1st Platoon to return to our lines. A little while later Cahill, who had to be carried, and the rest of his platoon returned. They brought back their dead, too.

That night a new corpsman cracked up. He began moaning and sobbing. My gunnery sergeant settled him down. No one else said anything. We didn't know where the enemy was, how many there were, or what his intentions were. Our perimeter was strong. It was also small. The wounded were told to keep their weapons and that if attacked, we'd need them. They were Marines—no problem.

19 August 1950

The remainder of the night passed quietly in company sectors.

SPECIAL ACTION REPORT, 3/5

1st Lt. ROBERT BOHN
G/5

At first light we reestablished contact with How Company. Following a heavy mortar barrage, they attacked and took their objective. By that time there was all kinds of activity around us; artillery fire and air strikes pounded the vicinity of the river. The enemy tried to cross the river any way he could. It became a rout.

Pfc. FLOYD AKINS
B Company/5th Cavalry

After the firefight the American air strikes hit the North Koreans on either side of the river. The planes dropped napalm and the artillery laid in white phosphorus. The North Koreans were screaming. We heard them, and we were a mile or more away.

At 0845 in compliance with orders from Brigade the 3d Battalion was ordered to patrol assigned areas to the brigade boundary and forward to the river. No enemy activity was reported.

SPECIAL ACTION REPORT, 3/5

HAROLD MARTIN
The Saturday Evening Post
The general [Craig] stood . . . on a point of land . . . and looked across the tawny river to the western hills where all that was left of the North Korean 4th Division hid, nursing its wounds.

He just looked at the hills beyond the river where the enemy lay, and the hills behind that his men had cleared at so great a cost in blood, and said, "Well, it was a pretty good little two-day operation after all, I guess." *

Pfc. **DOUG KOCH**
D/5
We came down off the hill and met the Army unit that was replacing us on top of Obong-ni. They had sleeping bags and all kinds of equipment; looked like they were going out on maneuvers and were planning to take life easy. As I passed one platoon I heard a lieutenant say to his men, "We're going to the top of this here hill. If anyone gets tired on the climb, fall out and catch up later." This tough old gunnery sergeant from our 1st Platoon was walking alongside. He muttered, "Them goddamn Army guys'll never hold this hill. We're gonna be back up there."

Pfc. **FRED DAVIDSON**
G/5
I talked to one of the young Pfcs from the Army unit that came to relieve us. He told me he had been in almost constant combat since the first week in July. He and his buddies looked spent and tired. I really felt sorry for them.

---

* Martin, *Post.*

Pfc. HERBERT LUSTER
A/5

All the way to Pusan, the other casualties and I took turns asking for water. One of the nurses, from the deep South by her accent, scolded me. "You should be ashamed of yourself. Some of these boys are hurt real bad, and you only have a broken arm."

"Sorry, ma'am," I apologized, "I didn't know I was causing so much trouble."

In the early-morning darkness, I felt sick all over. I was tired, but could not rest; I was restless, but could not move. My right hand burned and there was no relief; I could not move it. How long could I last? I asked myself how much could I endure. My limit was fast approaching.

The train came to a stop. The side door slid open like a cattle car on the Southern Pacific. "Over here," someone called hurriedly. "This guy is in real bad shape—load him first."

Two Americans moved to me quickly and carried my stretcher to the door of the railcar. I was placed on the dock, and a line was lowered from the boom of a ship. The handles of the litter were fastened to the cable, and up I went—suspended in midair above the Pusan pier. In a matter of moments, I was lowered to the deck of the hospital ship, pried loose from the canvas litter, and rushed into a well-lit green room.

A man in green hospital clothing stood beside me and said, "Can you move your fingers?" I tried to open and close both hands. "The other hand," the man said gently. "Are you trying?" "Yes, sir," I replied. After a brief moment of decision, the man said, "OK, son."

At a nod from the doctor, people began moving around the table I was on. Someone placed a mask over my face. "Breathe deeply, please," came the matter-of-fact command. Time was gone, and I dreamed.

Somebody was moaning and groaning. My head moved from side to side. I recognized my own voice, and was quiet. I slowly moved my body in a stretch—all except my right arm. It seemed to be anchored to the bed, or the table, or wherever I was. I strained to look at it to see what was the matter. All I could see were clean white sheets.

My right shoulder was anchored to the hospital bed. A pulley with about five pounds of weight was where my arm used to be. I was alive, but part of me was gone.

[Except for mopping-up operations, the first battle of the Naktong was over. The destruction of the enemy bridgehead cost the Marines 66 dead, 278 wounded. The North Korean 4th "Seoul" Division had lost nearly all its heavy equipment and weapons and had been virtually destroyed. Enemy soldiers captured after the battle estimated that no more than 300 to 400 men were left in each of its three rifle regiments. Ironically, on 19 August, while it licked its wounds west of the Naktong, the 4th "Seoul" Division was named a "Guard Division" for its outstanding accomplishments in the battle of Taejon.

With the Naktong Bulge safe, at least for the moment, General Walker turned his attention to other fronts and other threats. The North Koreans had not quit and the Pusan Perimeter was still under siege. However, the men of the Marine brigade would receive several days of hard-won rest. The 1st Provisional Marine Brigade was released from 24th Division control and went into Eighth Army reserve.]

20 August 1950

Fifth Marine Regiment moved after daylight to an assembly area in the vicinity of Miryang. Shortly after its arrival orders were received to move to an assembly area in the vicinity of Masan. Movement commenced at 1910.

SPECIAL ACTION REPORT, 5TH MARINES

Pfc. FRED DAVIDSON
G/5

The train stopped and started a hundred times. Once we stopped near an Army supply train that was being guarded by two soldiers. They had positioned themselves at either end of what must have been a fifteen-car train. It took no more than three minutes to figure out how we were going to get into that train. Five Marines went down to one end of the train and began a commotion. The guard at that end, of course, had his hands full. The soldier at the other end ran down to help his buddy. He shouldn't have, 'cause the 1st Provisional Marine Brigade hit those unguarded boxcars like a school of piranhas. Had you been there you surely would have thought we were professional train robbers. Slick as could be, all the goodies from one train were moved to the other train. Of course, we didn't want to cause too much trouble or get anyone hurt, so when the soldiers got wise to what was happening and ran over to the corpus delicti, we ceased operations.

I ended up with two cases of Grandmother's Oatmeal Cookies. When I couldn't eat anymore, I traded the leftovers for some cans of grapefruit juice. It was share and share alike. Everyone had something.

Pfc. DOUG KOCH
D/5
Early one morning we arrived back near the same river where we'd bivouacked four days before. Of course, now there were a lot fewer of us.

Brig. Gen. EDWARD CRAIG
Commanding General, 1st Provisional Marine Brigade
Most of our tentage had been left behind, even the shelter tents. We had only our CP tents. Most of the men had ponchos which they rigged on stakes or rifles and in the Bean Patch these became their homes.

It was at this time that General [Lemuel] Shepherd [Commanding General, Fleet Marine Force, Pacific] came through and inspected the brigade. Although the men were living right on the ground, he seemed to be pleased. Morale was high and training—something General Shepherd was very keen on—was going on.*

Pfc. DOUG KOCH
D/5
I was made a fire-team leader and received three replacements. One kid's name was Billings, another's, Colt. I don't remember the third

*Craig interview, MCHC.

one's name. Billings was dark-haired, short, and stocky. Colt was from Compton, California, and, although he was older, looked like he was sixteen. These kids were originally from a stateside service battalion.

One day we went out on a training exercise; on another day we marched around. Those of us from the original company didn't need the training, but someone felt the new replacements did. We trained.

Capt. FRANCIS ''IKE'' FENTON, JR.
B/5

Some of the replacements we received had been in combat in the last war, but the majority had not. These men came from posts and stations all over the United States and had been performing guard duty or office work for the past two years. It was imperative, therefore, that we give them some training in tactics. We spent four hours every morning conditioning and whipping the men into shape. The old-timers—the combat veterans—of the company deserved a rest, but they dug right in and did their utmost to help these new men feel at home and work together as a unit.

At this time our equipment was in terrible condition. The web equipment was rapidly deteriorating from exposure to rain, heat, and occasional submersions in rice paddies. We had lost a lot of weapons. These losses were not due to negligence but to the fact that, when a man is hit, he drops his weapon or takes it with him. We were having a hard time getting Browning automatic rifles. Many of our BAR men had been casualties, and we were down to about three or four per platoon. You just couldn't get a BAR belt in Korea. Shoes were another big problem. We couldn't fit men with odd sizes like 8FF. 8FF is supposedly a rare size, but we had a great number of men in the company who wore this size. There were none available. We reached the point where we had men running around in tennis shoes. Dungarees were in bad shape. They had been brand-new when we left the ship at Pusan, but now they were beginning to get thin and crusty. Our packs, which had been dropped at Pusan and were supposed to have been brought to us by the rear echelon, never arrived. The only way we could get a clean suit of dungarees was to wash them or survey the supply at the laundry unit when we took a shower. There were some new sizes available, but they were all thirty-sixes and thirty-eights, and, while we might have had a few men who wore these sizes when we arrived in Korea, the heat and the marching had cut their waistlines to thirty or thirty-two. About our last week in the rest area, we were able to get enough socks so that each man had two pairs. A scarce item, however, was toothbrushes. Our PX allotment of toothbrushes was very small—normally about five or six per company every other day. The men were screaming for them, but none were available.

2d Lt. FRANK MUETZEL
A/5

While we were bivouacked in the Bean Patch, John Stevens told me to take a detail of walking wounded over to brigade headquarters, where Purple Hearts would be awarded. He also told me to try to make myself look presentable.

My leggings had been thrown away, my trousers were out at both knees, my right boot had two bullet holes in it, and my dungaree jacket had corporal's stripes stenciled on the sleeves. I grabbed a fast shave with cold water, hard soap, and a dull blade. Gene Davis loaned me a clean set of dungarees, Tom Gibson loaned me his second lieutenant's bars, and off I went with my troops.

First Lieutenant Bob Bohn acted as company commander and Nick Schryver and I as platoon leaders for a company of more than 100 men who were going to receive Purple Hearts. South Korean President Rhee arrived by helicopter, and after a short address he and General Craig awarded the medals. After the company was dismissed, T/Sgt. Ernie DeFazio (Recon Company's gunnery sergeant) and I were called over to the CP so we could be presented to President Rhee. Ernie, who had been wounded in World War II, was receiving his fifth Purple Heart. I received my first and second.* Both Rhee and the general were very kind. Later General Craig furnished DeFazio and me with an autographed photo of the presentation.

Back in the company area, I returned the bars and the clean

---

* For his actions of 17–18 August on Obong-ni Ridge, Lieutenant Muetzel was also awarded the Silver Star for gallantry in action.

dungarees, put on my own raunchy clothes, and in the shade of a shack wall took a nap. Big day.

Brigade headquarters sent the medals and photo to my girl. It would have been awkward carrying the medals in my hip pocket.

Pfc. DOUG KOCH
D/5

I know we lost a lot of guys on the Naktong. One day at the Bean Patch the casualty list for Obong-ni Ridge was posted. I looked down the list and recognized many names. One was Henry Thomas David LeBlanc. He was the man on the Greasy George who had had the premonition of his own death. Later I found a corpsman who told me how LeBlanc had died. First he'd been shot in the leg. The corpsman said, "He'd managed to crawl back almost to the aid station. He was no more than twenty yards from safety when the North Koreans shot him again."

Pfc. FRED DAVIDSON
G/5

On the 22nd George Company went on patrol. When we returned Lieutenant Bohn's tent was up. The rest of us put up shelter halves or little "shade huts" with whatever was handy—dungarees or field jackets and ponchos. The bamboo we used for the posts came from a large patch that grew along the river. I'm sure the few people who lived in the nearby village owned the bamboo. Unfortunately for them, when the rest of the companies saw how we had constructed our shade huts, all the bamboo suddenly disappeared.

The river had many uses. One was to cool down the beer we were being issued. Alas, it failed in this purpose.

A day or so later, the brigade's kitchen got set up and began dishing out hot chow. I was assigned to KP. I dished out a spoon of mayonnaise to each guy in line. The men shuffled by. Stick out your tray, get a blob of mayo—very routine. One guy was stargazing and didn't give me his tray. I looked up. Leroy Goulette! From home! The guy I used to play war with in the hills around Richmond, California.

We'd been together in the sixth grade. It was such a surprise. "Leroy!"
"Fred Davidson?" "Yup, it sure is."

He had just joined George Company as a replacement. That
evening Leroy and I attended a South Korean girl show that was being
put on for the troops. One gal sang, "Beg Your Pardon." When I was
in Korea in 1948, I swear the same girl sang the same song.

1st Lt. ED JAWORSKI
G/5

Col. Victor Krulak visited the regiment in the Bean Patch. Before the
war he had commanded the 5th Marines, so all the guys knew him.
The colonel is very short. As he walked through our company area,
a group of guys was standing around off to one side. One of them
yelled, "Hey, you little shit, get out of the hole." The guys then just
disappeared into the bushes. Krulak turned around. Who was standing there? This dumb lieutenant. He stared at me. What could I say?

Pfc. DOUG KOCH
D/5

One hot morning—it was before noon—word went around that there
was going to be a funeral service for all the men who had been killed
on the road to Sach'on two weeks before. Anyone interested in attending would be picked up and taken to the cemetery.

West of Masan the trucks left the main road and climbed up
through some low hills. Near a grove of trees they came to a stop.
We climbed out and walked along a dirt road; there were a lot of us,
probably several hundred. We ambled past a Graves Registration tent.
Here there were rows upon rows of stretchers; on each, covered by a
poncho, lay a dead man. Most of them belonged to Army units that
had been fighting in this area. The Graves Registration people were
trying to identify each body. We were a pretty quiet bunch of guys.

We walked higher into the hills. Finally, one guy said, "Goddamn, you die and they can't even bury you down on the flats, they
gotta bury you on the side of a hill. When I die I hope to God they
bury me on the flats." That's kind of the way we all felt.

At the top of a hill the trail split. Protestants were asked to go to one side, Catholics to the other. It was easy to recognize where a friend was buried. Someone he had known stood by his grave. Next to Lieutenant Reid's grave stood Captain [Kenneth J.] Houghton and Lieutenant Hanifin. At another grave two brothers stood where the third lay buried.

The men stood silently either on the slope of the hill or below it. The service didn't last long. The Protestant chaplain said a short prayer. The Catholic chaplain said a short prayer. Part of the service . . . After thirty years it's still hard to talk about some things.

A firing squad fired several volleys into the air and taps were sounded. It was very quiet. Up in the trees some small birds chirped. Somewhere far away an artillery battery answered a fire mission. No one moved. How long we stood there I have no way of knowing. Finally, the chaplains told the men it was time to leave, the trucks were waiting for us. We walked back down the hill, past the Graves Registration tent. Inside, men wearing little white masks tried to identify the new bodies that would end up in that cemetery on the hill.

[While the Marines in the Bean Patch rested, regrouped, and remembered their dead, the North Koreans struck at the Naktong Bulge once again.]

Capt. FRANCIS "IKE" FENTON, JR.
B/5
A funny story began making the rounds. The Army heard that the brigade had taken up positions to their rear. The soldiers felt it wouldn't make too much sense to fall back; if they did, the Marines had orders to shoot them.

2d Lt. TOM GIBSON
Mortar Company/5
A great deal of real animosity developed in Korea between Marines and soldiers. Over and over the Army units tied in on our flanks didn't do their job. As a result many Marines died. Because the Army had been unable to hold their positions at the Naktong, Marines had had to fight a bloody battle to regain it. Now we learned the Army again

had been kicked off ground Marines had died occupying. It made a man bitter.

[Throughout the last days of August, the enemy had continued to hack at the Perimeter's defenses. A series of thunderous battles had erupted along the line. Across the northern rim, General Walker's defenses were breached in several locations, threatening the ancient city of Taegu and the corridor that led from it to Pusan. In the south, east of Sach'on, the North Koreans crashed into the 25th Division and regained the miles of road Task Force Kean had seized three weeks before. Then, early on the morning of 1 September, alarming intelligence reached Eighth Army headquarters. As the morning hours passed the news darkened. The Communists were again across the Naktong in the area of Obong-ni Ridge. Parts of four enemy divisions were in the process of punching a hole six miles across and eight miles deep in the Pusan Perimeter.]

Pfc. EDWARD GREGORY, JR.
B Company/23d Infantry

For a full day the enemy built rafts and barges. That was on the 27th. Some of them made it across that night. We couldn't sleep. On the 28th the enemy hit us hard with heavy artillery and mortars. Air support was called in. The F-80s did a great job strafing the area of the enemy buildup and sending him back into the hills. Again and again the North Koreans tried to cross the river. Our artillery pounded away at them. Fighting continued into the night. More ammunition was brought up. Next day, all day, and throughout the night, we held the enemy attack back. On August 30 I turned eighteen. It would have been so nice to have been home for the celebration. Firefights sprang up and died out, mortar rounds fell on our lines. After sunset fighting went on without interruption. Large groups of enemy soldiers managed to cross the river during the night and enter our lines.

Pfc. JACK CARTER
C Company/23d Infantry
Sometime after midnight I awoke from the last normal sleep I would
ever have. All hell was breaking loose! We were being attacked by a
large enemy force. All that night we fought, ran, and fought again.
While the sun slowly came up over the hills, down in the valley where
three of us were hiding it was still dark. Without warning, two GIs
ran up to us. While we talked and tried to get our bearings, one of
the guys saw several silhouettes on the crest of a hill. Before we could
stop him, he shouted, "We're GIs, we're GIs!" Of course, the men
on the hill were North Koreans. We broke for the opposite hill. The
North Koreans fired and chased us. We ran into an area of mounds
that I realized were Korean graves only when I stopped. I must have
frozen because one of the guys yelled, "Shoot your damn rifle!" I did,
but there were too many of them. Two in my group were killed. We
knew we couldn't stay where we were and let them pick us off one
by one. Three of us dropped into a narrow gully. To my right a North
Korean raised his head and ordered us to surrender. Three times I
fired at him. My two buddies told me we had no choice but to give
ourselves up. I threw my rifle down. As I did I felt some warm liquid
on my neck. When I reached back to feel it, I realized I had been
grazed in the neck and was bleeding.

The North Koreans ordered us to return with them to the top of
the hill. I became very alarmed by what they had me do next. Although they took all of our dog tags, I alone had to give them my
boots. A little enemy soldier put them on. He must have been a six
and I was a ten. Although he looked comical, I tried not to smile.
One of them took my wallet. Finding my girl's picture, he made a
"jack-off" motion and said, "Pon-pon." I was both mad and frightened. For some reason the North Koreans seemed especially angry at
me.

They walked us down to a shallow river. Before I could cross, I
heard a command and looked back. A North Korean officer motioned to me. I walked over to him. He jumped on my back, stuck a
pistol to my temple, and urged me into the water. Carrying this enemy officer across the river was the most humiliating thing I've ever
done. The North Koreans around me chattered back and forth and

laughed. The water was never more than hip deep. Without shoes, the rocks on the bottom cut my feet. I wanted to pitch this North Korean into the water. My better judgment prevailed.

Pfc. EDWARD GREGORY, JR.
B Company/23d Infantry
All day the battle raged on. We received additional rations of ammo. The enemy surrounded our position. Thousands more crossed the Naktong River. The company was cut off. We tried to hold back their attack. We fought hard, hoping to hold our position until relief arrived. The situation became more and more critical. A lot of men were dead or wounded, our perimeter shrank. We did what we could with what we had.

Around sunset orders arrived: "Pick up your wounded, pull back." We had only the dark of night going for us. In the morning, with luck, reinforcements would come up and relieve B Company. Throughout that long night we heard the enemy all around us. We lay still and made very little noise. As daylight came we saw a tank with a white star and "USA" printed on it. Someone on the tank yelled, "Hey, Joe, over here." One of our sergeants was very cautious. We stayed down. The tank opened fire on us. We realized it had been captured by the enemy. The group I was with moved out of that area, regrouped, and tried to take up a new position. We were now being fired on from all sides.

Someone hollered, "Over here. Get in the hole!" I ran like hell and jumped into a deep rice-paddy trench, water up to my hips. Corporal Crumpus was with me in the trench. There were twenty of us left, all that remained of B Company. Surrounded and pinned down, we fired at the enemy from different holes. Crumpus fired toward the rear, I fired to the front. Bullets zinged overhead or hit in the mud. I heard a loud clang and a yell. I turned around. Corporal Crumpus had taken a bullet through his helmet. He died instantly. There were still a few Americans around me; I heard them yelling and shooting.

A bugle call cut the air. It was a banzai charge. To our rear, on the high ground, the enemy fired down into us. From the other direction, holding bushes in front of themselves as camouflage, the enemy charged. I fired my BAR. I hit some of them. I heard men scream.

I threw my last two hand grenades. From a different direction another group of North Koreans charged toward us. They carried bayonets on their rifles. I fired at them until the bolt of the BAR slammed home. My .45 pistol was also empty. In my trench, I did not know if I was the only American left alive.

I dropped my BAR and .45 into the mud at my feet and stood on them to bury them. Now I was really scared. Not wanting to take a bayonet in my neck, I climbed out of the trench and began running as hard as I could. I heard bullets snapping around me. One hit me in the rear of my right arm, throwing me to the ground. If possible, I was now more frightened than ever before. I tried to play dead, but my heavy breathing gave me away. They yelled and kicked me. One Communist grabbed my collar and yanked me to my knees. Another tried to slide a wire noose around my neck. I moved my head away from it.

When more North Koreans gathered around, I saw they had captured Sgt. Jose Fernandez, also of B Company. They made us sit down and remove our boots. I noticed blood running down my arm into my hand. I tried to tend the wound, but a North Korean took my first-aid pack away from me. Some enemy soldiers yanked off my watch and grabbed my wallet. Sergeant Fernandez leaned over and tied an old hankie around my wound. The blood stopped flowing.

More enemy soldiers appeared. They had three more American prisoners with them. We now started our hell march. As we moved out they prodded and hit us with their rifle butts. "Hubba, hubba, pally, pally."

We marched for about two hours when we were joined by a large group of captured Americans, 128 to be exact. Many were wounded, some seriously. We marched north through hill country. Everyone who could took turns carrying the badly wounded. Others let the wounded hang onto them as they walked. The North Koreans told us if the wounded held them up or slowed them down, they'd kill them.

Pfc. JACK CARTER
C Company/23d Infantry
After we crossed the stream and the North Korean jumped from my back, they made us sit and wait. A short while later some more North

Koreans appeared with four more American prisoners. At least one of them, a very tall man, was from my company. I wasn't sure if I recognized the others. A short, fat North Korean walked over and swung a wooden staff, missing my head by no more than an inch. After that we weren't mistreated. We stayed near the front lines for two days. It was difficult walking barefoot. During this time we were given nothing to drink or eat. I could understand not giving us anything to eat as they had very little themselves.

On the third day the North Koreans prepared an ambush for five American tanks. Two other captives and I were ordered to lie on the forward slope of a hill. The other GIs were kept on the reverse slope. There were about 125 North Korean soldiers. As they attacked, the tanks buttoned up and returned fire. Three American planes appeared from nowhere and strafed the hill on which I lay. With my bare hands I tried to dig into the ground. Praying to God, I promised if He'd let me survive I would be good for the rest of my life. Bullets tore up the ground around me. My buddy on the left was hit in the ankle, the one on my right was sliced open at the stomach, as clean as if a scalpel had done the job. Most of the North Koreans were killed in this battle. The few that survived made me return with them to the other side of the hill. The two wounded GIs (the one with the ankle wound I had bandaged with a T-shirt) were left on the hill where they'd been hit.

Below the hill a small hut sat near the road. All e unwounded American prisoners were left here in the hands of a ounded North Korean. The rest of the enemy force moved to anotl hill and dug in for the night. My two wounded buddies who'd been left behind began to call and cry for us to come and get them. Finally, unable to take it anymore, another GI and I used sign language to tell the guard that we were going to go off and bring the two men back with us. We weren't sure what he was going to do, but taking a chance we climbed up the hill. With some difficulty we managed to carry the two wounded men back to the hut.

For the rest of the night, we took turns caring for these wounded guys. We also talked of grabbing the guard's rifle and escaping. Unable to take the wounded with us, we figured we'd better stay put, at least for a while. During that long, dark night, huddled together, I learned that one of the other prisoners was from the mountains of my home state, North Carolina, and another from neighboring Tennessee. If we ever returned home alive, we promised to look each other up.

I must have dozed off. I awoke to gunfire. The sun was already up. Soon we heard voices. "We're GIs. Don't shoot," we yelled. An American patrol and a tank were on the road. The wounded North Korean guard had crawled into a nearby culvert. I ran out to the road and stopped our guys from killing him. He was badly wounded and he had, after all, let us go and get our wounded comrades. The patrol put us five ex-POWs on the tank and called in a jeep to remove the wounded men.

The tank dropped us off at our regimental CP, which at that moment was being shelled. A sergeant asked where my shoes were. I explained what had happened and where I'd been. He told me to get a pair of shoes and to pick up a rifle. In a nearby tent I found a big pile of boots. By the time I found a pair that fit, my buddies in captivity were gone. I asked the sergeant what I should do next. He told me Baker Company's mail clerk and driver were going back and I should ride with them.

They took me with them and below a small hill I found Baker Company. There a sergeant told me, "You'll find what's left of Charlie Company up there," and he gestured toward a nearby ridgeline. I climbed the hill and found the company. A sergeant told me, "Out of 201 men, you're the twelfth man back." This was September 3, 1950.

[Three days earlier, while Privates Gregory and Carter were fighting for their lives in the Naktong Bulge, the Marines were leaving the Bean Patch. With the Pusan Perimeter threatened everywhere, General Walker had made a crucial decision: he would spend his reserves at the Naktong. He called again for the Marine brigade.]

1 September 1950
Fifth Marines received a warning order to stand by for immediate movement, on order, . . . to reinforce U.S. Army forces. At 1100 orders were received directing 1st Battalion to prepare

for movement to Miryang to be used as 8th Army reserve for the
Naktong River area. At 1630 all units of this command boarded
a train in the vicinity of the bivouac area for transportation and
proceeded to Miryang.

SPECIAL ACTION REPORT, 5TH MARINES

Brig. Gen. EDWARD CRAIG
Commanding General, 1st Provisional Marine Brigade
I arrived in Miryang [1 September] and was told I would attack practically through the same area we had attacked through before. I con-
ferred with the commander of the 2d Division [Maj. Gen. Lawrence
Keiser]. At that time the Eighth Army's chief of staff [Col. Eugene
Landrum] was at the CP. I remember it was his idea to commit the
brigade immediately despite the fact that our air control units had not
arrived from Chinhae nor had one of the battalions. This is the only
heated discussion I had in Korea with the Army. I insisted that the
attack be delayed until all my troops arrived and I had my air support
properly coordinated. They finally gave in to this. Their reason for
wanting to attack at once was the critical situation then existing. Later
I found out that the situation was not serious enough to commit an
unprepared force to combat.*

Pfc. DOUG KOCH
D/5
Late in the afternoon [2 September] we loaded aboard trucks and
headed through the same territory we'd been through before. The first
time, west of Miryang, we had passed a 2d Division cemetery that
had been dug in a schoolyard. Passing it now we noticed how much
larger it was.

Our new company commander was a first lieutenant named H. J.
Smith. No one said it to his face, but he was known as "Hog Jaw."
He was kind of a young, slender guy, who turned out to be a pretty
good officer.

*Craig interview, MCHC.

The next day, just as it started to get light, the company walked up the road toward a village. Some Army unit over to our left opened fire and we knew immediately those kids were pretty green. Their machine guns fired tracers. It looked like the 4th of July. They really shot up a storm. They must have thought it looked pretty. We thought, you dumb fools, you're going to draw all the fire in the world down on you. Sure enough, in came gook artillery right on top of them. After it lifted, we heard the soldiers hollering and moaning. Tough lesson to learn.

[The Marine brigade returned to the Naktong Bulge and the scene of its battles of 17–18 August. The terrain, especially the looming bulk of Obong-ni Ridge, was all too familiar to Marines who had wished never to see it again. General Craig's mission, as it had been two weeks before, was to clear the Bulge and drive the North Koreans back across the river. As in the case of the first Naktong, the brigade was placed opposite the center of the Bulge with the 9th Infantry on its right. This time, however, the advance would not be with a column of battalions, but with two battalions abreast—1st Battalion on the left, 2d Battalion on the right. The counterattack began at dawn on 3 September under a sky dark with dense smoke and the threat of rain.]

3 September 1950
At daylight it was discovered that the enemy had overrun the proposed line of departure by approximately 1,000 yards, and the 1st and 2d Battalions were required to launch their attacks from their assembly areas.

SPECIAL ACTION REPORT, 5TH MARINES

[By noon the 1st Battalion, 5th Marines, had seized its first objective and the North Koreans in that sector withdrew to Hill 117. This high ground lay directly across from the 2d Battalion's line of advance, and it wasn't long before the battalion was receiving heavy machine-gun and mortar fire from that direction. Dog Company was ordered to seize the objective. On the hill two battalions of North Korean infantry waited for the Marines to attack.]

Pfc. DOUG KOCH
D/5
At the foot of the Hill 117 we stopped and waited for an artillery barrage to soften up the enemy. Down the road from the north rolled
four or five American tanks. Here comes help, I thought. We were
sure going to need their firepower. All of a sudden a machine gun
stitched a stream of fire across the company's rear. I rolled over on
one elbow and looked behind me. Someone yelled, "God, they're
shooting at us." Instead of firing on the top of the hill, the tanks chose
to fire at the bottom of the hill. I saw a puff of smoke. Just that quick
a shell landed near me. It rolled me over into a little gully. I lay dazed.
God, I thought, we're gonna get done in by our own goddamn outfit.
While I lay with my head down, three or four more shells hit nearby.
I again looked behind me. Down the road, some Marines, waving
their arms wildly, raced toward the tanks. It's a miracle they weren't
fired on.

In the gully the guy in front of me lay with his feet in my face.
He had the feet of the man to his front in his face. We were packed
in tight.

As soon as the shooting stopped, the call for corpsmen began.
Obviously, a lot of men had been hit. I felt myself all over and, except for a loud ringing in my ears, I was OK. I checked the kid in
front of me. His right side had been cut up by shrapnel and he'd broken his arm. I hollered for a corpsman. Then I checked the guy in
front of him. He was one of the replacements who had come in a
few days before with Billings and Colt. His name was Kennedy and
he was one of the new squad leaders. I saw he had a hole in the back
of his jacket. Cutting the jacket open I found the shrapnel hole in his
back. From the way he was wheezing and the color of his skin I knew
his lungs had been hit. He wasn't fully conscious. His left hand
clenched some dirt; he wore a gold wedding band. Rolling him over
I saw there was no exit wound. Sergeant Dodge ran over and told me
to take Kennedy's valuables and send them to headquarters. His wallet contained a photo of his wife and two kids. A corpsman worked
his way over. He found there wasn't anything he could do for Sergeant Kennedy. He began treating the kid with the broken arm.

This incident just took the starch out of the company. It was devastating to be shot up by our own tanks. Men moved around but the movement lacked purpose. Lieutenant Smith began shouting orders. Back on the road the tanks now were shooting at the top of the hill.

The officers finally got the men moving. We climbed up the hill, still disorganized, still in shock. A third of the way up, alongside a small Korean cemetery, Lieutenant Smith stopped us. He and the squad leaders again formed us into platoons and squads. A skirmish line went forward.

Second Platoon ended up on the company's right flank and my fire team became the platoon's right flank. My BAR man had been wounded in the tank attack and remained at the bottom of the hill. This left me with only the two replacements, Billings and Colt. The line I followed to the top of the hill lay along a crooked ridge. As we climbed up the hill, this ridge swung me away from the rest of the platoon. I dropped down into a shallow ravine. Billings and Colt were on my left and were supposed to keep me tied into the platoon. The ravine became quite steep. I looked back and there, slowly climbing behind me, were Billings and Colt. With no other place to go, we continued upward. Above, where the ravine opened up on the hill, I heard a machine gun firing.

I ran ahead a little, Colt followed. We were alone. Obviously, when the tanks had opened fire on the top of the hill, the North Koreans had run off. Colt and I jumped into a partially dug foxhole. We were both pretty pooped from the steep climb and the heat.

Colt began talking about Sergeant Kennedy, whom he had known before they joined the brigade: "God, that's too bad about Kennedy." "That's the way it goes," I said. "You win some, you lose some." Colt looked at me. "Don't you have any feelings at all?" "Yeah," I said, "I have them, but there's nothing we can do for him. You aren't gonna do a damn bit of good by feeling sorry right now. That comes later." Colt said, "You're kind of a hard case, aren't you?" I guess maybe to him I did look that way. "No," I said, "I'm not." "Well," he said, "if anything happens to me, I got a picture of my girl. I want you to make sure it gets back to company headquarters so they can send it back." I said, "Goddamn it, don't talk that way."

Billings, who had moved past us on the hill, slid down the slope and jumped into the hole. "Where's the rest of the company?" I asked. "God, they're way back." He was still panting. "They're back down the hill, forty, fifty yards down."

A North Korean machine gun somewhere below opened up. I figured the gooks had spotted the rest of the platoon and were now pinning them down. Billings, Colt, and I in the ravine had evidently slipped past them unseen. Now that we were behind them, we opened fire. As we were hidden by bushes and tall grass, the North Koreans had no idea where this fire came from. We drove them further over to the side of the hill. Unfortunately, from there they were still able to hold up the platoon. "Guys," I said, "I think we're in one god-damn big bunch of trouble. We're so far in front of the company they don't know we're here. We're surrounded by North Koreans."

About then we saw an enemy platoon come over a rise and move toward what had been their position and now was ours. "Boys, I think we've had it," I said. "At least I'm gonna get me that officer waving that sword." I fired at him. Billings and Colt also let loose. I hit the officer, BANG! Knocked him right down. The gooks scurried back over the knoll. Because of the heavy brush on the hill they didn't know where we were.

One of their men, guess it was the platoon sergeant, tried to carry the officer back to their lines. I hit him too. The rest of the platoon must have then figured out where we were because in a short while they charged us on the run. The three of us cut them down. I don't know how many we hit, but I know we got quite a few.

We lay hunkered down in the hole. I turned toward Billings. "Slide down the ravine and see how far back the platoon is. Don't get yourself blown away. See if you can get the company's attention, and let them know where we are. Find out if they're any closer."

Billings slipped out of the hole and crawled back down toward the ravine. Colt and I waited.

Far away, on a small trail on the reverse slope of the hill, we saw a unit of North Koreans walking in our direction. Each man was carrying two boxes that I figured must hold ammo for their machine guns or mortars. There wasn't time to adjust my sight so I put a little "Kentucky windage" on it. "I'll try to hit the front man," I said to Colt. "You aim for the guy behind him." Aiming at his chest, I fired.

I must not have done a very good job because one of the boxes he carried exploded with one hell of a loud bang. Colt and I were so surprised we didn't know what to do next. When the smoke and dust settled several North Koreans lay sprawled on the trail. The rest of the column was nowhere to be seen.

Before we could do anything else, Billings rejoined us. "The company's way down the hill. Over there," and he pointed a little ways down the hill, "there's another gook machine gun. They're so busy shooting at the company they don't know we're here."

Billings, Colt, and I sneaked through the grass and, sure enough, there in front of us about twenty yards was a machine-gun nest. "We'll raise up," I whispered, "and fire together. Aim for the guys working the gun." Getting up on our knees we cut loose. I saw one or two North Koreans fall over. My clip flew out. I leaned forward to grab another one from the bandolier. Bullets whipped around my head. I shoved the clip into the receiver. All of a sudden it became real quiet. I looked to the right. Billings was on the ground not moving. I looked to the left. Colt was on his side. Both had been hit. I flattened out. When I reached out to touch Colt, I saw he'd been shot in the neck. He had no pulse. I rolled over to Billings. He, too, was dead.

Below, the enemy machine gun opened fire. The gunner couldn't depress the barrel enough to hit me but brush and twigs fell around and on me. He traversed the gun back and forth. I knew I had to get out of there because I didn't have the firepower to shoot it out with him. Checking again to make sure Billings and Colt were dead I crawled flat on my belly back to the hole where the three of us had spent the morning. Then I moved down the ravine, climbed the spine of the ridge, and almost got myself shot by my own platoon. They were sure I was a North Korean.

Sergeant Dodge and Dick Fletcher ran over to me. I told them what had happened. Dodge asked, "Are you sure they're dead?" I told him I was sure. He told me he had wondered why one of the two machine guns that had the platoon pinned down had stopped firing. I said, "Well, that was Colt and Billings and me."

The company crept closer and closer to the top of the hill. Some of the guys threw hand grenades at the machine-gun nest that had shot it out with me. Through the rest of the day, the company dueled the North Koreans for possession of the hill. It became a contest. They couldn't push us off and we couldn't push them off. Casualties mounted. Neither side had enough men for an all-out attack.

Late in the afternoon Lieutenant Howard asked if there were any volunteers to help some of the casualties off the hill and to bring back ammo. Since there was no one left in my fire team I said I'd go. About then it grew dark and a light rain began to fall. Down on the road we met stretcher-bearers who took our walking wounded. At headquarters I reported to the first sergeant. He said that the company had already been resupplied with ammunition. "It's late," he said, "and too dark to wander around. You're liable to get shot. Stay here tonight." By then it was raining pretty good.

[Twelve hours earlier there had only been a threat of rain in the air and low-lying clouds and smoke had hung over the battlefield. At 8:50 A.M., under the gathering sky, Lieutenant Muetzel's A Company, 1st Battalion, in line with Doug Koch's D Company, 2d Battalion, began its attack.]

2d Lt. FRANK MUETZEL
A/5

When we crossed the line of departure and headed for the hill mass 700 yards to the front, the company immediately came under long-range machine-gun fire. Although the rice paddies were knee-deep in water, we marched through them for the cover they offered. The North Korean fire was inaccurate but frightening enough when a nearby hit threw up a column of water.

In the middle of the paddy, I ran across a small group of wounded soldiers who had been left behind in the earlier battles. They were petrified and begged for help. Because I had lost my corpsman at the first Naktong, Pfc. Ben Simpson, who qualified with his Eagle Scout first-aid training, was acting as the platoon's aidman. He immediately stopped and broke out his kit. Knowing I could not pause to take care of these men, I told Simpson to leave them. Then I told the soldiers that an aid station lay to our rear and they should make their way to it. I felt bad about leaving them, but I couldn't stop the assault to care for men who wouldn't care for themselves.

While we crossed the rest of the rice paddy to the foot of the hill, tanks and air strikes pummeled its crest. With the 1st Platoon in line and our machine guns covering us, we charged the hill, firing from the hip. The slope was really torn up. I passed many bodies.

The enemy pulled out and we easily took our objective. I set up a hasty defense, lit a cigarette, and waited for the CO and mortars to come up.

Without my knowing it, two privates, Weller and Reynolds, crossed the crest of the hill. Weller was picked off by a sniper. Then, when he went to Weller's aid, so was Reynolds. I first learned about this mess when I heard that Ben Simpson, who had gone out to help them, was down. After setting up the machine guns so they could fire on the next ridge, I had all three brought back to our lines. Weller and Reynolds were dead. Simpson, although wounded in the chest, was still alive. Without another corpsman we did what we could for him, then started him for the rear. He died on the way.

When Captain Stevens came up, I was in tears. Even when we attacked a hill properly, it was still sheer murder. The exec bucked me up and Stevens issued orders for the attack to continue.

A deep valley lay between where we were and the hill that was our next objective. My 2d Platoon would feint down the valley; George Fox's 3d Platoon would assault from the left. I moved into the valley and up the opposite slope. The machine guns laying down covering fire on top of the hill for us had to cease fire when we reached the area just below their targets.

I heard over the radio net that Fox was down and his 3d Platoon had stalled. My neck was out a mile and on the block. The platoon began receiving enemy grenade and rifle fire from the crest. I asked Captain Stevens to give me some mortar fire, and on the last explosion I would assault the crest. This was preferable to trying to pull back under fire. I also really believed I could take the hill. Four rounds of mortar fire were fired. Two hit the top of the hill; two hit among my platoon. Privates Warren and Selle were killed instantly. Pfc. Judy was scalped. Because the rest of us were lower on the hill, the blasts went over our heads. This saved the platoon from annihilation.

Then we took the hill and dug in for the night. In the rain we waited for the counterattack. I thought about Selle and Warren, the two men killed by the mortars. They had been with the company less than a week, had no friends, knew no one. They came, were killed, and were carried away. One of the old hands, Judy, had also gone down. I knew this couldn't keep up. No one even considered the possibility of getting whipped by the NKs. But there were a lot of them and few of us. We, me, all of us were eventually going to get it; it was just a matter of when and how bad. I was really chapped wondering where the rest of the world was. It was just a god-awful mess— inadequate replacements, insufficient ammo, worn-out clothes and boots. No one much gave a rap about anything. Outside discipline was no longer a threat. What could the brass do to us that was worse than what we were doing? Each of us withdrew into our family—the squad, the platoon, the company, the regiment, the brigade, the Corps. Everyone else, bug off!

The expected North Korean counterattack never materialized. It rained all night.

[The heavy rain continued into the next day, 4 September.]

Pfc. DOUG KOCH
D/5
In the morning another guy and I loaded up with bandoliers of ammunition and hand grenades and in a torrential downpour headed back up toward the company. We passed some stretcher-bearers coming back with the dead that had lain overnight on the lower part of the hill where the tanks had shot us up so bad.

On top of the hill the North Koreans had taken off. The company began to re-form. Late in the morning we received word that we were to pull back to the road and go into reserve. We were told to bring our dead with us. Some guys went with me to pick up Billings and Colt. I rolled Colt over and took the picture of his girl out of his wallet. She was very attractive. Then I helped load him on a poncho so he could be carried down to the road. Another kid and I picked up Billings and laid him on a poncho. Before starting down the hill, I walked over to where the body of the North Korean officer I'd shot the day before lay. I looked down at him and knew I was the one who had killed him. Three or four more bodies lay nearby. These were the ones Colt and Billings had gotten. I felt no anger or remorse. Then I went back and helped carry Billings off the hill.

Back at the village I made sure I gave the first sergeant the picture of Colt's girlfriend. I explained that Colt had wanted someone from the company, not Graves Registration, to return it to his family. Then, in the village, the company formed back up. *

2d Lt. FRANK MUETZEL
A/5

During the day South Korean police cleared a village to our front. The company moved down the road and in the process overran an enemy divisional headquarters. We also picked up several North Korean stragglers who I sent to the rear with one of my walking wounded. He took them around a bend and shot them.

At one point, a barrage of enemy high-velocity flat-trajectory artillery fire roared overhead and landed amid the battalion CP. The troops thought this was pretty funny. They said it was about time the CP got into the war.

We dug in early that day and watched the 3d Battalion swing around and come up on our flank.

[A little after 8:00 A.M. on the 4th, the 3d Battalion, 5th Marines, began their assault on Hill 117, the center of the North Koreans' resistance the previous day. Once they had cleared the hill, 3d Battalion's G and H Companies turned westward and attacked in the direction of Obong-ni Ridge.]

Pfc. FRED DAVIDSON
G/5

The rest of that day we traveled through several hot areas. Hill after hill, we moved forward. I cannot remember any specific firefights. Up one hill, down another.

---

* Second Battalion, 5th Marines, casualties for 3 September totaled eighteen dead and seventy-seven wounded, most of them from D Company.

Once, during the day, I went up to the point and found Leroy Goulette. After being up front all day he was ready to return to Hawaii, where he'd been before he joined the company in the Bean Patch. Without warning, a hell of a lot of rounds whistled overhead. Leroy and I jumped behind the mound of a Korean grave. We lay on our backs and looked at the gray sky. Enemy bullets whizzed above us. As long as we didn't stand up we were safe. Leroy said, "What do you think Al Carlen and Steve Randall would do right now?" I broke up. Back in the sixth grade Leroy and I had invented characters and made up stories about them. Al Carlen was the name of Leroy's hero, while mine was named Steve Randall. Al and Steve were members of the Royal Canadian Mounted Police and were continuously getting into trouble in the Klondike. I don't remember my answer to Leroy's question, but I know we both laughed a lot.

Occasionally, Sergeant Ryder spotted some Marine who wasn't keeping his head down. "You're not covered there," he'd yell. "Get behind some cover!" Eventually, the enemy's firing stopped.

During the early evening hours, one of the replacements bugged out. I was given the job of taking him down to the road and back to the first-aid station. I didn't know who he was or what platoon he belonged to. I led him down the hill by the arm. He cried hard each step of the way. This made me mad. I cursed him, called him "coward" and "crybaby." Of course, I was only eighteen and had no idea then what this poor bastard was going through.

[The Marines waited out the long night of 4–5 September; with the dawn they would have a second go at the battle-scarred slopes of Obong-ni Ridge.]

Capt. FRANCIS ''IKE'' FENTON, JR.
B/5
Nothing happened during the night. The next morning, September 5, we received the order to continue the attack. This time my first-phase line was to be Obong-ni Ridge.

It had rained all night and the men were soaking wet. The battalion managed to get some hot coffee up to us, but just when it arrived, we got the word to move out. We weren't able to distribute any of the coffee. This turn of events didn't do the morale any good.

But the men were getting anxious to get this thing over. We felt that we stood a good chance today, the 5th, of running the enemy right across the river. With any luck, we were going to break their backs. We started out about 8:00 A.M. and moved against scattered resistance—mortar fire, sniper fire, and an occasional burst of machine-gun fire. It was enough to slow us down and cause us to try an envelopment. In each case, the resistance fell back. Then we moved along rapidly, and, once again, A and B Companies worked in close harmony.

2d Lt. FRANK MUETZEL
A/5

The company moved across a valley and back onto the same hill where the brigade had launched the first Naktong fight two weeks before. On this hill we found soldiers who had been sent there to hold the position. They had been overrun and were still in their sleeping bags. I could identify an outpost by the location of the bodies. Most had been shot, a few bayoneted. Decomposition was setting in and it was difficult to tell whether they had been white or colored. Negligence had cost them their lives. There had been an aid station at the base of the hill. Bodies on stretchers still lay there. Some carried tags. We knew that when the Army abandoned them these men had still been alive. It was enough to make you sick.

[After securing a large hill in front of Obong-ni Ridge, B Company was ordered to stop where it was.]

Capt. FRANCIS ''IKE'' FENTON, JR.
B/5

About then a civilian journalist by the name of David Duncan was sent up to me. He was taking pictures for *Life*, and he was to go along with me. I had a lot occupying my mind, and the last thing I needed was to be responsible for a civilian. I laid it out for him point-blank:

"I don't have time to mollycoddle you! I don't have blankets for you at night. I don't have rations for your meals. If you wanna stay, don't get in my way. Hang around the background. And let me tell you one final thing. If you're gonna get hit, get killed. I don't have men to carry you back to an aid station. If you get killed, I don't have to worry about you."

A short time later the enemy launched a strong counterattack against my company position. This counterattack was supported by three enemy tanks, one of them camouflaged in such a manner that it looked like a half-track. I'd estimate the number of troops between 300 and 400. It was a well-prepared counterattack, preceded by a heavy mortar barrage and antitank high-velocity fire from Obong-ni Ridge. Intense enemy heavy machine-gun fire made it practically impossible for us to move. I sent a runner to the Army unit coming up on my right flank to find out if they had any artillery support and, if they did, to please call it down on the enemy to my front. Then I sent two runners back to the battalion commander to notify him of what was taking place. I sent a fourth runner to notify the attached tanks and caution them about the enemy tanks coming around the bend.

Our tanks were in the same positions they had been in during the first Obong-ni battle (when they destroyed three enemy tanks). However, this time the enemy caught our lead tank with its gun trained in the wrong direction. Just as our lead tank made the turn in the road, the enemy opened up and scored a direct hit on the tank's turret. Our second tank, making the same mistake the North Koreans had made in the last Naktong battle, tried to go around the lead tank. It, too, was knocked out.

In the meantime I began receiving the artillery support I had requested from the Army. It helped a great deal. My 3.5-inch rocket launchers had moved into a position from which they had clean shots at the enemy tanks. These rocket launchers later received credit for disabling and knocking out all three NK tanks.

Because of the heavy rain, visibility was greatly reduced. The North Koreans then launched another counterattack on B Company's position.

DAVID DOUGLAS DUNCAN
Life

Rain poured even heavier upon those Marines still unhit, pressed upon the top of the hill, fighting for their lives. The clouds came even lower and it seemed almost like night.

A corporal machine gunner, named Leonard Hayworth, slithered over the top of the hill. He had come back for more grenades. He was told that there were no more, nor was there more ammunition for his machine gun, nor reinforcements to take the place of the wounded and dead . . . not even communication with the rear.

In a voice almost impossible to understand, for he worked over each word as though it was nearly beyond his power to form it upon his lips, he choked brokenly, "Can't see 'em. Only two us still there. Can't see 'em. Rest dead . . . wounded. Grenades! Grenades! Can't see 'em. Can't see gooks in rain. Can't see! Keep killing us! Where hell mortars?" He just wanted something to take back to his buddy up forward still holding their position. The knowledge that he must go back empty-handed was more than he could bear. Then he reached into his pocket and found that even his tobacco can was empty.*

Capt. FRANCIS ''IKE'' FENTON, JR.
B/5

I kept receiving reports from runners all up and down the line that we were being assaulted by groups of North Koreans, 40 to 100 in number, and I found it necessary to place every man I had in the company on line. Rocket men, corpsmen, mortarmen, every available man went on line to stop this counterattack. To make matters worse I began running low on ammunition. I was practically out of hand grenades, and things didn't look too rosy for us. Just at this time Lt. Col. George Newton, my battalion commander, who had probably guessed my situation, sent a much-welcome platoon from A Company with five boxes of hand grenades. The enemy had closed so rapidly that we just took the hand grenades out of the case and

---

* David Douglas Duncan, *This Is War!* (New York: Harper & Brothers, 1951).

tossed them to the men on the line. They would pull the pins and throw them. The enemy closed to less than 100 yards. I managed to get one of my radios back into working condition and gave it to the 81 [-mm mortar] FO. We called for immediate 81-mm fire for effect, with the range only 100 yards to our front. When we broke up the counterattack, the 81s had but eighteen rounds of ammunition left. The counterattack had started about 2:30 P.M. and it was over at about 3:00 P.M.

Shortly after the counterattack was broken up, we observed the enemy moving back off Obong-ni Ridge to what had been Objective Two [Hill 207] in our last Naktong River drive. It looked like they were beginning to run for the river again. It was at this time that Dave Duncan, the *Life* correspondent, informed me that he had just heard from a litter-bearer that the brigade was pulling out that night and going to Pusan. I couldn't believe the news and wouldn't believe it until we were actually pulled off the line and in Pusan. It just sounded too good to be true.

THIS MY OPN ORDER 22-50 X COMMENCING AT 2400 5 SEPT BRIG MOVES BY RAIL AND MOTOR TO STAGING AREA PUSAN FOR FURTHER OPERATION AGAINST THE ENEMY X PRIOR TO COMMENCEMENT OF MOVEMENT 5TH MARS WILL STAND RELIEVED BY ELMS OF 2ND INF DIV COMMENCING AT DARKNESS . . . CONCEAL FROM THE ENEMY ACTIVITIES CONNECTED WITH YOUR WITHDRAWAL . . .

BRIG. GEN. EDWARD CRAIG

1st Lt. ROBERT BOHN
G/5
As soon as I learned we were going to pull out, I called in my platoon leaders and gave them the order: "We're not leaving a man! You have to get word to everyone in a foxhole and tell them what we're doing. Count them before you come off the hill. We'll count 'em again on the road."

That night we pulled out—fire teams, squads, platoons—just like the book says. Everyone formed up on the road as a company in extended route formation. It was raining and cold when we counted again. Damned if the count wasn't one short. Some kid had fallen asleep in his hole. His platoon leader went back and brought him down. I read a couple of years back that we then walked six miles to where the trucks were waiting. Until then I thought we'd walked thirty.

Capt. FRANCIS "IKE" FENTON, JR.
B/5
I waited for the Army unit that was to replace Baker Company. No one showed up. An hour or so went by. Hell, still no Army unit appeared. My communications were out so I didn't know what was happening. Finally, down at the base of the hill I heard, "B Company, where are you? B Company!" The men, all seasoned veterans, were not going to fall into this kind of enemy trap. Not one of them called out.

Eventually, an Army lieutenant staggered into the area. "B Company, why'n hell didn't you answer my call?"

"You're lucky you didn't get killed. Who are you?"

"I'm here with my unit to relieve you."

"Well, fine. Put a platoon up there, put another over there, and another on the other side."

"What are ya talkin' about, platoons? I've got fifty men."

I thought, Oh, boy, here we go again. Fifty soldiers coming in to relieve a company of Marines. To make matters worse they were short certain ammo, they didn't have wire to run between their mortar FO and their tubes—they didn't have anything. I gave them what I could. Over and over I said to myself, Please, God, let them hold for four hours so I can get the hell out of here. Don't let the gooks break through yet and come right in on top of us. I'll tell you, if the gooks had probed up there on that hill that night, they would have come through like water through a sieve.

2d Lt. FRANK MUETZEL
A/5
About 11:00 P.M. an Army first lieutenant appeared with about thirty men who'd been scraped together from a headquarters unit. These 30 guys were going to relieve approximately 120 Marines, six machine

guns, and six mortars. I took the lieutenant to the very crest of the
hill and had him dig in in a circle. He asked me to leave him our
ammo for a 57-mm recoilless rifle he had. Marines didn't have 57s,
so he had a weapon and no ammo. He asked his sergeant to bring up
their one machine gun. The sergeant told him it had been left back
at the CP. I left behind about four cases of hand grenades. We all
figured the soldiers would be gone at first light or first shot, whichever came first.

Then I found that B Company had pulled off the hill and not
told the attached platoons from A Company. I formed these men up
in single file, aimed them at the burning tanks, and marched down
to the road. There I held a nose count. When I was certain I had
everyone, I led the unit toward the rear.

About half a mile down the road, I met the battalion exec, Major [Merlin] Olson. He was all alone and, having missed us at the
checkpoint, was coming forward to look for us. Literally staggering
with fatigue, I was never so glad to see anyone in my life than I was
to see him.

Pfc. DOUG KOCH
D/5
The Army trucks waited for the company almost exactly where they
had dropped us off several days before. It was still raining and it was
cold. Lieutenant Howard and most of the 2d Platoon climbed aboard
an Army six-by. In convoy, with their lights off, the trucks drove away
from the river.

Rolling through a cut in one of the hills, our six-by slid off the
inside of the curve and ended up in a ditch. The rest of the convoy
sped right on by. The Army driver was pretty upset. He didn't like
the part about being left behind at all. As we pushed and pulled the
big truck out of the ditch, a sniper's bullet occasionally whizzed overhead.

Soon as we climbed aboard, the driver took off. The road was
now very slippery. Several times the truck almost slid off the pavement again. Under blackout conditions we were driving without
headlights. The kid driving was quite nervous. Rain beat on the

windshield. Finally, Lieutenant Howard told Sergeant Dodge, "Lean over, Sarn't, and tell that sonovabitchin' driver to turn his headlights on. I'd rather be shot by the gooks than end up in this truck goin' over a cliff." *

* The lst Provisional Marine Brigade's sixty-seven days in the Pusan Perimeter had cost it 148 men killed in action and another 730 wounded. It is estimated the enemy suffered a total of 9,900 killed and wounded. It would be safe to say that when the Marines withdrew from the Pusan Perimeter the night of 5 September, they left it in far better shape than they had found it.

INCH'ON

6 September-16 September 1950

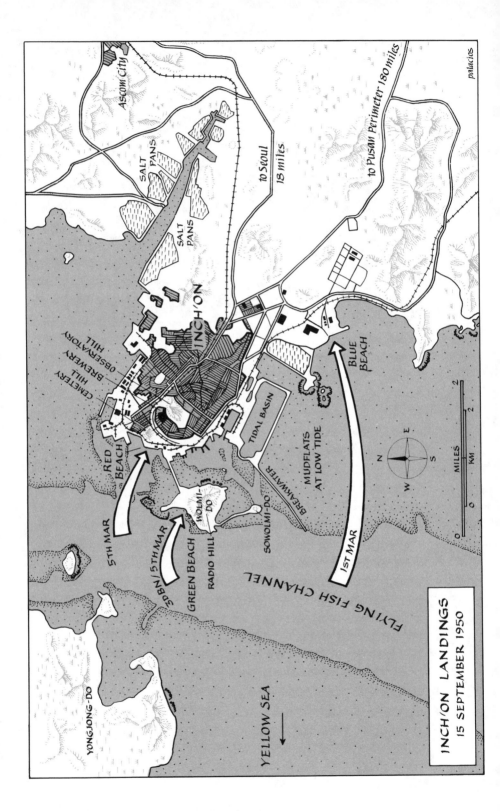

INCH'ON LANDINGS
15 SEPTEMBER 1950

The history of war proves that nine out of ten times an army has
been destroyed because its supply lines have been cut off. . . .
We shall land at Inch'on, and I shall crush them.

GENERAL DOUGLAS MACARTHUR

*In mid-July 1950, about the time General Dean's 24th Division was
being pounded at Taejon, General MacArthur conceived a plan to break
the back of the enemy's offensive. The operation called for a large amphibious landing far up the west coast of South Korea at the port of
Inch'on. Once ashore and in the enemy's rear, the American force could
then drive east and recapture the capital of Seoul. The use of a surprise thrust deep behind enemy lines followed the pattern of other sea-
to-land assaults the United States Navy, Marine Corps, Army, and
Air Force had perfected during the Second World War in the southwest Pacific.*

*From the beginning, however, MacArthur's Inch'on proposal met
with strong opposition. Naval and Marine specialists alike considered
Inch'on Harbor an improbable place for an amphibious landing. The
Navy was against it because the harbor's tidal range, at thirty-two
feet, was one of the most extreme in the world; at low tide, miles of
mud flats made an approach to the shore impossible. The Marines op-
posed the site because the landing force could be put ashore only during the hours of high tide. Fifteen September, the day of the next flood
tide, was mentioned as the best possible date for the landing. Unfor-*

tunately, the tide would come in just before sunset, leaving the rifle battalions precious little time to get ashore, consolidate their gains, and link up before nightfall. And no one wanted the Marines to have to do much maneuvering on an enemy-held shore in the dark.

In this dispute, of course, the man wearing the five stars prevailed. General MacArthur saw considerable propaganda value in capturing the South Korean capital, and the quickest way to Seoul was through Inch'on.

To accomplish the mission, Headquarters, X Corps, was activated and its command given to MacArthur's chief of staff, Maj. Gen. Edward M. Almond. The ground units assigned to the new corps were Maj. Gen. Oliver P. Smith's* 1st Marine Division and Maj. Gen. David G. Barr's 7th Infantry Division. The Marine division would be composed of the 5th Marines (after the regiment had been withdrawn from the Naktong front) and the 1st and 7th Marines, which had recently been activated and were on their way to Korea. The 7th Infantry Division, which had been on occupation duty in Japan, was brought up to war strength with the addition of 8,500 poorly trained and equipped South Korean soldiers.

On 20 August, MacArthur's headquarters in Tokyo issued orders forming Joint Task Force Seven, which would carry out the Inch'on landings. Vice Adm. Arthur D. Struble, commander, Seventh Fleet, was named task force commander. The responsibility of getting the invasion force ashore fell to Rear Adm. James H. Doyle and Task Force 90-Attack Force. Admiral Struble's flagship would be USS Rochester, that of Rear Admiral Doyle, second in command, would be USS Mount McKinley.

General MacArthur's flamboyance and penchant for grand gestures would never be more clearly shown than at Inch'on. To be successful, the landings would require audacity, genius, and, most of all, luck. For MacArthur, Inch'on was perfect.

---

* A 1916 graduate of the University of California, General Smith had served in World War I as a Marine second lieutenant. During the Second World War, he commanded the 5th Marines on New Britain, was ADC of the 1st Marine Division throughout the Peleliu campaign and deputy chief-of-staff of the U.S. Tenth Army on Okinawa. When Smith was given command of the 1st Marine Division the summer of 1950, he had been a Marine for thirty-three years.

Operation planned mid-September is amphibious landing of two division corps in rear of enemy lines for purpose of enveloping and destroying enemy forces. . . . Although the exact date of D day is partially dependent upon enemy reaction during the month of August I am firmly convinced that an early and strong effort behind his front will sever his main line of communication and enable us to deliver a decisive and crushing blow. Any material delay in such an operation may lose this opportunity. The alternative is a frontal attack which can only result in a protracted and expensive campaign to slowly drive the enemy north of the 38th Parallel.

GENERAL DOUGLAS MACARTHUR, CINCFE TO JCS, 23 JULY 1950

1. In general the coastlines of the city of Inch'on and the island of Wolmi-do appear to be well covered with a line of light and medium coast defense guns, AA guns, field artillery, and various types of emplacements. These installations are grouped in a series of strong points located on the key terrain features in the area. These strong points are connected by lines of open trenches, thus forming an almost continuous belt around the city and its adjoining island. However, there does not seem to be any significant depth to these installations, the largest percentage of which appear to be unoccupied at the present time.

2. Tides and Currents: The city of Inch'on has a tidal range that is one of the most extreme on record. It exceeds 27 feet and at mean low water a mud flat extends some 1,000 to 1,200 yards seaward.

3. Coastal and Beach Conditions: General beach conditions in the area are poor at best. It is to be noted that Beach RED [in front of the city] affords no natural beach at high water due to the seawall and only the precarious mud flats during low water periods. This cobblestone type seawall extends the entire length of the beach and has a gradient of five on one. This wall may be broken down by air and naval gun fire. Immediately behind the beach lies a three hundred yard zone of open ground traversed by a secondary road and a double

track railroad. Inland from this general line are railroad mar-
shalling yards and the beginning of the city buildings.

4. Terrain: The city of Inch'on lies on the tip of a small peninsula and is generally flat in the west and southern section with
the exception of Observatory Hill elevation 220 feet which
commands the entire city. Possession of Observatory Hill will
afford the holder observation over the city with the exception
of those streets on which are located two- and three-story
buildings. Immediately behind the left (north) flank of the
beach is a small hill, elevation 130 feet. Eastward of Observatory Hill are two hill masses within the city between which
run the main road to Seoul and a double track, standard gauge
railroad. Continuing eastward 3,000 to 4,000 yards, gently
rising, sparsely populated hills extend in all directions. The
main corridor leading to Seoul varies in width from 1 to 3
miles and parallels the Han River, the major north-south obstacle lying before the city of Seoul.

5TH MARINES, OPERATION ORDER

There is no question in my mind as to the feasibility of the operation and I regard its chance of success as excellent. I go further and believe that it represents the only hope of wresting the
initiative from the enemy and thereby presenting an opportunity
for a decisive blow. To do otherwise is to commit us to a war of
indefinite duration, of gradual attrition, and of doubtful results.
. . . There is no slightest possibility . . . of our force being
ejected from the Pusan beachhead. The envelopment from the
north will instantly relieve the pressure on the south perimeter
and, indeed, is the only way that this can be accomplished. . . .
This, indeed, is the primary purpose of the movement. Caught
between our northern and southern forces, both of which are
completely self-sustaining because of our absolute air and naval
supremacy, the enemy cannot fail to be ultimately shattered. . . .

GENERAL DOUGLAS MACARTHUR, CINCFE TO JCS,
8 SEPTEMBER 1950

We approve your plan and President has been so informed.

JOINT CHIEFS OF STAFF TO GENERAL DOUGLAS MacARTHUR,
8 SEPTEMBER 1950

Adm. ARLEIGH BURKE
Deputy Chief of Staff to Commander Naval Forces, Far East
Within four or five days after I got out of there [Japan], I think it was
August 10 or 12, some typhoons started to develop down in the South
China Sea. In reading the weather reports, I found anything could
happen with them. There was one storm [Jane] forming which was
just right. It was coming directly up the center of the typhoon channel. It could then go west or east or straight up to Japan. If it went
west, the typhoon would interfere with the advance of our fleet and
if it got up to Japan early enough, it could disrupt the loading of the
ships.

When I went over to see MacArthur about this I was not permitted to see him. Instead I was asked to talk to his chief of staff, Ned
Almond, who had X Corps and who was to be chief of land opera-
tions at Inch'on. He wanted me to talk to him instead of MacArthur.
"No," I said, "because somebody has to make a decision; I've got to
talk to MacArthur himself." Almond asked if I'd spoken to the G-3.
Again I replied, "I have to see the boss man. I think it's important."
I waited around for quite a while. Finally General Almond told me
to tell him about my concerns. "Well, I'm sorry, but I can't do that,"
I said. "I'll go back to my office."

By the time I reached my office I had a message waiting that I
could see MacArthur. When I saw him I explained, "If this typhoon
comes up and goes west, this landing won't occur on the 15th or 16th,
which it must because of the tides."

"What do we do, Admiral?"

"We sail early."

"All right. Please prepare the dispatches."

"I happen to have them right here."

They were issued immediately. If I'd gone through Almond, days
and days of discussions would have occurred, and if a decision had

been reached, it would have been too late. This shows the great combat intuition of MacArthur. He knew the importance of making a decision on time.*

[After they were relieved by an Army regiment, the last Marine companies left Obong-ni Ridge at midnight, 5 September. Although the trip back to Pusan was made in a cold rain, no one was sorry to see the last of the Naktong.

The 1st Provisional Marine Brigade was deactivated and the 5th Marines again became part of the 1st Marine Division. The regiment's missing rifle companies were waiting in Pusan and joined their respective battalions.† A celebration of sorts was held; for the first time in Korea, the 5th Marines was at full strength.‡ Other units that had been attached to the brigade, such as the engineer, medical, and tank companies, rejoined their battalions in the division. General Craig became General Smith's assistant division commander and the brigade's other staff officers were absorbed by the division.

Early in September, the Pusan dock area resembled an anthill that has been overturned. The battle-weary and bone-tired Marines, for the moment, could forget about the killing and dying on the hills above the Naktong. For eight glorious days, the regiment regrouped, refitted, and integrated replacements. The men rested, listened to scuttlebutt, waited, and made the most of some idle time.]

2d Lt. FRANK MUETZEL
A/5

The XO [executive officer] of Heavy Mortar Company [2d Lt. Tom Gibson] and I took an afternoon and went sightseeing in Pusan. We

---

*Adm. Arleigh Burke interview, Oral History, United States Naval Institute, Annapolis, Maryland. Hereafter, Burke interview, Nav. Inst.
†C Company joined 1st Battalion, F Company, 2d Battalion, I Company 3d Battalion—a total of 1,135 officers and men.
‡The 5th Marines numbered 3,611 men at this time.

came upon a photography shop and stopped in to have our pictures taken. It was a simple operation, an old camera and some flash powder. I was dressed in my old, worn-out combat utilities. I also had a three-day-old beard and I was tired. I was rather proud of the picture and I sent it to my mother. When I arrived home Mom said that when she saw how I looked, she cried for days.

Pfc. FRED DAVIDSON
G/5

Being back on the dock at Pusan was like being back at the Bean Patch. My diary entries read, "Got our cigarette ration this A.M.," or "Walked to Army PX and bought candy." My memory of that time only registers events which occurred outside the regular routine. Like the time Roy Goulette and I decided we'd go into town and get laid. It was around noon when we started out. We really didn't know where we'd find a whorehouse in Pusan, but we knew there had to be one somewhere. Since neither of us drank, we didn't go into any of the bars. Instead I would stop and ask Korean civilians where we could find some girls. After four tries we found a man who took us to a building on a side street. We climbed a flight of stairs and entered a dark room where we found four young Korean women. I gave the young man who had been our guide a handful of Korean paper money I had gotten from a Marine sometime after How Company blew the bank vault in Kosong on August 11.

I paid two girls in advance and they took Roy and me into another room. He laid down his M1 and began to take off his shirt. Neither of the girls was especially pretty. They lay down on hemp mats and lifted up their skirts. They weren't wearing panties. Suddenly, for some reason, I found the situation very funny. I began laughing. Roy was ready for some action but he never got to it. He, too, began to laugh. I collapsed next to one of the girls, laughing out of control. Both girls got scared and ran out of the room. After Roy got dressed we went back down to the street, found an ice-cream vendor, and had ice-cream cones.

1st Lt. ROBERT BOHN
G/5

When the company got back to Pusan, it was out of everything. A lot of our weapons weren't firing properly, especially the machine guns. We couldn't keep up with the barrels, which had to be changed constantly. You have no idea how many rounds we had put through them.

The men's clothing was a shambles. Utilities had rotted clean through from rain and sweat. All the camouflage was faded a pale green. Boots were falling apart.

2d Lt. FRANK MUETZEL
A/5

I needed a new pair of boots, badly. My right boot had two bullet holes in the uppers, and the soles of both boots were worn through. Since no Marine supply was available, I took a jeep to the Eighth Army Quartermaster to see if I could beg a pair. A throng of scruffy Marines in front of the building was being harangued by an Army major for begging and stealing. Everyone I could see, including me, looked like refugees from Coxey's army. The men eventually gave up and began to drift away. I decided to crowd my luck. I pushed into the building behind the major and faced him down. I was wearing a steel helmet, a dungaree jacket with holes in both elbows, a pair of pants with the knees out, and my two ratty boots. My shirt did have my bars pinned to the collar. I carried a submachine gun and wore a .45 on my hip.

This clean, neatly dressed major told me he had specific instructions to withhold the issuing of boots, which were being saved for some incoming airborne unit. I told him, simply, that I was just off

the line, I was going right back onto the line, I was an infantry platoon leader, I didn't have a hell of a lot to lose, and I wanted a pair
of boots right then and there! When he looked at my boots and noticed the bullet holes, he went right back into his stock and brought
out a new pair of Army parachute jump boots. This was the only time
I ever back-chatted with a superior, but I was ready to fight for those
boots and that major knew it.

10 September 1950
Position (moored).
35–06.2N   129–02.6E.
At 1820 commenced loading cargo and equipment of the 1st
Marine Division.

USS *HENRICO* (APA 45), CAPT. JOHN E. FRADD

Pfc. FRED DAVIDSON
G/5
You could tell at once that the troops fresh from the States had come
from somewhere other than the Naktong River sector. They looked
so young and clean. Even their dungarees were brand-new.

2d Lt. TOM GIBSON
Mortar Company/5
No one knows how difficult it is to be a replacement more than I.
During World War II, when I joined the 506th Parachute Infantry
Regiment, they were still fighting in Normandy. I was the new kid
on the block. You're really under the gun. The tough part is knowing
that no matter how well you produce, in the minds of the veterans,
you're not worth a shit because you could never be as good as Sergeant Jones, Lieutenant Smith, or whoever it is you're replacing. You're
unproven, the unknown quantity, and it's tough to trust your life to
someone who hasn't earned that trust. Once you get into a shooting
scrape and can prove what you're made of, you, too, become a veteran and are accepted. If a replacement can survive the early period,
whatever is thought of him at that time will eventually be forgotten.

The replacements who were waiting for us in Pusan had to face this tough period. Fortunately for them, the time to prove themselves was rapidly approaching, more rapidly than any of them could know.

Pfc. DOUG KOCH
D/5

There was a lot of commotion, caused by the replacements who were coming in to fill the spots left open by the men we'd lost in the Naktong River battles. As I had lost my whole fire team in those actions, I got three new kids. Although we were together about two weeks, I have to admit I can't remember their names. Maybe this is one way you start to protect yourself; you don't get friendly with people. I was accused of being cold and standoffish with these new men by one of the other replacements. Maybe those of us who had come with the original brigade, who had lost so many friends, might have been somewhat defensive with these new kids. Maybe we didn't want any more close friends we could lose. It was so painful to remember them.

I just don't remember the names of those new guys on the fire team. In my mind's eye I can picture them—two were short and stocky, like me; the other was a tall, blond kid, and kind of slender.

2d Lt. TOM GIBSON
Mortar Company/5

Because he had boxed at Annapolis, Baldomero Lopez was called "Punchy." When the Korean War broke out and the brigade left the States, Punchy was on orders to go to the Marine school at Quantico. Naval Academy and career guy and here comes Korea and Punchy's shunted off to some safe stateside school. He couldn't stand it. Before the brigade sailed, Punchy swore he was going to move heaven and earth and get out to us. And he did. We were delighted to find him waiting for us as a replacement. On the dock in Pusan Punchy Lopez couldn't wait to get at the bastards. It was like a game to him.

11 September 1950
Position (moored).
35-06.2N   129-06.6E.
At 1300 commenced loading troop ammunition of the 1st Marine Division.

USS *HENRICO* (APA 45), CAPT. JOHN E. FRADD

Pfc. DOUG KOCH
D/5
We heard a lot of scuttlebutt about where we were going to land. Lots and lots of names. The North Koreans had to know we were going to go in somewhere. We called this time in Pusan "Operation Common Knowledge."

Capt. FRANCIS "IKE" FENTON, JR.
B/5
While we were living in the dock area, the regiment circulated a mimeographed sheet about a landing beach at Kaesong. This information was put out, I believe, to mislead fifth columnists in the area. The papers were marked "Confidential," but we had orders to read them to the troops, and I do believe a copy or two managed to get lost.

2d Lt. FRANK MUETZEL
A/5
Only officers who were married were paid at this time. The rest of the officers in A Company pooled their funds and bought $150 worth of beer and $50 worth of ice from the Eighth Army PX. In 1950 you could buy an awful lot of export beer tax free for $150. All jeep trailers were emptied and the beer cans were stacked in them. Then ice

was poured on top and everything was covered with tarps. We let the beer chill for one day.

There was so much beer the troops stopped drinking water. Their behavior was great and no one got into trouble. When we still had beer left the next day, the off-duty sailors on the *Henrico* were unofficially invited to join us on the dock. This they did—in a big way. And when the rest of the regiment saw the 1st Battalion's party, they, too, got into the act. That's when it got noisy. Two Marines drove a jeep off the dock while being pursued by two MPs. Two others, who had gone over the fence, returned driving a Brockway bridge transporter. They abandoned it at the MP checkpoint. It plugged the entrance to the dock until a qualified driver could be found to remove it.

While we were waiting to board the *Henrico*, we were required to turn in all the captured vehicles we were driving. These were mostly motorcycles with sidecars and jeeps, but there was also an occasional truck. This left us unacceptably short of motor transportation. Consequently, vehicles were purloined from the Army. The worst offense I saw was the theft of the MP company commander's jeep. After a fast coat of green paint and phony numbers were slapped on, it was presented to Lt. Col. George Newton, our battalion CO.

Rather than give up all our Russian jeeps, one was saved and presented to Capt. John Fradd, the *Henrico's* captain. The last I saw of it, it was being winched to the bottom cargo deck of the ship.

1st Lt. ROBERT BOHN
G/5
As we waited to board ship, the company felt good about itself. We were veterans now, and very confident. We'd kicked the shit out of the North Koreans. If anyone had any reservations, it wasn't about the enemy. If we worried at all, it was wondering whether the Navy could get the next job done, and get us in, wherever that would be.

11 September 1950
On the night of 10 September 1950, all companies were alerted to make preparations to board ship on order because of an ap-

Taejon, the morning of the North Korean attack, 20 July 1950 *Source: Dan Cavanaugh*

Portions of Taejon burn during the battle, 20 July 1950
Source: Dan Cavanaugh

Brig. Gen. Edward A. Craig
(USMC) (left) and Maj. Gen. John
H. Church (USA) the morning the
Marines attacked Obong-ni Ridge,
17 August 1950
Source: Marine Corps Photos

Maj. Gen. Raymond Murray. In Korea in
1950, as a lieutenant colonel, he commanded
the 5th Marine Regiment.
Source: Marine Corps Photos

Marines on Objective Three move toward the
Naktong River, 19 August 1950
Source: Marine Corps Photos

Chow line at the Bean Patch, 24 August 1950 *Source: Marine Corps Photos*

Brig. Gen. Edward Craig awards a Purple Heart to Pfc. D.E.
McGuire after the first battle of the Naktong
Source: Marine Corps Photos

Marines swing wide around burning T34 tank west of Yongsan during second battle of Naktong Bulge, 4 September 1950 *Source: Marine Corps Photos*

H-Hour and the first wave of LCVPs heads for the beaches at Inch'on, 15 September 1950 *Source: Marine Corps Photos*

First Lieutenant Baldomero Lopez climbs out of an LCVP on RED Beach, Inch'on,
15 September 1950 *Source: Marine Corps Photos*

Two destroyed T34 tanks on the road east of Inch'on, morning
of 16 September 1950 *Source: Marine Corps Photos*

General Craig (right, front) confers with Colonel Puller (left) west of Yongdungp'o
Source: Marine Corps Photos

The battle for Seoul, 27 September 1950 *Source: Marine Corps Photos*

Item Company, 5th Cavalry Regiment, during a lull in the fighting on Hill 174, 17 September 1950 *Source: Don Pate*

"City Hall," or the I Company CP area, on top of Hill 174 with 1st Sgt. Arnold Mitchell in foreground, 17 September 1950 *Source: Don Pate*

Atrocities committed by the North Koreans discovered near Taejon, 29 September
1950 *Source: Dan Cavanaugh*

proaching typhoon. Actual embarkation of the battalion commenced at 1400, 11 September 1950. BLT [Battalion Landing Team] 1/5 and H & S Company, 5th Marines were the major units embarked.

SPECIAL ACTION REPORT, 1/5

Uniform and Equipment for Embarkation
(1) Individual arms and equipment (2) Utility with steel helmet camouflage cover, green side out, and leggings. (3) Field Transport Pack with following minimum content: 1 Belt, web, trouser, w/o buckle; 1 Buckle, metal, trouser, belt; 1 Cap, utility; 1 Coat, utility; 2 Drawers, cotton, pr.; 1 Jacket, field; 2 Shirts, flannel; 1 Shoes, field, pr.; 3 Socks, woolen, pr.; 1 Trouser, winter service; 2 Trousers, utility; 2 Undershirts, cotton; 1 Razor, w/blades; 1 Soap Box, w/soap; 1 Toothbrush, w/case; 1 Comb; 1 Soap, shaving; 1 Toothpaste; 1 Mirror; 1 Handkerchief; 1 Legging Laces; 1 Towel; 1 Sewing Kit; 1 Sleeping Bag, w/2 blankets.

ADMINISTRATIVE PLAN NUMBER 3-50, 1ST MARINE DIVISION

2d Lt. TOM GIBSON
Mortar Company/5
When we received word that we were going back aboard ship, everyone from the 1st Battalion, 5th Marines, hoped he would be back on the *Henrico*. When we sailed to Korea in July, on that three-week-long crossing from San Diego to Pusan, we went on the *Henrico*, which was known in the fleet as the "Happy Hank." By the time 1/5 got to Korea, the troops and the sailors were great friends. At Pusan we went ashore from the *Henrico*. We fought, were pulled back, and now, waiting to go back on board a ship, we hoped it would be the "Happy Hank"—and it was.

During the month we were away from the *Henrico*, the 5th Marines sustained heavy casualties—officers, NCOs, and snuffies [troops]. On the way over to Korea, the ship's officers and the battalion's officers began calling each other by their first names; so did their enlisted men and our enlisted men. Everybody knew everybody. It was a wonderful relationship. When we went aboard the *Henrico* after an

August of bitter fighting and heavy losses, the officers and men of the *Henrico* felt a great loss when they saw how few of us there now were. The men aboard that ship became very emotional.

12 September 1950
At 1300 completed embarkation of troops having embarked 1649 military personnel and 7 civilian war correspondents (Marguerite Higgins; John O. Davies; Richard Ferguson; Lionel Crane; Frede Vidar; Larry Keighly; John Shaw).

USS *HENRICO* (APA 45), CAPT. JOHN E. FRADD

USS *Henrico* sailed from Pusan, at 1450, 12 September 1950, and was underway for a period of three days. . . .

SPECIAL ACTION REPORT, 1/5

[The 5th Marines mounted out from Pusan; the 1st Marine Regiment, commanded by the legendary Chesty Puller, from Kobe, Japan.* The 7th Infantry Division and the other X Corps units not scheduled to make the assault landing sailed from Yokohama. The various parts of the invasion armada, divided into groups according to speed and roles, proceeded to Inch'on by different routes. Nearly 70,000 men were at sea, carried by 260 ships, including vessels from Australia, Canada, New Zealand, France, Holland, Great Britain, and the United States.

The command ship, Mount McKinley, with General Douglas MacArthur aboard, weighed anchor at Sasebo, Japan, a little after midnight on 13 September.

Plunging through rough seas from a nearby typhoon, the vast convoy steamed toward its objective. D day was two days away.]

2d Lt. FRANK MUETZEL
A/5
The voyage was the best I'd ever had on a Navy ship. The Navy was aware of where we'd been and where we were going. The food was good, little extras were made available, and harassment was kept to a

---

*The 7th Marine Regiment, still at sea, wouldn't arrive at Inch'on until 21 September.

minimum. Company officers were bunked together in the better staterooms, and the wardroom was made available twenty-four hours a day. Even the presence of Maggie Higgins, the female war correspondent, was tolerated.

Maggie went to Inch'on with us on the *Henrico* and occupied one of the few single bunk rooms. This created a domino effect with senior officers bumping junior officers until someone got double-bunked. She took her meals in the wardroom with the first sitting, which was reserved for senior officers.

Each day after the evening meal the wardroom would be cleared and the table turned over to the staff and supporting arms planners. In a short time the room would become hazy with cigarette smoke. To air the room out occasionally, the lights would be doused and the portholes opened. Everyone would remain seated in the pitch dark. Once the air had been freshened, the portholes would be closed again and covered. Only then would the lights be turned back on. One night a Marine captain entered the wardroom during one of the blackouts. After barking his shins on a chair, he unloaded a blast of profanity. "*Sshhh,*" someone said, "Maggie Higgins." The response went, "Fuck Maggie Higgins." Only then did this captain realize that the stewards were in the process of closing the portholes, and when the lights came on in another instant, he'd be the only person standing. When the lights went on everyone was sitting, except one Marine was sitting on some guy's lap.

Capt. FRANCIS ''IKE'' FENTON, JR.
B/5
All our available time on the *Henrico* was spent briefing our platoons, squads, and fire teams. During one of these briefings, a runner from the wardroom came down to me and announced that I was wanted. "By whom?" I asked. "By Miss Marguerite Higgins," I was told. "She wants to interview you, Captain." "Well, if Miss Marguerite Higgins wants to see me," I flippantly replied, "tell her to shag her ass down here. I'm busy briefing the troops." Well, the young runner returned to the wardroom and gave Maggie Higgins my answer exactly as I had given it to him. Needless to say, I never did get interviewed.

[On 13 September 1950 all units sailing for Inch'on were briefed on the mission of the 1st Marine Division. The holiday was over. Pusan was forgotten. It was time for the troops to get back to work.

Because of the extreme tides on 15 September 1950, the landings at Inch'on had to be carried out in two stages. The tactical key to Inch'on was the island of Wolmi-do, which sits about 500 yards off the central port area and is connected to it by a concrete causeway. Before the city could be assaulted, the hill on Wolmi-do had to be taken. If it was not, the main landing force would be exposed to close enfilade fire coming from the island.

With the morning tide, around 6:30 A.M., the 3d Battalion, 5th Marines, would storm Wolmi-do on GREEN Beach and secure it as quickly as possible. Naval gunfire and close air support would prevent the North Koreans from pouring reinforcements over the causeway. Once on the island, the 3d Battalion would have to sit and wait for the next high tide and the second phase of the landings to begin.

With the evening tide, the other two battalions of the 5th Marines would land over the sixteen-foot-high seawall of RED Beach and begin their direct assault on the city of Inch'on.

Three miles southeast of the city, Puller's 1st Marine Regiment would make its landing on BLUE Beach. Once ashore it would drive rapidly inland and prevent enemy reinforcements coming north from reaching the city.

The 5th and 1st Marines would have about ninety minutes of daylight to consolidate their positions. As soon as RED and BLUE Beaches were secure and before the flood tide began to recede, the large cargo-bearing LSTs [landing ship, tank], which carried ammunition, rations, water, and fuel, would begin arriving at RED Beach.]

Maj. MARTIN SEXTON
Aide-de-Camp to Maj. Gen. O. P. Smith
Basically, the plan was to have the 1st Marines and the 5th Marines seize limited beachheads, hold them during the night of D day, and then expand them on D plus 1. There was, of course, some concern about attacking an Oriental city under conditions of dark. If an actual heavy enemy disposition developed in the area, it could prove to be an extremely difficult task.

As far as I know, it was a fairly improvised plan. Though the regiments had made quite detailed plans for the night operations, time did not permit the precise planning and preparations that normally precede such an operation. There was not even enough time for landing exercises by the LVTs [landing vehicle, tracked]. Some of the LVT crews had not even had the opportunity to try their engines out in the water and paddle around.*

Ens. GEORGE GILMAN
Assistant Boat Group Commander, USS Mount McKinley
As soon as we pulled out of Pusan, we began to get briefings on the tide situation in the Inch'on Harbor area. As an assistant boat group commander, I was going to be responsible for some of the landing craft. We couldn't figure out how in the hell we were ever going to make any kind of an amphibious landing with those thirty-two-foot tides. None of us boat group officers had ever had any experience operating under such tidal conditions before, let alone ever having been involved in an amphibious landing. As the morning of September 15 approached, we realized we had all the ingredients for a disaster on our hands.

Pfc. DOUG KOCH
D/5
We saw maps and aerial photographs. D/5 drew RED Beach. On all the practice landings I'd ever made I had landed on a beach. Now, on the one that was really going to count, I was going to have to climb up a ladder out of an LCVP [landing craft, vehicle and personnel] and get over a seawall. It sure looked like we were going to be pretty well exposed.

*Major Sexton interview, on file at the Marine Corps Historical Center, Washington, D.C. Hereafter, Sexton interview, MCHC.

Lt. Col. HAROLD S. ROISE
2/5

Two things scared me to death. One, we were not landing on a beach; we were landing against a seawall. Each LCVP had two ladders which would be used to climb up and over the wall. This was risky, especially if the enemy had any forces nearby. It would also slow us down in getting all the troops ashore.

Two, the landing was scheduled for 5:30 P.M. This would give us only about two hours of daylight to clear the city and set up for the night.

Capt. FRANCIS "IKE" FENTON, JR.
B/5

Everyone was very apprehensive about this landing. It really looked dangerous. There was a finger pier and a causeway extending out from RED Beach which reminded us of Tarawa, and if machine guns were on the finger pier and causeway, we were going to have a tough time making the last 200 yards to the beach.

Our landing had to be made against a seawall which was about fifteen feet above the water level. That meant that we would have to use scaling ladders. However, a few boats in each wave would be able to locate holes in the seawall and not bother with the ladders. The holes were the result of aerial bombing that had been conducted earlier in the month and in late August. Using scaling ladders meant that only two men at a time could get out of the boats and climb up on the seawall. Equipment had to be lifted by lashing and lowering lines.

Once on the beach we would face a flat area of about 200 yards before we actually ran into the town itself. On the left side of the beach, our left flank, was a hill called Cemetery Hill. Approaching it by sea, it was a sheer cliff. The only good approach to the hill was from the east side, 180 degrees from the water side.

Just off to the right (east) of Cemetery Hill, there was a big beer factory, workshops, and a cotton mill. To the right of that and about 600 yards inland from the beach was Observatory Hill; the critical terrain feature in the area. It overlooked the entire landing area, and was the regimental objective.

On the right flank of RED Beach, the 2d Battalion's landing area, was a five-story office building. It was located right in the middle of their landing beach. The building was made of concrete and reinforced steel. The whole landing beach was dotted with emplacements and bunkers. Connecting trenches ran the entire length of the beach. Captain Stevens, whose A Company was going to land first, was quite worried about the trenches and bunkers. He knew that air, artillery, NGF [naval gunfire], and rockets were going to work that area over for two days, but he was wondering if we were going to be able to clear those bunkers out altogether.

Capt. JOHN STEVENS
A/5

Our experience, up to then, had indicated that if an officer or staff noncommissioned officer could make it through an initial firefight, his chances for continuing were good. Lieutenant Muetzel, platoon leader 2d Platoon, and Gunnery Sergeant McMullan, platoon leader 1st Platoon, were excellent examples of this. The assault plan at RED Beach called for Able Company to be deployed with two platoons up and one platoon in reserve. The 1st Platoon, under Gunnery Sergeant McMullan, and the 2d Platoon, under Lieutenant Muetzel, were selected as the two assault platoons. The 3d Platoon, under Lieutenant Lopez, who had just joined the company in Pusan as a replacement, was to be the reserve. I remember thinking that Lieutenant Lopez would have the least amount of exposure by being with the reserve platoon. Unfortunately, it didn't work that way.

2d Lt. FRANK MUETZEL
A/5

I almost stroked out when Captain Stevens briefed us on the schedule of maneuver. Third Battalion would land at dawn and take Wolmido. Then 1/5 and 2/5 would land at Inch'on on RED Beach at 5:30

P.M. in columns of companies. I really blew when he told me that A Company would land in a column of platoons and that my 2d Platoon would take the assault wave. Aerial photos showed us what the beach looked like, particularly the seawall. It looked like bad news for the assault waves.

We had all figured our chances of being in the assault wave were pretty slim. With the 1st and 7th Marines joining the 5th Marines in the division, our regimental chances of landing first were one in three. If the 5th did go in, the three battalions made it another one in three. Finally, if the 1st Battalion was committed, with the new C Company now on board, the chance of A landing first was another one in three. The odds were all in my favor. But it didn't work out that way. My squad was going into RED Beach on the first wave.

Everyone expected the first phase of the landing to be hotly contested and costly, but my platoon sergeant, Technical Sergeant Johnson, who had been at Tarawa, really came unglued. He became so upset I had to finally put him in my reserve squad.

I was only half in jest when I accused Stevens of trying to get me killed. After all, I was the sole surviving platoon leader. Stevens and Eubanks (the exec) assured me that the first wave was always the safest and that succeeding waves always caught it. No matter, I left Sergeant Johnson in the second wave.

Pfc. FRED DAVIDSON
G/5

We were told that the 3d Battalion's objective would be a small island in the harbor at Inch'on, and that our landing on Wolmi-do would take place on the morning of the 15th. Once we secured the island, we would wait until the rest of the 1st Marine Division landed on the mainland in the evening.

It never entered our minds that we would be in a very dangerous position waiting on this island until the tide had come back in and the rest of the division could land. Lieutenant Bohn and the other officers showed us fresh aerial photos of Wolmi-do and explained where we would land, what we would do, and what we could expect from the enemy. We were also shown photos of Kimpo Airfield. The Air Force, we were told, had bombed it so the enemy could not use it during the invasion. The photos showed a lot of bomb craters, but not one damn runway had been hit! That got me worrying about what they would do to Wolmi-do.

Maj. MARTIN SEXTON
Aide-de-Camp to Maj. Gen. O. P. Smith
The G-2 [Intelligence] section aboard the USS *Mount McKinley* was able to trace the development of the enemy's defenses by means of aerial photo interpretation, reports of agents, reports of refugees, and evaluation of many other sources. Daily progress and improvements were noted in the enemy's defenses of Wolmi-do and Inch'on. By D day they had become quite formidable.*

[*Reconnaissance reports indicated 106 hard targets already in place on Wolmi-do or along the Inch'on landing beaches. The island and the beaches would have to be softened up before the landing took place. The plan called for methodical naval gunfire preparation with closely coordinated air strikes launched from the carriers* Sicily *and* Badoeng Strait. *Attack squadrons were also available from Task Force 77—a fast carrier group sailing west of the main task force. The carrier-based attacks began on 10 September. Then, on the 13th, the JTF-7 destroyer element would hit Wolmi-do. Their mission was to close with the enemy in broad daylight and goad him into retaliating. Once all the North Korean guns on the island had been revealed, the U.S. cruisers* Toledo *and* Rochester *and the British cruisers* Kenya *and* Jamaica *would demolish them with their heavier guns.*

For the destroyers Gurke, Henderson, Swanson, Collett, De-Haven, *and* Mansfield, *Wednesday, 13 September, would be an eventful day. On Wolmi-do the North Koreans took the punishment meted out by the destroyers for nearly half an hour. They then obliged the joint task force planners and returned fire.*]

13 September 1950
0916 Formed column led by USS *Mansfield* (DD 728) and proceeded up Flying Fish Channel toward Inch'on, Korea.

---

* Sexton interview, MCHC.

Anchored in harbor. Adjusted heading at anchor to bring guns to bear.

1302 Commenced firing prearranged fire on targets, primarily gun emplacements.

USS *MANSFIELD* (DD 728), CDR. E. H. HEADLAND

13 September 1950

1302 Fire shifted to target area no. 2 but not before enemy commenced fire from that area. Within minutes there were at least 50 short and 50 over, plus continuous small arms fire.

USS *COLLETT* (DD 730), CDR. R. H. CLOSE

13 September 1950

1320 Observed shell fire being received by destroyers in the second section anchored south of Wolmi-do.

USS *MANSFIELD* (DD 728), CDR. E. H. HEADLAND

13 September 1950

1303 Commenced counter battery fire on target no. 2.

1308 *Gurke* (DD 783) asked where counter battery was coming from and *Collett* informed that it was in target area indicated on chart as "D."

1310 Received hit no. 1 (forward head).

1312 Received hit no. 2 (Steward's living space).

1326 Received hit no. 3 (Wardroom).

1335 Received hit no. 4 (Fireroom and Plot).

1336 Received hit no. 5 (Steward's living space).

1337 Requested permission from CTG 90.6 to get underway and shift our position. Our rate of fire was considerably diminished in local control as the smoke obscured the targets and necessitated frequent check of fires until targets again became visible. We did not seem to be giving as good as we were taking since some of the enemy guns had found the range and I hoped that the damage to the computer might be such that the guns could be put back in director control. . . . My request did not indicate a lack of initiative, but simply a consideration that part of our mission was to locate enemy batteries which we were still doing very effectively. I felt that a sound decision could be better made by someone with a broad view, mine having become somewhat limited by numerous splashes close aboard.

1338 Permission granted by CTG 90.6 to withdraw.

USS COLLETT (DD 730), CDR. R. H. CLOSE

13 September 1950

1350 Commenced firing main battery to starboard in accordance with D minus 2 day schedule at enemy positions on Wolmi-do.

USS ROCHESTER (CA 124), CAPT. EDWARD WOODYARD

13 September 1950

1400 Underway. Proceeding out of harbor at flank speed.

1415 Received counter battery fire from Wolmi-do. A total of twenty-five splashes were observed in the immediate vicinity of which five were close aboard.

USS MANSFIELD (DD 728), CDR. E. H. HEADLAND

Cdr. GEORGE H. MILLER
Plans Officer to Commander, Joint Task Force

A division of destroyers was sent forward to anchor close off Wolmido at point-blank range. The destroyers were to draw the fire of the shore batteries so those batteries could be destroyed by the big cruisers and by air strikes. The shore batteries did open up and were destroyed. The topside structure of one of the destroyers was shot up pretty badly. That night our ships withdrew to open water to return again the next day. I remember the destroyer squadron commander, Captain Allen, coming aboard late that night. He said to Admiral Struble, "They can't go back tomorrow. They've taken too much of a beating." Allen recommended that his destroyers withdraw to Sasebo. Struble glanced around the room. When he looked my way—I had only been on board ten days or so—I shook my head no. The hulls were still intact. After some more discussion Struble decided that the destroyer element should return to the harbor the next day except perhaps *Collett*, which had taken several topside hits. I called attention to the large number of moored mines that appeared on the surface of the channel at low tide and suggested that even though *Collett's* main battery was crippled, she could serve a useful purpose by moving in and destroying those mines with small-arms fire. Struble approved. The destroyers went back in on the 14th.

14 September 1950

0800　All engines stopped. All ships stopped in tribute to the gallant officer who was killed in action yesterday. Lt. (j.g.) Swenson, USN, being buried at sea with full military honors.

0930　Following movements of column leader, proceeding to D minus 1 bombardment Inch'on, Korea.

1140　Cruiser element opened fire.

1150　General Quarters.

1210　Cruiser element ceased firing.

1212　Air strike being made at Wolmi-do.

1216　Commenced firing at gun emplacements along waterfront.

1415　Ceased firing having received no counter battery fire.

USS *MANSFIELD* (DD 728), CDR. E. H. HEADLAND

[While the landing beaches were being worked over methodically by naval gunfire and air strikes, the transport elements of the invasion force rendezvoused outside of Inch'on Harbor. By the evening of 14 September, after five days of continual pounding, Wolmi-do and Inch'on were ready for the 1st Marine Division.]

14 September 1950

The battalion supply sections issued ammunition and rations to the companies for further distribution to the troops. During the afternoon of the 14th, a debarkation drill was held for all troops, and all boat teams of the first five waves were briefed in the use of the scaling ladders and cargo nets. . . .

SPECIAL ACTION REPORT, 1/5

2d Lt. TOM GIBSON
Mortar Company/5

The night before the Inch'on landing, we decided to finish off the beer we'd carried aboard the *Henrico*, but were confronted with the problem of how to chill it. One of the "Happy Hank's" officers suggested we use CO_2 from the ship's damage-control fire extinguishers. We took a trash can, filled it with cans of beer, wrapped a blanket around the business end of the extinguisher, and gave the big can a quick squirt. Instantly chilled beer. We used, I think, three fire extinguishers. If there had been a fire aboard the *Henrico* the next day, the only thing we could have done to put it out was piss on it.

2d Lt. FRANK MUETZEL
A/5

I spent the night before the landing in a stateroom belonging to Ensigns Herb Kindle and Richard Plank. Kindle was first boat wave commander and Plank the second. I was landing in Kindle's boat. We wrote our last letters home, checked field gear, and drank the two cases of beer I had smuggled aboard. We chilled the beer by blasting the cans with CO_2 bottles. I lunched on the *Henrico* in the spring of 1951, and the ship's carpenter really took a strip off me for emptying the bottles the night before action, but at the time I couldn't have cared less. It was time for the Navy to join the war.

A *Life* correspondent named Frede Vidar was there with a fifth of bourbon, so we helped him kill that and showed him how to load and unload his pistol. He was complaining that the correspondents were all landing in the same boat, and that he wanted to be on an earlier boat. I offered to take him in mine, but he declined when he found out it was in the first wave. Lopez came by, offered me a clean set of dungarees, which I needed badly, and had a beer with us. I'll always be glad he did.

Pfc. DOUG KOCH
D/5

Needless to say, we were pretty uptight. After chow there was a church service in the mess hall. A pretty good crowd of guys went to church that night.

You pray for your friends, that they might be spared. For yourself, you pray that if you're killed, it will be quick and merciful. You
never prayed, "Spare me, God, and I'll be good." It would sound
selfish if you prayed that you wanted to be spared.

Lt. (j.g.) PHILIP LEVIN
Commanding Officer, USS Osprey *(AMS 28)*
When I entered the harbor at dawn on September 15, a British light
cruiser [HMS *Jamaica*] was anchored in the harbor. They blinked a
signal to me, "Suggest you not proceed farther up channel. It is not
safe." My reply was based on a comment made by General Mac-
Arthur when he was informed that there could be foul weather the
morning of the invasion and that perhaps it would be wise to delay
the landing. The general's reply was, "We go." My response to the
cruiser was, "Orders are orders. We go."

*[On 15 September 1944, the 1st Marine Division had stormed ashore
in the Palaus, at Peleliu. Exactly six years later, one of nature's odd-
ities, the tides at Inch'on, brought that same division to the west coast
of Korea on a similar mission.*

*At 2:30 A.M. on D day, the ships carrying the 3d Battalion, 5th
Marines, began making their way up Flying Fish Channel toward
Wolmi-do's GREEN Beach. The first major amphibious assault by
American troops since Easter Sunday, 1945, at Okinawa was about
to begin.]*

Ens. GEORGE GILMAN
Assistant Boat Group Commander, USS Mount McKinley
Sometime after midnight we were told to man the landing craft and
be prepared to be lowered. Now the real terror set in. It was pitch-
black. As a matter of fact, I'd never seen a night as black as that one.
Here were six fuzzy-cheeked ensigns who had to get their landing craft
several miles up the channel to the USS *Fort Marion* (LSD 22), which
housed the commander of the advance attack force. The narrowness
of the channel up there was presenting all kinds of problems because
there was limited anchoring space for the amphibious force.

With a great deal of good fortune, we arrived on time at the *Fort Marion*. Our next stop would be Wolmi-do.

Lt. Gen. LEMUEL C. SHEPHERD, JR.
Commanding General, FMFPac
It was a beautiful morning, and as the first pink streaks of dawn broke in the east, my thoughts went back to other dawns when I had watched preparations for similar landings.*

Pfc. FRED DAVIDSON
G/5
Around 3:00 in the morning, the *Diachenko* stopped its engines. The compartment lights came on and reveille was played over the ship's PA system. Most of the men of George Company were already wide-awake.

lst Lt. ROBERT BOHN
G/5
There was some tension and a lot of excitement. Every rifleman knew what the plan of fire would be—naval gunfire, air, rockets, air. The Corsairs would be working over Wolmi-do seconds before the first wave landed. G Company was to land to the right of GREEN Beach in the assault, wheel right, and seize the dominant hill mass on the island, Radio Hill.

Everyone was up by 3:00. Then the shooting started.

---

*General Shepherd's journal, as quoted in Robert Debs Heinl, *Victory at High Tide* (New York: Lippincott, 1968), 89. Hereafter, Shepherd/Heinl.

Yn. 2/C JAMES PAGE
USS Rochester

The *Rochester* began pounding the enemy before first light. The roar of the big eight-inch guns was much easier on the nervous system than the piercing crack of the five-inch guns. Since the Korean War was fought before there was official concern over men losing their hearing, I watched the gunfire with my fingers stuck in my ears. The glow caused by the fires on Wolmi-do and the mainland was very noticeable. After about an hour the gunfire stopped and the carrier aircraft took over.

Maj. MARTIN SEXTON
Aide-de-Camp to Maj. Gen. O. P. Smith

The naval bombardment and the aerial saturation of the island were very thorough. The whole area for miles was obscured by smoke and burning fires.*

Pfc. FRED DAVIDSON
G/5

I found Roy, and as soon as chow call was sounded he and I went to the galley. I had heard many times that Marines who were about to make an amphibious landing on an enemy-held beach were always served a big breakfast of eggs, steak, bacon, and hot muffins. This certainly wasn't the case with us. The breakfast served George Company on the morning of September 15, 1950, consisted of scrambled eggs (powdered, of course), no meat (I would have remembered steak), and no hot biscuits. We did get toast, without butter, and some canned apricots.

* Sexton interview, MCHC.

I didn't realize just how nervous I was that morning until I stepped out of the serving line and began to make my way to one of the stand-up tables to eat. A sailor on mess duty accidentally bumped my tray and the apricots sloshed onto the scrambled eggs. "I'm really sorry," he said, and he meant it. I looked down at the eggs and apricots. "Goddamn it!" I said, and being a real asshole I dropped the tray. As it clattered on the deck, I stormed out of the galley. No one said a word. I don't know who cleaned up my mess—probably the sailor who bumped me. Since then I've often wished I could find that man so I could apologize for being such a shithead.

Out on the deck I lost all of my anger. As dawn broke, you could see, just dimly at first, where the Navy gunfire was landing. Because the island was completely covered in smoke, it was difficult to see anything too clearly.

Then it was time to get ready to board the landing craft. First, I remembered, buckle the helmet chin strap tightly so it can't fall on the men already in the landing craft. Second, climbing down the boarding net, place hands on the vertical ropes so the man above doesn't step on them.

1st Lt. ED JAWORSKI
G/5
Around first light we got into the LCVPs. As we circled it was like watching a combined arms demonstration. There were at least two LSMRs [landing ship, medium rocket] sitting out beyond us—nothing but five-inch rocket tubes. Just before we started in, they let go. It was like a continuous wave of fire. Wolmi-do, this little island, literally exploded. It was then that the landing craft headed toward the beach.

Pfc. JACK WRIGHT
G/5

I kept seeing in my mind the famous newsreel clip of the landing at
Normandy—the one where you're looking over the ramp and there's
the beach and a bombed-out house, and a hill off to the side with a
tree on it.

Ens. GEORGE GILMAN
Assistant Boat Group Commander, USS **Mount McKinley**

My boat was in the first wave and I felt naked as hell. We were on
the flagship and our captain was very taken with uniforms. All the
boat officers that morning in the various waves going into GREEN
Beach wore shiny black shoes, khaki uniforms, black ties, and very
bright shiny silver helmets with our ranks showing on them. The
Marines thought that was neat because they knew we'd draw the fire
and they wouldn't. As I got closer I took off my tie.

15 September 1950
0504 Commenced firing prearranged fire on Wolmi-do.

USS MANSFIELD (DD 728), CDR. E. H. HEADLAND

Pfc. FRED DAVIDSON
G/5

The Navy continued to pound the shore. Still far enough from the
island for it to be safe, I looked over the side. There were two LCVP's
on the right and three on the left. The closer we got to the smoke,
the louder the explosions became. Then it became possible to see the
explosions; the flashes lit up the smoke. Surprisingly, when I looked
to the right, the two LCVPs that had been there had dropped astern
and were trailing us. The same was true to the left, where now only
one landing craft was on line with us. I thought those four must have

been having engine trouble and couldn't keep up. The closer we got to the island, the more concerned I became. I didn't want to land and be the only target. All at once, we were in the smoke!

0629 Ceased all fire. Wave # 1 nearing GREEN Beach.
USS *DEHAVEN* (DD 727), CDR. O. D. LUNDGREN

Pfc. FRED DAVIDSON
G/5
It got quiet as hell. The only sounds were the LCVP's engine and the slap of water on the bow. There must have been fifteen seconds of this quiet. I imagined an enemy machine gun on the beach zeroing in on my landing craft's ramp.

1st Lt. ED JAWORSKI
G/5
Without warning the aircraft came in!

Pfc. FRED DAVIDSON
G/5
The roar of their engines hit us like a bomb. Those Marine Corsairs came flying through the smoke toward the beach not more than thirty feet over our heads! Hot, empty machine-gun shells fell on us. Talk about close air support. In front of me now I could see the beach. We couldn't have been more than twenty feet away.

1st Lt. ROBERT BOHN
G/5
The timing at Wolmi-do was superb. Everything worked—except me. As we approached the shore I cinched up my pack, a mistake that could have killed me.

1st Lt. ED JAWORSKI
G/5

Bohn and I were in the same boat. I was on the side of the LCVP
where the trip latch for the ramp was.

1st Lt. ROBERT BOHN
G/5

I turned to the men behind me. "Stand by to hit," I yelled.

1st Lt. ED JAWORSKI
G/5

The boat crunched to a halt. I dropped the ramp and leaped off one
side; Bohn jumped off the other. We both disappeared into ten feet
of water. Instead of the beach, the coxswain on the LCVP had hit an
old submerged hulk.

1st Lt. ROBERT BOHN
G/5

I went down like a rock. I reached upward and kicked as hard as I
could.

1st Lt. ED JAWORSKI
G/5

I thought I was going to drown. I kept going down. The carbine went
first. Finally, I got rid of the pack and bobbed to the surface.

1st Lt. ROBERT BOHN
G/5

Ed Jaworski was in the water with me. One of our sergeants, Harold
Beaver, had stopped the rest of the men from making the same mis-
take we'd made. I began swimming. When I finally made it to shore,
I looked to my left and saw Counselman's platoon hitting the beach.

Pfc. FRED DAVIDSON
G/5

Soon as I cleared the beach, I turned to my right and followed Lieutenant Westerman. It was hard to see because of the smoke. All the trees I passed had been blown down. I passed near a large unexploded shell. The first North Korean I saw was naked and had his hands on top of his head. There were several caves, which we cleared. We'd throw in a grenade and yell, "Fire in the hole!" After the explosion we'd wait for the North Korean troops to stumble out.

I started up the slope of Radio Hill. Halfway up, on a saddle, Lieutenant Westerman shouted to several of us to go toward the east. As we started to run in that direction, the rest of George Company continued to climb the hill. On the other side of the saddle, my group came upon a trench which had been cut across that side of the hill. We jumped in and set up a .30 light machine gun. From there we could look out at Inch'on. The Corsairs were busy making strafing runs. We also had a view of some buildings on Wolmi-do. As How Company approached them, we gave covering fire. Once How Company had occupied this area, we were ordered to rejoin George Company, which was now on top of Radio Hill.

Pfc. JACK WRIGHT
G/5

Surprisingly, our sector was hardly getting any return fire whatsoever. We got to the top of Radio Hill and found a great big bowllike depression. Everyone stopped for the first time since we'd hit the beach and began looking around. There was some shooting off down toward the beach on the Inch'on side of the island, but it didn't last for more than five minutes. All of a sudden, everyone, everything just went quiet. Standing there, looking around, it hit us all at once. The island was ours. We'd taken it!

> Captured forty-five prisoners . . . meeting light resistance.
>
> LT. COL. ROBERT TAPLETT, CO 3/5
> (RADIO MESSAGE TO *MOUNT McKINLEY*)

0703 Observed United States flag on top of Wolmi-do.
Landing highly successful.

USS *DEHAVEN* (DD 727), CDR. O. D. LUNDGREN

2d Lt. JOHN COUNSELMAN
G/5

My platoon guide was the one who brought the flag ashore. I'm not
sure I know how he happened to have one, but he did. On top of
the hill, not more than thirty minutes after we landed, the flag was
flying from a shattered, beat-up tree. I radioed Bob Bohn, "Our end
is secure."

Isherwood . . . Isherwood . . . This glove . . . Wolmi-do secured at 0800.

LT. COL. ROBERT TAPLETT, CO 3/5
(RADIO MESSAGE TO *MOUNT MCKINLEY*)

Maj. MARTIN SEXTON
Aide-de-Camp to Maj. Gen. O. P. Smith

As the first waves hit Wolmi-do, word came that they were landing
against very light opposition, and after one hour and thirty-seven
minutes the word was passed out from Wolmi-do that the island was
secured. The 3d Battalion, 5th Marines, was digging in, prepared for
further orders. General MacArthur, General Shepherd, General Almond, General Smith, General [Courtney] Whitney, Admiral Struble, and Admiral Doyle were up on the bridge observing the naval
bombardment and landing. General MacArthur smiled and seemed
quite pleased with the progress. Shortly afterward he went below to
his stateroom. It is my impression that General MacArthur's dispatch
stating, "Never have the Navy and Marine Corps shone more brightly

than today" was released after the seizure of Wolmi-do and prior to the landings on RED and BLUE Beaches.*

2nd Lt. JOHN COUNSELMAN
G/5
Suddenly, we began receiving a little sporadic harassing sniper fire coming from Sowolmi-do, that part of the island where the lighthouse was located.

1st Lt. ROBERT BOHN
G/5
Taplett ordered me to take Sowolmi-do. I sent Counselman over with a rifle squad from his 3d Platoon and some tanks.

2d Lt. JOHN COUNSELMAN
G/5
We went out on the little causeway—it was hardly wide enough to put two tanks abreast on it. We took some fire. There was a hill all interlaced with caves. We fired the 3.5s [bazookas] point-blank into them, then burned the rest with flamethrowers. It didn't even take two hours.

1st Lt. ED JAWORSKI
G/5
A lot of the North Koreans—those who had dug in on the back side of the hill and had thus missed being hit by the naval bombardment—began to swim for Inch'on. Hell, we had guys lined up like it was a rifle range, shooting at those bobbing heads.

*Sexton interview, MCHC.

1st Lt. ROBERT BOHN
G/5

By noon Wolmi-do was secure. As the tide receded we sat surrounded by a sea of mud. We became a little apprehensive; all of a sudden we weren't an island any longer. I sent a couple of Marines over to the mud flats to see if anything could cross on them. They came back and reported that nothing could.

Pfc. JACK WRIGHT
G/5

Later in the day, as the company runner I was ordered to go down to the beach to the battalion CP. I looked at my pack and got to figuring, "I'm gonna be back here in half an hour, why haul it around?" I turned to a buddy and asked him to keep an eye on my gear. "Sure," he says. When I got to the beach I was told to stay there and join the company later.

Pfc. FRED DAVIDSON
G/5

After the lighthouse was taken, most of the noise stopped. Occasionally, some hyper Marine would fire toward Inch'on. Because the distance, about 900 yards, was too far for my carbine, I didn't do any waterfront sniping. Besides, I never saw a human target and, to be truthful, neither did anyone else.

With nothing better to do we found places to sit so we could watch the main landing by the rest of the 1st Marine Division. It was a show no one wanted to miss.

Pfc. DOUG KOCH
D/5

There was a lot of tension aboard the *Cavalier* as we waited for information about Wolmi-do. Everyone felt that this would be an indicator. If Wolmi-do fell easily, it probably meant we would not have too tough a go on RED Beach that afternoon.

About ten o'clock the PA on the ship announced that the 3d

Battalion had secured the island, that resistance was moderate and, best of all, losses were very light. This news was greeted by a very loud cheer.

2d Lt. FRANK MUETZEL
A/5
We had issued ammunition and grenades, and were forming into boat teams when the PA system announced that Wolmi-do had been secured with no KIA and only fourteen wounded. For the first time I began to feel that I might have a chance to survive the landing. Up to this point we were all certain that we had another Tarawa on our hands. My antennae were really quivering. Never again in my life have I felt so aware of everything around me.

Pfc. DOUG KOCH
D/5
About eleven o'clock noon chow was served. It was cold cuts and canned fruit. Those of us who had fought at the Pusan Perimeter went down and had dinner. The replacements just couldn't eat. Everyone's stomach was in a knot.

> On the morning of 15 September 1950 all units completed last-minute preparations, and the battalion stood by to disembark on order. As the ship neared the transport area, all troops were ordered to their compartments.
>
> SPECIAL ACTION REPORT, 1/5

Yn. 2/C JAMES PAGE
USS Rochester
Aboard the "Roach-Catcher" (*Rochester*) all we could see of the target area was black smoke. The damage done by combining heavy naval gunfire with air strikes flown from the carriers was quite obvious. The shifting back and forth between naval gunfire and air attacks went on all day.

Planes were launched to conduct air strikes against shore defenses in the Inch'on area to prepare the beach for amphibious assault. The action was divided into two events (15 and 16). Event 15 consisted of a strike of twelve F4Us and five ADs. Event 16 consisted of a strike of seven ADs and ten F4Us. Pilots reported no enemy air opposition except some flak. No enemy concentrations were sighted.

USS *BOXER* (CV 21), CAPT. CAMERON BRIGGS

Pfc. FRED DAVIDSON
G/5
All afternoon the rocket ships, destroyers, and Corsairs did their work. Further out to sea, the bigger ships were also firing. I couldn't see them, but I could hear their big shells screaming overhead before they exploded far into the city. It wasn't long before the entire city of Inch'on was blanketed in one huge cloud of smoke. There was so much smoke that after a while the only indication we had on Wolmido that the shells were hitting their targets was the dim red or white flashes which we could see through the smoke cover.

1446 Executed signal "Land the Landing Force."
1526 Commenced debarkation of troops.

USS *HENRICO* (APA 45), CAPT. JOHN E. FRADD

Pfc. DOUG KOCH
D/5
They started calling the boats. I listened for mine: "One-three, starboard red." That meant first boat, third wave, was loading on the starboard side for RED Beach. I'd checked my rifle and pack and everything I could think of several times. We'd drawn our C rations earlier, and as we were about to go over the side, we drew our ammunition and hand grenades. As you climb down that net into the LCVP you're scared. What keeps you going is knowing this is what you have to do.

2d Lt. TOM GIBSON
Mortar Company/5

When Metz [2d Lt. Frank Muetzel] and I were stationed at Camp Pendleton we spent time together dating a lot of girls over on Coronado. We were on the *Henrico* together at Inch'on. As he went over the side, I shouted, "Coronado!" He looked up and smiled. "Coronado!" he yelled back.

2d Lt. FRANK MUETZEL
A/5

We boated up sometime around 3:00 P.M. I took a reinforced squad and the corpsman with me, and had a squad with rocket launcher and flamethrower in the boat on my right. Sergeant Johnson and a squad were in the boat behind mine.

Pfc. DOUG KOCH
D/5

The afternoon was overcast. With all the noise I could still hear the PA calling the boats away. On my side of the landing craft, I could see distant mountains. The sound of the cruisers and destroyers giving the beach a going-over was very distinct.

> 1539 Waves 1 and 2 loaded and dispatched to rendezvous area
> 1601 Waves 3 and 4 loaded and dispatched to rendezvous area
> 1619 Waves 5 and 6 loaded and dispatched to rendezvous area
> 1628 Waves 7 and 8 loaded and dispatched to rendezvous area
> 1639 Waves 9 and 10 loaded and dispatched to rendezvous area
> 1653 Completed debarkation of landing force
>
> USS *HENRICO* (APA 45), CAPT. JOHN E. FRADD

Lt. Gen. LEMUEL C. SHEPHERD, JR.
Commanding General, FMFPac

We watched the troops disembarking in small boats from the transports around us and their movement to the line of departure. It was overcast, and smoke from the burning city made it difficult to observe the final run to the beach. As H hour approached, the crescendo of fire increased. *

Maj. MARTIN SEXTON
Aide-de-Camp to Maj. Gen. O. P. Smith
As the first waves of the 1st Marines headed for their beaches and disappeared in the smoke, the second waves left the line of departure. A naval boat guide officer requested permission from AGC-7 to cease dispatching further waves because he could not determine, from personal observation, what was taking place with the two or three waves that had already been dispatched. Of course, permission was refused. †

MARGUERITE HIGGINS
New York Herald Tribune
We must have circled almost an hour, picking up the rest of the craft in wave number five. I was thoroughly keyed up, but the Marines around me were elaborately calm. Two of them played gin rummy on the wooden cover over the engine. They only stopped when the lurching of the boat scattered their cards all over the wet planks.

Finally, we pulled out of the circle and started toward the assault control ship, nine miles down the channel. It was an ear-shattering experience. We had to thread our way past the carriers and cruisers that were booming away at the beach, giving it a final deadly pounding. The quake and roar of the rocket ships was almost unendurable.

After twenty minutes we rounded Wolmi-do Island—it looked as if a giant forest fire had swept over it. Beyond was RED Beach. As we strained to see it more clearly, a rocket hit a round oil tower and big, ugly smoke rings billowed up. The dockside buildings were brilliant with flames. Through the haze it looked as though the whole city was burning. ‡

---

* Shepherd/Heinl, 100.
† Sexton interview, MCHC.
‡ Higgins, 142–43.

Pfc. DOUG KOCH
D/5
As we neared our final jump-off point, an M-boat pulled up along-side and transferred to us scaling ladders, extra jerricans of water, boxes of C rations, and ammunition. Dick Fletcher, my squad leader, came over to me. "Lieutenant wants the most experienced fire team to un-load this extra water, food, and ammunition. When we hit the beach, you'll be the last fire team off, and you guys are to unload this stuff on top of the seawall. Since you've been in a recon unit, you'll have a better chance of catching up with us than somebody without the extra experience." "Well, thanks a lot, Dick," I said. "You're kind of putting us in a bind." Fletch answered, "Well, you know your way around better than these replacements, and the lieutenant wants somebody with experience."

Maj. EDWIN SIMMONS
3/1
We had been told that a wave guide would pick us up and lead us to the line of departure. . . . Two LCVPS did come alongside our wave. The first was filled with photographers. The second was loaded with Korean interpreters. Two of these were hastily dumped into my LVT, apparently under the mistaken notion that I was a battalion com-mander. Both interpreters spoke Korean and Japanese; neither spoke English. Time was passing, and we were feeling faintly desperate when we came alongside the central control vessel. I asked the bridge for instructions. A naval officer with a bullhorn pointed out the direction of BLUE Two, but nothing could be seen in that direction except mustard-colored haze and black smoke. We were on our way when our path crossed that of another wave. I asked if they were headed for BLUE Two. Their wave commander answered, "Hell, no. We're the 2d Battalion headed for BLUE One." We then veered off to the right. I broke out my map and asked my LVT driver if he had a compass. He looked at his instrument panel and said, "Search me. Six weeks ago I was driving a truck in San Francisco."*

---

*Major Simmons letter, on file at the Marine Corps Historical Center, Washington, D.C. Hereafter, Simmons letter, MCHC.

2d Lt. FRANK MUETZEL
A/5

Smoke was boiling out of Inch'on, and aircraft were overhead. The gunfire bombardment had ceased except for an LSMR [landing ship, medium rocket] that had anchored to the front left of the boat lanes. The succeeding waves were circling behind us. All at once the LSMR opened fire and apparently emptied her magazines in one continuous ripple of five-inch rockets. The entire beach area simply disappeared in an enormous cloud of dust and smoke with only the occasional glare of a rocket burst showing. It was really awesome. When the LSMR ceased fire, the boats moved forward to the PC [submarine chaser that acted as the line of departure] just in time for the fool thing to open fire with its sole three-inch gun. The dang thing nearly deafened us. My guess is that the skipper decided to get his licks in for the sake of his crew, even though he wouldn't do much damage.

The landing craft lined up in waves abreast the PC, and when the signal flag dipped, motors were gunned and all surged forward toward the beach.

Pfc. FRED DAVIDSON
G/5

Late that afternoon I first saw them. The LCVPs. Here was the rest of the 1st Marine Division slowly making their way toward Inch'on. From where I sat on top of Radio Hill on Wolmi-do, I could see both landing sites. This was fantastic! It was just like watching a John Wayne movie projected on an enormous 3-D Cinemascope screen. Not everyone can say they actually witnessed a Marine division making a landing on a beach. It was simply beautiful!

When the LCVPs passed below, every crew-served weapon on Radio Hill opened fire on Inch'on. Even individual Marines opened up with their M1s. I sure wished I had something more than a carbine.

1708 Shifted main battery . . . and fired on large gray building after observing machine gun fire from Wolmi-do Marines. Area became quickly dark at H hour due to heavy overcast and smoke. Commenced firing 40-mm and 20-mm along entire seawall on RED Beach and Cemetery Hill. First landing wave heading in to beach.

1726 Ceased firing all guns due to naval aircraft strafing entire beach area.

USS DEHAVEN (DD 727), CDR. O. D. LUNDGREN

2d Lt. FRANK MUETZEL
A/5

All of a sudden four Skyraider ADs made a last run down the beach from south to north with 20-mm cannon fire. The timing was excellent, ricochets were flying over our heads. It was *really* close air support, and it was Navy!

I had all the troops squat or sit on the deck as doctrine taught, but stood upright myself to continue my assessment of the developing situation. Kindle was standing on top of the engine housing with signal flags, keeping the other boats abreast. It was a brave but very foolhardy thing to do. I really didn't pay too much attention to the boats other than being aware that the LCVPs on the right and left were abreast.

Pfc. DOUG KOCH
D/5

RED Beach was getting closer now. It made me feel very small and insignificant. I thought I could be somewhere else and no one would ever miss me. The noise got louder. We began to take small-arms fire.

2d Lt. FRANK MUETZEL
A/5

As the boat approached the seawall, the hole appeared dead ahead and Kindle took us right into it. On the rim of the wall to the north was an earthen bunker with the barrel of a machine gun protruding. I was hoping the machine gunner on the boat would take it under fire, but apparently he didn't see it. The bunker never did open fire, but if it had, we were all through.

By prearrangement, as the ramp of the boat dropped, only my squad leader and I threw a grenade from the boat over the wall and into the enemy trench. No one moved till they exploded. Then we went over the wall, into the trench, and fanned out left and right. The gun crew from the bunker was pulled out. The trench was clear except for them.

Capt. JOHN STEVENS
A/5
Lieutenant Muetzel and part of his platoon landed with no casualties. To his left, half of the 1st Platoon was delayed offshore by a boat breakdown. The remainder of the platoon scaled the seawall and immediately ran into heavy fire coming from their left and from a bunker directly to their front. They were unable to advance more than just a few yards inland. At this time, the 3d Platoon, under Lieutenant Lopez, landed.

2d Lt. TOM GIBSON
Mortar Company/5
There's a famous photograph of the Marines landing on RED Beach. Taken from the rear of an LCVP, it shows a lot of Marines waiting to climb over the seawall. One Marine, however, is already on a ladder. His right leg is on the seawall, his right arm, in which he's holding his rifle, is steadying him on the ramp, his back is hunched. The Marine is Punchy Lopez.

Moments later he took out a North Korean bunker. A second bunker remained. Lopez began to attack it. Before he could throw the grenade he held in his hand he was hit. The grenade dropped to his side. To save the men of his platoon he rolled over on top of it. Punchy won the Medal of Honor right there on the beach. On the dock at Pusan, he couldn't wait to get at the bastards.

"A" Company, with the mission of taking battalion objective No.
1 (Cemetery Hill) . . . landed amid heavy small arms fire and
intermittent mortar fire coming from trenches and bunkers on
the beach, from the exposed left flank, and from Cemetery Hill.
SPECIAL ACTION REPORT, 1/5

2d Lt. FRANK MUETZEL
A/5

We moved across the flat ground south of Cemetery Hill toward the rail yards and a series of metal buildings. Knowing we were ahead of anyone else because of delays with scaling ladders, I wanted to clear the area quickly. We rousted and shot an enemy running toward a building, but on finding the buildings padlocked from the outside, we disregarded them, crossed the rail yard, and advanced till we reached the first street. I was in front of a red-brick church and knew I was on the company's extreme right flank. We dropped grenades into spider holes dug into the street and veered left behind Cemetery Hill. Directly behind the hill we took a 90-degree turn and went up a hilly street toward the Asahi Brewery, the platoon objective. All of the above had been done on a dead run in a very short time. To this day I don't recall a single sound other than shouted instructions to the troops.

[Wave after wave of Marines continued to pour ashore. Landing areas became congested. Dense, rolling smoke added to the confusion on both RED and BLUE Beaches. The tide was about to go out and the sun to go down. Everyone was in a hurry.]

Lt. THEODORE B. CLARK (USN)
BLUE Beach Control Officer

While the initial waves of LVT(A) [landing vehicle, tracked (armored)] and LVT were milling around BLUE Beach control vessel [USS *Wantuck*], mortar fire was received in the immediate vicinity. This created some confusion until a destroyer spun around on her anchor and silenced the battery. This was the beginning of the end of the well-planned ship-to-shore movement for BLUE Beach. *

The BLUE Beach control officer was unable to contact LVT wave commanders or wave guide officers by radio at any time during the initial assault. The control officer was aware that waves or groups of LVTs and boats were landing at the wrong places but was helpless to

---

*Lieutenant Clark letter, as quoted in Lynn Montross and Capt. Nicholas A. Canzona, USMC, *The Inch'on-Seoul Operation*, vol. 2 of *U.S. Marine Operations in Korea, 1950–1953* (Washington, D.C.: Historical Branch, G-3, Headquarters, U.S. Marine Corps, 1955), 103.

prevent it without communications. As a last resort Casualty and Salvage landing craft were dispatched to assist the initial wave guides (members of UDT 1) in rounding up vehicles and leading or directing them to BLUE Beach.*

Lt. Col. JACK HAWKINS
1/1
He [the boat group commander] insisted that we were at BLUE Beach, but if we wanted to land somewhere else, that was up to me. He then departed in his boat and I did not see him again. †

LCdr. CLYDE ALLMON (USN)
BLUE Beach Primary Control Officer
When the ramps went down, the Marines, being Marines, debarked in a hurry. The sailors, seeing their boats empty, and being sailors, retracted and headed seaward in a hurry. ‡

Maj. WILLIAM BATES, JR.
Weapons Company/1/1
The battalion was not properly landed. The errors were cumulative, and exactly where they started is hard to say. I was to land in the twentieth wave. There were vehicles aboard the boats in this wave, the first to be landed, since the assault battalions had landed from LVTs and had not brought any vehicles ashore.

My wave was to attempt to land on BLUE Beach 3, a protected beach behind a seawall, which aerial photographs indicated might be used as a vehicular landing beach. The boat wave commander (who was in my boat) had an improperly functioning compass. That, of course, was bad, since it was getting dark and visibility was none too

---

* Ibid., 120–121.
† Lieutenant Colonel Hawkins letter, on file at the Marine Corps Historical Center, Washington, D.C.
‡ Lieutenant Commander Allmon letter, on file at the Marine Corps Historical Center, Washington, D.C.

good because of haze and the smoke from the naval and aerial bombardment. As we proceeded toward the beach, darkness fell. The wave commander requested a bearing from the control vessel, and asked for a searchlight beam to point out our course. Following that bearing, we found ourselves coming to what I considered to be the wrong beach. Fortunately, some spectacular pyrotechnics lighted up an area to the south, and I saw two small islands on our right which should have been on our left flank as we made our approach. The boat wave commander came about, and we went back out to sea a short distance and rounded the islands, looking for the proper beach. I established radio contact with the battalion commander, who had landed on BLUE Beach 3, and tried to guide the wave in by the fires that were burning, which by this time were about the only recognizable terrain features. We gradually began to feel our way toward the proper beach. We were receiving a negligible amount of small-arms fire coming to seaward, but not particularly close. We finally found our way into the beach, made our landing, and found that BLUE Beach 3 was a fine beach for vehicles.*

Capt. FRANCIS ''IKE'' FENTON, JR.
B/5
There was a great deal of confusion on RED Beach from H hour to H plus 180 minutes due to the failure of the coxswains to land in their assigned areas. Units were intermingled and unit commanders had difficulty organizing their commands. I believe the coxswains' failure to land at the proper beach was in part caused by enemy fire from Observatory Hill and the beach itself, which pushed them a little off course. But I also feel that the coxswains of the boats had not been well briefed about the beach itself. They knew where RED Beach 1 was, but they had no idea where RED Beach 1 and 2 met. I think they were only concerned with getting everyone on RED Beach, wherever they could find an opening.

---

*Major Bates interview, on file at the Marine Corps Historical Center, Washington, D.C. Hereafter, Bates interview, MCHC.

Pfc. DOUG KOCH
D/5
My boat was the farthest left in our wave. We ended up way, way north of where we were supposed to land. At the seawall the coxswain had to gun his engine continuously to keep the LCVP tight against it. The wave action was bouncing the LCVP up and down and it took some time for everyone to climb up and over the wall.

Then it was my team's time to unload. I climbed to the top of the ladder and told the other three guys in my fire team to begin handing the spare cans and boxes up to me. I was standing with one foot on the seawall, the other on the ladder. The boat was going up and down, and the Navy coxswain was screaming at the top of his lungs for us to hurry. He was scared. I could tell by the look on his face. We unloaded as fast as we could, but with the motion of the boat it probably took us ten to fifteen minutes.

We followed orders. We didn't bust open the ammunition and draw any more. We stuck with what we had. We figured, heck, we might need it here on the seawall if things turned bad.

Capt. JOHN STEVENS
A/5
When I heard of Lieutenant Lopez's death, I asked First Lieutenant Eubanks to take over on the left and get that platoon organized and moving. At the same time I radioed Muetzel, who had already reached the Asahi Brewery, and asked him to bring the 2d Platoon back to the beach to help out.

2d Lt. FRANK MUETZEL
A/5
As we were catching our wind and preparing to enter the brewery, my radio operator relayed a message that the rest of the company was stalled on the seawall and that Lieutenant Lopez was dead. This was the first indication that other units had not had my luck. I got on the phone and John Stevens told me to return to the beach and attempt to pressure the enemy from the rear. I didn't like the sound of that at all.

We turned around and started back down the hilly street toward the base of Cemetery Hill, but on the way I made the snap decision to hit the hill from the rear. In planning, Cemetery Hill had given us the most trouble. It was unscalable on three sides. It looked like a miniature Gibraltar, and we expected great difficulty with it.

On reaching the base of the hill, I shook out a skirmish line right and left, which pretty well covered the hill. I left the corpsman and prisoners at the base. As I only had about twelve men, I could make no provision for support on fire and maneuvers. I counted on surprise, and we either took the hill or we didn't. No support was going to be available to us. I figured we'd better not miss any enemy and leave them in our immediate rear. All of this was reflex action. Believe me, I didn't stop to rationalize any of it. I just did it!

We moved up the rear of Cemetery Hill in a skirmish line and, sure enough, we caught the Reds in their holes looking forward. We didn't fire a shot, just disarmed them and sent them back down the hill to the corpsman and the prisoner bag.

Halfway up I heard a shout from the left to watch for an officer with field glasses heading north and trying to get around the line. I needed those glasses badly, having lost mine in the Perimeter. I waited alongside a stone caretaker's shed with my nerves twanging. I didn't know if he was armed and ready. We both stepped around the corner of the building simultaneously. I was so keyed up I let him have a burst from my M3 submachine gun at close range. Point-blank, let's say. My first reaction was that I must have blasted the glasses, but they were intact. I took them off his neck and continued up the hill.

We were approaching the crest, where a stone wall stood. Trenches had been dug outside the wall, and a tunnel under it. I never did get a good look at the beach. Just after securing the hill, I reported my location to Stevens and let him know the hill was secure. He told me to stay put, that they [A Company] had broken out and would join me.

Then I remembered the corpsman. I had no idea how many prisoners we had, but I knew he only had a pistol with one magazine, and that he was unfamiliar with the weapon. So I raced back down the hill where I found a mob of North Koreans squatting on the ground and a white-faced corpsman holding a .45 at arm's length in both hands. It was funny.

Capt. JOHN STEVENS
A/5

On the left side of the beach, Eubanks had cleaned out the bunker in a grenade duel, followed by a flamethrower attack. He then took the 1st and 3d Platoons out of their pocket and drove inland to the edge of the city where he made contact with the 2d Platoon. At 1755 I fired an Amberstar cluster indicating Cemetery Hill was secured. The thirty-minute fight in the area of the 1st and 3d Platoons cost us eight killed and twenty-eight wounded.

MARGUERITE HIGGINS
New York Herald Tribune

The sun began to set as we lay there. The yellow glow that it cast over the green-clad Marines produced a Technicolor spendor that Hollywood could not have matched. In fact, the strange sunset, combined with the crimson haze of the flaming docks, was so spectacular that a movie audience would have considered it overdone.*

Pfc. DOUG KOCH
D/5

The first wave had gone on into Inch'on and began to take their objectives. When the naval gunfire lifted, more and more North Koreans began to wake up on the beach. As we finished unloading our LCVP, we began to catch more fire from the beach.

I knew we were at the extreme end of RED Beach when we should have been only halfway up. We began running diagonally across the beach, hoping to catch up with our platoon. Soon we began drawing a lot of small-arms fire. We hit a shell hole and decided we'd hunker down and wait there for a while. More boats were landing all the time.

The smoke got thicker. It started to get dark. That's when the LSTs began arriving—big and ponderous. When they hit the seawall, they caused a lot of water to rush over it. The waves generated by

* Higgins, 145.

one LST washed over some wounded, who were lying in a shell hole, and carried them back out into the harbor. The ramp of another LST was dropped on some wounded who were waiting to be taken off.

It got darker, and a fine mist began to fall. We watched one LST just forty yards from us. The guy in front was firing his 40-mm into the hills. We knew there were probably Marines up there.

2d Lt. FRANK MUETZEL
A/5
Just at the time I was trying to move back to the beach, a shout came down the hill that we were taking fire on the crest from the 40-mms on the LSTs. I shouted back to clear the crest and move to the rear slope.

Capt. FRANCIS "IKE" FENTON, JR.
B/5
The confusion was compounded when a beached LST arrived shortly after the ninth wave and started firing over the heads of the troops into Cemetery Hill. I imagine that the gunners on the LST thought that Cemetery Hill was probably occupied by the enemy. However, A Company had reached the top, and the LST's 40s and 20s were shooting into them.

Brig. Gen. EDWARD CRAIG
Assistant Division Commander,
1st Marine Division
The LSTs practically landed right behind the 5th Marines. On one of them I noticed a sailor firing his bow machine gun directly into the beach and the Marines who were on it. Then he traversed the gun and fired directly across our front.*

* Craig interview, MCHC.

Lt. Col. HAROLD S. ROISE
2/5

After landing we came under fire from our own LSTs. These ships were coming in early, about 6:30 P.M., to get to the seawall at high tide. They came under fire from enemy mortars and machine guns. Gun crews on some of the ships reacted by opening up with their 20-mm guns. These shots were fired to our front and right flank where the battalion's H & S and Weapons Companies had set up their perimeter. The casualties in the two companies were more than in the three rifle companies combined. If we hadn't moved H & S to the other side of the Nippon Flour Company building, the casualties would have been greater. Weapons Company was more forward and, therefore, exposed to the firing. At one point Weapons Company asked if they could shoot back at the LSTs. I said no, as this would cause them to shoot even more at us.

All the LSTs were in their berths by 7:00 P.M. When they got to the seawall and made contact with the infantry, the firing stopped.

2d Lt. FRANK MUETZEL
A/5

It was getting very dark and was beginning to rain by the time the company CP joined me on Cemetery Hill. Stevens told me that C Company control had been disintegrated, and that B Company had landed and was going to link up with us and the 2d Battalion to our right. Our total defensive perimeter would shrink a bit, leaving the brewery outside. He told me to take my platoon off the hill, and extend my flank on the lower part of the hill. I linked up with B Company.

Capt. FRANCIS "IKE" FENTON, JR.
B/5

Because of the difficulty C Company was having in reorganizing, the battalion commander deemed it necessary to commit his reserve. I received orders to pass through C Company, continue the attack, and seize Observatory Hill. In passing through C Company, I found that darkness was more of an aid to me than to the enemy. And the cover and concealment that the town afforded helped me greatly in obtaining the objective. The men had been very well briefed; they knew all the streets, knew where each house was. So even in the dark, they were able to make their way with good speed and seize the objective. We managed to get to the top of the hill around 8:00 P.M., but it was not until approximately 11:30 P.M. that we were tied in with the 2d Battalion on the right and A Company on the left.

2d Lt. FRANK MUETZEL
A/5

Civilians started coming out of their homes and gathering in the street to our front. This was dangerous, so I called Stevens, who called up the ROK Marines to clear the area, which they did, promptly and brutally. On my way back up the hill to the CP, I was challenged and almost shot by one of the heavy machine guns from Weapons Company that had been placed in my line without my knowledge. While that indicated growing strength, it almost caused me to shoot off my foot with an accidental discharge from my pistol. I was getting goosier and goosier.

I went to the company CP, which was in a covered bunker, to get out of the rain and to have a cigarette. I was still happy and keyed up.

Pfc. DOUG KOCH
D/5

We began to move again in an attempt to find our company. The depot was burning firecely. We got into the railroad yard. By then it had begun to rain. "It looks like we're not going to find the company tonight," I told the fire team. "There's too much shooting going on. Let's find a place to spend the night. We'll catch up with 'em tomorrow."

About that time we found Fox Company. They said we could spend the night in their perimeter. It was raining pretty hard now. The four of us crawled under a railroad car, and used a rail as a headrest. I could still hear some rifle fire and occasionally a machine gun would open up. Inch'on was burning real bad.

Lt. Col. HAROLD S. ROISE
2/5

I was concerned about Dog Company. One of their platoons had run into a small enemy group and there had been some almost hand-to-hand fighting; one man was killed and several wounded. This was on the hill on our left flank. I went up the hill to check on Dog Company. I was close to the company's executive officer when he was hit by some small-arms fire. The shooting lasted only a short time. Then it became quiet.

Capt. U. S. GRANT SHARP
Fleet Planning Officer (for Inch'on invasion), Staff, Commander 7th Fleet

Although the troops were well ashore, there was still quite a little fighting along the beach close to the landing. Admiral Struble proposed to General MacArthur that they get in a boat and go along the landing area and inspect the state of the landing. Well, he asked me to go along and, as I remember it, the flag lieutenant, who was the boat officer, was supposed to take care of the boat.

General MacArthur and Admiral Struble were sitting in the stern talking, and every now and then they indicated they wanted to get in closer to the shore. It was dark, pitch dark. Sensing that the flag lieutenant was having trouble with his navigation, Admiral Struble told me to go up and take over. I hadn't really looked at the shallow water but was tossed the job anyway.

We were feeling along up close to the seawall and could see personnel carriers or tanks going along the beach. The admiral and the general were looking over the situation with great interest. Suddenly, somebody on the seawall yelled at us, "Get the hell out of there. We're going to blow up the wall in a few minutes!" With that, General MacArthur's and Admiral Struble's curiosity abated a little and we headed back out to the open water, much to my relief.*

---

* Adm. U. S. Grant Sharp interview, Oral History, United States Naval Institute, Annapolis, Maryland. Hereafter, Sharp interview, Nav. Inst.

Maj. WILLIAM BATES, JR.
Weapons Company/1/1

The battalion began its reorganization close to BLUE Beach. It was there that we took our only casualties, not from enemy fire, but from an explosion set by elements of the shore party to demolish the seawall as an aid to further vehicular landings. No one was killed. A couple of men were wounded; one was evacuated.*

Chaplain GLYN JONES (USN)
1/1

They had to blow up the seawall to bring in reinforcements and supplies, but they blew it up too soon. Huge chunks of concrete ranging from the size of a TV set to the size of a large room started to come down. We lost some people, and I lost the one important thing any chaplain has. Unfortunately for me, one of those chunks landed on and demolished my communion set. †

Our losses are light. The clockwork coordination and cooperation between the Services was noteworthy. . . . The command distinguished itself. The whole operation is proceeding on schedule.

DOUGLAS MACARTHUR, CINCUNC TO JCS, 15 SEPTEMBER 1950

[It had taken only eight hours. By 1:30 A.M. the beachhead was firm and all major objectives taken. Thirteen thousand Marines, their weapons, equipment, heavy vehicles, and armor were ashore. Despite the darkness, the tides, and the confusion along the beaches, the landings had been made on time, objectives had been captured, and the

---

* Bates interview, MCHC.
† Chaplain Jones interview, Oral History, United States Naval Institute, Annapolis, Maryland. Hereafter, Jones interview, Nav. Inst.

enemy hit so hard and swiftly that he was not able to recover or resist. American casualties for the day totaled 196.

Murray's 5th Marines occupied a significant portion of the city. Puller's 1st Marines had advanced one mile inland and held the Inch'on-Seoul highway. It is reported that both regiments passed the night quietly.]

Pfc. FRED DAVIDSON
G/5

After the main landing George Company left Wolmi-do and followed How and Item Companies across the causeway into the smoke of Inch'on. What had begun as drizzle now turned to rain. By the time we arrived in Inch'on, it was pitch dark.

Pfc. JACK WRIGHT
G/5

After we crossed the causeway and stopped to get organized for the night, I went looking for this buddy of mine to retrieve my pack. I found him. "Hey, I'm sorry, Archie, your stuff's still on the island. I just couldn't bring your gear and mine, too." I had just learned one hell of a lesson: under no circumstances ever go off and leave your gear. So there I was, and all I had to my name were the clothes on my back and a rifle. Wouldn't you guess it, it started to rain hard. I spent a night that was long, wet, cold, and miserable.

2d Lt. FRANK MUETZEL
A/5

Prior to the landing, the battalion commander, Lt. Col. George Newton, told me that if I took the brewery intact, we could have all the beer we wanted. It was said in jest, of course. As the brewery ended up just outside the defense perimeter—even though I had had it at one time—mortar fire set it afire and it burned all night. We were close enough to hear the barrels exploding.

Capt. FRANCIS ''IKE'' FENTON, JR.
B/5

I had to relieve myself. Climbing out of my hole, I walked about twenty yards to an empty foxhole the enemy had used earlier in the day in defending Observatory Hill. I stood over it, broke out "old Purdy" and began urinating. All of a sudden out jumped a North Korean who began bowing and scraping and chin-chinning to me. Talk about getting scared out of your wits. I damn near jumped out of my shoes.

Pfc. FRED DAVIDSON
G/5

The darkness and low-hanging smoke combined to make it difficult to see more than ten feet in front of us. The rain continued to fall. I had no idea where in Inch'on I was. George Company hadn't moved very far from the causeway when orders were received to secure for the night.

A few minutes later Lieutenant Westerman was ordered to send a squad to his front to guard against a night attack. Unfortunately, I was ordered to go with this squad. Once we left the safety of the company perimeter, it was a matter of trying to walk in the darkness without falling into a shell hole or bumping into some ruins. We moved forward in a skirmish line. To our front, in the distance, we could hear sporadic gunfire. Our sector was quiet except when one of us would step into a crater. Occasionally, a flare would brighten the darkness. We used these moments to check out the path we were on and to spot any obstacles that would be in our way. I couldn't figure out whether we were safer in the dim light provided by the flares or when it was totally dark. We had been out on patrol for nearly an hour, and I kept waiting—as the rest of the squad did—for the squad leader to tell us we'd gone the 500 yards ordered by Lieutenant Westerman.

From somewhere to our left, without warning, small-arms fire whistled down on us. As I began to run, my feet were knocked out from under me. Only about fifteen shots were fired. No one returned the fire as it would have given away our position. The squad leader yelled, "Anyone hit?" No one answered. My right leg hurt. I figured I'd tripped over some corrugated steel that had been blown onto the street. "Let's get out of here," the squad leader ordered. We got to our feet and plunged back down the street, making all kinds of noise as we went. Returning to George Company, the squad leader noticed I was limping. He asked if I'd been hit. I told him I'd tripped, but was OK.

Back with George Company I found a place for the night. I took off my right shoe and legging and noticed the legging was torn. I felt blood on it. Too tired and wet to care about the pain, I covered myself with a poncho and went to sleep.

Chaplain GLYN JONES (USN)
1/1
We had gone through the city without much opposition and stopped outside. Our regiment was deployed on either side of the main road to Seoul. The 5th Marines was on our left. My battalion, the 1st, was on the line that night. I sat in a ditch beside the road, my poncho over my head. The night passed and the rain continued heavy. The water draining into the ditch started to rise and in a few hours it was over my knees. Everyone was too pooped to move. Also, I didn't want to move for fear some young Marine replacement would unload on me. I spent a cold and miserable night on that road outside Inch'on.*

2d Lt. FRANK MUETZEL
A/5
Sometime during the night my platoon sergeant told me that two men from the 1st Platoon, who had become separated from their unit, had taken a shortcut back to their platoon by going in front of the north face of Cemetery Hill, and had been shot from a cave in the north face. I had missed that cave because of its inaccessible location and because it was between me and the beach.

From the north crest I could see their bodies in the darkness but couldn't locate the cave. They were alive and calling for help. We

*Jones interview, Nav. Inst.

couldn't fire or grenade because of their position and time slipped by while I tried to figure out what to do. I couldn't order someone to pull them out, and I was afraid to do it myself.

In desperation I got a ROK Marine officer to go with me as far forward as I dared, and to shout to the North Koreans in the cave to surrender. If they wouldn't, I was prepared to have a tank pull up in front of the cave with lights on and blow them out. Once the squad of enemy troops had surrendered, we were able to retrieve the two Marines. One was dead and the other, Pfc. Wilson Bingaman, died while awaiting transfer off the seawall to a hospital ship.

I was becoming exhausted and emotionally drained. It stopped raining, and as it grew lighter I found I had not evacuated the dead Marine, but had only covered him with a poncho. I had him taken to the beach and went back to the CP for instructions. I found the CP group gathered around the NKPA officer I had shot the previous day on Cemetery Hill. He was alive and his eyes were open. I got so mad I tried to kill him again, this time with my pistol. The company gunny, Sgt. Stanley Millar, stopped me, for which I will be forever grateful. But I did jerk this officer to his feet and make him walk back to the seawall. I just couldn't bring myself to have Marines carry him out.

Pfc. FRED DAVIDSON
G/5

Around daybreak the pain in my right ankle woke me up. I couldn't believe what I was seeing. My lower leg was swollen and black and dried blood covered the whole area. I tried to stand but couldn't. A corpsman came along and cleaned the foot. He told me I'd been shot. SHOT! I had a gunshot wound. The hole was plainly visible. Lieutenant Bohn ordered me back to one of the LST(H)s [landing ship, tank (hospital)] for treatment. As I hobbled back to the beach to look for a doctor, George Company, going in the opposite direction, moved out on the road to Seoul.

SEOUL

16 September-6 October 1950

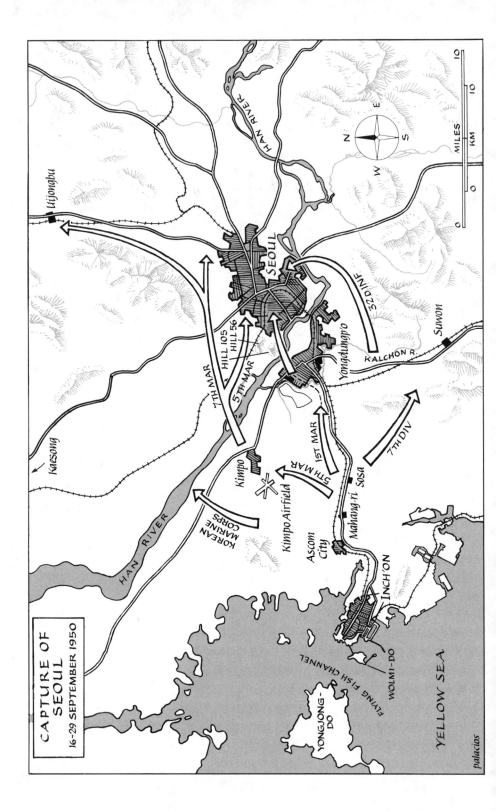

CAPTURE OF
SEOUL
16-29 SEPTEMBER 1950

Uijongbu

HAN RIVER

SEOUL

32D INF

Suwon

KALCHON R.

HILL 105

HILL 56

7TH MAR

5TH MAR

Yongdungp'o

Kaesong

1ST MAR

5TH MAR

7TH DIV

Kimpo

Mahang-ri Sosa

KOREAN MARINE CORPS

HAN RIVER

Kimpo Airfield

Ascom City

INCH'ON

WOLMI-DO

FLYING FISH CHANNEL

YONGJONG-DO

YELLOW SEA

N
W   E
S

MILES

KM

palacios

Col. LEWIS B. PULLER
1st Marine Regiment
Goddamn, fifteen minutes after we went over the seawall at Peleliu
there was a pile of dead Japs on their side of the wall and a pile of
dead Marines on our side. After ten days our outfit had 63 percent
enlisted Marine casualties and 74 percent officer casualties. The Japs
were real fighters. These fellers up here at Inch'on are second-stringers.

[*Ahead lay Ascom City, Kimpo Airfield, and Yongdungp'o. The Han
River was twenty-five miles away and across it, farther still, Seoul.
The 1st Marine Division would carry out the main drive on the capi-
tal, the 7th Division would cover the Marines' right, or southern, flank.*

*It was no secret that large bodies of North Korean troops were
also converging on the city. Mile by mile, ridgeline by ridgeline, hill
by hill, as the Americans fought their way toward the capital, enemy
resistance would stiffen. If the North Korean second team had been at
Inch'on, their first team would be waiting for the Marines in the streets
and alleys of Seoul.*]

Pfc. DOUG KOCH
D/5

The rain had stopped. At first light we were up [16 September]. Fox Company had already pulled out. We began walking inland, the four of us, two on each side of the road. In just a little while we caught up with our company.

Lieutenant Howard and Sergeant Dodge thought we'd probably been shot on the beach since we hadn't caught up earlier. Nothing bad happened to us, not even a chewing out. As soon as we caught up, we were told to form up and head for Kimpo [Airfield].*

We started down the road that morning. Then, those of us in Dog Company branched off the road and followed trails the rest of the day. We drew sniper fire from time to time, but not enough to slow us down.

2d Lt. FRANK MUETZEL
A/5

After going through Inch'on, we advanced at a leisurely pace in a column into the countryside. We stopped for the night on the out-skirts of Ascom City.† We'd seen no enemy and heard no shots.

---

*Kimpo, Korea's largest airfield, was ten miles northeast of Inch'on and one of the primary objectives of Murray's 5th Marines.
†Ascom City lay five miles east of Inch'on on the main highway to Seoul.

Capt. FRANCIS "IKE" FENTON, JR.
B/5

During the day, moving along the Inch'on-Seoul highway, the 1st Marines were on the right, the 5th Marines on the left. By nightfall the regiment had traveled a number of miles east of Inch'on. Just west of Ascom City, on the high ground, we tied in with the 1st Marines.

Pfc. DOUG KOCH
D/5

Just as it got dark and I'd finished scratching out my foxhole, Dick Fletcher and Sergeant Dodge came over and said the lieutenant wanted a listening post in front of our perimeter. "Yeah," Fletcher said, "and you got the most experience, so you know who gets the job."

I set up with my rifle team in a ditch down almost to the road about forty yards in front of the 2d Platoon. Nothing too much happened through the night. The 11th Marines,* way behind us, would fire star shells over, which would lighten things up. But, mainly, it was pretty quiet.

Along about four o'clock I heard a truck coming down the road from Ascom City heading toward our lines. I hollered up to the hill where the platoon was dug in and asked whether we should stop it. "Naw," came the reply, "we got tanks behind us. Let them stop it."

Just before sunup I turned my watch over to one of the other guys in the fire team. I pulled up my camouflage poncho and went to sleep.

The next thing I knew, one of my guys was shaking me awake. "I hear something," he said. As soon as I woke up, I heard something, too. I heard tanks! You can't mistake the low rumble of their

---

* Two battalions of artillery landed at Wolmi-do at the same time the rifle regiments were storming ashore at Inch'on. The artillery landing was completed on the morning of 16 September. Plans for the drive inland called for the artillery battalions to fire in direct support of the 1st and 5th Marines.

engines and the clanking of their treads. It was just starting to get light. I took a look down the road toward Ascom City; I could see the outlines of some Communist T34s. I knew then it was too late to run.

"If we jumped up now," I said to the other guys, "they'll see us sure. Pull your poncho over you and lay still in the ditch." If you ever wanted a helpless feeling in your gut, this was it. Lay and pray they didn't see us, that's all we could do.

I watched six tanks and about 200 North Koreans go by—some riding, some walking. They were silhouetted against the brightening sky. As the tanks rolled by, the ground shook almost as much as I did. I didn't know what I was going to do. One BAR and three M1s were no match for them. The NK troops were talking to each other.

Luckily for me, the guys in the platoon on the hill also let them pass without firing a shot. After they turned the curve south of us, the guys in my fire team moved back some ten, fifteen yards from the ditch and the road. Soon the Marine tanks down the road, our recoilless rifles, and the entire battalion up in the hills opened up.

No sooner had the firing begun when some of the North Koreans who had been with the tanks came running back around the curve. We let them get close to us—about ten, twenty yards away—then let them have it. We got ten or twelve, maybe fifteen. It was just a turkey shoot. We didn't get to see the tank battle, but it didn't last too long either.

When we went back up the hill we could look down to the other side of the road. All six of those tanks were burning and there were dead North Koreans lying all over. That was quite a sight. We sat around on that hill and told what had happened to us. There was a lot of excitement, everyone discussing where they'd been, what they'd seen, what they'd done.

2d Lt. FRANK MUETZEL
A/5

When we didn't jump off at first light, it was obvious that something had happened to our front. Traffic began backing up on the road. There had been a nip in the air that night, and for the first time in Korea many of us had slept in our field jackets. It was full sunup and warm when word finally filtered back that an enemy tank counterattack had developed in front of the 2d Battalion and been beaten off.

When my platoon reached the site of the battle, I saw several knocked-out Russian T34 tanks by the side of the road. Some were still burning. Bodies of North Korean infantrymen still lay on the rear decks and many more were sprawled out in the surrounding rice paddies.

A cavalcade of vehicles approached from the rear carrying a lot of brass. It was a good-sized body of people and they were a little too close to the lines for comfort. Particularly so, because a little earlier, the 4.5 rocket battery had fired a ripple and had drawn fire to the clouds of smoke and fire it created.

Pfc. DOUG KOCH
D/5
We were sitting on a little hill eating C rations when down the road comes a couple of jeeps. When they got past the tanks and were below us, they stopped. All these officers—we could see their eagles and stars—jumped out and began talking to the guys along the road. Here we were, sitting there eating, not knowing whether we should jump up and throw a salute or what. This one guy was real tall. He walked closer to us. It was General MacArthur. Boy, we were, you know, well, it was the thrill of a lifetime. MacArthur! Pretty soon they jumped back in their jeeps and went down the road.

Soon a kid from the village near us came over and started jabbering to our interpreter. Then the interpreter went over to a lieutenant and talked to him. The two of them climbed down to the road right where General MacArthur had stood and the interpreter hollered into a culvert. A moment later seven armed North Koreans came out of the culvert, all with their hands on their heads. Just think how famous one of them would have been if he'd lobbed a hand grenade onto the road a few minutes before and hit our generals.

The rest of the day was kind of uneventful.

2d Lt. FRANK MUETZEL
A/5

After the general was escorted to the rear, we moved forward again. After passing through the last cut in the hills east of Inch'on, the road entered the flat Han River delta country.

All that day I hadn't seen Captain Stevens, my company commander. All communication with him had been by radio. I learned that the 1st Battalion would be veering to the left, extending past the 2nd Battalion, and would move toward Kimpo. The 3rd Battalion was going to clear the built-up area known as Ascom City.

Sometime that morning my luck ran out. A bullet from a Russian machine gun tore off the calf of my right leg and then hit and killed Cpl. Tom Callison from A Company's machine-gun platoon. I raised the company commander on the radio, handed over my maps and submachine gun to Tech Sergeant Johnson, my platoon sergeant, and passed out. Cpl. Henry Adame and T/Sgt. Dan Carroll fashioned a tourniquet around my thigh with my trouser belt and kept me alive till a corpsman arrived and put a surgical clamp on the severed popliteal artery. I kept coming to and fading out while all this was going on. While I was aware that Callison was dead, I had no idea how serious my own wound was.

I was loaded onto the lower rack of a jeep ambulance, right under Callison's body, and driven to the aid station where we were checked. Then we were driven to the division hospital on the seawall at Inch'on. There I gave my new army jump boots to a corpsman to make sure my personal gear didn't disappear. Because Callison's blood had dripped down all over me, I was a pretty gory sight.

I had to wait all day because of the tide for a boat to take me out to the USS *Consolation*. When the tide came in, so did the boat. Because I was losing too much blood, the boat carrying the casualties off-loaded me on the USS *Henrico*, which was closer to shore than the hospital ship. I handed over my pistol and Russian field glasses to Ens. Richard Plank and Ens. Herb Kindle, who had been the boat wave commanders taking me in to RED Beach. Plank told me months later that he threw up when he saw me on the stretcher literally covered with dried blood.

After receiving several pints of whole blood on the Happy Hank, I was put on a boat about 10:00 P.M. and delivered to the *Consola-*

tion. There, when I was being checked on the quarterdeck, a live hand grenade was found in my jacket pocket and promptly thrown overboard. All afternoon and evening I kept going in and out of a haze. I was taken to a private room where I was given intravenous whole blood in both arms and my left leg. I was told I would lose my right leg.

[On the Inch'on-Seoul road, the Marines at first moved rapidly against scattered resistance; it was evident the enemy was withdrawing eastward toward the Han.]

Maj. Gen. OLIVER P. SMITH
Commanding General, 1st Marine Division
Except for the press, Murray [5th Marine Regiment] had the situation well in hand. The command post was overrun with correspondents and kibitzers. Though the American people are entitled to know what is going on, this should not extend to the point where correspondents look over the shoulder of the commander while he is making plans. *

2nd Lt. TOM GIBSON
Mortar Company/5
During the march on Seoul, which was a very mobile stage of the war, we began collecting a lot of war correspondents and photographers, so much so that they became a problem. They stole our rations and filched our equipment. You'd come back in from being on the line, drop your pack, and go off and do something. When you came back, some correspondent had taken your chow, unrolled your bedroll, and happily fallen asleep.

---

*Gen. Oliver P. Smith interview, Oral History Collection, Marine Corps Historical Center, Washington, D.C. Hereafter, Smith interview, MCHC.

[While Murray's 5th Marines drove toward Kimpo, on their right Puller's 1st Marines advanced along the main road toward the industrial suburb of Yongdungp'o.]

S/Sgt. LEE BERGEE
E/1

The road from Ascom City ran along the south shoulder of a flat corridor and on the west side of this road ran a railroad track. The railroad eventually slices through a belt of ridges and hills near Yongdungp'o. The road was dusty, the hills covered with scrub pine and brush. Bordering the road were poplar and sycamore trees and off on the hillside were round mounds of ancient tombs.

After jumping off from Ascom City at 0700 [17 September], E Company hit its first resistance just west of the mud village of Mahang-ri.* The enemy had placed a roadblock on the right flank of a large hill complex known as Hill 208. Our company outflanked the roadblock and ran into some North Korean diehards on the outskirts of the village. We killed twenty of the enemy, who were entrenched in a hedgerow. I remember well how I would toss a grenade only to have three thrown back at me.

We received reinforcements around noon. Most of the village was now afire. Some tanks attached to our battalion drove down the hedgerow and helped eliminate the North Korean position. I spotted the barrel of an 88-mm gun sticking out from one of the huts. Running over to a tank, I took the intercom phone out of the box and told the tank commander of my find.

---

*Two miles east of Ascom City.

S/Sgt. CHESTER BAIR
Heavy Tank Company/32d Infantry

One of the crew members began screaming over the intercom, "Enemy tank behind house at two o'clock!" A moment earlier I had seen what I thought was a leaning telephone pole near one of the huts about 400 yards away, then thought nothing more about it. Now I saw it was a cannon barrel and it was slowly turning in our direction. I ordered the loader to load one shell. While he did I turned the turret to bring my cannon to bear. When we were in position, I aimed and fired. A miss! I was about 100 yards short. The enemy T34 tank fired its 88-mm cannon at us. Their round missed us by inches and exploded nearby. The tank immediately behind us fired and its round went right through the hut and into the enemy tank.

S/Sgt. LEE BERGEE
E/1

The mud hut flew in all directions and the T34 hidden inside blew up before the crew could aim at us.

In the midafternoon, after securing the village, we ran into a well-defended enemy position on a ridge that ran across the road. It was at this moment that our Marine tanks began to run out of gas. They had not had a chance to refuel. While the tanks used hand pumps from drums brought up in a truck, the North Koreans had an opportunity to really dig in and fortify their position.

The Communists launched a counterattack just as our battalion began to advance across a field toward the ridge. The North Koreans charged us with fixed bayonets. My platoon dropped down behind an embankment beside a rice paddy and opened fire on the attackers. Our fire was "rifle-range aimed" and we cut them down one by one.

Some Corsairs zoomed in with rockets and cannon blazing. With this support, we resumed our advance north. The North Koreans had used antitank guns and the road was blocked with knocked-out Marine tanks. The enemy finally broke and ran. That evening, after facing our stiffest opposition since landing at Inch'on, we dug in. My company had been fighting since 0700 that morning.

The following morning we attacked again. During an artillery concentration by our own guns, two Marines from the 2d Battalion were killed and three wounded. The rounds had fallen short. I recall cursing out loud at this misfortune.

We took Sosa* at noon [18 September] against heavy mortar fire from the Reds. The North Koreans used their large, 120-mm mortars, and they were wicked. It was during this attack that I had my canteen blown off my cartridge belt and that evening, when we began to dig in, I grabbed for my entrenching tool only to find the handle gone. This action took place on Hill 123, or what we called "Shrapnel Hill."

[On their fourth day ashore, the 5th Marines captured one of its major objectives; after a sharp, bitter clash on the morning of 18 September, Kimpo Airfield was taken and the surrounding villages secured.]

1st Lt. DAVID PEPPIN
D Company/1st Engineer Battalion/1st Marine Division

As the infantry moved into Kimpo Airfield, the engineers moved onto the runway. Although there was some barbed wire and other obstacles on it, the runway wasn't in too bad shape. Down at the far end of the airfield was a hangar. Careful of booby traps, we pulled the hangar doors open with ropes and there inside were several North Korean aircraft, all in first-class condition.

---

*The market town of Sosa lies midway between Inch'on and Yongdungp'o.

Pfc. JACK WRIGHT
G/5

There were quite a few Russian fighters sitting around. One kind had a turret directly behind the cockpit. They seemed to be in perfect flying condition except somebody had collapsed the landing gear and they were sitting belly down on the ground.

1st Lt. DAVID PEPPIN
D Company/1st Engineer Battalion/1st Marine Division

Then a crazy thing happened. The runway had just barely been cleared when this Corsair appeared, throttled back, flying overhead. The field was still closed but this Corsair was there, landing! The pilot climbed out of the airplane and he was hooting and hollering. Even though the field was still off limits, he had the honor of being the first to land a plane on Kimpo.

Capt. U. S. GRANT SHARP
Fleet Planning Officer, Staff, Commander 7th Fleet

About four days after the landings, Admiral Struble suggested we get off the ship and look around the beach. The skipper of the *Rochester*, Eddie Woodyard, and I thought this was a good idea. On shore we found lots of activity. They were getting ready to cross the Han River.

We stopped an empty truck and told the driver we'd like to go up to Kimpo Airfield. He said he'd be happy to take us. So we got in the back of this two-and-a-half-ton truck, and went dashing up the road. After a while we noticed that the Marines were going along on each side of the road with their rifles ready, acting as though they were looking for snipers. This made us wonder if we were really on the road to Kimpo. Then we passed some howitzers near the road that were firing over a hill. Finally we asked the driver, "How many times have you been to Kimpo?" "This is my first time," he answered. "OK," I said, "let's ask somebody where we are and whether we're on the right road." We finally stopped and asked a noncom if we were on the right road for Kimpo. He said, "No, you're on the road to Seoul and you're just about to pass over into enemy lines." We turned around and eventually ended up at Kimpo.*

Pfc. FRED DAVIDSON
G/5

Trying to get back to George Company, I had to catch several different rides during the day [19 September]. One of them took me past Kimpo Airfield. There was a great deal of activity in the area as a steady stream of Corsairs took off and landed. Toward evening I finally found the 3d Battalion's aid station and a wounded man told me the location of How Company. I knew if I could find How, George would not be far away. I was right.

I reported to Lieutenant Bohn and told him I'd been released from hospital that morning and was ready for duty. It was now very dark and in spite of all my activity that day , I had a lot of trouble getting much sleep. There seemed to be a hell of a lot of activity on the road below the hill where George Company was billeted.

Pfc. PAUL MARTIN
Reconnaissance Company/1st Marine Division

Sometime after midnight on the 20th, according to the plan, a small team of swimmers from Recon Company would cross the Han and,

---

* Sharp interview, Nav. Inst.

if they found no enemy present, would signal for the rest of the company to cross in LVTs. Once across, the 1st and 3d Platoons would seize Hill 125, which dominated the river on the enemy's side. The 2d Platoon would move farther inland and block the main road and rail connection going to Seoul. With the bridgehead in place, the 5th Marines would cross the river and pass through Recon Company in the assault.

At midnight the swimmers entered the water and safely made it across the river. Finding their side of the river quiet, Captain [Kenneth J.] Houghton radioed the rest of Recon Company, "The Marines have landed and the situation is well in hand." This was our order to cross. The amtracs [amphibious tractors] took an hour to reach our embarkation point. The noise these nine LVTs made was deafening, and I'm sure it alerted the enemy to our plans. I was with the 2d Platoon and could see the dark silhouette of Hill 125 directly across from our position. I thought our crossing would be unopposed until, about halfway across, I saw one muzzle flash from the crest of the blackened hill. He must have fired too soon. Shortly afterward, all hell broke loose! We were told that in the case of a firefight we would withdraw to the south side of the river. This was easier said than done. Several amtracs, including mine, became stranded in the middle of the river on some mud flats.

We took a lot of small-arms fire and some mortar shells landed near us. Our own artillery began leveling Hill 125. Through all this noise I heard a train whistle. I figured the enemy was bringing in more troops to defend the area.

After three hours we climbed out of the tractors and began wading, sometimes in waist-deep water, sometimes around patches of quicksand, back to the south side. Every time an amber cluster exploded, we froze. The firing died down. On reaching the riverbank and regrouping, we patrolled until all the swimmers were accounted for.

Returning to Kimpo around dawn, I saw the 3d Battalion, 5th Marines, assembling near the LVTs for their daylight crossing, which would begin in several hours.

Pfc. FRED DAVIDSON
G/5

At first light on the 20th I saw that the company was within spitting distance of the Han River, and the activity I'd heard the night before was caused by LVTs converging near the river. I was told to cross with Lieutenant Counselman's platoon. The Han at this point was about 300 yards wide. It had been churned up by LVTs crossing ahead of ours and was a dark, muddy color.

Nearly all the enemy's firepower was directed at the vehicles that were in front of mine, although several times I heard the clank of a round hitting my LVT's armored sides. By the time we beached on the opposite side, all the small-arms fire had died away and we were home free. We didn't stop but continued our ride in the LVTs for some time. We passed a small, deserted village. There were no planes in the sky and the air was growing hot. We did a lot of stopping and starting. Everyone was covered with the dust thrown up by the vehicles in front.

We stopped some way from the river, disembarked, and headed for a hill on the left side of the road.

1st Lt. ROBERT BOHN
G/5

We climbed it without incident. On top was a sight that occurs once in a Marine's lifetime. In the distance, from the direction we had just come, I could see the Han and all the activity of the crossing. Closer to home, though, below and behind us, in a large area of rice paddies, were a thousand North Koreans, maybe more, maybe less, moving toward us in the open. I remember thinking at the time that there were a lot more of them than us. My artillery FO, Sergeant Callow, was already on the radio talking to a battery from the 11th Marines, asking for time on target. The artillery people had trouble when they realized we were asking for an artillery attack to be brought in behind us. They didn't understand that we hadn't walked to our location, but had traveled by amphibious tractors. I got on the radio and convinced the battery commander that the target was exactly where Callow said it was. Suddenly, the radio net lit up. I think every artillery piece the 11th Marines had within range got into the act. You could see the stuff come in. First salvo came in. After the smoke and mud settled, there were still some NKs who were able to get up and run. Second salvo came in. After the third salvo landed, there was no one left to run. It was really super.

[*The day after the 5th Marines crossed the Han, the 1st Marine Division's last rifle regiment, the 7th, landed at Inch'on. This unit had been hastily formed out of Marine Regulars stationed throughout the world* * *and civilians in the organized Reserve. At the beginning of the summer of 1950, the civilian Marines had been worrying about mortgage payments and the family car's next tune-up. In July the bleak news coming out of Korea changed all that. Suddenly, domestic cares and routine were replaced by a chance for travel and adventure; many of the men saw the call-up as their opportunity to star in a real-life war movie.*

Commanded by Col. Homer L. Litzenberg, the 7th Marine Regiment began coming ashore at Inch'on on 21 September. When Litzenberg asked the division commander what troops should be unloaded first, General Smith answered, "An infantry battalion." "And what next?" "Another infantry battalion," answered the general.

The regiment would spend its first days in Korea patrolling and protecting the division's left flank. Once this short period of seasoning ended, it would swing above Seoul and be on line northwest of the capital. Thanks to extraordinary staff work in solving problems of organization and equipment, the 7th Marines was ready to enter the battle for Seoul just twenty-three days after it had set sail from San Diego.]

---

* The regiment's 3d Battalion had been a unit of the 6th Marines stationed afloat in the Mediterranean, and didn't join the 7th Marines until it arrived in Japan in September.

Pfc. FRANCIS KILLEEN
A/7

Having lost one set of bagpipes in World War II, when we shipped out for Korea I decided I was not going to lose another. The night before 7th Marines went aboard the ships in San Diego, I had the Red Cross send them to my family. In the morning the captain, David Banks, said, "Hey, my outfit goes aboard with the pipes." I told him, "I've shipped them home with the Red Cross." Captain Banks sent Sgt. Red Donovan out on a mission. Damned if he didn't come back with them. I played the 1st Battalion aboard ship. People all over the dock were waving and cheering.

At Inch'on [21 September] I still had my pipes. The landing was rather uneventful with the exception of my playing the outfit ashore. This time nobody was on the dock waving and cheering.

Pfc. JOHN BISHOP
I/7

We walked inland and found a train. It looked half the size of the trains in the U.S. We were told to climb aboard the flatcars. Everybody rushed aboard to get a good place and to take the heavy gear we were carrying off our backs. Then we found that the little engine couldn't pull all our weight and we were ordered off. We began walking again. On the march we were told to watch out for land mines. I don't know how the others felt, but as for me, looking out for mines plus looking out for gooks made me as jumpy as a cat.

Pfc. JOSEPH SALUZZI
D/7

After we landed we were shuttled to an assembly area near the Han River. On the way we passed some trucks filled with weary Marines from the 5th Regiment going in the opposite direction. Greetings were exchanged on the fly. They were glad to see us. I felt funny seeing them and not being battle-tested myself. I looked at those Marines with great admiration.

Pfc. FRANCIS KILLEEN
A/7

Everyone was scared stiff and obeyed orders without hesitation. We did great against empty houses and dugouts which the 1st and 5th Marines had already taken. When we stopped, every shovel was busy. By the end of the second day, we had dug up half of Korea and had not fired a shot. With all the trucks blowing dust in our faces, everyone got their first lesson in water discipline. Most of the young ones had drunk their canteens dry. "From now on, no one drinks without permission, and then only a sip. Don't drink from these streams, you don't know where these people shit. You old-timers, don't think you can rip off a quick one with these girls. We're here to save them." "Save them for what, Sergeant?"—a young voice in the rear. "Save them for me. I need a fan and a cold drink before I get warmed up."

The road which led from Inch'on to Seoul was long, and we were hot and dry. The company was very tired, and the men were getting careless. We walked along ridgelines, overexposed ourselves. Then it happened. One shot. A Marine fell—got it right above the ear. A cold evening breeze came up and we started to button up. There were no more wisecracks.

Hospitalman 3/C WILLIAM DAVIS
B/7

We were trying to cross the Han and had found some place where the water was low and the river was narrow. There was a village on the other side. Every time we tried to cross, a machine gun would fire at us. I was squatting next to a Navy fire-control officer who was talking to one of the big ships out beyond Inch'on Harbor. If I remember correctly, it was the *Missouri*. To this day I can hear him say, "OK fire for effect." A few moments later we could see the shells coming in. They sounded like freight trains going over. The village was there. Then there was a gigantic boom. When the smoke cleared, the village no longer existed. In its place was a large, shallow lake with a little straw from the village roofs floating in it. That's when I knew I wasn't in any John Wayne movie.

Pfc. JOSEPH SALUZZI
D/7

The following day [22 September], moving closer to Seoul, I saw my first dead bodies. They lay in grotesque positions along the route.

When we reached the Han River, we were assembled near an area covered with litters of dead Marines. Their boondockers and leggings were sticking out from under the blankets or ponchos that covered them. I was afraid to look but eventually forced myself to. Only hours before those Marines had been joking and telling sea stories. It was then that the full realization of what was to come struck me. I saw myself covered by one of those blankets and remember thinking, When it comes, let it be quick and without pain.

Later we crossed the Han and dug in for the night. Somewhere, not too far in front of me, some dogs began to howl. No one slept well that night. There were no incidents, only a heightened awareness of what was to come.

Pfc. FRANCIS KILLEEN
A/7

I will never forget our first real firefight. There was all kinds of small-arms fire up ahead. We heard Lieutenant Horvath on the [SCR] 300* calling for help. We fanned out to the left of the formation and lined up on a rise in the middle of a rice field, everyone in the prone position. We spotted a small party of soldiers, the rest we took for guerrillas. We opened up. Soon a white flag appeared. Cease fire. The Koreans started toward our line. It was a sorry sight for our first engagement. Women, children, and some Korean Home Guards who were trying to lead those poor civilians to safety. Our corpsman did what he could. One Korean civilian, a man wearing a neat white shirt—he seemed to be the leader of his village—stood, crying uncontrollably, holding a little wounded girl in his arms. He handed her to Doc, waiting for some sign. Doc Woods took the little one from him, laid her on the ground, and covered her with a poncho.

"We got no time here—move out!" So our first contact was one for the other side. The captain was really mad. Lieutenant [James] Stemple, our platoon leader, caught it that night. "What the hell," some felt, "they were gooks, too." The Marine veterans had little experience with civilians. Saipan, Cape Gloucester, Peleliu, "the canal" [Guadalcanal]—there were only good guys or bad guys, no civilians. It was a real down feeling, that I might have been the one who put the slug through that kid's heart.

Cpl. MERWIN PERKINS
B/7

The company was above Seoul when we ran into our first fight. We were moving at night; I thought we were lost. Green tracers were

---

* A short-range company-to-battalion pack-set radio.

coming in, red tracers were going out. It was real confusing, the first night, real confusing. I didn't know what was going on. I was very scared. I pretty much hugged the ground.

I was nineteen when I got activated. My group traveled from Minnesota to Camp Pendleton on a troop train. It took five days. I had been in the Reserves. I never had any boot camp, just summer camps where we mostly goofed off. When we went through the line at Pendleton some sergeant asked, "How many summer camps?" I said, "Three." He wrote "CR"—combat ready! My company landed in Korea on September 21, one month to the day after I had left civilian life in Minnesota.

Outside Seoul we were all scared. I didn't even know how to dig a foxhole. Hadn't any idea. A gunnery sergeant told me how. "Make it like a grave," he said.

Pfc. JOHN BISHOP
I/7
I don't know how long it took to get to Seoul, but sometime on the way, up on a mountain, we spotted a gook FO. About twenty of us shot the shit out of him. It made me feel good because I was in on my first kill.

[As Litzenberg's 7th Marine Regiment moved into position northwest of Seoul on 22 September, Murray's 5th Marines across the Han and outside the captial began a series of ferocious hill battles.]

Pfc. JACK WRIGHT
G/5
After we crossed the Han I began growing up. Starting in Seoul I finally found out there is no glory in war. It's cruel, miserable, dirty, and nothing worth bragging about.

1st Lt. ED JAWORSKI
G/5

The day following the big artillery shoot, 3/5 passed through Hal Roise's 2d Battalion. We had some tanks with us. G Company was in the lead. There was a curve in the road. Bohn wanted to send a fire team out. Ace Ryder and I took four guys out to see what was around the bend. We got down to the railroad tracks. All of a sudden we got hit by machine-gun fire. The six of us went down—bing, bing, bing! Ryder was hit really bad. I got it in the arm. Those of us who could move a little tried to drag the others behind the railroad embankment. We began yelling for corpsmen. None came. No one wanted to go out in that fire. Back behind the curve John Counselman jumped on a tank, gathered some corpsmen, and came out to get us.

2d Lt. JOHN COUNSELMAN
G/5

I got behind a tank and had it move out to where Jaworski and the other Marines were hit. Then I took a ricochet. A round skipped off the side of the tank and hit my leg. It hardly drew blood, but my leg immediately turned blue black. A corpsman had my pants down around my ankles. I looked around and, oh, God!, there was Maggie Higgins. Every time you looked around, there she was!

This was the second time I was wounded, but it wasn't even bad enough to leave the platoon. The next time I was to be hit, it would be a different matter.

1st Lt. ED JAWORSKI
G/5

If the North Koreans had waited another fifteen or twenty minutes, George Company—perhaps the entire 3d Battalion—would have come around that curve and entered the ambush. The day was bad enough, though. Two hours or so after Counselman and I were wounded, Bob Bohn got hit.

1st Lt. ROBERT BOHN
G/5

Soon after crossing the Han, we were ordered to attack Hill 236. I was with the 3d Platoon. There was a little wooded area down to the left. They let us get by, then they hit us. I don't think there were more than ten or fifteen of them. A couple of guys got hit. Then I did. A machine-gun bullet tore through my thigh just an inch below my balls. The corpsman slipped my utilities down and looked. "Jeez, boss. Missed them by half an inch."

I made sure that some guy got my weapon and my water. You do those things automatically. I knew I was going someplace where I wouldn't need them.

Pfc. DOUG KOCH
D/5

As we drew closer to the hills around Seoul, the company began taking more fire. On the afternoon of the 23rd we moved up along some railroad tracks. A machine gun opened up. Dick Fletcher went over to talk to the lieutenant. I lay along the railroad. The day was still warm. Someone hollered, "Fletcher's hit!"

When I got to him, he was on the ground with shrapnel in both legs. From some civilians who were lying in a culvert I grabbed a blanket and wrapped Fletch in it. I said, "Aw, you lucky sonovabitch. Looks like you're gonna get out of here." "This makes you the last guy left from the 2d Platoon," he answered. "Now that I'm gone, you'll be squad leader."

The lieutenant ran by. "Leave Fletcher here! He'll be safe. We're gonna have to cross the road and get up those little hills over there," and he pointed. When we'd established a toehold on Hill 56, we really began drawing a lot of fire.

Back from where we had come, Fox Company was fighting the North Koreans in the trenches that had been dug around the hills.

Being in a position to do so, we laid down a good base of fire in front of Fox Company.

At this time the kid next to me got hit in the chest. I rolled him over and cut open his jacket looking for the bullet wound. A slug had gone right through his lung: in the front, out the back. There were no corpsmen up to us yet. The kid began to wheeze and I knew his lung had collapsed. I spat on both my hands, then placed one on the entry wound and the other on the exit hole. After a few minutes of holding him like this, he started breathing better. He was still conscious. I asked him if I could do anything more for him. A corpsman came up and began bandaging his wounds. "I don't know whether he's gonna make it." The sun began to go down and the shadows grew longer. The kid whispered, "Would you read to me out of my Bible?" Fox Company was still fighting across the road. We were pinned down. I read to him from his Bible. Some stretcher-bearers made their way up to us and carried the kid away. I accidentally put the Bible in my pocket. Inside was the name "A. W. Lawson." I've often wondered whether the kid made it or not.

[While the 5th Marines advanced hill by hill toward Seoul, Puller's 1st Marines, still south of the Han, continued its furious attack on the grimy suburb of Yongdungp'o.*]

S/Sgt. LEE BERGEE
E/1
Yongdungp'o was surrounded by a moat on one side, by a wide rice paddy on the west, and by high ridges on the southeast. Staring at the sooty chimneys of the city, I wondered how many of us would be killed taking this dirty town.

Our battalion crossed a rice paddy that ran alongside the road. One of our tanks was hit and was instantly engulfed in smoke. One of its treads whipped the air. My platoon began receiving intense mortar

---

* Yongdungp'o is to Seoul as Jersey City is to Manhattan. Astride the main Inch'on-Seoul road, the industrial suburb is bordered on the west by a tributary stream, the Kalchon, and on the north and east by the larger Han.

and machine-gun fire that came from a knoll off to the right. To our front the enemy had sown a field with wooden box mines. These could not be detected using the normal means and each one contained fifteen pounds of high explosives.

Due to the heavy gunfire and the minefield the company stalled in its advance. Marine air and artillery methodically worked the Communists over. Corsairs dropped napalm and fired bursts from their 20-mm cannons. We finally took the knoll. That night the company dug in and waited for the inevitable counterattack. It came after midnight.

They came at us with T34 tanks. In the darkness I listened to their clinking clatter and goose bumps rose all over my body. Pvt. Oliver O'Neil's shouted challenge was met by a loud blast of machine-gun fire. O'Neil fell wounded.

An enemy truck came down the road. We held our fire and allowed it to pass into our defensive position. Soon afterward it ran over one of our mines. It blew up with a loud roar. The truck had carried ammunition, and for a while the night looked like the 4th of July.

The T34s cut loose. Because they were armor-piercing, their shells ricocheted off the ground and rocks without exploding. Marine mortars and antitank weapons entered the battle. Enemy infantrymen sought shelter. I heard them yell and scream. Illuminated by the mortar bursts, the T34s jerked and tried to turn around. Bazooka teams closed in for the kill. The lead tank was hit. In the orange glare I saw one Marine step into the open and fire. The man was hit instantly by a machine-gun burst. His round, however, found its mark. This hero destroyed two tanks before he died. His name was Monegan [Walter C., Jr.]. Two tanks managed to escape, a third surrendered.

When dawn broke over the eastern hills, I looked around the area. There were more than 300 North Koreans lying dead on the road and in the ditches. Enemy weapons and equipment were strewn everywhere; the enemy truck still smoldered on the road. Monegan's two tanks stood silent and charred. The night had been quite a nightmare.

For the sixth consecutive morning, our company began the day by attacking. We jumped off at 6:00 A.M. and fought North Koreans all the way to the Kalchon River. The Reds pulled back across the river to a ridge south of the road. At noon, Colonel [Allen] Sutter, our battalion CO, ordered a halt. We then dug in on a piece of high ground overlooking the river and the bridge.

Yongdungp'o was literally infested with North Korean troops. All afternoon we observed them fortifying their ridge. Artillery, heavy mortars, and our Corsairs pummeled Yongdungp'o that afternoon. The 4.2s [mortars] fired white phosphorus, setting sections of the city ablaze. One of our planes dropped napalm on a block-long fuel dump. Flame and smoke rose a mile and a half into the air.

Sometimes before dark General MacArthur stopped by for a visit. He was surrounded by brass and correspondents. Although he didn't stay long, we were all allowed to see the "Great General."

Night fell and our artillery really cut loose. It must have been a terrible ordeal for those North Koreans in the city. I didn't feel sorry for them, though!

Chaplain GLYN JONES (USN)
1/1

While the rest of the 1st Marines lay stalled outside Yongdungp'o, one rifle company managed to get into Yongdungp'o [21 September]. Capt. Bob Barrow's Able Company found an opening and knifed right into the heart of the city. He dug in on both sides of a railroad passing. That night the North Koreans found out he was there. They attacked. But Barrow was very securely situated with machine guns on either flank and he cut those people down. He ended up holding out. At one point, the North Koreans were regrouping behind some buildings for another assault and they were being harangued by an officer who was building them up to blood pitch. The Marines could hear this but didn't know what he was saying. Barrow called down to the end of the line, "Can anybody see this character? What's he doing?" Nobody could, so a Marine at the end of the line slithered down the bank and on his belly went across, still in the darkness, until he could see this man. He was standing on a small rostrum making a speech to his troops. The Marine zeroed in and shot him, then returned to his position. Barrow had heard the shot and shouted, "What the hell happened?" The boy who had done the shooting yelled back, "Captain, that poor bastard just talked himself to death." *

S/Sgt. LEE BERGEE
E/1
The next morning [6:30 A.M., 21 September] we launched our attack against Yongdungp'o. The battalion faced the bulk of the enemy defenses and we had a difficult time. E Company got beat to death trying to cross the Kalchon River bridge. Enemy machine-gun fire forced us into the river, where we waded to the other side. Deploying to the right alongside a railroad embankment, we were in the open and exposed. Soon we were forced back to the road. After we dug in around an old brick factory, I helped send back the dead and wounded. Among piles of bricks and rows of kilns we waited for orders.

Soon a flight of Corsairs bombed, rocketed, and strafed the area in front of us. While they plastered the railroad embankment, we hugged the ground. In a little while we were up and again moving forward.

[If there had been doubts before Yongdungp'o, afterward there would be none; in Seoul, the North Koreans were going to fight for every street. No longer content just to delay the Marines, they now intended to beat them.

The 5th Marines was about to meet opposition such as it had not encountered since the landing on RED Beach a week before. The struggle for the western approaches to the capital began around a complex of interlocking hills that furnished the North Koreans with a natural defensive barrier they would use with bloody efficiency. The battle began in deadly earnest on the morning of 22 September.]

* Jones interview, Nav. Inst.

Capt. FRANCIS ''IKE'' FENTON, JR.
B/5
Hill 105 was very barren and looked like an egg that was flattened on the top. We were subjected to a great deal of fire from the ridgeline that the enemy still held, and also from the high ground in Seoul, which was to our immediate front. The enemy was firing a great deal of antitank and high-velocity fire at us, and the ridge was continually swept with machine-gun fire. It was unsafe for the men to venture out of their holes during daylight hours.

During the night the North Koreans counterattacked up the eastern slope of the hill and overran a platoon of C Company, killed a machine-gun crew, and took their gun before being driven off. The enemy started moving down to the base of the hill and around the hill, firing the captured gun into our lines to draw fire. When no fire was returned, the enemy got a little bolder and started back up the hill. When the enemy got closer, every Marine on line cut loose with a hand grenade. This discouraged the enemy and he withdrew. We estimated that the counterattack consisted of approximately fifty men.

Throughout the following day we were ordered to remain in position. We were subjected to enemy small-arms fire and sporadic mortar and high-velocity fire. Movement was impossible during the daylight hours. Water, rations, and ammunition had to be supplied to us after dark, when the enemy small-arms fire subsided. During the early hours of the 24th, we had another counterattack in the same spot as the previous one. This counterattack force was practically wiped out to a man, and we counted a little more than fifty dead when daylight arrived.

Pfc. DOUG KOCH
D/5
Although the sun was up, the ground was covered in thick fog. The lieutenant called us in. "We've been going east, but today we got to swing out and go up to the top of this hill. Koch, you're the squad leader of what's left here. Take your squad and lead out. First platoon will be behind you, and the company will follow." This was September 24.

I turned to the kids who were left in my squad. They were all replacements who had joined the company on the dock in Pusan. The sun had begun to burn through the mist. It was growing brighter. I picked up my rifle. "Follow me. We're going to start up this hill. The platoon will follow us." I was the first guy to start to cross a little terrace. I was about halfway across. All of a sudden it felt like I got kicked in the hip by a horse. I went flying backward. I knew immediately I'd been hit. I couldn't move my legs. The two kids in my fire team ran up alongside me. "Can we help you?" "No," I said, "keep moving. You know where you're going. The lieutenant will be right behind you. I'll be all right." The rest of the platoon ran by me.

I tried to collect my wits. I was lying out in the open. There was nothing else around me. I lifted my arms and took my pack off. As carefully as I could, I rolled over on my back, took out my knife, and cut open my pant legs. After you're on the line for as long as I'd been on, you expect your luck to run out someday. My left leg looked as if someone had slapped a large patty of raw hamburger on it. I sprinkled sulfur on it, but the bandage I carried was too small to cover it.

I didn't feel any pain. The shock at the beginning numbs you. But this only lasts a short while. For half an hour I lay there. I kept trying to figure where everybody else was. Where were the North Koreans? There was some noise around me. Suddenly, I got hit again. It rolled me right over onto my stomach.

I continued to lie out in the open. If I remained still, I was left alone. If I moved, I was shot at. I tried to see where the sniper was. Another slug went through the sleeve of my field jacket.

As time passed the shock of being wounded wore off and I began to feel a tremendous amount of pain. I can't describe how much pain I felt. There was so much I thought I could crawl into it and be covered by it. Occasionally, I hollered for a corpsman. I knew I shouldn't. They were busy and I was pinned down. During this time I did a lot of praying, a lot of swearing, and a little bit of crying. God, how I hurt.

The morning wore on. It got warm. Then it got hot. I was in an area that nobody could get to. The terrace was covered by the North Koreans. I tried to pull myself up with my elbows. Two bullets zinged by. Another time I raised my head and hollered for a corpsman. A round landed in front of my nose. I picked dirt out of my face.

Sometime in the early afternoon the North Koreans were driven off the hill and a corpsman managed to get to me. It happened to be a guy I'd known ever since we'd gotten to Korea. Doc Downs was his name. First thing he did was roll me over and try to bandage me as best he could. I yelled, "To hell with the bandages, Doc, give me a shot of morphine!" This he did. Then he bandaged me. Some other Marines ran over to us and began to move me onto a door they had wrenched off a hut somewhere. The morphine had not yet begun to work on me. When they tried to lift me I screamed. They laid me back down and covered me with the door.

Downs finished filling out my tag. The morphine began to take effect. He leaned over me. "There can't be much left of Dog Company. There's a lot of guys lying out up there. I gotta go."

I lay there on my back. The door had fallen off me. I dozed off. An hour or so later I woke up. There were some stretcher-bearers running by. I hollered. "Well, for God's sake, we thought you were dead. That's why no one's picked you up." "Hell, no," I answered, "I ain't dead." The morphine was still working on me and I wasn't hurting that bad. They picked me up and we started down the side of Hill 56.

Pfc. JACK WRIGHT
G/5

The assault on Seoul began. The company headquarters' unit had set up in a ravine. Three or four of us runners were sitting nearby, including my buddy Casanova. When they called for the first runner of the day, since it was his turn, Casanova got up. "See ya later, Archie." "Yeah, take care."

Five minutes later they called for another runner. It was my turn. I got up and received instructions to deliver a message to the battalion CP. They vaguely pointed me back toward Inch'on. Off I went. I cleared the ravine, stepped out into a rice paddy, and there's two Marines kneeling over a dead Marine. The dead Marine was Casanova. A sniper had nailed him. It suddenly dawned on me that I was taking his place.

I couldn't stop. I hit a road with some buildings and temples, cut to my left, and started climbing a hill. Just then I passed a burning building. Two South Korean soldiers waited nearby. I turned and saw four North Koreans, three with hands on their heads and one crawling on all fours coming out of the smoke. These ROKs never batted an eyelash. Once the North Koreans were clear of the building, they gunned them down.

I was out all day, going on a zigzag course, heading in the direction where I thought I'd find battalion. Nothing else spectacular happened. It was a whole day wasted. It was hot. Off toward Seoul I could hear the sounds of battle. Once in a while artillery shells would whiz overhead. I found the CP at sundown. When I delivered my message, I learned battalion had received the same message by radio about the time Casanova had been killed.

[Seoul in Korean means, simply, "capital." The city sits in a mountain-rimmed basin, the site having been chosen 100 years before Columbus discovered the New World. Old-fashioned and somewhat shabby, Seoul in 1950 was a city of contrasts; modern office buildings overlooked 500-year-old palaces with their manicured lawns and gardens. Broad boulevards connected the ancient with the modern—Kyongbokkung Palace (built in 1394) and the Anglican cathedral, the Great South Gate, and the Chosun Hotel. At the time of the North Korean invasion, the city had a population of roughly 2,000,000 people, many of whom were still in their homes on 24 September 1950, fearfully awaiting the battle that would clear their doorsteps of the invader.]

Pfc. JOHN BISHOP
I/7
When we got to the top of one of the hills, I'll never forget the sight I saw. Down below was a very big city. It looked at the time as big as New York. Up until then, walking for days and days, all we'd seen was dirt, rocks, hills, farms, and old shacks. I was surprised they even had a city.

Smoke was coming from everywhere. Buildings and houses were on fire. You could see Corsairs dive down from the sky, then swoop back up, leaving behind a puff of black smoke and a dull explosion. From the top of that hill, it looked like I was watching a movie right before my eyes. Except it was for real.

S/Sgt. LEE BERGEE
E/1

Our battalion crossed the Han River and entered the outskirts of Seoul on the morning of September 24. We had been nine days on the road from Inch'on and we were tired. I looked toward our company front and saw crowded slums, a railroad yard, and many roadblocks. It wasn't going to be easy!

The enemy roadblocks were made from hunks of concrete, streetcar rails, steel beams, and large rocks. We destroyed many of the roadblocks with bulldozers. It seemed that every building in Seoul housed an enemy sniper. We cleaned out doorways and rooftops; we went from street to street, house to house. Inside some of the houses, we knocked holes in the walls and then tossed grenades through the openings.

Pfc. WIN SCOTT
C/5

The fighting in Seoul was different than most of the fellers had seen, even in World War II. Some of our NCOs had been officers then, and they thought that only on Okinawa had they seen the kind of fighting we were seeing now.

Seoul is a big city, and there was a lot of resistance in many parts of it, especially in the streets the enemy had barricaded with tanks. The fighting was mostly done at the platoon, squad, or fire-team level. First we laid down as much fire as we could in a certain area to find out where the opposition was. Four guys, two on each side of the street, would work a leapfrog thing. We'd cover for each other. One group would fire into a building while the other two would work their way next to it. Then these two would toss grenades through the windows to clear the inside and rush it. The teams would then reverse positions. The two who had taken the building would cover the other two across the street and the process would be repeated,

building by building, street by street, sector by sector, until the entire
city had been cleared. The best weapons we had were grenades, pistols, and shotguns.

Pfc. FRED DAVIDSON
G/5
George Company was on one of the main streets which led through
the outskirts of the city. I was about halfway back in the column and
on the right. It seemed as though all of the fighting was on the point,
with an occasional round hitting here or there. As I'd come up a side
street or alley, I'd take a careful look around the corner before I crossed
the open area. At one such crossing I thought I saw a head and rifle
barrel in the window of a small, one-story building. A wooden fence
ran around the building. I ran over to the fence. Not being able to
see anything from there, I sprinted to the building. When I peeked
around the corner, I saw the doorway. I crept up to it, wishing I had
a hand grenade. It never occurred to me that the head I'd seen belonged to a civilian. Not having a grenade, I decided to jump into
the building and spray the inside with my carbine as I did. There
were no other Marines around to cover me. Taking a deep breath, I
jumped through the opening. As I landed inside, I saw there was indeed an armed North Korean in the room. When I pulled the trigger
of my carbine to spray him, only one shot fired. The damn thing had
jammed. Fortunately, the one round caught him as he began to run
to another part of the building. This one bullet hit him in the left
buttock, exited his right buttock, and managed to hit his right hand,
where it tore off three fingers and most of his palm. He dropped to
the floor and began screaming and crying. I tried to clear the jam
while I walked over to him. He was about my age. I kicked his rifle
away from him and looked into the room he was running to. There
was no one there. I cleared the jam and decided to kill the North
Korean by shooting him in the head. I stood over him. Just then two
Marines came in through the doorway. They had seen me go in and
had decided to give me a hand. We looked at the enemy soldier. He
wore a pair of dark brown trousers and a light brown shirt. He did
not have a cap. A rope acted as a belt. His tennis shoes were low-

cuts. His rifle had a five-round clip in it. There was no other ammunition on him. Five rounds of ammo. No extra!

By this time the room had become crowded with other Marines who came to see what all the excitement was about. A Navy corpsman began working on the man's wounds. I sort of drifted on out to the main street, leaving the corpsman and a couple of Marines with the prisoner, who was by now naked. All I could think about was what that small carbine bullet had done. It was amazing. I had used a carbine in the Pusan Perimeter and knew it could be effective when used at full automatic. This was the first time I'd seen a single exit wound left by it. I was impressed!

Pfc. JOHN BISHOP
I/7
We came upon people waving small Korean flags. One old man shuffled over to my group and said in broken English, "America, number one." One of our guys pointed his M1 at him. "Fucking A, buddy," he replied, "and don't you forget it!"

Pfc. WIN SCOTT
C/5
The city was full of civilians. Some of them might have been armed. We didn't trust anyone. We couldn't. Civilians were a big problem. Suddenly, in trying to get away from a firefight in their neighborhood, hundreds of women and children would mob into our area, blocking us off.

Chaplain GLYN JONES (USN)
I/1
I remember a curious thing that happened in the city. Because fire was coming down the streets, I passed the word that I'd be celebrating Holy Communion out of the line of fire behind a certain building. (I'd gotten a new communion kit from the division chaplain almost as soon as I lost the one on the beach at Inch'on.)

I began to celebrate Holy Communion on the back of a jeep. I was in my fatigues, but I wore a stole and had a chalice. The Marines began to gather, and out of the holes of the buildings came Koreans, Korean Christians. They understood what was happening. I celebrated Holy Communion, and they received. I would say twenty-five Marines were there and I'd guess about fifty Koreans. They didn't know me, I didn't know them, but they knew what was happening. As soon as they received, they disappeared. *

Pfc. JACK WRIGHT
G/5

I can remember going down this street and coming to an intersection. Later, we called it Blood and Bones Corner. At first it didn't seem different. One of our fire teams made it across without problems. It was when the next team tried to cross that all hell broke loose. The intersection was situated in such a way that the only riflemen who could get into the fight was the Marine at the corner. As soon as he went down, another man moved up and took his place. That's the way it continued. Another runner and I kicked down the door to a building and climbed to the second story. We figured we might be able to snipe at some of the North Koreans who were holding us up. We spotted a column of North Koreans moving up on a connecting street. This other Marine and I were at windows which formed a 90-degree angle. He nailed 'em on one block, I nailed 'em on the other. We got into a rhythm: let four go, pop one, let four go, pop one.

We were called back and told to get out of there. When we pulled back, it wasn't a very happy company. The fire team that tried to get back across the street was wiped out except for the squad leader, who somehow lived. He just sat around for days afterward, depressed and guilt ridden. No one could convince him that it wasn't his fault, which it wasn't.

There at Blood and Bones Corner, in that short amount of time, we took more casualties than at any time since the battle of No-Name

* Jones interview, Nav. Inst.

Ridge down in the Perimeter. We found out street fighting wasn't all that easy.

When we got back to that corner after the North Korean machine gun had been outflanked, South Korean civilians came from someplace and helped us carry our wounded. When we ran out of stretchers, they carried our men on doors. For a people who could, at times, be so cruel and so crude, there were other times when they could be very gentle. A mother couldn't take care of her baby better than those civilians took care of our wounded.

Pfc. WIN SCOTT
C/5
The city was dirty. There were animals running wild and junk everywhere. Some battles were fought around barricades formed by trolley cars. Pictures of Stalin hung on some of the buildings. Communist propaganda was all over.

Once, my squad came across a large parking lot full of cars all in perfect line—it was outside the telephone exchange. One bazooka team fired a round that went right through each of these neatly lined-up autos. I won't forget that time. Except for that, however, I remember only that there was quite a bit of fighting. There was no front and no rear. Thank God we had tanks with us. Without them we'd still be fighting there.

S/Sgt. CHESTER BAIR
Heavy Tank Company/32d Infantry
My tank company in Seoul, where I was a gunner on an M4 Sherman, was assigned to the Marines. Inside the city the enemy had set up strong defensive positions. They had artillery and plenty of T34 tanks. There were roadblocks at almost every city block.

It would take about thirty minutes to break through one roadblock. As soon as one had been eliminated, there would be another. After a tank overran three or four of them, it would be replaced by another one. In this manner each tank could refuel, clean its guns, receive ammo, and allow the crew to work and do maintenance.

The T34 was faster than our M4 and armed with an 88-mm cannon. While the Sherman had only a 76-mm gun, its turret was electronically operated and we could sight faster than the Russian tank with its manually operated turret. The Marines used tanks very well. They would use the telephone located on the rear of each tank which talked to the commander inside. In this way the Marines acted as our eyes. Buttoned up inside, depending on a periscope, our vision was very limited. Working outside in the streets, the Marines tremendously increased our ability to close with the enemy and to direct our firepower.

One time, as we rolled down a street, expecting to see one of our own tanks, a T34 swung around a corner. Both of us stopped. Our cannon fired first and ripped their turret completely off. The Russian tank burst into flames, and the shells inside its hull began exploding. It was one of those times to shoot first and ask questions later.

Pfc. JACK WRIGHT
G/5

About noon one day we were walking carefully in columns of file down both sides of a street in a residential neighborhood. The streets were terraced one above the other. A firefight broke out. A group of us cut up to the road above the one we had been on. I sneaked around in back of this one house, and there below me were two North Koreans. I shot one, then ducked behind the house. When I leaned around again, I got the other one. Back on the street I told a squad leader what had just happened. "Yeah, yeah, Archie. Everyone's seeing gooks." Right then I spotted three more coming up to where we were crouched. I didn't get a shot at the first two, but I did nail the third one. "I got him," I yelled. "I got him!" This sergeant turned. "Well," he said, "don't get so uppity over it, Archie. The next one might get you." That got me to thinking.

Chaplain GLYN JONES (USN)
1/1

We continued to work our way through the city. There was a kind of competition about raising American flags in places. We ended up outside the city, in defensive positions, waiting for the Army to come up from the south.

I'd seen a lot of corpses in the city. I was told they'd been killed by the enemy. But then I came to have reason to believe that this was not entirely the case.

One afternoon our battalion CO went off to a conference. Jack Hawkins is a very unusual man. He had been captured on Corregidor with the 4th Marines, but had escaped and gone into the hills to conduct guerrilla warfare against the Japanese.

I was up on a hill that day at a machine-gun position with a master sergeant named Barber. We saw this long procession of people coming toward our line. I said to Barber, "What the devil is happening here?" He said, "I don't know." So I said, "I'll go and see." I went down and found that this was a group of about 100 civilians, all carrying shovels and picks, being escorted by South Korean officers and men. They were being taken to some place where, after digging their own graves, they were going to be executed. They were people who were alleged to have supported the enemy in the city. This was civil war, which is very unlike any other war. There were kids there, some no older than eight, who were going to be shot because they had carried messages for the North Koreans for a stick of gum. Pregnant women were going to be shot; so were old men, ignorant of the issues. All these people were going to be murdered.

When the South Korean in charge of the group saw me come down, he stopped—probably thought I was a Marine line officer. Anyway, they soon saw the cross and knew I was a chaplain. I said, "You cannot advance any farther until the Marine CO comes down and authorizes it. You must stay here." The South Korean captain in charge said, "I operate under my own orders, and we are planning to execute these people." I pointed out Sergeant Barber's machine gun and said, "Do not move. It is very dangerous if you do."

Everybody sat down and waited. Jack Hawkins came back in due course. I explained the situation to him. At some risk to himself, he got the civilians away from the South Koreans and took them to a safe place. This kind of thing happened all over the front.*

---

* Jones interview, Nav. Inst.

S/Sgt. CHESTER BAIR
Heavy Tank Company/32d Infantry

Two ROK soldiers were searching the never-ending line of refugees which streamed past our roadblock. On top of the tank I could see everything happening. An old papa-san with a small horse and two-wheel cart filled high with his belongings was stopped and everything was searched. The two ROK soldiers discovered a small crock of money. Next thing I noticed is that they had, on the street, divided the money into two equal piles. It was obvious what they meant to do. The old man was begging them to return the money to him. I got very angry. I shouted at the soldiers, and gestured that they should return the money to the old man. They acted as if they didn't understand me. I threw a round into the .50-cal machine gun mounted on the turret and pointed the barrel in their direction. Without hesitation, they returned the money to the crock, and sent the old man on his way. Old papa-san knew what had happened. He continued to bow to me all the way down the road for as far as I could see.

[*The 26th of September found the units of the 7th Marines in the rough hill country northwest of Seoul's city limits. It would be a day of long marches and exhausting climbs. For D/7, however, a different kind of day was in store.*]

Pfc. JOSEPH SALUZZI
D/7

Our first major action came on the morning of September 26. Our mission was to approach Seoul from the north and join the 5th Marines in securing the city. The road was lined with civilians who cheered us all along the way.

Entering the northwest corner of Seoul, having passed Hoengjeoe-ri, we approached Sodaemun Prison. Just opposite the prison we came under heavy enemy fire and found ourselves trapped. Our company CO, Capt. Richard Breen, and my platoon leader, 1st Lt. William Goggin, were wounded. The machine-gun section, headed by S/Sgt. John O'Neill, a very brave man, went forward to assist in the assault on the prison grounds.

The company began to receive fire from the slopes of Hill 296, which was on our right, and Hill 338, which was on the left. Sergeant O'Neill was shot at point-blank range, and died within a few minutes. Immediately, Sergeant Ralphs, my squad leader, put our gun into action. After spraying a tower, where some enemy fire was coming from, our gunner was wounded. As assistant gunner, I took over the weapon. Within a few moments I, too, was hit, first in the right arm, then in the chest. It felt as though I'd been hit in the chest by a sledgehammer. I could not breathe. Somehow, I gasped for air and lay panting until the initial shock wore off. To this day I remember the pain and horror of those moments.

Our squad was pinned down and couldn't move. The gunner and I kept screaming for the corpsman, but even he couldn't get through. Both of us lay in an exposed position. The North Koreans who shot us knew that we were alive and that they could pick off any Marine coming to our aid.

We lay there for what seemed like an eternity. My breathing became more difficult because my chest was filling with blood. After what must have been a few hours, Cpl. Frank Brennan and Pfc. Mark Valetta from one of the rifle platoons crawled to us with a blanket. The gunner was bleeding heavily from the mouth but still hanging on. Using the blanket as a stretcher, they moved him first, and came under heavy fire. The gunner was hit again, this time a round grazed his head. I passed out. The next thing I knew, it was night. I was still out in the open.

At this point I went through my second horror of the day. The prison came under heavy artillery bombardment. Since I lay near the wall, I was right in the middle of it. The pain was unbearable and I couldn't move. I passed out. When I came to, the ground around me was erupting, and bricks and steel were falling around me. Miraculously, I was not hit. I passed out again.

When I came to again, the sun was up, and staring at me in disbelief were four South Korean boys. Around me I noticed several dead North Korean soldiers. The boys gently placed me on a straw mat and carried me back to the company CP. Lieutenant Goggin was there to greet me. The word went down the line, "Saluzzi's alive." Hospitalman Schlansky dressed my wounds, and the chaplain came over to give the last rites. He handed me a crucifix to hold. As I brought it to my lips to kiss, I broke down and cried.

Seoul, the capital of the Republic of Korea, is again in friendly hands. United Nations forces, including the 17th Regiment of the ROK Army and elements of the U.S. 7th and 1st Marine Divisions, have completed the envelopment and seizure of the city.

UNITED NATIONS COMMAND COMMUNIQUÉ, 26 SEPTEMBER 1950

Three months to the day after the North Koreans launched their surprise attack south of the 38th Parallel the combat troops of X Corps recaptured the capital city of Seoul. . . . The liberation of Seoul was accomplished by a coordinated attack of X Corps troops. . . . By 1400 hours 25 September the military defenses of Seoul were broken. . . . The enemy is fleeing the city to the northeast.

X CORPS COMMUNIQÚE, 26 SEPTEMBER 1950

[The day Seoul was "liberated," fierce fighting continued in the heart of the city. The North Koreans fought stubbornly from roadblock to roadblock, house to house. Units of the 1st and 5th Marines slowly ground forward. Streets in the shattered, burning city were shrouded in a heavy gray cloud of smoke. The heat was nearly unendurable.]

DWIGHT MARTIN
Time
This morning Ma-Po [Boulevard] wore a different look. The burned and blackened remains of the boulevard's shops and homes sent clouds of acrid smoke billowing over the city. Buildings still ablaze showered sparks and ashes high into the air to cascade down on red-eyed, soot-faced Marines.

A group of Marines waited behind a wall, tending three of their wounded and a wounded enemy soldier. The corpsmen shouted for an ambulance. A Marine from the other side of the street replied, "Bring 'em out on litters. The major says we've lost four ambulances, seven corpsmen, and four drivers since last night. We ain't got the ambulances to replace 'em."

Further along, behind a barricade just seized by the Marines, we saw another amazing sight. Less than fifty yards away, through dense smoke, came forty to fifty North Korean soldiers. They dragged a light antitank gun. Apparently, they thought the barricade was held by their side. The Marines first stared in disbelief, then opened fire with every weapon available. The Reds screamed, buckled, pitched, and died on Ma-Po's pavement. *

S/Sgt. LEE BERGEE
E/1
As we fought yard by yard up Ma-Po Boulevard, tanks led the way. I saw a North Korean soldier lying in the street. He'd been hit by a burst of white phosphorus. His body was still burning. I watched one of the tanks roll over him, crushing and grinding his body into the pavement. During this period our battalion lost four ambulances; seven corpsmen and four drivers were killed.

I remember one day during "Almond's mopping up" when our battalion gained exactly 1,200 yards. At each barricade we had to annihilate the enemy, then reorganize, evacuate casualties, and wearily go on to the next. At the railroad station we found the still-warm bodies of women and children—hostages massacred by the North Korean secret police.

Pfc. PAUL MARTIN
Reconnaissance Company/1st Marine Division
Mail finally caught up with us while we were attached to the 7th Marines in the hills and gorges north of Seoul. The fighting had been pretty heavy, so it seemed appropriate to receive a letter from a friend who had lost touch with me and whose opening line was, "Hope you're enjoying sunny California." Copies of the *Pacific Stars and Stripes* also arrived announcing in bold headlines: SEOUL LIBERATED. The issue was dated September 26. It was news to us.

---

* Heinl, *Victory at High Tide*, 240.

S/Sgt. LEE BERGEE
E/1

My own personal recollection of the actual day Seoul fell was September 27. There comes a time in battle when you know that you have won. On this date I felt at last we had won a hard-fought victory.

Around 11:00 A.M., on the 27th, we raised a French flag over France's deserted embassy. Then there was a hot fight just west of Duksoo Palace. My platoon straddled the streetcar tracks.

We reached the Russian embassy and found it abandoned. E Company tore down the Hammer and Sickle and ran up the Stars and Stripes. We then advanced to the American embassy, where we found knee-high weeds and all the furniture gone. As members of my company started to raise the American colors, a sniper fired. The whine of the ricochet made us all duck. One of the men killed the sniper and he fell from his perch on the rooftop of Duksoo Palace. Shortly afterward our battalion made contact with G Company, 5th Marines, and I realized the end was near.

Pfc. JACK WRIGHT
G/5

Sometime early afternoon the company moved down a wide boulevard toward the Capitol building. You could see the dome when the wind whipped the smoke back and forth. We hit the gate outside the compound on a run and charged across an open area right up the steps of the Capitol. It was room-to-room fighting. We made one mistake; we started at the bottom and worked up. The North Koreans on the upper floor were trapped. If you ever saw a man fight, it's when he's trapped. We had one hell of a fight on our hands.

After we cleared it, we went back out and watched a bunch of guys forming a human pyramid so they could reach and untie the rope which held the North Korean flag on the pole. Someone came up with one big, beautiful American flag. Needless to say, everybody cheered.

We mopped up after that, and were told to assemble in the back of the Capitol. I climbed up a wall and looked over a beautiful park which did not seem to have been touched by all the fighting. Off to the side of the Capitol was another imposing building which I was told was the Koreans' equivalent of the Library of Congress. Well, me, I've always liked books, so I went on over. There were books scattered over all the floors and out in the corridors. I began looking at many of these volumes, and because they were written in Korean or Japanese, all I could do was look at the pictures. One book I found very interesting was full of pictures from what I figured must have been a war the Japanese had with Russians years before. I got carried away, and time slipped by.

When I returned to my unit, I found a couple of guys who, while going through the rooms in the Capitol, had come across one where medals were on display. When they got back to the platoon, they looked like a couple of Russian generals. As the saying goes, the Marines came and took Seoul. When they left, they took Seoul with them.

S/Sgt. CHESTER BAIR
Heavy Tank Company/32d Infantry

Not far from the railroad station we discovered a brewery. After dumping the water from our five-gallon cans, we filled them with beer. Next we drove around to a neighborhood bank. We blew open the front door. The vault was also locked. After driving up the stairs, we fired an armor-piercing shell into the vault door. Found nothing but some papers we couldn't read. The perfect bank robbery, but the robbers left without any valuables.

Pfc. JACK WRIGHT
G/5

We sat behind the Capitol for a day. We got word that there was going to be a big ceremony when MacArthur returned Seoul to the South Koreans. Well, we never got to see it. We were pulled off and moved to an area about a mile from the Capitol where we set up a defensive perimeter.

[An elaborate ceremony was held in the smoking ruins of Seoul at noon on 29 September. Fourteen days after the landing at Inch'on, General MacArthur returned the capital of South Korea to its president, Syngman Rhee.]

Col. EDWARD S. FORNEY
Deputy Chief of Staff, X Corps
Occasional falls of glass from the dome, and drifting smoke and ashes, were part of the scene. Unheeded noise of rifle shots punctuated the talks. Grim Marines from Puller's regiment surrounded the seated audience. The youth of the guards was offset by the tall, gray-haired figures of Generals Smith and Barr at the front of the audience.*

Mr. President: By the grace of a merciful Providence our forces fighting under the standard of that great hope and inspiration of mankind, the United Nations, have liberated this ancient capital city of Korea. It has been freed from the despotism of communist rule and its citizens once more have the opportunity for that immutable concept of life which holds invincibly to the primacy of individual liberty and personal dignity.

GENERAL DOUGLAS MacARTHUR

Pfc. JACK WRIGHT
G/5
After the ceremony was over, we saddled up and went back to the Capitol. Boy, were we ever disappointed. The building that was supposedly the Korean Library of Congress had been set on fire and was badly damaged. I don't know if it's true, but we were told it had been burned to give a dramatic background for MacArthur's speech. It's a big disappointment when you take something and it's in one piece and then some joker comes along and burns it down just to make a show for somebody. That don't set so good.

7th Marine Regiment—To advance rapidly and seize blocking positions in the vicinity of Uijongbu.

OPN O 14-50, 1ST MARINE DIVISION, 30 SEPTEMBER 1950

[The 7th Marines would now spearhead a drive to capture the vital road and rail junction at Uijongbu, sixteen miles north of Seoul. Lo-

*Montross and Canzona, *The Inchon-Seoul Operation,* 284.

cated at the end of a natural corridor, which runs through a range of mountains, the city was an important key in preventing the retreating North Koreans from reaching and crossing the 38th Parallel.

At 6:30 A.M. on Sunday, 1 October, Litzenberg's regiment jumped off. There was every indication that the retreating North Koreans would not fight for Uijongbu. The indications were wrong.]

Pfc. FRANCIS KILLEEN
A/7
We came up on a hill and set up positions. Enemy troops were moving in a column some 500 to 600 yards away. Our platoon commander was eyeballing them: "Hey, boys, that's them!" We had three former team shooters in our company including a former Lauchheimer Trophy winner. We immediately adjusted sights and hasty slings. It is amazing what three Marines can do to an enemy when they get their zero. Before the North Koreans could recover from the shock of sudden accurate rifle fire, panic set in. Their commander lost control; we got him, too.

Hospitalman 3/C WILLIAM DAVIS
B/7
Our battalion and the 3d mounted out on October 1 to capture the high ground on both sides of the road leading from Seoul to Uijongbu. We accomplished this mission fairly easily, although we were under artillery and mortar fire throughout the day. Early on the morning of October 2, the entire battalion mounted out to advance on the east side of the road through hilly terrain with several high peaks. In the early afternoon we were approaching one of these peaks when we came under mortar and machine-gun fire from bunkers on the slope and at the top of the peak. I was in a company-size unit at the time, and upon receiving fire we took cover at the base of the hill. My platoon was in a forward position directly in front of a bunker about fifty to sixty yards up the slope of the hill. We were receiving machine-gun fire from the bunker.

After the origin of fire had been located, the platoon leader [Lieutenant Graeber] was ordered to send out fire teams to assault the bunker. We laid down covering fire and three fire teams advanced on the left, right, and center. The teams on the flanks had some hill and brush cover, but the center fire team was exposed. After advancing for about ten to fifteen yards, the four men came under direct fire from the machine gun and all were hit. I buckled my helmet strap, and, dragging my first-aid bag, began to crawl and run to the fire team. Covering fire from the platoon was focused on the bunker, but the area was still receiving fire from either this bunker or another emplacement. When I examined the first casualty, I found he was hit in the legs, so I dragged him back to the shelter of the mound where the remainder of the platoon was located. I left the man and returned to the other three casualties. The next man I examined was dead, so I proceeded to the last two, who were close together. They had both received several wounds and I carried or pulled each in turn back to shelter. By this time another corpsman arrived and we were able to administer first aid to the three wounded men. The fire from the bunker or perhaps from several locations continued. I remember quite clearly the zipping sound of the bullets and the dirt kicking up around me. Several mortars were brought up as I was treating the wounded, and they finally silenced the bunker, which was then taken by the two fire teams that were on the left and right flanks.

1st Lt. LAWRENCE SCHMITT
F/7

After our week around Seoul we pushed on north, expecting each day to run into heavy resistance. A combined tank/infantry attack was planned. The road we traveled on was heavily mined and a tank hit one of them. Just about then the Marines took heavy North Korean artillery and mortar fire. We had a rough afternoon. Fortunately, as always, we had Marine Corsairs on station and they knocked hell out of the enemy positions. There was a Marine aviator who traveled right with the frontline troops and he had radio contact with the planes at all times. He could have them on target in less than two minutes.

That afternoon outside of Uijongbu, the Corsairs really put on a show for us.

Pfc. JACK WRIGHT
G/5

Directly in front of us our route was blocked by a long, low hill line. Word had it that there was a company or two of North Koreans waiting behind it for us. An air strike was called in. It proved to be something worth watching. We sat on the ground and enjoyed the show. A Corsair would dive down on the left and disappear behind the hill. The plane would then climb out on the right leaving behind a big, black column of smoke. Really quite a good show. One Corsair came down, dove behind the hill, the smoke came up, but the Corsair didn't. If you ever wanted to see a bunch of men suddenly go quiet—we just looked at one another. The other Corsairs came back but didn't do any more diving behind the hill. They flew low as if they were looking at something. A patrol was sent out. When they returned they told us of finding the slopes of the valley littered with enemy dead. The Corsairs had really done a job. But in that valley was our downed Corsair. The plane was burnt, the pilot dead. One pilot for an estimated enemy company. The odds didn't mount up. We figured we were the losers.

1st Lt. LAWRENCE SCHMITT
F/7

The battalion dashed madly into town and took it. Uijongbu had been so badly bombed and shelled that the gooks had taken off for the hills. We dug in. One night a gook truck drove up to our lines. Thinking it was friendly, my platoon let it pass. A half hour later the same truck returned, now towing an artillery piece. One feller was sharp enough to be suspicious. He challenged the driver. When the truck stopped, an interpreter asked the occupants who they were. There was some confusion. Suddenly, the interpreter grabbed a rifle and shot two of the men on the truck; thirteen more surrendered. They proved to be Reds who had returned to the town to collect a field piece they'd hidden.

Shortly afterward we moved north to about ten miles from the 38th Parallel. We dug in again. Later a ROK unit came through and relieved us. Apparently, they then crossed the Parallel and continued moving north.

A successful frontal attack and envelopment has completely changed the tide of battle in South Korea. The backbone of the North Korean army has been broken and their scattered forces are being liquidated or driven north with material losses in equipment and men captured.

GENERAL DOUGLAS MacARTHUR, 6TH REPORT OF THE C-IN-C,
UNITED NATIONS COMMAND, TO THE SECURITY COUNCIL
OF THE UNITED NATIONS

Pfc. PAUL MARTIN
Reconnaissance Company, 1st Marine Division
The sweet smell of victory was in the air when we learned Army units had reached the 38th Parallel. We were ordered to return to division CP in Seoul. Rumors of the 1st Marine Division returning home, and of parades awaiting us in San Diego, Los Angeles, and maybe even New York, floated through the air. We could be home in time for Thanksgiving dinner and the football games; then we'd get a thirty-day Christmas leave.

All these rumors were discarded when we were issued cold-weather sleeping bags and sent back to Inch'on for loading.

At 1130, 5 October 1950, the Battalion upon order of 5th Marines entrucked in preparation for movement to 1st Marine Division Assembly Area at Inch'on, Korea. At 1245, the last serial was underway and by 1600 the last had arrived at the new assembly area. The Battalion was billeted in buildings of the Jinsin Electrical Works. On 6 October 1950, 1/5 remained in the assembly area and began reorganization and resupply.

SPECIAL ACTION REPORT, 1/5

Pfc. JACK WRIGHT
G/5

Back at Inch'on we were given liberty. Curious as a cat I headed into town. It was interesting to walk down a street in a city I'd helped liberate. The older guys knew where the bars and the houses that had the females were. Being young and naive, I never found a thing. I just went sightseeing.

[The total number of casualties sustained by X Corps during the Inch'on/Seoul campaign was 3,161 men killed or wounded. In light of the victory and achievement, this was not considered excessive. Enemy dead was rounded off at 14,000, and POWs taken at 7,000.

A solemn ceremony dedicating the military cemetery at Inch'on was conducted on 6 October. After the invocation and a short speech, wreaths were laid on the graves of four unknown servicemen. Volleys were fired and a bugler sounded taps. A small band played the national anthems of the United States and the Republic of Korea.]

Brig. Gen. EDWARD CRAIG
Assistant Division Commander,
1st Marine Division

Back at Inch'on we held a ceremony at one of the new cemeteries which held the remains of the men killed at the landings. When the Marines learned that the only flag to be raised would be the UN's, they complained and demanded that an American flag, too, be raised. This was done.*

---

* Craig interview, MCHC.

ITEM

6 September-21 September 1950

6

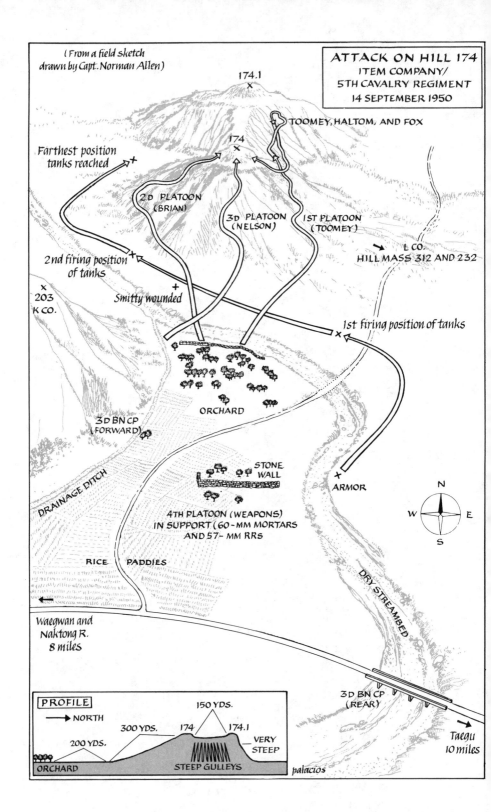

(From a field sketch
drawn by Capt. Norman Allen)

ATTACK ON HILL 174
ITEM COMPANY/
5TH CAVALRY REGIMENT
14 SEPTEMBER 1950

174.1
×

174
×

TOOMEY, HALTOM, AND FOX

Farthest position
tanks reached
+

2D PLATOON
(BRIAN)

3D PLATOON
(NELSON)

1ST PLATOON
(TOOMEY)

L CO.
HILL MASS 312 AND 232

2nd firing position
of tanks ×

×
203
K CO.

+
Smitty wounded

1st firing position of tanks
×

ORCHARD

3D BN CP
(FORWARD)

STONE
WALL

4TH PLATOON (WEAPONS)
IN SUPPORT (60-MM MORTARS
AND 57-MM RRs)

×
ARMOR

N
W   E
S

DRAINAGE DITCH

RICE   PADDIES

DRY STREAMBED

Waegwan and
Naktong R.
8 miles

3D BN CP
(REAR)

Taegu
10 miles

PROFILE
→ NORTH

150 YDS.

300 YDS.   174   174.1

200 YDS.   VERY
STEEP

ORCHARD   STEEP GULLEYS   palacios

In early September, while the Marines readied themselves for their historic invasion, General Walker's Eighth Army was still locked in a deadly struggle with the North Koreans along the Pusan Perimeter. By mid-September, however, at the time of the Inch'on landings, the threat to most of this line had eased. In the northern sector the ROK Army had stopped the Communists in the mountains; to the south the 25th Division had held the enemy at the gates of Chindong-ni. The one exception was around Taegu, where for two weeks some of the most solid fighting of the war took place. Like an old fighter going on instinct, the North Koreans were taking a final whack at ending the war. If Taegu fell, so, too, would Walker's Perimeter, leaving the corridor to Pusan wide open. In the hills and valleys surrounding Taegu, the U.S. 1st Cavalry Division fought for its very existence. Many engagements were fought simultaneously, but in this chapter we will follow the course of one battle and describe the actions of a single rifle company. Numerous battles like the one on Hill 174 were waged. Some were larger, some smaller; for the 1st Cav's troopers, the fighting was everywhere the same.

In late August the regiments of the 1st Cavalry Division received their third battalions from the United States. The 5th Cavalry Regiment's 3d Battalion, consisting of Companies I, K, L, and M,* ar-

---

* These companies had originally belonged to the 14th RCT.

rived in Korea from Camp Carson, Colorado, where it had undergone extensive training in mountain climbing and cross-country skiing.

Item Company's commanding officer, Norman Allen, sat a horse well and enjoyed a good fox hunt. Old enough to serve in World War II, the handsome Californian had campaigned in the Pacific. He had made the Army his life, and by the time war in Korea broke out, he had had command of I Company for more than a year.

Growing up in the old "Soo" in Ontario, Canada, Victor Fox's only experience with battle had been playing "guns" and other boyhood games. Out of work in 1948, he had decided to see something of the world and had enlisted in the American Army. He arrived in Korea as one of I Company's many inexperienced foxhole GIs. He was eighteen years old. Back at Camp Carson, Fox had asked his platoon sergeant why he had not yet been made a squad leader. He was told, "You'd probably get everyone killed."

The 2d Platoon leader, Adrian Beecher Brian, was related on his mother's side to Harriet Beecher Stowe, the author of Uncle Tom's Cabin. A recent graduate of West Point, Lieutenant Brian was sent to Korea in early August 1950, as a replacement. Two weeks later, to give it his "seasoning and experience," he was assigned to the 5th Cav's I Company. Everyone in the company called him "Beech."

Born in Cudahy, Wisconsin, on Halloween, Jerry Emer was the seventh son and thirteenth, and last, child born to John and Teresa Emer. He graduated from high school in 1945 and was immediately drafted into the Army. The Japanese surrendered before Emer saw any combat. He left the service in 1946, but in less than a year had reupped. During the Korean War he served in Lieutenant Brian's platoon.

Item Company's most reliable machine gunner, Donald Pate, was a combat veteran of the Second World War. After serving as an MP in Japan with the Army of Occupation, he shipped home and was assigned to a unit helping in the reburial of American servicemen killed in the war. In Korea Pate was a squad leader in Item's 3d Platoon.

Around the time the Marine brigade was withdrawn for a second time from the Naktong Bulge and trucked back to Pusan to await orders for their Inch'on adventure, the newly arrived Company I, 3d

Battalion, 5th Cavalry Regiment had been on the line in one of the Perimeter's quieter sectors for one week.

Capt. NORMAN ALLEN
I Company/5th Cavalry

Several hundred yards back from the enemy's side of the Naktong lay a lateral road lined with tall trees. In a nearby open field stood a lone, tall, leafy tree. Because we could adjust artillery fire from it, my FO used this tree as a convenient registration point.

One breathlessly hot afternoon in the first week of September, I went down off my hill to take a little catnap. I had been asleep a short time when the FO called, "Hey, Cap'n, you better come up here. We've got enemy moving to our front." When I joined him by the spotting scope, I saw a company-sized enemy unit marching in open column on that tree-lined road across the river. I at once called the CP and alerted all my crew-served weapons for a possible fire mission. Then I called the lieutenant whose platoon was closest to the river and told him to hold his fire.

The FO and I took turns on the scope. Suddenly, he said, "Holy Christ, you won't believe it. My God, they are!" I grabbed the scope. It *was* unbelievable. The head of the enemy's column had halted in the shade of that tall tree and the rest of the unit was closing on it. God . . . My heart pounded; what an opportunity. Clumped together under the shade of one tree stood more than a hundred North Koreans. Although they were a mile away, the FO and I spoke in whispers. I could see some of the enemy drinking water, others relieving themselves. The FO picked up his radio. "Fire mission," he said. "Registration point 106. Give me T-O-T." Time on target, TOT, is when all the rounds of a battery are fired so they strike the enemy at the same time. Usually only the first few seconds of artillery fire on an unsuspecting enemy are really effective. After that, the enemy hits the ground and it takes real pounding to take them out. Most casualties are taken in that initial salvo. I gave the target to our crew-served weapons as well. I told them to fire on the artillery splash-down, then, after thirty seconds, to walk their fire right and left from the big tree and up and down the road. That should catch anyone who hadn't been hit at first and was now jumping for cover.

The FO and I held our breath. The North Koreans were completely oblivious to our presence. Finally, when the anticipation became too much, the FO turned and grinned, "Well, Cap'n, whaddaya say we drop 'em in their shit." I was so excited I couldn't talk; two wars and I'd never before been presented with such an opportunity. I nodded. "Fire for effect!" the FO shouted over his radio. I heard the immediate tinny response from the battery CO to his gunners, "FIRE!" Then to us, "On the way!" The FO counted down. "Eight, seven, six," the enemy never moved, ". . . four, three," never moved, ". . . one, SPLASH!" Around the tree the earth erupted in flames. Clumps of mud and bodies flew into the air. Plumes of dense smoke blanketed the area where the tree had stood. It was beautiful. I grabbed the FO's mike and yelled to the firing battery, "You did it, right on the button. You got over a hundred." In the valley below I heard the gun crews cheer.

As soon as it was dark, a patrol slipped across the river. It returned within a half hour. They confirmed that we had done right; there were dead North Koreans all over the area. I told the men to turn in and get some shut-eye—there was always tomorrow. Alone, I walked back to the CP. I was pretty satisfied. We'd hurt the enemy bad and not been hurt ourselves. This had been a good day for I Company.

A few days later [9 September] I received orders to be prepared to move back and occupy the high ground to my rear. It went on to say that in the north, where the division front joined the ROKs, the action was increasing and that the division intended to tighten its front in our sector. I received an overlay showing me the company's new zone of responsibility and was astonished to find that it had increased from 6,800 yards to 10,800. Certainly in this instance the 1st Cavalry Division's plans had no relevancy to the 5th Cav's I Company.

I prepared plans for a night-phased withdrawal. I also sent a lieutenant with several men from each platoon to survey our new positions. Shortly after dark, in a heavy rain that was very disagreeable but helped screen us from the enemy, the company commenced its movement. I was most anxious to slip out from our forward positions undetected. It is pointless to shed blood over a position you're in the process of abandoning.

The night was very dark. After midnight the rain became a torrential downpour. But the company's withdrawal and occupation of its new positions were accomplished without difficulty. Lieutenant [Robert] Geer and I managed to erect a small pup tent. Shivering with cold and soaked to the skin, we crawled under it and took advantage of the meager protection it offered.

Pfc. VICTOR FOX
I Company/5th Cavalry

The monsoon rain was miserable. The 3d Platoon to which I was attached settled into its new positions. Nearby we discovered one of the regiment's signal groups. These people were equipped with powerful transmitters and generators and other sophisticated radio equipment. The men in this outfit let us come in out of the rain and listen to radio reports they were monitoring. We heard actual reports from Cav units north of Taegu that were engaged in heavy fighting. Sometime during the night we heard the broadcast of the enemy's Seoul City Sue. This alluring voice spoke about the glories of Communism and of intervention by the American imperialists. She also read the names of American POWs, their units, and hometowns. What surprised many of us was how much she knew, not only the locations of other units, but where the 1st Cavalry Division was and where along the line its regiment's rifle companies were. Amid all this extraordinary news she played current American hits such as "Good Night, Irene" and Nat King Cole's "Mona Lisa."

Capt. NORMAN ALLEN
I Company/5th Cavalry

Midmorning the rain slowed to a downpour. I told Geer to ditch the tent and find us a better position while I went out and checked on the rest of the company. As soon as I crawled from under the tent, I noticed a man, poncho over his head, hunkered down in a pool of water. A more miserable sight I don't believe I've ever seen. I walked over and tapped his helmet. A soft, miserable voice moaned, "Jesus Christ, leave me the fuck alone." It was my "top" [M/Sgt. Arnold Mitchell]. I identified myself and squatted beside this poor drowned rat. Obviously, my work was cut out for me. I prayed the other platoons were in better shape than the one I was in now. Somehow Sergeant Mitchell and I had to get these men up. Not only did they have to protect themselves better from the rain, but they had to establish a perimeter they could defend against an enemy attack. For the rest of the day, Mitchell and I cajoled, laughed, sympathized, and, where necessary, kicked ass.

That night the sky was clear and studded with stars. The moon wouldn't be up until after midnight. I did some pretty heavy patrolling to see if the enemy had occupied the company's old positions. They had not.

The next morning Colonel Treacy* gave me a warning order to be prepared to move out in late afternoon. I asked what we could expect in the new location. "We'll be moving north," he replied. "Battalion will be there when you arrive. One more thing, Norm. We'll be moving into a real hot spot."

I sent Geer and half a squad on ahead to reconnoiter our new positions. Then I moved around the company alerting the men that we would shortly be leaving the position. I was going to write a few letters and I thought they might want to also. I really had a bad feeling, call it a premonition, about where we were going. I knew 3d Battalion was in considerably better shape than the regiment's other battalions. We'd had our time in a relatively quiet sector. We'd drawn blood and had a little drawn on us. I felt the company had settled down very well. It was just a question of time before we were thrown

---

* Lt. Col. Edgar Treacy commanded the 5th Cavalry's 3d Battalion. In conversation, lieutenant colonels are called "colonel."

in to plug a gap or take a tough enemy position. I sat on the hill kind of reflecting on my life.

11 September 50*

Dearest Mother:

All the miseries of war have been present the last three days. Boiling sun by day, cold rain at night, trying to sleep sitting in a foxhole with four inches of water in it, covered by a poncho, wet clear to the bone, sand in our weapons and cartridge clips. Yesterday and today have given us a chance to get our clothes, socks, and shoes dried out and though our clothes are very muddy we manage to be pretty comfortable. The only "old" officer left in my company is Lieutenant Geer, my exec. The others were transferred to units that had been badly mauled and lost their officers. They themselves are casualties now. Bob Geer and I found a little ankle-deep pool on the edge of the mountain I am sitting on and washed, shaved, splashed around, knocked five days of whiskers off and eight days of dirt. Raised our morale considerably.

We are standing by today alerted to move to another sector of the front. The battalion is being committed piecemeal.

Everyone is holding up fine, still hear occasional laughter and a song, though I have to admit the majority of it is mine.

My command post is on a high ridge about five miles south of Waegwan, just a little shelter half-tent over a foxhole, but it seems like home. The men are cleaning weapons, a few are shaving or carrying water. Two mile hand carry for drinking water and eating cold rations but still the front in our immediate sector is quiet. My company now has 10,800 yards of front, that's just short of six miles. So you can see how thinly spread we are. Things should look up before too darn long. I certainly hope so—a little of this goes a real long way. Might be ages till I have another chance to write.

Hello to the rest of the family and all my love to you.

Norm

* On this day the 5th Marines began embarking at the port of Pusan for the Inch'on landings.

Along about 3:00 P.M. [11 September] an officer from 1st Battalion called me and said that my "deuce-and-a-halves" [two-and-a-half-ton trucks] were scheduled to arrive within a half hour and the company should move on down and pick them up.

Pfc. VICTOR FOX
I Company/5th Cavalry
The long drive took us through Taegu. It was there the company mess picked up and adopted a little ten-year-old Korean boy they named "Smiley."

North of Taegu the trucks climbed over a large hill mass. Coming down on the other side, the road twisted and turned every which way until it leveled off on the floor of a deep valley. Near a bridge that spanned a narrow stream the trucks stopped and I Company dismounted.

It was already dusk when the order came to saddle up and move out. We passed through a beat-up company. One of their guys said, "See if you can stop 'em. We can't."

Capt. NORMAN ALLEN
I Company/5th Cavalry
The sun had dropped down behind the mountains. We found ourselves in a bowl with high hills all around us. Shadows were beginning to lengthen. I contacted Lieutenant Geer and he pointed out the hill the company was to occupy. I stopped the men and walked over to battalion. Colonel Treacy appeared very busy and told me to get on with it as K and L Companies were already in their positions. I again asked Geer where we were going, and he kind of pointed to a dark hill mass to the right front.

To reach the foot of this hill, the company first had to cross a rice paddy. On the hill the slope quickly grew very steep. I was huffing and puffing and I could hear around me the men panting with exertion. I decided we'd drop our full field packs that included bedrolls and secondary items the men carried but weren't essential to survival.

I asked Geer, "Can you tell me exactly where we're going? Can you guide me?" He replied, "No. I haven't been up this far. It's all dark now, and I really don't know where we are." I thought, Christ

Almighty! We dropped rolls anyhow. I told the men to be quiet and not to smoke. Starting out again, I figured that when we reached the summit we'd dig in and prepare our defensive perimeter.

We climbed another forty-five minutes before cresting out on top of the hill. When I turned around I discovered I had only eight or nine men with me. No one else. The trail below was deserted. What in hell had happened to the rest of the company? I couldn't figure it out. I sent Sergeant Mitchell down the hill to see if he could find the rest of the column. In about a half hour he was back, alone. "Well," I said, "what did you find out?" He told me, "I can't find nobody." As Mitchell had been the last man to reach the crest, I asked, "Well, goddamn it, what about the man who was supposed to be right behind you? When did you last see him?" Mitchell answered, "When we dropped rolls, you said move out. I started up. When I turned around the guy behind me was bending down tightening his boot-lace. I kept on climbing. I stopped and looked back a couple of times but nobody was behind me. I figured the guys were coming along."

Here I was with less than a dozen men on top of a bloody hill that was supposed to be occupied by an entire company. I don't need to tell you the pucker strings were pretty tight. After reporting the situation to battalion, I set up a tight little defensive perimeter. We spent the night nervous. I don't mind saying, very nervous.

12 September 1950

Enemy concentrations were being built up during the night in the draw between Hills 203 and 174. So numerous were his forces on hand that small groups could be heard moving over the entire regimental front. Facing the 5th Cavalry at this time was the 3d North Korean Division, assisted by elements of the 13th Division and the 105th Armored Division, a formidable force for a half-strength regiment to engage.

UNIT HISTORY, 1ST CAVALRY DIVISION

Capt. NORMAN ALLEN
I Company/5th Cavalry
At first light I searched down the slope and into the rice paddy with my glasses, trying to trace last night's route. On my left I spotted L

Company on nearby Hill 174. On the road below I made out the battalion CP where the night before I had stopped to talk with Colonel Treacy. Some tents and a few vehicles were in the area. Then, suddenly, in the rice paddy, I noticed heads looking around, then dropping down. It looked like a bunch of young turkeys in a draw. After watching for a while, I figured this was the rest of Item. As I had all the company radios with me, I asked battalion to send someone over to the rice paddy and, if my company was there, to send it up to me.

Along one of my flanks, maybe 4,000 yards to my right, on a very high ridge, I spotted some movement. Battalion told me it was no doubt the 8th Cav's left flank. If this was so, there was then a huge gap between the 8th Cav and the 5th Cav. There was no way I could do any more than just patrol up to that ridge. Later in the morning I did send a patrol out. It came back and reported that there were GIs on top of the ridge, and since I knew they weren't from a 5th Cav unit, I assumed they belonged to the 8th Cav and left it at that.

The better part of the day [12 September] I spent organizing the company's defenses—getting the machine guns in, checking the men's sector of fire.* In the afternoon I concentrated on watching Hill 174 and a firefight L Company was involved in. Further off to their left, where I assumed K Company was, I could hear additional firing.

It was customary to leave the FO artillery party in a particular area and not have it move with any specific unit. I had left my first FO party on the Naktong, and in the early evening a new FO party (usually four men) came up and introduced themselves to me. The leader of this group was a first lieutenant, an older feller who probably had some enlisted time behind him. We conducted our business. Then I went around the company's perimeter to make sure we were set for the night and to check that the men had had a hot meal. Before I turned in, I made one last visit to the FO party. The older lieutenant followed me away from his position and told me he wanted to talk a little bit. He seemed quite apprehensive about something.

---

* On the 12th, the 1st Marine Division sailed for Inch'on.

We discussed the basic fire plan again. The guy kept looking about and I knew something was bothering him. "Well, I'm getting ready to go back to the CP," I said. "You got anything else?" "Yes, sir," he replied. "What I want to know is what will your signal be." "What signal?" I asked. "Signal for fire, or for what? We've just discussed this. What do you mean?" "Well, no," he answered, "I mean the bug-out signal." I said, "What do you mean, bug-out signal?" "Well," he said, "I've had companies bug out before and forget to tell me." "Goddamn it," I shouted, "I'm sick and tired of hearing about this 'bug out.' I don't know where you've been, but I'll tell you, this company is not bugging out anywhere. You just plan on hanging in here and doing your job because that's what all of us are gonna do. You roger that one?" He said, "Yes, sir," and returned to his position. I returned to the CP and settled down for the night.

D/T [date/time]
13/1650: Elements of L Co reach top of 174.*
13/1715: King 6 to Blue 2 [K Company CO, Capt. Ralph Curfman, to 3d Battalion]—Need of 60-mm mortar ammo—Will be delivered immediately from rear OP [outpost]. Observed about 15 NK side of Hill 203.
13/1720: Arty 3 to Blue 2 [1st Cav Division Artillery to 3d Battalion]—Ammo restriction lifted. Fire all possible targets.
13/1745: L-6 to Blue 6 [L Company CO, Gerald Perry, to 3d Battalion CO]—NK filled in all holes—getting casualties from 120-mm mortars. Do not know how long we can hold.
13/1910: Swing 2 to Blue 3 [5th Cav Regimental HQ to 3d Battalion]—Notified us that there are 60 to 70 NK assembling on N edge of Hill 174. He is putting 81-mm mortar on them.
13/2005: Blue 6 to Swing 3 [3d Battalion CO to 5th Cav Regimental HQ]—Gave Love [Company] permission to come in. L can't organize his position because he is in

*On this day the Marines were informed of the Inch'on landing details and the destroyer element of JTF-7 bombarded Wolmi-do.

fire fight and under mortar fire from Hill 203. L to
move back and tie in with King's [Company] right flank.
14/0010: L Company under Banzai attack.

S-2/3 JOURNAL, 3D BN, 5TH CAVALRY

Capt. NORMAN ALLEN
I Company/5th Cavalry
When I heard all this firing and noise, I figured it had to be coming
from L Company's position. I moved up to the FO's position to get
a good view of the battle. God almighty, there was all sorts of crashing and booming, lots of lights flashing. I could see tracers. No question, it was very heavy contact. I alerted my men, figuring whatever
had hit L Company might slip around and include us. I ordered, "No
firing whatsoever unless you've got a target right smack in front of
you."

Pfc. VICTOR FOX
I Company/5th Cavalry
We could pick out by their tracers all of L Company's automatic
weapons. Our artillery really lit up the front of L Company's positions on 174. It was very noisy and most of us felt for our comrades.
It was a rare experience to witness a fight as intense as this and not
be a part of it.

D/T
14/0015: Blue 3 [3d Battalion] called for arty [artillery].
14/0050: L Company reports attack repulsed but second build-
          ing up.
14/0100: L Company reports 2d attack and stronger than first at-
          tack.
14/0105: Blue 3 called for arty support.
14/0130: L Company reports second attack repulsed.
14/0145: Love 6 to Blue 6 [L Company to 3d Battalion CO]—
          Can't hold position. Blue 6 gave OK to fall back.
14/0145: Blue 3 to Swing 3 [3d Battalion to 5th Cavalry Regi-
          mental HQ]—Enemy attack forced L Company to

evacuate position—due complete exhaustion of ammo and heavy casualties.

S-2/3 JOURNAL, 3D BN, 5TH CAVALRY

Capt. NORMAN ALLEN
I Company/5th Cavalry
Along about 3:00 A.M. it got quiet. I went back to the CP and tried to get a little shut-eye.

14/0845: Item Company notified to assemble unit and prepare for attack.

S-2/3 JOURNAL, 3D BN, 5TH CAVALRY

Capt. NORMAN ALLEN
I Company/5th Cavalry
About 9:00 A.M. I called battalion and asked Capt. Robert Humpries, the new assistant S-3 on loan from regiment, to meet me on a small draw some 100 yards from battalion in a half hour, as I had some things I wanted to talk to him about. Mainly, I wanted to know what exactly was driving Company L from Hill 174, what their current strength was, and generally what was going to happen next? I was beginning to see the handwriting on the wall—it wouldn't be long before I Company would be going after that sonovabitching hill. Taking a radio operator, I walked down from my hill to the meeting place. Humpries just kind of shrugged when I asked what was driving Company L off the hill and informed me their strength was down to probably eighty or ninety. He said I had doped things out correctly; if regiment insisted Hill 174 be taken—over Colonel Treacy's resistance—then I should accept his remarks as a warning order to attack that day. He returned to battalion and I sat for about half an hour and formed my course of action. It was just before 10:00 A.M. when I returned to my company position. I issued a warning order to Bob Geer to be prepared to move in a couple of hours and asked him to make sure the company was heavily supplied with ammo and grenades, that the men got some good hot chow—not the C rations we usually had at noon—and that they write any letters they had paper for. Finally,

I told him to *stay loose!* With that, I again moved down the hill with a radio operator and proceeded to the battalion OP [observation post].

[In four days of punishing battle, Hill 174 had changed hands seven times. On 14 September it would be up to the men of I Company to make it eight.]

Pfc. VICTOR FOX
I Company/5th Cavalry
I Company gathered near battalion headquarters and the narrow stream for its assault on Hill 174. We had something to eat. The North Koreans were shelling right up to the highway bridge where the trucks had dropped us off two days before. Everyone filled his canteen. Lieutenant Geer briefed the platoon sergeant [M/Sgt. Wally Nelson], who was the acting platoon leader, and the four squad leaders on the attack. [Sgt. Steve] "Blackie" Furlan then gave his 3d Squad the scoop on how it was expected to assault the hill and what support it would receive. This is SOP. The idea of telling an infantryman what he is to expect and do is a good one. Unfortunately, the mess and confusion of combat are things that don't easily lend themselves to planning.

2d Lt. ADRIAN B. BRIAN
I Company/5th Cavalry
I was told my 2d Platoon would be on the left of the company. We were to attack through the rice paddies between 174 and 203. Once across the paddies, and on the left of 174, we would climb the hill and join the rest of the company on the top. We would be accompanied by two tanks which would move along a trail that skirted 174 on the west.

Capt. NORMAN ALLEN
I Company/5th Cavalry

I had originally wanted the tank platoon to split into their two sections and have one section support the company in the attack on the left, the other on the right. The tank CO refused to split the platoon. Not much I could do then but alter my plan. The tank platoon would start on the right and bring any enemy on that side of the hill under fire. It would then cross over to the left and support the other two attacking platoons on that side.

Shortly before 2:00 P.M. the tanks began to draw enemy 120-mm mortar fire and some AT/SP [antitank/self-propelled].* They rumbled back and forth to avoid what they could of it. Their CO questioned me about when I would jump off. I had been promised an air strike and was waiting for it to arrive. The enemy mortars began to find the apple orchard and my 3d Platoon that was waiting there. I kept asking battalion about the status of the air strike and they kept telling me to hold on, it was coming.

Pfc. JERRY EMER
I Company/5th Cavalry

We assembled at the foot of a hill near a small grove of peach and persimmon trees. The slope in front of us was almost a cliff. Nearby on the road were several Army vehicles. I stood near a ditch with [1st] Lieutenant [Joseph] Toomey, the 1st Platoon leader, and his runner, and was told to watch for the arrival of my platoon and, when it arrived, to point out to the men the path they should follow. Suddenly, there was a loud *whooosh;* we flattened out—BLAAM! Branches and sod rained down on us. Within seconds, two more shells fell a little farther down the ditch—BLAAM, BLAAM. Lieutenant Toomey said, "Damn, they're close." His runner and I nodded; I felt very weak and

---

* About this same time, off Wolmi-do, the destroyers of the Inch'on landing fleet reported that the enemy's guns had been silenced.

shaky. Lieutenant Toomey and the runner moved off toward the hill.
I was alone.

The whole area was now being shelled. I spotted members of my
platoon, hunched over, running toward me. I shouted and pointed
out the route they were to take to the foot of the hill. "That way!
That way!" One of our KATUSAs* ran by. *Whooosh.* BLAAM! The
KATUSA was hurled into the ditch a few yards from me, terribly hurt.
He began mumbling and whimpering. I crawled to him. One of his
arms, near the elbow, had a huge, ugly tear; there was also an irregular gaping wound which ran down his rib cage to his hips. Other
lesser injuries dotted the rest of his body. The webbing of his cartridge belt was smoking, apparently because several clips had been set
off by the explosion. I tore the belt off him. His first-aid kit was nowhere to be seen. I used my own bandage to try to stop the blood
flowing from the arm wound. I was shaking badly and didn't do a
good job. The Korean, I believe, was trying to tell me something, but
I couldn't understand him. I grabbed his canteen, which hadn't been
damaged. It was heavy. Great, I thought, I'll at least wet his lips and
be able to take a slug myself. (My canteen was already bone-dry. War
is a thirsty business.) I found his canteen was full, not with water,
but with granulated sugar. I half laughed, half cried. "The poor miserable bastard," I muttered. "Mother of God. Poor miserable bastard.
Oh, God, help me." Meanwhile, more men from my platoon ran
by. (Later, they were surprised that it wasn't me who'd been hit, covered as I was in the Korean's blood.) I shouted at one of our sergeants, "Where's the medic? Where's Smitty?" He yelled back,
"Coming. Not far behind." To my great relief I finally saw Smitty's
skinny figure hustling toward me. "Over here," I shouted. "Over here,
Smitty!" He jumped in the ditch and took over. Doyle Smith and I,
in the few weeks we'd been together, had become close buddies and
I was glad to see him. He was from a small Illinois farm town and as
American as apple pie. Lean, sandy-haired, he looked like where he
came from—the corn belt. He was engaged to a Japanese girl. He'd
shown me her picture. The Korean still mumbled and whimpered.

---

* KATUSAs (Korean Augmentation to the United States Army) were South Korean soldiers assigned to fill out American Army units.

Smitty said, "No sense wasting a bandage on that side wound, he's a goner. I'll give him a shot of morphine." In a few seconds the Korean became quiet and still, his eyes glassy. Smitty said, "OK, let's go. I'm the last of the platoon."

What a relief it was to get out of that ditch, to be moving again. We passed several dead Korean farmers, their white clothes splattered red. Another minute or two and we reached the area of our line of departure. Lieutenant Brian told me an enemy mortar had just killed two machine gunners dug in on the edge of a small grove of trees. I thought Smitty was going to have a busy day. I found water somewhere and refilled my canteen. I also washed the Korean's blood off my face and hands as best I could. I thought of Pontius Pilate.

2d Lt. ADRIAN B. BRIAN
I Company/5th Cavalry

Prior to moving out, the platoon received some mortar fire and I was concerned we might get hurt when we moved through the paddies. The rice was about waist-high and would not offer concealment to anyone walking through it. (It would, unfortunately, conceal someone lying down.) I therefore directed the men in my platoon to spread out in a more-or-less line and, when the word came, to dash quickly to the bottom of the hill. I had a full platoon, as I recall—about forty men, plus about fifteen KATUSAs.

Capt. NORMAN ALLEN
I Company/5th Cavalry

I was forward by the stone wall and orchard, watching the artillery prep on the hill, when Sergeant Nelson grabbed me. "They're pasting us in the orchard, Cap'n. We'll get knocked out before we go." I was scared as hell myself; knew we couldn't stay and continue to take it where we were. Hated like the dickens, though, to go without an air strike. Didn't know what to do. Moved the tanks up to bring direct fire on the forward slope of 174. Enemy mortars again found the range and the tanks wanted to withdraw. I ran over to their CO and yelled at him that he had all that goddamn armor around him when all we had was our fatigue jackets, and that he damn well better stay in there.

Suddenly, Colonel Treacy was there. He shouted, "Why haven't you jumped off? It's after 2:00." I explained about waiting for the air strike. He said, "Norm, you've got to go now. You can make it. I've just come from there." "Come from where, for God's sake?" I asked. "From Hill 174," he replied. "The enemy is not occupying the near knob."

Unexpectedly, four F-80s showed up and treated us to a real supporting air strike, quite a show. (First time I realized the new jet fighters could offer us close air support; I had thought they were strictly air-to-air fighters.) The jets ripped into that hill with rockets and .50-cal. I mean, they moved trees!

I called battalion and said I wanted a signal when the strafing run had been completed because I wanted to jump off immediately to take advantage of the shock effect upon the enemy. Battalion answered they would have the artillery fire a WP [white phosphorus] round, then commence their supporting fire. The fighters left, the WP came in. I yelled, "OK, let's go!" And off we went.

Pfc. VICTOR FOX
I Company/5th Cavalry
We dashed out of the orchard and across the rocky streambed. Through very heavy enemy small-arms, mortar, and artillery fire, the platoon began to climb toward the summit of Hill 174. The main thrust of the company's attack appeared to go along the streambed and then up the hill's left side. My 3d Platoon went up slightly to the right of the hill, on either side of a ridge that led to the summit.

From the streambed that was now behind us, tanks fired their cannons and machine guns on the objective. Artillery whooshed and moaned overhead, then crashed on the hill's forward slopes.

Pfc. JERRY EMER
I Company/5th Cavalry
When we entered the rice paddies, we were urged to keep in a skirmish line and not bunch up. Because of the heavy rains in early September, the paddies were filled with water and footing was very soft. Loaded with extra ammo and grenades, we sank into the stinking muck

with every step. As fate would have it, the day was bright, hot, and humid. It wasn't long before we were all panting and gasping for air.

Capt. NORMAN ALLEN
I Company/5th Cavalry
Things weren't too bad for about the first 150 yards—good progress, some mortar fire. We were pretty much shielded from direct fire by the near knob of 174. But, as Toomey's and Beech's platoons cleared the direct shield of the knob, enemy fire increased in variety and intensity, and became very heavy. Toomey's 1st Platoon was somewhere on my right and out of sight. On the hill I looked down on Beech's platoon in the rice and saw men falling right and left.

Pfc. JERRY EMER
I Company/5th Cavalry
The North Korean mortars began to hit among us. A real barrage. Soon I heard cries all around me, "I'm hit. Medic. Medic." Beech Brian called to me, "Stick with Sergeant Odom."

2d Lt. ADRIAN B. BRIAN
I Company/5th Cavalry
The going through the rice was slow. We had barely started when the mortars found us in the open. With their first shells they were among us. One landed about ten yards to my left front. The blast folded me over from the waist as if I had run into a hidden wire. A KATUSA near me was severely wounded, and shrapnel tore a hole the diameter of a silver dollar in the lower stomach of my platoon medic, a kid we called Smitty.

When I saw how severely Smitty was wounded, I sent my platoon runner, Covington, back to guide up some litter-bearers. (He went back and told the bearers where the wounded were in the rice, but did not guide them himself. He stayed with the company kitchen people. All this I was to learn later.) Smitty cried with pain and fear. "Don't wanna die." I told him not to worry, that I had sent back for help. When I tried to raise him to wrap a bandage around the wound, he screamed with pain. He told me he felt sick to his stomach and he stuck a finger down his throat. As soon as he did, his stomach heaved and the pressure on his muscles forced about a foot of intestines to spill out the hole in his belly. I didn't know what to do. My main responsibility was my platoon and I knew I had to join them before they got too far ahead of me. I draped a bandage over the wound to keep the flies off, then strung a linen bandage from Smitty to the nearest rice-paddy dike. There I tied the end to Smitty's carbine (in Korea medics carried weapons since the NKs didn't respect the Geneva Convention) and laid the weapon on the dike so the litter-bearers Covington was bringing up would be able to follow the bandage back to where Smitty lay hidden in the rice. I checked on the wounded KATUSA and found him unconscious but close enough to the dike to be seen.

I then moved forward. Maybe five minutes had elapsed. I caught up with the remnants of my platoon, about twenty men, huddled at the base of the hill. I got them moving again on up the hill.

Capt. NORMAN ALLEN
I Company/5th Cavalry
Battalion began to press me for information. I had to tell them to clear the net so I could handle my supporting fire. Battalion insisted, said regiment wanted to know our progress. "Fuck regiment," I yelled. "If they want to know what's going on, tell the bastards to come forward, look for themselves. I'm being hard-pressed, everyone's into it. Clear the goddamn net so's I can manage my fire! Out!"

I was about twenty yards short of the crest of the near knob and saw the lead squad make the top only to be swept away by a volley of artillery fire, which I have always suspected was our own 155-mm. A second squad quickly followed into that havoc, only to be swept from the objective as well. I knew there wasn't much left of Nelson's 3d Platoon. We finally rushed for the crest and jumped into prepared shelters. Beech joined me from the left and I asked him how many men he had left. He replied, "No more than fifteen, if that!" I knew I could not expect him to continue the attack and instructed him to hold with Nelson.

Pfc. VICTOR FOX
I Company/5th Cavalry
Third Platoon went into a skirmish line. Machine guns and BARs laid down heavy covering fire. A North Carolinian, Bill Haltom, and I were on the point. Sergeant Furlan stayed close. I have no idea what happened on either side or behind me, but I did hear the loud noise of a large firefight going on to my left. Enemy fire around my platoon was heavy and we returned this fire. Near the top we dashed to the summit with fixed bayonets, firing all the way. We found the enemy had pulled back. I glanced around quickly and saw a narrow ridge or spine that led 300 to 400 yards to another hilltop which was designated 174.1 on the maps. The North Koreans had withdrawn there. The ridge that bridged the two summits was gouged by deeply eroded gullies or ravines that cut to the base of the hill. This moonlike landscape was partially covered with dusty shrubs and brush. The tops of both hills were rock bare.

Experienced World War II veterans had cautioned that once an objective has been gained, the assault team must continue to move forward as the enemy will certainly lay down artillery and mortar fire on it. On 174 he did. Haltom and I moved forward. On the right of the spine connecting the two hilltops, we crawled from one gully to another. We got so close to the enemy that we could easily see the muzzle flashes from their rifles and machine guns. We were literally under their gunsights. Because they were concentrating on their left where I Company's main attack was slowly proceeding, they failed to notice Haltom and me.

We stopped and looked around us. Except for Lieutenant Toomey, who was crouched in another gully, we were alone. I noticed the lieutenant had a worried look on his face. All around a terrific battle was taking place. Oddly, no friendly artillery fire fell on the enemy's position. Maybe they knew we were there.

Capt. NORMAN ALLEN
I Company, 5th Cavalry
Toomey was in front of the enemy's position and over the radio argued with me about sending the rest of the company forward to where

he was. He felt from there we could take the whole hill. It was a tough call. I understood his reluctance to give up what he had won, but he didn't know the condition of the rest of the company. Our front was being raked by enemy fire and any attempt to advance down the ridge would have been murder. The terrain on the left was more broken than on the right. The men were exhausted and running low on ammunition. I realized it would be tough to hold what we had, let alone grab more. I ordered Toomey to withdraw.

Pfc. VICTOR FOX
I Company/5th Cavalry
The lieutenant crawled over and told us to "haul ass" out of there. Haltom and I—remember, we were both just kids—thought we could take 174.1. Reminding us that we were without grenades (which we'd used clearing the first hill) and support from the rest of the company, the lieutenant convinced us to pull back.

We skittered down, over and through the gullies we'd used in our advance. The North Koreans finally spotted us and paid us some attention. It took quite some time for us to get back. We had to time our leaps and runs very carefully. One of our machine guns helped cool off the enemy's fire. I learned later it was being fired by one of the company's World War II veterans, Sergeant Pate. His covering fire was laid so low that if we three retreating soldiers hadn't kept down he would have given our butts another hole. After this I had a lot of respect for Pate.

Sgt. F/C DONALD PATE
I Company/5th Cavalry
During the attack my squad's machine gunner, Cpl. Bill Taylor, was wounded in the head by mortar and rock fragments. I picked up the gun, leaving the tripod with Taylor. I managed to fire the gun during

the rest of the attack by bracing the pintle against whatever rocks were nearby.

2d Lt. ADRIAN B. BRIAN
I Company/5th Cavalry

On top of the hill we did our best to dig in while trying to get cover in little folds in the rocky surface. All we could really do was build small rock walls out of loose shale, which covered the ground. You couldn't get a tool into the ground if your life depended on it, which it did.

Pfc. VICTOR FOX
I Company/5th Cavalry

Back on the forward slope of Hill 174, as we were scrambling around for position, the enemy laid some heavy mortar fire on us. This went on for hours. Many men were wounded. Once Sergeants Furlan, Nelson, and I were crouched in a wedge of a ravine when a mortar round landed nearby. I felt a burning sensation on my shoulders and back. "I'm hit," I yelled. Sergeant Nelson grinned and brushed off some hot shell fragments. "You're all right," he said. It appeared that the men I saw during this bombardment were punch-drunk from the concussion of the explosions that rained around us.

Sgt. F/C DONALD PATE
I Company/5th Cavalry

The damn hill was made of rock covered by a few inches of soil. This made preparation of a gun position or digging a foxhole very difficult, as the rock had to be broken up and taken out in layers. In abandoning the hill the night before, one of our companies [L] had left behind a quantity of ammunition which we now collected and prepared to use. I gathered many parachute flares which could be fired from a rifle and a fair number of high-explosive fragmentary grenades. We also gathered some North Korean concussion grenades, which looked like a can of beans with a detonator. I showed the men in the squad how to rig grenades with trip wires so anyone moving at night in our area would blow themselves to pieces. Enemy fire continued to fall all around the company.

Pfc. VICTOR FOX
I Company/5th Cavalry

Constant machine-gun and small-arms fire drove what was left of I Company over the skyline of 174 and back down on the reverse slope. There we had a breather from the enemy's bullets but not from his mortars. I wanted to see what was happening in front of me and looked over the rim. Sergeant Furlan warned, "Fox, better keep your head down." I ducked my head and an enemy machine gun, just like in the movies, clipped the ground above me.

Word came that we would again have to take the forward slope. Timing was everything. The men scampered back over the skyline, all wildly looking for holes to dive into. One- and two-man holes had already been dug by the enemy. Because the ground was solid rock, it was hard to dig them deeper or widen them. On the forward slope, the only way the enemy's damnable mortars could get anyone was if they landed right in the hole with him. Sometimes this happened and it was an awful sight.

Item Company's perimeter defense did not seem to cover a large area. Each soldier concentrated his firepower on the field of fire he was assigned. Recoilless riflemen crawled near our positions to get off decent shots, then scampered away when the enemy responded with heavy and rapid fire. We guys in the holes were left to take it. The 57-mm RR is a one-man walking artillery piece. When it is fired it makes a hell of a noise, belches fire and smoke from its muzzle, and, what's worse, raises clouds of dust and dirt from the backblast. The enemy notices this. Everyone wants RR supporting fire. It's just that he wants it from someone else's location.

Before I Company arrived on the scene, Hill 174 had changed hands many times. You knew the North Koreans were under heavy pressure when they did not remove their dead. The summit was covered with enemy dead. In front of Haltom's and my hole sprawled about twenty North Korean bodies in grotesque positions. This was just in our immediate area. In the days ahead the total would grow. Haltom and I were by now fairly immune to the sight of dead bodies. We had to live, so while a couple of dead gooks glazed coldly at us, we ate our C rations. Let it be said that there is nothing more dead than a dead human body. Period.

14/1620: To Blue 1 [Administration, 3d Battalion] Get as many litters here as quickly as possible.

14/1625: Item 6 to Blue 1 [Captain Allen to 3d Battalion] Have arty moved forward . . . last fire landed in our troops. Arty notified.

14/1638: I Company request all available MG ammo be sent forward immediately.

S-2/3 JOURNAL, 3D BN, 5TH CAVALRY

Capt. NORMAN ALLEN
I Company/5th Cavalry
When I scanned the valley and slope the company had used in the attack, and saw the number of wounded and dead that lay there, I was sick, sick and frightened over what had happened to us. I knew the only thing we were capable of doing now was holding on to what we had. I had to get help for the wounded, but couldn't spare anyone myself.

2d Lt. ADRIAN B. BRIAN
I Company/5th Cavalry
After we secured the hilltop and Captain Allen set up his command post, I went back to it to assure myself litter-bearers had come up for Smitty and all the others. (Back to the CP was about fifteen to twenty yards behind the forward foxhole.) When the company CP moved forward they laid field wire so they'd have telephone contact with the battalion CP. The first sergeant told me medics had come forward and had already picked up wounded from the route of my platoon advance through the rice paddies.

Capt. NORMAN ALLEN
I Company/5th Cavalry

About 5:00 P.M. the shadows lengthened and, because of higher hills
around us, the light began to fade. I told Blue [3d Battalion] they
would have to get carrying parties with ammo and water up to me at
once. I explained I couldn't spare a man to go after it. I also told
them that Heavy Weapons Company and Headquarters Company
would have to form carrying parties to get my wounded off the field
and back to the aid station. At this, Major [Edward] Mayer [3d Battalion executive officer] asked how many wounded I had. I answered
that near as I could tell I had between eighty and ninety. He replied
that he didn't realize we had taken this sort of a beating and asked
why I hadn't reported it during the attack. "Jesus Christ, Ed," I said,
"I couldn't keep looking for Blankenship [my communications sergeant who carried the radio]. I was too busy hitting the ground, jumping
up, firing my weapons, and throwing grenades to think about informing battalion of anything except shifting fire support. A good part of
the time getting on top of this goddamn hill it was every man for
himself." He understood and immediately got cracking on the resupply and carrying parties for the wounded. I told him he would have
to get the carrying parties out as quickly as he could. If he didn't, the
light would fade before all my wounded in the high grass could be
found.

Darkness fell before all tasks were accomplished and that put an
end to things. As I could no longer adequately cover the litter parties,
they withdrew. There was one man in the valley to the left they could
not see or get to; I believe to this day that we got all the rest. When
I asked "Top," the first sergeant, if he thought we could get to that
man, he replied, "Sir, we can't spare a man to go and we couldn't
cover him if we did, and, besides, the guy's probably dead anyway."
I pursued it no further. We were all suffering from the trauma of the
ferocity of the attack; we had sustained eighty-nine casualties, including some of our new KATUSAs, who were not officially reported beyond battalion level.

I returned to Lieutenant Geer's position, where I had intended
to put my CP, only to find we did not have a true position, only a
very shallow erosion ditch on the line. I was too tired and exhausted
to complain, and lay down ahead of Geer, his head at my feet.

Pfc. VICTOR FOX
I Company/5th Cavalry

Once the sun went down I knew they would begin to probe. Haltom's and my front-hole position was a risky place to be. We laid out grenades which had the pins partially pulled.

During the night, when we weren't under actual attack, our artillery randomly laid down fire in front of I Company's positions. We soon realized that white phosphorus was what we wanted. With all that white stuff lying on the ground, the gooks could easily be detected crawling across it. The artillery also fired flares that really lit up the area. These had a problem, though; for long minutes afterward a flare destroys night vision.

With quiet efficiency the enemy used the gullies and crevices Haltom, Toomey, and I had used earlier in the day. It was pitch-dark and you could imagine all sorts of things happening in them. The enemy tried to spook us into firing our weapons to reveal our positions. It was the last thing we wanted to do. An enemy grenade would end the shooters' chances of surviving until morning. Throughout the night our machine gunners worked their bolts back and forth. This sound seemed to freeze even the enemy's breathing. The air was filled with tension. The North Koreans are a patient people and they waited for their opportunity. At times I swear I heard them whispering. I know I smelled the odor of garlic.

Capt. NORMAN ALLEN
I Company/5th Cavalry

The night was darker than a whore's heart. The company lay on a rocky, barren hilltop. We were 700 yards from the nearest friendly troops and surrounded by gooks who lay in the dark waiting for us to move.

Before we had jumped off in the attack, I'd told the company we would not withdraw. We were going to hold our holes and fight. When morning came, I told them, maybe dead, maybe alive, we would be on that hill. It was our only chance. If we got shoved off, we'd only have to fight our way back and that was more deadly than holding and fighting.

Nevertheless, the night of September 14–15 was a real hell—a month long, dark and cold. Dear God, I hope I never spend another as terrible. My eyes peered into the darkness until they ached, even my goose pimples ached. My ears rotated like radar dishes.

14/2340: Item 6 reports a small banzai attack on Item CP area.
S-2/3 JOURNAL, 3D BN, 5TH CAVALRY

Capt. NORMAN ALLEN
I Company/5th Cavalry
We repelled the first attack. The next one succeeded in getting into my CP. A gook stepped on my back. Knowing he had hit something soft, he knelt behind me and tried to figure out what it was. In the dark his eyes looked like a nest of young owls. My carbine lay just two feet away; I could have easily stretched out and reached it. I was too afraid to move. He was silhouetted against the dark sky. I sneaked my hand very slowly to my shoulder holster, pulled the slide of my .45 slowly, slowly back, and aimed over my left shoulder. The .45 exploded. I'm sure I almost blew my left ear off. The shot went true.

14/2355: Item 6 to Blue 5—Some casualties from attack on CP but otherwise all OK.
15/0015: Item 6 called desiring info about casualty evacuating of litter cases. Told to wait 'til light.
15/0045: Item 6—Things are rather quiet.
S-2/3 JOURNAL, 3D BN, 5TH CAVALRY

Capt. NORMAN ALLEN
I Company/5th Cavalry
What truly made the night a horror was one of my mortally wounded men who lay all night not twenty yards from me. Wanting a doctor, wanting off the hill, wanting water, he continued to cry out throughout the long night. I sent the medic out time after time and later crawled down to him myself. All we could do was make him as comfortable as possible.

15/0215: Called Item 6—Reports he is drawing small arms and
grenades sporadically in CP area.*

S-2/3 JOURNAL, 3D BN, 5TH CAVALRY

Pfc. VICTOR FOX
I Company/5th Cavalry
It is impossible to know how many enemy died that night. All night
long we exchanged grenades—the heavy WHOOOMP of the North
Korean concussion grenades against the explosive ZINNNG of our
fragmentation grenade. Once in a while from the darkened crevices
I could hear the sound of some enemy soldier catching the full force
of the blast. Then would come the muffled sound of the wounded
soldier being dragged away.

Bill Haltom and I developed into a good team. I kept my eyes
peeled for creeping enemy movement. Haltom, with his longer arms,
batted or swept grenades away from our hole. All night I heard other
GIs around us doing the same thing.

Capt. NORMAN ALLEN
I Company, 5th Cavalry
We begged the wounded lad to our front to hang on until morning
when we'd be able to take him off the hill. With the first gray light
the man lay quiet, then he was still. I lay there helpless, numb, sick
clear through. I asked God in his infinite mercy, "Why so long?" The
man died a little boy, wanting his mother, crying for her, asking for
his God. That night has left a long, deep scar.

Pfc. VICTOR FOX
I Company/5th Cavalry
When daylight came into its fullness the heavy exchanges of long-
range machine-gun fire from both sides resumed. Near misses sounded

---

*About this time, aboard USS *Diachenko*, the 3d Battalion, 5th Marines, was awakened and
began preparing for its landing on Wolmi-do.

like cracking whips. It left my ears ringing. Enemy small-arms fire rained down on our positions. Corpses left in the open were hit time and time again. Then, along with their mortars, the enemy brought up SP [self-propelled] guns and let go at us with them. BANG when they fired, WHEEEYOWWW when they hit. I could hear Captain Allen yelling into the radio for counter battery fire to neutralize these guns. BANG! WHEEEYOWWW! My eyes rolled in their sockets. If anything, enemy fire intensified as the morning moved along.

> 15/0835: Blue 6 to Item 6—Plan for an eventual withdrawal if necessary to wall [3d Bn CP].
> 15/0925: I Co expects heavy attack. . . . Request arty on valley to left front.*
>
> S-2/3 JOURNAL, 3D BN, 5TH CAVALRY

Capt. NORMAN ALLEN
I Company/5th Cavalry
I could see large groups of North Koreans in the valley between us and K Company. They milled around like they didn't know what to do. They also began to move down the valley on our right, and in smaller numbers along the high ridge that ran parallel to 174 and 174.1. They must have been very confused when Hills 127 and 203, which they assumed they held, opened fire on them. Around 10:00 A.M. I had more targets than I could get fire missions for.

I reported to Colonel Treacy that the enemy was so bold and careless in their efforts to seek cover and concealment that they must be part of a large force. I stated that I believed if I and K Companies were not withdrawn, and soon, to the bridge in the valley where a roadblock could be established, the enemy would simply bypass the hills and continue their attack along the road. Colonel Treacy asked if I could hold until 11:00 A.M. I told him it might be touch and go, but I would try. I passed the word to the company that we would soon be in one hell of a fight and would have to hold until 11:00, no matter what!

---

* An hour and a half earlier, 3d Battalion, 5th Marines, signaled that Wolmi-do had been secured.

> 15/1056: Blue 6 to Item 6—Prepare to execute BAKER [withdrawal back down to the road].
>
> S-2/3 JOURNAL, 3D BN, 5TH CAVALRY

Capt. NORMAN ALLEN
I Company/5th Cavalry
I counted the minutes and kept up as much fire as I could. A little before 11:00 I reported to Colonel Treacy that it was apparent to me the enemy was about to launch a daytime attack in force against us and that sizable forces on both sides were about to outflank my position. "It's gonna be a real squeeze. When I pull back it will be a last-minute thing. Everybody back there better understand, we'll be moving fast like a sonovabitch."

> 15/1105: To Item 6—Execute BAKER.
> 15/1106: From Blue 3 to Love 6—Prepare to cover I withdrawal.
> 15/1108: Blue 3 to King 6—Assist I withdrawal if possible with fire.
>
> S-2/3 JOURNAL, 3D BN, 5TH CAVALRY

Capt. NORMAN ALLEN
I Company/5th Cavalry
It was important to move quickly and, under the circumstances, in good order. To delay even an unnecessary minute for the sake of organization could mean disaster. My orders were simple, brief, and, no doubt, sketchy. I wanted off fast. We would cover as best we could 1st Platoon [Toomey's], which was by itself on the right side of the hill. Then when they were clear, the two platoons on the left [Nelson's and Brian's] would leapfrog their way to the bottom.

As 11:00 approached I was damn glad I hadn't agreed to trying to hold out any longer, for the enemy was detected moving close up on the right, almost within grenade range of Toomey's platoon. Minutes were becoming critical. At 11:00 straight up, I radioed battalion, "I'm coming off, now!" And gave the order to move back in order,

but to move smartly! No one had to be told twice. I don't think there
was much running, but there was a lot of jogging for damn sure!

Pfc. VICTOR FOX
I Company/5th Cavalry
No one ran and no one had the "Bug Out Blues." We still had the
capacity to fight. The noise was tremendous. With L Company and
K Company also under attack on adjacent hills, the noise reached a
crescendo. Third Platoon vacated its positions under heavy enemy fire.
Once around the right side of 174's summit, the platoon was free from
enemy small-arms fire. Their mortars, however, continued to punish
us.

> 15/1115: I Company surrounded. 150 enemy to east & 200 en-
> emy to west.
> 15/1120: CP burning maps and documents in preparation for fight
> out of area.
> 15/1120: Mortars ordered to shoot the works in covering retreat
> of I Company.
>
> S-2/3 JOURNAL, 3D BN, 5TH CAVALRY

Pfc. VICTOR FOX
I Company/5th Cavalry
Someone shouted, "It's every man for himself!" I thought, What'n
hell do I do now? I remembered, or someone told me, to get back to
the streambed, wall, hamlet, orchard road. About halfway down that
damnable hill I found myself alone. The North Koreans must have
closed in right behind us. The world was again filled with air-crack-
ing fire; my ears rang with it. I did not run—my wits told me that
would lead to panicking—but I sure as heck didn't dawdle, either.

Near the bottom of Hill 174 and not too far from the streambed, I came across a wounded GI who could no longer make it on
his own. Although I didn't know his name, he knew mine. "Fox,
please don't leave me here." "Don't worry," I told him, "if you get
it, we'll both get it." I could not see the enemy behind me. This didn't

prevent me, however, from emptying two clips in their direction. For the moment the deadly whipping noises around my ears stopped. I took the arm of this young GI, put it around my shoulders and together we stumbled toward the streambed. Suddenly, I heard a man's voice say, "Don't worry, Victor, don't worry. Everything is going to be all right." I never learned if the wounded GI also heard this voice. Maybe my nerves were approaching that "1,000-mile look" or I was simply going batty, but this soothing voice gave me renewed vigor to keep going.

15/1155: Item Company 150 yards from wall and closing fast.
S-2/3 JOURNAL, 3D BN, 5TH CAVALRY

Capt. NORMAN ALLEN
I Company/5th Cavalry
We came off 174 man by man. There was no one route down the hill that was better or worse than another. Every man found his own way. We held up at the stone wall to catch our breath and so that I could make a rough head count. I also wanted to be sure K Company was off 203. What to do next? That goddamned SP and a dug-in North Korean tank made the most horrible-sounding firing noises. One round hit a dead tree next to the wall and sprayed us. It was then, 100 yards apart, that we moved out on the run.

Pfc. VICTOR FOX
I Company/5th Cavalry
When the wounded GI and I arrived at the streambed, a terrific fight was being fought near where the company had launched its assault the morning before. In broad daylight the North Koreans were attacking in mass down the streambed.

15/1214: Switchboard being removed. P & A [Pioneer and Ammunition] Platoon will hold gray wall until "I" is in position.
S-2/3 JOURNAL, 3D BN, 5TH CAVALRY

Pfc. VICTOR FOX
I Company/5th Cavalry
Guys from battalion headquarters ran up and took the wounded man off my hands. I next found myself behind the headquarters position near the edge of the hamlet by the base of Hill 203. With all that was happening, I expected K Company to come streaming off Hill 203 at any moment. K Company held.

> 15/1216: I Company clears thru CP. Further ordered to place unit on high ground across river to cover bridge.
> 15/1320: From Swing 3 [Regimental HQ CP]. Must hold present position.
>
> s-2/3 JOURNAL, 3D BN, 5TH CAVALRY

Pfc. VICTOR FOX
I Company/5th Cavalry
Along the base of 203 a path ran next to a mud wall. I found many of the men from the company gathered along this path. About this time 3d Battalion got everyone up on the line—cooks, clerks, truck drivers, radio operators.

Capt. NORMAN ALLEN
I Company/5th Cavalry
It looked for a bit like the gooks were going to come all the way to the bridge. That would have given us a very bad time. Our tanks under the bridge and the 4.2s [mortars] really poured their fire on them. The heavy machine guns did their job, too. This is when the North Koreans broke off their attack.

Pfc. VICTOR FOX
I Company/5th Cavalry
I ran across a buddy, Joe Blunt, from Minneapolis. Blunt sat off the path and appeared to be in shock. His face was the color of the wall— gray. I asked him how he was doing. He answered, "Oh, God!" A

few steps farther I found John Irons, another buddy. He lay on the ground and gasped for air. I looked around for my 3d Platoon. Then I heard a sudden rush of air, nothing else. A dozen GIs stood nearby. In front of me there was a flash of light. Silence. The stone wall buckled, then smeared like a stained watercolor picture.

I next remember Sergeant Nelson kneeling over me. I lay on a stretcher. I do not know why, but I was angry. I struggled off the stretcher and wobbled to my feet. Captain Allen wanted me evacuated. I refused. I wanted to rejoin my squad. All around were dead and wounded GIs. A man stood directly in front of me. Obviously in shock, his face looked serene. He stared at me. One of his arms hung from the shoulder by ribbons of flesh. It matters very much that today I cannot remember which arm it was.

Sometime in the afternoon a group I was with headed to the battalion's right flank. Haltom was with me. Fifty yards away a group of GIs, which included John Irons, was bracketed by enemy mortar fire. Three rounds seemed to explode at once. Irons appeared to be in the middle of the explosions.

Capt. NORMAN ALLEN
I Company/5th Cavalry
About 4:30 in the afternoon Colonel Treacy called me on the radio and told me I would have to retake Hill 174 before dark. The men, myself included, were exhausted, hungry, thirsty, and mentally fatigued. I told him that to do so he'd have to come up and whip my ass, because to get my men to go back that afternoon I would have to whip each of theirs. The order was one of those so often typical of regiment. This time it must have been their reaction to the news earlier in the day of the Inch'on landings.* Colonel Treacy said that he would intercede with regiment about attacking that afternoon, but I could bloody well plan on going the next morning.

---

* At Inch'on, an hour later, the 1st Marine Division landed on BLUE and RED Beaches.

Pfc. VICTOR FOX
I Company/5th Cavalry
When night arrived I was somehow still in the vicinity of the streambed
and mud wall. Around me was one of M Company's 81-mm mortar
sections. This was the front line. The mortars fired furiously and never
stopped. Since I was in no shape to help them, the mortar men let
me sleep.

Before first light [16 September] some SOB kicked me awake,
informing me I had it easy and should stay awake. When the sun
came up, I Company—what was left of it—gathered for another go
at Hill 174. We heard that B-29s were going to prep the enemy for
us. Later we heard the cloud cover was too low and the bombing
mission had been scrubbed. Sometime that morning the regimental
history reports that we learned the Marines had successfully landed
behind the enemy at Inch'on. I don't remember receiving this information.

Capt. NORMAN ALLEN
I Company/5th Cavalry
Colonel Treacy came up a little before 1:00 P.M. and sat with me.
We watched as the men formed up and moved down the trail toward
Hill 174. Colonel Treacy pointed to one of the men. "That man
doesn't have a weapon. Why doesn't he?" I ran over to the man.
"Where's your weapon, soldier?!" He glanced at me, then dropped
his head: "What the fuck does it matter, sir? I'm gonna be killed anyway." I unslung my carbine and roughly thrust it at him. "Goddamn
you, take mine. Knock that shit off." He took it and plodded away,
his head still down. I figured as soon as someone shot at him he'd
shoot back. I returned to Colonel Treacy and picked up an M-1 from
the stack collected from wounded men who'd been evacuated. I explained my plan of attack to Colonel Treacy. He said, a bit wearily,
"Norm, what does it matter? You took that damn hill for the eighth
time two days ago; this will be the ninth. The enemy has every possible approach covered and registered. God go with you."

When it was time to hit the hill I called the platoon leaders together and issued a very brief order: "OK, we're gonna hit 174 from
a slightly different direction, platoons in the same order as yester-

day—Toomey right, Nelson center, Beech left. Stay in close. When
we get on top, have each man occupy the position he had the night
of the 14th. Be ready to repel a counterattack. When I give the order
to go, everyone'll go like hell from right here. Don't stop for anything; casualties we'll get later. You won't know where anyone is, so
no grenades. This is gonna be a balls-to-the-wall go. Remember, no
man stops! Questions? OK, take five. We'll wait here five minutes.
I'll put down a TOT, then walk it along the crest. Hot chambers [a
round in the chamber] and fixed bayonets."

Pfc. VICTOR FOX
I Company/5th Cavalry
As far as 3d Platoon goes, the attack on the 16th up Hill 174 followed
the identical route as the attack on the 14th had. This time, however,
the company received tremendous artillery support, more thunderous
even than two days before. Tanks moved up the streambed and, unlike the first attack, they stayed and plastered the top of the hill. Enemy opposition was light. What was left of the 3d Platoon made its
final charge on the summit with fixed bayonets.

Bill Haltom and I raced to the same two-man open fighting hole
we had occupied earlier. We leaped in feet first and landed on a spongy
bottom. The North Koreans had buried one of their dead in the hole
and covered him with a spoonful of soil. (As far as I know, that body
still lies on Hill 174.) Around our positions the enemy dead lay in
terrible positions. Most had been badly mangled by artillery fire.

All day, long-range firefights erupted between the summits of 174
and 174.1. The North Koreans pounded our positions with heavy
mortar and lots of SP fire.* The day was very hot. The same dead
North Korean lay near the rim of Haltom's and my hole. Now he
was black and swollen. The stench he gave off, combined with that
of the other corpses, became stifling. In all the time I spent on 174,
there was never an opportunity to remove the corpses that surrounded
us. The continual, deadly firefight made any such venture an impos-
sibility. (As a matter of fact, unless you could wait until darkness, you

---

*On the Inch'on-Seoul road the Marines ambushed the enemy tanks outside Ascom City and
Frank Muetzel was wounded and evacuated.

relieved yourself where you crouched.) While eating our C rations amid this human carnage, Haltom and I had time to contemplate how the human body is put together from the brains to the feet. There were certainly enough dissected examples lying about for close-up analysis.

The night was cool. In the darkness I still could make out the North Koreans crawling out of the gullies and into our perimeter. Throughout the night the two sides bombarded each other with grenades. Between midnight and 4:00 A.M., our artillery helped keep the enemy at bay.

In one of the aprons of white phosphorus that lay around us, I discovered a dark form. I stared at it interminably. It seemed to move ever so slightly. When early sunlight revealed the dark form to be a North Korean, the question arose, was the body dead or alive or booby-trapped? Word arrived that if alive, the CP wanted it for questioning. Who now would leave his hole and drag the body back? Haltom and I, like everyone else, had already strained the law of averages to the breaking point and were not about to volunteer. A GI finally ventured out and dragged the enemy soldier in. The enemy did not open fire, which led us to believe that they wanted us to take their man and not for any humanitarian reasons either. The last I recall of this North Korean was that he was alive and being taken back to battalion.

I had experienced moments of giddiness ever since I'd been mortared. Now, in the morning [17 September],* I shattered my glasses on my M1 rifle sight. Being nearsighted, I was useless to I Company without glasses. This, coupled with my injuries of the day before, helped Captain Allen decide I should leave the hill. Men left Hill 174 at their own risk. They were on their own until they reached 3d Battalion HQ on the other side of the stream. This is how I finally left Hill 174, by myself. When I reached the aid station, I was still carrying my rifle. The next thing I recall is coming to on a blood-soaked stretcher in the Taegu railroad station.

---

*The day the 1st Marines fought through the roadblock at Mahang-ri.

Capt. NORMAN ALLEN
I Company/5th Cavalry
K Company passed through us [17 September] and attempted to take
174.1. Just short of the objective they were turned back and left five
dead under the brow of the hill. For the next three days we had to
stare at these five bodies, arms outspread, stranded against the rocky
crest. A terrible sight, but there was nothing to do but look. At this
point I believe the men in I Company learned to hate. It is very important for infantrymen to hate; it's easier to meet the enemy when
you do, when you're at the end of the rope—hungry, desperate,
sleepless, mean, angry. That's when you concentrate your emotions
on them, the sonovabitches that got you there. If you can't hate, you
might hesitate before pulling the trigger and the hesitation could kill
you.

Colonel Treacy told me to hold tight to what I had of Hill 174
and not try again for the far end of the ridge [174.1]. The next three
days were miserable. On the 18th they poured 120s [mortars] on us.
Our mortars and artillery returned the fire. On either side of the ridge,
machine guns fired at anything that moved.

Sgt. F/C DONALD PATE
I Company/5th Cavalry
There was damned little division artillery support and the company
relied heavily on the mortars from the company, battalion, and regiment. Rounds for the mortars were somewhat limited and occasionally we were told we could only have one or two shells at a time.
This produced many comments among the troops like "What a hell
of a way to fight a war." At least it gave us something to bitch about,
and that's always good for morale.

The mortar fire from the enemy intensified and we continued to
have difficulty getting counterbattery fire. We did receive a resupply
of ammo for our weapons, and some peanut-butter-and-jelly sandwiches were sent up from the kitchen. Those sandwiches were more
welcome than the ammunition. Next to a letter from home, food is
always on a combat soldier's mind. Also, the pocket Bible many of
us carried got a lot of use while we waited in our foxholes for the
enemy to do something or for orders to attack.

Capt. NORMAN ALLEN
I Company/5th Cavalry

We used to have one man out of a platoon (which at this point was
no larger than a squad) gather canteens and run to the rear to a small
stream for water. It was about 500 yards to the stream and the man
would run like hell, all the time being worked over by enemy small-
arms fire. He'd run down and back, ducking, dodging, cutting. We'd
all watch and cheer him on. It was our morning soap opera. We all
realized how important and dangerous the mission was, so the runner
really held center stage. First time or two, men were somewhat reluctant to volunteer, but, thereafter, not. Frequently they would return to the perimeter laughing; they'd outfoxed the enemy and that
was a real achievement. There would be great rejoicing and backslapping. Each man would be the star of the hour and he'd enjoy every
moment of it. One stalwart soul, as he was running back, stopped
and pointed for the enemy's benefit to where he was going to run
next. He then cut the other way and an enemy burst struck where he
had pointed. I told the man's platoon leader not to send this bird again,
as he was making too much of a game out of it. The game he was
playing was against death, a game he couldn't win.

I remember another time—it was on the 18th—I was sitting on
the reverse slope of the hill away from the small-arms fire. Sergeant
Wilson was shaving nearby and had his mirror propped up against
some rocks. He had a great sense of humor and when things got tense
he always managed to say something cheerful. With death and dying
all around, Wilson would grin and shout to me, "Hey, Cap'n, I eat
this shit up." I'd laugh at this. He always found a way to lighten the
load on my shoulders. On the morning of the 18th, I chided him
about shaving: "A good soldier, Sergeant, oughta shave in his hole."
"A good soldier," Wilson replied, "should neither shit nor shave in
his hole." Shortly afterward I heard a mortar shell coming in. I fell
backward into my hole. My left foot didn't make it and caught a fragment. I crawled out and looked for Wilson. He was slumped over. I
couldn't find a mark on him. I ordered him tagged WIA, so a doctor
could examine him, but the medic refused, said he was dead. I blew
my top, nearly drew my pistol on the medic. The guys around us
intervened and told the medic that if he knew what was good for him,
he'd tag Sergeant Wilson WIA. I wouldn't accept that Wilson could

be dead. It was too personal, too tragic. Wilson was carried down the hill tagged WIA.

I had too much on my mind that day to worry about my foot and soon forgot about it.*

That evening I received word from the aid station. A needle-sized sliver of steel had penetrated Sergeant Wilson's skull at the hairline and he had died instantly.

On the morning of the 19th, we sat taking a terrible mortar pasting. I called Colonel Treacy and asked him to give the reverse slope of 174.1 a heavy pounding with our 4.2 mortars that night. I had figured out a way of taking the hill and wanted to attack the next morning. He approved, and that night [19–20 September] our mortars gave the enemy hilltop an all-night pounding. At first light I moved two assault platoons to just short of the far summit. They were covered by fire from the rest of the company. Below the summit each man in the attacking platoons threw two grenades, and before the gooks could get back into their fighting holes we had taken the hilltop. The plan worked because the attack went off like clockwork. It also worked because during the night, except for the dead they couldn't carry, the enemy had withdrawn.

Later in the morning, before we pulled off, we spent some time writing down the location of all our dead for Graves Registration. I don't know what happened to the dead North Koreans. There was no soil on top of the hill for them to be buried in.†

2nd Lt. ADRIAN B. BRIAN
I Company/5th Cavalry
It turned out that on the first day of attack the litter-bearers and medics had missed my corpsman Smitty. Several days after the battle was over and the Graves Registration people were combing the area, they found Smitty's body. I was fit to be tied, especially after one of the people in the CP told me he had seen someone standing in the rice

---

*On the 18th the 5th Marines captured Kimpo Airfield.
†As Item Company left Hill 174, 150 miles to the northwest Murray's 5th Marine Regiment crossed the Han River and advanced toward Seoul.

the day after the attack, but, assuming it was a North Korean, he didn't mention the sighting to anyone. What a tragic error.

Capt. NORMAN ALLEN
I Company/5th Cavalry
Early the next morning [21 September] the battalion moved out. Hill 174 receded behind another hill and was left behind. We traveled in a wide semicircle. Around 10:00 A.M. I Company topped a low ridge that looked out over a wide, flat valley which ran about a mile and a half to the Naktong River. The battalion was spread out below. To the left, 500 yards away, was K Company; to the right, closer, was L Company. Strung out on the road was Battalion Headquarters and Headquarters Company; behind them, M Company. It was great to see us all together again. I made a rough count and discovered the battalion numbered about 300 men. Three weeks before, when we arrived in Pusan, it had numbered nearly 900.

BREAKOUT

16 September-8 October 1950

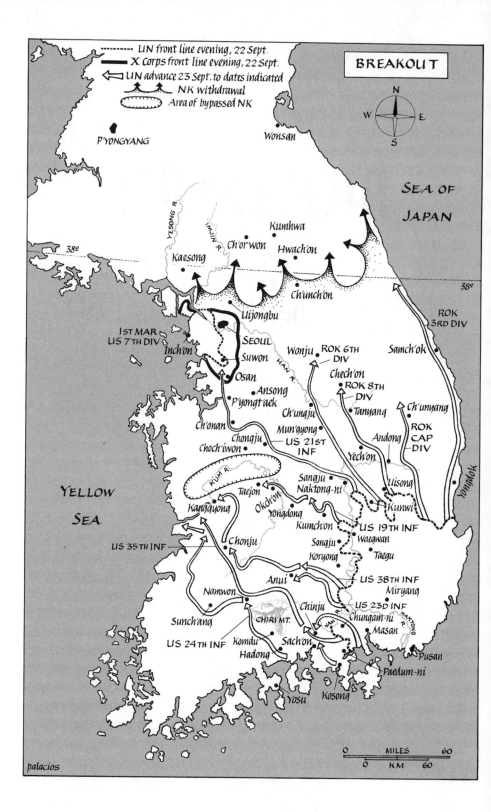

The day the survivors of Captain Allen's Item Company marched off Hill 174, the 5th Marines crossed the Han River. The 1st Marine Division had been ashore at Inch'on for five days and was preparing to battle the North Koreans for Seoul. As soon as X Corps had landed in the enemy's rear, MacArthur put into action the second phase of his audacious plan—Eighth Army's breakout from the Pusan Perimeter and its advance northward to link up with the Marines, 150 air miles away. The attack by Eighth Army and the ROK divisions in the Perimeter was set for 9:00 P.M., 16 September, one day after the Inch'on landings.

Pfc. LEONARD KORGIE
G Company/21st Infantry *

The platoon sergeant told us to assemble up forward. Colonel [Richard] Stephens, the regimental CO, was going to clue us in on the

---

* In late August the 34th Infantry, which had been so severely punished in the battles of July, had been reduced to paper status. Of the 2,000 men who landed in Korea with the 34th in early July, 184 were left. On 31 August, these survivors were transferred to the other regiments

next chapter of our infantry careers. He stood on top of a truck and looked tough. His address was spirited. "OK, men, we're done farting around with these gooks, we've had enough of their shit. In the next couple of days we're going to rack their asses. You guys are *infantry!* The infantry closes with and destroys the enemy. We're going across that river, bust through the resistance, and go north. If they try to stop us, we're gonna bayonet the sumbitches right in their holes."

The colonel fired us up. We weren't going to worry anymore about our flanks or rear. If I went down, at least it would be while charging forward. We were going to kick some ass now. I noticed everyone moved with some vigor and spirit. It was a far cry from those days when we dragged ourselves like whipped pups down the long road from Taejon and into the "stand or die" positions of the Pusan Perimeter. I noticed in myself—behind the fear of going back into combat—a little excitement, a little feeling of adventure. Hell, we were going to move into enemy territory. We slicked up those rifles, sharpened those bayonets, and made sure we had plenty of ammo. The whole thing was getting a little heady. The only thing that cooled our ardor was that a number of us had the runs again. We'd eaten too many of those apples in the orchard where we were billeted.

[*General Walker's plan was simple—a general attack all along the Perimeter that would achieve a dual purpose: prevent the enemy from rushing reinforcements to Seoul and break the iron vise that had held the Eighth Army for six weeks. The success of the Inch'on landings did not at first affect the combat efficiency of the North Koreans who surrounded the Perimeter.* With victory in the air, however, General Walker's forces slashed away at the enemy cordon.*

---

in the 24th Division. The troops of the 1st Battalion, 34th Infantry were transferred to the 3d Battalion, 19th Infantry; the GIs of the 3d Battalion, 34th Infantry, (including Leonard Korgie), were transferred to the 2d Battalion, 21st Infantry. The 34th Infantry's CO, Colonel Beauchamp, was reassigned to command the 32d Infantry, 7th Division. The 5th RCT, which had helped comprise Task Force Kean, was transferred to the 24th Division and replaced the 34th Infantry.

*At the time of the breakout, North Korean strength around the Perimeter was put at 70,000 (of whom only one in three were veterans of the June invasion); the strength of Eighth Army was 85,000, the ROKs 73,000.

A *battalion of the 38th Infantry crossed the Naktong near Ch'angnyong on 18 September, the first permanent crossing by any unit of Eighth Army in the breakout. The next day another battalion was pushed across. To support these units west of the river, on the 19th Army engineers constructed a floating bridge downstream from the crossing site.]*

Cpl. MARIO SORRENTINO
2d Engineer Combat Battalion/2d Division

The approach to the Naktong was along a wide, level strip of sand. Across the river American aircraft strafed and napalmed the high ridge that overlooked the proposed bridge site. Our tanks pulled up around us and offered some protection. North Korean bodies either floated in the water or lay about the beach. It was obvious from the carnage that in the act of trying to cross the river, an enemy battalion had been caught by our air force. It must have been a slaughter. Scattered among the dead were several women wearing North Korean uniforms. One I saw must have been very young. She was naked from the waist down. Her head lay toward the river. She had had her stomach ripped open. I felt so degraded. Flies covered the gaping wound. It was horrible. It wasn't that I felt sorry for her, it was her lying there so exposed.

As soon as the bridging equipment arrived [19 September], we began to unload the trucks. Engineer assault boats loaded with infantry paddled across the river. Then a boat carrying a drum of one-inch cable made the trip. We would use this cable line to anchor the bridge. Downriver small units inflated pontoons attached to rafts that would ferry tanks across. (All day long armored vehicles would be pushed across the river.)

Once the steel cable was fastened to a large tree on the opposite bank, it was drawn tight by cable pullers. Next, rafts were tied in to the taut cable. Once a raft was attached to the growing bridge, tie lines would fasten it to the anchor cable. Upstream from this activity a log boom that would prevent large obstructions from smashing into the bridge was being constructed.

All during this hectic time our aircraft rocked the ridge opposite. Artillery poured round after round into it. A heavy firefight went on. Control of this ridge was essential. The Sabre jets were beautiful. Their timing was remarkable. They dove on the ridge in a continuous circle: soon as one climbed away, another would drop its napalm, and another, higher up, would begin its dive.

As soon as the bridge reached the far shore, tanks and trucks began to cross. MPs stationed on either side directed traffic. Vehicles flowed across it. Occasionally, traffic moving north would be stopped and ambulances carrying men wounded in the battle for the ridge would cross in the opposite direction.

Throughout the night we continued to work to strengthen the bridge. Pins anchoring its various parts were driven home. I must have hammered a thousand of them.

Next day a flood of vehicles crossed the bridge. The roads leading to it were crammed with anything that had an engine and four wheels. I'd never seen so many vehicles before in one place.

Sgt. WARREN AVERY
G Company/21st Infantry
The day we crossed the Naktong we took a hill.* As the North Koreans ran off we knocked down quite a few. They left behind a wounded officer. Our officers asked for volunteers to carry him off the hill. Of course, no one volunteered; we had all heard about atrocities the North Koreans had participated in. After a little bit of an argument about what we should do with this wounded officer, the platoon leader went over to him and shot him between the eyes with his .45.

*The 21st Infantry's 2d Battalion crossed the Naktong early on the morning of 20 September. The regiment's other two battalions had crossed on the 19th.

Pfc. LEONARD KORGIE
G Company/21st Infantry

Once we were across the Naktong our company CO, Captain Syverson, sent a fifty-man patrol over the hills to get behind Waegwan.* When I was told I was going on this patrol I figured it could be a bitch. Our objective was a large hill several miles away. To reach it we would have to cross several other heavily wooded hills. In spite of the adrenaline and my excitement, I was scared. God, fifty men, all those hills! We stood a chance of being cut to ribbons. In that heavy foliage we could walk right into the North Koreans' laps and not know it until it was too late. What the hell, the Marines had landed at Inch'on, the end was in sight. Besides, the patrol would be led by Lieutenant Williamson. Battlefield commission, former first sergeant of L Company, 34th Infantry Regiment, he was a soldier's soldier. Had guts to burn.

Off we went [20 September]. In the first village we passed through we found a large square of recently turned earth. Through an interpreter, the villagers told us it was a mass grave.

We moved carefully through a thick forest for several hours. Near our objective we drew NK fire. The brush was so heavy, no one could see where it came from. The enemy was somewhere below us in a valley dense with foliage. Us kids were battlewise and mean. We were also anxious to keep moving. After two months of eating shit, we were now getting goofy with the smell of victory. A giddy kid next to me lifted his head to see if he could spot the North Koreans. *Brrrr! Brrrr!* A machine-gun burst caught him. The carnival atmosphere of having the enemy in a shooting gallery ended right there.

Lieutenant Williamson decided to march down the hill. Down we went—yelling, swearing, and firing like hell. Some North Koreans jumped from their holes and immediately went down; others raised their hands in surrender, but stupidly held onto potato-masher grenades. We didn't hesitate—tore their heads off! We didn't take any prisoners on this patrol; no one surrendered in acceptable style.

Off we went again. In a small clump of trees we spotted two T34

---

*The 21st Infantry was to attack north until it reached Waegwan, where it would turn west and strike out towards Kumch'on.

tanks. Lieutenant Williamson called back to Captain Syverson and gave him the coordinates. The first artillery round came in. BOOM! Williamson walked the rest into the trees. WHAMMO! WHAMMO! Both tanks went up in splashes of fire. It was fabulous.

We climbed several more hlls before coming in sight of our objective—a hill about three city blocks long and 700 feet high. The lieutenant looked it over through his binoculars. "Hell," he exclaimed, "there's nobody there. The holes are empty." God, this was heady stuff. I was beginning to enjoy myself. We ran over to this big bald-ass hill and found the holes. They were beautiful. Down and in, big enough to sleep in. And, indeed, empty.

Sometime later the North Koreans came down the road to retrieve the holes they'd left earlier. We could hardly restrain ourselves. When they were half a football field away, we popped up like Jacks-in-the-Box, and poured it at 'em. I remembered the long road from Taejon to the Perimeter. I fired until there was no one else to shoot at. I had a ball!

Rations were brought up. We waited for a counterattack. It never came. Next morning the road below was covered with American tanks and trucks; everything we had was rolling north.

[The breakout gained momentum and the American trap began to close. Between the anvil held in the north by X Corps and the hammer wielded in the south by Eighth Army, the North Korean vise would loosen, then let go. At first it was a matter of erosion, then disintegration.]

Sgt. WARREN AVERY
G Company/21st Infantry
After we crossed we went real hard. The push toward Seoul was on. We spent the second night after the breakout in a dry riverbed, where we were heavily shelled by mortars and artillery. Because we were exhausted, no one had taken time to dig in. When the artillery started landing, everyone tried to dig a hole. For each scoop I took out, two fell back in. For quite a while there was a lot of chaos.

Capt. NORMAN ALLEN
I Company/5th Cavalry

Mother darling:
Started again this morning and after 2,000 yards met my vehicles and got a wonderful hot breakfast, our first in nine days— powdered eggs, franks, crackers, coffee, and juice. The enemy has withdrawn . . . and we are following. Will make contact again soon, probably. Received your letter today with the envelopes and paper. Really grand of you to think of it. Sprained my ankle, same one I got a rock and shrapnel bruise on the other day. It is badly swollen and I can hardly walk, but we have to keep forging ahead. That damn Hill 174 had been taken seven times before our Bn hit the sector. Eleven attacks for a damn rocky, sandy hill. "L" Company lost over 100 men on it and "I" lost 80.

Wish all units were advancing with as little opposition as we have had so far this morning and yesterday afternoon. After such a hard, slow fight it is real nice to be able to push ahead. I will send some souvenirs if I can get them mailed. Have a couple of NK bayonets. It is hard to carry them, particularly when we are taking with us only what's on our backs. Have stripped down to really the minimum—fifty sheets of toilet paper, two pencils, notebook, toothbrush, two brushes and can of oil for my weapon; the rest is weapons, ammo, compass, canteen, shovel, grenades, helmet, field glasses, field jacket, extra pair of socks, map, and one can of cold rations. Captain Curfman always brings me a couple of cans of beer. On the 17th, when he brought his company up to attack through my position, we lay behind a small bush and rock making our plans, enemy bullets snapping six inches overhead, each of us drinking a can of beer. What a war.

Pretty worried about my ankle, just can hardly stand walking on it but couldn't stand to leave the company for even one day.

Holding here now on the side of a little rice paddy while the 7th
Cav reconnoiters for a divisional river crossing. So guess we start
going again and just as soon keep driving until we hit the 38th
Parallel. My lads are all in good spirits but we are tired. Need a
good barber to get this damn beard off. The division commander
says any officer that doesn't shave daily goes to a rifle company.
Ha! What can he do to me? Haven't had enough water for coffee, let alone shave in, so to hell with them.

Next day.
     Spent the night on the Naktong River again, a lot of people
around us now. Moving north up the Naktong. Just hope the
5th Cav doesn't get in the rat race to Seoul. They get eager, move
too fast, and people get hurt. I still can't walk so am with the Bn
CP while my exec, Bob Geer, is taking the company. Crawled
into my bedroll last night. Slept warm for the first night in many,
and broke my fever. Should be able to hoof it again. Shaved this
morning.
Love to all. . . .

The enemy was adjudged to be making a withdrawal. The sudden assumption came as a surprise, but reports were received that
groups were withdrawing to the North. Facts were further sub-
stantiated by fanatical, die-in-place fighting.
                              NARRATIVE REPORT, 5TH CAVALRY REGIMENT

Capt. NORMAN ALLEN
I Company/5th Cavalry
From time to time we could see gooks on the high hills in the distance. They didn't particularly try to hide, nor did they bother us. As
a matter of fact, they were so conspicuous that many of the men
thought they were friendlies. I knew these were no friendlies this far
forward. I would occasionally call in a map-coordinate fire mission
on them, then continue moving down the road, often not even
watching to adjust the fire I had called in. Really figured that if the
company could advance for about two days, it would be in a position
to knock them on their asses when they tried to get past us. About

dark the company halted and dug in at the bottom of a ridge on the edge of a small, narrow valley. I was pretty confident that the NKs would do everything possible to avoid a fight—they wanted out of there too bad.

The next morning the battalion surgeon cut a piece of metal from my ankle and bandaged me up. (This was the sliver I'd taken on the 18th when Sergeant Wilson was killed.) Afterward I could hardly get my boot on. Colonel Treacy saw me struggling with the laces and ordered me back to the hospital. I argued. He said, "Norm, if you go now, you'll be back in ten days. If you hang around here, the foot will get infected and you'll be gone for a month or more. What do you want?" I allowed myself to be evacuated.

[At the time of the Pusan breakout, the large group of American POWs (including Edward Gregory) that had been captured by the North Koreans during the Second Naktong Offensive was still on the road and still in South Korea. Throughout September the American Air Force controlled all the roads and the POW column was forced to march at night. The prisoners were weary and hungry, the wounded had received no care. They did not know what had happened on the Perimeter. As far as the POWs knew, North Korea was still winning the war.]

Pfc. EDWARD GREGORY, JR.
B Company/23d Infantry

I began asking men near me whether they wanted to try to escape. Most thought I'd never make it back to our lines. A sergeant named Jamison said, "Good luck, soldier, but I don't think you'll make it." I had made up my mind anyway: I was going to try. When we stopped for a five-minute break, I rolled down off the side of the road and lay quietly in a ditch until I heard the column move off. I lay for another half hour or so. I didn't want to be picked up by a trailing guard. When I felt I was alone, I took off and began making my way south.

When I became too tired to continue, I lay down under a big tree, covered myself with loose brush, and went to sleep.

At daylight I started out again, unaware that the North Koreans had sent out a patrol to try and find me. I made a mistake and openly walked near a small farm. I believe the farmer saw me and gave away my location to the North Koreans. They spotted me and fired several shots. I knew I was trapped. I froze. Three North Koreans ran up to me. One of them hit and kicked me until I fell down, then all three hit me with their rifle butts. My body hurt all over. Then they marched me back in the direction from which I had come. Once in a while one of the North Koreans would crack me with his rifle. We came to a little village. The guards yelled and hollered at the people lining the street. I didn't know what they shouted, but it sure didn't look good for me. The South Koreans began throwing rocks at me. They hit me with sticks and spat on me. I was never so glad of anything as I was to get out of that village.

We walked for several more hours. When we stopped, the guards began to talk among themselves. One of them put a bayonet on his rifle and jabbed at me. "Hubba, hubba" and off we went. Two guards left and I was alone with a very young North Korean. He spoke a little English and somehow he got me to sing the national anthem. It was wonderful to sing it, but under the circumstances it felt strange.

Eventually, we came to another village, larger than the last one. The guard put his bayonet in my ass and pushed me into a building. I was taken to a room where I was questioned by an officer. He told me if I, or anyone else, tried to escape again, they would shoot ten prisoners. When he noticed I still wore my rosary beads, he ripped them and my dog tags off. He called me a Christian pig. A guard then took me to a dungeon where the rest of the prisoners were being held. I was very happy to see them again. Sergeant Jamison came over to me: "I told you you wouldn't make it."

[*Private Gregory might not have made it, but his friends and colleagues in the south had, and in a big way. After several days of stiff resistance, the enemy cordon around the Pusan Perimeter had been smashed. By 23 September the North Koreans were streaming northward. Eighth Army, motorized and led by armored spearheads, advanced along all the corridors leading away from the Perimeter. Two hundred years earlier Marshall Comte de Saxe had written, "If the officer you have ordered in pursuit prides himself on the regularity of his formations and the precautions of the march . . . there is no use in having sent him. He must attack, push, and pursue without cease."]*

Enemy resistance has deteriorated along the Eighth Army front permitting the assumption of a general offensive from present positions. In view of this situation it is mandatory that all efforts be directed toward the destruction of the enemy by effecting deep penetrations, fully exploiting enemy weaknesses, and through the conduct of enveloping or encircling maneuver get astride enemy lines of withdrawal to cut his attempted retreat and destroy him.

OPERATIONAL ORDER, EIGHTH ARMY

[The North Koreans were being chased over the same ground on which they had pursued General Walker's 24th Division some two months before. Now the Communists were the hare, Eighth Army the hound. It was the enemy's turn to go hungry and shoeless, to wonder if they were trapped, to be harassed, surrounded. In late September American infantrymen found the taste of revenge to their liking.]

Pfc. LEONARD KORGIE
G Company/21st Infantry
We had the enemy in a squeeze and intended to smash the hell out of him. All of a sudden we were winning the damned war! I began to feel like a normal human being again. Even Captain Syverson was smiling. We went down the roads, sometimes marching, sometimes on tanks—Patton style.

Once in a while we hit a pocket of resistance. A platoon would be sent around to envelop the roadblock; suddenly the traffic was moving again. Our interpreters would shout into megaphones the Korean words for "come here." Down from the hills the gooks would come. We shoved them to the rear, where they had time for prisoners. Most of the time the POWs were meek. Once in a while we'd get an arrogant bastard. I'd get the uncontrollable urge to jump on the SOB and choke him.

One day we passed the hill I'd been chased off of in July when the gooks had us on the run. Graves Registration teams were bringing the bodies down. That heat of July and August had baked the corpses coal black. There were a lot more of them than I realized.

Pfc. VICTOR FOX
I Company/5th Cavalry

The wreckage of the North Korean Army was strewn all along the roads. Weapons, ammo, supply crates, rice sacks—everything to sustain a field army—even jeeps, trucks, and T34 tanks. Much of it was salvageable. Sergeant Huber, the company's supply sergeant, managed to get a North Korean truck which he badly needed. What sticks in my mind is how surgically clean the North Koreans maintained their artillery pieces. A lot of equipment was destroyed by the enemy themselves, but most had been strafed, napalmed, or bombed by the American Air Force. From the wreckage of North Korean convoys caught on the roads, it certainly appeared the enemy had enough equipment to continue the war for a long time.

I had left a Swedish-operated hospital in Pusan a few days before. After being treated for cuts and bruises, having my glasses replaced, sleeping lots, and eating good hot chow, I was sent to a "Repl Depot" for processing back to I Company. I spent two or three days in the company of other combat returnees and recently arrived Stateside replacements. The former were brooding and quiet; the latter, excited and talkative.

One day we were assembled in a large, open dirt area. Each individual's name was called out, as well as the unit he would join or rejoin, whichever the case. Every time the 1st Cavalry Division was announced, loud "oooohs" and "aaaahs" of condolences went up from the gathered throng. This was the first inkling any of us in the Cav had of just how terrible the fighting outside Taegu had been for us. Having never experienced any other combat, we kids thought what happened on Hill 174 was normal and could be expected every time we fought.

The train going north seemed to take forever. In Taegu I saw hundreds of what appeared to me to be freshly inducted South Korean troops on their way to the front. Rumor had it that these troops did not go through an American-style Selective Service route. Instead, they had been picked up off the streets, given uniforms and rifles, and sent north. What fascinated me was the song these troops sang. The melody was very stirring and gave me a feel for the Korean people. The music is long forgotten, but the emotions I felt when I heard it remain with me.

The train continued north. No refugees made this trip. It was packed with GIs and supplies going to the front. We line troopers wondered about the supply of riches the train carried. Little did we know just how little would reach us in the weeks ahead after we crossed the 38th Parallel.

Somewhere after Sangju but before Suwon, I finally caught up with I Company. After being in the rear area with hundreds and hundreds of troops, I Company looked so small. With the exception of us replacements, the troopers in the company looked a mess.

Prisoners were captured in droves. The 24-hour total numbered 776.

NARRATIVE REPORT, 5TH CAVALRY REGIMENT

Cpl. LACY BARNETT
Medical Company/3d Battalion/19th Infantry
To break the monotony of the push, a couple of us decided to count the number of destroyed U.S. and North Korean trucks and tanks that were within sight of the road. Between Taejon and Suwon the count reached 788.

PW states he is from 3d NK Division. PW captured at Munui. PW heard that all units in the south are to make their exodus northward through the Sobem Mountains. PW states the 3d NK

Division started climbing through the Sobem Mountain Range on 27 September. He claims an estimated 20,000 North Koreans, both organized and disorganized, are using this range for escape routes. PW says that the NKs are traveling day and night.

S-2/3 JOURNAL, 5TH CAVALRY REGIMENT

Cpl. MARIO SORRENTINO
2d Engineer Combat Battalion/2d Division
The area we drove through had already cleared and we met no opposition. If it had not been for the dust, it would have been similar to a lazy ride on a country road. Here and there we saw the results of battle. Vehicles of every description littered the roadside, many Korean homes still smoldered. The area was pretty flat; only a few small rolling hills broke the monotony. Rice paddies on both sides of the road were beginning to dry up and looked like checkerboard squares. Everything was turning a grayish brown. There were a few trees. Every mile or so we passed through small farming hamlets.

Convoy driving is a bore. Your speed is determined by the lead vehicle of the serial and the speed of that vehicle is determined by traffic and road conditions. Korean roads, if you can call them that, are at best similar to the secondary roads you find in Wyoming and Utah. They appeared to have been cut by road graders and covered with stone or rock. These were the better roads. Getting off the major road was something else. Then you would find trails wide enough only for an oxcart. The typical Korean, namely a farmer, had no use for roads; they had no vehicles and walked wherever they wanted to go.

The Koreans I saw appeared haggard and frail. They were simply worn out. Their clothes all looked the same. Women wore ankle-length skirts; the bodice appeared to be folded over the breast; sleeves were worn down to the wrist. The men wore baggy trousers. Men's and women's clothing was white, which, I was told, was the color of mourning. It struck me, boy, did they pick the wrong color. It was beyond me how anything in that country could stay white.

At times the roads were just clogged with civilians carrying all their possessions. Men carried wooden A-frames on their backs, women

The 1st Platoon, I Company, 5th Cavalry Regiment, sometime after the men crossed the Imjin River *Source: Lee Carpenter*

Lt. Gen. Walton H. Walker (USA) (left) with his son, Capt. Sam Walker, who commanded a company in the 19th Infantry, in early October 1950
Source: William Menninger

The railroad bridge, looking toward the enemy shore at P'yongyang, seen from the island in the Taedong River, 19 October 1950 *Source: Norman Allen*

Troopers from I Company, 5th Cavalry, clear a dugout in P'yongyang, 20 October 1950 *Source: Norman Allen*

An Item Company patrol walks
through streets of North Korean
capital the day city fell
Source: Norman Allen

GIs from the 19th Infantry advance northward toward the Yalu River,
late October 1950 *Source: William Menninger*

Chinese Communist prisoners captured near Sudong-ni, 5 November 1950
Source: Marine Corps Photos

Col. Homer L. Litzenberg (USMC) somewhere along the MSR. General Craig is on the left with hands in his pockets. *Source: Marine Corps Photos*

Rugged terrain along the MSR occupied by Marines of the 1st Marine Division, early December 1950 *Source: Marine Corps Photos*

View toward Rocky Ridge from Pfc. Ernest
Gonzalez's fighting hole on Fox Hill, 28
November 1950 *Source: Ernest Gonzalez*

Marines wait for a roadblock to be eliminated between Yudam-ni and Hagaru-ri,
1 December 1950. Two weeks remain before the Marines will embark at Hungnam.
Source: Marine Corps Photos

Elements of the 1st Marine Division south of Koto-ri about to descend through
Funchilin Pass, 10 December 1950 *Source: Marine Corps Photos*

Maj. Gen. O. P. Smith (USMC)
congratulates Raymond Murray on his
promotion to full colonel
Source: Marine Corps Photos

Winter in western North Korea. A squad from I
Company, 5th Cavalry, tries to keep warm around a
small fire. *Source: Norman Allen*

A convoy of 2d Division trucks driving north seen from the bivouac area of A Battery,
61st FA Battalion, late afternoon of 25 November 1950. The hill called Chinaman's
Hat is on the right. *Source: Jimmy Marks*

"A" Battery, 61st FA Battalion and one of their 105-mm howitzers, early December 1950 *Source: Jimmy Marks*

Taking a break during Eighth Army's long retreat from North Korea, December 1950 *Source: James Cardinal*

carried bundles on their heads. The fortunate ones pulled large carts which in better days had been pulled by an ox.

It was a pitiful sight that brought back memories of those grim days along the Perimeter. I recall one day finding this little girl who couldn't have been more than eight, trodding down the road crying hard. In her hands she carried a rusty tin of water. We tried to stop her because she was entering a dangerous area. She tried to get away from us; her screaming broke our hearts. A chaplain appeared on the scene and through an interpreter he learned she was returning to her village, where she hoped to find her parents who had been separated from her. Everyone in war suffers. Children, however, suffer the most. They don't understand. Try explaining it to a child. They are terrified, dirty, and hungry. Without the solace of parents or anyone else, they're lost. The chaplain took the little girl with him when he drove off.

Mile after mile, the convoy drove north. Many thoughts went through my mind. I remembered what death smells like, a putrid stink like no other. I remembered how anxious I was to get to Korea. I was eighteen and couldn't wait to see combat. That lasted until the first firefight. Afterward it was, Please, God, don't let me get hurt. If I do, please let it be small, something that will get me home in one piece. Time went by, the road seemed endless. Thoughts of the war faded and I would doze off. A pothole or another stop kept the naps short.

Sgt. ROBERT DEWS
E Company/21st Infantry *
The awful sights we saw along the road staggered the imagination: tanks and trucks, some undamaged, some with their engines still running. E Company traveled forward each day. There were no living enemies to be seen. The terrain was covered with craters from the American bombings—it was a land of the dead.

The wary and cautious 24th Division went more slowly than the recently arrived units. It had sold this real estate with the lives of its

---

* In the Pusan Perimeter Sergeant Dews had been transferred to the 21st Infantry.

own brave men and did not intend to let the enemy get behind it again.

> Seven miles north of Choch'iwon, old position 3d Battalion, 21st Infantry, found considerable American dead.* Some evidence of execution. Will establish guard over area, request graves registration team also.
>
> S-2/3 JOURNAL, 5TH CAVALRY REGIMENT

Pvt. JAMES CARDINAL
I Company/5th Cavalry

Dear Folks:

It's Sunday in Korea. We are dug in on the side of a cemetery. It's a quiet sunny morning. Down a little ways they are holding Protestant services and it's well attended. Yesterday we went out on patrol scouting an enemy convoy that had been shot up a few days ago. It was about four miles long with vehicles about every thirty feet. Most had been burned and were off the road. The vehicles that would run were brought back to use ourselves.

Yesterday, fifty miles from here, a whole battalion of Americans that had been murdered two months earlier was found. The bodies, now skeletons, were still in their foxholes where they died.

Korean prisoners are constantly streaming in and some are horrible messes. Don't think the GIs don't get even with them too. We had 160 of them sleeping in a room 20 feet by 30 feet. They practically had to sleep on top of each other. The stink was worse than the Chicago stockyards. One who had white phosphorus had maggots all over him. You can't imagine how terrible he looked.

You people would get a laugh if you saw how we live here. I

---

*The 3d Battalion, 21st Infantry, had been overrun outside Choch'iwon on 11 July.

haven't taken a bath in ten days. We never wash before we eat because there's usually only water to drink unless we're near a river or a stream. The most uncomfortable thing is sleeping in these damp foxholes and nearly freezing to death. I don't really mind it. I just wish it were a little more active. I haven't seen too much fighting, and probably won't now that the war is almost over. . . .

The regiment ran its total of captured trains to three when it located two today. One flatcar contained a combat-loaded T34 tank.

Handling of prisoners is fast proving to be an obstacle. Six hundred forty-one were taken today.

NARRATIVE REPORT, 5TH CAVALRY REGIMENT

Pvt. JAMES CARDINAL
I Company/5th Cavalry

Dear Folks:

We are right outside the city of Suwon, a big city south of Seoul. We've been moving continuously north towards the 38th Parallel against no opposition except occasional snipers. It's unbelievable how wrecked and bombed the countryside is. In the last five miles I counted twelve wrecked North Korean and two American tanks as well as hundreds of trucks and other vehicles. All the bridges are blown up, railroad tracks are torn up, and the centers of cities and villages are leveled.

I'm pretty well contented with things, although it is sort of cold at night. I can frankly say I'm very glad I came as it is an experience I'll never forget. . . .

Pfc. VICTOR FOX
I Company/5th Cavalry

The huge entrance gate leading into Suwon was decorated with evergreen garlands and boughs and large banners written out in English. Civilians waving South Korean flags and shouting "man se"*

---

* A Korean cheer, literally meaning "long life."

lined the streets of our advance. Some troopers wondered whether the people held North Korean flags in their other hand—just in case. From what I could see, the civilians looked genuinely happy to see us.

[The American pursuit managed to catch up with Pfc. Edward Gregory outside Seoul just in the nick of time, ending his month-long ordeal.]

Pfc. EDWARD GREGORY, JR.
B Company/23d Infantry
Taken from the dungeon by our North Korean guards, we were again marched north. The wounded we carried began to get weaker and the column began moving more slowly. We tried, but in vain, to keep our wounded moving. The guards began shooting the men who were most unable to keep up.

Often the North Koreans would place their rifle barrels at our temples and pull the trigger. *Click.* There had been no bullet in the chamber. They enjoyed watching us flinch.

Near the end of September, the column of prisoners had been whittled down to eighty-eight Americans. A corporal by the name of Simmons had a bad leg wound; maggots ate away at it. He was always in pain. To the rest of us he became an inspiration. If he could continue, we certainly could.

We were kept in a big barn. Our march had taken us 160 miles away from the Perimeter. The nights were cold and the only way we could keep warm was by huddling together. We lay on a dirt floor. Our clothes and bodies were covered with lice. A day or so after we reached the barn, Corporal Simmons asked to go outside to relieve himself and get a little sun. He was allowed out of the barn. We heard a plane flying overhead—sounded like an observation plane. Next, several shots were fired. One of the guards told us the plane had shot Simmons. We knew better. Those lousy North Koreans shot him. Later in the day they gave us some rice and told us we'd be moved north by trucks.

The next day the guards came in and took out eleven South Koreans who were with us. After making them dig their own graves, they shot them. The guards came back and told us they were going to move us. Ten men had their hands tied behind them. We knew then the guards planned to shoot us ten at a time. With nothing to lose we decided to rush and overpower our guards. Suddenly, we heard something that sounded like tanks. The sound grew closer and closer. The North Korean guards took off but closed the barn door. One of the sergeants yelled for everyone to hit the ground and stay there. Somebody looked through a crack, "They're American. There's a black soldier with them." We prayed one of the tanks wouldn't put a round into the barn. A voice outside shouted, "Any GIs in there?" Those were the greatest words I ever heard.

Pfc. LEONARD KORGIE
G Company/21st Infantry
Somewhere near Seoul the company ran into elements of the 7th Division which had landed at Inch'on. Now I knew the war was over. I was going to survive. Then we came across some Marine units getting ready to pull out. It was then I decided I wanted to be a Marine. All that big equipment and lots of it. Go in, shoot the works, capture the objective, pull out, go back on ship, eat three squares a day, sleep in warm bunks—and probably be home in three weeks. What a wonderful way to fight a war. I envied them.

1st Lt. CHARLES PAYNE
*3d Battalion/19th Infantry**
Just before Seoul there was a slow-up. I found a party with a MASH unit. I learned that some 190-proof medical alcohol will flat do away with any notions about romance—but who cared?

---

* Along with the other survivors of the 34th Infantry, Lieutenant Payne had been transferred on 31 August.

Sgt. ROBERT DEWS
E Company/21st Infantry
All roads now led to Seoul—the largest city in the world without underground sewage. The smell of Seoul even in good times used to sicken Westerners when their ship entered Inch'on Harbor. Now death and decay added to the usual smells. It seemed that everything in the world was trying to get onto the road leading north. Military traffic in the South Korean capital was snarled with all kinds of vehicles.

Pfc. VICTOR FOX
I Company/5th Cavalry
I'm not certain whether fighting was still going on, but Seoul was still burning. Smoke and devastation covered the route we took through the capital. As our motorized column passed the shelled-out main railroad station, we passed a weary Marine unit, fully combat-ready, sitting on what was left of a street curb. One of the Marines noticed the 1st Cav Division markings on the bumper and yelled out, "Hey, where's your horses?" Blackie Furlan jumped to his feet and shouted, "We ate 'em waiting for you bastards to get here!" Even the Marines thought that was a good one.

Item Company, 5th Cavalry Regiment, did not stop in Seoul; we only passed through.

3 October 1950
Orders directed a 5th Cavalry Regimental move north of Seoul to the vicinity of Munsan-ni, and to establish a bridgehead across the Imjin River for the 1st Cavalry Division.

NARRATIVE REPORT, 5TH CAVALRY REGIMENT

Pfc. VICTOR FOX
I Company/5th Cavalry
The scene was in a wild ravine. First I saw piles of brightly colored silk gowns and black conical hats. Many of the corpses also appeared to wear Western-style clothing. In these mounds of ruffled clothing,

I could also see parts of bodies, a head here, an arm there. While the company was somewhere between Seoul and Munsan-ni, word had been passed that we should divert several miles east of the main highway and check out reports of a massacre. The company had entered a hilly wilderness area. Even before we arrived at the designated location, we knew something terrible had taken place from the horrible stench of decaying human bodies that polluted the breeze. I learned later that an estimated 200 civilians were executed at this site. Someone found out many of the murdered were professional and business people, educators, artists, politicians, civil servants. The dead appeared to include entire families, from children to the very aged. The company did not tarry long in this area. After about two hours flank security was pulled in and the company returned west to meet the main highway, where we continued our march north to Munsan-ni.

2d Lt. ADRIAN B. BRIAN
I Company/5th Cavalry

On the day we entered Munsan-ni, Item Company was leading the regiment, the division, and Eighth Army in the advance and my platoon was leading I Company. The marching orders were clear: "Follow this road." We had been leapfrogging our way along for an hour when we approached the outskirts of a town. From experience I knew that if there were civilians along the road waiting to greet us, there were no NKs nearby. Along this road there were lots of civilians at the edge of town. They bowed, raised both hands in the air, and shouted "Man se!" When I saw this celebration, I stopped the leapfrogging business and moved smartly along the road. The crowd swarmed out and stopped us. Someone pushed a twelve-year-old boy toward me. The kid smiled and said something in what I believe he thought was English. To me it was unintelligible. Anyway, I smiled and put him on the hood of my jeep. All the Koreans cheered some more and thought I was being a loving and gentle liberator. My motives were not that pure. I knew the civilians wouldn't let the kid ride with me if the road ahead was mined.

The rest of Eighth Army, which, I presumed, was following me, advanced through the village as easily as my platoon had. Down the road a mile or so I took a fork in the road and proceeded east, the 1st Cavalry Division in my wake. For the only time in my life I was in the first jeep on an advance and was the first American soldier leading the division and Eighth Army into enemy-held territory. What a thrill! About half a mile down the road, I received a frantic signal to stop. I was leading Eighth Army down the *wrong* road. What a blow to my ego. What fun we had turning the entire regiment inside out along that narrow country road. I don't know why they didn't just have someone else at the rear of the column turn around and become the point, but they didn't. I had to resume the lead and the regiment had to back-and-forward its way until every vehicle was turned around and following the one it had followed before my gaffe. I passed everyone until I was again in the lead. I did not always understand Colonel [Marcel] Crombez [5th Cavalry Regiment CO], but, after all, I was only a second lieutenant. Eighth Army's password that night was "Wrong Road."

5 October
The Imjin River, a tidal stream, is one of the widest in Korea. There was no bridge near the designated area for the 3d Battalion crossing.

NARRATIVE REPORT, 5TH CAVALRY REGIMENT

2d Lt. ADRIAN B. BRIAN
I Company/5th Cavalry
The next day [5 October] it was Joe Toomey's 1st Platoon's turn to lead Eighth Army's advance. Joe and I were classmates at West Point. He was taller than I, better-looking, smarter, more popular, and I was jealous. The only thing I had more of than Joe was luck. Time and again, when it was my turn to go on patrol, cross a river, take the point, lead an attack, things would be quiet. When Joe did these things, all hell broke loose. This day was no exception.

Pfc. VICTOR FOX
I Company/5th Cavalry
The company arrived at the Imjin River on a sunny but cool early
October day [5 October]. In our sector the rapidly flowing river was
about 150 yards wide. The bank on our side sloped gently into the
water. On the enemy's side the bank rose steeply, about 100 feet to a
ridgeline that extended along the north shore. Beyond was an area of
high hills. A blown-out highway bridge lay tangled in the water a few
hundred yards to our left.

> The Blue Commander [Colonel Treacy] asked for artillery and
> assault boats to facilitate the crossing. He ordered Item Com-
> pany to ford the stream . . . and protect the balance of the bat-
> talion elements crossing.
>
> NARRATIVE REPORT, 5TH CAVALRY REGIMENT

2d Lt. ADRIAN B. BRIAN
I Company/5th Cavalry
We didn't know it at the time, but the river was affected by the tide
and the bottom was covered with slimy mud and, in places, with
quicksand. Joe Toomey was ordered to ford the Imjin where the road
led down to the water and where in normal times I presume a ferry
met it.

Sgt. LEE CARPENTER
I Company/5th Cavalry
This was our first river crossing and, in addition to the normal apprehension, some of the guys were really worried because they couldn't
swim. Our platoon was not informed that there was anything unusual
about the river. It wasn't long after we jumped off that we realized
the damn river bottom wasn't solid. If you didn't keep moving, you'd
sink. I realized it was quicksand. The closer I got to the opposite shore,
the deeper the water became. Being a short person, the water got high
on me fast. I held my rifle over my head and practically tiptoed along
the bottom. I began contemplating swimming the rest of the way but

realized it would be awkward with my rifle and a full load of ammo. Just as I was about to choose between my rifle and my life, one of the Aussies,* who had reached the enemy shore, saw me struggling and pushed an old "gook" boat or raft out to me. He probably saved my life and, for certain, my pride, because a few more steps and I'm sure I'd have dumped my rifle and ammo into the river.

Once I hit the shore, I headed uphill. Lieutenant Toomey was also heading in that direction and we continued to climb. Near the top the lieutenant and I realized we were alone, and looking down toward the river, I saw most of the platoon just leaving the water. I began yelling and motioning for my squad to get their rears in gear. Lieutenant Toomey stopped for a short breather and took his helmet off to wipe his forehead. He was above me on the hill, maybe ten yards. I turned to look at him and saw this gook grenade with a long handle come arching through the air. The damn thing hit Lieutenant Toomey on the head and bounced off—it went one way, the lieutenant the other. The grenade never went off, but Lieutenant Toomey suffered a large gash on his head.

2d Lt. ADRIAN B. BRIAN
I Company/5th Cavalry

The cut in Joe's head wouldn't stop bleeding and he asked Lieutenant Geer over the radio to send another officer to relieve him. In spite of having a concussion and being blinded by the blood running into his eyes, I think he should have "faked it." There were only three officers in our company at the time—Joe; our exec, Lieutenant Geer, who was the temporary CO until Captain Allen returned; and me. I was sent from my nice, safe hilltop and ordered to cross the river.

The water at first had been only two feet deep. Now the tide was coming in and it was waist-high and rising. While I crossed I got caught in some quicksand. I couldn't move. Some NKs evidently got into a better position or something because bullets began splashing in the

---

*To get into the fighting sooner, two Australians had left the 3d Battalion, Royal Australian Regiment (which had arrived in Korea on 28 September), and joined I Company before the Imjin River crossing.

water around me. A hundred things went through my mind. I wore two grenades attached to my cartridge-belt suspenders, my carbine was held above my head in my right hand, my left hand, too, was above my head keeping my wristwatch dry. The muck was now about to my knees, the water to my chest just below the grenades. It came to me I couldn't keep everything dry and that I had to do something *fast!* I transferred the carbine to my left hand and reached down with the right and pulled my right ankle into a kneeling position. I then reversed the procedure and lifted my left knee with my left hand. Once I got into a kneeling position, I had enough surface on the bottom to keep from sinking farther. My head was just out of the water. I began moving again and finished the crossing on my knees. (Later in the day, when I could count noses, I found that three men, two KATUSAs and an American, had been caught in the river and drowned.)

Pvt. JAMES CARDINAL
I Company/5th Cavalry

The attack was temporarily postponed until we could safely find a way to get the other platoons across the river. Lieutenant Geer asked for volunteers to cross the river and bring back a raft Toomey's platoon had spotted. Logsden, a big farmer from the Missouri Ozarks, and I volunteered. There being no other volunteers, Lieutenant Geer sent us on our way.

The crossing was very difficult. The river bottom dropped quickly and we were soon swimming, holding our rifles above our heads. We eventually reached the raft, which was just at the shoreline. By now Logsden was exhausted. Because he felt he could not make it back across the river, he decided not to return with me. Despite all my arguments and pleading, he left me to get the raft safely across the river by myself. Leaving him behind, I pulled and tugged the raft until I had recrossed the river. I ended up somewhat downstream of where Logsden and I had started. When I returned to the platoon, I was about dead with exhaustion.

I was then ordered to go with the next platoon scheduled to cross the river. The raft was quickly loaded with our equipment and we began to cross. We immediately came under small-arms fire. An occasional mortar round landed in the river. By now I was so exhausted

I could hardly move. Struggling in water up to my knees, I stepped into a patch of quicksand. The more I tried to shake myself free, the deeper I became embedded. The water reached my shoulders, the muck was at my waist. It was then that Jerry Emer and Sergeant Lee noticed my danger and came to my rescue. They endangered their own lives in doing so, as they became excellent targets for the North Koreans in the hills across the river. They managed to pull me free and avoid the quicksand that had grabbed me. I was pushed and shoved onto the raft, where I lay flat and tried to regain my breath and strength. (No doubt, Lee and Jerry Emer saved my life. Next day I spoke to Lieutenant Geer about their bravery and asked him to recommend them for medals. He showed no interest at all.)

Pfc. VICTOR FOX
I Company/5th Cavalry
The 3d Platoon entered the water in full combat gear, each man held his weapon above his head. A GI in front of me [Pfc. Leonard Shipp] was hit and his body floated out of sight. Near the north side of the river, I stepped into deep water and, being a small man, went over my head. In great alarm, while fully submerged, I frantically thrashed around trying to reach bottom. I knew in my hysteria that I was drowning. With gratifying relief my feet touched bottom and I was able to push off to more shallow ground. I was so spent from pulling myself out of the river and moving toward the cover of the riverbank, I paid little heed to the small-arms fire that hit around me. In the lee of the riverbank, it became apparent that the enemy was firing at us from a high hill that rose to our left and in front of the demolished bridge.

Before any of us fully recovered our breath, 3d Platoon was ordered to attack this hill and silence the enemy's fire. We raced at full speed across an open space the length of two football fields and at the foot of the hill began to climb. We assaulted the summit in a skirmish-line wedge, firing all the time we walked forward. The hill extended through tree cover for some distance. Making sure the North Korean dead did not spring back to life, we next advanced along the evergreen-covered summit. We had advanced about 200 yards when someone shouted, "They're behind us! They're coming!" The dreaded words caused us for the first and last time to "bug out." Excited and confused at the sight of a lot of guys running away, my buddy Haltom and I joined them. A hundred yards from the summit, Sergeants Nelson and Hughes grabbed running troopers. With loud cursing and much kicking of ass, they managed to turn the platoon around. We did not advance much farther after that, however, and dug in for the night where we were. Everyone was a bit ashamed of his behavior. We were, after all, combat veterans. While we dug in, no one talked much.

[*Eighth Army crossed the Imjin and paused for several days below the Parallel while, in General MacArthur's words, "logistical difficulties" were sorted out. Headquarters' staffs and company clerks used the hold to catch up on all the work that had gone unattended while the Army raced pell-mell for the border. The foxhole GIs stopped where they were and enjoyed the respite. For some it was the first rest they'd had since early July.*]

Pfc. LEONARD KORGIE
G Company/21st Infantry
Much time was spent bullshitting. Talk was of home. We did not have any idea what MacArthur was going to do next and didn't care. Food had top priority in our bull sessions. We smoked like fiends. Surprisingly, some of the conversations turned to sex. Up to then the only sexual references I'd heard were those obscenities hurled at the enemy. Everyone was too drained emotionally and physically to have a sex drive, much less talk about it. On the Parallel, with prospects of Japan, home, and safety, came the stories—stories of seductions, conquests, Japanese girlfriends, hometown sweethearts. While we waited to find out what would happen next, some wonderful events reminded us of home: sleeping in a bed with sheets, having a roof overhead, sitting on a stool, and defecating in a bathroom. I thought to myself, When I get home I'll never bitch about another thing for

the rest of my life. Whatever years my Creator has left for me I will consider bonus time. Never again will I ever be afraid.

Pfc. VICTOR FOX
I Company/5th Cavalry

One of the first things anyone noticed was that the days and certainly the nights were growing colder. One morning north of the Imjin there was frost on the ground. Sergeant Huber used the lull to issue us field jackets to cover our summer fatigues.

Much of this time was spent shooting the breeze with guys from other units, especially guys from the other two cavalry regiments. In late August, fresh from the States, our 3d Battalion had stepped right into the front lines and ever since had been slugging it out with the enemy. Now we had a chance to catch up on Cav gossip. We learned, for example, that the 1st Cavalry Division, which went back to the old horse cavalry days, was General MacArthur's favorite. After the end of World War II, the division had been the general's "palace guard" in Tokyo. We heard that the reason the 1st Cav got into some of the worst fighting was because MacArthur felt it could handle anything. We sort of figured the general was not exactly doing I Company any favors.

Another story we heard had to do with a memorable Tokyo brawl between the Cav and the 11th Airborne. Back at Camp Carson I had heard that the Airborne boys had cleaned up on the Cavalry. Now, on the Imjin River, we had a chance to talk to one of the Tokyo occupation GIs who stopped by to shoot some bullshit. Without us bringing up the story, he talked about it himself. His version had the Cav stomping hell out of the 11th Airborne.

Pvt. JAMES CARDINAL
I Company/5th Cavalry

The men in the field felt the war was over. After all, the enemy's army had been virtually destroyed and prisoners streamed in by the thousands. All that remained was the trip home and the big victory parade.

I was very disappointed that I had seen so little action. At one point during this period, I asked Lieutenant Geer for a transfer to the 2d Division, which was rumored to be involved in fighting in another area. He never even answered me—just walked away. Later, Lieutenant Brian explained that Geer thought I was nuts because I was always volunteering for patrols and other dangerous activities. (In fact, as I look back upon it after thirty-four years, my behavior must have seemed somewhat bizarre.) I was beside myself with frustration at having seen so little combat. Time went by slowly. Life became boring. It was wait, wait, wait. Mail call was heaven, except, of course, for those unfortunates whose names were not called.

Some time was taken up guessing how long it would take Hollywood to produce in glorious Technicolor the first Korean War movie. Names like Tyrone Power, Errol Flynn, John Wayne, and Gary Cooper were put forth as prospective heroes. There was in these discussions a certain cynicism which grew in intensity in the bleak, cruel months that lay ahead.

2d. Lt. ADRIAN B. BRIAN
I Company/5th Cavalry

Very strong bonds of friendship developed at this time. I became very close to two of my men—Jerry Emer and James Cardinal. We used to sit next to our pup tents at night and talk for hours about all topics imaginable. Jerry was short but powerful and could throw a hand grenade farther than anyone I'd ever seen. He was the youngest of thirteen children and often amused us with stories about his childhood. He was quiet and let the world roll by without getting emotionally involved. Jim wanted to be a New York City police sergeant. His greatest desire was to be a hero so his war record would help him advance in the police force.

I used to think it was not right for me to like these two so much. I was afraid it would compromise my leadership role or result in my playing favorites, but it never did. I think the combat situation makes the need for a clear line of authority so obvious that no one would think of challenging it. Each frontline infantryman looked to his leader for his safety and well-being. I had heard stories of officers being shot by their own men or being "fragged" by a grenade tossed into their tent. This is hogwash! It sure as hell never happened in Korea in the frontline outfits.

Capt. NORMAN ALLEN
I Company/5th Cavalry

Mother darling:
Arrived from the hospital yesterday to a company which handles replacements and hospital returnees.

The ROKs have been across the 38th Parallel two days now and report that the Reds have withdrawn, so how far they intend to withdraw and where they plan to make their defense is the problem. There are so many possibilities—back to a junction with the Chinese Reds or to a point where the Chinese can reinforce them. Time will tell, just hope it doesn't take too long.

Next day.
Today wrote personal letters to all the parents and wives of my KIAs, giving them some of the details of the action the man was killed in. I also told how well-liked the man was and some of the outstanding things he had done while in the company for which he will be remembered. It brought Hill 174 all back and was kind of heartbreaking.

The cold weather is really beginning to hit. Three blankets are not enough on the canvas cot I am sleeping on now. Golly, you know the ground is going to be worse. Everyone is really praying this doesn't turn into a winter campaign. That would really be rough.

On the front lines the very little things, extra water, some gum, a few cigars, and maybe an occasional hot meal and the men are insanely happy. Troops in the rear with cots, roofs over their heads, hot-water showers, bitch and raise hell cause they don't get enough beer. Actually it's not so unreasonable, just the troops at the various echelons live at such varied standards. What it takes to please the frontline soldier with the lowest standard, wouldn't even faze a rear-line soldier. A little thing like a night without fear is looked upon as a golden apple and about as rare.

Should be able to rejoin I Company tomorrow. It will be nice to see the lads again. . . .

PURSUIT

9 October-31 October 1950

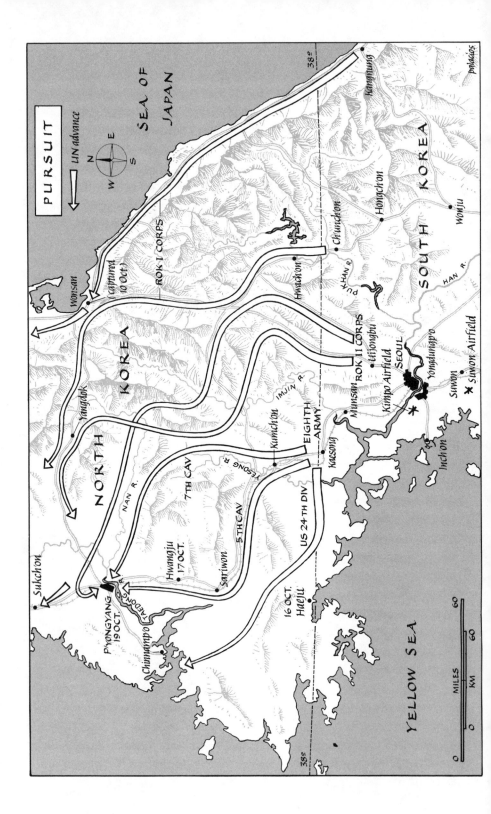

By midsummer there was a growing consensus in Washington that Eighth Army should cross the 38th Parallel and reunite Korea. During August the U.S. ambassador to the United Nations, Warren Austin, raised the idea of unifying Korea in the Security Council. In early September the National Security Council prepared a paper, which President Truman approved, recommending that General MacArthur be authorized to operate in North Korea on the condition that the Soviet Union or Communist China did not intervene before the Parallel was crossed. The Joint Chiefs of Staff (JCS) sent the recommendation to MacArthur on 15 September, the day of the Inch'on landings, and advised him that a directive would be forthcoming. The directive reached Tokyo on 27 September. It authorized MacArthur to go north on the conditions approved by the president, and said he would be sent armistice terms he could broadcast to North Korea. The JCS asked the general to submit his plans for operations in North Korea. He sent them on the 28th and they were approved by the JCS the next day.

The Marines had stormed ashore at Inch'on and Eighth Army had broken out of the Pusan Perimeter; it was apparent to everyone the war would soon be over. There still remained, however, the necessity of pressing and destroying the North Korean Army. After weeks of cautious and concerned debate, the General Assembly, in a vote at Lake Success on 6 October, approved a plan for the UN forces to cross the Parallel. If there had been any doubt about what would happen at Lake Success, there was none at all about what Syngman Rhee's South

Korean government would do. On 1 October ROK units marched over the border and the next day set up command posts in North Korea. General MacArthur, too, had never been vague about his wishes. The day the South Koreans crossed the Parallel, he sent a message to Department of the Army:

I plan to issue and make public the following general directive to all elements of the United Nations command at 1200 hours, Monday, 2 October, unless I receive your instructions to the contrary. "Under the provisions of the United Nations Security Council Resolution of 27 June, the field of our military operations is limited only by military exigencies and the international boundaries of Korea. The so-called 38th Parallel, accordingly, is not a factor in the military employment of our forces. To accomplish the enemy's complete defeat, your troops may cross the border at any time, either in exploratory probing or exploiting local tactical conditions. If the enemy fails to accept the terms of surrender set forth in my message to him on 1 October,* our forces, in due process of campaign will seek out and destroy the enemy's armed forces in whatever part of Korea they may be located."

GEN. DOUGLAS MacARTHUR, COMMANDER IN CHIEF,

UNITED NATIONS COMMAND

The plan of attack north of the 38th Parallel called for Eighth Army to advance in the west and for X Corps, which had been withdrawn from the Seoul/Inch'on area, to make an amphibious landing on the peninsula's east coast at Wonsan and march north toward the Chosin Reservoir and the Yalu River. For the next phase of the war, these two independent field commands would be separated by seventy-five miles of high, nearly impenetrable mountains.

Eighth Army would proceed in the west along the railway line and main highway that linked Seoul with the North Korean capital

---

*Not only were they not accepted, they were ignored. The terms were obviously heard by the Chinese, who warned India's ambassador to Peiping on 3 October that China would enter the war if the UN forces crossed the Parallel. New Delhi passed the warning to Washington, D.C., where it was evidently dismissed.

of P'yongyang. Its advance would be spearheaded by the 1st Cavalry
Division. The 24th Division and ROK 1st Division would protect the
flanks and form the reserve.

Pfc. VICTOR FOX
I Company/5th Cavalry

We were told to saddle up for the ride into North Korea. When we
neared the border, a World War II combat veteran announced, "Remember this day, you guys. We're makin' history." The spontaneous
reply, delivered in unison, "Buuulllshit!"

Pfc. LEONARD KORGIE
G Company/21st Infantry

Our dreams of a short war were shattered the morning of October 9
when we were awakened by the clank of tanks and the roar of trucks.
What the hell was this?! We learned the boys in the 1st Cav were
crossing the Parallel. We were told we were going to cross, too. No
one knew why or how far we would go. The news wasn't all that bad.
Most of the enemy's main battle divisions had been overrun at the
Pusan Perimeter, the rest had been scattered at Inch'on by the Marines. What was left couldn't amount to much; they'd either surrender or become civilians.

Sgt. WARREN AVERY
G Company/21st Infantry

We'd followed the North Koreans all night. Every four or five miles
our lead tank would shut off its engine and we'd hear the North Ko-

rean tanks in the distance down the road. Before first light, right in front of us, at the foot of a mountain, we saw a town. We attacked at dawn. It was like being back in combat school. As we moved across the rice paddies, just like clockwork, the Air Force strafed the town. Then our tanks and artillery opened fire. Everything hit the town all at once. We blew it to smithereens! We found half a dozen dead North Koreans and three destroyed T34s. The rest of the North Koreans escaped around the next mountain.

Pfc. LEONARD KORGIE
G Company/21st Infantry
The civilians were so happy to see us. I was thrilled for them. They wanted to *give* us eggs and produce, not like the South Koreans, who tried to sell them to us. They lined the road in their villages, looking like they'd been relieved of a heavy burden—silent, happy, meek as lambs. I guess five years of Communist rule would do that to a people.

The 1st Cav rode ahead of us in trucks, we marched on foot. A day or so into North Korea we uncovered a small but grisly scene. I've seen it in my dreams a thousand times. Some signal unit from the 1st Cav had been ambushed by North Korean guerrillas. Obviously spread out on the road, this unit had been picked off and destroyed. The enemy must have attacked at close range. The GIs scattered into the ditches. The North Koreans charged and finished them off. Then the Communists poured gasoline over everything and set it on fire. We walked among the smoldering bodies. Some guys still clutched letters from home. The North Koreans had finished off anyone who wasn't dead. On this calm day the smell of burnt flesh hung over the scene. There was nothing we could do. It was over and we went on. For hours no one said a word. *Now* we were on our guard. The enemy was alive and well and in the hills around us. No longer did we move with impunity.

Sgt. WARREN AVERY
G Company/21st Infantry
We battled in the mountains with North Korean guerrillas who had been left behind. We had one terrific fight around an abandoned gold

mine the enemy was using as a stronghold. Around dusk they hit us, came out through the mine's entrance. It was then I really found out what a BAR can do. I dueled all night with a North Korean. He shot green tracers at me; I shot red tracers at him. He fired, I ducked; I fired, he ducked. About 2:00 in the morning, I finally hit him. The sluiceways caught fire and the North Koreans were silhouetted in front of the flames. It became a shooting gallery. By morning it was all over.

Pfc. VICTOR FOX
I Company/5th Cavalry
A genuine wonder was the way so many units made their advance. Footpaths on any kind of acceptable terrain feature were quickly worn and widened by hundreds of wheeled and tracked vehicles passing over them. And in some of the damnedest places. Many of these "new" roads needed only a bit of grading to rank with the North Korean so-called main highways.

2d Lt. ADRIAN B. BRIAN
I Company/5th Cavalry
After we crossed the 38th Parallel, we really started moving. There were only pockets of resistance here and there. We got into a race for P'yongyang; everyone wanted to be the first unit to get the enemy's capital. From time to time there were arguments over who would have road priority. One time we were rolling along a narrow dirt track, large enough for an ox-drawn cart but hardly wide enough for a two-and-a-half-ton truck or a tank, when we had a run-in with a solitary British soldier who was having trouble with his armored personnel carrier [APC].* The thing had broken down at a critical spot on the

---

* The British 27th Infantry Brigade, a unit of regular troops comprising the 1st Battalion of the Middlesex Regiment and the 1st Battalion of the Argyll and Sutherland Highlanders, arrived in Korea on 29 August 1950.

road where there was no way around it (there were drops on both sides). The entire 5th Cav stopped behind the British soldier and his vehicle. Colonel Crombez worked his way forward and got into a shouting match with this Tommy. The Brit was not about to let Colonel Crombez push his vehicle off the road. We were held up for about an hour. We all were quietly cheering for the British soldier, who won the confrontation.

[The long motorized columns were constantly vexed by supply problems, mined roads, and enemy roadblocks. The advance stopped, started, and stopped again with metronomic regularity. Where you were in the column, and when, determined what piece of the war you saw or participated in. Often the ride was tedious, at other times wildly exciting. It was like riding a roller coaster: the climbs put you to sleep, the drops woke you up—screaming.]

Pfc. VICTOR FOX
I Company/5th Cavalry
Day and night there were long periods of stop and go, stop and go. No matter when or where the stops were made, I Company piled out of its trucks and secured the road flanks. We slept in full combat gear. During the pursuit there was little time for eating. Hot chow never caught up with us, though we heard it was ready.

One morning a group of wailing women near a cluster of huts ran toward us. They were accompanied by a young North Korean Army nurse who surrendered to us. She was put in my truck, in the front of the truck bed, so she could not escape. Pretty soon some guys at that end began molesting her. I knew then why the women on the road were crying. Guys around me spoke up: "Lay off!" "Come on, you guys. What d'ya think we're here for in the first place?" "Hey, knock it off!" It wasn't that the rest of us were Puritans, but under the circumstances it didn't seem like the right thing to do. Besides, many felt that if harm came to this girl, divine retribution in the form of a night ambush would descend upon us. After a few hours the girl was turned over to a POW collecting point. I don't know if she still had her pants on.

Later in the morning, about fifty yards ahead of our platoon, a half-track touched off a mine. A terrific blast jolted the vehicle upward, blackened it, and blew a neat hole right through the hood, killing the two GIs riding in the cab. Everyone hollered frantically. The trailing vehicles immediately pulled off to the side of the road.

The North Koreans were so harried they often left their land mines fully exposed on the road. This, of course, caused much derisive comment. It did look like a futile gesture—until the sun went down and we drove at night without headlights. Then, every bump along the darkened road caused a wince. A definite pucker string situation. GIs gladly volunteered to walk the road in front of the vehicles. Infantrymen and engineers crawling on their hands and knees, probing, oh, so c-a-r-e-f-u-l-l-y for mines, can really slow down a good drive.

13 October 1950

The enemy had established a continuous mine field on the road between Yugadong and Kumch'on, employing an extremely large number of wooden AT mines. The road march was temporarily held up by 300 enemy at Yonghap-tong. These obstacles were dispersed as fast as fire power could be brought into position.

NARRATIVE REPORT, 5TH CAVALRY REGIMENT

Pvt. JAMES CARDINAL
I Company/5th Cavalry

Somewhere east of Kumch'on, forward elements of the regiment had run into a roadblock and the column stopped. The North Koreans were chased off and because we were in the middle of the column, it took us a while to reach the scene of the firefight. A little off the road lay several North Koreans who had been wounded in the fighting. It so happened it was at this spot that my platoon stopped and broke out the C rations. Jerry Emer and another guy ate canned hamburger, a meal I detested so much that no matter how hungry I was, I refused to eat it. A platoon of tanks hove into view. When they got closer, I saw the lead tank was led by a lieutenant wearing a

Western-style moustache, goggles, and a baseball cap worn backward. He stood up in one of the hatches. When he spotted the wounded North Koreans, he leaned forward to shout into the tank. This tank, followed by the other three, swerved off the road and clanked over the enemy soldiers. Shrill screams were quickly blotted out by the roar of the engines. A cloud of dust, mixed with blood, guts, and pieces of bodies, swirled in the air. The tanks returned to the road and were soon out of sight. Emer was a hardy soul and never missed a bite of his cold hamburger. The other kid vomited all over himself.

A day later the company stopped in the road alongside a small village. A couple of guys from 1st Platoon threw lighted matches on the straw roofs of the huts. In no time at all the village was an inferno. I expect these are common occurrences in all wars. Man has an infinite capacity to be bestial to his own kind.

15 October 1950
Rainfall and muddy roads made travel virtually impossible when the Regiment assembled to move out. . . . The Regiment moved to Hanpa-ri then west a few miles before muddy roads halted the column.

NARRATIVE REPORT, 5TH CAVALRY REGIMENT

Pvt. JAMES CARDINAL
I Company/5th Cavalry
Near P'yongyang the food and cigarette shortage became unbearable. A typical meal at this time was a slice of Spam and a half canteen-cup of grapefruit juice—once a day. We stripped the countryside bare in our search to find anything edible. There is a popular belief, circulated mainly by Hollywood, that combat soldiers talk about nothing but sex. This is totally false. In fact, as we grew hungrier and hungrier, we talked of nothing but food. We had reveries about food in the day and dreams about food at night. It obsessed us. We titillated each other dreaming up meals we would prepare if we got home. This is when I became very fond of lamb, a meat my mother never used to serve in our home. An Armenian American in 2d Platoon talked of nothing but lamb: roasted, broiled, baked, on rice, with potatoes, smothered in herbs—lamb, lamb, lamb. (It was the first meal

I ordered in a Tokyo restaurant on an R and R trip in July 1951, and when I rotated home in September.)

The craving for cigarettes was partially satisfied by smoking dried leaves wrapped in C-ration toilet paper. The irony of it all, as in every war, is that just a few miles behind the front, rear-echelon troops have all the food and cigarettes they could possibly want.

Another problem was the weather, which grew colder. We still had not been issued winter uniforms. I will never forget my disgust with Lieutenant Geer when he ordered me to remove a fur cap I had taken off a dead North Korean soldier. He told me it was unsoldierly, that I would have to be satisfied with my fatigue cap and helmet.

Cpl. MARIO SORRENTINO
Task Force Indianhead

I had volunteered in early October for a special mission. They needed demolitions experts and, knowing nothing more than that, I volunteered. Much speculation went on about what we would do. Rumors had us blowing a bridge or tunnel. A tall lieutenant colonel with a crew cut eventually filled us in on the mission. Called "Task Force Indianhead" (from the 2d Division's patch, which shows an Indian wearing a warbonnet), our job would be to liberate American POWs or capture Russian personnel found in the North Korean capital, P'yongyang. I never blinked. As far as the capital went, I could hardly pronounce it, let alone be afraid of what I'd find there. I couldn't have cared less about the danger or seriousness of the mission. I was eighteen at the time. If it was exciting, I was all for it.

Pfc. VICTOR FOX
I Company/5th Cavalry

Once we rode down out of the mountains and reached the plain leading to P'yongyang, the race really picked up. Enemy delaying tactics all but vanished. We were aware that the ROKs on our flanks were moving very fast and could well beat us to the capital. To slow the South Koreans down, the rumor went, Cav units would fire on them— accidental-like.

18 October 1950
Orders from the commanding general, 1st Cavalry Division, were received for the 5th Cavalry to pass through the 7th Cavalry Regiment and lead the 1st Cavalry Division into P'yongyang. The advance was to be made in a column of battalions.

NARRATIVE REPORT, 5TH CAVALRY REGIMENT

Pfc. VICTOR FOX
I Company/5th Cavalry
The trucks drove in blackout condition—no headlights. It was raining hard. Third Squad, augmented with some South Koreans, dozed the best they could. Most sat propped up by the press of bodies. Suddenly, everything went topsy-turvy; felt like we were in a washing machine dropped from a building. The truck lay upside down, most of us lay pinned beneath it. Momentary silence. People tried to move, to crawl out. Some shithead yelled, "Fire!" Threatening voices got the panic-head calmed down. Everyone eventually managed to crawl out in an orderly manner. Flashlights and spotlights from up on the roadway shone down in the gully where the truck lay. It was difficult just scrambling back up to the road. It was a miracle none of us were killed. Our nerves were shot to hell.

Capt. NORMAN ALLEN
I Company/5th Cavalry
About dawn I came upon a deuce-and-a-half with I Company markings off the road upside down. Some men were pulling other men out from under the truck. I was returning from the hospital (actually was sick of medics and just walked out), caught a ride and had ridden

about 100 miles. A lieutenant named Tomlinson, an older, country fellow, whom I had never seen before, was standing by. Told me he was with I Company. I identified myself and with his help got four or five of the injured men into a medical vehicle and sent to the rear. We distributed the uninjured men in 5th Cav vehicles with instructions for them to join us when they could.

Pfc. VICTOR FOX
I Company/5th Cavalry
We were told to hop a ride on any passing vehicle. Most of my squad climbed on the back of a deuce-and-a-half carrying fifty-gallon drums of gasoline. We were badly shaken and lit up cigarettes. After a while the driver stopped and took a look at what he had suspected. He turned deathly white. Afterward, the driver was so unnerved, the officer with him had to take the wheel. First, though, this officer really ass-chewed all of us. Said he was going to write us up, wanted the names and unit "that has this bunch of stupid bastards in it." Most likely we gave the officer the name of another unit. I cannot remember Captain Allen ever mentioning it to us.

Capt. NORMAN ALLEN
I Company/5th Cavalry
I finally caught up with the regiment and found 3d Battalion leading the column. When I located Colonel Treacy, I asked which company was on the point. "Guess," he replied. I requested permission to resume command of I Company. He approved, and I drove on. Beyond K Company I found I. Told Lieutenant Geer that I was again taking command. He didn't seem to mind.

Cpl. GEORGE CAMPBELL
3d Battalion/Royal Australian Regiment
I was evacuated near Sariwon on the grounds of suspected appendicitis. Had I not arrived so late at the casualty clearing station, I would have been flown out immediately.

In the morning I felt much, much better and persuaded the doctor to let me go back to my unit. I hitchhiked at first, then continued on foot until nightfall, when I was given shelter by an American artillery unit.

The next day [18 October] I continued my journey toward the front and reached the advance company of the United Nations forces, Item Company, of the 5th Cavalry Regiment. Its commander asked if I wanted to be returned to their headquarters or stay and take part in the forthcoming attack on the North Korean capital. I replied I would like to stay, but had only five rounds of .303 Lee Enfield ammunition with me. Captain Allen gave me the carbine of a sergeant who had recently been killed.

Cpl. MARIO SORRENTINO
Task Force Indianhead

Our task force commander drove directly to the head of a long convoy of vehicles belonging to the 1st Cavalry Division. There he was told by some colonel in no uncertain terms that our task force would not enter P'yongyang ahead of the 1st Cav. The rest of the day we bided our time and crept slowly toward the capital. By late afternoon we had reached the outskirts of the city. Twisting and turning down narrow streets, we halted before sunset alongside some railroad yards. We spent the night there.

[P'yongyang is the oldest city in Korea. When the war began, it had a population of nearly 500,000. Located forty miles from the Yellow Sea, the capital sits astride the broad, swiftly flowing Taedong River. On the south side of the river is a large, sprawling, industrial suburb; on the north side is the old city and all the governmental buildings. In 1950 two railway bridges and the main highway bridge connected the two areas.

The 5th Cavalry Regiment's 3d Battalion was ordered to seize and occupy the part of P'yongyang that lay north of the Taedong. To Captain Allen's Item Company would fall the task of forcing the river and establishing a bridgehead on the northern bank for the rest of the battalion.]

19 October 1950

A hot meal on a cold, frosty morning instilled new energy in the impatient Cavalrymen. They were ready to travel by 0700 hours, at which time the advance began.

NARRATIVE REPORT, 5TH CAVALRY REGIMENT

Capt. NORMAN ALLEN
I Company/5th Cavalry

At dawn it was still raining. A pretty fair breakfast of pancakes was brought forward. Second Battalion passed through us and took the point. Later in the day we found dead and wounded gooks lying by the road, indications the 2d Battalion was doing a fine job. We rolled behind them for several miles before we stopped at a dike on the edge of a small cluster of houses that marked the southern outskirts of P'yongyang. General Gay and Colonel Crombez [division and regimental commanders] were on the left of the road. General Gay's aide, the son of one of his old friends, had just been shot and lay dying. Gen. Frank Allen, the 1st Cav's ADC, was in the road and waved us through. A hundred yards farther down the road, I ordered a halt and realigned the column. Then I pulled my jeep to the front and the column began to wind its way to the railroad bridge that was our objective. Drawing no fire, we proceeded until stopped by the Taedong River.

I dismounted and ran to the dike to see what I could. No more than five feet away, I looked into the eyes of a North Korean soldier. He turned to run and I dropped him. Excited about getting out of that one and of hitting the sonovabitch, I failed to notice an enemy machine gun off to my right along the riverbank. It was only when I turned to wave the lead platoon forward that from the corner of my eye I caught the gun's movement as it shifted toward me. By this time I was a little ways down the reverse slope of the dike and didn't know what to do. I froze. The machine gun suddenly swung away from me and engaged another target, then moved back to me. Just then, M Company's CO, a redheaded Texan named Walt Watts, charged down into them, waving his .45. Swinging left and right, hitting here, banging there, he captured the entire enemy crew without firing a shot. For more than an hour Captain Watts marched these North Koreans up and down the road until I'm sure the entire regiment saw them. (He received a Silver Star for the episode—deserved it, too, for he had surely saved my ass.)

When the covering tanks, machine guns, and mortars were in place, we began to cross the Taedong River over the railway bridge. Second Battalion [E and G Companies] moved with us on the highway bridge to our right. The North Koreans then blew that bridge. A moment later they blew the far span of our railroad bridge.

[Earlier in the day the 5th Cav's Fox Company had crossed a portion of the railroad bridge and stopped on an island in the middle of the river. When Captain Allen's I Company went to relieve them, the North Koreans attempted to blow the bridge. Fortunately for everyone but the Communists, only the span connecting the enemy's side of the city to the island was destroyed. The span connecting the American-held side to the island remained intact.]

Pfc. VICTOR FOX
I Company/5th Cavalry
A Sherman tank astride the railroad track covered us while we made our way along the bridge. The distant sounds of machine guns and the accompanying twinkling lights meant the North Koreans were on the other side and trying to stop us. Fire zinged overhead. Damned if the North Koreans weren't finally making a stand.

Pvt. JAMES CARDINAL
I Company/5th Cavalry
Just before we started across to the island, I spoke to a guy named Baer. He had two bandoliers of ammo crisscrossing his chest and four grenades dangling from various pockets. I cracked a pun about how he looked like he was loaded for bear. When I reached the island, I stumbled upon his body, which lay in the underbrush. He had been shot through the head.

19 October 1950

The entire city of P'yongyang south of the river was secured by the end of the day. The 1st Battalion followed the 3d Battalion and deployed along the Taedong River in the vicinity of the railroad bridge, preparatory to crossing the river. Enemy artillery and small arms fire continued to harass 5th Cavalrymen throughout the night.

NARRATIVE REPORT, 5TH CAVALRY REGIMENT

[Alone on the island in the middle of the Taedong River, the men of Item Company had much to do before the sun rose. Nothing that happened to them on the wet, cold night of 19–20 October was routine or expected.]

Capt. NORMAN ALLEN
I Company/5th Cavalry
Once night fell, Colonel Treacy came up to tell me I Company would attack next morning across the river. Boats would be brought up and the company would go over at dawn.

Pvt. JAMES CARDINAL
I Company/5th Cavalry
We lay huddled behind a dike and waited for the boats. As time passed we grew more apprehensive. Occasional harassing enemy fire kept our heads down. It was cold and wet and dark. Imagining what might happen at daybreak kept us awake. Lieutenant Brian suddenly emerged from the darkness. He casually sauntered along the beach in front of his platoon. Sporting a magnificent moustache he seemed, at that moment, the reincarnation of a Civil War officer preparing to lead his men, saber in hand, in a bayonet charge. His bravery had a calming effect on each of us.

Cpl. GEORGE CAMPBELL
3d Battalion/Royal Australian Regiment
Rather than sit in the mud, I sat in my helmet and covered myself
with a poncho, a trick I learned in World War II in New Guinea.
The sergeant waking the next batch for guard duty by giving them a
kick on their bottoms kicked my helmet and remarked, "Christ, but
you've got a hard ass." I said, "Have I?" He answered, "Oh, you're
the Aussie."

Pfc. VICTOR FOX
I Company/5th Cavalry
Third Squad was ordered to the south side of the island to set up security and guide the 8th Engineer groups, which would come from
that direction to our position. Haltom, Sergeant Furlan, Sergeant
Nelson, and I positioned ourselves just below the skyline of the embankment that led up to the railroad bridge. Worried we might be
cut off while on the island, the machine gunner, Sergeant Pate, also
set up.

     It rained hard and the damp cold went through us. Because of
harassing fire coming from the other bank, we could not light a fire.
Forgot when we'd eaten last. Hours went by.

2d Lt. ADRIAN B. BRIAN
I Company/5th Cavalry
There were a couple of freight cars abandoned on the bridge about
fifty yards offshore. I thought we should check on them but had done
nothing about it because of the danger. If there were North Koreans
lying in ambush in the cars, anybody checking them would be a dead
duck, because there was no place to take cover. I was thinking out
loud about the problem when Jim Cardinal volunteered to check the
cars. This bothered me because I never ordered anybody to do something I would be afraid to do. If I had to send out a patrol in a dangerous situation, I would lead it in spite of my fear. In this case, I
just couldn't do it. Anyway, Jim started down the tracks toward the
cars. As he disappeared into the blackness of the night, I began to
pray.

Pvt. JAMES CARDINAL
I Company/5th Cavalry
Visions of glory danced before my eyes. I was eager to make a name for myself, to be cited for heroism. I had to prove I was as good, if not better, than my father.

I was warned that an enemy machine gun was sighted along the bridge and I should be very careful and extremely quiet. It was pitch dark and very cold. I stripped down to my shirt and trousers. Because it was too dark to see clearly where I was going, I groped my way along the bridge, feeling for the ties, on which I placed my hands and knees. Far below, the river raced by. Occasionally, an enemy machine gun fired in my direction, its tracers flying overhead.

I crawled for what seemed an hour. A flare went off and illuminated the entire area. I flattened out. More flares burst upstream. In their light I saw that the abandoned railroad cars were empty. I returned as quietly as I could to the island and reported this news to Captain Allen. He thanked me and promoted me on the spot to a squad leader in the 5th Platoon, which was made up of KATUSAs.

Pfc. VICTOR FOX
I Company/5th Cavalry
Finally, from the darkness below where we lay, we heard sounds. Had the enemy worked their way behind us? We tightened the perimeter. When our platoon sergeant called out, he was answered by an American voice. Even though we had made contact with the engineers, we remained wary of all those Korean porters who lugged the assault boats onto the island. One of the engineer GIs bragged that he could have picked some of us off the embankment. We told him we considered a 5-to-1 kill ratio in our favor to be acceptable. Then we found out the goddamned engineers forgot to bring all the paddles.

Capt. NORMAN ALLEN
I Company/5th Cavalry
The boats took all night to come up, and when they did, the five boats had but one paddle between them. A brand-new engineer, second lieutenant, right out of West Point (I learned later he'd graduated

in June), came with them. When he reported, he asked how I intended to employ the boats. "To cross the river in," I barked. "What'n hell did you think I was gonna do with them?!" When I calmed down, I told him I was going to need some information and wanted him to get it for me. Because I'd heard that the Taedong had a very fast tidal current, I wanted to know *how* fast and from what direction it flowed at dawn. I also wanted to know how much river there was between the island and the enemy-held shore. Because this information would tell me the time needed to reinforce the first wave, I considered it particularly important. Once I knew the amount of time it would take to cross the river, I could decide how large the first wave needed to be. I guess this was a big order for the youngster, but he said he would try to find out for me. Then I received a radio message that this officer was expected to report back to regiment immediately. What bullshit! I told him, "To hell with what regiment wants. You figure out what I asked you. We're making the crossing, not the fucking regiment!" Poor kid didn't know what to do. He stayed. Guess he figured I was closer and meaner.

That night it rained and was cold as hell. After conferring with Colonel Treacy, who had come out to the island, I returned to the problem of crossing the river. As a Boy Scout I had learned how to measure the height of a tree by using a right triangle. I wondered now if I could apply the same technique to a horizontal problem. I spotted the engineer platoon sergeant and walked over to him; figured he might not savvy the mathematics, but might have the experience to figure something out. I was not about to put my entire trust in a green second lieutenant. The sergeant was coiling a wet rope and counting to himself. From the river I saw a soaking-wet and freezing lieutenant walking toward us. "What'n hell is going on?" I asked. He was shivering and his teeth chattered. He replied, "S-sir, I only knew one w-way to make sure of the w-w-width of the r-river." The sergeant jumped in. "He swam it, sir, and I'm measuring the line he took with him." I believe I remarked that after four years of West Point, and in engineering at that, there had to be a better way to measure a river—jeez, or words to that effect. It took some courage, though, to swim that damn cold river. If he had suspected how many gooks were waiting in the trenches on the far side, he would really have turned purple. Unfortunately, regiment again insisted that he return, so I never learned his name nor saw him again.

Sometime before sunrise I tackled another problem. First Lieutenant [Lester] Blevins, who had joined the company a week before, got into a squabble with division artillery, which insisted on firing 155s in our support. I had asked Blevins to tell arty that they should not fire on the river dike, but on the built-up area that lay behind. I wanted to leave the dike to our 4.2s, which were a hell of a lot more accurate and responsible. Some goddamn regimental artillery captain told Blevins, "You don't tell us what to fire, we tell you." I'll never forget that. I grabbed the mike and yelled at the sonovabitch that he had already dropped short rounds on my company on Hill 174. "If you drop one short on me this time, no matter how long it takes, I'll find you and kill you!" He turned off his radio and I was left howling into an empty mike.

Just before the first wave was due to leave the island, by God, if they didn't drop another short round, this time right on the platoon CP! It wounded several men, including Lester Blevins. When I got to him, he was lying on his back, spread-eagled. He'd been hit in the groin. Top Mitchell pointed to a cordlike thing that stretched out from him about twenty feet. "What'n hell's that?" Top whispered, "Testicles." "Holy Christ!" I had never seen anything like it. Top said, "I'll cut it off up close." "Hell, no," I said, "let's roll the stuff up and stick it in his crotch bandage. Let some doctor make that decision."

2d Lt. ADRIAN B. BRIAN
I Company/5th Cavalry

One of the other platoons had the honor of being the first to cross; the engineers did the paddling. They took off in five boats with only a few paddles. I thought how ironic it was that our great nation could only provide a few boats for an assault across a river in the heart of the enemy capital.

Pfc. VICTOR FOX
I Company/5th Cavalry
The 1st Platoon piled into the assault boats and slid off across the dark water. Our sergeants yelled over and over to keep our supporting fire concentrated on the embankment skyline. It would be a court-martial for anyone lowering his aim. Our artillery really pounded the far shore.

2d Lt. ADRIAN B. BRIAN
I Company/5th Cavalry
The assault boats were to land by the base of the railroad bridge opposite our position. Fortunately, the current swept the boats downstream about 100 yards, because the area where they had been scheduled to land was protected by at least one NK machine gun. Heavy fire broke out as they reached the shore. We heard some rebel yells and shouts among the sounds of firing, so we knew our people were in a pretty tough fight.

Pfc. VICTOR FOX
I Company/5th Cavalry
From the far embankment we heard a shout like a rebel yell. Our officers and NCOs on the island ran around frantically kicking ass: "Cease fire, goddamn it. Cease fire. Our guys are ashore." We stopped firing. The enemy didn't.

> Heavy automatic fire came from the buildings and the dike running southwest of the railroad. Determined troopers in the boats and with support from the 2d Battalion enabled the assault force to gain the northern shore. As the boats returned for more personnel, artillery disabled one of the craft. Crossing was slow because of the boat shortage. . . .
>
> NARRATIVE REPORT, 5TH CAVALRY REGIMENT

Capt. NORMAN ALLEN
I Company/5th Cavalry
The engineer sergeant, an old, white-haired soldier (well, guess he wasn't so old; probably had premature white hair and had been run hard and put up wet a few times), insisted he had to remain on the island to manage the boats. I told him if the boats were in the river or on the far side, then that is where he should be. Don't know if he went or not. Of course, the engineers didn't want to make repeat trips into that hell. Think only one or two of them braved the fire on the initial wave. The rest busied themselves running about saying they were trying to get additional boats and paddles, but I'm sure they only did this when we were looking at them. The rest of the time they were doing what the rest of us would have liked to have been doing— heads down, digging like hell. Screw the goddamn business of crossing a wide, wild river in teeny-weeny rubber boats while being shot at. Christ, what a way to earn a living.

Pvt. JAMES CARDINAL
I Company/5th Cavalry
When the boats came back to the island, I jumped into one that contained several dead bodies. While the boat rose and fell in the current, bloody water sloshed back and forth. After the bodies were unloaded, the boats took us across the river under heavy fire. I looked at the landing area. The shore ran 100 feet before it met a precipitous fifteen-foot-high dike. I dropped into the water and waded toward the beach. It was like a dream many of us have had: we are wading through water, trying to escape some evil monster, and our feet move in slow motion. It seemed forever before I made the shore and ran to the dike. A concrete blockhouse lay in my path. I tossed a grenade through a narrow aperture. A muffled explosion followed. I didn't stop to find out if there had been anyone inside.

At the dike I saw my KATUSAs were disorganized and beginning to falter. They were as brave as the next man, just needed firm leadership. Cursing and kicking, I got them back on the firing line.

Once on top of the dike, we looked into the city. Below, dozens of North Korean soldiers ran between buildings. We poured our fire into them. Smoke covered the city. There were many casualties.

Pfc. VICTOR FOX
I Company/5th Cavalry
The assault boats returned. Third Platoon jumped in. We used rifle stocks and hands to paddle across the swiftly flowing river. We were told to crouch low and stay that way, no matter what. About midway a redheaded kid stood up for some reason. He was immediately cut down. His body splashed into the water and was gone. He'd been a good kid, but worried so much that he went around with the look of death on him.

More sunlight illuminated the scene. My boat touched the embankment. I glanced up. Second Platoon was chasing North Koreans off the top of the levee. We jumped ashore and climbed forward. For the "light resistance" advocates, there were sure a lot of dead North Koreans behind the embankment.

Item Company pushed forward and gradually enlarged the bridgehead. They had secured 700 yards of the dike centering on the railroad bridge by 0938 hours.

NARRATIVE REPORT, 5TH CAVALRY REGIMENT

Pfc. VICTOR FOX
I Company/5th Cavalry
We crossed the embankment in full daylight. The first houses we came upon contained air-raid shelters. At the entrance to one, we shouted down for anyone there to come out with their hands up. Soon an old papa-san, women, and children emerged. They were badly frightened. Our interpreters told us these civilians expected us to put them to death, as that's what they had been told by the Communists. Their fears turned to happy confusion when we offered them cigarettes, chewing gum, and chocolate bars. I think we also gave them some of our canned rations. Looked like they needed them more than we did.

In many sections of the city, snipers, automatic weapons, and some antitank guns greeted our arrival. Each strong point was promptly wiped out and the enemy killed or driven north. By

1430 hours, 3d Battalion had secured their zone of the city and made contact with British and ROK forces. . . .

NARRATIVE REPORT, 5TH CAVALRY REGIMENT

Cpl. GEORGE CAMPBELL
3d Battalion/Royal Australian Regiment
I met a jeepload of Australian war correspondents who had been with a South Korean unit and had come into the capital from a different direction. They were put out to find they had not been the first Australians into P'yongyang.

Pfc. VICTOR FOX
I Company/5th Cavalry
In the afternoon we cleared the downtown and business sections. The streets were cleverly arranged in mazes of sandbags and other barriers. There was the expected sniper and occasional harassing fire but nothing in the way of all-out street-to-street, door-to-door fighting that had gone on in Seoul. On the sides of many buildings were interesting and different posters, all depicting the evils of Western imperialism. One showed a lustful GI with a Dracula face sporting wristwatches clear up both arms. Another poster showed the Communists' own armed forces in the usual heroic and angelic poses. What made it curious was that all the North Koreans looked like blue-eyed WASPs. It drew the typical GI response.

2d Lt. ADRIAN B. BRIAN
I Company/5th Cavalry
We were on patrol when we came across an intoxicated ROK walking down the road all by himself. In his condition I don't know how he managed to stay alive. He had a bottle of champagne, which was obviously a hazard to his health. I saved his life by relieving him of it and sending him down the road toward our position. After a while my patrol climbed to the top of a hill overlooking the city. We stopped to rest and Emer and Cardinal and I shared the champagne with a

couple of other guys. We had grandstand seats to watch an air strike about half a mile away. We toasted the brave heroes of the Air Force.

Pfc. LEONARD KORGIE
G Company/21st Infantry

P'yongyang must have been carpet-bombed by B-29s. It was really battered. We found eight wounded NKs lying in the display window of a store. Each had a leg wound that prevented him from retreating with the main garrison. They were very frightened. Once they realized they weren't going to be executed, they talked freely. Through an interpreter we learned their Russian advisers had left the day before. It was always the same. We couldn't catch one of those bastards.

I was at the head of the column with Captain Syverson. We moved down several streets. Machine-gun fire to our rear stopped us in our tracks. Syverson sent several of us back to find out what had happened. We were told the eight wounded North Koreans had been shot. We asked around but no one seemed to know anything more.

Guys kept looking for Kim Il Sung's [Premier of the Democratic People's Republic of Korea] residence. I had visions of being part of a capitulation ceremony, something like Lee surrendering to Grant at Appomattox or MacArthur accepting the Jap surrender on the *Missouri*. My fantasy was soon destroyed. Kim and his boys had apparently flown out with the Russians. My chances of being a part of history went down the drain.

If we didn't find the government, we did find factories. Alas, they were empty. I asked civilians where the machinery was—the studs were still in the floor. I learned the machinery had gone north along with Kim Il Sung.

Cpl. MARIO SORRENTINO
Task Force Indianhead

I had no idea what to expect. Entering the city wasn't a problem. We encountered several barricades consisting of fifty-five-gallon drums filled with stone and rocks. At one corner a twin-barreled anti-aircraft gun pointed down the street.

The city was dirty and had a lot of unpaved streets. The store-fronts were shabby and reminded me—of course, without the traffic and lights—of Chicago's skid row district.

We drove into a schoolyard. Sitting on the ground were well over 1,000 North Korean POWs. They sat in rows of about fifty with their hands clasped on their heads. In front of this mob, South Korean officers sat at field tables. It looked like a kangaroo court was in session. ROK officers and NCOs walked between rows of prisoners. Occasionally, one of them would beat on or kick a POW. To one side several North Koreans hung like rag dolls from stout posts driven into the ground. These men had been executed and left to hang in the sun. The message to the prisoners sitting on the ground was obvious. At the time none of this affected me, not in the slightest. Little did I know then that this scene would stay forever in my memory.

The school building was not large—one story with several wings. I was shocked to find in one classroom the names of sixty-five Americans written on a blackboard. I distinctly remember the last name was Galvin. The school, I assume, was a holding area for prisoners of war. Nowhere, however, do I remember seeing bars or barbed wire.

From this school we drove to the city prison. A long stone building, it looked exactly like what it was. Inside, the cells were small and empty. A safe in one of the offices contained nothing but NK officer shoulder boards. We could not tell if American prisoners had been held there. Someone ran in and yelled that a well full of bodies had been found. We dashed outside. At the end of one cellblock there was a circular cement well. It was not deep—well, I don't know, it might have been. It was filled with the bodies of civilians. They lay one on top of another. We left. Our job was to find American POWs. I assumed people responsible for this kind of thing would take care of it.

Pfc. VICTOR FOX
I Company/5th Cavalry
Somehow, later in the day Company I came upon the Russian embassy. It was a two- or three-story Western-style brick building set in a spacious, fenced-in, tree-shaded compound. We really hoped we would nab the *true* Communists, the Russians. Instead, we found the

building stripped as bare as a bride on her wedding night. Just as clean, too. It sure made us feel good to be in a building like this one, with its thick walls and solid roof, especially in this impoverished and woe-begotten land.

Not far from the embassy, a company patrol happily discovered fully stocked and intact warehouses. In one we found all kinds of canned goods, and, best of all, great quantities of Russian booze. As in the embassy, much time was spent looking for booby traps. But the time consumed in probing and poking proved to be well spent. Guys then tore into the food and gorged themselves. That evening Captain Allen threw a tight guard around the warehouses, especially the one with the booze.

21 October 1950

Hanson Baldwin [*The New York Times*] reported from Korea that an increased concentration of Chinese Communist troops near the Korean frontier had been observed during the past week. About 450,000 Chinese troops were believed to be in Manchuria, including 250,000 near the frontier. Baldwin said that this concentration was not viewed too seriously and that it was thought that the time for Chinese intervention had passed.

DEPARTMENT OF STATE CHRONOLOGY

Pfc. JAMES CARDINAL
I Company/5th Cavalry

General MacArthur announced that we would be home by Thanksgiving. We believed him. Life seemed good in P'yongyang. Morale was sky-high.

I had six South Koreans in my squad. I called them by American names: Jesse, James, Dick, Pop, Siam, and Big Stoop. They were all fairly reliable. One day, in spite of the Russian food, which had quickly disappeared, leaving us as hungry as we'd been before, I asked James to scout around and return with something to eat. I had in mind a chicken or perhaps a calf that we could butcher. Three hours later he returned with the most pathetic, emaciated mutt I'd ever seen. The poor pooch was covered with scabs and whimpered with fright. Since eating dogs was common with the South Korean soldiers, I'm sure James was pleased with his find. Despite his generosity, I declined the dog. Later we learned the Koreans had killed and eaten it. I'm sure they received a belly laugh out of my squeamishness. Little did I realize that in just over three weeks I would be so hungry I, too, would eat a dog and enjoy it as much as any Korean.

Sgt. F/C DONALD PATE
I Company/5th Cavalry

One day we kidnapped the swans from the P'yongyang Zoo and one of our KATUSAs cooked them in Russian wine. Our brand-new platoon leader was 1st Lt. Ark Tollefson, a teetotaler, and he got "drunker than Cooter Brown" on the broth. Those damned birds had to be old because they were like bubble gum to chew.

Sgt. WARREN AVERY
G Company/21st Infantry

When we hit P'yongyang we got a rest. We spent a lot of time trying to open a safe in one of the big banks. To blow it we used 3.5s and satchel charges and anything else we could scrounge up. Finally, we got it open. It was full of North Korean money which did us no good at all.

22 October 1950
Colonel Crombez, the 5th Cavalry Commander . . . was appointed Civil Assistance Officer to direct Civil Affairs for the 1st Cavalry Division. Lieutenant Colonel Treacy, 3d Battalion Commander, assumed command until arrival of the new regimental commander, Lt. Col. Harold K. Johnson.

NARRATIVE REPORT, 5TH CAVALRY REGIMENT

Pfc. VICTOR FOX
I Company/5th Cavalry
We knew, naturally, that once the rear headquarters group found out about it, the lavish quarters afforded by the Russian embassy would not be given to a company of infantry mudslingers. But until the "mistake" was discovered, we made the most of our civilized surroundings.

Cpl. GEORGE CAMPBELL
3d Battalion/Royal Australian Regiment
Item Company's headquarters was in the building housing the Russian embassy. At the end of a very elaborate concrete bomb shelter, I discovered a study. Inside, I found boxes of stationery containing American embassy letterheads. I set fire to these. Paneling in the study also caught fire and the room was destroyed. When asked why I did this, I replied, "I think the bastards will be back."

23 October 1950
A new Z/R [Zone of Responsibility] was assumed, as well as a different mission. The zone included a twenty mile radius. The 5th Cavalry was confronted with collection and stockpiling of weapons and instruments of war, burying enemy dead (using PWs and indigenous personnel), and vigorous patrolling throughout the assigned northwestern section of P'yongyang and westward.

Lt. Col. Harold Johnson, veteran of Bataan, assumed command of the 5th Cavalry Regiment and Lt. Col. Treacy resumed command of the 3d Battalion.*

NARRATIVE REPORT, 5TH CAVALRY REGIMENT

Capt. NORMAN ALLEN
I Company/5th Cavalry
When we found the booze, battalion asked us to share it with the other companies. Colonel Treacy came by and asked what I planned

---

*Johnson, a survivor of the Bataan Death March, eventually became a chief of staff of the Army.

on doing with it. I told him Curfman and I had agreed that our companies would protect each other while we alternated getting sloshed. Seeing that Ralph and I had already agreed to this and that this was a better solution than both companies getting bombed together, the colonel thanked me for the cognac I gave him and departed, not to return for at least two days.

Pfc. VICTOR FOX
I Company/5th Cavalry
It was probably during the night hours of October 23–24 that I Company really got smashed on the booze from that warehouse. Since some other teetotalers and I elected not to drink, we were told to keep an eye on the festivities. We sober guys were surprised at times how otherwise normal men, when loosened by vodka, expressed personal thoughts. In different drinking groups the same kinds of war stories were told, so were thoughts about home and loved ones. On this one night everyone became buddy-buddy, *including* Captain Allen! The South Koreans proved happy drinking groups are the same the world over.

That night the area around the Russian embassy became a highly dangerous area to be near. Heavy drinking and armed men do not mix. Guys tossed grenades over the wall without knowing whether anyone was on the other side. Small arms were fired. Eventually, the party turned into just plain, unrestricted hell-raising. It must have been something like this in the Old West when a trail gang, after eight weeks of herding longhorn, rode into Dodge. No one interfered or tried to. As far as I can recall, no one was killed or even injured. The following day I Company had all its excess ammo and hand grenades taken away.

24 October 1950
Life was relatively pleasant for the battle-hardened troopers presently enjoying the comforts of improvised stove-heated buildings.

NARRATIVE REPORT, 5TH CAVALRY REGIMENT

Cpl. MARIO SORRENTINO
Task Force Indianhead
One day I struck out on my own and drove to the center of the city.
Downtown P'yongyang did not strike me as a metropolis. A large rotary shunted traffic down several boulevards. Propped against the wall
of the city hall were enormous portraits of Stalin and Kim Il Sung.
Side by side, they'd been placed there by some ingenious soldier, whose
reason for doing so succeeded beyond his wildest dreams. All day long
trucks carrying troops from one place to another drove past the two
portraits. Each soldier did his best to spit on the paintings as he passed.
I would say half the 1st Cav and thousands of ROKs paid their re-
spects in this manner.

A dead enemy soldier still lay near where the truck traffic entered the rotary. At first, I noticed these vehicles turned to avoid hitting the corpse. Later, one vehicle drove over it. Then, it became
like a game; everything—jeeps, trucks, half-tracks, tanks—rolled over
it. I watched that body become a wet splotch, then totally disappear.

25 October 1950
Fires occasionally ignited rubbish or buildings in the Z/R. Almost every unit at some period during the occupation of the city
was called upon to extinguish a blaze.
NARRATIVE REPORT, 5TH CAVALRY REGIMENT

Pfc. VICTOR FOX
I Company/5th Cavalry
The find was made in an area a few miles north of P'yongyang. The
scene appeared to be in a wide irrigation ditch or possibly a prepared,
open burial site. The civilian dead were again in national dress or
wore Western clothes, and were people from the upper social level.
All appeared to have died from automatic-weapons fire. The dead here
appeared to be more densely packed than those in the site outside
Seoul.

Pfc. JAMES CARDINAL
I Company/5th Cavalry

Dear Folks,
I have seen the most terrible sight of my life and I felt I had to write about it.

I've seen many horrible things, bodies heaped in piles, arms and legs blown off, friends just killed being carried to the rear, etc., but what I saw this afternoon makes that seem like nothing.

Just before our company took the capital the Communists gathered together all the opposition leaders, those friendly to America, and beat them terribly. Then they tied their hands behind their backs and shot them. More than fifty lay all over a small field in front of a school. When I got there relatives were claiming the dead and washing and cleaning and wrapping the bodies. That was the saddest part of it, mothers, wives, and children crying and screaming. The sight of death doesn't bother me anymore, but to see the women crying made me feel very bad.

You can believe everything you read in American papers about how miserable the Communist leaders treat the people behind the Iron Curtain. If any American Communist ever tells me when I get home that America was the aggressor in this war I think I'll kill him on the spot. When I think of the young kids who've been killed in the company while American Communists shout off about it makes me sore.

There's a rumor going around that the 1st Cavalry Division is returning to Japan pretty soon, now that the war is over. I certainly hope so. I'm sick of this country and this war. I've seen all I want of it. If I'd only known three months ago what it was like I think I'd of hidden in a mountain cave to keep out of it.

Believe me, sleeping in foxholes in a drizzling rain, cold and waiting to attack, dodging bullets, and going for three or four days with one small meal is not as romantic as the movies make out.

I'm glad I've gone through the experience but believe me, never again. . . .

26 October 1950*
Morale was excellent in the regiment. Giving everything possible, the 1st Cavalry Division provided a movie projector with
several films—the first movies available since sailing from Japan.
NARRATIVE REPORT, 5TH CAVALRY REGIMENT

Capt. NORMAN ALLEN
I Company/5th Cavalry

Dearest Mother:
We must really be getting to be rear echelon; saw a movie in our
company area tonight, *Nina Goes West.* Boy, did those well-built
American gals look good.

Two days ago we worked a trade with a hospital outfit of some
gook rifles for a radio. So we are really living. Liberate some
chickens occasionally. It's awful good living compared to a week
ago this time.

Held our battalion's memorial services. When the colonel read
the list of our lads KIA it was long and grim. Sure hope it gets
no longer. We constantly pray the old infantryman's standby,
"Please, God, just a little wound." When the action is heavy
each and every foxhole is an altar getting heavy business.

I've got the best damn fighting company there is—we opened
the gate to P'yongyang, crashed the river alone, spearheaded the
division, held Hill 174 for five days and nights (the longest anyone else stayed on it was one day and night). So if the enemy
comes, they better bring their lunch and plan on staying all day.
But God willing, they will not come again. . . .

---

*On this day, eighty statute miles east of P'yongyang, the 1st Marine Division began an ad-
ministrative landing at the port of Wonsan. They were met by the ROK I Corps, which had
advanced rapidly up the east coast after crossing the 38th Parallel. Three days later the U.S. X
Corps put its final component ashore 178 road miles above Wonsan when the 7th Division
landed unopposed at Iwon.

Pfc. VICTOR FOX
I Company/5th Cavalry
I Company ended up north of the capital near the main road, billeted in a rather new, two-story brick building. Captain Allen, through Top Mitchell, lost no time cracking down on the company by enforcing military courtesy. We began saluting again, something the officers were kind enough to overlook on the battlefield. Garrison soldiering again became the order of the day.

No time was lost in putting up the Army's usual OFF LIMITS signs. The fabled chickenshit of the 1st Cavalry Division was verified when yellow paint was distributed, with which the company areas were marked out. Moustaches on men under twenty-one were ordered cut off. Full field inspections and, I believe, formal guard mounts were held. Everything a garrison soldier endured in the States became routine again—everything but KP. There was just too much available cheap native labor around to replace GIs performing this drudgery. The chow still seemed to be skimpy.

The large expanse of a surrounding field became a parade ground and eventually the location of several military ceremonies. Second Platoon's Jenkins was awarded a Distinguished Service Cross for his heroism on Hill 174.* Decorations always brought up talk among the men. Everyone was honestly glad for men who earned a medal, as long as that individual did not intentionally kill himself or endanger the lives of others. Teamwork is so vital in combat that an act of individual heroism usually comes more as a surprise than as a contrived action. This left out the John Wayne types. Action often comes down with such sudden violence that there's usually no time to do anything except wonder how you got into it.

One day I Company fell out for some kind of ceremony and "passed in review." When lined up together the platoons looked no larger than squads. We became quite emotional. We asked ourselves, "Is this all that's left?"

---

*On the afternoon of 15 September, Jenkins had climbed on an American tank and, under withering fire, directed its guns on the North Koreans who were attacking along the dry riverbed.

26 October 1950

It was reported that North Korean prisoners had said that the enemy had been reinforced by 20,000 to 30,000 Chinese Communist troops. Headquarters doubted that the Chinese People's Republic would intervene on such a small scale at this stage of the war.

                                    DEPARTMENT OF STATE CHRONOLOGY

Pfc. VICTOR FOX
I Company/5th Cavalry

There was a foot-operated pipe organ that had been tossed outside our building. I drove guys nuts constantly playing one chord over and over.

Something many of us found strange was our lack of interest or curiosity about baseball or football games played back in the States. In Korea American sports seemed worlds removed from what we were doing. We couldn't have cared less about who had won the World Series.

27 October 1950

Maj. Gen. Yu Hae Heung, commander of the ROK 2d Corps, said 40,000 Chinese Communist troops had recently crossed the Yalu. It was disclosed that Chinese prisoners had been taken by ROK forces in the Unsan-Onjong area.

                                    DEPARTMENT OF STATE CHRONOLOGY

27 October 1950

The greater portion of the day was spent patrolling, attending [winter] clothing instructions, and enjoying the Bob Hope Show. The two hour comedy show . . . was thoroughly enjoyed by all in attendance.

                            NARRATIVE REPORT, 5TH CAVALRY REGIMENT

2d Lt. ADRIAN B. BRIAN
I Company/5th Cavalry

We learned that Bob Hope was going to put on a show for the whole regiment. At the proper time we loaded up in our jeeps to return to the company area so we could see the performance. (My platoon had been given a sector to patrol and we had moved into a building away from the company area.) About halfway back I saw an armed civilian run into a building. I knew if I had any sense I would ignore him and continue on to see Bob Hope. However, not having that sense I stopped the platoon and went to investigate the situation. What we stumbled into was a North Korean guerrilla headquarters. We fanned out and searched the surrounding buildings and discovered dozens of rifles and other weapons. I went alone into a small, enclosed backyard and spotted an NK disappearing over a wall. I fired but missed him. I saw another duck down a hallway. I chased him into a room and discovered, to my amazement, about twenty men sitting on the floor with their legs crossed. I had apparently interrupted a staff meeting. I wasn't sure what to do. I pulled out a big .45-cal automatic. I don't know why I did that, except maybe I believed it looked more threatening than my carbine. Although alone, I pretended to talk to some of my men. After about twenty seconds of this imaginary conversation, a couple of my troops arrived to investigate the shot I had fired. We gathered up the prisoners and moved them to the entrance of the building. We collected more of them than we had room to transport in our jeeps, so we loaded the captured weapons in the vehicles and marched the North Koreans with their hands over their heads to the company area. Once we got there we sent the NKs to a POW collection point. Never did get to see the Bob Hope show.

Pfc. JIMMY MARKS
A Battery/61st Field Artillery Battalion

No one who saw it will forget Marilyn Maxwell's sweater, the Taylor Maids' acrobatics, the wit of Jerry Colonna, the music of Les Brown, and, most of all, the great man himself. It was hard to imagine that Bob Hope was actually in P'yongyang.*

Cpl. MARIO SORRENTINO
Task Force Indianhead
I spent most of my time in P'yongyang sitting in a jeep, watching the military traffic stream past. A lot of the traffic consisted of ROK trucks. Down one street I spotted a South Korean soldier on a bicycle weaving back and forth across the road. A deuce-and-a-half truck coming from the opposite direction slammed on its brakes to avoid running the bicyclist down. As it was, the poor guy ran into the truck. Two South Korean soldiers leaped from the cab, rushed to the downed bicyclist, and dragged him back to the passenger side. A ROK officer jumped down and began screaming at the guy. Then he slapped him. What happened next was unbelievable. The officer pulled his pistol and right there and then shot the bike rider. The two soldiers threw the body on the back of the truck, climbed into the cab, and, with their officer, drove off.

28 October 1950
An intelligence officer at MacArthur's headquarters said that To-kyo G-2 [Intelligence] was not in a position to confirm or deny that Chinese had entered Korea. It was believed, however, that they might turn out to be Koreans who had previously served with Chinese Communist forces. MacArthur said, "There is no positive evidence that Chinese Communist units, as such, have entered Korea, although incomplete interrogation of these prisoners of war indicates that possibility."

DEPARTMENT OF STATE CHRONOLOGY

28 October 1950
The 5th Cavalry Regiment was notified that the Z/R boundary lines might be extended as far north as Anju. Representatives from

---

*Three days earlier, Bob Hope's USO show had entertained the 1st Marine Division at Wonsan.

the 9th Regiment and 2d Regiment visited the CP relative to their possible assumption of responsibility for the 5th Cav's area in the city. All indications pointed to a departure from the ancient city in the near future.

NARRATIVE REPORT, 5TH CAVALRY REGIMENT

Capt. NORMAN ALLEN
I Company/5th Cavalry

Dearest Mother,
We got a movement order today, just the alert. Don't know when we'll go and I was just about making up my mind that this fracas was over for us. . . .

29 October 1950
Orders came through about 1700 hours that the 5th Cavalry would guard the MSR [Main Supply Route] from Anju north. Preparation for the move was complete by nightfall.

NARRATIVE REPORT, 5TH CAVALRY REGIMENT

Cpl. LACY BARNETT
Medical Company/3d Battalion/19th Infantry

We moved seventy miles north, and on the evening of 30 October set up in a rice paddy. That night there was a lot of rifle fire between our forces and what was thought to be NK troops. It was discovered in the morning that the firefight had been between our battalion and another American unit. There were no casualties. The incident seemed to be an example of the confusion that was prevalent at that time. We would often not know what unit, if any, was tied in to our flanks. It was at this time that everyone, including our commanders, thought the war was over. To reach the Yalu all you had to do was get on the road and drive north until you got wet.

Sgt. ROBERT DEWS
E Company/21st Infantry
Cold, dirt, mud, and rain were the big enemies now—the latter three
were eventually absorbed by a new enemy, snow. The name of the
game was to keep from freezing while the drivers tried to stay on the
road. Both were hard to do. Plenty of men froze and plenty of vehicles ended up in a ditch or over a mountain.

Pfc. VICTOR FOX
I Company/5th Cavalry
The mountains rose higher and the temperatures dropped lower. Morale also dropped. Everyone remembered how close we'd come to being
sent to Japan.

[*Eighth Army had begun what it thought would be the last, brief phase
of the war—the pursuit of the enemy to the northern limits of North
Korea. This final drive was a continuation of the one begun at the
Pusan Perimeter just six weeks before. UN forces fanned out above
P'yongyang and drove for the border. Everyone hoped the swift advance to the Yalu would bring peace before that implacable enemy of
all infantrymen, winter, really had a chance to clamp down.*

*At first the hunt went well. The British Commonwealth Brigade,
followed by the U.S. 24th Division, had little trouble in crossing the
Ch'ongch'on River, the last great water barrier before the Yalu. On 29
October the Commonwealth Brigade fought its way into Ch'ongju. The
next evening the 21st Infantry Regiment passed through the British
unit and continued the chase. They were about fifty miles from the
Yalu. A bright harvest moon lit up the road.*]

Pfc. LEONARD KORGIE
G Company/21st Infantry
The column was stretched out for a mile. Second Battalion spear-
headed the drive. I rode on the second tank. We were very near the
Yalu. In the moonlight I could see a high range of hills to our front.
A gook suddenly jumped out into the road and fired at the lead tank.
A machine gun tore his head off. Another gook ran up to the col-

umn; he was unarmed and yelling his head off. Word was passed he told our officers not to go any farther—the Chinese were crossing the Yalu by the thousands. After a short pause the column jerked forward. We hadn't gone very far when a hellish firefight broke out. The infantry hit the road and spread out behind a high dike. The trucks and tanks stopped where they were. We had been ambushed. Although the histories say the 2d Battalion fought the NKs that night, the trap was so beautifully organized I believe we were hit by a Chinese unit. Because of the terrain the tanks were road-bound. The fire we received was as intense and well directed as any I had experienced. They had picked a beauty of a spot.

The night was clear, cold, and bright. There was a great artillery duel. Incoming fire looked like balls of fire flying through the air. I really got psyched and shot my ammo as fast as it was brought up. I fired so much I had to fill ejected clips with single rounds. I thought we were going to do a night charge. I hoped so. I was ready to go for broke. The total volume of sound and fire was tremendous! Then our artillery hit one of their dumps. WOW! Fourth of July.

Before first light, word came down we would assault the enemy's position. The sun began to rise. We leapt up and charged, each man yelling, swearing, firing. Level ground. No cover. Two F-80 jets dove at us. We could use the air cover. Shit! They fired on us. Right in the middle of this open field. I stopped and waved off the planes. I felt very lonely out there. Guys got up and the charge resumed. The jets came in again and this time their rockets and machine-gun fire landed in the trees on the hill. Their shell casings rained down on us. On the hill, we discovered the enemy had pulled back. They had even taken their wounded with them.

Back on the road, weary from the all-night battle, we sat by the side of the road as Colonel Smith of Task Force Smith fame and his 1st Battalion passed through our unit and continued the advance.

[The 1st Cavalry Division had also advanced rapidly and was within a day's march of the Yalu. On the evening of 31 October two of its regiments were northeast of where the 21st Infantry had been ambushed the night before. The 5th Cavalry Regiment was bivouacked at Yongsan-dong and the 8th Cavalry, farther north, was at Unsan. It was Halloween.]

Capt. NORMAN ALLEN
I Company/5th Cavalry

Hi Mother:
Have advanced seventy-two miles and am about thirty miles from the Yalu. I told the men that by tomorrow afternoon we'd be lined up pissing in it.

Expect to live under combat conditions for some time, but unless the Chinese come in it should be on its last legs. Have had frost in the morning and it's bitter cold. Don't have enough tents for all the men so can only pray it doesn't rain or snow. I'd much prefer to spend the winter in troop billets in Japan than in a foxhole in Korea. Must chow down and check to insure we are ready to move. . . .

31 October 1950
The battalions were alerted at 2030 hours of an attack plan, if necessary, along the MSR to Unsan.

NARRATIVE REPORT, 5TH CAVALRY REGIMENT

31 October 1950
A spokesman for MacArthur's headquarters told reporters that while Chinese prisoners had been taken it was not yet known whether Chinese units as such were involved in the fighting in Korea. He pointed out that the appearance of Soviet tanks and guns showed that the enemy was receiving arms from across the Manchurian border, and that it had always been known that the North Koreans received men from Manchuria who had been trained in Chinese Communist units.

DEPARTMENT OF STATE CHRONOLOGY

Pfc. ROBERT HARPER
Headquarters Company/3d Battalion/
19th Infantry

For two or three days prior to Halloween, the radio operators on the line had been picking up a lot of enemy radio talk. They said it sounded like Chinese. No one knew what the hell was going on. One night battalion decided to send out a company-size patrol to see if it could find out anything. There was to be no radio communication, so battalion sent along a wire team, which included me, to lay a landline from the patrol back to headquarters.

Our team followed one of the rifle companies off the hill and into the valley. We waited while a small recon patrol disappeared into the night. It was Halloween and colder than a witch. No one had been issued winter gear yet. Nobody said anything. Our phone line back to battalion had been hooked up earlier. We waited and froze. It was very dark.

The patrol came back and reported finding a large enemy force in front of us. We withdrew very quickly back up the hill to our own positions. We went up faster than we'd gone down and entered our lines about daylight. It had been a long, cold night. But it hadn't been as long, nor as cold, as the nights to come.

SETBACK

1 November-23 November 1950

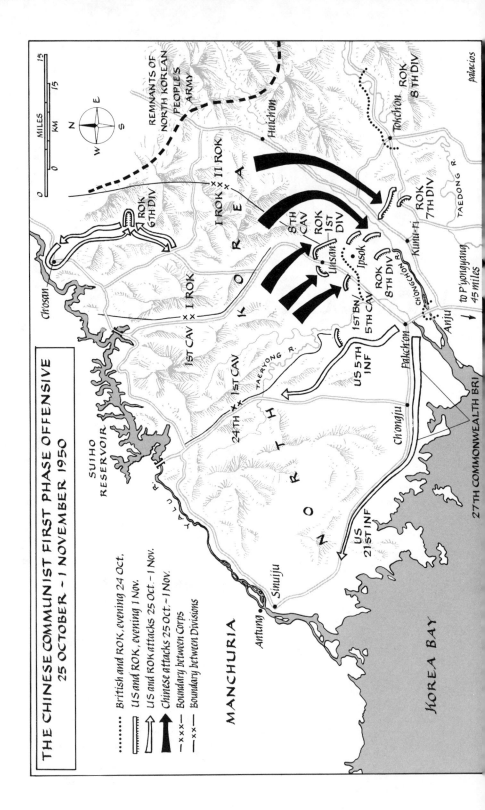

THE CHINESE COMMUNIST FIRST PHASE OFFENSIVE
25 OCTOBER – 1 NOVEMBER 1950

.... British and ROK, evening 24 Oct.
▭▭▭ US and ROK, evening 1 Nov.
⇨ US and ROK attacks 25 Oct.– 1 Nov.
◆ Chinese attacks 25 Oct.– 1 Nov.
–x x x– Boundary between Corps
–x x– Boundary between Divisions

MANCHURIA

Antung
Sinuiju

KOREA BAY

27TH COMMONWEALTH BRI

N O R T H   K O R E A

SUIHO
RESERVOIR

Chosan

ROK
6TH DIV

I ROK × × II ROK
I ROK × ×

REMNANTS OF
NORTH KOREAN
PEOPLE'S
ARMY

Huichon

Tokchon, ROK
8TH DIV

ROK
7TH DIV

TAEDONG R.

8TH
CAV

ROK
1ST DIV

Unsan

Ipsok

Kunu-ri

1ST CAV × × I ROK

ROK
8TH DIV

CHONGCHON R.

Anju

to P'yongyang
45 miles

1ST CAV

TAERYONG R.

24TH × × 1ST CAV

1ST BN/
5TH CAV

Pakchon

US 5TH
INF

Chongju

US
21ST INF

palacios

Pfc. LEONARD KORGIE
G Company/21st Infantry

We followed the 1st Battalion into Chonggo-dong [1 November] and now were only eighteen miles from the Manchurian border. The town was beautiful. Food was still on the tables of the houses we entered. Huge posters with the faces of Stalin, Lenin, and Kim Il Sung hung in all the public buildings. Neat picket fences surrounded wood-frame houses. I found some newspaper cartoons showing Truman and Acheson dropping bombs on North Korea. Our engineers blew the bank vault and found nothing. We slept soundly that night in a dry, cozy, well-built schoolhouse. Next morning we received hot chow—pancakes and coffee. Heck, North Korea was all right. Things were definitely looking up.

Then the shit hit the fan. Around 9:00 in the morning [2 November], we were ordered to saddle up, we were moving again. This time it would be south! Word rapidly spread that on our right, troopers from the 1st Cav had had the stuffings knocked out of them. We'd have to move fast or we stood a chance of being cut off. The Chinese were in North Korea in force. Shit!

Sgt. ROBERT DEWS
E Company/21st Infantry
It was a blustery cold but bright day. The snow had ceased to fall and
everyone was in good spirits. About ten miles up the road the convoy
slowed down and then came to an abrupt halt. It got colder and colder,
the men became restive. All kinds of rumors drifted back down from
the head of the column. Then came the real dope. Everyone was to
dismount, our vehicles were to be used to take the wounded and dead
back to Seoul. Everyone wanted to know, what wounded, what dead?

The men of Easy Company secured their gear, tightened their
belts, and moved in combat formation along the vehicle-choked road.
Soon, in the frozen rice paddies along both sides of the road, they
passed bodies stacked like cordwood. It didn't take a genius to figure
out that one of the 1st Cavalry's units had pulled another Custer.

*[The air had rapidly grown colder, the days shorter. One of North Ko-
rea's most bitter winters lay around the corner, just how bitter no one
could even imagine. In late October several ROK divisions were badly
thrashed in their race to reach the Yalu by what was reported to be
Chinese combat troops. It was unclear, however, whether the enemy
units were made up of volunteers fighting with the North Koreans, or
if Communist China had formally entered the war. Any question
General MacArthur's headquarters had about who or what mauled the
ROKs was answered on 1 November when a Communist Chinese division slammed into the 8th Cavalry Regiment at Unsan. Two other
Chinese divisions then dove in behind Eighth Army's open right flank
and threatened to cut off the 1st Cavalry Division. Since the 5th Cavalry's responsibility included protecting the rear of the 8th Cavalry, its
3d Battalion was ordered to take up a defensive position about ten
miles below Unsan.]*

Capt. NORMAN ALLEN
I Company/5th Cavalry

We hit the road on November 1 and the MPs pointed south. We swung in a looping turn that took us southeast, crossed a high bridge, traveled along a ridge, and in the valley below saw the remnants of an artillery battery that had been overrun. Bodies of dead artillery-men lay about the guns.

Pfc. VICTOR FOX
I Company/5th Cavalry

Stove smoke still floated over the large section tents. The 155s and their tractors were neatly arranged in a defensive ring; other vehicles were parked haphazardly about the area. Not one live American GI could be seen anywhere.

Capt. NORMAN ALLEN
I Company/5th Cavalry

Somewhere around the walled city of Yongbyon the 2d Chemical Battalion, which had also been overrun, fell in with our column. These men looked mighty sad. I talked to a lieutenant who had taken com-mand after his captain had been killed. His eyes were as wide as sau-cers and he acted as if he was in shock. Later in the day we ran across thousands of ROKs fleeing southward. I unexpectedly recognized a captain I'd known at [Camp] Carson who was now an adviser to the South Koreans. I asked him what the hell was happening. He told me no one had believed him, but his unit had been fighting the Chinese for a week. I told him I was going to find a choke point in the valley, and if the Chinks tried to come through it, I was going to knock them on their asses. He began to move off down the road. The retreating ROKs and their vehicles kicked up a lot of dust. My old friend turned and hollered back, "Good luck, Norm, hope you do. They're not coming down the valleys, they're running the ridges." I looked up at the high ridgelines on either side of the road and my confidence slipped away.

[*In the early hours of 2 November, the 3d Battalion of the 8th Cavalry south of Unsan discovered it was surrounded. In the darkness a fierce hand-to-hand battle was fought around the battalion CP. The Chinese were finally driven out, but not off. When the sun came up, the Americans were still surrounded.*]

Capt. NORMAN ALLEN
I Company/5th Cavalry
At 11:00 P.M. Colonel Treacy informed me he had been ordered to form a task force to help rescue the 3d Battalion, 8th Cavalry, which was known as "Scrappy Blue." I was told I would command the force (made up of I and L Companies and four platoons of tanks) that would actually go down the road and bring out the battalion. Colonel Treacy and I then went up to the 1st Battalion's [5th Cavalry] position, which was farthest north and closest to the surrounded unit.

From a hill we looked over a long valley that skirted a deep river. The 3d Battalion, 8th Cavalry, which had come on the same ship with us to Korea, was now about eight miles north of where we stood and cut off from the rest of their regiment. On our left were two prominent ridges. One of them was to become known as "Bugle Hill." I could see our 1st Battalion fighting for the first ridge. Once they had succeeded in taking it, the 2d Battalion [5th Cavalry] would take the next, Bugle Hill. When this ridge was secured, my task force would race down the road into the Scrappy Blue perimeter, collect the men, and race back. I was told the last five miles of road into the perimeter would be uncovered, in other words, without protective fire. I didn't relish the mission. It would be hairy, to say the least.

Tentative jump-off time was 2:00 P.M. Around 1:00 P.M. I had all tanks crank up and told the tankers they would go in clean of infantry. That way they could bust into the perimeter and bring out the 8th Cav's guys on the tanks. The infantry would follow in trucks and hold the road junction that was some 300 yards from Scrappy Blue's alleged position.

Two o'clock came and went. So did 3:00. I told Colonel Treacy I felt I needed two hours of daylight to effect the rescue. Any attempt to do it under cover of darkness would prove to be a hell of a lot more of a disadvantage for me than the Chinese. *They* knew where they were; I didn't. Nor did I know, for that matter, where Scrappy Blue was. I could just see the confusion trying to get the survivors out of their holes and onto the tanks in the dark. Colonel Treacy reassured me he understood. He told me that if the second ridge [Bugle Hill] wasn't at least under heavy attack by 4:00 P.M., the task force mission would be scrapped. While we waited to go, the wounded streamed up the road past our position. It was obvious that some real tough fighting was going on up ahead.

Near to 4:00 P.M. I had the tanks and trucks again turn over their engines. Colonel Treacy came up and told me the 1st Battalion had not been able to seize the first ridge, even after the 2d Battalion had been thrown in to help out. The mission was canceled. I was told to be ready to cover the withdrawal of the two battalions, which had just been ordered to break off contact with the enemy.

It was during this withdrawal that we first experienced that business with the wounded. Walking wounded captured by the Chinese were allowed to return to our lines. They told us the Communists would allow us to pick up our other wounded, that they would be placed along the road, and vehicles coming for them would not be fired on. One medic said, "Give me a jeep. I'll go." He was joined by other guys. I placed two tanks across the road and told them to cover the jeep. If anyone fired on it, they were to plaster the areas on either side of the road. A few minutes later the jeep returned carrying four or five wounded. These poor souls were dropped off. The jeep spun around and again raced down the road. This time it was followed by several others. The wounded told of being carried by the Chinese to the road on stretchers marked "Donated by the American Red Cross." The jeeps rushed back and forth until it became quite dark. Then we fell back and went into a regimental perimeter.

That night the rest of the 8th Cav pulled out of the line. The

poor devils in their 3d Battalion remained in the trap. We were told
they would have to get out themselves any way they could. No more
help would be forthcoming. The following morning we fell back about
twenty miles.

*[As soon as General Walker realized he was being attacked by a new
and powerful enemy, he ordered Eighth Army to withdraw and re-form
behind the Ch'ongch'on River, the first natural barrier south of the
Yalu.*]*

Pfc. LEONARD KORGIE
G Company/21st Infantry
I sat shivering on the last tank in the column. The tank commander
had orders to turn his turret to the rear and shoot hell out of anything
that looked suspicious. We couldn't have missed the Chinese by much.
I kept thinking, How come MacArthur didn't know China was coming into it? Where had our Air Force been?

We drove through heavy rain. One tank slid off the road and fell
like a boulder down the side of a mountain. I was cold and soaked to
the bone. One night I burrowed into a haystack and slept with just
my head out in the air. The lice dug into my skin like peanuts in a
shell. When I got warm, my body itched terribly. I scratched and
scratched until I bled. But what a relief.

It wasn't too long before we stopped and set up a perimeter.

1st Lt. CHARLES PAYNE
3d Battalion/19th Infantry
Seems as though we were almost in sight of the Yalu when out of the
blue came orders to get south fast, no questions. It was bitter cold.

---

*The Ch'ongch'on, with its two tributaries, the Taeryong and Kuryong, flows in a southwest-
erly direction and empties into Korea Bay at Anju.

We were so mad. Why in hell should we turn around when we were
so close to the river? We followed orders and turned around. I was
out front of the column. We moved cautiously and were scared. We
had learned the Chinese were over the river and running around North
Korea. On the road in front of us sat a small American convoy. Quiet
as hell! With my two scouts covering, I moved in. The convoy had
belonged to a division medical battalion and included dental vans,
everything. It had been ambushed at a roadblock. There were lots of
dead around. Some still sat in the vehicles with their carbines on their
laps. Didn't know how to use them, I'm afraid. We located one half-
mad lieutenant colonel who babbled about our looting his trucks. He
was in shock. The convoy I was with now knew how vulnerable it
was to hit-and-run ambushes. We continued to move south. It took
us a day and a half, maybe two, to reach the area we were ordered to
occupy. I had been riding with an Air Force liaison officer. He had
had his radio on and liked his music played loud. I stepped out of
the jeep and fell face down. I was out. Too much sipping on a canteen of 196-proof medical alcohol.

Capt. NORMAN ALLEN
I Company/5th Cavalry

4 Nov

Dearest Mother:
Today is *cold*. Rain last night and this morning, cold wind and
really mean.
Our regiment yesterday moved 56 miles back SE to Sunch'on. I watched civilians moving out; women carrying what they
could on their heads, kids strapped to their backs, those a little
older walking alongside or running to keep up. All are hungry
and poorly dressed. My God, how awful if it were our kids doing
that. If we are fighting to keep our kids from running like that,
our women, our old men, then we have a reason for being here.
It's not the long stream of refugees that sticks in my memory, it's
the cute little three year old jogging, trying to keep up, her mother
carrying a crying baby, their few possessions tied in a blanket

balanced on the mother's head. I remember one old woman, bent over, lagging behind. Everyone for herself.

I am now in a battalion area, no more than muddy rice paddies, awaiting word what we do next. Everyone is wondering what all this means. The UN forces were extended in their move to the Yalu and the strong Chinese attacks on the ROKs forced their withdrawal which has resulted in us all falling back. I thought at first it might be a political decision, move our bombing time down and deliver China an ultimatum to get out or else. But now I believe it's a military move to regroup and straighten the line, then determine where the enemy is and in what strength. Make our plans and then go back and hit him hard.

It's a nasty realization with the casualties returning on jeeps and tanks, that the war is still on and we are still in it. We see issues of *Time* and *Newsweek* stating, "War over—only mopping up—troops in Japan for Thanksgiving—home by Christmas." Wish the people who write this were over here now. This is certainly no time for optimism. It's mean and nasty; elements make living difficult—muddy ground and rain do not make for good bedfellows. Being in a fight makes it just that much worse. Still sleep with our boots on. When we do sleep it's only for a few moments. The rattle of rifle fire means someone nearby is having a rough go.

The battalion has been fortunate that so far the "ginks" haven't hit us. I'm told the enemy is well trained and organized. They speak Chinese and were born and raised in China; they'd never even heard of Korea before now. Anyone who says they aren't Chinks is crazy! Things now are beginning to shape up to be as grim as those days in September around Taegu. . . .

[The night Norman Allen wrote that letter, the Chinese moved to cut off the British Commonwealth Brigade on the Taeryong River. The U.S. 61st Field Artillery Battalion had set up south of Pakch'on, two and a half miles away. It was between the Americans and the Commonwealth Brigade that the Chinese intended to cut the road.]

Pfc. JIMMY MARKS
A Battery/61st Field Artillery Battalion

It was plenty dark when we pulled off the road and started setting up, and one of those nights [4–5 November] that started you shivering. We lit no fires and only got warm when it was time to crawl into a sleeping bag. We were attached temporarily to the 27th British Commonwealth Brigade and had been on the road all day traveling to a new location.

Before anyone had a chance to fall asleep, we were buzzed by Bed Check Charlie, a small single-engine North Korean plane that flew only at night and dropped grenade or mortar shells on units he spotted. Once this little activity ended, most of the 61st went to bed.

M/Sgt. ALLAN STANBERRY
A Battery/61st Field Artillery Battalion

I was up all that night running trunk lines and FDC [Fire Direction Center] lines, then troubleshooting this old wire that had been run over and cut up so many times. I laid the FDC line four times until I finally got a good one in. Throughout the night refugees filed past in a steady stream. This seemed unusual, but I was too cold and miserable to think much about it. Somewhere in the mountains a pack of dogs barked continuously. Finally, with all the lines in, I found a couple of blankets and tried to go to sleep. My carbine was covered with dirt and dust. I should have taken the time to clean it. I didn't.

Pfc. JIMMY MARKS
A Battery/61st Field Artillery Battalion
Daybreak was crisp and cold. The cooks had been up early and were preparing a breakfast of powdered eggs, bacon, toast, and coffee. Some of the cooks burned trash in a hole and kept feeding it discarded powder-charge bags. Most of the gun sections had small warming fires going.

With the first light of day, we saw we had spent the night on either side of a harvested rice paddy. The road was paralleled on both sides by a wide drainage ditch, deep enough to hide a man. Mountains rose to the north and it looked as if a small village lay at their base. A river, and a bridge that carried the road over it, was a little to our right. Sergeant [Charles] Roy's ammo section, their trucks laden with 105-mm artillery shells, was camped down in that direction— close enough to service the guns and far enough for the rest of the battery to survive a direct hit on the trucks. The half-track of the 92d AAA Battalion with its four .50-cal machine guns and a 37-mm cannon was parked near the FDC, about 150 yards west of the river and bridge.

Once breakfast was finished and mess kits washed, most everyone went about their assigned tasks. In the gun section the maintenance of the 105-mm howitzers always had priority. Pretty much the same kind of activity was going on at B and C Batteries, which had parked down the road east of us.

Allan Stanberry had gotten up and scrounged a scalding cup of coffee from the mess crew. Private Bryan Myler and several other ammo bearers were out searching for firewood. FDC, with Private Boler and me on duty, opened for business. Boler had the gun phones, I was on the battalion line.

Without warning, several pistol shots rang out. A British sergeant had been on the road near our position when he noticed that the ditches along the road were crawling with enemy troops. He had immediately opened fire. It didn't take long before the Englishman's shots were joined by many others, until the firing became a din.

M/Sgt. ALLAN STANBERRY
A Battery/61st Field Artillery Battalion
To me it was unreal; the very idea that anyone could have approached this close without being discovered was unbelievable. In less than three seconds, we were all in the game.

Pfc. JIMMY MARKS
A Battery/61st Field Artillery Battalion
Myler and the rest of the ammo section out looking for firewood ran smack-dab into a squad of enemy troops. Sergeant Roy and all but one of this group were captured. (They were never heard of again, although Roy's .45 would later be taken from a dead Chinese.) The only man to escape was Private Myler. He'd dropped his wood and taken off running—didn't stop until he hit A Battery's position.

M/Sgt. ALLAN STANBERRY
A Battery/61st Field Artillery Battalion
Myler ran up to [M/Sgt.] Max Wood. He was beside himself. "Sarge, them sonovabitches shot me. Look, they got me in the leg." Wood told him to go down the road a piece and find the battalion aid station. Myler, true to his name, totally unaffected by his wound, ran another mile for treatment.

The firefight was now hot and heavy. The enemy was obviously well equipped, well organized, and, for sure, superior in size to our battalion.* One of the cooks, a big, fat GI, climbed up on one of the ranges in the mess truck and from this vantage point opened fire on the enemy. One of them must have spotted him. A burst of fire splattered the truck, pulverizing large cans of mustard, ketchup, coffee, and everything else. These burst all over the cook. God, did he look a mess!

I was in a ditch in front of the battery. From there I alternated between trying to beat my carbine into firing order with my fist, and field-stripping and lubricating it with a shaving brush covered with

---

*The Chinese force was later estimated to be battalion size.

lubricating oil thick as molasses on a cold morning. I was very busy. The firing had developed into a full-scale battle. I looked up and there on the road stood Rex Gunnell [A Battery's CO], calm and cool as usual. "Come on over here, Stanberry," he says, "you can get some good shots from here." "Cap'n," I said, "the sonovabitch won't fire."

Pfc. JIMMY MARKS
A Battery/61st Field Artillery Battalion
Captain Gunnell had been an infantry officer during World War II and always had complete control of himself. He was an inspiration to all of us. On the road, amid the firing, Captain Gunnell strolled about the area, occasionally relighting his Sherlock Holmes–style pipe that was filled with Mixture 79. Enemy troops advanced in a dogtrot all around the battery's perimeter. He puffed on his pipe. I heard him say, "Hell, they look like Chinks." This was the first I learned that the war had suddenly gotten bigger.

For several hours we battled 500 Chinese troops armed with automatic weapons and mortars to a standstill. Down the road, C Battery was completely surrounded. Their CO, Captain [Howard] Moore, ordered the trail of his howitzers lifted so they could be fired at the Chinese at point-blank range.

In our perimeter, Lieutenant [John] Kean rallied the troops, and in the ditch organized a firing line made up of FDC and wire-section personnel. Boler, who'd been on the gun phone relaying Captain Gunnell's voice commands to the gun pits, was hit. I crawled fifteen or so yards to him and picked up the job of relaying orders to the guns. M/Sgt. Earl Collette, A Battery's salty first sergeant, stood fully exposed and calmly emptied his .45 into the Chinese. When he ran out of rounds for this weapon (he kept the last one in the chamber, saying later he had no intention of being captured), he grabbed an M1. In the classic offhand position, he squeezed off round after round in a manner that would have pleased the most demanding rifle-range instructor.

Stanberry had gotten his carbine to function, and he and three other GIs were across the road in the rice paddy, which, not surprisingly, they shared with the Chinese.

The AA crew had opened up with their quad .50s. When the

barrels turned cherry red, they jammed. Now the crew was picking apart corn shocks with the 37-mm cannon. Each time they hit one, a Chink would fly out. Twice during the long battle, Lieutenant Kean personally led those half-track antitank guns to new positions. He stayed with them, continuously pointing out new targets and directing fire.

Private Calhoun climbed up on a truck and cocked the bolt on one of the ring-mounted .50-caliber machine guns. While his right index finger was extended, it was cleanly shot off. Calhoun opened fire with a vengeance.

Everyone began to run short of ammo. In anticipation of being returned to Japan, the 61st had turned in all the extra ammunition it had over basic loads. With battalion lines cut, Captain Gunnell was unable to raise battalion. He ordered Sergeant Stanberry down the road and told him to get battalion to send more ammo and men. Stanberry and another man took off. An incoming mortar round knocked Stanberry to the ground. Regaining his feet, he resumed his journey. He realized he was now alone. Arriving at battalion, Stanberry was unable to find the CO, who was out on the lines. He delivered his message instead to Major [Paul] Fisher [the battalion executive officer]. Fisher said they would do the best they could.

Stanberry started back to A Battery by another route. He encountered a firing line from B Battery. From them he conned two canisters of carbine ammo. When he finally stumbled into A Battery, he was near exhaustion.

M/Sgt. ALLAN STANBERRY
A Battery/61st Field Artillery Battalion
Almost as soon as I returned, I was told to go and help out on the river corner of the perimeter. There I ran into Lieutenant Jack Sadler and Corporal Joe Bevins. I told Sadler, "By God, there's gotta be a better way than this to make a living. If I ever get out of this bend in the river, I'm sure as hell gonna find it." An incoming mortar round landed almost on top of us and buried itself in the mud. When it exploded, we were covered in thick muck.

Pfc. JIMMY MARKS
A Battery/61st Field Artillery Battalion
After several hours of all-out fighting, a company from the 1st Argyll
and Sutherland Highlanders, accompanied by American tanks, managed to battle its way down the road and enter our perimeter. An hour
or so earlier at battalion, the Scottish commander had asked Major
Fisher, "Can your chaps hold a bit longer?" Fisher replied, "I guess,
by God, we can. We've been holding them for four hours." The next
day we were told what happened next. The Argyll's senior NCO asked
his CO, "Shall we attack in packs, sir?" The CO answered that the
lads could remove their packs and put them by the side of the road.
He added, "But see that they are aligned neatly." GIs standing around
watched in disbelief. Once the packs were placed along the road (definitely neatly), the Argylls advanced down the road as nonchalantly
as if on morning police call.

When the tanks appeared on the road, the Chinese pulled back
and disappeared. The Argylls moved in. The British commander reported the success of his mission to his headquarters. Standing nearby
I heard what he told his Scottish radioman. The radio operator relayed the good news in a long string of unintelligible "burrrs" and
"ochs."

Dead and dying Chinese lay all around the outside of our perimeter. Down the road around C Battery seventy dead enemy soldiers were counted. Men who went to look them over reported that
many of the dead Chinese carried American money. The 61st had
just been paid.

Before long the 61st received orders and was again on the road.
No one did much talking. We weren't in any mood to pat ourselves
on the back. After a while we relaxed somewhat, but we were never
the same again. I remembered later what the commander of the Argylls had told us. He had said he thought our defensive position looked
like a scene right out of the Napoleonic Wars.

*[Eighth Army's piecemeal advance, which was to have ended the war
before Thanksgiving, had been stopped. Across the mountains, X Corps's
advance up the east coast had also been delayed. UN forces once again
found themselves on the edge, holding on. By the end of the first week*

of November, it was clear Communist China had entered the Korean War. It was as if one war had ended and another begun.

Working with scraps of intelligence, Far East Command in Tokyo and Department of Army in Washington estimated the size of China's intervention far below what it actually was. Only later would the full extent of the Chinese involvement be learned. At first it was thought they had committed no more than twelve divisions. In reality they had committed thirty: eighteen in the west, twelve in the east. In other words, by mid-November there were 180,000 Chinese infantrymen massed in front of Eighth Army and 120,000 in front of X Corps.

These enemy troops had crossed into Korea from Manchuria during October and early November. Traveling by night, hiding by day, they had managed to avoid being spotted from the air. Somehow, incredible as it may seem, no one saw 300,000 Chinese troops cross the Yalu River. Since late October much of this force had been lying coiled in the cold, hard, high country of Korea waiting for General MacArthur to make his next move. When Eighth Army and the ROKs moved northward out of P'yongyang and pushed toward the Yalu, the Chinese had fallen on them and whipped them soundly. After driving Eighth Army behind the Ch'ongch'on and slowing X Corp's advance, the Chinese Communist forces (CCF) suddenly broke off contact and withdrew back into the mountains.

By 10 November the front lay quiet, and until Thanksgiving Eighth Army would advance slowly against moderate resistance and rearguard activities. The war was entering its most quiet period.]

Capt. NORMAN ALLEN
I Company/5th Cavalry

9 Nov 50

Dearest Mother:

We moved early morning [6 November] from Kumch'on to two miles north of Kunu-ri into the defensive line. Another case of too damn much real estate for close in and proper defense. Have made platoon strong points with little connecting outguard posts to cover the intermediate valleys. Days are fairly quiet, but nights

are freezing as usual. Somebody on our right or left catches a
prisoner who states his unit is going to attack during the night
and we all stay on the alert all during the hours of darkness (6:00
P.M. to 7:00 A.M.).

It is colder than the Arctic. The sun doesn't burn through the
haze until 11 or 12 and today appears to have a little overcast
which will keep it cold all day. (Writing with gloves on—a little
cumbersome). We are sweating out day or night attacks, but of
course can see during the day and have a little more warning
than we do at night. U.S. Air is active during the day and hits
whatever it can see. But at night, of course, it can't do a thing.
We have much artillery backing us up and if we can see or hear
the enemy we can paste him hard before he gets in close. But at
night he can crawl up close, jump in, yelling, and charge into
your position before you even know he is on you. Don't know
the big picture but the local division paper says Commies all over
China are volunteering for No. Korea. Hell, morale is kinda low,
we can't fight all those damn Chinese.

Sure hope Stalin or the UN or Truman—somebody, anybody, tells them to go on home. I was hoping it was all about
over.

I've been getting my men 3 hot meals a day, but we are all
out of cigarettes and that is really mean. Division says they don't
have any, why—I don't know. We can do without food sometimes for a day, and sleep, but not being able to let off the nervous tension with cigarettes is *really* missed. They should be getting some in a week or so, but the men have whittled pipes out
of corn cobs and smoke anything. Really quite comical, everyone going around with the damn corn cobs, calling each other
Mac, looking for dark glasses and saying "I have returned." What
a bunch of nuts!

Yesterday and day before, our early morning security patrols
have found three soldiers each day from the 3d Bn 8th Cav which
was cut off near Unsan. It's like seeing them back from the dead
and after they have walked, crawled, hidden from detection for
7 days and 23 miles, looking starved and weary, sometimes
wounded, they are really glad to see us, hugging and kissing the

patrol. It's been a tough ordeal for them. If there were a lot of troops over here or things were about over, they could look forward to a rest in Japan or in the States. But the way the picture is now, it looks like a short rest in a rear area for a couple of days, then back into the line, is all they can look for.

Just sitting and waiting, hoping, sweating, and praying. Sure have got our fill. Course, they can't do more than kill you. . . .

[On the thirty-second anniversary of the end of World War I, the war that was to have ended all wars, the 5th and 7th Cavalry Regiments established fresh bridgeheads across the Ch'ongch'on River.]

Pfc. VICTOR FOX
I Company/5th Cavalry
Just before dawn [11 November], 1st Platoon conducted a recon on the hill the company was ordered to secure. The patrol actually got near the top before the enemy forced them back. With heavy fire all around, the men hightailed it down the cliffside of the objective and splashed back across the Ch'ongch'on River at a dead run. The platoon leader told us the hill was teeming with gooks, and they were so well dug in they could hardly be seen.

Capt. NORMAN ALLEN
I Company/5th Cavalry
General [Hobart] Gay [CG, 1st Cavalry Division] asked Colonel Johnson to send him with one of the attacking company commanders for the jump-off, and the colonel sent him off with me. We sat in my foxhole overlooking the Ch'ongch'on and chatted for about two hours while we waited for the air and artillery to soften up the high hill that was our objective. The general told me he had been Patton's chief of staff. I asked whether he remembered a master sergeant named Mims who had served under me in Japan and who before that had been Patton's driver. Gay told me that of course he remembered Sergeant Mims. We spent the rest of the time chatting about Patton.

Cpl. JERRY EMER
I Company/5th Cavalry

Seeing General Gay caused a stir among the men. I'd been in the war long enough to know that generals don't often become personally involved in the operations of a company. It was comforting to know, I thought, that if we needed anything—from tactical air support to medivac helicopters—the general was right there. Even a company CO as persuasive and forceful as Captain Allen might, on occasion, be turned down when asking for extra rounds of 155 to soften up an enemy-held hill, but never a divisional commander.

Pfc. VICTOR FOX
I Company/5th Cavalry

While the rest of I Company received the scoop on the assault, a flight of twin-engined B-26s banked out of the clouds and, like P-51 Mustangs, dive-bombed the hill. They really put on a show. Additionally, heavy-artillery impacts and air bursts billowed all over the high ground.

Capt. NORMAN ALLEN
I Company/5th Cavalry

Received a dumb order that day from regiment or division to fire three rounds from all weapons at 11:00 to celebrate Armistice Day. Real bullshit and I ignored it; we had a battle to fight. I planned on firing plenty of ammo in preparation for the attack, but not rifles, machine guns, mortars, or recoilless rifles—we'd save them for the close fighting.

L Company made the initial crossing, but got pinned down by machine-gun bullets. I Company then passed through them.

Cpl. JERRY EMER
I Company/5th Cavalry

The company objective was a moderately high hill shaped something like the prow of a ship. In front was an expanse of flat farmland. The harvested field still had a few scraggly rows of sorghum and some scattered corn shocks.

Sometime in the afternoon the artillery began its concert and we entered the chilly waters of the Ch'ongch'on. Lieutenant Brian shouted the usual: "OK, don't bunch up. Keep moving! Keep moving!" As on the Imjin River crossing, enemy bullets began to hit around us. I saw a burst of three or four hit nearby. Obviously, at least one enemy machine gun was firing from the "prow." Fortunately, this time the river bottom was solid, the current moderate, the water pretty damn cold.

Pfc. VICTOR FOX
I Company/5th Cavalry

Once on the enemy's side, long-range machine-gun fire ricocheted off some rocks and a few troopers went down. Despite our terrific artillery cover, enemy fire harassed us all the way to the base of the hill.

Capt. NORMAN ALLEN
I Company/5th Cavalry

Crossed 300 yards with machine-gun bullets kicking up sand all around. Then 700 yards of a dirt field, through a corn and bean patch, and to the base of a high hill. It looked as if the climb was going to be straight up.

Pfc. VICTOR FOX
I Company/5th Cavalry

The objective did not afford a broad front. In fact, the ridge allowed only two platoons to maneuver. On the right, 3d Platoon scaled a steep section of the hill. About the midway point we again came under small-arms fire, to which grenades were added. No one could pinpoint the source of this fire, only that it was coming from above. In a way, the steepness of the slope worked for us, as it seemed that a lot of fire and grenades harmlessly went over our heads.

Capt. NORMAN ALLEN
I Company/5th Cavalry
The gooks on top of the hill had to get up and expose themselves to fire down on us. Sergeant Pate really proved himself this day. His machine gun delivered such a volume of accurate fire at extreme range that he kept the gooks' heads down.

Pfc. VICTOR FOX
I Company/5th Cavalry
We could not have asked for better close-in artillery support. At times the bursts were just to our front. They walked with us right up to near the summit. You always worry about a short round, but this doesn't lessen the feeling of care and protection they afford.

A GI hollered, "Here they come. Watch it!" A flight of F-80 Shooting Star jets made a run on the enemy's positions. We stopped and watched in amazement. They began their run from a great distance. Then within seconds they roared overhead—their noise has to be heard to be believed. Understandably, they did not drop napalm, but their hailstorm of machine-gun fire was awesome. With their engines roaring and whining above, we hunched down. The expended shell casings rained down on us like a hot metal blanket.

Cpl. JERRY EMER
I Company/5th Cavalry
The noise was tremendous, the planes on top of the artillery. Beech Brian shouted in my ear to leave the radio I was carrying and catch up with Cardinal's squad to tell them to stop short of the crest of the hill and wait for reinforcements. The lieutenant was also worried they might run into their own supporting artillery fire.

Pfc. JAMES CARDINAL
I Company/5th Cavalry
We were strafed and rocketed by jet planes, and shelled by our own artillery. WP and HE fell among us. We screamed down the hill for someone to call the jets off; they were hitting no more than twenty feet in front of where we lay. Then we yelled for the artillery to raise their sights.

Capt. NORMAN ALLEN
I Company/5th Cavalry
I brought artillery and air very close, which gave the men excellent cover almost to the summit. Colonel Treacy told me later that General Gay had remarked, "My God, but that support is close. Better lift it." Treacy answered him, "I always sweat it out, too, sir, but Norm likes it close and tells me when to lift it."

   I had learned in WWII to bring in artillery right up to our positions. When the shit really hit the fan, I felt it might be necessary to take some casualties among my own men, but in the long run they would catch less hell than the enemy. The artillery and air support the company received this day were a bit closer than I really wanted, but it did save our ass.

Pfc. VICTOR FOX
I Company/5th Cavalry
Incredibly, the enemy continued to stubbornly defend the ridgeline. Near that imaginary, critical "line" where the final charge is begun, a trooper was killed in a way that disgusted us. He took a gunshot wound in the leg. This was a million-dollar wound, one that wasn't serious enough to do permanent injury, but bad enough to get him evacuated, maybe even to Japan. Instead, this poor GI went into shock and died. It seemed such an unnecessary death.

Close to the summit we discovered what had so badly shaken the 1st Platoon earlier in the morning. The gooks were in beautifully camouflaged one-man holes. You practically had to step on one before you knew he was there.

Cpl. JERRY EMER
I Company/5th Cavalry
The enemy had somehow managed to survive the jets and artillery, and now popped out of their holes and began hurling grenades and firing burp guns. Cardinal and others threw grenades back, and for a while the battle became a grenade-throwing contest. This was one of the few times I made an aggressive suggestion before Jim: "Let's get 'em!"

Pfc. VICTOR FOX
I Company/5th Cavalry
A gook opened up at point-blank range on Haltom, Sergeant Furlan, and me. He really pinned back our senses. Somehow he missed us. I emptied a full clip, then hit the ground. I, too, missed. Next, he threw a grenade in our direction; it landed well behind us.

Pfc. JAMES CARDINAL
I Company/5th Cavalry
The underbrush was so thick that Jerry and I got only about ten feet from a gook's hole when an arm came out of it and lobbed a grenade in our direction. It landed right next to me. It was a dud.

Pfc. VICTOR FOX
I Company/5th Cavalry
I yelled to Sergeant Furlan, "I know where the sonovabitch is," and with that threw a grenade that landed behind him by about a city block. Everyone lay flat. I realized I was going to have to charge this hole to kill the gook. Just then a GI named Cardinal brushed by me.

Pfc. JAMES CARDINAL
I Company/5th Cavalry

I moved toward the gook's hole and got within five feet of him. When he started to throw another grenade, I shot him between the eyes. It was him or me. I killed another enemy soldier later with a hand grenade. These were the first two men I know I actually killed.

Pfc. VICTOR FOX
I Company/5th Cavalry

My nerves were really on edge now. I moved off to the left of the summit. At the edge of a clearing I saw some brush move. I emptied another clip and skidded to the ground. A moment later a couple of GIs climbed out of the brush white as a sheet, wondering who'd shot at them.

Capt. NORMAN ALLEN
I Company/5th Cavalry

Gooks began to squirm out of their tiny homes, putting their hands on their heads as soon as they could. [Cpl. Mark] Leachman [a squad leader in the 5th Platoon] was lining them up and peering into their faces. I asked him who he was looking for. "One of these fuckers tossed a grenade at me, then threw up his hands to surrender. I'm trying to figure out which one it was. When I do, I'm gonna cram this bayonet clear through 'im." When he couldn't identify the man for sure, he suggested it might be a good idea to throw all of them over the cliff. I told him he could only do so to the gook who'd thrown the grenade. He continued to peer into their faces. After a few moments of this, I said, "OK, Leachman, come on. There are still some more gooks on the hill. Let's go!"

I had been looking around a short time when I suddenly spotted a group of about 35 North Koreans not more than fifty yards away. They didn't seem to know whether to turn tail or jump us. Another group, a larger one of about 300, moved in good order up a nearby slope. I couldn't let that bunch get away or remain this close to us. I threw Sergeant Blankenship to the ground and grabbed the radio he carried. I shouted to the battalion's exec, Major Mayer, to get me artillery real quick. "I'll adjust after the first splashdown. Just give me a battery, two or three rounds, thirty yards forward of my position!"

"Norm, I can't give you artillery for five minutes; all guns have shifted to other targets. We all thought you had the objective."

"I do have it; it's a question of keeping it. There is a large group of gooks fifty yards away thinking of coming back and taking it from me."

"Norm, I have four flights of F-80s on air cover itching to have a go at it. Can you use them?"

"Yes, any goddamn thing, but I need it right now. I repeat, right now! Do you know where we are?"

"I have the ALO [air liaison officer] right here with me. He's been watching the action and tells me he knows where all your men are."

"Bring 'em in, and pray they shoot good and straight."

The F-80s made a tight turn, then came in slow and low. The lead aircraft in each flight poured its .50s and 20-mm on the North Koreans. Brass fell around us and down our jackets. We danced like demons, not only from the hot brass but because the jets screamed in right over our heads. The bunch of gooks nearest us was torn to hell. The jets then pulled right up into the late-afternoon sun, banked, and dove smack into that larger group. Each plane fired everything it had and kept coming back until it was out of ammo. It was a beautiful show and, for my money, the Air Force never looked better.

I then returned my attention to the prisoners we'd captured. I didn't want to keep them on the hill, so sent them down with a detail with orders to turn them over to the cooks, who could escort them back to battalion once hot chow came up. The cooks apparently didn't understand what they were supposed to do with the POWs and, in the confusion of getting chow up, they left them unguarded.

Pfc. VICTOR FOX
I Company/5th Cavalry
As evening approached, Haltom and I were sent to bring back the rest of the squad's sleeping bags, which, after the attack had succeeded,

had been carried to the foot of the hill. With the company under no imminent danger, it was normal for two men from each squad to bring forward the rest of their unit's bedrolls.

It was dark by the time Haltom and I climbed down off the hill and reached the heap of bedrolls. In this pile we were lucky to recognize our own, let alone the rest of the squad's. All of a sudden I sensed we were not alone. Looking around I discovered, squatting nearby, the large group of enemy prisoners that had been sent down earlier in the day. Clad only in their cotton uniforms, they sat shivering in the cold night. There were no guards in sight and no other GIs in the area. The POWs looked at us balefully. I had come off the hill with only a .45, Haltom had his M1. Among the pile of bedrolls we discovered a BAR. Laying these weapons out in front of us, we stared back at the North Koreans. It was so cold we could see our breath in the air. Neither Haltom nor I knew what to do. We didn't want to leave the prisoners, nor did we want to spend the night watching them. They could have rushed us at any time, and some certainly would have reached us. Haltom and I had earlier vowed never to be taken prisoner, especially by the North Koreans. In their hands, we felt, our deaths would be particularly bad. This looking game with the prisoners went on for nearly half an hour.

It was a great relief to see another group of GIs coming off the hill. When we did not return promptly, this group had been sent down to check on us. They took charge of the prisoners while Haltom and I climbed up to the CP to report what we had discovered. By the time we talked to Captain Allen, we had a bad case of the shakes. What with bullet holes in our clothes from the morning and being left alone with a large group of POWs in the evening, we were really shook up. First Sergeant Mitchell, a decorated and fearless veteran of World War II, somehow found our story a bit amusing.

Capt. NORMAN ALLEN
I Company/5th Cavalry
A number of guys were very upset over the bedrolls. Men had gotten out of the habit of tying the identifying knot into their ropes. That night men looking for their rolls scattered gear all over the place.

Several fistfights broke out. The next morning some more punches were thrown. I had to rattle the chain of command all the way down to straighten things out.

[The brief spell of Indian summer, which had arrived at the same time as the Chinese offensive, disappeared, and toward the middle of November temperatures in North Korea tumbled. Eighth Army continued to probe, continued to try to find out where the Chinese had gone.]

Capt. NORMAN ALLEN
I Company/5th Cavalry

Darling Mom:
Moved forward [12 November] about 2,000 yards. We should move forward again tomorrow, probably just ridge running.

It's been very cold. Have set all day huddled around a fire in an effort to stay warm.

Everyone praying for some sort of arbitration, it's the only way any of us can see an end to this constant fight to keep warm. Been getting a few cigarettes, but still short. No winter clothing present in front line units and we are in dire need of some. It was below zero last night, 15–20 F all day. Just can't write more, too cold. . . .

Sgt. WARREN AVERY
G Company/21st Infantry
We had not been issued any winter equipment. I guess MacArthur figured since we were going to be home for Christmas, why bother with it. All each GI had was a poncho and a blanket. To keep warm, three of us would place two ponchos on the frozen ground to lie on. Then we'd cover ourselves with the three blankets and the remaining poncho. This way we got a fairly comfortable sleep.

Pfc. VICTOR FOX
I Company/5th Cavalry
We felt the presence of the Chinese all around. We heard stories about hordes of them appearing suddenly on all sides, decimating units, then breaking contact and mysteriously fading away into the wilderness. Item Company never came to grips with the Chinese, although some aggressive patrolling ended up in wild, short firefights.

On one such combat-size patrol, 3d Squad took most of one day to scale a towering hill mass. By midafternoon I could barely make out the thin thread of a railroad line in the valley far below. When the squad scrambled the final few yards to the summit, we were surprised to find three or four North Koreans waiting to surrender to us. Maybe they were Chinese, but whatever they were, they were peaceful. At this time, as in all cases, our orders were, if we made contact or drew fire, we were to clear out fast.

Capt. NORMAN ALLEN
I Company/5th Cavalry

15 November

Dearest Mother:
Read your last letter by a little candle stump Lieutenant Geer had. It lasted through the letter, then pifted out. Got probed afterward by an enemy patrol. After a short, heavy volley they turned away. This last attack, my usual shakes were noticeable by their absence. Always get that little knot in the pit of my stomach, but teeth didn't chatter, knees didn't knock. My pulse stepped up when the MGs started whipping up sand and I could hear the death bees cracking around my ears, but just wasn't frightened as I had been before. Hope it's not a sign I'm getting used to this business.

Lines have straightened up now, aggressive patrolling is taking place.

This is a terrific fight, living in a hole, a little pup tent pitched over it, trying to stay warm. Of course, it isn't as bad as if we had to do a lot of moving around or the enemy was in such force we couldn't light a fire. The wind today has gone down but there is an overcast and a real threat of snow. Took over a little gook house, had it cleaned up and warmed and let a platoon at a time move down to wash and change clothes, at least underwear. I haven't made it yet but hope to tomorrow.

The prospect of a winter campaign looks very real. The only solution I see is stabilize somewhere, dig deep bunkers, build fires in them and wait for spring. Curfman and I have drafted an ultimatum to the Chinese that we will furnish them transportation to carry all of us to New Guinea to carry on down there.

Waking moments, lay huddled in the sack, daydream about home, warm bedrooms, football games, long drives, and thousands of other luxuries. . . .

16 November

Mother:

A fairly quiet night. Someone tried to probe and rattled our noise-maker cans that we have strung around the position. A few shots and they went away. No word to move yet, can't just realize what's in the offing.

Got two lads out on division General Orders for the Silver Star for Gallantry in Action. They are the first ones awarded in the battalion. They are quite proud of them and certainly rightfully earned them.

Bye for now, must get out a few administrative reports and can only write a few minutes at a time before fingers get numb. . . .

Pfc. VICTOR FOX
I Company/5th Cavalry
Hunger and cold became a way of life. From all the climbing we also found we were constantly thirsty. One day, coming down a steep incline covered with trees, the company discovered a narrow, deep-flowing, winding stream. It seemed all of us, thirsty and crusted in filth, fell or flopped headlong into the clear, cold water and drank our fill. Soon a patrol that had been out to our front returned. With them they brought word that upstream, just around a bend, there were dead and bloated horses, cattle, and oxen floating in the water. Only then did we notice the stench.

At remote road junctions we'd come across lone military police-men who would give the company its route directions. These solitary MPs appeared to be miles and miles from anywhere. We often wondered later, in light of what was to come, what had become of them. In asking around, we would learn that most had simply disappeared.

One day, in the mountains, the company rested in a quiet glade surrounded by tall, dark evergreens. Without warning, a small deer bounded onto the sun-filled slope of a nearby ridge. His long, silent leaps appeared to be in slow motion. It was so unexpected and the animal was so graceful. We sat quietly and absorbed all that we saw.

Pfc. JAMES CARDINAL
I Company/5th Cavalry

19 November

Dear Folks:

It's 5:30 in the afternoon. The sun has gone down behind the mountains and it's starting to get cold. Of course it's cold all day long but the nights with a howling wind are *really* cold. I'm sitting next to a campfire with my buddy Jerry Emer. In all directions the scenery is spectacular. The distant mountains are covered with snow and the scene reminds me of Italy. The Korean soldiers in my squad are singing native songs. All together it's a very touching and sentimental scene. Something known to you back in the States as a quiet day on the front. It's something a soldier doesn't soon forget. However, I would trade it all for home and some of Mom's cooking.

Most of the time now when we are not climbing hills to set up new positions (about every other day) we spend waiting—waiting for chow, for mail, for cigarettes, for candy, and, most of all, for news. It's all very boring. . . .

Cpl. LACY BARNETT
Medical Company/3d Battalion/19th Infantry
General MacArthur told everyone there would be one more push and
that we would all be home for Christmas. In our bull sessions we
concluded that Russia and China would not sit idly around while one
of their friends was replaced by one of its enemies. They just would
not permit South Korea to gain control over the north. The Communists were not that dumb. However, we all felt maybe General
MacArthur knew something we did not know and, in fact, we *would*
be home for Christmas.

Word was out: the Chinese had withdrawn back north of the Yalu.
It was with some surprise then that our Item Company on patrol one
day had had a firefight with a Chinese unit mounted on horses.

1st Lt. CHARLES PAYNE
3d Battalion/19th Infantry
I watched as one of our units came in contact with some Chinese
horse cavalry. It was terribly one-sided, what with our machine guns,
mortars, and artillery. Lots of screaming horses and dying Chinese; it
didn't seem real. Reminded me of World War II, winter of 1944–45
in the Apennine Mountains, when some German artillery got in on
the mule trains bringing us supplies and replacements.

Pfc. LEONARD KORGIE
G Company/21st Infantry
Our battalion made some sort of contact with the Chinese just before
Thanksgiving. At this time we also received MacArthur's "Win the
War Offensive" message. No one could figure out how we Americans
were going to effectively handle the millions of Chinese when we were
right across from their backyards.

It was at this time I was called to battalion and asked if I wanted to be a clerk typist. Why hell, yes! Anything to get out of those cold foxholes; this would mean living in a big, warm tent. It also meant a promotion to corporal. I'd finally gotten a break.

Pfc. VICTOR FOX
I Company/5th Cavalry
Late in the afternoon of Thanksgiving eve [22 November], the company was relieved "in position" by a company from the all-black [except for its officer] 24th Infantry Regiment, 25th Infantry Division. I Company at the time was about five or seven miles north of the Ch'ongch'on River in the vicinity of Yongbyon, where the 3d Battalion, 8th Cav, had been destroyed. We occupied a long ridgeline that was not, for a change, in rugged terrain.

Capt. NORMAN ALLEN
I Company/5th Cavalry
I accompanied Lt. Col. Russ Blair, who commanded the 3d Battalion of the 24th Infantry, while he walked our position. The company that replaced us had a strength of about 230, and we had dug positions for about 140, which is all the men I Company had.

After we moved off the ridge, we assembled in a tiny village, actually just a cluster of seven or eight houses at a bend in the road. We stopped and had some hot chow that had been brought up. We then heard some firing from our old positions. We moved about a bit, still chowing down, but alert now. We hadn't had any action in that position, though patrols exchanged fire with the enemy on an almost daily basis. We knew the enemy was there, just hadn't pressed us—yet.

Pfc. VICTOR FOX
I Company/5th Cavalry
We were very happy to hop on the trucks and get the hell out of that area. Everyone sensed something was in the air, that something was about to happen. It was a bad feeling.

23 November 1950
In Pyongmyon the regiment became Army reserve. Here troopers observed Thanksgiving Day. An excellent turkey dinner was provided with accent on both quality and quantity.

NARRATIVE REPORT, 5TH CAVALRY REGIMENT

Pfc. JAMES CARDINAL
I Company/5th Cavalry

23 November
Dear Folks:
Well, here it is Thanksgiving afternoon. We've finished eating our turkey dinner and a very fine dinner it was indeed. Every man had all he wanted to eat. It's about time. We had turkey (frozen, shipped from the States), sweet potatoes, corn, stuffing, gravy, olives, pie, and candy. We were very lucky we got all this as we were only relieved from the line yesterday.

We also had another pleasant surprise this morning. Every man in the company took a hot shower and received a change of clothing. I can't tell you how much this means to combat troops. I hadn't taken a real shower since September 22. The feeling was wonderful, beyond description. . . .

The regiment also planned for a ceremony to present decorations of valor to members of the 5th Cavalry.

NARRATIVE REPORT, 5TH CAVALRY REGIMENT

Cpl. JERRY EMER
I Company/5th Cavalry
During the presentation a motley band which had been dug up from God knows where played march music. One of the songs they played we all knew and spontaneously began to sing: "In her hair she wore a yellow ribbon, she wore it for her lover who was in the cavalry. CAVALRY! CAVALRY! She wore it for her lover who was in the cavalry."

At that moment I felt close to Custer and his "long knives." It was goofy the way I felt. Others said they felt the same thing. How could we get so caught up in all that Hollywood corn? But we did. The emotion rubbed off on our South Koreans. They hummed along, but joined in on the chorus. When they sang it, it came out, "CAW-VAH-REE! CAW-VAH-REE!"

Capt. NORMAN ALLEN
I Company/5th Cavalry

Mother dearest:
The parade now over was very impressive. As General Gay was trying to pin the Silver Star* on my field jacket he said, "Hope I don't give you another Purple Heart, son." The regiment was all assembled and afterward the adjutant read off the Battle Streamers on the regimental colors—Civil War names like Bull Run, Cold Harbor, Wilderness; Indian Campaigns—Apaches, Nez Perce, Sioux; the last war—Luzon, Leyte, Japan. It made us all think back on the many shivering troopers who down through the years have stood in similar regimental formations.

These rest periods are heaven, but it's an effort to keep everyone keyed up with the proper mental attitude for combat. Going back is always hard. . . .

---

*Captain Allen received the Silver Star for his actions on Hill 174.

CHOSIN

23 November-14 December 1950

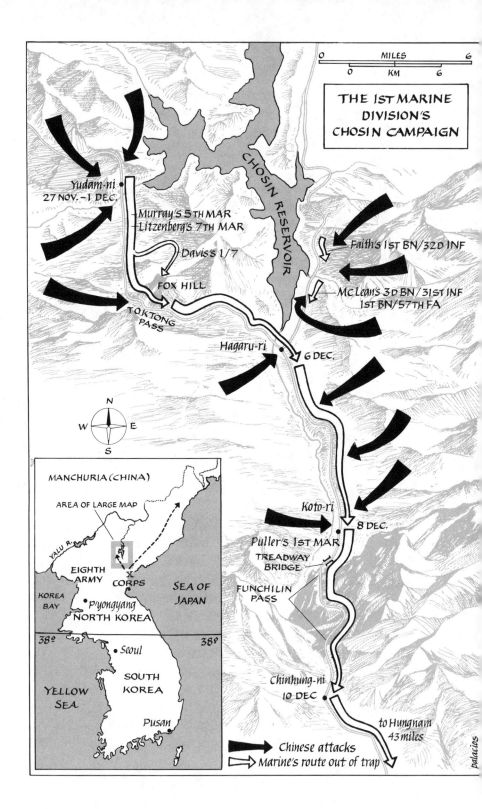

MILES
0   6
0   KM   6

THE 1ST MARINE DIVISION'S CHOSIN CAMPAIGN

CHOSIN RESERVOIR

Yudam-ni
27 NOV. – 1 DEC.

—Murray's 5TH MAR
—Litzenberg's 7TH MAR

Davis's 1/7

Faith's 1ST BN/32D INF

FOX HILL

McLean's 3D BN/31ST INF
1ST BN/57TH FA

TOKTONG PASS

Hagaru-ri   6 DEC.

N
W   E
S

Koto-ri   8 DEC.

MANCHURIA (CHINA)

AREA OF LARGE MAP

Puller's 1ST MAR
TREADWAY BRIDGE
FUNCHILIN PASS

YALU R.

EIGHTH ARMY

CORPS

SEA OF JAPAN

KOREA BAY

P'yongyang
NORTH KOREA

38°   38°

Seoul

Chinhung-ni
10 DEC

YELLOW SEA

SOUTH KOREA

Pusan

to Hungnam
43 miles

➡ Chinese attacks
⇨ Marine's route out of trap

palacios

23 November 1950

Thanksgiving services were held at H & S Company, 1st and 2d Battalion areas. The Thanksgiving dinner of turkey, cranberry sauce, shrimp cocktail, vegetables, dressing, fresh potatoes, pumpkin and mince pies, coffee, fruitcake, candies, nuts, oranges, apples, and other items was served to the 1st and 2d Battalions and H & S Company and attached units.

HISTORICAL DIARY, 5TH MARINE REGIMENT

Lt. Col. RAYMOND DAVIS
1/7

I talked [Col. Homer] Litzenberg into letting us have a day off for our Thanksgiving meal. As we had gone out of Hagaru-ri before the turkeys arrived, I knew we would miss them. I also knew the men needed a lift. When the turkeys caught up with us, there were stacks of them, but unfortunately they were frozen hard as could be. I couldn't get the cooks to guarantee that the birds would be thawed in time for dinner. It was so cold no one could figure out how to do it. Everyone, from the chief cook on down, said it couldn't be done. The night before Thanksgiving one of the headquarters officers finally came up with an idea. He made a mountain of the frozen birds around two field kitchen stoves that had been fired up. Next he covered the whole thing with two pyramidal tents that he sealed tight with snow and brush. By morning the birds were thawed enough for them to be cut up and cooked. *

S/Sgt. LEE BERGEE
E/1
Our company had Thanksgiving dinner in an apple orchard near a small stream. Each day it had gotten colder. To the north and west I could see high, snowcapped mountains. We ate turkey and all the trimmings. The night before, I watched the cooks working, their area illuminated by truck headlights. Before dinner I refereed a tackle-football game on a field two bulldozers had leveled for us. In the afternoon Colonel Puller pinned decorations on the chests of men who'd won them at Inch'on or Seoul. He pinned each on with deep sincerity. One corpsman with our battalion shook his head from side to side while they read his citation for bravery. I washed some clothes in the stream; the water was very cold. Each night was below freezing. I hoped we would be out of Korea before the worst of winter fell on us.

Chaplain CORNELIUS GRIFFIN (USN)
7th Marines
We held our Thanksgiving feast. I told the mess sergeant to save the red cellophane the frozen turkeys came wrapped in from the packer and, once dinner was over, to wrap all the bones he could find in it.

---

* Gen. Raymond Davis interview, Oral History Collection, Marine Corps Historical Center, Washington, D.C. Hereafter, Davis interview, MCHC.

"My God," he asked, "what do you want with that junk?" I said, "When we get up farther north, if we have to, we can boil the hell out of those bones in melted snow and make some damned good turkey broth." As it turned out, that is exactly what we would do later in the week. Then we took the red cellophane and reused it a second time to cover all the holes and loose corners in the sick bays during blackouts.

Pfc. JAMES GRAHAM
F/5

Thanksgiving dinner was served in an abandoned schoolhouse which had been pressed into service as a mess hall. I ate in the second shift. When I was through, it was getting dark and I prepared to return to the line. An Army six-by-six truck was parked near the school. Since it was the only one in sight, I figured it must be loaded with food. I unstrapped one corner of the tarp covering the truck bed and, sure enough, I saw cases of canned food. I looked around quickly and found I was alone. I grabbed one of the cases and headed up the hill to my foxhole. The next morning, at first light, the guys in my fire team gathered around to see what treat I had obtained for us. The case was large; we thought of inviting the entire squad. I opened it. No one shouted with joy. The case contained six one-gallon cans of pea soup.

Hospitalman 3/C WILLIAM DAVIS
B/7

It was very, very late when we got back to the company and found the field kitchen there preparing Thanksgiving dinner. It was actually the day after Thanksgiving, but no one minded. We were served turkey and all the things that go with it on tin trays, just like aboard ship. Darker than pitch. We turned on the lights of jeeps and stood or sat on the hoods of the vehicles and ate our meal. I didn't give a good-sized damn because it was food and we hadn't had honest-to-God food in a long, long time. You had to eat fast because everything was turning cold. The gravy and then the mashed potatoes froze first. The inside of the turkey was still warm. Boy, you ate fast. And all the time the snipers were shooting at us.

Pfc. PAUL MARTIN
Reconnaissance Company/1st Marine Division
We enjoyed a nice Thanksgiving dinner with plenty of leftovers. It
was at this time that I read an issue of the *Pacific Stars and Stripes*
that showed pictures of well-bundled-up generals and colonels standing with what it said was the Yalu River in the background. I read
that Eighth Army, across the mountains on the west coast, was about
to make the final push to the Manchurian border. We were told by
the X Corps commander that when we reached the border, we would
be replaced by ROK units, that we were not to let a bunch of laun-
drymen stop us. The sweet smell of victory was again in the air. Recon Company received orders to move north and join the 7th Marines at Yudam-ni. Because of a lack of antifreeze and tire chains,
the company was delayed one day in departing. This was all that kept
Recon Company from being up around the Chosin when the Chinese
sprang their trap.

[*On Thanksgiving in 1950, of course, no one knew, nor could anyone
have guessed, that to the Pantheon of Marine battles, to the legends
of Guam and Saipan, Tarawa, Peleliu, Iwo Jima, and Guadalcanal,
the Corps would soon add the Chosin Reservoir. As many great moments in history do, the campaign that saw the Marines reach the
Chosin had begun quietly enough.*

*In late October, while Eighth Army temporarily rested in the en-
emy capital of P'yongyang and prepared to push to the Yalu, X Corps,
the same force that had landed at Inch'on and recaptured Seoul, had
been put ashore midway along Korea's northeastern shore at Wonsan.* Major General Almond's command consisted of two ROK divisions, a commando group of British Royal Marines, the U.S. 7th and
3d Divisions, and the 1st Marine Division. Its mission was the same*

---

*The 1st Marine Division landed at Wonsan without incident on 26 October.

as Eighth Army's: to prevent the further withdrawal of the North Korean Army. With little chance of the enemy unconditionally laying down his arms, MacArthur authorized General Almond to use whatever forces were necessary to secure all of his sector of North Korea. Once ashore at Wonsan, the Marine division was ordered to the port of Hungnam and then to the area of the Chosin Reservoir, some sixty-five miles to the northwest, where they would relieve ROK units already in the area.

At first the Marine advance into North Korea's bleak, mountainous heartland was uneventful. The weather was pleasant: warm days, cool nights—Indian-summer weather. But October became November; the evenings grew chill, the mornings misty, the blue sky changed to gray, and the first snow the Marines were to know in Korea whitened the surrounding mountains. The north wind from Siberia blew more blustering and searching. It grew steadily colder.]

S/Sgt. LEE BERGEE
E/1
I recall being told that a North Korean winter struck quickly. There would be no autumn; it would go from summer heat to winter cold. I went to sleep on my sleeping bag one night in the middle of a cabbage patch. When I awoke I was freezing and frost covered the field and me. Winter arrived that suddenly.

Pfc. DAVE KOEGEL
B/7
In the subzero temperatures many weapons refused to operate or did so only after much cursing and kicking. There was little we could do to keep them firing. Many men, however, found an ingenious way to keep dirt, snow, or moisture from getting down the barrel—they covered it with a condom. Especially useful were the "reservoir"-tipped

models whose narrow ends fit snugly over the barrel. Removing the condom was done more hurriedly than the recommended rolling method shown in the VD training films.

Pfc. ROBERT EZELL
F/7

The cold was something else. Guys from the cold states like Minnesota used to razz us Californians for not being able to handle the cold. They, however, were some of the first to get frostbite from being careless.

One morning we had hot chow for breakfast. They poured warm milk on my cereal. I walked over and sat on a stump to eat. The milk had frozen.

Pfc. DEAN WESTBERG
B/7

I had my feet checked for frostbite and was sent back for treatment to the division hospital near Hungnam. The doctor asked, "Where you from?"

"Minnesota."

"Oh, I thought you guys up there knew how to take care of yourselves."

"First off, we come in out of the cold. We don't usually sleep outside when it's twenty degrees below. We're smarter than that. Second, we have the right kind of clothes and enough of it."

Pfc. FRED DAVIDSON
G/5

We had "warming tents" set up on the reverse slope of every hill we occupied for the night. There were so many of us and so few tents that it became impossible to stay in the tents long enough to even approach getting warm. It was always time to leave and go back on the line so someone else could use the tents. The days and nights rolled into a blend of light and dark. There was always a hill to climb and it was always cold! When it snowed it was cold. When the sun shone it was cold. When we marched north it was cold. When we marched south it was cold. And I was tired. I'd been in combat since August 2 in the Pusan Perimeter; I'd been twice on the slopes of Obong-ni Ridge; I'd landed at Inch'on; I'd crossed the Han and fought in Seoul. I was tired and damned near ready to give up the ghost.

[During the 1st Marine Division's advance into the North Korean highlands, it encountered a new enemy—the Chinese. In early November, at the very time General Walker's Eighth Army was ambushed above the Ch'ongch'on River, the 7th Marines fought a sharp night battle with the Chinese at Sudong—and defeated them. The enemy then withdrew into the surrounding mountains.

One must assume that General MacArthur's headquarters in To-kyo had been alerted to the dangers this new enemy presented. But, as he had done at Inch'on, MacArthur decided to gamble. He had succeeded before; why not try again? Unable to link the two wings of his command, now separated by seventy-five miles of high mountains, MacArthur permitted Eighth Army in the west and X Corps in the east to proceed independently to the Yalu River. Once they reached the border, there would be time to consolidate their positions. Shrugging off the Chinese attacks of early November, MacArthur ordered a final offensive to crush what was left of the North Korean People's Army before it managed to escape across the Yalu into Manchuria. This accomplished, the five-month-old war would be ended.]

Col. HOMER LITZENBERG
7th Marine Regiment

This campaign in North Korea was novel insofar as the Marine Corps was concerned. It was mountain warfare and we had not been particularly trained for it. We had to improvise as we went along. The roads in North Korea generally follow valleys; hence, we were usually proceeding up a valley. The hills on either side of the road averaged 1,000 or 1,500 feet above the valley floor. Usually, there was a rocky streambed in the valley. These shallow streams were fordable almost anywhere. Beyond each hill lay another that seemed higher. We had to struggle against the tendency to go out and take over the highest ground. If we had taken the highest hills, we would have overextended ourselves. We had to accept that we would always be under observation from the enemy. There was little concealment from the heights, which were occupied by the enemy.*

[At first the Marines marched along a section of the two-lane paved road that traverses forty-three miles of gently rolling terrain from the supply port of Hungnam to Chinhung-ni. Above Chinhung-ni the terrain changes dramatically. The road becomes narrower and, rising steeply for 2,500 feet, twists and turns through Funchilin Pass until it reaches Koto-ri. On one side of the road, there are vertical drops; on the other, granite walls. After Koto-ri it levels off and cuts through eleven miles of rugged tableland. At Hagaru-ri the road divides. The right fork follows the Chosin Reservoir's eastern shoreline, the left climbs 4,000 feet over Toktong Pass, west of the reservoir, then drops into Yudam-ni, a small village of mud huts that sits in a broad valley 3,500 feet above sea level. The view from Yudam-ni in every direction is of ridges and mountains. The seventy-eight miles that link the bustling port city of Hungnam to the remote mountain village of Yudam-ni were known to the Marines who traveled it in the winter of 1950 as the main supply route or, simply the "MSR." †]

---

*Col. Homer Litzenberg interview, on file at the Marine Corps Historical Center, Washington, D.C.
† Distances in road miles between points along the route are: Hungnam to Chinhung-ni, 43; Chinhung-ni to Koto-ri, 10; Koto-ri to Hagaru-ri, 11; Hagaru-ri to Yudam-ni, 14.

Pfc. DEAN WESTBERG
B/7
We'd walk all day along the MSR. At dusk we'd climb to the top of
a hill, set the mortars, then go back down to the road and bring up
the ammunition and water. Then we'd dig a foxhole, eat cold C rations, and sleep in a hole. In the morning, when the sun came over
the mountains, the pattern would begin again.

We pretty much knew what to expect. We knew the weather was
going to be miserable. We knew we would hit the Chinese in the
daytime if we found them; we knew the Chinese would hit us at night
if they wanted to. We tried to sleep. Some nights we got set early.
Others, we wouldn't begin to set up until late—nine or ten o'clock.

*[The 7th Marines occupied Hagaru-ri on 15 November. That night
the temperature plunged to four degrees below zero.]*

Pfc. DEAN WESTBERG
B/7
I remember the first night in Hagaru-ri was pitch-black and cold. Cold!
The company was on a 100 percent watch. Rumors said there were
thousands of Chinese in the hills. I was about to spend the most mis-
erable night of my life.

A field kitchen was set up in Hagaru-ri, and earlier in the evening I had eaten a generous helping of dehydrated corn-beef hash.
Before it could be cooked it had to soak. Even with the soaking, the
diced potatoes and hash were hard as little bullets. But we were also
served fresh-baked bread. My buddy Perk [Cpl. Merwin Perkins] and
I were chowhounds. That night, in the hole he and I ate bread and
finished everything off with a can of peaches.

The temperature was well below zero. A howling wind blew the
snow and cold into the foxhole. We were like cats. You know how
cats hate to be out in the wind because they become disoriented; the
noise of the wind makes it seem danger is lurking everywhere. That's
the way Perk and I felt. And there were the Chinese, who were probably all around us. We crouched in our foxhole to get away from the
gale.

Perk didn't look too good. "I'm sick. I'm going to throw up."

"Get out. Put your mouth up there over the edge."

"I can't. My stomach's knotted up. Can't move. I'm gonna throw up. Gonna throw up." He lay on his back next to me.

"Perkins, get your head out of the hole." I grabbed him and tried to lift him. He was as stiff as a board. I got a shoulder under him and shoved. As his head cleared the foxhole he threw up. All those peaches.

I lay there and by now I knew I had diarrhea. Oh, God, I thought, let me hold on, just until morning, let me hold on. I couldn't. I had to get out of the hole. I walked toward the front line. The wind felt like a hurricane. Everyone was skitterish. The password was "Salted"; the countersign, "Peanuts." I had my shovel, but didn't know what I was going to do with it in the frozen ground. Every step I took seemed like someone wanted the password. "Salted." "Peanuts." I had to go so bad. "Salted." "Peanuts." The wind blew so hard. Down the hill I scrambled. "Salted." "Peanuts." No moonlight. It was the end. It really was. Everything was wrong. I was as miserable as I could get. Upset, mad, angry, I cried with frustration. The wind howled, the cold got colder. The tears froze on my cheeks.

I completed my runs—almost. A shot rang out below me. The Chinese *were* there. I stopped and tried to pull up my layers and layers of pants. I couldn't. My hands were so numb I couldn't zip or button my pants. I tried to hold everything up and not drop my rifle and shovel. I tripped several times. My hands felt like footballs.

Back in the foxhole I put my hands under my armpits and tried to thaw them. If I was going to get killed, this would have been the perfect time. I'd at least have gotten it over with. I didn't want to survive this night only to be killed sometime later.

[The 7th Marines waited at Hagaru-ri while the village was transformed into a forward base. Work on a small airstrip began on 19 November. General Almond believed it might be a good idea, in the event of some winter emergency, to be able to land small planes at Hagaru-ri and bring in supplies or take out casualties. The worry would not go away. If General MacArthur and his staff were not overly concerned by the presence of those Chinese hidden somewhere in the nearby mountains, the commanders in the field were. In mid-November, with the 1st Marine Division spread along most of the MSR, Maj. Gen. Oliver P. Smith and his regimental commanders—Puller, Murray, and

Litzenberg—grew more cautious and deliberate. How many Chinese were there? Would they attack again? Where? When?]

Maj. Gen. OLIVER P. SMITH
Commanding General, 1st Marine Division

What I was trying to do was slow down the advance and stall until I could pull up the 1st Marine Regiment. I was unable to complete this plan until November 27. By that date the 1st Marines had broken loose from its commitments in the south, and I was able to put one of their battalions at Hagaru-ri, another at Koto-ri, and the third at Chinhung-ni. They were to guard our main supply route.

Earlier in November Litzenberg had gone up the road and met the Chinese below Chinhung-ni [at Sudong, 2–3 November], where he had quite a fight. Litzenberg had forty-four killed and a couple hundred wounded, but his regiment decimated the 124th CCF [Chinese Communist Forces] Division. Then we took it slow. With winter approaching, I was hoping the division wouldn't have to get up on that high plateau and, on that one road, advance beyond Koto-ri.

I was told to occupy a blocking position at Yudam-ni with the 7th Marines after Thanksgiving, and to have the 5th Marines go up the east side of the Chosin Reservoir until it hit the Yalu. I told Litzenberg not to go too fast. He didn't want to go over the Toktong Pass and into Yudam-ni because of that tremendous open flank in the west.* But the pressure was put on me to get going. I finally had to tell Litzenberg to occupy Yudam-ni.†

[The 7th Marines was ordered to Yudam-ni on 23 November. During the next two days, Lt. Col. Ray Davis's 1st Battalion advanced

---

* There were nearly eighty miles separating Eighth Army from the 7th Marines.
† Smith interview, MCHC.

methodically over Toktong Pass, scattering small enemy units as it went.]

2d Lt. JOSEPH OWEN
B/7

Our first objective was the spike of rocks that marks Toktong Pass. It was more than a mile ahead of us and we moved in parallel columns spread along each side of the twisting, frozen-mud road. Able and Charlie Companies covered our flanks. They were positioned in the high, snow-buried hills that rose in endless rows around us. Except for occasional thick pine forests near the road, the hills were snow and bare rock.

We moved out in colorless dawn, and the men in the subzero darkness beat their hands against their sides after the finger-numbing ordeal of strapping gear and checking weapons. They were helmeted, shapeless figures in their long, hooded parkas, showing only a small patch of face to the north wind that could numb exposed flesh in seconds.

"Nothing but Chinamen from here to Mongolia," muttered a rifleman, walking backward for shelter from the wind. There was little response from his comrades, perhaps a few listless profanities. Until we met the Chinese, the cold was our enemy.*

Pfc. DAVE KOEGEL
B/7

The company had taken the point on the advance along the west side of the Reservoir. Two columns, one on each side of the road, trudged toward someplace called Yudam-ni. I carried two chests of machine-

---

* 1st Lt. Joseph Owen, USMC (Ret), "Chosin Reservoir Remembered," *Marine Corps Gazette*, December 1980, 52–55. Hereafter, Owen, *Gazette*.

gun ammo. The metal chests or cans could be gripped by handles secured to them by clips. Experienced carriers improvised web slings to carry the cans over their shoulders. I was new and not so equipped. I plugged along the road with the fifteen-pound cans dangling from my hands. Each step jostled my shoulder sockets and elbows. I managed, however, to keep in the column—that is, until one of the clips broke. For a time I struggled to carry the can under my arm. "Fix the handle, dummy," someone said. I sat by the side of the road and did the best I could. By the time my makeshift repair was complete, the column had moved around a bend and was out of sight. Somehow I had to find the extra energy to make up the distance between me and the company. It was with great relief that I saw a jeep come up from behind me. When it drew near I recognized Baker Company's first sergeant. He'd give me a ride to my section. I explained why I had dropped out of the column and expressed happiness at the help I was about to receive and from someone in my own company. Probably in an effort to build character and self-reliance in a new replacement, the sergeant said, "Well, better get moving." He left me in a spray of ice and gravel.

2d Lt. JOSEPH OWEN
B/7
The Chinese defending Toktong Pass took us under fire from 200 yards. They were embedded around the high rock pile, and dug in on the slope facing us. Their machine-gun and rifle fire was slow at first, sporadic, but would soon intensify. Their frequent failure to open up with concentrated fire on designated targets was always puzzling.

Reflexively, the leading rifle platoon deployed in skirmish lines off both sides of the road and returned the fire. One of the mortars set up behind 1st Lt. Hank [Harrol] Kiser on the right, and almost immediately the tube was thumping in response to Cpl. Hugo Johnson's raucous direction. Enemy fire was heavy now as the second platoon climbed behind the hill to extend our left flank.

Captain [Myron] Wilcox, the CO, moved forward up the road. Even during firefights he maintained an easy, ambling gait. His large tortoiseshell glasses gave him an academic look that was incongruous with the shouting Marines rushing about him. He set up his CP in the ditch just behind Kiser's platoon. The crackle of the SCR-300 communicating with battalion added to the sounds of battle. Soon, too, there were the urgent cries of "Corpsman! Corpsman!"

The cold had been forgotten. We sweated heavily with the strain of moving quickly through the deep snow.

"Keep your toes wiggling!" was the strange command shouted by squad leaders to their men firing from the prone position. Sweat-soaked socks inside airtight shoepacs would freeze within a few minutes of inactivity and cause frostbite. Frostbite discipline had become a primary responsibility for every unit leader.

Plt/Sgt. Joseph R. King, of the 2d Platoon, was crouched among large boulders several yards above me to the left of the road. He had spotted a target near the tower of rocks, but I could not hear his directions. King motioned for me to join him.

Running up a steep, snow-buried hill with weapon, pack, parka, shoepacs, and several layers of clothing was laborious effort. My runner, Cpl. Robert F. Kelly, and I made slow progress, slipping frequently, falling to our knees, scrambling upward again. Our struggle through the snow attracted enemy attention, and we were suddenly targets of opportunity. With Chinese ammunition whining about us, our progress accelerated and I have a clear memory of prodigious upward bounds over the snow and into the sheltering boulders.

Just below us Cpl. Alphonzo Burris had found a rock-rimmed pit for his gun and was soon throwing [60-mm] HE mortar shells. Unfortunately, our HE had little effect on the well-emplaced Chinese. Their position was good, and even with artillery support it appeared that we would be in for a long, hard day.*

Pfc. DEAN WESTBERG
B/7
Joe Owen, the mortar section leader, was a real Marine. We had asked, "Where you from, Joe?"

"Here."

"Naw, Joe. Where's home?"

---

* Owen, *Gazette.*

"Right here. Wherever the Marines send me, that's home."

We thought Joe was odd because he was so gung ho. He was a Regular, we were Reservists. He should have had a platoon with the 5th Marines. He had us Reservists instead. Our weapons platoon sergeant, Don Wright, said one time, "When Joe wants a volunteer, I want you guys to get out there and volunteer. Joe really likes that." We thought, You crazy or something? This had happened a few days before. We were pinned down now near a big outcropping of rocks by a Chinese machine gun. It was near the top of the Toktong Pass. Joe called for volunteers. Silence. I said to [Hugo] Johnson, a kid from Texas, "Let's do it." "OK," he said. We ran up. "Waddya want, Joe?" "Get out there. Start firing on the gook gun up there." I couldn't believe my ears. It was a wide-open space, no cover anywhere. "And get moving. Now!" This was in his booming voice. We jumped out there and set the mortar while we crouched as much as we could. We had a pretty good idea of the range. I sighted, Johnson dropped the first mortar round in. PLOOMP!

2d Lt. JOSEPH OWEN
B/7
We were joined amid the boulders by the forward air-control officer. With his radioman, he had covered the same near-vertical slope, the two of them hauling their heavy communications gear under thickening fire. The Chinese had now realized the purpose of our position. The fire that they concentrated on us filled the air with ricochets and chips of boulders.

The air officer was able to call in a flight of Corsairs, and within minutes they were circling above us.*

Pfc. DEAN WESTBERG
B/7
Out of the corner of my eye I spotted the Corsair. It came in low, right over the outcropping. I stopped and watched and could see the

---

*Owen, *Gazette*.

pilot clearly. Johnson had his back to him. Poor kid hadn't heard or seen him—yet. Just as the Corsair closed on us, the pilot cut loose on the Chinese with his rockets. Poor Johnson nearly died. He was sure he'd been hit from all sides at once. The noise was tremendous. The Corsair climbed straight up, looped, and came in again.

2d Lt. JOSEPH OWEN
B/7

Friendly napalm, precisely laid against a stubborn, dug-in enemy, is a spectacle of beauty to a rifle company in the assault. The red flames and black smoke billowed against the white snow. There was a sudden silence. I think we were all awed by the power of that close-in napalm strike.

Then I heard Hank Kiser shouting to his men to move out. The air officer congratulated his pilots on a good strike. Runners radiated to the platoons from Captain Wilcox's CP, and the skipper walked forward along the road again, trying to make direct contact with his platoon leaders on the ever erratic walkie-talkies.

There was no further resistance as we crossed the open slope to the high ground covering Toktong Pass. When we arrived there were several charred Chinese bodies, but the enemy had withdrawn in good order, taking their wounded and their weapons.

Toktong Pass, going north, had been an easy fight, thanks to air. We would return to this position within several days. By then it would be known as Fox Hill, and we would have a much more difficult time. *

[On 25 November, the day the 7th Marines entered Yudam-ni, the Marine division was ordered to reorient its northward advance and provide more assistance for Eighth Army, seventy miles away across the mountains in western Korea. The Marines would be the right arm, Eighth Army the left, of a gigantic pincer movement that would envelop the enemy before he had an opportunity to flee across the Yalu. The 5th Marines, once they'd been relieved east of the

---

* Owen, Gazette.

Chosin Reservoir by units of the U.S. 7th Infantry Division, would pass through the 7th Marines at Yudam-ni and lead the advance west to Mupyong-ni.]

Maj. Gen. OLIVER P. SMITH
Commanding General, 1st Marine Division

Apparently, pressure was put on General MacArthur by the Joint Chiefs of Staff in Washington to get some kind of contact between X Corps and Eighth Army. He devised a new plan that rushed some troops from the 31st and 32d Infantry Regiments [7th Division] east of the Reservoir to relieve the 5th Marines. The 5th would then move over to Yudam-ni and with the 7th Marines attack northwest to link up with Eighth Army. Those poor devils from the 31st and 32d Infantry came to me to get liners for their parkas and other equipment. "Look," I said, "we only have one parka per man ourselves." I warned them, "Now see here, don't go out on a limb up there. Take it easy." *

[Marine operations east of the Reservoir came to an end at noon on the 25th, when Murray's 5th Marines was relieved by the 1st Battalion, 32d Infantry, 7th Division.†]

Capt. EDWARD STAMFORD (USMC)
ANGLICO Team/1st Battalion/32d Infantry ‡

The Marine units started moving out on Monday morning [27 November]. As soon as the Marine units cleared the area, we moved up and took their old positions, which were approximately twelve miles north of Hagaru-ri. We moved onto the high ground on both sides of the road. Earlier, the commanding officer of our battalion [Lt. Col. Don Faith, Jr.] made a trip to the regimental CP of the 5th Marines and was given all information on what patrols had been sent out and

---

* Smith interview, MCHC.

† The next day this battalion was joined on the east side of the Reservoir by the 3d Battalion, 31st Infantry, and the 1st Battalion, 57th Field Artillery.

‡ Marine Captain Stamford was attached to the 1st Battalion, 32d Infantry, as a forward air controller, the Marine Air and Naval Gunfire Liaison Company (ANGLICO).

what they knew about the area. While we were in our bivouac, we also sent patrols out to our east and northeast to see if they could contact the enemy, but they were largely unsuccessful. Our battalion S-2 [Intelligence] questioned civilians through his Korean interpreter and learned the Chinese were saying they were going to take back the Chosin Reservoir.

Everyone more or less pooh-poohed the idea. *

S/Sgt. CHESTER BAIR
Attached 1st Battalion/32d Infantry
My truck was taken to the forward perimeter. The ammo-bearers descended like flies and removed my cargo. I could tell the infantry guys were getting nervous. We all knew we were in China's backyard. All I wanted was to get in my truck and head back to Hamhung. When Lieutenant [Hugh] May [the motor transport officer, 1st Battalion, 32d Infantry] walked past at one point, I asked when I was leaving. He told me some of the supply trucks would be leaving next morning, but he would let me know when I would be going back.

Everyone was griping about the cold and bitching about the steep hills that had to be climbed. Some of the vehicles were having mechanical problems caused by the temperature. As I was a trained mechanic, I went to work.

Rumors began to fly. The one we all feared we heard the most: we had walked into a trap; we were surrounded by the Chinese.

[On Sunday evening, 26 November, X Corps command was startled to learn that the left wing of MacArthur's pincer maneuver, Eighth Army, had been attacked by a massive Chinese force and the ROK

---

* Stamford interview, on file at the Marine Corps Historical Center, Washington, D.C. Hereafter, Stamford interview, MCHC.

divisions guarding its right flank had broken. News of the disaster did not make its way down the ranks to the Marines around the Chosin Reservoir, who still believed, as they began their advance, that they would soon be on the Yalu.

The last two battalions of Murray's 5th Marines left the east side of the Reservoir on Monday morning, the 27th, and were trucked south to Hagaru-ri, then north across Toktong Pass.]

27 November 1950

The MSR from Hagaru-ri to Yudam-ni was frozen but passable. The grade and sharp curves made it very dangerous. Control points were required because it was usable only to one-way traffic in many places. Because of the extreme cold and bad road conditions ten trucks were rendered temporarily unserviceable. The weather was bitter cold.

HISTORICAL DIARY, 5TH MARINE REGIMENT

Pfc. JACK WRIGHT
G/5

We pulled into Yudam-ni, which is in a wide, flat valley with steep hills on both sides. At the northern end the valley narrowed and was crossed by a dike. We saw Marines in fighting position along that dike. Directly in front of them was a large hill that came to a point and looked like an upside-down cone. The Marines [3/7] were firing at the hill and some Corsairs were literally blowing the hell out of it.

We were very curious about all this. After we set up, an officer came around and gave us the scoop. "The regiment will jump off in the assault. It will pass through the 7th Marine Regiment, which is on line right now, and push northwest until it meets Eighth Army units. We will then be relieved by an army of occupation and go into X Corps reserve. You will probably meet scattered North Korean units. They have no artillery, no automatic weapons, very little ammunition and food. The only reason they'll bother you is to steal your supplies. We expect to be on the Yalu in ten days. Thank you, gentlemen."

We walked away to our platoon areas still wondering why those Marines were blasting hell out of the cone-shaped hill.

[When the last two battalions of the 5th Marines arrived at Yudam-ni on the 27th, the regiment's 2d Battalion, which had reached the village the evening before, had already jumped off in the attack. Supported by units of the 7th Marines, which were disposed in the perimeter around Yudam-ni and overlooked the route of attack, 2/5 had at first advanced without meeting opposition. The situation changed in midmorning. Around 9:30 A.M., Corsairs providing aerial reconnaissance and close air support began reporting enemy sightings. The Chinese, as General Smith had suspected, lay in strength in the mountains west of Yudam-ni and had every intention of blocking the Marines' advance.]

Lt. Col. HAROLD EISELE
VMF-212 *

We made a predawn takeoff and were directed by Devastate Baker †
to search an area southwest of the Reservoir. We saw two Marine platoons walking west. We flew low over them but were unable to establish radio contact. Ahead of them and over a ridge we discovered many footprints in the fresh snow. These ended at a ridge that lay two or three miles ahead of the Marines. We flew low back and forth along the brush-covered ridge but could not detect the enemy. I reported this to Devastate Baker and it advised that it would contact the patrol about our discovery. We were then directed to a target near Yudam-

---

* One of the Marine fighter squadrons of the 1st Marine Aircraft Wing.
† Devastate Baker was the call sign of the Marine Tactical Air Control Squadron-2, and was under the operational control of the 1st Marine Division.

ni. Before leaving the area I flew back over the Marine patrol and fired a few rounds of 20-mm in the direction of the ridge. We then attacked our assigned target and returned to Yonpo.*

The rest of the day was hectic. We flew many missions attacking targets around the Reservoir. Some of them were troops we caught in the open.

[The Chinese were all across the front, well dug in and, seemingly, in great numbers. The Marine attacking force was heavily engaged throughout the rest of the day. Baker 7's patrol action was typical of the bitter battles fought that day in the rugged hill country around Yudam-ni.]

2d Lt. JOSEPH OWEN
B/7

By noon we had climbed into the high ground [south ridge], a mile west of the road, and three miles south of Yudam-ni. It was a gray day and the temperature was far below zero, but the incessant cold was nearly forgotten as we struggled upward through the deep snow. Baker Company was alone that day.

We had encountered no enemy since leaving the road more than an hour before. But Kelly, my runner, insisted. "There are gooks all around us. I can sense them," he told me, but I saw no sign of them.

The men sprawled in the snow on either side of the trail broken through by the forward platoons. They fumbled and complained over their ration cans. Lieutenants and NCOs ranged the halted column, checking for frozen weapons and frostbite. Body heat, trapped inside several layers of clothing, kept us warm until we saddled up again.

"Up there! Look!" Kelly nudged me. A ridgeline 500 yards southwest was crowded with Chinese soldiers looking down on us. We had all seen them by now, and the men scrambled to the ready. Before our mortars could begin to thump, there was the sound of heavy fire from our front. 1st Lt. Woody Taylor's platoon was taking most of it.

---

* Yonpo is south of the port city of Hungnam and was the location of a modern airfield.

Taylor attempted to move forward, to higher ground, in order to take pressure off the leading tip of the company. Captain Wilcox passed the word for the remainder of us to create a perimeter. The walkie-talkies were working, for the moment.

The Chinese maneuvered as if they were executing a well-planned trap. They formed close on all sides of us, running across the snow in squad columns. They took positions among the boulders or prone in the snow, facing us. Corporal Johnson spotted a moving column at 300 yards. Without a bipod he "led" his target with the mortar tube and dropped a round of HE. We watched the shell arc, then saw it fall precisely in the middle of the Chinese squad. But the direct hit was another dud. The men cursed in disgust. Johnson spat brown tobacco juice in the snow.

Now we were fully surrounded, and the Chinese fire was intense. Several times the enemy charged at our line, but they made no significant penetration. We fought them off, mostly with small-arms fire and grenades.*

Sgt. SHERMAN RICHTER
B/7

When the Chinese attacked I was frightened to death until I pulled the trigger on my machine gun. If you don't do nothing, you're gonna stay scared through the whole onslaught. Don't tell me about heroes. Everyone is very afraid. The enemy comes at you from every direction. You don't know what will happen. Once the battle begins you stop thinking, your mind goes berserk. For however long the battle goes on, you stay crazy. Why else would I have continuously pumped round after round in bodies that I knew were deader than a doornail? To me, they weren't dead. I'd seen Chinese kill my buddies, I knew they were trying to kill me. I pumped bullets into them. I mean, how

*Owen, *Gazette.*

many times can you kill a guy? Until the battle is over, until you stop pulling the trigger, you're crazy. When you stop, you return to reality.

2d Lt. JOSEPH OWEN
B/7

Pfc. John J. Gallapo, Hank Kiser's runner, spotted a machine gun at 200 yards, and he called for fire from Cpl. Merwin A. Perkins's mortar. Under heavy fire, Gallapo stood as an aiming stake, shouting range and deflection until the Chinese gun was neutralized. Several times during that long afternoon he repeated this aiming technique.

Light began to fade, and we were concerned about our dwindling supply of ammo. There were no friendlies between us and Charlie Company, a mile back at the road. More Chinese moved into position, but since their fire did not further intensify, we assumed they intended to wait until dark, then run over us.

Amid the cries of "Corpsman!" someone yelled out that Captain Wilcox had been hit. He had taken a bullet in the face, and [1st. Lt.] Joe Kurcaba became CO.

Woody Taylor had long since brought his platoon back in to form the western edge of our shrinking perimeter. Corpsman [William] Davis had been hit, but he still tended the wounded in the center of the position. Otherwise, all hands were prone in the snow, facing the enemy. There was only one man on each mortar; the rest of the section filled in the line with rifles and BARs picked up from casualties. Unit leaders now imposed strict fire discipline in anticipation of an overnight battle.

Joe Kurcaba had just passed the word that we were to make ready to attempt a breakout at the eastern edge of the perimeter, when there was a sudden clearing of the clouds. Almost simultaneously, there were three Corsairs overhead. They showed an excellent understanding of our situation, for they immediately scathed the long, deep valley that runs east to the road. The Chinese at our end of the perimeter were silenced. Joe Kurcaba yelled, "Move out!" Hank Kiser's platoon, with the mortarmen in the center, charged forward and broke through the first enemy position blocking our way. This sharp forward thrust gave us momentum, and Kurcaba quickly formed the remainder of the company in two parallel columns. Firing to both sides and the rear, they moved out behind us. For the remaining few minutes of light, the Corsairs continued to make covering passes and held the Chinese to their positions.

Darkness came quickly, though, and our progress was slow. Now we were slipping and stumbling downhill. Stretcher-bearers in the center of the column strove to protect the wounded from rough falls. Flankers were out on the shoulders of the hills on each side of us, but the forward elements took little Chinese fire. Woody Taylor's platoon fought off a few trailing attacks. Strangely, the Chinese seemed to let us slip from their grasp.

It took several hours for Baker Company to make its way to the road. Our battalion commander, Lt. Col. Davis, had brought elements of Charlie Company out to meet us. There were trucks waiting for us at the road, and we loaded our dead and wounded. The men were silent, spent from the cold and brutal day. And, Captain Wilcox had been a good skipper.*

[While the attacks on Baker 7 and the 2d Battalion, 5th Marines, to the northwest were in full progress, Fox Company, 7th Marines, left Hagaru-ri and rode north toward Yudam-ni. Its mission was to occupy a hill overlooking Toktong Pass and protect the vulnerable MSR between the two villages from there. Once Fox 7 dug in, it would be seven mountainous miles from the friendly perimeter at Yudam-ni and another seven from the one at Hagaru-ri. The 240 officers and men of Fox 7 would be on their own.]

1st Lt. ROBERT McCARTHY
F/7

The CO, Capt. William Barber, who had preceded the company to the defensive position with the battalion commander, Lieutenant Colonel [Randolph] Lockwood, met the company as it was detrucking [27 November]. The captain made his reconnaissance of the area with the platoon leaders and issued the company order. Fox Com-

---

* Owen, *Gazette.*

pany was to set up a defensive perimeter as security for the main supply route, and was to remain in the position for some five days.* Patrols would be sent out during the daylight hours as guards for the
main supply route.

The hill that Fox Company was to organize for defense rose
sharply from the road, its lower half covered with small trees, the upper half barren except for some low brush at the summit. North from
the high point of the hill, a saddle extended some 900 yards to a ridge
running in an arc from the northwest to the east of Fox Hill. Only
on the northwest portion, which was very rocky, was the elevation
higher than Fox Hill. The saddle extending to the north fell away
sharply on both its east and west slopes. Except for the narrow top of
the saddle, Fox Hill was well separated from the other high ground
in the area.†

Pfc. ERNEST GONZALEZ
F/7

When we arrived at Fox Hill, it was starting to get dark. Having waited
in the cold before being told where to dig in, the men in my fire
team were tired and angry. We were finally told to climb to the top
of the hill and join Lieutenant McCarthy's 3d Platoon. Angry, I decided to stay with a squad that had dug in at the base of the position.
I finally joined my team when the BAR man told me to go up. There
were two foxholes up there. I don't know who had dug them. The
BAR man took one hole, I took the other. We were connected by a
trench. My foxhole was large enough to lay out my sleeping bag and
still have room to build a fire to warm my C rations. The BAR man
took the first watch. I went to sleep.

---

* Fox Company was augmented by heavy machine gun and 81-mm mortar sections of Weap-
ons Company.
† Capt. R. C. McCarthy, "Fox Hill," *Marine Corps Gazette*, March 1953, 16–23. Hereafter,
McCarthy, *Gazette*.

1st Lt. ROBERT MCCARTHY
F/7

By 9:00 P.M., Fox Company, with no prospect of getting into warm-up tents, had settled down in its sleeping bags. A full moon rose at about 11:00 P.M. and the night was clear, bright, and miserably cold. Half of the company was alert, if that is possible in weather well below zero. Except for the traffic on the road, all was quiet.*

[On the night of 27 November, the 25,000 men of the 1st Marine Division were positioned all along the MSR. Farthest south, two battalions of Puller's 1st Marines guarded the route at Koto-ri and Chinhung-ni. Most of another battalion, with two batteries of artillery, defended the supply base and airstrip at Hagaru-ri. East of the Chosin Reservoir, two rifle battalions and a field artillery unit from the 7th Infantry Division were bivouacked along the road. West of the Reservoir, fourteen mountainous miles above Hagaru-ri, Murray's 5th Marines and Litzenberg's 7th Marines held Yudam-ni. Ten understrength rifle companies occupied the hills above the village, while the two battalions which had arrived at midday on the 27th from the east coast of the Reservoir had taken positions in the valley. Four miles away a rifle company, C/7, watched the MSR where it began to climb Toktong Pass; Fox Company, 7th Marines, alone, but not forgotten, was dug in on top of the pass.

Twenty-five thousand men, strung along a track calling itself a road, in an obscure corner of a remote section of the world, on a night colder than any of them could remember. No doubt history would have taken little notice had it not been for the Chinese. The enemy had positioned 120,000 of his best troops throughout the mountain vastness of northeastern Korea, surrounding the scattered American and South Korean divisions of General Almond's X Corps. Twelve enemy divisions—three field armies—had crossed the Yalu at the same time as the Chinese armies that had attacked General Walker's Eighth Army and had hidden in the eastern mountains undetected. They had been waiting for many weeks, and on the night of 27 November were ready

_____
* McCarthy, Gazette.

to launch the second phase of an offensive they hoped would this time not only defeat the Americans but also annihilate them.

The Chinese had been particularly careful in setting the trap that would catch the 1st Marine Division. Eight enemy divisions, 60,000 Chinese, had left their places of concealment and converged on the bleak mountains and snow-covered hills that rise above the Chosin Reservoir. From Yudam-ni to Hungnam, only one road, the MSR, led southward, and the Chinese had made sure most of its seventy-eight miles were covered. From Hagaru-ri to Chinhung-ni, and everywhere in between, the Chinese waited for the Americans. But it was around Yudam-ni that the enemy was especially eager to catch his prey and kill it.

On Monday, the 27th, finding progress in the western hills increasingly costly in human life, the Marines discontinued the attack in midafternoon and deployed in defensive positions. Night fell quietly on Yudam-ni; the temperature tumbled. The men of the 5th and 7th Marine Regiments hunkered down in their icy fighting holes or hid behind whatever shelter they found and waited for the dawn. It was a long time before any of them would be warm again.]

Pfc. DOUG MICHAUD
Headquarters & Service Company/1/5
The bugles were the first thing I remember. Then the chaos. There didn't seem to be any sense of order. I was in my sleeping bag snoozing with my BAR. A guy who'd been on watch grabbed the bottom of the bag and began dragging me down the hill. He kept hollering, "They're here! They're here!" A lot of guys must have been caught with their boots off. I saw them running in their stockings. It all happened so fast.

Pfc. JACK WRIGHT
G/5
During the night the guy on watch woke us all up. "Hey, you guys oughta see this." Our fire-team leader asked him what in hell was going on. The guy answered, "Man, the hills all around on both sides

are lit up like Christmas trees. There's tracers, there's WP, the whole works going up. Not only that, but bullets are hitting all around out here, too." Our fire-team leader told him not to worry about it: "Don't wake us again unless the platoon leader orders a fall-out." The BAR man chipped in, "Don't wake us up unless they drop an atomic bomb. In that case don't worry about it because it'll be too late anyways."

I don't know how much later, but sometime during the night we got the word to saddle up. When we picked up our gear, we assembled at the platoon CP. The guy on watch had been right—those hills were really popping!

Pfc. FRED DAVIDSON
G/5
An incoming white-phosphorus shell exploded about twenty-five yards to my left. White-hot shrapnel whizzed in every direction. The next WP shell exploded twenty-five yards in front of me. The third one landed twenty-five yards to my left but right in line to where I lay. I was on the extreme left edge of George Company's perimeter. None of the shells had hit among the unit. I began to figure fast and realized the gun was being fired in increments of twenty-five yards and that the next round would land on top of me. I jumped up and ran. The fourth shell landed right behind me. Even though I didn't feel much push from the explosion, I nevertheless was slammed facedown into the snow. No question about having been hit, but it took a few seconds before I realized I was being burned by the white phosphorus. I tried to get to my back and couldn't reach it. I yelled for help. A couple of guys ran over. They tore through my clothes and packed my burns with snow. My back was badly mauled. The quick action by the guys shoving snow on the burning holes put out the phorphorus. A Navy corpsman came up and did what he could. I don't remember any kind of injection for the pain. And the pain was real bad. I was helped down to the road and back to the battalion aid station.

[Hounded and beset from three sides, the Marines began a series of local counterattacks just before sunrise. In order to give themselves

breathing room, it was vital that they force the Chinese off the hills surrounding the village.]

2d Lt. JOHN CAHILL
G/5

They called [2d Lt. Dana] Cashion's and my platoons out to retake a hill [1384]. It was well below zero and the moon was out. We went up the hill in a skirmish line. The Chinese wore white uniforms that blended into the snow. They began lobbing concussion grenades. An old machine gunner next to me yelled, "Gas!" The guy was a maverick no one else wanted, but I'd taken him in. Our gas masks were with our armored vests, back in camp. I hit the guy over the head.

Pfc. JACK WRIGHT
G/5

We started out in a skirmish line. The man directly in front of me got it, his whole front went off like a flashbulb. When the platoon hit the base of the hill, the Chinese fired at us like all get-out. On the hill the Chinese cut loose with grenades. Down we went. I lay, cussing my buttons because they wouldn't let me get closer to the ground. I hollered for a buddy, Don Murrell. He yelled back, "You hit?" "No. Just want to make sure I'm not alone." "We're all here, Wright. Don't worry."

I can't say if it was on a signal or not, but suddenly all the Marines on the hill jumped up and charged the crest of the hill. Directly in front of me was a bunker with an open back. I saw the silhouette of a man firing to one side. I fired my rifle at him, then, when I ran by, dropped a grenade in. We cleared the hill. The entire crest was littered with dead Chinese. There was a row of them, maybe six, down on their knees, doubled over with their faces in the snow. They had died in that position. Old .45-caliber Thompson submachine guns lay everywhere. Looked like a gangsters' convention. These were guns the U.S. had given the Chinese Nationalists. The Chinese Communists were returning them to us.

2d Lt. TOM GIBSON
Mortar Company/5
Colonel Murray had just come out of his CP at Yudam-ni. It was pitch-black. Murray had had a conference with some of his people and his eyes were not completely adjusted to the darkness. Feeling his way along the trench, he bumped into me. "Who's that?" he asked. I said, "Lieutenant Gibson, sir." "Hoot," he said, "you have a hell of a talent for getting yourself surrounded." In a split second he had remembered that during the Second World War I was at Bastogne. "Yes, sir," I replied, "It's a talent I wish I didn't have."

Pfc. WIN SCOTT
C/5
One of our units, Easy 7, was hit pretty hard. We went up on Hill 1282 and relieved these men. There were a lot of dead Chinese lying in front of the lines. They had evidently attacked frontally in waves. We used some of their frozen bodies to brace our crew-served weapons. There were so many of them that when our turn came and the machine guns tried to fire down the slope of the hill, they hit these piled-up corpses. I actually went out and moved bodies to clear our fields of fire.

When they hit us . . . Well, it's hard to describe because a firefight doesn't describe well. It's all one big chaotic event, especially when it's really coming at you. War is 90 percent boredom and 10 percent sheer fright. When they came, I remember Chinese leaping over my hole. They were so close. You'd shoot some, miss some. When it happens, a manual can't help. You have to know instinctively what to do, then do it. Burned out a barrel on the .30-caliber machine gun that night.

Morning came and I breathed a sigh of relief. First you see the horizon becoming a little less dark. It's not light and it's not dark. I knew if we could hang on an hour more, we'd make it to morning. Once daylight arrived we knew our air cover would be overhead. Exhausted. Had to hold on; if we did, we could make it.

28 November 1950

The MSR from Hagaru-ri to Yudam-ni was severed by enemy action during the night.

HISTORICAL DIARY, 5TH MARINE REGIMENT

[Captain Barber's Fox Company had settled in on the top of Toktong Pass for what the men felt would be a freezing, miserable night. Nothing unusual had taken place in the early hours of the evening and trucks still made the long climb going to, or returning from, Yudam-ni and Hagaru-ri. A full moon had risen before midnight. Fox Hill was quiet.]

1st Lt. LAWRENCE SCHMITT
F/7

Captain Barber acted as if he expected to be attacked. God bless him. Once he'd checked the perimeter, and made sure ammo had been given out and sound-powered phones were in between the CP and mortars, the captain returned to the tent. He wasn't through quite yet. "I think we're set up OK for tonight. But I want a watch on the phone. There will be an officer or NCO on it at all times during the night." In the tent were three officers—the skipper, the exec [1st Lt. Clarke Wright], and me—and three sergeants. This meant one-and-a-half-hour watches for each of us between 10:00 P.M. and 7:00 A.M.

(The tent also housed a corpsman, radio operator, wireman, and Korean interpreter.)

My watch came first. I sat on an ammo box and stoked the fire in a small stove while I took the "all clear" reports each half hour from the three platoons. At 11:30 I nudged Sergeant Groenwald. "Take over, buddy, it's time." I slipped off my shoepacs and scooched down in my sleeping bag. The day had been very active and I must have been asleep by the time the zipper reached my neck.

"Cap'n! Cap'n!" I woke up. The sergeant on the phone was nudging Captain Barber. "Second Platoon says there are some natives coming up the road." "Hmm? What time is it?" A voice off to the side said, "O-four-hundred." "Cap'n, there's natives in the road." Barber said, "Hold 'em until we can question them. Mr. Chung [the interpreter], get down to the road and check those people." I thought to myself, Glad I'm not a wheel. I wouldn't get out of this bag for anything. At that instant a burp gun and some rifle fire let go; it was a quick volley.

Pfc. ERNEST GONZALEZ
F/7
I woke up and heard the whizzing of bullets just like on a rifle range. Crawling out of my sleeping bag, I found two other Marines in my foxhole. One handed me his rifle and asked if I would unjam it. When he had a target, he borrowed my rifle. I unjammed his, finally, and had mine returned.

1st Lt. ROBERT McCARTHY
F/7
I was awakened by heavy firing to the north, west, and south sides of the company perimeter and by Corporal Ashdale shouting, "Here they come!" Lt. Joe Brady and his mortars were hit at practically the same moment as were my 3d Platoon and Lieutenant Peterson's 2nd Platoon.*

---

* McCarthy, *Gazette.*

1st Lt. LAWRENCE SCHMITT
F/7

Slugs tore through the upper half of the tent. In an instant the ten men in that tent squirmed out of their bags and in the darkness grabbed for their boots. I was using mine as a pillow. I yanked them on, didn't bother to lace them, just wrapped the rawhide around the ankle and knotted it. Captain Barber shouted, "Where'n hell are my boots? C.B., you got 'em?" Lieutenant Wright answered in his southern drawl, "No, suh." The skipper was frantic. His boots were gone. Out of the corner of my eye I saw him throwing his bedding around desperately looking for his boots. The Chinese were attacking and, from the sounds of the battle, weren't very far away. No one thought of going out of the tent in that subzero temperature and snow without his footgear. The captain let out another shout. "Goddamn it, C. B., here yours are under your bag. You've got . . . Never mind, I'll use yours." There was no more confusion. "Wright, take over the CP. I'm going to see what'n hell is going on. Schmitt, get on the phone and stay on it. Gunny, come with me." I grabbed the sound-power and sat near the flap of the tent looking into the night. I tried to make contact with the mortars but the phone apparently was dead. The radio operator sat next to me trying to raise battalion. "Bilgewater, this is Bilgewater Fox, do you read me? Over." Pause. "Damn this contraption." "Keep trying," I said. I tried the sound-powered phone again. Nothing. A good-size firefight just over the knoll to the left of the CP was in progress.

Pfc. ERNEST GONZALEZ
F/7

I saw a squad of Chinese moving to my left. I aimed, the light of the moon reflected off the rifle barrel, and fired. A man went down. Every time I spotted a grenade I yelled a warning and ducked. Some exploded, some didn't. In front, I saw the flickering light of a Chinese automatic weapon firing in my direction. I could not get a shot at it and had no grenades. I saw a second Chinese squad to my right rear. I fired and another man went down. The Marines in my foxhole warned me not to fire as it drew fire from the enemy. I thought, What the hell are we here for but to fire on the enemy when we see him?

The BAR man was wounded by a grenade but continued to fire. More Marines joined us. There was an explosion. I turned and saw a Marine behind me bleeding from his forehead and mouth. He had shielded me from the blast. My fire-team leader was in a foxhole on my left with a machine gun. Throughout the night I saw the Chinese trying to reach him with grenades. Finally, some of them were able to get into his foxhole. The Chinese left him for dead and made off with the machine gun. A grenade went off in the connecting trench. I saw the flash and felt the shock wave. Several Marines were wounded by it. I was protected by the curve of the foxhole. Of the six Marines with me, I was now the only one not wounded. Whenever I killed a Chinese, I wanted to cheer, but realized if I did so, I might get careless. I had butterflies in my stomach and my shivering was not caused by the cold.

1st Lt. ROBERT MCCARTHY
F/7

The 3d Platoon was under extremely heavy attack. The front two squads and the machine-gun section of the platoon were overwhelmed by sheer force of numbers. Of the thirty-five Marines in these units, fifteen were killed, nine were wounded, three were missing, and only eight were still effective. One gunner stood up after his gun had jammed and shot six Chinese with his pistol. These units were withdrawn to the area of the 1st Squad, across the rear of the 3d Platoon's area. The left and center fire teams of Corporal [Thomas] Ashdale's 1st Squad were now heavily engaged. Grenade and small-arms fire was intense. The whole hilltop was alive with grenades, both ours and Chinese. Pfc. [Harrison] Pommers had three grenades explode in his foxhole and a fourth on the top of his helmet, the latter knocking him out. When he regained consciousness he continued to direct his fire team. Pfc. Smith's fire team was having a bitter contest on the platoon's left. Two men from the 2d Platoon joined this fire team when their fire-team leader and BAR man were killed. One of these Marines, Private [Hector] Cafferata,* was directly responsible for

---

*Private Cafferata, who fought through the night in his stockinged feet because there had been no time to put on his boots, was subsequently awarded the Medal of Honor for this night's work.

stopping what might have been a breakthrough just to the left of the 3d Platoon. Cafferata stood up, completely exposing himself to the heavy fire of the enemy, and shot two M1 rifles as fast as a wounded Marine could reload for him. Cafferata also grabbed one Chinese grenade, threw it out of the trench, and pushed two others from the parapet.*

1st Lt. LAWRENCE SCHMITT
F/7
I saw five Marines about ten yards up the slope huddled behind a hut. Even with all the noise, I heard them shouting to each other. "To hell with the phone," I said to no one in particular and, grabbing my carbine, I sprinted up the slope to the hut. "What's going on here?" I recognized the 81-mm section leader and four of his men. "Jonesy said to get out of there and we left." A glance showed me the 81-mm mortars had been abandoned. I knew we needed them. "Shut up," I screamed. Then, in a low voice that surprised me by its calmness, I said, "Listen, the mortars might be our only artillery. We've got to get them and carry them up the hill." The men stood silently now. It was vitally important we carry these mortars from the clearing near the CP to the center of the perimeter. "We're going out to get those guns. Don't leave any parts or ammo. Remember the goddamn bipod isn't any good without the tube and none of it is any good without ammo." There were now about eight Marines huddled in the lee of the hut. "Who's a gunner here?" "I am." "OK, you and these three men," and I gestured with my carbine, "will get the left mortar. The rest of us will grab the other one. Ready? Then let's go!" I turned and ran for the clearing. We covered the ground on the slope of the hill in a few seconds. An experienced mortarman released the tube from the bipod and started up the hill. A second guy grabbed the bipod and took off. A few stray shots or richochets flew in our direction. Bullets hitting the snowy, icy ground made a thudding sound. The last Marine with me and I grabbed the baseplate and yanked. It didn't move. "It's froze to the ground," he yelled. I found an entrenching

---

* McCarthy, *Gazette.*

tool and a few raps with it jarred the baseplate loose. "Take off," I ordered. Luckily, the ammo was on a carrier and I was able to drag it. The group reassembled by the hut. Only a few minutes had gone by, but we were all panting like racehorses. "Let's get up the hill and get 'em set up." Each man with his heavy load slipped and struggled up the hill.

I stopped near the summit when I found a slightly level area. The trees were far enough away for clearance. "Section Chief," I yelled. "Yes, sir." A little feller with a tube cradled in his arms staggered over. "Take over and get those guns set up." In a little while I heard the "PLOOOP" from the top of the hill as the mortars began registering fire on the targets called back by the platoons.

1st Lt. ROBERT McCARTHY
F/7

The 2d Platoon was heavily engaged along most of its front, particularly higher up the hill. The light-machine-gun crew and two Marines of the fire team between the gun and the 3d Platoon were killed. Lieutenant Peterson, while trying to reorganize that particular section of his line, was shot through the shoulder. After receiving first aid, the lieutenant returned to his platoon and fought the remainder of the night. The 2d Platoon had pulled the lower portion of its line up into the trees about fifteen yards above a ten-foot bank that ran along the lower portion of Fox Hill, tying in with headquarters section.

Captain Barber made continuous inspections of the company perimeter all during the attack. He was exposed to murderous small-arms fire, two company runners being wounded while accompanying him.[*]

[The Army battalions bivouacked east of the Reservoir were particularly hard hit the night of the 27th. The 3d Battalion, 31st Infantry, and the 1st Battalion, 57th Field Artillery, were in a perimeter near

---

[*] McCarthy, Gazette.

Singhung-ni. Five thousand yards farther north was Lt. Col. Don Faith's* 1st Battalion, 32d Infantry.]

Capt. EDWARD STAMFORD
Attached, 1st Battalion/32d Infantry

About midnight or soon after, I heard some shots and Captain [Edward] Scullian [CO, A Company] yelling in our direction. Just after this and before we could get up to see what was happening, we heard some chattering outside of our bunker. The poncho was pulled aside; I saw a fur-rimmed face in the moonlight and fired at it from a sitting position, but he had already dropped a grenade, which blew up between my feet on the sleeping bag. One man was wounded. We fired back, but upon receiving rifle fire withdrew into the slit trench, where we remained for about three minutes. Our own MG fire cleaned off the top of the bunker and we were able to get out. I immediately organized my men and others in the vicinity in defense of this position. Captain Scullian was killed in the attack. It was his first action in Korea.†

Pfc. JAMES RANSONE, JR.
A Company/32d Infantry

It seemed like I had been asleep only a short time before all hell broke loose. I looked around. Some of my buddies, who were in an outpost line on the upward slope of a hill to my right, were being overrun. In the light of flares that exploded overhead, I saw Chinese soldiers jumping in the holes with the GIs. There was panic in the area. The Chinese turned their attention to us. Everyone fired wildly. I didn't

---

* Faith had distinguished himself in the Second World War as aide to Maj. Gen. Matthew Ridgway, then commander of the 82d Airborne Division.
† Stamford interview, MCHC.

know who I was firing at. Middle of the night. An awful lot of people
on both sides got killed.

S/Sgt. CHESTER BAIR
Attached, 1st Battalion/32d Infantry

The Chinese attacked us in full force, wave after wave. Some companies on this first day of combat were reduced to the size of a platoon. The 1st Battalion, where I was, held fast its perimeter.

Casualties flowed into our perimeter and overflowed the aid stations. Wounded men told the most unbelievable stories of what was
happening on the lines. I began helping with the wounded. From
what I saw, all walking wounded were returned to the line to fight.
They were joined by rear-echelon troops going forward.

Capt. EDWARD STAMFORD
Attached, 1st Battalion/32d Infantry

One officer (I believe it was Lieutenant Ortinze of Dog Company)
approached me as I was directing some troops to better positions and
said, "Well, Captain, you are the next senior man. I guess you have
the company." I seized this opportunity and immediately dispatched
one of my Marines to obtain reports from the other platoons and made
the executive officer platoon leader of the 1st Platoon. After finding
that that was the only place we were hit, I brought the 2d Platoon
down to strengthen our line and proceeded to clean out our CP area
of Chinese. With this accomplished, we were in fair shape and repulsed many more attempts in force to overrun the CP. About dawn
they found our weak spot and started an end run, but the 2d Platoon
succeeded in getting back to their original position with little effort
and repulsed the attack on our flank.*

[When dawn finally broke on Tuesday, 28 November, the Marines and
soldiers, although completely surrounded, were still holding out. The
MSR had been severed in several places, splitting the Marine division
into beleaguered perimeters at Koto-ri, Hagaru-ri, and Yudam-ni. While

* Stamford interview, MCHC.

the Army battalions east of the Reservoir and Fox 7 beat back Chinese attacks, the 5th and 7th Marines continued to counterattack. Colonel Murray and Colonel Litzenberg met and decided to realign their regiments around Yudam-ni. Once this had been accomplished, they could get on with the business of relieving Fox 7 and breaking out to Hagaru-ri.]

Pfc. DOUG MICHAUD
Headquarters & Service Company/1/5
In the morning casualties lay all over the place. We dragged the dead down the slope like you would deer—slipped a rope around their boots and dragged. At the road the bodies were stacked in six-bys. Word was passed we were going to fall back. I believe those were the orders—"fall back," not "retreat." Marines were dependable. Goddamn, you want something done, you send the Marines. They got it done. All of a sudden we learned we were going to fall back. I cried. I cried. I couldn't believe it. Of course, I didn't know the big picture. If I had, I might have cried for a different reason.

Pfc. JACK WRIGHT
G/5
When we returned to our old position—we'd been relieved on the hill by another outfit—we found our sleeping bags had been shredded, our shelter halves had been torn and ripped by shrapnel, our rations had holes in them.

The ground was so hard we couldn't dig in. The engineers decided to blow holes in the ground for us. This didn't last long. They blasted a few holes and the rock and flying dirt took out more men, including my BAR man, than had the Chinese the night before.

Someone then got the idea to thaw the ground by building a fire on it. This worked like a champ. Each man built a fire over the spot he wanted to dig his hole. Once the fires went out, we dug our holes in the thawed ground. It still took some time to hack through the frozen area. The minute we hit soft ground they called for us to assemble.

We went to the platoon CP and then over to the company. We

were told we were going back up in the hills to take positions. They also told us we had been hit by a couple of Chinese divisions and were not completely surrounded. We would hold till further orders.

Pfc. WIN SCOTT
C/5

I remember the order: "When you come off the hill, carry your dead with you." It had become fairly quiet and you could stand up now and walk around [Hill 1282]. Once in a while a sniper fired a shot, but no one bothered about him. I couldn't find a body to carry, so I lugged the .30-caliber machine gun. The M1 was strapped across my back and the machine gun was over my right shoulder. I started down the hill. All of a sudden—it happened quick—artillery. From a distance I heard a rumble. Then nothing. BOOOM! A shell landed down the slope in front of me. Yudam-ni was farther down in the valley and I could see all the activity in that direction. It was incoming! You get used to it, so it's not the most upsetting event ever. BOOOM! Closer this time. They were walking a barrage toward us. I thought, If I can get to the ridge there, I got it made. Well, I didn't. WHAAM!

I woke up facedown in frozen brush. My ears rang. I shook my head. I had no idea where in hell I was. My back felt wet and the wet was spreading. I thought my back must be blown wide open. I took a quick inventory: right hand, left hand. There was a hole in my mitten and I could feel liquid. That was nothing. It was the thing on my back, and I couldn't tell what it was or how bad. I was more scared right then than I have ever been in my life. I'm dying, I thought, and there's nobody here. Here I am in this godforsaken country and I'm going to die alone. I yelled, "Corpsman!" I yelled again. Then again. Then I lost count. A Marine came over the ridge. "Hey, buddy, I'm not a corpsman, but can I help you?" I said, "Get me a corpsman!" He went away. Above, artillery explosions continued to hit the reverse slope of the hill. A corpsman ran over to me. "Doc," I said, "give me a shot." He carried the morphine in his mouth so it wouldn't freeze. He cut away my clothes and gave me a shot in the shoulder. I was next placed on my poncho and dragged down the hill. I passed out. When I woke up I was lying on my stomach on a stretcher inside a tent. I thought I was in heaven. My God, they even had a stove in there.

Later, the wounded poured into the tent, most of them worse off than I. I was taken outside and placed on the ground. The sun was shining. It wasn't snowing and it wasn't blowing, but it was cold.

Some C-119 cargo planes flew over and dropped supplies. I got scared again. These planes came over about 500 feet above my head. The guys up there opened the back door and pushed cargo out. Jesus, I'm going to be hit and crushed, I thought. One of those chutes isn't going to open; survive all this and get killed by my own guys. I felt the cargo cases hit—boom, boom, boom—and the ground shook.

Chaplain JOHN CRAVEN (USN)
7th Marines
Taking care of the wounded during this period presented problems to stagger the imagination. During the first two days of heavy fighting at Yudam-ni, we suffered so many casualties that we ran out of tents in which to place them. I had a working party gather hay from the scattered stacks and spread it out on the courtyard of a native house. We placed the wounded foot to foot on the straw and covered them with a large tarpaulin. This arrangement helped to conserve on our tentage and also facilitated our ministry to the wounded. *

28 November 1950
The regimental aid station moved to join the 7th Marines aid station in a relatively less exposed position. Evacuation of patients was impossible except that a few of the most seriously wounded were taken out by helicopter. Shortly after noon patients began to come in by the truckload and the medical sections were rapidly swamped. The tents and courtyard of the aid Station area were filled. Patients eventually filled twenty-two tents, four civilian houses and the remainder were put in straw and

---

* As quoted in Capt. Clifford M. Drury, USN, *History of the Chaplain Corps*, vol. 6 (Washington, D.C.: U.S. Navy), 38. Hereafter, Craven, *History*.

covered with a large tarpaulin. It was estimated that nearly 500
were being held by midnight. About dark battalion aid stations
began holding patients instead of evacuating them to the regimental aid stations. . . . Seventy-four bullet holes were counted
in the 5th Marines aid station tent after the previous night's action. Personnel report for the period 6:00 P.M. 27 November to
6:00 P.M. 28 November: 16 killed in action, 136 wounded in
action, 2 missing in action, 91 non-battle casualties, 8 returned
to duty, 4 prisoners taken.

HISTORICAL DIARY, 5TH MARINE REGIMENT

From: CO 5th Marines   Date/Time/Group: 28/1815/I
To: 1/5; 2/5; 3/5; 1/11; H & S Co.; 4.2 Mortar Co.
All hands make sure that every shot counts.

[*The morning of the 28th, while Litzenberg and Murray realigned their
regiments at Yudam-ni, the 1st Battalion, 7th Marines, set out to retrieve Charlie Company, which guarded the MSR four miles south of
the village, and Fox 7, which was still holding out on Toktong Pass.*]

Pfc. FRANCIS KILLEEN
A/7

I really did not know where we were going and was at the tail end of
the platoon file when I should have been up front with Lieutenant
Stemple. My leg had been giving me trouble, but this was minor
compared to what some of the guys were hiding. My feet were still
good; a lot of the guys were already limping with frostbite. It was about
10 degrees below that morning, warm for North Korea. No wind and
very bright. When I caught up with Stemple, I found out just how
bad things were. He told me the Army on the other side of the ice
[Chosin Reservoir] had been really cut up. Our battalion's Charlie
Company had gotten hit by a Chinese battalion and was now under
heavy attack. There were many casualties. My best buddy, Vito Ju-

nivicious, was with Charlie. He was a good Lithuanian who tried to learn Irish songs. We pulled a lot of liberty together at the Brooklyn Navy Yard. He'd come there a sergeant and within two weeks was a Pfc. He was a fine Marine but could not stand Stateside liberty. When I was in the hospital in Hungnan, the guy managed to call me via the company-to-battalion hookup. "You lucky Irish bastard, you'll probably go home. Tell me how to catch those million-dollar wounds." I had not seen him since Sudong.

Colonel Davis [1st Battalion, 7th Marines CO] moved out with Baker Company. Able would guard the flank. Suddenly, a lot of firing broke out up ahead. The echo of it put any creep show to shame. A terrible sound, like what hell must be like on election night. Then silence. We waited. Word came back: Charlie was relieved. Some of their wounded passed to our rear. I slid back and asked about Vito. "Yeah, caught one in the shoulder." Now it was the Lithuanian son-ovabitch that was going home.

[*The 1st Battalion, 7th Marines, with Charlie Company and its forty-six wounded in tow, returned to the Yudam-ni perimeter late in the day on the 28th. Fox 7 had not been relieved and remained marooned on its hill overlooking Toktong Pass. Tuesday was a very busy day for the men in Captain Barber's company.*]

1st Lt. ROBERT McCARTHY
F/7

At daybreak [28 November], in the direction of Hagaru-ri, we saw several flights of planes. We were not sure where they were going, but we hoped they were coming to our assistance. As they flew closer to our positions, we could see they were our own gull-winged Marine Corsairs. As the drone of their motors swelled in volume, the men of the 3d Platoon started to cheer. The Chinese must have thought we were going to attack because for a quarter of an hour they ceased firing completely. The planes flew on toward Yudam-ni, but the very sight of them had given our morale a considerable boost.

By 6:30 A.M. the Chinese had received so many casualties that the attack could no longer be considered organized. Few Chinese remained alive near the company perimeter. Individual Chinese continued to crawl up and throw grenades. A Marine would make a one-man assault on these individuals, shooting or bayoneting them. The company ammunition supply was becoming dangerously low and grenades were practically nonexistent. The mortars had less than ten rounds of ammunition; however, by this time, the only enemy troops in the area were trying to withdraw. The attack could be considered over, although three Marines, one being Private Cafferata, were hit by rifle fire at 7:30 A.M. We received small-arms fire intermittently during the day, but no attack.*

1st Lt. LAWRENCE SCHMITT
F/7
We collected the wounded at the abandoned hut near the old CP. Whatever sniping there was came from the direction of the 3d Platoon, which was on the northern rim of the hill. Captain Barber decided to move the wounded and put them in two tents that would be pitched in the center of the perimeter.

1st Lt. ROBERT McCARTHY
F/7
The corpsmen, with the assistance of Gunnery Sergeant Bunch and a detail of Marines, set up two tents in the trees as an aid station. With nothing but morphine and field bandages, the corpsmen tended the wounded. The corpsmen of Fox Company were to work day and night keeping our wounded alive. By candlelight they changed the bandages, slipped men in and out of sleeping bags, warmed C rations for the men, and melted the morphine Syrettes in their mouths before the injections. Because the plasma was frozen, the corpsmen had to watch men die for the lack of it.

Captain Barber had requested an air strike on the rocky ridge to the northwest of Fox Hill. At 10:30 A.M. eight P-51 Mustangs arrived on station. We were a bit surprised to have someone other than Marine pilots coming to our assistance. The captain called to Hagaru-ri

---

*McCarthy, Gazette.

via SCR-300 radio, as we had no radio capable of direct contact with the planes, and the Hagaru-ri station directed the planes to make the strike. The P-51s were from an Australian squadron and they turned out to be a red-hot outfit. When they made their runs on the rocky ridge, several of them would pass Fox Hill much lower than the top of the hill. They bombed and rocketed the ridge very effectively. Then they strafed the valley along the Yudam-ni road. Some of the Aussie pilots appeared to be low enough to chop kindling wood with their propellers. After the air strike there was very little Chinese activity.

On the afternoon of November 28, Marine transport planes (R5Ds) arrived and started dropping medical supplies and ammunition into the area near the two houses at the base of Fox Hill. The drop was excellent; just where we had called for it. The supplies were not scattered. Sergeant Smith, company supply sergeant, started at once to collect the supplies.*

1st Lt. LAWRENCE SCHMITT
F/7

Sergeant Smith was outside the perimeter down near the road collecting parachutes which had dropped food and ammo to us. The crates had already been recovered, but Sergeant Smith wanted the parachutes for the wounded to lie on. A single shot rolled him into a ditch. "He broke my leg," he yelled.

I grabbed a litter. "Three men come with me. Let's get him." We reached Smith and put him on the litter. I took about three steps toward the hill and felt my leg snap like a dry branch. I said, "I got the same medicine as Smitty."

My first impulse was to get out of there. I tried to crawl on my knees but didn't get far. Two guys grabbed me under the arms and carried me up the hill and into the tent where I'd spent part of the night before. On the way I asked the two guys to pick up my carbine. While I lay in the tent, one of the Marines came back and handed it to me. A corpsman came by and gave me a shot of morphine. [First Lieutenant] Joe Brady, who was also wounded, gave me a precious

---

* McCarthy, *Gazette*.

shot of Scotch he'd been hoarding since he joined the company as a replacement three weeks before. The corpsman set my leg with two sticks. The skipper thought it better if Smitty and I were taken to the aid tents that were higher on the hill. When I arrived in the new tent, I counted fifteen men already there. In the days to come, more would arrive.

Pfc. ERNEST GONZALEZ
F/7
Word was passed to kill all enemy wounded. I found one Chinese curled up, lying facedown. He had a head wound shaped like a perfect pie-cut that exposed his brain. I fired into his midriff. He turned slowly and looked at me as if saying, "Why must you make me suffer more?" Although it remained a common practice on both sides, I never again killed another wounded Chinese soldier.

I walked down to the base of our position and saw what had happened to the squad that had dug in there, the one I had almost spent the night with. The squad leader was still in his sleeping bag. Some lay dead along what had been a defensive line. Due to the frozen ground, they had only been able to dig in about six inches. I looked for a former fire-team mate but could not locate his body. One Marine lay wounded; his sleeping bag was riddled. A stretcher was brought up and another Marine and I carried him to the company aid station.

I ate some C rations, then went behind a bush to satisfy nature. This proved to be quite an operation. Once I finally peeled off all the multiple layers of clothing I wore, a Chinese sniper fired at me.

Later, I returned to the base of the hill where I ate another C ration. Then I began picking through the dead Chinese that lay around. I picked up a camera, two rolls of film, an enemy rifle with bayonet and ammo, a bowl, some rice, and an enemy pack. This last item contained boots with steel spikes, a special cold-weather rifle oil, a folder showing all of Red China's leaders, and photographs of the dead man and his family taken in some Chinese city.

I found the Chinese weapons could use American ammo, but ours couldn't use theirs.

The dead all looked like wax dummies, that light-brown color of frozen flesh.

Later in the day two Marines and I sniped at what was known as the Rocky Ridge. With binoculars we could see the Chinese lying in an exposed position. A bullet hit in front of my face. I played dead, then jumped up and got back to a foxhole. I lost all my souvenirs except the bayonet and camera.

At dusk, all the walking wounded volunteered to return to front lines. I was ordered to take up a new position, one that was near the first Chinese I killed the night before. I was in a two-man foxhole and my new buddy was Freddy Gonzalez (no relation) from San Pedro, California. Our foxhole looked like an armed fortress. We had six rifles, plenty of ammo, and two grenades. Some Marines, to make sure their weapons still functioned in the extreme cold, fired stray rounds. When the sun went down, we waited.

1st Lt. ROBERT McCARTHY
F/7

At sundown on November 28 the company perimeter was about the same as on November 27 except for the 3d Platoon's area. The 3d Platoon, having twenty-two men effective, extended in one line across the top of the hill instead of two squads up and one back. Lieutenant Campbell called in harassing fires from How Battery [at Hagaru-ri] all during the night. Pfc. [Lloyd] O'Leary, under Captain Barber's direction, harassed the rocky ridge to the left front with the 81-mm mortars. The 60-mm mortars were registered on the saddle to the north of Fox Hill. Half of the company was on the alert.*

Pfc. ROBERT EZELL
F/7

Jerry Triggs and I tried to dig a hole in the frozen ground with limited success. The machine gun was below to our left, another squad was across the top of the hill on our right. Snow lay on the ground and more was falling lightly. Firing began, and up the hill to our front came the Chinese.

* McCarthy, *Gazette.*

Pfc. ERNEST GONZALEZ
F/7

We fired at the Chinese whenever we had a clean shot. I covered 180 degrees on one side, Freddy covered 180 degrees on the other. Once a bullet struck the frozen mound right in front of my face. When one or the other of us had to urinate, we would check to see if the other guy had at least three rounds in his rifle. We didn't want to have to reload when the other guy couldn't cover the position.

When the grenades landed, I'd yell a warning and duck. We were bombarded by some kind of red explosive. The night went on.

An explosion on my right ripped off my helmet and glasses. "Fred, I've been hit. I can't open my eyes." I eventually forced my eyes open and found I wasn't wounded, just covered with dirt.

Pfc. ROBERT EZELL
F/7

Triggs and I had two hand grenades each. We could've used a boxful. Because of the cold, before we threw one we had to pull the pin and lift the spoon. If we hadn't, the spoons, which were frozen, might not have released. We threw every grenade we had at the closest groups of rushing Chinese. They didn't slow down and soon were running by on either side. We had our M1s, but in the cold they seized up and would only fire single shots. The return lever would catch on the next cartridge and I would have to push the lever to get the round into the firing chamber. It was also very difficult to load new clips with bulky gloves and cold hands.

Pfc. ERNEST GONZALEZ
F/7

During one lull in the fighting, Fred and I wearily sat down. In that instant we heard a noise. Fred jerked around and fired his M1. I saw he'd hit a Chinese who was charging toward us. The round caught the enemy soldier squarely in the head. His fur hat flipped in the air, he uttered a disappointed low groan and fell not more than three feet in front of the foxhole. Fred had saved my life. I would have been the first one caught by the enemy's burp gun.

Pfc. ROBERT EZELL
F/7

One time, while I was trying to push a clip down on the loading spring, a Chinaman got up on the other side of the rocks. I could hear him rustling around. Just as I stepped around the rocks to go after him, a grenade went off between Triggs and me. I flew through the air but never felt myself hit the ground. It knocked the air out of me. My pack and sleeping bag must have absorbed much of the shock and force of the explosion. A metal shard tore into my lower leg. I never lost consciousness, but I knew I couldn't move. Besides this, which was bad enough, we were overrun.

After the Chinese overran our position, they used it as a gathering point. I lay quietly, breathing down into my field-jacket hood, my eyes half open. It was very dark. I heard the Chinese talking and shadows moved past me. Every now and then they would blow their bugles.

A Chinaman sat down near me. Because my head was turned away, I couldn't see him. He slipped my gloves off and looked for a watch. (Triggs told me later the guy had done the same thing to him.) Thankfully, that's all he did to me.

After a while, they moved to attack what I later found to be our mortar section. I could hear the sound of a battle. One of the Chinese buglers was hit in mid-note.

1st Lt. ROBERT McCARTHY
F/7

The Chinese were bunched up, chattering, and blowing their bugles. One of the light machine guns in the 3d Platoon's area was turned about and heavy fire was brought to bear on the Chinese with deadly effect. Lieutenant Peterson also brought fire to bear on them from the 2d Platoon, and most of the Chinese were killed. The right of the 3d Platoon's line was shifted slightly to face the Chinese on the right flank and was able to contain them. With a gap in the lines on both flanks, the 3d Platoon withdrew about twenty yards. Pfc. Richard Bonelli, manning one of the platoon's light machine guns, carried gun, tripod, and belts of ammunition from firing position to firing position all alone. I was trying to contact the 1st Platoon on the right, just after the captain had arrived to see how the situation was, when both the captain and I were hit in the legs by a burst of fire from the right front. Platoon Sergeant John Audis assumed command of the 3d Platoon.

The 2d Platoon, after the initial attack and after the line was restored, maintained contact with the 3d Platoon.[*]

Pfc. ROBERT EZELL
F/7

I lay and didn't move for a long time. Flares exploded in the sky and floated to earth; it was like a fireworks show. Sometime later I heard Gleason holler, "Fire some mortars up by the rocks, there still might be Chinamen up there." I yelled, "There's Marines up here!" "Is that you, Zeke? Can you move?" "I don't know. I'll try." I rolled over with some effort. On my belly now I pulled myself through the snow. My legs wouldn't work. I reached the trees. "Triggs is still up there. Don't know how he is." A sergeant from a rifle squad picked me up and helped me to the aid tent.

The tent I was put in was crowded. They had me lie on my left side. I was next to the side of the tent. It was cold there and during the rest of the night I received severe frostbite in my left foot.

Pfc. ERNEST GONZALEZ
F/7

Once we heard two Chinese down the hill on the left talking to each other. I tossed a grenade but it didn't go off. The Chinese continued to chat away. I threw another grenade. This one exploded and the talking stopped.

Throughout the night we had shouted to our platoon CP to ask whether we should pull back or stay put. We never received an answer and believed, therefore, since the Chinese were all around us, that it had been overrun.

[*] McCarthy, *Gazette.*

I saw a Chinese in the early morning near the area of the platoon CP. I fired and he disappeared. Fred and I had between us now a total of five rounds of ammo. We did not want to be taken prisoner and decided to try for the company CP. Each of us spent a moment saying our act of contrition. I crawled out of the foxhole and was met with machine-gun fire. I slid back into the hole. Fred and I waited for the final Chinese attack. We heard firing behind us. A Marine counterattack reached the platoon CP. We yelled, "Hey, over here! We're Marines!" The guys below were surprised to hear from us. They had spent part of the night hollering to us, but Fred and I had failed to hear them.

1st Lt. ROBERT McCARTHY
F/7

At sunup, Platoon Sergeant Audis led the 3d Platoon in an attack and reoccupied its original position on the crest of Fox Hill. Chinese opposition was not heavy and only two Marines were wounded. One was Pfc. [Harrison] Pommers, who had withstood the grenades in his foxhole the night before. Although Pommers was seriously wounded in the neck, he remained with his fire team until the platoon's position was secured.

This second night cost the company 5 dead and 29 wounded, one of the wounded being Captain Barber. The Chinese lost about 150 dead and many wounded. Their cries rang out until the extreme cold silenced them.*

[*Fox 7 was not the only enemy target the night of 28–29 November. Seven miles south of Fox Hill, the Marine base at Hagaru-ri was brought under heavy and repeated attacks. With its supply depot, medical facilities, and airstrip, it was vitally important that it be held.*]

---

* McCarthy, *Gazette.*

Sgt. VINCENT MOSCO
H Battery/11
About midnight [29 November] three red flares burst overhead and
the Chinese, who could clearly be seen against the snow, charged
our position. They ran screaming and yelling at us, blowing whistles
and bugles. We received the command, "Fire at will." It is a command that comes rarely to an artillery battery. For several hours we
loaded, fired right, left, loaded, fired, up, down, loaded, fired, until
there were no more Chinese to fire at. We were then ordered to cease
fire. The few Chinese who reached the bottom of the hill were picked
off by the rifles of a nearby antitank company.

I had the ammo corporal account for all the rounds expended
by our howitzer. The count came to 105 rounds. We had quite a job
removing all the brass casings from the gun-pit area. Around sunrise
the sergeant in charge of the 1st Service Battalion area walked over
to the battery and gave each man a big cigar. There was a lot of
handshaking and backslapping. Then it was back to work. There was
a new day to face and much to do before morning chow.

[*The Chinese had attacked Hagaru-ri with a full division, only to see
it thrashed by a bobtailed rifle battalion and two batteries of artillery.
Fox 7 had also come through the night in one piece. The company,
alone on its hill above the Toktong Pass, spent Wednesday, the 29th,
receiving airdrops. Sniping continued throughout the day. Life went
on and the men on Fox Hill found a routine to it.*]

Pfc. ROBERT EZELL
F/7
Captain Barber limped by and checked our position. He then moved
on up the hill. I was assigned to lead a man without glasses down to
the aid station. Near the aid tents I saw several dead and wounded
Marines lying about. One guy had had his ankle nearly severed.

I saw a few people I knew, then climbed back on top of the hill.
When I reached the squad area, it was no longer there. The machine
gun had been moved to the rocks near the top of the hill. As I walked
to this new location, Sergeant Elrod tumbled down the hill. I knelt
over him and saw he was wounded in the hip. He asked, "Does your

rifle work? If it does, then get up there," and he motioned toward the summit with his head. Before I left him he gave me his binoculars. "Take these; I won't need them anymore." I saw one of the lenses was smashed, probably from whatever caused his wound.

I moved to the new position where half a dozen or so Marines had gathered. About the time I arrived, a Chinese soldier jumped up about ten yards away. He held a burp gun in one hand, a grenade in the other. Someone yelled, "Duck. Grenade." I fired three rounds. The Chinese soldier tumbled backward.

A short time later about ten Chinese who were trapped in front of our position raised their hands. "Don't shoot 'em," someone hollered. "Take prisoners." When the Chinese reached our lines, we searched them, then had them sit apart until they were escorted down the hill.

An ammo carrier named Bernard was wounded in both legs. In a little while a corpsman came up with a stretcher. He'd been running for a long time. There were a lot of casualties. Four of us were assigned to carry Bernard down to the aid tent. It was a hairy trip. We crossed open areas that were under sniper fire. With our weapons, the heavy stretcher, the snow and rough ground, we didn't move very fast. We slipped in one of the open areas. "Everyone OK?" "Yeah." "Sure." We counted to three and took off and didn't stop until we reached the aid tent.

Later I returned to the rocky hilltop. Our machine gun was located in an area of some trees and boulders. A Marine named Valerie and I were put out on one of the flanks. Sniper fire came through the bushes and trees and knocked twigs on us. We were to closely observe the dead Chinese that lay in front of our position and to shoot any we thought might be playing possum. The dead looked like sagebrush in the desert. I didn't count them, but there were a lot.

Eventually, we were ordered to collect the weapons from the dead Chinese that lay nearest our position. We gathered up some Thompson submachine guns and burp guns and others, including wooden rifles with bayonets attached. We were all young kids—I was nineteen—but these dead Chinese, and the prisoners I'd seen earlier, looked to be about thirteen or fourteen years old.

Sniper fire took its toll. In my little area it killed one and wounded three others. One of the wounded was Valerie, who was grazed in

the head. Once he left to go down to the aid tents, that left just four
of us from the original squad—Al Dytkewicz, Bill Gleason, Jerry Triggs,
and me.

In the afternoon Triggs and I were together on the rocky top.
We spent the time sniping at Chinese stragglers in the valley who
were trying to get back to their units.

1st Lt. ROBERT MCCARTHY
F/7

At about 5:00 P.M. on November 29, Captain Barber called all the
platoon leaders together and informed them that other Marine units
were under heavy attack and not to expect relief that night; in fact,
he told them to prepare for even heavier attacks. There were no com-
plaints. Some of the wounded asked for grenades or a rifle. Booby
traps and trip flares had been placed around the company perimeter
during the afternoon and the foxholes had been dug deeper.*

[Eighteen miles south of Fox Hill, the Marines at Koto-ri were also
being told to expect an enemy attack, the first the Chinese would launch
against the village. Second in importance only to Hagaru-ri as a base,
Koto-ri was jammed with Marine and Army troops unable to get past
the enemy roadblocks to the north. All day on the 29th, the Chinese
had shown themselves in the hills above the village. Toward sunset
Marine air strikes hit the swarming Chinese troops. When the sun set
the Corsairs returned to their base and the Chinese moved down off
the high ground. Easy Company, 1st Marines, dug in along the perimeter's northern rim and waited for them.]

S/Sgt. LEE BERGEE
E/1

I could see many silhouettes walking toward our line. Then the machine guns opened up and the Chinese screamed and charged. It was
as if someone had kicked over an anthill. Everywhere I looked I saw

---

* McCarthy, Gazette.

Chinese soldiers running at me. Flares were fired and illuminated the entire area. Tracers burned the air overhead; I clearly heard the crack of near-misses. Grenades exploded, shrapnel whined. Sergeant Music's machine-gun platoon hammered away with great intensity. Music had been captured on Corregidor by the Japs during the Second World War. I can't imagine his thoughts that night at Koto-ri.

Sgt. M. J. VANDERVEEN
E/1
A few of the enemy broke through our line over a silenced machine-gun position and headed directly for the warming tents and battalion aid station. I saw the shadowy figures firing point-blank through the walls of the tents before they were gunned down by Marine fire. In the morning Chinese dead covered the area in front of our company's lines, frozen in the position in which they died.

S/Sgt. LEE BERGEE
E/1
The Chinese withdrew into the surrounding hills. I walked over to one of the warming tents. It had been riddled. Inside, sunlight streamed through the many tears. The tin chimney on the stove, too, had its share of bullet holes.

[*Several hours after the Chinese attack had been beaten off, the Marine division's Recon Company managed to slip into Koto-ri and was immediately put into the line.*]

Pfc. PAUL MARTIN
Reconnaissance Company/1st Marine Division
In Koto-ri our officers told us we were surrounded. The Chinese were in front and in back of us. Airdrops would supply us. A gung-ho gunnery sergeant next told us how lucky we were to be able to make names for ourselves during our first enlistment. Some Marines, he told us, spend their time in the Corps during peacetime and feel they've never done anything. We would now be able to show off with campaign

ribbons and battle stars. I thought back to Camp Lejeune and how I had felt. Corporals with combat ribbons had more prestige than senior NCOs who didn't. I even thought privates wearing ribbons were better than many staff sergeants I'd seen without them.

A major talked to us, told us the Marines were back on center stage. "The whole world will be watching. Your friends and neighbors will read about you. This is your big chance to show the world what a Marine is."

That night I had the first watch. It was bitterly cold. Toward Hagaru-ri I heard the thump of artillery and saw flashes from exploding shells. I became very depressed. There were snow-covered hills all around and the wind bit into me. Just two months earlier Inch'on had seemed to be *the* big campaign. Now, no one ever talked about it, and it was as if it had never taken place.

When my watch was up I woke my buddy. "Anything happen?" "Not yet." I climbed into my sleeping bag. For a while I stared at the stars. Around 3:00 A.M. I woke up. The moon had risen and lit up the valley. I looked toward the gully where earlier in the day I had seen enemy activity. I thought about grade school, how we children had been asked to contribute a quarter to help a baby in a Christian mission in war-torn China. My mom had given me a dollar to contribute. I wondered if one of those babies who had grown up waited now in the gully across the valley to kill me.

[*While the Chinese concentrated on breaking the Marines' defensive perimeters at Koto-ri, Hagaru-ri, and Fox Hill, they did little at Yudam-ni but probe for weaknesses. Unlike the night of the 27th, which saw fierce fighting all around the village, the remaining days of November were relatively quiet ones for the 5th and 7th Marines. Bitterly cold weather, however, continued to punish the men of both trapped regiments.*]

By 28 November it was known that the enemy had cut the MSR between Hagaru-ri and Yudam-ni. The commanding officers of the 5th and 7th Marines in joint operations consolidated positions at Yudam-ni. The 2d Battalion, 5th Marines was withdrawn from its advance position and other subordinate unit positions adjusted to form a perimeter around Yudam-ni.

The night of 28–29 November was free of any strong enemy attacks. However, on the 29th the 3d Battalion and 1st Battalion were pressed continuously throughout the day. "I" Company repulsed three strong enemy attacks. Air strikes by Marine aircraft aided materially in breaking up these attacks.

HISTORICAL DIARY, 5TH MARINE REGIMENT

29 November 1950
Approximately six inches of snow fell during the night which delayed operations until 0850. Thirty-four Close Air Support and two reconnaissance sorties were flown in support of X Corps.

HISTORICAL DIARY, VMF-212

1st Lt. WILLIAM DAVIS
A/7
When I was on some high ground and could look into the flats, I saw Chinese units attacked by aircraft. It was something to see. They didn't run or scurry around, but kept going in a straight line. It was just like they didn't know the planes were there. I don't know how they did it. Once, the 1st Battalion was advancing up a road and one of our Corsairs came up behind us and flew low, right down the line. He couldn't have been more than twelve feet off the deck. The whole battalion, 1,000 guys, one after another, fell to the ground like a collapsing house of cards. I thought later, What if that had been an enemy plane? It must be awful to be on the receiving end of an aerial attack. The things you fear the most are the things you understand best. The Chinese didn't have air cover or support. Maybe they just didn't know what it could do.

29 November 1950
A total of thirty-one sorties and 75.7 hours were flown. All thirty-one flights were sent to the Hagaru-ri area. On the first flight in the morning . . . ridges containing a heavy concentration of Communist troops were hit and all armament expended. Very

little reconnaissance work was done as all of the planes were needed to fend off the Communist attack with Close Air Support.

HISTORICAL DIARY, VMF-312

Pfc. DOUG MICHAUD
Headquarters & Service Company/1/5
I stood by the TACP [Tactical Air Control Party] radio. The guy on the ground was talking to a pilot: "What'n hell you guys shooting at?" The pilot said, "You won't believe this. We've got Chinese walking five abreast. We're throwing everything we got in the cockpit at them and they won't break. They will not break ranks. Almost out of fuel, but we'll be back." And in a little while another flight was.

As long as the Corsairs were flying overhead, you felt good about the situation. The sun was out and we had an umbrella above us. When the sun went down, the icy feeling would return, that empty feeling, the fear of what you knew was coming at night. Then it was man to man. During the day we were the big shots, we had the clout. At night it was their ad.

30 November 1950
Snow still covered the runway [at Yonpo] except a narrow strip down the center which had been blown clean by the previous day's operations. Forty-six Close Air Support sorties represented the day's efforts in support of the X Corps elements in contact around the Chosin Reservoir.

HISTORICAL DIARY, VMF-212

Lt. Col. FREDERICK DOWSETT
7th Marines *
At Yudam-ni it was not unusual for us to be on one side of a mountain ridge and the Chinese twenty or thirty yards away, on the other. We'd bring in air support about thirty yards in front of our lines. One

---

* Dowsett was the 7th Marine Regiment's executive officer.

night we asked that strike groups be put on station because, with the snow and bright moonlight, we felt we could safely run night Close Air Support. (We learned later pilots of the 1st Marine Air Wing volunteered for these night strike groups.) The moon came up about 10:30 P.M. From then until daylight the rifle companies had at least four planes on station. In some instances the men built little fires to mark their frontline position.*

Lt. Col. RAYMOND DAVIS
1/7

Our Forward Air Control officers had been pilots with the squadrons that were flying support. One time when the situation was tense, I overheard a casual conversation between my FAC and a flight leader. When the squadron dropped all its napalm and expended all its ammunition, it wheeled and began to leave. The flight leader said calmly, "See you tomorrow morning, buddy." The FAC yelled, "Damn you! There's two hours 'til dark. You're going to see me again before dark. You get your asses back up here." And they did.†

30 November 1950

A total of thirty-one sorties and 824 hours were flown.

HISTORICAL DIARY, VMF-312

Pfc. FRANCIS KILLEEN
A/7

One of the craziest sights was to stand on a mountaintop and look down at Corsairs making strikes against the enemy. The place looked like one gigantic Christmas card, except most of it was on fire. You could watch this speck move down, then the orange glow of a napalm bomb. "Give 'em hell, wing-whippers!." There were days when the overcast hung over the mountains and I don't know how they did it. We'd be on top in this cloud, and one of those nuts would fly over

---

* Lieutenant Colonel Dowsett interview, on file at the Marine Corps Historical Center, Washington, D.C. Hereafter, Dowsett interview, MCHC.
† Davis interview, MCHC.

trying to get a bearing. He'd be so close you could reach up and touch
his wings. Often we led them in with tracers. They were great. When
they made a run they were deadly. You'd see them go into a valley,
then wait awhile, and see them come out the other side. They left
smoke wherever they went. Once we went through someplace where
there were all these dead Chinese—I mean hundreds—and their quilt
uniforms were still smoldering. One Marine said, with a twinkle, "Here
we get these guys all corralled in one place where we can get them
and this flyboy comes along and messes everything up."

Maj. Gen. OLIVER P. SMITH
Commanding General, 1st Marine Division
I received an order from X Corps to displace a regiment to return to
Hagaru-ri and rescue the Army outfits east of the Reservoir. My God,
at that time we were ourselves being attacked by three or more enemy
divisions.

For two days we received no orders from X Corps to withdraw
from Yudam-ni. Apparently, they were stunned, just couldn't believe
the Chinese had attacked in force. Every four hours we sent a report
of what was going on. It took Corps two days before they told us to
withdraw to Hagaru-ri.*

30 November 1950
During the night 29–30 November minor enemy action was encountered in vicinity of Yudam-ni. On 30 November, 5th Marines subordinate units moved to new positions replacing elements of the 7th Marines. The two regiments received orders from
division to expedite return by way of the MSR to Hagaru-ri. Enemy occupies positions to NW, NE, and SW of present 5th and
7th Marine positions. Capable of cutting MSR and from any direction. 5th and 7th on 30 Nov and 1 Dec adjust positions to
protect Yudam-ni and conduct operations to clear MSR to
Hagaru-ri.

                                    HISTORICAL DIARY, 5TH MARINE REGIMENT

* Smith interview, MCHC.

1 December 1950
Orders issued to segregate litter patients from those able to walk in preparation for the trip to Hagaru-ri.

HISTORICAL DIARY, 5TH MARINE REGIMENT

Pfc. JOHN BISHOP
I/7
Our officers told us to destroy anything that wouldn't work or we couldn't take with us. Trucks had their engines destroyed. One kid fired his M1 into a jeep radiator and the ricochet hit him in the leg. I even saw a guy take a pickax and try to punch a hole in a two-wheeled water carrier.

I saw a six-by truck full of frozen bodies waiting to move out. It looked like a load of meat going to market. I saw a Marine strapped over the barrel of a howitzer. He was covered by a poncho, all but his stiff legs. It reminded me of a deer carcass tied to the top of a car.

Pfc. FRANCIS KILLEEN
A/7
Somebody kicked me in the back of the head. It was Thompson. That long drink of water was moving down the hill all saddled up. "They want you down at the CP. We're pulling out."

Lieutenant Stemple stood next to our radioman. The CO came out of the warm-up tent. Lieutenant [Eugenous] Hovatter told us, "There are four or five Chinese divisions moving in on us." I looked up and to my left saw an air strike in progress. An artillery battery on the main road began to really open up. Across the road junction I saw tents burning and long lines of Marines coming in across the frozen fields. "We're going to attack in another direction. We're moving south. Puller is waiting for us at Koto-ri. The 5th and 7th will take turns guarding the flanks and breaking through roadblocks. Trucks, jeeps, and tanks will move out with us. We will take our dead and wounded with us. I'm gonna leave a detail here to destroy whatever we can't carry. I mean destroy. We're gonna leave nothing for those slant-eyed sonovabitches. Get saddled up."

After the lieutenants went back into the tent, 1st Sgt. Red Donovan came out. He now wore a battle dressing tied like a bow over his right foot. He spotted me and Price, another China Marine about my speed. "Killeen, you know radio and can read a map. I want you to take charge of cleaning up this mess. Between you and Price I know you can think up a couple of good ideas." We were given about six other Marines to help us, most of whom were replacements. I did not know these guys or how they would behave, so Price and I made like Parris Island.

We found about seventy cases of C rations, thirty cases of grenades, and many cases of 60-mm mortar. Every man would carry a full cartridge belt plus two bandoliers and four grenades. We opened the C rations and took out the fruit cocktail, the only thing worth eating. We also grabbed fistfuls of bouillon cubes. Then the cocoa powder was passed out. Tins of machine-gun ammo would be rotated among the men. Everything else, including tents, would be destroyed.

I took the radio; we were "Able 10." I looked at Price and the six guys looked at us. "Where do we begin?" I picked one guy to act as lookout. "When you see that line of Marines reach that bridge, let me know." I picked another kid to watch in the other direction. He was a Mexican kid. Price said, "Looks and sounds like he's one of Pancho Villa's regulars."

Doing away with the tents was easy. We had plenty of heating oil. It was the chow and the grenades . . . We then came up with a great idea, best of the war. Place a grenade in each C-ration box where we had removed the fruit cocktail. Pull the pin, wedge the spoon against the side of the box or put the box back upside down, close the cover, replace the box in the case. "When the Chinks run through here, they'll make a dive for the chow. When they bend over to pick up their noodles, WHAAAM, instant fricassee." We were almost tempted to stay and watch.

Everything was burning nicely. The column of Marines was way down the road and fading fast. Price yelled up the hill to the Mex, "Vamoose, Pancho." We started marching southward. All of us limped on the same foot; at least we were in step. The Chinese mortars seemed to follow us out of the village.

Maj. Gen. OLIVER P. SMITH
Commanding General, 1st Marine Division
I've tried to explain many times to people that "Retreat, hell" business.* You can't retreat or withdraw when you are surrounded. The only thing you can do is break out. When you break out, you attack. That's what we were doing. †

[*The attack southward toward Hagaru-ri commenced on Friday morning, 1 December.*]

Pfc. DOUG MICHAUD
Headquarters & Service Company/1/5
We held our positions above Yudam-ni until the Corsairs came in and gave us cover. The word flew along the line and we came down the slopes running like hell. The Chinks were right behind us. On the road we turned and stopped. The Chinese weren't behind us anymore. They had stopped and were scavenging through the burning tents for food and clothing. They'd been out there in those damn mountains for a long time. They were cold and hungry.

[*The plan of attack called for one Marine battalion to advance cross-country to rescue Fox Company and secure Toktong Pass. Since the wounded could not be carried up and down the mountains, the rest of the Marine force, including the vehicles carrying the wounded and dead, would have to fight its way along the fourteen tough road miles of the MSR from Yudam-ni to Hagaru-ri. Col. Robert Taplett's 3d Battalion, 5th Marines, on the point of the main column, would attack and clear the enemy's roadblocks. Lt. Col. Raymond Davis's 1st Battalion, 7th Marines, was selected to climb over the mountains and rescue Fox 7. It was hoped that Taplett and Davis would reach the summit of the pass at the same time.*]

---

* In reply to questions from newsmen about the withdrawal, General Smith answered, "Retreat, hell, we are just attacking in a different direction."
† Smith interview, MCHC.

Pfc. DOUG MICHAUD
Headquarters & Service Company/1/5
Companies cleared the ridgelines on either side. Only the most severely wounded, and of course the dead, were permitted to ride. Guys
with Hollywood wounds—shoulders and minor stuff like you see in
the movies—walked. The dead were stacked in trucks like so many
cords of wood. When they ran out of truck-bed space, they laid the
dead on fenders, across hoods, tied on the barrels of artillery pieces.
God, there were a lot of them.

Pfc. WIN SCOTT
C/5
For the breakout I was placed on a trailer pulled by a jeep. There
were four stretchers in the back of the jeep and two on the trailer.
Guys walking on the road alongside would help me. A priest came
by once: "How you doing, son? Anything I can do?" Each day he
would check on me.

It was very cold. I wasn't always conscious. I looked into a valley
once and watched a flight of Corsairs drop napalm. I watched them
swoop down, drop their loads, and fire their rockets. I could hear the
firefights up ahead or in the hills above. The convoy stopped often.

Chaplain JOHN CRAVEN (USN)
7th Marines
When we left Yudam-ni for Hagaru-ri, we had about 600 wounded
in trucks and strapped to jeeps. (When we would arrive at Hagaru-ri,
fourteen miles away, about three days later, we had over 1,000
wounded.) Chaplain Orlando Ingvoldstad [regimental chaplain, 5th
Marines] and I worked closely together in ministering to these wounded.
During periods when the convoy was held up by heavy fighting, we
filled the large native cooking vats which were a part of the kitchen
stoves with water and heated the C-ration cans to feed the patients on
stretchers. While this heating of food was going on, we permitted
ambulatory patients to come into the rooms of the native huts to warm
on the radiantly heated floors. After twenty minutes these men would
be turned out and another group which had been standing outside in

the cold admitted. Occasionally, the chaplain had to get a little rough with some of the men who wanted more than their share of the heat.

The most heartbreaking experience came when trucks or weapons carriers turned over on icy roads in the middle of the night, and the already wounded men would be killed or receive further injuries. Trying to pick up these wounded men and find places for them on other vehicles previously loaded with casualties, while the bluish-green Communist machine-gun bullets flew around, was a nightmare I shall never forget.*

Lt. Col. FREDERICK DOWSETT
7th Marines

We made it a policy never to move out and attack until 8:30 or 9:00 A.M., which gave the men an opportunity to build a fire, warm their rations, get squared away, and receive ammunition.

The 7th Marines subsisted entirely on C rations. In the extreme cold these rations in our supply dumps were frozen solid when they were issued to the men. We had no means of setting up field ranges and the one-man Coleman stoves were inoperative. The men tried to eat twice a day. At daybreak they'd build a fire and throw in a can of field rations. About the best they could hope for was that it would thaw by the time they moved out.†

Pfc. WIN SCOTT
C/5

It snowed one night and in the morning, when they removed the tarp, I saw the ground was all white. Some of the days were gray and overcast. Sometimes the sun shone brightly. One of the wounded guys on the jeep whimpered. He never shut up. I talked to him at first.

There was a lot of debris left by the side of the road, some abandoned trucks and jeeps. A lot of it was on fire. The Marines carried out a lot, but they left a lot. There was crap all along the road.

---

*Craven, *History*, 40.
† Dowsett interview, MCHC.

The road was narrow and rough. We stopped and started, stopped and started.

Bodies were strapped on the barrels of artillery, on the sides of trucks, across hoods, anywhere there was space. They were stiff. Sometimes I'd see feet sticking out of a bag, sometimes there wasn't a bag and I'd see the whole corpse. The second day out of Yudam-ni the guy next to me died.

Maj. Gen. OLIVER P. SMITH
Commanding General, 1st Marine Division
It never occurred to me and I don't think it occurred to any man in the division that we wouldn't get out. The only time I was concerned was when the 5th and 7th Marines were fighting their way out of Yudam-ni and around midnight I received a dispatch from Litzenberg: "Situation grave." I didn't like that at all. It was followed within the hour with another that reported the situation was in hand.*

Pfc. JACK WRIGHT
G/5
Item [Company] took the hills on the left, How [Company] the hills on the right, and George [Company], with a tank and a bulldozer, cleared the road.

We marched a few miles and came to a halt. At sundown I heard one hell of a fight up on the hill [1520] where Item Company was. It lasted all night long. There would be a lot of firing. It would die out. Then it would flare up and die out again. All night this went on. No one on the road knew what was happening.

Around sunup five or six Marines came down off the hill. No one else. We figured they'd been sent down to pick up supplies. George Company was ordered to fall in. We started up the hill the Marines had come down. We figured we were going to relieve Item. We figured wrong. We went up in a skirmish line. No one knew why. I found out. When we neared the top of the hill we found the area

---

* Smith interview, MCHC.

littered with dead Marines. Item 5 had been all but wiped out. The guys who had come off the hill were a few of the survivors.

We didn't make it all the way to the top. Didn't try. We stopped about fifteen yards below the crest and set up two lines: one faced east up the hill, the other faced south toward Hagaru-ri.

We began taking incoming mortars and had some casualties. We stayed on the hill the entire day. Once in a while, a Chinese on the ridge above would get up and make a run for it. Most made it. A few didn't.

In the afternoon I received a lesson about bunching up. Two Marines sat side by side. A sniper with one bullet hit both of them. The first Marine died hard. He grabbed himself, rolled over, grunted, rolled some more, grunted again, got up on all fours and crawled in a circle. Then he caved in on himself. That's when our platoon leader said, "OK, there's a good lesson for you. Don't bunch up." Once we knew the Marine was dead, some of the guys crawled to him. One guy took his ammo, another his rifle, another his bayonet and grenades. When someone was hit we took what gear we needed. Might sound heartless, but it was survival.

Later—it was in the afternoon—we were ordered to take the top of the hill. We started up. Below the crest were three deep foxholes. A Chinese soldier jumped out of one of them. I tried to bayonet him. With all the clothes I was wearing and his quilted uniform I couldn't make a dent in the guy. Another Marine behind me shot him. Down in these foxholes we found about five Item Company Marines who had been captured the night before. Their hands had been tied behind them with wire and had turned black. None of them were in a very healthy condition. Our corpsmen untied their hands and got them down to the road where they were put on a truck.

We were then ordered to move forward and take the next hill. I noticed something. My feet felt like they'd gone to sleep and I wasn't feeling the cold in them anymore. I stumbled along trying to wake my feet up, to get some circulation going in them. It felt like I was walking on someone else's feet. Instead of stepping over rocks, I tripped over them. I was tired. I was hungry. I was thirsty. We all carried water and C rations; only thing was, you couldn't drink or eat them. They were frozen solid. The last real sleep we'd had was days before in the valley. I continued to stumble along. Every time I fell, the guy next to me would stop. Pretty soon people were hollering at me to keep going. This is when I realized I was the left guide, and when I stopped, the entire skirmish line stopped. I noticed other Marines stumbled like I did.

The line finally reached the top of the hill. We found one Chinese. Couldn't have been more than sixteen years old. His unit had abandoned him. His feet had froze up and burst open. He lay quietly. I couldn't tell whether he was crying or growling. The noise he made was weird. Our corpsman looked, then shook his head. I walked away. There was a shot. This was the first time I knew a prisoner had been shot out of mercy and not meanness.

The squad leader came over. "Wright, what'n hell is the matter with you? Why couldn't you stand up?" "Well, my feet are asleep." "Stand up here. Stomp 'em." I stood up and stomped. Almost fell on my face. He called the corpsman over. "Keep moving around, Wright, and see what happens." I moved around until I realized I was on the ridgeline. "Oh, hell . . . " I sat down, but moved my legs and feet and all that stuff. Nothing happened. The corpsman walked over with the platoon sergeant. The sergeant said, "Wright, go down to the convoy and turn yourself in." "Aw, hell, Sarge, ain't nothin' wrong. My feet went to sleep, that's all." "Wright, get your ass down to the road. Maybe if enough of you people turn in, they'll get some relief up here for us."

I found our company corpsman at the bottom of the hill. "Yeah, I know," he said. Didn't bother to check me, just wrote out an evac tag and hung it on me. "What the hell's that for?" "Don't you know what's wrong with you?" "My feet went to sleep. Big deal." "You got frozen feet, Wright." I just stared at him. "Frozen feet?" "Yeah. Consider yourself evacuated." "Now, how'n hell am I gonna get evacuated?" He pointed to the long line of trucks strung out along the road. "Take your choice."

Right in front of me was a jeep pulling a trailer that had three Marines riding in it. One of them told me to hop on the trailer. One old guy got out of the jeep. I'll never forget him. He looked like he'd been born in the Corps and been a Marine since 1776. He said, "Take your boot off." I took my boot off. Hell, I wasn't going to argue with that guy. When I pulled the socks off, a layer of skin also came off.

The old guy unbuttoned his parka and dungaree jacket and took my foot and placed it on his bare belly. That's how one Marine will take care of another, even if he doesn't know him. Told me to wiggle my toes. I wiggled. He stood for a minute. Then he growled, "Wiggle your toes." "I am." "Oh, damn," he said, "that this should have to happen." Out of his pack the guy produced two pair of nice, clean ski socks. The socks I'd been wearing I'd worn since they were issued to me down on the coast, an eternity ago. He had me put on the new socks, then my shoepacs. He said, "Shoepacs are the most useless damn things the government ever dreamed up." It was true. Shoepacs were darn good as long as you didn't move. Once you did, your feet sweated, the sweat couldn't evaporate, and your feet froze.

From that point on, I joined the walking wounded.

[*While the 3d Battalion, 5th Marines, shoved the Chinese off the hills above the MSR and led the way for the main column, the 1st Battalion, 7th Marines, began its rescue mission. Lt. Col. Ray Davis's force, with Baker Company on the point, climbed into the mountains east of the road the night of 1 December and set off overland for Fox Hill.*]

2d Lt. JOSEPH OWEN
B/7

As soon as we completed digging in and night registration fire, Joe Kurcaba summoned his officers to the CP. I walked over with Hank Kiser, and we conjectured that one of us would pull a night patrol. We mutually wished each other the privilege of the assignment.

The word that Joe Kurcaba had for us was: "Baker Company will move out in a half hour. Colonel Davis has determined to move the entire battalion, under cover of darkness, through the Chinese positions facing us. Baker Company will take the point, and our direction will be marked by star shells fired at five-minute intervals. Silence is essential, for hopefully we will walk through the defenders without them hearing us or seeing us."

1st Lt. Chew Een Lee, who had been wounded three weeks earlier at Sudong, had escaped from the hospital and rejoined us. As a reward, Joe Kurcaba gave him the company point.

The men were lethargic from cold, physical exertion, and lack of rest. Before we moved out in column we had them double-time in place. This let us check for noisy gear, and it got their blood moving.

The azimuth we followed was over a series of sharp rises and dips. The mortars were in section behind Lee's platoon, and Kurcaba's headquarters followed us. At first the pace of our column was slow but regular. Later, though, as we descended into the dips, we were unable to see the guiding star shells, and the point was halted until Lee was able to check his bearings.

The hesitation at the point caused the column to accordion, and our vital silence was threatened with muffled curses and the sound of men colliding in the dark.

Joe Kurcaba, with the whisper of an enraged bull, repeatedly passed the word up the column to "Keep moving! Keep moving!" To us it was miraculous that the Chinese did not detect our column, for by now we could hear them clearly talking among themselves in quiet tones. If they were aware of us, as they must have been, it was most likely they thought we were a detail of their own people moving back.*

Pfc. DAVE KOEGEL
B/7
I carried the thirty-three-pound light machine gun over one shoulder and, like everyone else, floundered in the deep snow. There's been talk that we were guided that night by a star. I don't see how this could be true, since visibility was only a few feet in any direction. I lurched from side to side. The machine gun seemed to gain weight. At times I thought I could hear the Chinese talking to each other— probably complaining about the cold. Ordinarily, changing the gun from one shoulder to another was no problem, but that night I did not want to make any noise. Eventually, I was forced to shift the gun from one shoulder to the other. Unfortunately, as careful as I tried to be, the pintle pin swung free like the clapper of a bell and struck the receiver. The ringing chimed on and on, or at least in my mind it did. If the profanities that were whispered at me could have killed,

* Owen, *Gazette.*

I would have been riddled. The Chinese took no note of my "chime."
I staggered on.

Lt. Col. RAYMOND DAVIS
1/7

Up on the ridge we were exposed to the wind, and the cold was just
plain numbing. I would hunch down in an abandoned Chinese foxhole to check my compass. Because we didn't want the enemy to know
where we were, when I used the flashlight I covered myself with a
poncho. When I was sure of the direction, I would turn out the light,
shift out of the poncho, and stand up. I would be dazed by the cold.
Two or three people standing around would say something. By the
time I answered them, I'd forgotten what I'd done with the compass
and map and I would have to go down and repeat the entire process.
We were absolutely numb with cold. It was hard to believe.

The route we climbed crossed some ridges that ran parallel to
the valley on our east. Because this valley was under fire from our
own artillery, it was natural for the men to slide in that direction.
Because of the deep snow and ice, the going was very difficult. To
make any time at all the men followed each other in single file. Since
I had no radio communication with the head of the line, when it
drifted off course I passed the word along the column to halt until I
could get things straightened out. I found my orders didn't get beyond seven or eight Marines before someone said, "Shut up the noise!"
That was the end of my order. I then had to beat my way to the head
of the column to get it stopped. When I finally arrived I could hardly
breathe.*

2d Lt. JOSEPH OWEN
B/7

At one point, as I moved back along the side of the column with
word from Lee to Kurcaba, I collided with a Marine churning forward through the snow. As we both recovered our balance, I recog-

* Davis interview, MCHC.

nized Colonel Davis. He had run forward, concerned that we had veered off our azimuth. The men, not recognizing the colonel in the darkness, hissed at him to keep down the noise.

1st Lt. WILLIAM DAVIS
A/7

We couldn't believe it. Here was Colonel Davis going up and down the column. I was in good shape and I was dying. All the eighteen-year-old kids were moaning and groaning. And here was Davis humping up and down. He was phenomenal. When he first took command of the 1st Battalion, 7th Marines, at Pendleton he gave a speech. He said, "Whatever we do, whether it's playing football or ping-pong or fighting the enemy, we are going to be the best!" He was a very unassuming man. He wasn't a runner, he wasn't an athlete, he was just a doer. Just a doer. Halfway to Fox Hill here was Davis going back and forth. I was dying and I'd kept myself in shape. I couldn't believe anyone was in better shape than I was. Well, I'll tell you, Ray Davis was.

Lt. Col. RAYMOND DAVIS
1/7

I had a big sergeant in my S-2 section named Schaeffer. On one of the snowy ridges we climbed that night he came over to me and said, "Come with me, Colonel, I wanna show ya something." He reached down into the snow and pulled out of a hole a solid chunk of ice that was a Chinese soldier. I asked, "Is he dead?" Schaeffer said, "No, sir, his eyes are moving." We walked around and found half a dozen more Chinese frozen solid in their holes. It must have been some kind of little outpost. Every enemy soldier we found, except that first one, had frozen to death.*

---

*Davis interview, MCHC.

2d Lt. JOSEPH OWEN
B/7

The stopping, starting, and standing still and silent in the snow for long moments began to tell on the men, who had long ago passed the point of exhaustion. They were functioning now on instinct. Officers and NCOs ranged the column, silently prodding Marines who slumped into the snow during a halt. That night Marine Corps discipline was a final resource and a saving grace.*

Lt. Col. RAYMOND DAVIS
1/7

We finally reached the summit of a very difficult, tortuous ridge which we had climbed on our hands and knees, holding onto roots to keep from sliding back down the trail. The moon came out from behind the clouds and illuminated the scene. I saw we were about 1,500 yards from Fox Company's position. It was about 2:30 or 3:00 A.M. Because I didn't have adequate communication with F Company, I decided to hold tight where I was until daylight. No sense in getting into a firefight with our own people.

When the troops were told to hold where they were, they fell over like frozen flies. They just couldn't stay on their feet. I became very alarmed, so much so I had each company organize teams of NCOs to go around and keep some of the men alert for the few hours we had to pass before sunrise.

I decided to take a short nap. I crawled next to a small rock formation to get out of the wind. I had just pulled a poncho over me when an enemy machine-gun bullet grazed my head. I was not seriously injured, though.†

2d Lt. JOSEPH OWEN
B/7

Finally alerted to us, the enemy opened up, but their fire was erratic and confused. Lee added to their confusion by calling out to them in

---

* Owen, *Gazette.*
† Davis interview, MCHC.

Chinese. Several times they revealed themselves to him, to be quickly eliminated by our men, who had come alive again, instinctively pressing the advantage of surprise in the night.

The fight on the snowy, rocky, dark meadow was short and sharp. The astonished Chinese were unable to organize. Much of the fighting was man to man, with the Marines enjoying momentum. Corporals Bifulk and Perkins took possession of a rock-barricaded position by attacking its occupants with entrenching tools. Grenades were our common weapon until enemy resistance ceased.

The men of Baker Company slipped exhausted into vacant Chinese holes. There would be three hours' rest before we jumped off again at first light. Fox Company was still holding out, less than a mile from us.*

Lt. Col. RAYMOND DAVIS
1/7

In the morning we raised Fox Company and Bill Barber made his classic remark when he asked whether he might send some of his troops out to help us into his perimeter. I declined the offer.†

1st Lt. ROBERT MCCARTHY
F/7

At noon the 1st Battalion, 7th Marines, commanded by Lt. Col. Raymond G. Davis, was in radio contact with Fox Company. Captain Barber warned that the rocky ridge to our left front was still occupied by the enemy. At 2:00 P.M. Fox Company sent out a patrol to keep the Chinese on the rocky ridge engaged. The rocky portion of the ridge was still held in such force that seizing it was impossible. However, the Chinese were diverted enough by the patrol to allow the 1st Battalion, 7th Marines, to move in from the right and drive them out.

*Owen, *Gazette.*
†Davis interview, MCHC.

Lieutenant Colonel Davis and his battalion arrived at Fox Company's position at 4:30 P.M., 2 December.*

Pfc. ERNEST GONZALEZ
F/7
I saw a column of men coming from the right side near the base of "Rocky Ridge." We challenged them. They shouted back that they were our relief. Word went around it was a unit from the 7th Marines. Fred was then able to go down to the aid station and have his frostbite taken care of. (I would not see him again until the next month, when I bumped into him at Santa Margarita Hospital at Camp Pendleton.)

Pfc. ROBERT EZELL
F/7
When we were relieved, all the dead and wounded were carried down to the trucks on the road. The Chinese prisoners were used as stretcher-bearers. I heard one of the Marines tell a guy lying next to me, "Good job, buddy."

I was placed in the front seat of a jeep. Stretchers were placed across the back and on the hood. I could move my legs a little. I asked for a weapon and was given a carbine.

Pfc. ERNEST GONZALEZ
F/7
With Freddy gone I was now alone. A Marine came over later—I think he was one of the men from Colonel Davis's 1st Battalion—and dug himself a foxhole in which he went to sleep.

That night I had difficulty sleeping and spent most of it listening for movement to our front. I needed to throw a tarp over myself to keep warm.

* McCarthy, *Gazette.*

1st Lt. ROBERT MCCARTHY
F/7

Baker and Charlie Companies, 1st Battalion, 7th Marines, moved through Fox Company's area and set up defensive positions for the night on the high ground across the valley to the south. Headquarters Company and Able Company, 1st Battalion, 7th Marines, bedded down in Fox Company's area for the night. All the rations that Fox Company had were turned over to the 1st Battalion. The medical officer of the 1st Battalion stayed up all night caring for the wounded and advising the corpsmen about some of the more seriously wounded. Some of the Fox Company wounded told the doctor if he didn't get them to a hospital soon, they would be healed up and ready for duty. There was no Chinese activity on the night of 2 December.

Just before the 1st Battalion moved out on 3 December its doctor [Lt. Peter Arioli, USN] was giving the corpsmen instructions. A sniper suddenly fired four rounds and the doctor and one corpsman were killed, and another corpsman was wounded.

The last elements of the 1st Battalion, 7th Marines, cleared Fox Company's area by 10:00 A.M., 3 December. They left their wounded and dead with Fox Company, because they were assigned the mission of clearing the left side of the road to Hagaru-ri.

One battalion of the 5th Marines was pushing the Chinese ahead of it on the south side of the Yudam-ni road. Lieutenant Campbell called in some very accurate fire from How Battery, which inflicted heavy casualties on the Chinese. The 3d Battalion, 5th Marines, preceded by an M26 tank, arrived on the road at Fox Company's position at 3:00 P.M., 3 December. This was the advance guard of the column of the 5th and 7th Marines. Instructions were received to burn excess equipment and to place the dead and wounded on the trucks.

Captain Barber supervised these final arrangements of his company, caused the company to fall in beside the road, and turned it over to First Lieutenant Peterson for the march to Hagaru-ri. Though Lieutenant Peterson had been hit twice, he was the only officer left with two good legs, so Fox Company was now his.*

---

*McCarthy, *Gazette*. Fox 7 was not engaged at any time between its old position on the hill and Hagaru-ri. What was left of the company marched into Hagaru-ri at 1:30 A.M., 4 December. A week before, it had numbered 240 Marines. It returned to Hagaru-ri with 122 Marines

Approximately one hundred additional casualties were loaded on passing vehicles near the top of the pass between Yudam-ni and Hagaru-ri while many walking wounded accompanied the column. Most of these casualties came from F/7 which had been isolated . . . for several days. Others had become casualties during the attack to capture Toktong Pass and from snipers along the way. Approximately 900 casualties were brought out in the convoy. Subsequently, about 80 percent of all casualties were found to have frostbite.

NARRATIVE HISTORY, 5TH MARINE REGIMENT

Pfc. DOUG MICHAUD
Headquarters & Service Company/1/5
All the way from Yudam-ni to Hagaru-ri it was, "Five more miles, guys; warm buildings, hot chow. Just five miles, guys." "Four miles more, keep going. Got hot chow ahead. Come on! Come on! Just four to go." Hell, I thought, the war's over at Hagaru-ri. No one suspected that it would get worse there.

4 December 1950
The column was halted several times by defended roadblocks that were cleared. The battalion continued to move until 1530 at which time B and C Companies were set in position to cover the withdrawal of division elements. H & S Company, supply train and Weapons Company proceeded on to Hagaru-ri arriving there at 2100.

SPECIAL ACTION REPORT, 1/5

At 2:00 P.M. on 4 December the last elements of the rear guard, 3/7, entered the perimeter and the four-day operation passed into history. Some 1500 casualties were brought to Hagaru-ri, a third of them being in the non-battle category, chiefly frostbite cases. It had taken the head of the column about fifty-nine hours

---

still effective. Six of its seven officers had been wounded. The seventh, 1st Lt. John Dunne, would be killed on the road to Koto-ri, 6 December.

to cover the fourteen miles, and the rear units seventy-nine
hours.

U.S. MARINE OPERATIONS IN KOREA

[*The 5th and 7th Marines had successfully fought their way out of the
massive trap set at Yudam-ni by the Chinese, ending the first phase
of their attack to the south. The three Army battalions of the 7th Infantry Division, which had been attacked east of the Chosin Reservoir
eight days before, were not as fortunate. Their ordeal too had ended,
but not successfully, and, for most of the soldiers, not at Hagaru-ri.
Survivors of the five days of continuous fighting east of the Reservoir
who eventually escaped over the ice told of a disaster that had begun
the night of 27 November, the same night the Chinese had come out
of the hills around Yudam-ni. The 7th Division battalions were separated by about three miles and a frozen inlet of the Reservoir. Col.
Allen MacLean, commanding the 31st Infantry, had the 3d Battalion
of his regiment and the 1st Battalion, 57th Field Artillery, in a perimeter near Sinhung-ni. Lt. Col. Don Faith's 1st Battalion, 32d Infantry, was along the shore farther north in a separate defensive perimeter. Soldiers in both perimeters had been hard-pressed during the night
and, when the sun rose above the eastern mountains on 28 November,
they found themselves hemmed in on all sides and growing desperate.*]

Pfc. JAMES RANSONE, JR.
Task Force Faith*

Somehow we had held. In the morning [28 November] I checked a
foxhole in front of my position. I found a Chinese soldier. He had
his burp gun pointed toward the ground. If it had been pointed in
the other direction, I would have shot him. He dropped his gun and
raised his hands. Then he put one of his hands inside his quilted jacket.
I watched close, afraid he'd have a pistol there. He slowly took out a
small wallet and handed it to me. Inside I found a picture of a woman

---

*At the time of the Chinese attack, Colonel MacLean had been visiting Colonel Faith's
battalion. When he tried to cross the inlet and rejoin the 3d Battalion, 31st Infantry, he was
wounded and captured by the enemy. Colonel Faith eventually fought his way to the perimeter
at Sinhung-ni. The combined force then became known as Task Force Faith.

and child. I guess it was his family. I thought I would have done the same thing to keep from being killed.

Eventually, we rounded up all the prisoners and organized the wounded. The dead we put on trucks. We withdrew to another position and set up a perimeter. There were quite a few men here. Our morale was real bad. We knew we were trapped and couldn't expect help. We didn't know what to do. It looked like Custer's Last Stand was going to be reenacted.

Capt. EDWARD STAMFORD
Task Force Faith
I reverted to my job of FAC and gave support to the battalion [1st Battalion, 32d Infantry] all day on the 28th. I have no idea of the number of strikes run, but it was considerable. The planes were coming both from Yonpo and from carriers. Division was cognizant of the fact that great numbers of aircraft were going to be needed by both the Marines and by me and they made every effort to keep as many aircraft on orbit over the Hagaru-ri area as they could.*

The ground unit in the most danger from Communist attack was a large group of approximately 2,500 from the 7th Army Division [Task Force Faith] who were cut off from the main group and had advanced up a canyon of the southeast side of the Chosin Reservoir. Their controller, Boyhood 14 [Stamford], called for all the help he could get. Hills on all sides of his position were covered with Communist troops, some of whom were growing so bold as to stand up defiantly in their foxholes. Napalm, rockets, strafing, and bombing were all used on phosphorus-marked positions. It was evident that the friendlies were receiving heavy resistance from all sides from greatly superior numbers.

HISTORICAL DIARY, VMF-312

* Stamford interview, MCHC.

Lt. Col. HAROLD EISELE
VMF-212

Colonel Faith's forward air controller was Capt. Ed Stamford, and I flew several missions under his control. I remember one of them. He directed my flight of four Corsairs. When he announced that we appeared to be on target, I could see in my gunsights as many American Army troops as Chinese. I made a second pass, but again I could not fire. I told Ed we had seen large masses of enemy troops in the surrounding hills and we would attack them. Our F4U-5s [Corsairs] carried four 20-mm cannons. Every third round was high-explosive ammunition and we used these against large concentrations of troops with great effectiveness. With our rockets and napalm, we killed many Chinese on this and subsequent strikes in the area.

S/Sgt. CHESTER BAIR
Task Force Faith

The Chinese in their white uniforms faded into the gullies when our air support arrived, which usually came in low and fast across the ice. Once the planes left, the Chinese came right back at us.

The enemy had no heavy weapons (like us) other than their 82-mm mortars, which they used with great accuracy. The dead and wounded began to mount up. I stacked my truck with the dead.

Within the perimeter there were a few warm-up tents, but men could only stay in them a short time. The mess halls were trying to serve hot coffee and soup, but I believe most of the men did not know this. Whenever GIs came past my truck, I directed them to the mess and warming tents. Most men seemed surprised they existed.

No one caught more than three or four hours' sleep. The time was spent fighting, working, or guarding. One night my buddy, who had been wounded, and I stood guard. I talked away about the good old USA. When our relief came, my buddy didn't move. I shook him. He fell down. Sometime during the night he had died and I did not know it.

Supplies we desperately needed were air-dropped to us. Because of the strong winds and the smallness of the perimeter, much of it unfortunately drifted into the hands of the enemy. This affected us greatly as we later ran out of ammo and medical supplies.

Air support was reduced and our artillery had a difficult time firing.

A helicopter arrived at our CP. We were told that General Almond, who was on board, awarded Colonel Faith a Silver Star for heroism. After the helicopter carrying General Almond left the area, I saw Colonel Faith rip the medal off his uniform and throw it on the ground.

Maj. Gen. OLIVER P. SMITH
Commanding General, 1st Marine Division
General Almond flew into Hagaru-ri a couple of times. The first time he came he was full of beans—wanted our schedule for rescuing TF Faith by 6:00 that evening. Major General [David] Barr, who commanded the 7th Division—he was a pretty good egg—came with him. We talked it over. I said, "We can't do anything about going up there for those people until the 5th and 7th Marines fight their way back to us. Then, maybe we can do something." Barr agreed.*

[Lt. Col. Don Faith's 1st Battalion, 32d Infantry, fought its way down the road and arrived at the Sinhung-ni perimeter on 30 November.]

Capt. EDWARD STAMFORD
Task Force Faith
When we joined the 3d Battalion, 31st Infantry, we found the dead were everywhere. The FAC of the 3d Battalion, 31st Infantry, had been killed during the first attack and his radios put out of commission; consequently, they had no close support until the 1st Battalion, 32d Infantry, joined them.

Colonel Faith had taken command of all three battalions now, and Major Miller was CO of 1st Battalion, 32d Infantry, which had the responsibility for the southern sector of the perimeter. The 3d Battalion, 31st Infantry, had the northern sector, and the 1st Battalion, 57th Infantry, was in the center, its guns capable of covering the

---

* Smith interview, MCHC.

whole perimeter. With the amount of ammunition available, the supporting arms did a very good job of supporting the troops. The enemy seemed to have three avenues of attack: one from the north through a shallow draw in the vicinity of the bridge; one from a draw leading to the high ground on the southeast; and one along the road and railbed from the southeast.*

Pfc. JAMES RANSONE, JR.
Task Force Faith
I felt better when I saw Colonel Faith in the middle of the perimeter. Here was a lieutenant colonel in the middle of everything. Usually, a CO is back in regiment and regiment is not close to the front lines. When the men saw Colonel Faith, their morale picked up some.

We were under fire during the day and during the night. My foxhole was next to the railroad and close to the road and bridge. I was fortunate in having a small boulder out in front of my hole. It didn't give much shelter, but some was better than none. A ROK private shared the hole with me. I kept telling him to keep his head down. He would not. Maybe it was curiosity, but, whatever it was, he continued to look out of the hole. He took a bullet smack between the eyes. I was surprised that he didn't die instantly. I pushed him into the hole and called a medic. Last I saw him he was being carried to the aid station.

It wasn't too long before a Chinese soldier tried to crawl in the foxhole with me. It was at night and I spotted him looking around the boulder. He decided to get me and crawled on his hands and knees toward the hole. I got him with a round from my rifle.

More Chinese crawled along a ditch next to the railroad. My foxhole overlooked that ditch. There's no telling how many Chinese were killed right there. I don't have the slightest idea. They lay on top of each other, in some places ten deep. They came and they came. They were everywhere. Only thing I can figure is they were hepped up with something, opium or whatever. They blew them bugles and hollered and screamed. They came in hordes of human beings, flow-

---

* Stamford interview, MCHC.

ing toward us. I never saw human beings like them. There was no fear in them, like they were wild.

Finally, we found out there would be no relief.* We'd have to do the best we could ourselves. We had very little to eat and drink. Our water was frozen. We ate snow. Most of us had frozen tongues. My own tongue was completely numb. When we weren't fighting we put our rifles next to our bodies to keep them from freezing. We also changed our socks whenever we could. I tried to keep my feet in good condition. I'd been taught my two main assets as a fighting man were my hands and my feet. I put the socks I'd just removed inside my long johns and my body heat would dry them. I changed socks this way three or four times a day.

The situation in the perimeter was terrible. You couldn't leave your hole to use a latrine. We used our helmets instead and threw the human waste outside the holes. Supplies were short. Planes dropping things to us would miss the perimeter and the Chinese would end up with them. Nothing was working out. We were being shot up bad. We were just in a terrible situation. We were being annihilated.

[On the night of 30 November and morning of 1 December, the Chinese attacks increased in intensity and the perimeter came under heavy mortar fire. It was during this period, when all hope of relief or reinforcements had faded, that Faith decided to break out toward Hagaru-ri.]

Pfc. JAMES RANSONE, JR.
Task Force Faith
It was rumored the night before we broke out that we would have to fight our way back to Hagaru-ri. I figured there were ten miles of Chinese between me and safety. We would do our own fighting; soldiers couldn't expect help from Marines.

The morning broke dark and dreary. There was about a foot of snow on the ground. The first thing I remember on that morning is Colonel Faith walking past my foxhole. He wore a shiny helmet with

---

* A relief force of company strength, made up of 31st Infantry units around Hagaru-ri and supported by Army tanks, was attacked on 29 November and turned back.

a silver oak leaf on it. His parka looked brand-new, so did his riding pants. He wore a backpack harness and had two grenades attached to the upper part of his parka. I noticed he carried a .45 in his right hand. He looked outstanding and stuck out from the rest of us. He was a sitting duck for a Chinese sniper. He looked directly at me: "Men, out of your holes, let's go!" I climbed out and stood up.

S/Sgt. CHESTER BAIR
Task Force Faith

The plan was to attack southward and join up with a rescue team coming to meet us. The Chinese were all around us and letting us know it in more ways than one. Many of the vehicles that were to have made the breakout were now out of action.

Around noontime, four Corsairs showed. This flight miscalculated the distance and dropped napalm on the head of our column. A wall of flames about twenty feet high shot down the column, burning men and destroying vehicles and equipment. I was just out of its reach but could feel the heat from it.

Pfc. JAMES RANSONE, JR.
Task Force Faith

About the time the column was organized and getting ready to move out, an American plane dropped a napalm bomb short. It hit and exploded in the middle of my squad. I don't know how in the world the flames missed me. In my lifetime I'll never know. Men all around me were burned. They lay rolling in the snow. Men I knew, marched and fought with, begged me to shoot them. It was terrible. Where the napalm had burned the skin to a crisp, it would be peeled back from the face, arms, legs. It looked as though the skin was curled like fried potato chips. Men begged to be shot. I couldn't. The medics arrived and did what they could. It wasn't much.

Later, the platoon moved down the ditch toward the bridge. I noticed Chinese hiding under it. Maybe they were playing possum because they didn't look like they'd been shot. We took care of them and advanced farther down the road.

I lost all sense of time. I can't tell how long it took to get to the larger bridge. We were pinned down much of the time.

[Task Force Faith fought its way south all day Friday, 1 December. Tragically, just four and a half miles short of Hagaru-ri, Lieutenant Colonel Faith was mortally wounded.* Discipline then evaporated and the men struck out on their own.]

S/Sgt. CHESTER BAIR
Task Force Faith
After Colonel Faith was killed, it was everyone for himself. The chain of command disappeared. Some men sat down and refused to move. Those in fairly good physical condition looked around for others who would join them either in escaping over the ice [Reservoir] or in fighting down the road. I heard that such a group had formed at the head of the column and was going to make a mad dash toward the south in the hope of running into a rescue team. I declined to join this group.

My luck had died. I got out to help a wounded GI. Behind me I heard machine-gun fire. It was close. Back at the truck I saw the windshield had shattered. My driver, in attempting to get out of the cab, hung over the door. He was dead. Water gushed out of the radiator, oil spilled and stained the road. I looked toward the rear of the column. Chinese troops were on the road. They seemed to be checking the dead with their bayonets. Men who were still alive were made to stand by the side of the road.

Cpl. JACK CHAPMAN
Task Force Faith
What remained of my unit was overrun. I first saw the Chinese on the skyline moving toward the road. The line seemed to go on forever. When they reached us they grabbed our weapons, ammo, medical supplies, and food.

---

* Lt. Col. Don Faith, Jr., was posthumously awarded the Medal of Honor.

Although wounded and in a daze, I clearly recall one incident. The Chinese, who were not familiar with the 75-mm recoilless rifle, while examining it, accidentally fired it. Several of their troops watching in the rear were caught in the weapon's terrible backblast and were killed. I wanted to laugh.

I also recall one GI who lay on the road next to me. He had half his stomach blown away. He cried and screamed for help. A Chinese soldier came by and rolled him into a ditch where he was left to die. I remembered the man had told me he had just been married before being sent to join the company in Japan.

We were herded like sheep into a farmhouse which lay some distance from the road. Because I was only half-conscious from the bleeding and shock, I do not know precisely how long we were kept in that building.*

S/Sgt. CHESTER BAIR
Task Force Faith
I had decided earlier I would not be taken prisoner, not me. I was surrounded by deep mortar craters. I selected one that had several dismembered and shattered GIs lying in it. I crawled in with the corpses. I got as close as I could to the dead so I would also appear dead.

The enemy passed by and continued moving toward the head of the column. I crawled over and hid in some rocks near the base of a hill. I must have looked awful. I had already been covered in blood. Now I must have looked worse.

Capt. EDWARD STAMFORD
Task Force Faith
I caught the lead truck about 400 yards down the hill from a road-block and found they had picked up Colonel Faith, who was very seriously wounded in the body. I led the convoy down the hill by walking in front of it and held them up at the bottom while I checked

---

* Corporal Chapman remained a POW for the duration of the war.

a bridge ahead to see if it was passable. I made a thorough recon-naissance and found the bridge blown. I came back along the rail-road, which was intact, and found a path leading to the road over which we could move the vehicles. I held a conference with those around me as to my plans. We went into a small building on the side of the road and I lit a cigarette as I talked. I saw a lieutenant colonel and a few other officers; none made any attempt to take over com-mand. I became peeved and started out to lead the convoy. I led them over the railroad and found a place to cut off onto the road. Once on the road, I stayed about 200 yards in front of the lead vehicle on the point with a few men. I walked about a half mile or more when we were suddenly surrounded by the enemy and taken prisoner.*

Pfc. JAMES RANSONE, JR.
Task Force Faith
Because fire on the road was so intense, I ran to a cornfield on the left side of the road. I worked my way over the snowy ground, found a large corn shock, and joined fifteen or twenty GIs hiding behind it. I knew this many men would eventually draw the enemy's fire. The group of men broke up. I ran across the field. A bullet went through my canteen, another hit my ammunition belt, one tore my parka, one cut off my bayonet scabbard. The fifth round went through my left arm. I never saw so much enemy fire in one place. In that corn-field, bullets fell like rain. It was impossible to be in that field and not be hit. I believe I was the only man from that large group behind the corn shock who managed to get back to the road.

I saw four or five American tanks on the side of the road that had been knocked out in trying to reach our perimeter. I stood by one of these tanks. A lieutenant—he was a dentist—was hit by a shell that took half his head off. Next I saw my company commander and an artillery FO, Lieutenant Barnes, running down the road toward me. I asked them to check my arm to see how bad I'd been hit. My CO glanced my way, but paid me no more attention and kept run-ning. Lieutenant Barnes stopped and looked after me. "I don't think

* Stamford interview, MCHC.

you're hit very bad. It looks like maybe a flesh wound. Not bleeding. It'll be all right." I appreciated his taking the time. I didn't think too much of my company commander. In a situation like that you never know who will do what.

I walked past the tanks and around a bend in the road. I stayed to the side because there was a lot of fire directed at the road. I stumbled on five Chinese trying to unjam a machine gun. Couldn't have been more than twenty yards from them. They were so engrossed in their work they didn't notice me at first. When they did, they grabbed their rifles and bayonets and took off after me. I'd lost my rifle in the cornfield and was now unarmed. All I figured I could do was outrun them. I ran as fast as I could. Down a ravine, then zigzagging, I knew I had to outrun them. They never fired at me, just stayed on my trail. I hit the bank that dropped to the frozen Reservoir. I slipped over the edge and slid to the ice. I picked myself up and tried to run on the ice. It seemed for every step I took I slipped back two. I slid and fell. Finally, I said to myself, If they're going to get me, they're going to get me. I thought, however, that if I took off my galoshes, I might be able to get better footing. I'd try again. The Chinese stopped at the edge of the ice and remained there. They never fired at me. Perhaps they too had run out of ammo. Once I removed my galoshes, my legs felt so light I had trouble moving them. It was the oddest sensation. I went out on the ice as far as I could. The Chinese were left standing, watching me. Eventually, I passed out from exhaustion.

S/Sgt. CHESTER BAIR
Task Force Faith
I climbed a small hill. Reaching into my coat I drew out my pistol. The time of truth had arrived. I would not be taken a POW. With this bitterly cold weather and this deep in enemy territory, I didn't stand much chance of escaping. How had I gotten myself in this situation?

I heard a movement close by. I saw an Army officer. Soon afterward a Pfc and a Marine captain joined us. The four of us decided to try to make our escape over the frozen Reservoir.

A little while later the Chinese captured us. Fortunately, some heavy firing broke out nearby. Our captors ran for cover. I ran in the other direction and fell over the top of the ridge. I slid, fell, rolled to the bottom, and ended up in a snowbank. When I figured things out, I got up and noticed two GIs walking toward the ice. I shuffled toward them. When I reached them I saw it was two of the men I'd been with before. Around us, other GIs were walking southward on the ice. It was better not to clump up; too many men moving together would draw enemy fire. We also saw some Chinese troops. They made no effort to capture us. Maybe they were as cold as we were.

Night fell. Traveling south, we passed GIs lying on the ice. We did not stop to see if they were dead or alive. We kept moving south. I thought to myself, In all that fighting I never fired my pistol.

Capt. EDWARD STAMFORD
Task Force Faith

The soldier guarding me wanted me to lie down on the side of the road. Evidently, I didn't move fast enough or he was scared, too, and discharged his rifle in my face. We had a guard behind us and one across the road with automatic weapons. The enemy sent one man out to reconnoiter, and a morter fired a couple of rounds from a position alongside the road about 300 yards farther on. There were enemy on the high ground also. Someone fired several bursts with a weapon from the convoy and it passed over our heads. Soon after this, the lead truck ran the blockade and seemed to draw little fire. The man beside me said he was going to try to escape at the first opportunity and I told him I'd try, too. The guard behind us moved off, firing at someone coming at him, and I took this opportunity to leave, telling the man beside me to go. I crossed the road and railroad and ran about 300 yards west, cutting south into a line of scrub for concealment. I then started moving south to the next town about a mile away, hoping to find help. I reconnoitered the town and found it dead. I continued south as I started over a saddle on a path I saw someone coming. I changed direction and he pursued me, so I went into some scrub pine and over the roughest terrain I could find. I came down the other side and injured my ankle. I then worked my way toward Hagaru-ri, being careful to stay off the road because it showed signs of being heavily traveled by foot troops. I infiltrated the Marine lines at Hagaru-ri and was picked up on the perimeter by the 105-mm battery [H/11] under Captain [Benjamin] Read, at 2:25 A.M. on December 2.*

Maj. Gen. OLIVER P. SMITH
Commanding General, 1st Marine Division
[Lt. Col. Olin] Beall † took a jeep and drove up on the ice [of the Reservoir] to see what was going on. He said it was pitiful. Some of these men from Faith's outfit were dragging themselves on the ice, others had gone crazy and were walking in circles. He began to rescue them. One day [2 December] he brought back 319 of them. ‡

Pfc. JAMES RANSONE, JR.
Task Force Faith
The next thing I remember is lying in a big Marine six-by. In the aid station at Hagaru-ri, I learned my fingers and toes were frostbitten and I had a flesh wound. I would be airlifted to Japan.

S/Sgt. CHESTER BAIR
Task Force Faith
I was disoriented, exhausted, nearly frozen, hungry, and vomiting blood. The temperature at night was 20 or more degrees below zero. The wind was so strong it was hard to stand or walk on the ice. In the early morning hours, my group ran into a Marine outpost at the southern end of the Chosin Reservoir. The Army officer, an artilleryman, tried to explain what was taking place farther north with Task Force Faith. The Marine said they were doing all they could to get themselves out of the trap and he was sorry. Around us were a few

---

* Stamford interview, MCHC. Captain Stamford was evacuated on 3 December to the 35th Station Hospital in Kyoto, Japan.
† Lieutenant Colonel Beall commanded the 1st Motor Transport Battalion, 1st Marine Division.
‡ Smith interview, MCHC.

other escapees off the ice who had already been picked up. We were debriefed, asked if we had seen others on the ice. We told them what we knew. They took us to an Army unit. From there we were taken to Hagaru-ri.

There everyone was packing up, tearing down tents, preparing to move out. I was turned over to the medics. I did not see a doctor or receive treatment for my condition. A medic looked at my tag and put me on a truck.

> A company-size task force of Army troops from Hagaru-ri, supported by tanks, moved out that day [2 December] to bring in any organized units of three shattered battalions which might have been left behind. Known as Task Force Anderson after Lt. Col. Berry K. Anderson, senior Army officer at Hagaru-ri, the column met heavy CCF opposition and was recalled when it became evident that only stragglers remained.
>
> [Lieutenant Colonel] Beall and his men kept up their rescue work until the last of an estimated 1,050 survivors of the original 2,500 troops had been saved. A Marine reconnaissance patrol counted more than 300 dead in the abandoned trucks of the Task Force Faith convoy, and there were apparently hundreds of MIA. The 385 able-bodied soldiers who reached Hagaru-ri were organized into a provisional battalion and provided with Marine equipment.
>
> U.S. MARINE OPERATIONS IN KOREA

[About the same time the last survivors of Task Force Faith trickled through the Hagaru-ri perimeter, the lead elements of the Marine regiments from Yudam-ni began to arrive in the village. Once the 5th and 7th Marines closed on Hagaru-ri, the area crackled with activity. For several days the Chinese made few attempts to interrupt this bustle; both sides used the time to get ready for the next phase of the campaign. Hagaru-ri was eleven miles from Koto-ri and sixty-four from Hungnam and safety.]

2d Lt. JOSEPH OWEN
B/7
After we went into Hagaru-ri, we were called back out. We'd been
rear guard all the way [from Fox Hill], so being the last guys in, we
were closest to the road. Apparently, some gooks had formed on a
hill mass northeast of town. Chew Een Lee's platoon went up and I
brought the mortars in after him. We walked the mortar bursts about
fifty yards in front of Lee's platoon.

When I came back down the hill, I saw Gunny Foster lying dead
in a ditch. Naturally, I felt very bad about losing him. Nearby was
another Marine who'd been killed. I had seen him briefly earlier in
the day. He was one of the replacements who'd been flown in and
assigned to Baker Company. When I saw him lying at the bottom of
the hill, I asked if anyone knew his name. No one did. The kid joined
us that day, went up the hill, got killed, and now lay at the bottom
of a hill in a ditch. That was one of the sad days. I felt bad about
Gunny, but it struck me about the kid.

Chaplain ROBERT SCHWYHART (USN)
1st Marine Division
I checked on the chaplains of the 5th and 7th Marine Regiments and
was glad to learn they were well. They were dreadfully tired, though,
having been without sleep for two or three days and nights.

Chaplain JOHN CRAVEN (USN)
7th Marines
I worked all one night at Hagaru-ri with two British Navy hospital
corpsmen attached to the British Royal Marines. The three of us had
four tents and two native houses filled with stretcher cases to care for
as best we could.

We were isolated from the large field hospital, and no doctor
could be spared to stay with us. The next morning I secured a large
utensil filled with hot cakes and a gallon of jam. We spread jam on
the cakes, rolled them up, and passed them out to our patients. I don't

suppose anyone ever appreciated homemade jelly rolls as much as they did.*

Pfc. WIN SCOTT
C/5

It must have been in Hagaru-ri. A guy came around and unloaded the litters. Maybe I was out when he did, maybe he confused me with the kid who had died next to me. In any case, I found myself in a sandpit by the side of the road with nothing but corpses. They were all frozen. Some of the positions they were in were grotesque, arms or legs sticking out or bent. I couldn't hear anything. They're leaving me, I thought. I'm not dead. I yelled and yelled. Some guy came by and told me to take it easy.

I was so thirsty. I couldn't get anything to drink. A Marine came by. "You want a can of juice?" He had a can of fruit juice, one of those big quart cans. It was pineapple juice. He held me up. I twisted around. My back didn't hurt right then. The juice ran all over me. I drank all I could.

1st Lt. LAWRENCE SCHMITT
F/7

I was placed in a hut in Hagaru-ri and waited several days to be evacuated. The medical attention I received consisted of a shot of penicillin given by a British commando corpsman. I asked, "How are things in merry old England?" He answered with proper accent, "They ayn't so bloody merry these dyes." †

Pfc. JACK WRIGHT
G/5

I was told to report to sick bay. I found it set up in a Korean house. I was assigned with eight others to a little room. Believe me, those

---

*Craven, *History*, 40.
†Lawrence Schmitt was evacuated from Hagaru-ri and arrived in Fukuoka, Japan, on 6 December.

Korean houses can get awfully hot. I got my first night's sleep since that night in Yudam-ni when we watched the fireworks in the hills.

The next day I fell in line to see the doctor. He read my evac tag and told me to take off my gloves. It had never dawned on me to take off my gloves. I'd kept them on for a week at least, maybe more. When I pulled them off, half the skin on my hands came with them. The doctor chewed me up one side and down the other, told me if I'd washed with hot, soapy water every day like I was supposed to, this wouldn't have happened. I couldn't believe what I was hearing. Hot, soapy water . . . There'd been no water except that which could be chopped out of a frozen stream. Where in hell had this doctor come from? Could anyone have been in the rear that long not to know what was happening? I let him chip his teeth for a while. Finally I said, "Yes, sir," and walked out. Hot, soapy water . . .

I went looking for my outfit. No one seemed to know where George 5 was.

2d Lt. JOSEPH OWEN
B/7

At Hagaru-ri Colonel [Raymond] Davis called all the officers in the battalion together and explained to us the difficult situation we were in. I stood next to [1st Lt. William] Red Shea, who was with Charlie Company. "Bad Luck Charlie," we called him, and I was afraid to even stand next to him. Red had a severely sprained ankle. I don't think he'd been shot. He carried a staff and really hobbled when he walked.

Colonel Davis said, "If any of my officers don't think they can make it all the way, the planes are leaving right over there. You can just sign up and fly out." We were all Regulars. Jesus, wouldn't it look great on the old record. Yuk, yuk, Colonel. Everybody looked over at Red Shea. Red wasn't about to fly anywhere. He walked out, all the way.

Maj. Gen OLIVER P. SMITH
Commanding General, 1st Marine Division
The landing field at Hagaru-ri was nothing more than a bean field,
but it was frozen to a depth of eighteen inches, so all we had to do
was scrape it smooth. It was finished enough on December 1 for a
transport plane to get in and take out some wounded. The fourth plane
in was overloaded with ammo and its landing gear collapsed. This
finished the strip for that day. The next day we got it back to full
speed.

What we worked on first was removing the Task Force Faith
casualties. I'm afraid, though, some flew out who weren't in too bad
a shape—frostbitten fingers and so forth. What those Army jokers did
was to go down to the strip with a blanket and lay down on a stretcher
and groan a bit. The corpsmen would come along and onload them.
It was probably our fault. The Air Force sent up what they called an
"evacuation officer," and our doctor assumed this officer would see
that only the proper people were put on board the planes. But this
was not the evacuation officer's function at all. He thought only in
terms of planes, not what flew in them. Once we got a handle on the
situation, no one was evacuated who didn't have a ticket.*

5 December 1950
Litter patients continued to be evacuated by air during the day.
A "screening" line was set up for walking patients to determine
the seriousness of their wounds or illnesses and only those considered not able to make the remainder of the move were given
air evacuation. Total evacuation for the day by all units was 1,300.
                    HISTORICAL DIARY, 5TH MARINE REGIMENT

Pfc. WIN SCOTT
C/5
I lay near a runway. I could hear airplane engines. There was a fire-
fight going on nearby. My stretcher was out on the ground and there

---

* Smith interview, MCHC.

were a lot of other guys lying out there on stretchers. There was an
air strike in progress off to one side. Marguerite Higgins was there
interviewing guys. She'd kneel down to talk to them. I lay on my
stomach and didn't look presentable. She walked over to me, told me
she wanted to talk to me. I told her to go to hell.

Pfc. JAMES RANSONE, JR.
Task Force Faith
They loaded thirty-three wounded men on the two-engine cargo plane.
Our morale was real high. We thought everything was OK. I wasn't
too badly wounded, but I had an evac tag and I was going to be
flown somewhere. I didn't know where, but anywhere was better than
Hagaru-ri. The village was surrounded and I didn't want to do any
more fighting. My arm gave me some pain and I didn't have any feeling
in my toes or fingers. My tongue was numb and I hadn't tasted the
good meal I'd been given.

The plane took off. I waited for it to level off. It never did. It
began to dive. I panicked. The plane was going to crash! I watched
from the window. The propeller hit the ground first and flew off. I
was thrown against the bulkhead. Men fell all around me. There
weren't any straps or seat belts. Panic! That high-octane fuel would
burst into flame and explode! The plane slid to a halt. There was no
explosion or fire. Someone kicked the cargo door open. I hadn't broken
any bones, but was bruised all over. We unloaded the three litter patients. Everyone managed to get off the aircraft. Our boots had been
removed in the aid station back at Hagaru-ri so we stood by the crash
site in our stocking feet. We were in knee-deep snow, behind enemy
lines and with three wounded GIs who couldn't walk. It was a hell
of a fix. It seemed almost as soon as we climbed out of the wreck we
had air cover. The planes attacked the mountains on either side of
the valley we were in, then attacked them again. Those of us who
could walk carried piggyback the men who couldn't. Eventually, we
made it back to Hagaru-ri, where another plane evacuated us to
Hamhung.

Pfc. DOUG MICHAUD
Headquarters & Service Company/1/5
The airstrip at Hagaru-ri was used to fly out casualties and fly in replacements. Can you imagine what a horrible thing it must have been
to be a replacement? One day you're fat and sassy and living in Japan;
the next, you're in Hagaru-ri, it's 30 below, and a million Chinks are
shooting at you. I'm not sure they would have gotten me on the plane.

Pfc. EDWARD DAVIS
G/5
I was in a planeload of about forty Marines flown into Hagaru-ri as
replacements. The first thing I noticed when I stepped off the plane
was a 105-mm artillery battery firing at about 10 degree elevation at
a hill to our north that was no more than 1,000 or 1,500 yards away.
Hagaru-ri was in a flat valley with high ground encircling it. Off the
end of the landing strip there was a wrecked Corsair. Across the valley an air strike was in progress. Us replacements were lined up on
the road and processed. I watched a Corsair drop a napalm canister
which didn't go off. The plane circled around and came back strafing. One of its tracers set off the napalm in a mushroom of flame
and black smoke. Another Corsair dropped a few bombs. Then both
planes flew away.

Oddly enough, while we waited in line on the road, one of the
other replacements was hit in the wrist with something. After a short
while he was put in a plane that carried wounded men and flown
out. He didn't look that badly hurt. I remember thinking how lucky
I thought he was.

The weather was gray and overcast and it was snowing lightly.
Around dusk eight or ten of us were assigned to George Company,
3d Battalion, 5th Marines. So there I was, in a rifle company. I wondered if I would get out alive.

Maj. Gen. OLIVER P. SMITH
Commanding General, 1st Marine Division
While we were still in Hagaru-ri, we knew the bridge over the pen-
stocks below Koto-ri had been destroyed by the Chinese. Partridge [Lt.

Col. John, CO, 1st Engineer Battalion] knew this and was already planning what to do about it. He flew a light plane back and forth over the chasm where the bridge had stood and made notes and estimates while he figured out how to replace the bridge.

South of Koto-ri there was a power plant in the valley below the road. Four tremendous penstocks, or pipes, carried water down off the mountainside to the power plant. Where the penstocks cut the road, there had been a concrete bridge about thirty feet long. The Chinese blew the bridge, which left a sizable gap in the road. There was no possible way to get our vehicles around the gap—a cliff on one side, a precipice on the other—without a bridge. We knew if we were to get back to Hungnam, we had to put a bridge across the gap. It was as simple as that.

Partridge was kind of a grouchy guy. He came to me with a plan. He'd talked to the Air Force and had decided what he wanted to do was drop treadway bridge sections by parachute at Koto-ri. He intended to put this treadway bridge over the gap in the road. He admitted the Air Force had never before dropped treadway bridge sections—each one weighed 2,500 pounds. The Air Force, he told me, was willing to make some test drops to see if it was possible. I asked Partridge a few questions. "Now, look. Do you *know* this will work? Have you tried it before?" Then I asked, "Suppose one of the four sections is damaged when it's dropped? Have you any provisions for that contingency?" "Yes," he answered. "I've ordered double the number of sections I'll actually need." I kept on. "If all this treadway stuff fails, are you prepared to put in a trestle bridge?" (If we had had to do this, we would, of course, have lost our tanks.) He said, "Yes, I know where to get the timber." I could see Partridge was getting mad. He told me, "I got you across the Han River. I built you that airstrip out there [Hagaru-ri]. I'll get you a bridge!" "OK," I said. "I'll take that." *

---

* Smith interview, MCHC.

Pfc. JACK WRIGHT
G/5

When I heard we were going to move out again, I teamed up with another Marine, name of Lee, who was also wearing an evac tag. The truck we hitched a ride on carried eight dead Marines. At the time Lee and I couldn't have cared less.

Pfc. ERNEST GONZALEZ
F/7

We were allowed to carry any extra food we could find. I picked up a large K ration of powdered chocolate, small portions of which I knew I could mix with snow in my canteen cup. We were told if we had frostbite to have it checked before we left. I found an aid station and showed a corpsman one of my feet. He said it was all right. Unfortunately, I showed him my left foot. Later, at Masan, I discovered my right foot was much worse than my left.

Pfc. EDWARD DAVIS
G/5

The first thing I did with my new rifle company was help set up a perimeter. Soon, machine guns next to me opened fire on the south end of the valley. I joined in the firing. Tracers flew around for a while; then the firing died out.

About midnight we moved down the road in the direction we'd been firing in. No one slept that night, or the next one.

[The Marine attack to the south resumed at first light on 6 December. The 7th Marines was ordered to lead the advance along the MSR to Koto-ri. The 5th Marines would cover the movement out of Hagaru-ri, then protect the rear of the main column.

The regiments had used the two days in Hagaru-ri to rest their weary riflemen, fly out their casualties, and receive more than 500 replacements. The enemy had used the time to strengthen his positions along the MSR. A few weeks before, on their advance northward, the Marines had covered the eleven-mile hump between Koto-ri and Hagaru-ri in a matter of a few hours—morning chow in one village,

*lunch at the other. It would now take 10,000 Marines and more
than 1,000 vehicles thirty-eight hours to travel the same distance.]*

6 December 1950
1st Battalion—to move out at 0430 to clear the ground to the
right of the river;
2d Battalion—supported by tanks, to attack as advanced guard
along the MSR;
Provisional Battalion (31/7)—to clear the ground to the left of
the MSR;
3d Battalion—to bring up the rear of the regimental train, with
George Company disposed along both flanks as security for the
vehicles.

7TH MARINE REGIMENT, OPNO 14-50

Sgt. VINCENT MOSCO
H Battery/11
The battery continued to fire in support of the 7th Marines until it
was our turn to join the column moving south to Koto-ri. It was about
5:00 P.M. when the howitzers began to roll. Each section had its men
put a piece of white cloth on their backs. Each man then took his
turn walking in front of the blackout light on the vehicle. This system
helped in the pitch dark to keep the drivers on the road. The word
had been passed that everyone but the most severely wounded would
walk to Koto-ri.

Pfc. DOUG MICHAUD
Headquarters & Service Company/1/5
Just beyond Hagaru-ri we stopped and watched them blow the town.
Explosions ripped the area apart, all hell broke loose. The Chinese
would find nothing they could use in Hagaru-ri.

6 December 1950
The weather was bitterly cold as the convoy moved out and the
5th Marines fought a heavily contested rear-guard action all night
to protect the rear of the division train.

HISTORICAL DIARY, 5TH MARINE REGIMENT

Pfc. EDWARD DAVIS
G/5

The Chinese held the road in both directions and the hills on either side of it. Battalions took turns breaking roadblocks. The Chinese were never far away and the company got in a couple of good firefights. One was outside Hagaru-ri, near a small bridge we had to cross. The line stopped, and word was whispered back that Chinese troops were hiding under the bridge. Everyone opened fire on the bridge, then toward a steep ravine. The firing lasted a few minutes; then the column moved on again.

It was cold and the wind was vicious. Around my face I wore a scarf that my breath quickly turned to ice. The road was full of Marines, trucks, jeeps, and tanks. Whenever possible we huddled around exhaust pipes and tried to get warm. One place on the road we passed a convoy of trucks that had been ambushed and overrun.* Trash was everywhere. I remember a mailbag had been torn open and envelopes lay everywhere. There were also a lot of dead men lying around.

Pfc. DOUG MICHAUD
Headquarters & Service Company/1/5

We passed a convoy that had been ambushed. Hordes of dead Chinese were stacked up on either side of the road. The scene reminded me of one I'd seen often in the movies, the one where the wagon train is ambushed by the Apaches. Everyone was dead. The drivers still sat behind the wheels of their trucks. Footlockers had been pried open, mail satchels ripped apart, and the envelopes lay where the wind had blown them. We couldn't help ourselves; we bent down and looked at names and addresses. Personal effects were thrown everywhere. All this, frozen in time. There was no gore; it had all frozen. There was nothing but death. Some joker put a pack of cigarettes in the hand of a dead Chinese. Looked like he was offering you a butt. Another

---

* Task Force Drysdale had been sent from Koto-ri on 29 November to reinforce the garrison at Hagaru-ri and had been ambushed the same day. It was named for Col. Douglas B. Drysdale, commander of the 41st Independent Commando, Royal Marines, a reconnaissance unit assigned to the 1st Marine Division in early November.

Marine pushed a lighted cigarette in the mouth of a dead Chinaman.
It scared the hell out of me at first. The whole scene was eerie.

Maj. Gen. OLIVER P. SMITH
Commanding General, 1st Marine Division
I had quite a time with the Army people—they had no spirit. We
helped them as best we could. We flew in weapons for them, as they'd
thrown theirs away. They wouldn't put up tents; expected us to take
care of them, feed them, put up their tents. We disabused them of
this idea. Eventually, we salvaged 385 of these men and with other
soldiers formed a provisional battalion.* I attached it to Litzenberg.
It was pitiful. Litzenberg gave them the task of guarding the left flank
of the column in the breakout from Hagaru-ri to Koto-ri. Whenever
the Chinese attacked, the soldiers simply went through the column
to the other side.†

2d Lt. JOSEPH OWEN
B/7
From Hagaru-ri to Koto-ri, 1/7 had the right flank and that provisional Army battalion had the left. We constantly had to stop and
wait for them to come up. We took casualties because our left flank
was often in the air. Those "doggies" wouldn't move. When I was up
in the hills, I looked down on the road and saw groups of soldiers
sitting around. Nobody was telling them to move forward. When they
did, they didn't have any idea how to clear a roadblock or take a hill.
They did nothing.

Lt. Col. FREDERICK DOWSETT
7th Marines
We saw some troops over to the right of the road. In checking on
them, we found these Army troops, both ROK and U.S., had moved

---

*This provisional Army unit, made up of 7th Infantry Division soldiers including survivors of
Task Force Faith, was attached to the 7th Marines and is sometimes referred to as 31/7.
†Smith interview, MCHC.

over to the right of the road and were between the column and our right flank battalion. This meant there was nothing on the left side of the road. The movement of these troops was made without any authority. They still had their orders that had been given them previously that they would move to the left and rear of our 2d Battalion, which was astride the road.

These soldiers were needed to attack the Chinese who were firing on the convoy and making rushes with grenades. The Army officers said they didn't have control of their troops and couldn't get them to move. The ROKs wouldn't move, weren't organized, and there wasn't any way to move them to their proper position on the road. I then sent word back to the Army officers that if they didn't get their troops back to where they belonged, I would get a Marine unit to chase them there. If they still didn't move, we would open fire on them.

About 4:00 P.M. Lieutenant Colonel [Berry] Anderson* came up to the jeep I was riding in and told me he had lost control of his battalion, that he had no communications with any of the units, that he didn't know where any of his units were except that they were somewhere along the road, and that, because it was dark, it would be impossible to regain control of the battalion. We had already employed our 3d Battalion over on the left flank and had taken over the mission assigned to the Army unit. We thought, Let them follow along the road and get the hell out of the way. Everything would then go along more smoothly.†

Pfc. ERNEST GONZALEZ
F/7

We marched in two columns, one on each side of the road. We were told to keep a six-foot interval between us and the man in front and not to bunch up.

Sniper fire fell among the column. Everyone scattered for the ditches. We were immediately ordered back on the road. "It's only

---

*Lieutenant Colonel Anderson, USA, commanded the Provisional Army Battalion.
†Dowsett interview, MCHC.

snipers. If you get hit, there'll be a corpsman along shortly. Keep moving!"

All of a sudden a machine gun opened up. I dove for a nearby ditch, then moved to some better cover afforded by mounds of dirt. On the frozen ground near the road I saw the Marines who'd been hit. I recognized some of them. An officer nearby asked if we could find an officer from Fox Company. I volunteered. I ran from tank to tank looking for one of our platoon leaders. When I found one he was wounded. I returned and reported this to the first officer. Then I sat down with several other Marines next to a tank. There was a sudden explosion and an orange flash. A 90-mm shell casing flew out of the tank and smashed one of the Marines in the face. Everyone shouted at the men in the tank to let us know the next time they fired.

Someone ordered me to use my BAR and help break the roadblock. I ran to the ditch on my left and attempted to fire on the hill that rose from that direction. The BAR wouldn't fire. No matter what I did it wouldn't function. What the . . . After carrying the damned thing all the way from Fox Hill, I find it won't work! Disgusted, I threw it away, even forgot to field-strip it.

I watched our platoon sergeant draw a bead on an enemy soldier. The Chinese was on the run and going uphill. He was a long way away and looked the size of an ant. When our sergeant hit him with his first shot, we shouted with glee and slapped him on the back. We couldn't know it then, but in about half an hour, he, too, would be dead.

I made my way back across the road and began to look for a weapon. I crawled past a big sergeant who was standing up without a helmet and barking orders. He was hit in the head and fell next to me. He lay on his back, vapor came from his mouth. When I crawled past, I took his M1. "Sorry, Sarge, I need your weapon." I thought sure he was dead or soon would be. Then minutes later I overheard some guys talking about their sergeant who'd been shot in the head. He was still alive, they said, and mad with rage. He was quoted as saying, "Some blankety-blanky-blank stole my rifle!"

I ran back to the east, or left, side of the road. Fox Company had orders to attack the hill to our front. The signal to attack would be a white-phosphorus shell exploding on the hill. I was handed a

grenade, which I put in my parka pocket. I dropped my pack and
sleeping bag and said an act of contrition. The WP went off and I
started to run toward the objective. I was the last man on the left. In
a ravine I stumbled on Chinese who were hiding in one-man foxholes. A Chinese in front of me threw up his arms in surrender. I
motioned for him to approach, but he was shot by a Marine standing
next to me. The word was, no prisoners. I moved to my right. A shot
fired from a bunker across the ravine landed nearby. I dropped. Another slug landed in front of my face. I jumped up and ran (the best
I could) around the ravine. I dropped to the ground and looked around.
I noticed a trench to my left leading to a bunker. A Chinese stood
up and threw a grenade. It landed next to my head. I turned my head
away and waited. It never went off. I turned back and stared at the
damn thing. I was afraid if I touched it, it would go off. Someone
yelled to us to use our own grenades. I reached for mine but couldn't
find it; must have lost it when I ran around the ravine. A lieutenant
ran up and wanted to know where the Chinese grenade had come
from. I pointed to a foxhole near the trench. We approached the hole
together and found a Chinese who looked like he was dead. Both of
us knew he was playing possum. I fired at his chest, the lieutenant at
his head. Another shot, this one fired from the bunker, hit the lieutenant in the stomach. He fell. When I reached him he lay on his
back and had already lit up a smoke. We were relieved shortly afterward by an Army unit. I told a machine gunner about the bunker.

Near the base of the hill were five Chinese prisoners of war. The
word was to take no prisoners, but here were these five. One of them
was very tall and thin. Frozen blood hung from his nose like red ici-
cles.

Back on the road I learned that our platoon sergeant had been
shot in the heart.

I resumed walking to the south toward Koto-ri. I could see how
small Fox Company was. On my left were some ROK troops. We
left the road again and formed a skirmish line. Any houses we saw
were to be destroyed. Nothing was to be left for the enemy to use.
When we found an old hut, we told the ROKs with us, using sign
language, to burn it. When they set fire to the straw roof, the owner
rushed out. We left him yelling and screaming.

Toward evening I was back on the MSR. The sun was about to go down. The column stopped again and I rested beside the road and waited for something to happen.

Pfc. DOUG MICHAUD
Headquarters & Service Company/1/5
Between Hagaru-ri and Koto-ri, I got dysentery. I had earlier kicked in a hole in some ice next to a body to get some water. I was so thirsty. I couldn't do anything but foul myself. When one of the layers of clothing got to be too bad, I just cut it out. There was nothing anyone could do for me. Who in hell was going to go over to a corpsman who had spent the last week, day and night, trying to keep guys alive, and tell him you needed help with your runs?

They didn't want you to lie down at night to sleep, felt you'd freeze to death. If you lay down, someone was sure to come along and kick you until you stood up. My two buddies from Duluth and I found an ingenious way to get some sleep. Standing up and at a slight angle we put our heads together like a tripod and leaned on each other. Wasn't comfortable, but we did get some rest.

Hunger was a terrible problem. I came across four Marines huddled around a pathetic little fire trying to thaw a can of rations, four guys sharing one can. I said to Jerry Malone, "You know, I shouldn't feel this way, but I do. I'm almost ready to shoot those guys to get that can, I'm so goddamn hungry." "You hungry?" he said. "Ha, ha," and he starts laughing. Reaches down to the bottom of his parka and comes out with a can of C rations, chicken and vegetables, frozen like it had been in a deep freeze. "What the hell?" I said. "I'm starving to death and you're saving this?" We didn't have any problem building a fire of little sticks because we didn't build one. We just took our bayonets, ripped the damn can open, chopped the chow up, put the frozen pieces in our mouths, and let them thaw there. When I asked Malone why he had saved this one can, he said, "I was waiting for a special occasion!"

Lt. Col. RAYMOND DAVIS
1/7

Water was always a problem. It made no difference that the ground was covered with snow. We constantly ate the stuff to get our thirst under control. It didn't help much. Even when we added a little sickbay alcohol to our canteens, the water in them remained frozen. One of my runners was determined to get water somehow. In his efforts he would gather twigs and anything else lying around and try to start a fire. Every time we stopped, he'd build one of these little fires. Then he'd pack his canteen cup with snow. When it melted he'd add more snow. The little fire would go out and he'd have to get it going again. He'd work, work, work until I finally said to him, "You can't melt enough snow to make the effort worthwhile." He, too, eventually reached that conclusion and just gave up.*

2d Lt. JOSEPH OWEN
B/7

A round hit on the road. Ice and frozen road splattered us. Bifulk ran up to me: "I'm hit, Lieutenant, I'm hit. I'm going back."

"Where in hell you hit?"

"Right here, on my back. Right here."

"Show me blood."

"Well . . . Look, I've got a right to go back. I'm wounded and want to be treated."

"Let me see the blood. That's not . . . just ice and dirt. Get back in the column."

"Jesus, Lieutenant, goddamn . . . " And he shuffled off mumbling. I had to laugh.

Pfc. FRANCIS KILLEEN
A/7

There was a little elbow that stood out, a good spot to cover the company's withdrawal. Our platoon got the job. The Mexican was put

---

* Davis interview, MCHC.

out on the listening post. I'd been on the go for two days and nights. All of a sudden I had a pressing urge. Now this was a real work of art. In the wind and cold I was going to shed eight layers, drop my pants, squat, and go. This was probably the most courageous act in my entire career. When I started, I couldn't stop; this thing smoking in the snow must have been three feet long. I duck-waddled away from it. Like a good Marine I grabbed my entrenching tool and went to cover it. Sergeant Kline walked up at that moment. "Leave it, Killeen. When the Chinks get up here they'll think we got giants."

Pfc. JOHN BISHOP
I/7

Joe Unnuzzi, Nick Falcone, and I were walking together. The convoy moved very slowly. Stop and start, stop and start. Lucky if we went 100 yards an hour. Snow lay everywhere and it was very, very cold. A haze covered the moon. Somewhere Joe found a bottle of booze. I believe he found it in a pack someone had dropped or in one that belonged to a dead guy. Since we were going so slow, we decided to step into one of the abandoned houses that we occasionally passed and split the bottle. After each of us had a few good belts, Joe decided to light up a cigarette. Either the gooks, or our own guys, saw the match. Bullets flew around us. Something slapped my face. Nick yelled, "I'm hit. Oh, my God, I'm hit!" I took off my glove and felt my face and found blood and flesh from Nick's hand that'd been hit. Joe and I went out to the convoy and located a corpsman, who gave Nick a shot of morphine and bandaged his hand. Joe and I walked with Nick the rest of the night. In about a half hour, Nick told us whatever the corpsman had given him was making him feel good. He complained, though, that his thumb felt funny. We looked at his bandaged hand. The slug had caught him in the heel of the palm and exited through his thumb. In the dark the corpsman had bandaged Nick's hand the best he could. He had, however, left the thumb uncovered. Because it was frozen now it was numb. It sounds crazy, but Joe, Nick, and I got a good laugh out of that.

Pfc. FRANCIS KILLEEN
A/7

Then it was our turn to really get nailed. We'd been moving along at a good pace and there was talk we were a short way from Koto-ri and Chesty Puller's 1st Marine Regiment. It was night. We had long ago discarded our packs and were carrying sleeping bags over our shoulders, Spanish-American War style. The best weapon we had was our entrenching tool. We were walking on the reverse side of some godforsaken ridge. Suddenly, there were the Chinese! They seemed as surprised to see us as we were to see them. Their burp guns, no matter how cold it was, always seemed to work. I fired point-blank at one guy. Sparks came out of his ears. I swear it. The next one came right at me. Trying to balance on the slope of an ice-covered hill is no small trick. I lifted the rifle and noticed the operating arm had separated from the bolt. In eight years of training with a pig-sticker [bayonet], all I ever used it for was opening cans of beer. Here it was, like it or not. The Chink came in with a high off-the-shoulder thrust. I dropped to a crouch and parried his blade. It went past my ear. I caught him in the pit of the stomach. He said, "Ooofff." We went ass over. He got up first and ran down the hill. My damn bayonet hadn't gone in, just knocked the wind out of him. I grabbed my entrenching tool and waited. On my right I saw the big frame of Paul Yeasted. He looked awesome; with all those clothes on, he looked four feet taller than he was. A Chink saw him, too. He stopped, and began to run in the other direction. Paul had a clip of tracers that he used to help pick targets for the machine guns. He put one round between the Chink's legs, another past his ear.

Then I got knocked flat on my tail and felt an awful pain in my right side. I tried to get up, tried to get my breath. I kneeled in the snow on all fours. I heard the Mexican kid's voice. "You all right? You better git. Better git. Here they come again." If I needed motivation to get off that hill, I couldn't have thought of more inspirational words. I made it down that mountain in nothing flat.

Chaplain CORNELIUS GRIFFIN (USN)
7th Marines

The regimental train stopped outside of Koto-ri in the early hours of the morning [2:00 A.M., 7 December]. Sgt. Matt Caruso, my loyal clerk, and I climbed into a small ambulance to see if I could help anyone. The column was hit by enemy fire. Sergeant Caruso threw himself around me and screamed out, "Look out, Father! Look out!" Those were his final words, as he was killed right there. More bullets smashed through the windshield. One struck me in the jaw and went out my back. I fell on top of Sergeant Caruso's body. Dr. Bob Wedemeyer yelled, "Watch him." I asked whether I was bleeding to death. Bob said, "Don't let him exsanguinate!" (This meant, in Latin, "run out of blood.") I told him I'd forgotten more Latin than he ever learned. A corpsman [Chief Pharmacist's Mate Peter Ciani] told me to shut up so they could go to work. Bob Wedemeyer then ordered Sergeant Caruso's body removed from the ambulance. I protested. He said to me, "Padre, this ambulance is for the living, not the dead."

[The 2d Battalion, 7th Marines, was first to arrive at Koto-ri and, by 5:00 P.M. Thursday, 7 December, the entire regiment was inside the perimeter. The Chinese then closed in on the MSR from both flanks and attacked the main column, which was still extended along the entire length of the route. Characteristic of these engagements was the one fought by How Battery, 11th Marines.]

Sgt. VINCENT MOSCO
H Battery/11

About 10:00 P.M. [6 December] Lieutenant [Wilber] Herndon accompanied by Sergeant [H. E.] Blizzard ran up to me and told me to move my truck and howitzer forward. At this point we were just a couple of miles south of Hagaru-ri. It took some time to weave my way around all the vehicles that were stopped on the road. The rest of How Battery followed me but fell far behind. Sergeant Blizzard guided my section to a point where Captain [Benjamin] Read waited for us. As soon as I reported, he pointed to a draw alongside the railroad tracks and told me the enemy was hiding in it. My crew and I unlimbered the howitzer and prepared it for direct firing. Two vehicles in front of the gun were driven off the road.

By this time the Chinese were really pouring everything they had at the road. Mortar rounds, rifle and machine-gun fire, grenades and rifle grenades fell like hail. Because of the frozen ground, I believe the antitank rifle grenades were the most deadly. They'd fly over the convoy like so many flocks of birds. When they hit the frozen road, the shrapnel flew in every direction.

We began firing at the Chinese in the draw with a charge-four. Because the spades could not dig into the road, we realized this was too large. We reduced the charge to a one and resumed firing. Our casualties grew. My crew was reduced to three. Someone grabbed my arm and shouted in my ear to use a charge-seven. I turned and told the man that because we could not dig the spades in, the gun would recoil too fast for us to hold it. He shouted over the firing, "I don't give a damn about the difficulties, I want you to use a charge-seven." I hollered right back, "Who'n hell d'ya think you are?" and asked to see his horsepower. He flipped up the visor of his Mongolian piss-cutter [a fur-lined cap] and there, smack-dab in the center of it, was a silver oak leaf. He told me curtly he was Lieutenant Colonel [Olin] Beall [1st Motor Transport Battalion]. I asked him whether he'd take responsibility for damages caused by firing this large a charge. "Hell, yes," he shouted, "fire away."

I loaded the gun with the larger charge and hollered to everyone standing nearby to get away from the trails. Private Bender pulled the lanyard and we both jumped on the trails. The howitzer roared and away we went down the road. The left trail spade hit the radiator of a truck and the gun bounced to a halt. Colonel Beall ran up, told us he was sorry about the truck, and pitched in to help us return the gun to the railroad tracks. Some say you can't fire a 105-mm howitzer at a range of seventy-five yards without injuring the crew. We sure did that night, and survived the experience.

Around dawn [7 December] I could see the action occurring up and down the column more clearly. Our battalion executive officer [Maj. Norman Miller, Jr.] ran up and told me the skipper had spotted some enemy officers on a hill just east of our position. We turned the gun in that direction. There was no time to worry about elevation

or deflection. With Lieutenant Herndon spotting for us, I sighted over
the tube and cranked off a round. It fell long. The second round was
short and to the right. The next was right on target. So was the one
after that.

Someone came up and told me Sergeant Blizzard and the captain [Read] were down. I ran to where the stretchers lay and tried to
cheer Blizzard up with some silly remark. He was in a great deal of
pain. The battery corpsmen were doing the best they could. There
were just too many wounded.

We continued to fire our gun at targets of opportunity we spotted across the railroad tracks and down in the ravine. I spotted a number
of Chinese hiding behind a pile of railroad ties. I grabbed a round
without noticing the type and fired it directly into the pile. What a
fireworks display: white flame, smoke, splinters, and bodies flew into
the air. I had fired a round of white phosphorus.

The section continued to fire until Colonel Beall ordered us to
cease firing. He told us later he never wanted to hear anyone say again
that the artillery couldn't keep up its end of a good firefight.

Everyone helped load the wounded onto trucks, then we hooked
up the howitzer, which was still warm, and the convoy continued on
to Koto-ri.

*[Around midnight on 7–8 December, the last elements of the 1st Ma-
rine Division entered Koto-ri. Colonel Puller's already overcrowded perimeter now teemed with men and activity. With the arrival of the 5th
and 7th Marine Regiments, more than 14,000 men were crammed into
the village. Unlike Hagaru-ri, there would be no pause here, and before the last Marines trudged into the perimeter, orders were cut for
the advance to resume at first light on the 8th. This leg of the attack
would cover the ten twisting miles down the Funchilin Pass to Chinhung-ni.]*

Pfc. PAUL MARTIN
Reconnaissance Company/1st Marine Division
When the guys from the 5th and 7th Marines reached Koto-ri, they
looked terrible. Tired, dirty, hungry, cold—they had had it. I began
looking for friends. Found most of them had been killed. I overheard

one major say, "I have over fifty Medals of Honor to recommend. I don't know anyone's name, though. There was no time to get them or write them down."

1st Lt. WILLIAM DAVIS
A/7

The company marched into Koto-ri at dawn on the anniversary of Pearl Harbor [7 December], and though we were tired, as usual, most of us checked through the other rifle companies of the battalion to see how many old buddies were still with us. The 1st Marines manned the perimeter. Judging by the number of bodies outside, and some inside, they had been a trifle busy of late. After downing four or five meals of "Cs" [rations], I climbed into my beloved sleeping bag for a fifteen-hour snooze. When I awoke I was ready to charge again. In this Marine Corps it's good to feel ready to charge, because the opportunity always seems to be there waiting for you.

2d Lt. JOSEPH OWEN
B/7

By the time we reached Koto-ri, we were beat. They had warming tents for us. It was a big deal. They destroyed us—everyone just completely relaxed. All the company officers were in one tent. Jeez, someone came in to get us out. The warmth was wonderful. I couldn't move. The guys coming around getting us out were tough. One of them said, "Get out, you sumbitches, or we'll shoot you." Hank Kiser was so sick, we literally had to pull him off the deck. It was tough to get moving that day.

Pfc. EDWARD DAVIS
G/5

Once the company was settled in at Koto-ri, I walked over to an aid station. I'd been nicked slightly in the last firefight. It was full of seriously wounded men lying on stretchers. There were so many of them, they overflowed the tent and were placed outside in the cold. I returned to the company.

Groups of Marines huddled around little fires. Planes called Flying Boxcars dropped supplies to us. I made a small tent out of one of the parachutes. Despite enemy snipers, I managed to get some rest.

Pfc. FRANCIS KILLEEN
A/7

I found an aid station in a house by a frozen river. I saw a familiar face. It was Father Killeen, one of the boys from home but no relation. "Clansman, how badly hurt are ya?" By the time they got around to looking at the wound in my side, the good father had given me my last rites and a slug of sick-bay brandy. My cartridge belt had evidently been hit with a slug and two magazines had exploded. All I had were brass filings embedded in my side. They were trying to kill me in pieces. At this rate I'd last a hundred years.

Father came back and we chatted awhile. He told me Father Griffin had been shot in the mouth but it looked like he'd survive. I asked whether my buddy from Charlie Company, Vito Junivicious, had made it out before the trap snapped closed. "I'm afraid Vito didn't make it. They overran the aid station where he was. They shot everyone." That was a tough one to take. He was a good buddy. I thought of the time he made me go on a date because his girlfriend had a friend. God, she was two ax handles across the beam and weighed about 300 pounds. I almost killed him. "Get some shut-eye," the padre said. "You can check with battalion in the morning."

I was asleep when the fire began. When I woke up, the house was burning. It must have lit up the whole valley. On the way out, a sergeant grabbed a head or a foot and dragged. I was too dazed to get organized at once. I saw a sleeping bag and dragged it out. The building collapsed in an explosion of flame and sparks. The sergeant walked over to check the guy I'd dragged out. "Great! You pulled out a dead one."

Pfc. JACK WRIGHT
G/5

Lee and I found a bunch of soldiers preparing to burn a spare tent. We talked them into letting us have it and promised we'd destroy it before we left the village.

All well and good. We had a place to stay. Lee went scrounging and returned with two cases of C rations and an Army corporal. I can't remember his name, but believe he said he was with F Company, 31st Infantry. He'd been his company commander's driver and, as far as he knew, the only survivor of his company.* He had a jeep with a .50-cal mounted on it and a trailer full of mail sacks and personal gear which was to be sent home when he got down to the coast.

In a little while we heard a tap on the outside of the tent. I hollered for whoever it was to come in. A British Marine corporal came in and asked if it was OK if he billeted about twelve of his troops with us. "Sure," we said, "go right ahead. We'll appreciate the company." The Brits dropped their gear outside and entered the tent. The first thing they did was clean the place up. They tore the stove apart and cleaned it, then gathered up all the litter and threw it out. Lee, the Army corporal, and I took one look and headed outside. We were ashamed because we looked so cruddy. The Brits looked like they had come right off a parade.

S/Sgt. LEE BERGEE
E/1

Days earlier, the engineers had leveled off a runway north of E Company's perimeter. The runway was eventually extended [6–7 December] to accommodate transport planes. Sometimes these planes landed on the frozen runway in a blowing snowstorm. When the 5th and 7th Marines finally fought their way through to Koto-ri, planes used this runway to take out the casualties by the hundreds. Many of these casualties were, of course, wounded, but many others suffered from frostbite and intestinal disorders caused from eating frozen C rations and snow. Many of the latter suffered from diarrhea. Some men evacuated had pneumonia.

---

*This, of course, was not the case.

Lt. Col. FREDERICK DOWSETT
7th Marines

The Air Force and Navy transport pilots did a magnificent job in flying out the wounded. The strip at Koto-ri was an OY [a light observation plane] strip that had been built along the road. It was under constant enemy small-arms fire. I was evacuated out in a TBM [an Avenger Torpedo Bomber] that landed on it.* Later, at the hospital in Yokosuka, I saw men who had flown out in an Air Force C-47 that had landed and taken off from this little strip. †

N. HARRY SMITH
War Correspondent

I noticed that Marine and Army artillery pieces all along the perimeter defenses were lobbing an endless stream of shells into the hills to the north and discouraging the enemy from venturing too close to the encamped Marines. "When are we going to stop shelling those hills?" I asked a colonel.

"They haven't stopped for the past two days," he replied. "The reason we haven't slackened up on this cannonading is because we have more shells with us than we can possibly find vehicles to carry when we start marching out of here. Instead of blowing up all those shells, we decided to give the Chinese a bellyful of them. What's left over will be blown up tomorrow by Lieutenant Freudenberger and his disposal team.

"You see," the colonel went on, "we had tons and tons of shells of all types dropped to us by airlift during the time we have been up here, and prior to running into any large enemy concentrations. The amount dropped to us was nothing more than what would normally

---

*Lieutenant Colonel Dowsett had been wounded along with Chaplain Griffin during the attack on the 7th Marines regimental train in the early hours of 7 December.
† Dowsett interview, MCHC.

be required in any such offensive operation. But when we got hit heavy and ordered south, we loaded up with all the ammo we could carry and disposed of the rest of it. This is the best way to dispose of it: give it to the enemy in the manner they like least."

The hills surrounding the encampment were pockmarked with patches of every conceivable color. The patches were parachutes that had been used to drop ammunition and supplies to the fighting Marines. This was one of the great feats of the Korean War. The airlift established a lifeline for the Marines, who could not have survived otherwise. Cargo command had performed a superb job in the execution of the airlift. It never slackened its load drops until it became evident that our forces would have to about-face and fight south to Hungnam. It then became apparent that the continuation of such drops would prove a burden to the Marines, and might prove advantageous to the enemy. Therefore, only the absolute necessities were dropped once the push south started. Nylon had proven its worth. It looked as though Du Pont had moved into this frozen wasteland lock, stock, and barrel.

Pfc. ERNEST GONZALEZ
F/7

In Koto-ri the Air Force dropped supplies. Some parachutes didn't open and their crates crashed in the town. Some crates had contained boxes of C rations. We roamed in groups looking for certain types of food. My favorite was wieners and beans. I didn't find any. My least favorite was pork and lima beans. I found plenty of those.

S/Sgt. LEE BERGEE
E/1

Some of the most precious articles the Air Force dropped to us fell just east of the company perimeter. These were eight 2,500-pound sections of a large treadway bridge. Without them we would not have a way across the Funchilin Pass. The bridge we had used going north had been destroyed by the Chinese.

Maj. Gen. OLIVER P. SMITH
Commanding General, 1st Marine Division
It took one Flying Boxcar to carry one section of the treadway bridge.
We needed four sections, so we had the Air Force drop us eight. In
order not to kill anyone in Koto-ri, we dropped them outside the perimeter. One section fell into Chinese hands. We still had seven and
we didn't kill anyone.

Fortunately, General Almond, in one of his optimistic moods,
had the idea of establishing an advance Corps HQ at Hagaru-ri. He
had sent up a young lieutenant with tents and other stuff that included treadway trucks. These trucks had a special winch used to handle
the sections. It could have been done with a bulldozer, but the trucks
were better. *

1st Lt. DAVID PEPPIN
D Company/1st Engineer Battalion/1st Marine Division
Lt. Col. Jack Partridge [CO, 1st Engineer Battalion] asked me if I
knew the M-2 steel treadway bridge. I did. "Tomorrow morning," he
said, "we are going to lay this bridge across a chasm by the Changjin
Power Plant Number 1." The old bridge, he told me, had been destroyed by the Chinese and, before the Marine column with its trucks
and other vehicles could safely get down to Hungnam, another bridge
would have to be laid.

Pfc. PAUL MARTIN
Reconnaissance Company/1st Marine Division
The Catholic chaplain said mass. And what a crowd. Many men I
believed were atheists prayed and sang the loudest. If there had been
a collection, I believe the men would have given everything they
owned, little as that now was. The men lowered their heads and the
padre gave general absolution. His sermon was about the number of
martyrs and saints who had died for their beliefs.

Afterward the company received orders to follow the 1st Marine

---

* Smith interview, MCHC.

Division out of Koto-ri. You didn't need to be in the Marines long
to know this was a nice way of saying, "Recon Company will stand
rearguard action."

While the guys from Yudam-ni and Hagaru-ri passed through
our lines, I thought about the honor it was to protect the division's
rear.

Pfc. JACK WRIGHT
G/5
The British Marines left in the morning. Didn't see them again until
down on the coast. When they marched out of Koto-ri, they wore their
berets, and they were as cocky as all get out.

The Army corporal got his jeep ready to move. Lee and I went
out to see if we could find some more chow. We didn't. We gathered
instead all the ammo we could pack. When I was in sick bay at
Hagaru-ri and had walked out on the doctor, I'd left my gear behind.
I picked up somewhere an M2 carbine and another cartridge belt,
also a couple of canteens heavy with ice. We all met back at the tent.
We poured gasoline on it and set it afire. Then we joined the convoy
leaving Koto-ri. I rode shotgun beside the corporal; Lee climbed up
beside the .50.

*[The 7th Marines was ordered to attack south from Koto-ri at 8:00
A.M. on 8 December. A well–dug-in Chinese division held the high
ground that commanded Funchilin Pass and the MSR. The day began with a swirling snowstorm that dropped visibility to fifty feet. There
would be no air cover for the Marines until the snow stopped falling.]*

Maj. Gen. OLIVER P. SMITH
Commanding General, 1st Marine Division
We had to get the bridge site away from the Chinese. For Litzenberg
it was pretty slow going trying to take the hills on either side of the
road south of Koto-ri.*

---

* Smith interview, MCHC.

2d Lt. JOSEPH OWEN
B/7

We fought an unseen enemy the morning of the 8th. Their small-arms fire was heavy, rifle and automatic weapons hit us from the front and from the high ground to our left. The Chinese advantage was that we must pass through their well-placed zones of fire, but in the blinding whiteout we could not locate their positions. Progress was very slow and casualties rapidly reduced our already depleted numbers.*

1st Lt. WILLIAM DAVIS
A/7

We went 100 yards before we hit a frozen stream about 25 yards across. The first three men to dash across the ice made it; the fourth was cut in half by automatic fire.

All we needed was a little clearing of the skies and we could call up the equalizers—air and artillery. The snow never let up. I stood in a ditch and tried to look across the road. No dice. The artillery FO was going berserk, trying to get an estimate of range for his battery of 105s. Normally, a quick pass by a Corsair, or two or three artillery rounds, and this bottleneck would evaporate. But here, as long as the snow continued to fall, the Chinese had us.

Snow or no snow, we couldn't stay where we were for long. We all knew the longer the wounded stayed on the trucks the easier it was for frostbite to set in. All it took to get the old juices flowing was a glance at some of those wounded guys lying on the back of a six-by-six truck.

2d Lt. JOSEPH OWEN
B/7

Joe Kurcaba and I stood by the road as he traced on his map a route for my platoon to attempt a climb around the Chinese firing down

---

* Owen, *Gazette.*

on us from the left front. We were to locate and clear those positions that were holding back our advance.*

Cpl. MERWIN PERKINS
B/7

There was a lot of snow blowing around and the Chinks were really close. It wasn't as if they were three blocks away. Somebody hollered, "Mortars, up front!" That meant Bifulk and me. Someone yelled again, "MORTARS, UP FRONT!" Bilfulk and I went up. Nearby, I saw Lieutenant Kurcaba talking on a phone to a tank commander. There was a lot of fire coming in. He stood like he was at a church picnic. I shouted, "Kurcaba, get down!" Other people also hollered. All of a sudden, the lieutenant dropped. He was a good man, knew what he was doing and was all business. Never thought he was going to get hit. But you can stick out your neck too far, too.

2d Lt. JOSEPH OWEN
B/7

The bullet had pierced his forehead, just below the rim of his helmet. He fell forward, against me, and I put him softly to the ground. Joe Kurcaba, the old mustang, had led us well in many battles. He had been a good friend in difficult times.

Chew Een Lee was with his platoon on the right front, by the road. I told him he was now company commander, and he directed us to make the flanking movement that Joe Kurcaba had assigned.

We lost radio contact with Lee almost immediately after we began our climb. My miniature platoon reached the high ground without casualties, but before we could close with the enemy, a runner

---

* Owen, *Gazette.*

came gasping through the snow up the steep hill. "Lieutenant Lee's been hit. Lieutenant Taylor wants your platoon back down the hill."

Woody Taylor was waiting at the base of the slope. He had a tank coming up frqm battalion, and we would use it to cover a frontal assault. The snow had stopped and visibility had improved. There was a long, low ridge that began to rise fifty yards from the road, and we had glimpses of the enemy firing down on us from its crest.

Taylor ordered me to meet the tank at the road on our right flank. Moving along the line I counted twenty-seven men, Baker Company's remaining "effectives." They were firing prone in the snow, or from behind trees and rocks.

There was a man huddled behind a tree. He was not firing his weapon, nor was he facing the enemy. He was a teenage Reservist who had been with us since Pendleton. The fuzz on his face had collected a layer of frost that gave him the look of a bearded old man. I prodded him with my shoepac and told him to resume firing. His eyes showed no response, but, robotlike, he rolled over on his stomach. Facing the enemy, he began firing his rifle.

The Pershing [M26] tank was waiting at the road. It was buttoned up against the heavy fire, but I could talk to the commander on the handset aft. We threw a round of cannon along the ridge, then let them have the .50s. Enemy fire quickly diminished and the tank moved toward the incline.

Baker Company rushed forward on a line with the tank. Its treads broke a path for me through the snow and up the rising slope, and its guns kept the enemy pinned down. The men were firing and moving forward in quick rushes. Most were running, even though the snow was knee-deep. We wanted this hill fast.

Abruptly, the handset went dead, and I lost communication with the tank commander. At the same time, inexplicably, the tank veered sharply to the right, firing straight ahead. The enemy, less than twenty-five yards above us, popped up in their positions and resumed firing down on us. We were caught in the open.*

---

* Owen, *Gazette.*

Cpl. MERWIN PERKINS
B/7

Lupacchini and I were lying in the snow next to each other. He said, "Cover me," and he got up and ran forward before he dropped in the snow. Then he covered me while I ran forward. Next he said, "I'm gonna go to those rocks. Cover me." When he got near the rocks, he dropped again. I ran up and flopped next to him. "OK, Lupacchini." He didn't say anything. I touched him. His body gave off a smelly gas. It was right after that I heard someone yell, "Joe's down."

2d Lt. JOSEPH OWEN
B/7

A burp gun caught my left shoulder, spun me, then hit my right elbow. Then I was on my back in the snow.*

Cpl. MERWIN PERKINS
B/7

I carried Joe to the road, where I left him with some South Korean stretcher-bearers.

2d Lt. JOSEPH OWEN
B/7

My last memory of Chosin was a brief, lucid moment when I came to consciousness. I was lying by the road and a tank stood near me. I was warm and still, from the morphine. Then I remembered to wiggle my toes against the frostbite. Discipline stays with you all the way.†

Pfc. ERNEST GONZALEZ
F/7

When it began to get dark, I buddied up with another Marine. We borrowed picks and shovels when they could be spared and took turns

---

* Owen, *Gazette.*
† Owen, *Gazette.*

trying to dig into the frozen ground. We were not able to dig too deep a hole. To keep warm, we covered ourselves with a canvas. Machine-gun fire flew around. The tracers seemed to go right overhead. During the rest of the night, I heard Marines nearby trying to dig their holes deeper.

1st Lt. WILLIAM DAVIS
A/7

When night fell we pulled our numerically fewer troops into a perimeter below the crest of the ridge. Word was passed to pick off the Chinese when they charged over the hill. The plan worked well. The snow stopped falling, and the Chinese contrasted beautifully with the bright, snow-covered deck. Time and time again they rushed the perimeter, and our M1s picked 'em off like targets on a rifle range at Pendleton. Once the skies cleared our artillery FOs worked their radios. The whistle of "outgoing mail" told us the situation was no longer in doubt.

[The morning of 9 December dawned bright, clear, and cold.]

On this date the 1st Marine Division was poised on the top of the plateau in preparation for the hazardous trek down through the Sudong Gorge. As the first echelon of Marines started down the hill, flights of four planes hit Communist troops on either side of the canyon.

HISTORICAL DIARY, VMF-312

Maj. Gen. OLIVER P. SMITH
Commanding General, 1st Marine Division

Litzenberg finally moved down the road to his second objective. We started the bridge train behind him. It was necessary to get the bridge to the chasm as soon as possible. I believe we had two trucks. Mortar fire hit the road and Litzenberg worried the darn trucks would be hit. He told Partridge to go back up the road out of range of the Chinese mortars. He would send for the trucks later. Partridge went back up the hill. Off to the side of the road he saw what looked like a flat field. There were some tanks in the area which would give him protection. He backed one truck into the field with no problems. The second broke through an icy crust and was slightly damaged. The trucks stayed in this area until Litzenberg captured the bridge site. *

1st Lt. WILLIAM DAVIS
A/7

Complete despair was my reaction when I looked down from the high ground and saw that chasm between us and Chinhung-ni. Here was the great divide, this Korean mini–Grand Canyon that could cancel everything the Marines had achieved up to this point. The troops could climb down and then up the steep walls of the precipice and gain the road on the other side, but I knew there would be no way to carry the truck-bound wounded with us. To leave them was unthinkable. We were so close to breaking out. The company took up a defensive position above the proposed bridge site. Every man, I'm sure, shared my thought. "Let's go, Engineers!"

1st Lt. DAVID PEPPIN
D Company/1st Engineer Battalion/1st Marine Division

The Army trucks carrying the treadway bridge sections had turned around and backed down the road to the chasm. The power plant lay far below in the valley. Water from the Chosin Reservoir was fed into four large pipes and these pipes ran down the side of the mountain to the turbines in the power plant. Where before there had been a bridge that carried the road over the four pipes, there now was a wide gap. Off to the side I noticed a pile of bridging timbers engineers call "dead men." The Japanese had prepositioned them there many years before and they were a part of a system that made nearby villagers responsible for road or bridge repairs. It was not unusual in Korea to find a stack of them along the road, near a bridge, and I thought nothing more about it.

I decided to check the width of the chasm. Without a tape mea-

---

* Smith interview, MCHC.

sure, I carried some communication wire and crossed on the mountain side of the gap. When we ran out the wire and then measured
the distance, we discovered the bridge we had would be too short. It
wouldn't span the chasm. "Jesus Christ, what are we gonna do?" One
of the platoon sergeants got the idea. "Why don't we build a crib on
this little shelf? If we lay the bridge from the crib to the other roadway, it will fit. It ain't a good shelf, but it's a shelf. Build the crib
and lay the far end of the bridge there," and he pointed to the road
across the gap. The crib could be built with the pile of "dead men"
I'd seen up the road. Hell, it was a terrific idea. The Chinese prisoners were put to work carrying the timbers down the road to the site.
The timbers were measured and cut and the crib was constructed.
Colonel Litzenberg came up. "What's the delay? What's taking so
long?" "The bridge doesn't fit, Colonel. We're building a wooden crib
to extend the bridge and make it fit." "How long will it take?" "About
two hours." He looked at his watch. It was 1218. "All right, we cross
at 1418."

Within the hour the crib had been built: good timber, good perch.
The Army trucks backed down and dropped the bridge sections across
the gap. Once the treadways were laid, they were hooked together.
This part went fast. The treadways were far enough apart so that a
tank's treads would fit on them. A truck will not fit because the
wheelbase of a truck is shorter than the width between a tank's treads.
So, plywood boards were placed between the steel rails or treadways.

I had been ordered earlier, as soon as the bridge was in place,
to advance along the road and remove a steel railway bridge the Chinese
had managed to drop across the MSR. As soon as a battalion from
the 7th Marines crossed the treadway bridge, I went across with a
bulldozer. I asked some riflemen on a nearby ridge whether they could
see this new obstacle. They reported that it was there, all right.

I expected the obstacle to be defended, so wasn't completely surprised when a mortar barrage of twelve rounds racked both sides of
the road. The operator and I dove for cover under the bulldozer. After
a short while we crawled out from underneath and, when nothing
else happened, we drove down to the railroad bridge.

It was a great big thing. What in the world was I going to do
with it? It was just sitting there. The Chinese had simply dropped it
from its perch over the road. It seemed I had two choices. I could

blow it into sections and bulldoze them off the road or use a winch
to pull it off. Either way, a lot of time was going to be spent removing this obstacle. What the hell, I thought I'd try something. I ordered the dozer operator to give the machine full power and push the
bridge. If that bridge had been dropped on an American highway, a
bulldozer wouldn't have been able to budge it. But on that narrow,
humped, icy road, by God if the bridge didn't begin to slowly move.
I stopped the operator and got him to move the dozer to one end of
the bridge. The operator gunned the engine again and, damn, if the
bridge didn't slowly swing off the road. Beautiful!

On my way back up the road to report that the obstacle had been
removed, the dozer was bracketed by another mortar barrage. I believe this time the mortars were not Chinese, but American. A piece
of shrapnel hit the guy driving the bulldozer. The bridge was easy;
the mortars were hard.

*[Throughout the night a flood of people and vehicles, stretching back
to Koto-ri, crossed the fragile treadway bridge.]*

Lt. Col. JOHN PARTRIDGE
1st Engineer Battalion/1st Marine Division

The sensation throughout that night was extremely eerie. There seemed
to be a glow over everything. There was no illumination and yet you
seemed to see quite well; there was artillery fire; there was the crunching
of many feet and many vehicles on the crisp snow. There were many
North Korean refugees on one side of the column and Marines walking on the other. Every once in a while there would be a baby wailing. Everything added to the general sensation of relief, or expected
relief, and was about as eerie as anything I've ever experienced in my
life.*

*[At 2:45 A.M. on 10 December, advance units of the 1st Battalion,
7th Marines, arrived at Chinhung-ni. The rest of the division poured*

---

*Lt. Col. John Partridge, as quoted in Lynn Montross and Capt. Nicholas A. Canzona, USMC,
The Chosin Reservoir Campaign, vol. 3 of *U.S. Marine Operations in Korea, 1950–1953*
(Washington, D.C.: Historical Branch, G-3, Headquarters, U.S. Marine Corps, 1957), 323.

*down the winding mountain road in a seemingly endless stream of troops
and vehicles. By that afternoon the last Marines in the perimeter began leaving Koto-ri.]*

N. HARRY SMITH
War Correspondent

From the top of the hill, we had a bird's-eye view of the convoy-
forming operation of the camp. Huge parachutes had been used to
drop supplies to the embattled Marines at Koto-ri, Hagaru-ri, and
Yudam-ni. These parachutes had been cut away from their loads and
used by the Marines to cover tanks, antitank guns, cannon, and ammunition dumps as protection against rust, corrosion, and frost. Now
there was no longer any use for them. The parachutes were thrown
away and were now caught by the windswept air currents—ghosts in
the wind.

The convoy showed signs of being ready to move. Marines who
were designated convoy flank guards were jumping up and down, first
on one leg, then the other, in a futile effort to fight the bitter wind
and cold.

The Marine command knew that the Chinese were in the hills
to the north of us, observing our every move, yet not trying to halt
our loading and assembling operations.

My jeep had been assigned to the convoy about one-quarter distance from the tail end. In front of us was a large truck carrying mortar and machine-gun ammunition, and to our rear was a jeep. The
view further back was obliterated by the personal gear that was stacked
to the height of the jeep driver's head. Behind the jeep came the heavy
mobile equipment—dual-wheel International trucks, antitank guns,
reconnaissance trucks with .50-caliber machine guns mounted on
them, a long line of 105-mm and 155-mm cannon—followed by a
few jeeps and tanks bringing up the rear.

The train was organized to move out in sections, each section
having adequate firepower for its own tactical operation. Each section
of the train was spaced a quarter-mile interval from the next. Each
vehicle in the column was likewise spaced about fifty yards from the
vehicle directly to its front and rear. This gave added assurance that

the enemy would not be able to exact wholesale destruction of an entire section if they attacked the convoy.

High on the mountain ridges, on both left and right flanks of the road, we could see Marines and GIs moving south, keeping pace with the train. These patrols had been detailed the night before to take up positions serving as phase points Able, Baker, Charlie, and Dog. During the night a number of pitched battles took place between these patrols and the enemy, who had tried to dominate the ridges so they could cover our train with fire.

Orders to the effect that the driver *only* was to ride in each vehicle of the convoy assured further safeguard against excessive loss of life should the train come under enemy fire. This order also augmented the strength of our immediate column guards, swelling the ranks of the walking Marines.

Each man looked like a walking arsenal. Aside from the rifles they carried, hand grenades were strung over their chests, around their waistlines, and even upon the sleeves of their parkas. Someone in the column had remarked that they looked like a "walking army of Christmas trees."

I noticed that many of the men walked with a peculiar gait resembling men treading barefoot across a plank studded with spikes. They looked like light-footed marionettes; they kept bouncing off the balls of their feet. These Marines were walking upon frostbitten feet and had refused to turn themselves in to the doctor for fear of being evacuated by air as so many of them had been. Others were too proud to complain. Their pride kept them in the designated category of "walking casualties."

Pfc. PAUL MARTIN
Reconnaissance Company/1st Marine Division
Our position was in the eastern sector of the town. As the division passed through, Koto-ri became more and more empty. It wasn't long before I felt I was in a ghost town. The sun began to cast long shadows on the hills. The last tanks rolled south. My teeth banged together and I felt colder than I'd felt before. Our gunny came around checking on us. "No matter what happens, I'll be here with ya. We're

Marines. We'll stand to the end." I think he was as frightened as the rest of us, but was doing a good job fighting it. The only sound now was that of the wind. In the distance I saw Marines coming down off the western hills and starting to hike southward. My buddy said, "Something must be wrong. Maybe the division's forgotten about us." I thought about the chaplain's sermon the day before. We began to receive some mortar fire and long-range small-arms fire. It looked as if we were going to be pinned down. Sniper fire from the western hills that had just been abandoned by a rifle company flew overhead and kicked up snow and dirt. My buddy said, "I don't care if we leave later. Let's have it out with them bastards once and for all. Let's kill each other. Tired of waiting, walking, climbing, freezing. Let's get on with it." Maybe this explains how many scared men become heroes. What better choice did we have?

Korean civilians poured through Koto-ri. Many were screaming. Our officers yelled, "OK, let's get out of here. We should be out of here." The small-arms fire was heavy now. Most of it was long-range and wasn't causing us any difficulty. A round bounced off my buddy's helmet. We leapfrogged, gully to gully: when one unit dashed to the rear, another covered it. We left Koto-ri in this manner. It was now very dark. Down the road a little ways, we ran into a platoon of tanks that was holding the civilians back. I ran up to the first one to call in fire on the hills from where we knew the Chinese were shooting at us. The phone box was empty. I couldn't believe it. It was like going to a police box to report an emergency and finding no phone. I ran to another tank and began directing fire on our old positions. Next thing I remember, I was lying in the snow bleeding from the nose. That's when I learned the concussion one of those tank's 90-mm cannon blasts has. I was put on a jeep and driven to the top of the pass.

N. HARRY SMITH
War Correspondent
I was determined to see the dumps blown up, and the only way I could do this was to join the tanks at the top of the hill. Having decided upon my action, I told the lieutenant what I intended to do. He explained that tank commanders were a breed all their own; they

did not tolerate any unnecessary burdens in any of their operations, and I might be considered such a burden. He suggested that I receive prior OK from the tank commander in charge of the coverage operation.

There were about twenty-five tanks at the end of the column, their crew members bursting with activity: walking around the lumbering monsters with wrenches in their hands; working on the treads; assembling and disassembling machine guns; and adjusting radio communication antennas.

Captain [Bruce] Williams, commanding officer of B Company, 1st Tank Battalion, was talking to a gun captain when I walked up to him. My request confused the captain. It was clear that he had never before been confronted with such a request, and, after passing silent judgment, said, "I'll assign you to the last tank. I'm not vouching for your safety, but you'll be in pretty good hands because the boys on that tank are my best."

It was 3:30 in the afternoon before the entire train had cleared the campsite and begun its course south as a whole unit upon the road. Nothing remained in the camp now but bonfires from which billowing streams of smoke rose skyward. What had once been an orderly, compact village was now a large patch of snow- and ice-covered tundra.

We crossed the shallow stream at the southern exit of the camp and rolled to a stop at the top of the first hill on the road. We had assumed a position 1,000 yards from the demolition team and were abreast of the two tanks that had preceded us.

To the northeast we could see the four tanks that had been guarding the refugee group. They were now racing across the snow-field at high speed to join us at the top of the hill. The tanks passed the ammunition dumps, churning up a cloud of snow that momentarily obliterated the view to their rear.

Riflemen clinging to the top of the onrushing tanks, the muzzles of their rifles pointing in the direction from which they had come, jumped to the ground in a wide leap as the charging tanks joined us with a clanking, jarring stop. Jumping down from the tank I was seated upon, I joined the men who had taken up kneeling positions with rifles cradled in their arms.

In the distance we saw the mass of refugees running toward the ammunition dumps and the road. As they came closer their howling, near-savage, and pitiful cries for mercy pierced the air.

The demolition-team jeep was now racing across the snow toward us, Major Williams the sole occupant. As he rolled to a stop alongside the tanks, he shouted to the battalion tank commander, "Where in the hell is the guy who is meant to give us the word when to let her blow?"

"I don't know who he is or where he is," the tank commander shouted back at him. "Let the sonovabitch blow! We're covering you. You can't wait any longer." With that, the major turned the jeep around and raced back across the snow to the dumps.

The group of refugees by this time had come to within 500 yards of the dumps, stopped, and were crouching in the snow. Lieutenant Freudenberger and his men had opened fire with their rifles, and were shooting over the refugees' heads in order to hold them back until the fuses at the two dumps had been ignited. Then the men would run for their jeep.

"Jesus!" yelled the Marine kneeling at my side. "There must be a million of the bastards!" Out of the hills to the northwest poured hundreds of Chinese soldiers. Like ants running toward a drop of honey, they came shouting, shooting rifles and burp guns, crawling on their stomachs, stumbling, running toward the ammunition dumps.

"Clobber the bastards!" shouted a Marine. Another Marine to my right ran ten feet out into the snow, fell flat to the ground and opened fire with his rifle.

WHOOOM—WHOOOM—WHOOOM. The 90-mm gun on the tank directly above me spit shells with an angry roar. The earth at my feet heaved slightly, then settled down with a soft, convulsive spasm. Now all the tanks had turned their big guns upon the hills, lobbing shells into the onrushing horde of Chinese. The shells swished through the air, struck the ground with a thud, then exploded, sending gushers of snow, dirt, and flesh flying through the air in all directions. Wherever the shells hit, they killed Chinese in droves.

The flatland at the foot of the mountains was swarming with thousands of the enemy—still running, screaming, and shooting. One Chinese soldier hesitated a second amid the confusion, took a few steps, and dropped dead. Blood gushed in a great fountain from his short, stubby neck as he took the last few steps into eternity. He had no head. Tankmen opened fire with their machine guns, spraying the field from left to right, then from right to left.

Wherever one looked along the base of the mountains, the ground was covered with huge heaps of brown-clad, quilted, enemy dead. Extending to within 400 yards of the dumps was a solid field of them, the snow barely visible any longer. And still they kept coming.

Flat upon my stomach by this time, I crawled around to the front of the tank to get a better view of the activities. Racing across the snow, with bullets puncturing the white blanket at the churning wheels of the rolling jeep, the demolition team joined us at the top of the hill. No longer threatened by the rifle fire of the demolition team, the refugees began running toward the dumps to gain access to the road.

"Hop in!" Lieutenant Freudenberger shouted to me as the tanks began to move into column position and disappeared over the crest of the hill, racing to join the rest of the regimental train. As I jumped into the front seat of the jeep I landed on top of Sergeant Lynch and Major Williams. Turning my head to the rear as we disappeared over the top of the hill, I heard a loud CRRRRRWOOOM— CRRRRRWOOOOM! The two dumps went up in a gigantic earth-shaking roar, the refugees still a safe distance from the explosion.

We were receiving small-arms fire from the hills to our right, bullets swishing past our ears as we crazily careened up and down the narrow, hilly road. The enemy were breaking out of the mountains in groups, jumping up and down in jubilation. Their happiness was not justified. We had taken a terrific toll on their army in the space of a few minutes.

Pfc. PAUL MARTIN
Reconnaissance Company/1st Marine Division
Near the treadway bridge, the company re-formed into teams that were to accompany the tanks through the pass and down into the valley. My nose had stopped bleeding, but was frozen, and I had difficulty breathing. All the trucks had gone past. The tanks had taken up a blocking position on the road. I rode on the lead tank. Just before we reached the bridge, we learned the last tank in the column had stalled, then been engaged in a firefight. Recon Company was ordered back

to help out. Rather than move around the winding road, we took a straight path across the hills. We climbed and slid and saw nothing. Orders were received to hurry back to the bridge.

N. HARRY SMITH
War Correspondent
Slowly, inch by inch, our jeep moved down the steep grade until it came to the north side of the treadway bridge, where it was stopped. "Now take 'er easy, driver," said one of the engineers directing traffic over the steep structure. "Come on. . . . Easy now . . . Got t'keep those wheels of yours 'tween the markings. . . . That's it. . . . You got it made now. . . . Over! Now for the next sonovabitch!"*

"Wow!" exclaimed Sams as he rolled the jeep to the south side of the bridge. "One little itsy-bitsy slip and this bouncin' betsy would have gone down there," pointing to the floor of the deep canyon lying 2,000 feet below to our right.

Deep in the canyon we could make out the outlines of the snow-covered cables that shimmered in the air and penetrated the blackness like a graph drawing of a radiological wave. They broke off at the gigantic electric turbines, which were not visible. We had negotiated the pass as far as the first power plant. We now had only a few miles of traveling down the mountain before we would come to the second power plant and the flat country.

"Now do ya believe we'll make it?" said Sams, delighted in his successful navigation of the jeep over the bridge. "I don't think there's much to worry 'bout from now on. Only, ya can't tell. Those gooks are liable to pop out of the thin air. Don't trust those bastards, no-how!"

---

* Partridge, in laying the beams of the bridge, had to compute minimum widths so that every vehicle—from wide-tracked tanks to narrow-width jeeps—could cross. The result was about a one-inch inboard clearance for tanks and a one-inch outboard clearance for jeeps.

Maj. Gen. OLIVER P. SMITH
Commanding General, 1st Marine Division

Finally, the Reconnaissance Company was the last to cross the bridge. They shouldn't have been. Lewie's [Puller's 1st Marines] should have been last out. When the last Marine crossed and Partridge verified they were the last, he ordered the bridge blown. Afterward, Partridge said in an interview, "I had a sense of well-being after everyone had crossed over and I'd blown the bridge." *

[South of the bridge Marine units in the hills began discovering large numbers of Chinese troops too dispirited to fight, too numb and cold to run.]

Pfc. PAUL MARTIN
Reconnaissance Company/1st Marine Division

After we had crossed, we were told to climb the next ridge and make contact with the rifle company defending the road from that position. We reached the crest around daybreak and found the position deserted.

Next we saw about twenty unarmed Chinese soldiers slowly walking toward us. Farther back on the ridge more Chinese with hands over their heads waited for us. They looked frozen and numb. I couldn't find it in my heart to hate them. They were there for the same reasons we were there: orders.

Sgt. M. J. VANDERVEEN
E/1

South of Koto-ri, 2d Platoon, Easy Company, was given the job of guarding the flank for the column. We moved off the road up into the hills. As we climbed above the road, I came across two Chinese soldiers squatting in the snow. They were frozen stiff in their padded cotton uniforms and tennis shoes. They must have died as they tried to escape the numbing and deadly cold of that Korean winter night.

---

* Smith interview, MCHC.

S/Sgt. LEE BERGEE
E/1

Several exhausted Chinese we captured told our interpreter they had
hiked hundreds of miles from western Korea. They wore mustard-
colored quilted uniforms and tennislike rubber shoes. They would run
at night along the ridges, sweat, and the sweat would freeze. I saw
some prisoners whose feet were the size of footballs. Some of them
had to have their fingers broken in order for us to take the rifles from
their frozen hands. They suffered from the cold as much as we did.

Once, when I was on a ridgeline walking flank guard, I came
upon a Chinese soldier. He sat on his haunches, his rifle leveled right
at me. I almost fired, then I saw he was dead—frozen stiff in that
position. His skin was all puffy and glossy black.

Sgt. SHERMAN RICHTER
B/7

We began to capture a lot of Chinese. It was snowing, there was no
air cover, we were out of food, we climbed hill after hill. Now we
had prisoners. Down on the road battalion sends a message: "Send
the prisoners down for interrogation." We said, "Fine." The Chinese
were lined up and shot. A message was sent back down to battalion:
"The Chinese tried to escape and we shot them." We had no time
to bring prisoners down to the road.

*[Along the MSR the long column of men and vehicles snaked down
toward Chinhung-ni.]*

Pfc. ERNEST GONZALEZ
F/7

My feet were bad and I was lucky to get a ride in a jeep. A sergeant
also jumped on with me. Because of the road's icy condition the jeep
slipped and slid in every direction. Finally, after a mile of this, the
driver ordered one of us to get off, said he was overloaded. The sergeant and I stared at each other. Neither of us spoke a word. I slid
off. My feet hurt worse than ever.

N. HARRY SMITH
War Correspondent

As we progressed through the pass, the high bank on our right gradually leveled off even with the road, revealing a sheer drop of 2,000 to 3,000 feet. The road bank to our left rose in a straight perpendicular line for hundreds of feet, against which both men and vehicles clung in shrinking terror.

Inch by inch and yard by yard we progressed, the vehicles traveling about five miles an hour. The drivers sat hunched over the steering wheels trying to negotiate the blind turns and the razor-sharp, snow-covered rocks that protruded in clusters like so many daggers. Tears of strain rolled out of their eyes and dropped at their feet in tiny crystals of ice.

In the distance to the right, the mountains rose in jagged peaks, the tempest of the howling wind swirled the snow across the open canyon and spent its force upon the moving column. Nothing froze but the already frozen; nothing remained in this area but frozen mountains, freezing marching men, and sputtering, steaming vehicles.

Water became an acute problem. Canteens were frozen solid, their plastic caps shattering into dozens of pieces. Food was out of the question. Rations were solid chunks of ice. Men hungered, thirsted, and froze. But the train always moved southward, closer to the bottom of the pass and the flat country below.

I thought to myself, Thank the good Lord for this opportunity to walk upon my frozen legs. I didn't want to ride in *any* vehicle over this hellish road, down a mountain that never leveled off into flatness. I didn't want to be seated in the jeep, holding on to it in prayer, praying every second that we would not run over a small stone in the road, slip, and be catapulted into the ravenous emptiness.

Men were shouting abuse upon the enemy and the elements as they trudged along. "The sonovabitch is bleedin'," spoke the man in front of me. The wind had cut his bearded face to ribbons.

[In front of the tanks that guarded the column's rear, Marines plodded southward. Although occasional enemy ambushes would still have to be fought off, the big battles were left behind. Most Marines passed

*through Chinhung-ni without incident, the mountains surrounding the
Chosin Reservoir receded into the distance. The MSR was now under
the protection of the 3d Infantry Division. Ahead lay Sudong-ni, Majon-dong, Oro-ri, Hamhung, and finally the port of Hungnam, where
the Navy waited. From Chinhung-ni to the sea, it was just a matter
of putting one frozen foot in front of the other. Forty-three miles to
go.]*

Cpl. FRANK BIFULK
B/7

Walked down the mountain. It's hard to believe but, honest to God,
when we hit the valley it was like going from Minnesota to California. Boom! It wasn't cold anymore.

Cpl. ROBERT KELLY
B/7

I was walking, walking, and so tired. I wasn't with anyone else from
Baker 7. I finally had to sit down. A corpsman came by. "What's the
matter, buddy?" "I can't walk no more. My feet give out." He started
to laugh. "What the hell's so goddamn funny?" "You dumb asshole,
you're shot." "You crazy?" He took a bayonet and cut my shoepac
off my right foot. There was blood in the snow. My feet were so frozen I'd walked and not known I'd been hit. To this day don't know
when or where.

Pfc. JACK WRIGHT
G/5

We raced down the road. It's amazing how all hell can break loose
in one place and somewhere else nearby it's as calm as a summer's
day. The armored personnel carrier I rode in pulled into an Army

outpost about a mile below where we'd hit a roadblock. There was a lone soldier out in front of a little Korean house. The rest of his outfit was up in the hills. We asked him if we could wait there until the rest of the convoy caught up. "Fine," he said.

We went inside the house to warm up and found the treasure of all treasures—water that wasn't frozen. Five gallons of it. We nearly drank the tub dry. I also unearthed some Army five-in-one rations, stuff Marines seldom, if ever, saw. Unfrozen food! Well, the cans were too big to stuff inside my pockets, so I couldn't steal them. I did find a box of chocolates, though. I cleaned it out, took every bar. It was probably a hell of a thing to do to a guy who had invited us in out of the cold, but we were hungry.

When the convoy finally broke through the roadblock and pulled up outside the Army outpost, we mounted the personnel carrier and drove off. The soldier ran out onto the road hollering about someone stealing his food. I kept my mouth shut. Down the road five miles or so I pulled out the candy and passed it around.

M/Sgt. THOMAS BRITT
Headquarters Battery/3d AAA Battalion/3d Division
Our task force made contact with the Marines and was able to keep the road open, enabling them to pass through us on the way to safety. Cold chills still go up my spine as I recall watching Marines, themselves frozen from head to foot, meticulously caring for their wounded and bringing back the dead bodies of their comrades. The Marines were battle-scarred, but still looked as if they could do battle. It reminded me of pictures I've seen of General Washington's frozen troops at Valley Forge.

2d Lt. JOHN CAHILL
G/5
We got right into the 3d Division's lines; they never even challenged us. Somebody came around with a string of trucks. "Do you wanna ride into Hamhung?" I yelled, "No, no. We've walked this far, we're gonna walk the whole way." No better way to freeze than get on a

damn truck and sit. I'd find kids sitting by the side of the road or trying to ride on a tank. "Hey," I'd say, "you wanna lose a leg, wanna lose an arm? You gotta keep moving." That's all you needed to say and the kids would get up and start walking.

Pfc. DEAN WESTBERG
B/7
I was in a unit, scrounged from men in the hospital at Hungnam, that held a defensive position on the MSR through which the division eventually passed. The guys looked grubby, hadn't washed or shaved. They straggled along the road in groups or individually; some here, some there. There didn't seem to be any organized units marching together. I went down to these people and asked for information about my unit, Baker 7. No one knew anything, only about himself. Trucks carrying the dead and wounded streamed by.

Pfc. PAUL MARTIN
Reconnaissance Company/1st Marine Division
We reached the low ground and slowly passed through a defensive line the Army had established. We expected to turn around here and set up a defensive perimeter. Instead, our officers told us we were going to Hungnam for hot chow and then aboard ship.

Pfc. ERNEST GONZALEZ
F/7
It was getting dark when an officer got my group into a truck and we rode to a railroad siding [at Majon-dong]. What was left of Fox Company boarded a gondola car which had no roof. The more hardy and curious stood up and looked around. I huddled in what little warmth I could find. I looked up at the stars and worried about being ambushed.

Lt. Col. RAYMOND DAVIS
7th Marines *

Down off the mountain a railhead had been established. From it, a train shuttled back and forth between the base of the mountain and a reception area near the coast. In getting off the mountain, a lot of strays wandered in and out of our group. When the train pulled in to carry us down into the valley, we were somewhat disorganized. I grabbed a few officers and NCOs.

I was beginning to get the situation sorted out when over on one side of the train a soldier uncovered a large stockpile of sweets that had been hidden by a canvas covering. He yelled out for everyone to hear, "Anybody want candy? Come over and get some." For a while we lost control. Here were piles of boxes of candy, and for the first time I realized how starved we were. The only way I could resolve the problem was to send some of my leaders around behind the stockpile and carry as many boxes as they could onto the train. Once we had transferred the candy to the train, the men crawled on the cars to get at it. When everyone was aboard, off we went. †

Cpl. FRANK BIFULK
B/7

Around the train guys were telling us where to go. Baker Company had a couple of cars reserved. We climbed on board. Inside were big cases of Tootsie Rolls. In the service you get used to robbing food. Merv and I filled our pockets. We must have looked guilty or something. A lieutenant walked by. "You men don't have to steal that. It's all yours. Just help yourselves." I thought it was like being locked in a candy store. I felt like a kid.

Lt. Col. RAYMOND DAVIS
7th Marines

During the train ride, to my amazement, I ate five or six of these large Tootsie Rolls. When we arrived at the reception area, the men

---

* Davis had replaced the wounded Dowsett as regimental executive officer at Koto-ri.
† Davis interview, MCHC.

were immediately led to a continuously running chow line. In two hours I ate something like eighteen pancakes.*

11 December 1950
When the train arrived at Hamhung troops were disembarked, placed aboard Army trucks for movement to the regimental bivouac area, Yonpo Airfield. All personnel were billeted in the bivouac area . . . with tents, stoves, galleys with hot food, water, and a security guard. The remainder of the day and the morning of the following day personnel spent the time resting, reading mail, and making preparations for going aboard ship.

SPECIAL ACTION REPORT, 1/5

Cpl. FRANK BIFULK
B/7
When we got off the train, there were trucks to transport us the rest of the way to the port area where the troopships were waiting. There were four big deuce-and-a-halves waiting for Baker 7. What was left of the company didn't fill half of one of those trucks.

Pfc. JACK WRIGHT
G/5
We pulled into the outskirts of Hungnam. I asked an MP directing traffic the location of 3d Battalion, 5th Marines. He pointed away from the direction the personnel carrier was headed. I shook hands with the Army corporal, said good-bye to everyone else, and hopped off.

In a little while I picked up a ride going the direction I wanted to go in. Two hours later I found my outfit, or what was left of it. I reported in to my company first sergeant. He looked up from the papers on his field desk. "Wright, you're damn lucky." I asked him why, considering the shape I was in. He showed me a long list he'd been

---

*Davis interview, MCHC.

working on of men missing in action or killed in action. My name was on it. He asked what had happened to me. I showed him the evac tag I was still wearing. He asked, "Well, what are you gonna do?" I tore the tag off and handed it to him. "To hell with it, S'arnt. Ain't worth it." He told me where I would find my platoon area.

I hobbled down there, but didn't see anyone I knew. That afternoon they called a muster. Third Platoon fell in, all three of us—Robert Solen, Don Murrell, and me. We'd been the three runts of the platoon. Right there and then 3d Platoon went out of existence. We were assigned to 2d Platoon. That was it.

[The last elements of the 1st Marine Division rolled through Chin-hung-ni around noon on 11 December. Four and a half hours later they cleared Majon-dong. By 9:00 P.M. all units, except those in the armored column, were in their assembly areas around Hungnam. The tanks clanked into the port just before midnight.]

S/Sgt. LEE BERGEE
E/1
I barely remember the field hospital down in the valley at Hamhung. In the hospital tent I overheard a doctor tell a corpsman, "Put that one over there. He won't make it." How I prayed it wasn't me he was talking about.

S/Sgt. CHESTER BAIR
Task Force Faith
The day was very windy, snow and dust blew around the plane. The aircraft's engines stirred them even worse. The ambulance drove right out to the waiting C-47. A cargo hatch on the side of the plane swung open and steps were dropped so we could climb aboard.

When I looked up, I was amazed to see a pretty American woman wearing bright red lipstick reaching down to help me. I could not believe my eyes and began to cry. She thought I was in pain. I was rejoicing with happiness.

Pfc. PAUL MARTIN
Reconnaissance Company/1st Marine Division
Mail was waiting for me. Most of it was three months old. One letter hoped I was enjoying sunny California. Another reported, "I was at a football game Thanksgiving and the weather was so cold. I felt so sorry for the players out there on that frozen gridiron."

The Hungnam evacuation plan, as outlined in X Corps OpnO 10-50, issued on 11 December, provided for the immediate embarkation of the 1st Marine Division and the 3d ROK Division. A smaller perimeter than the original concept was to be defended meanwhile by the 7th and 3d Infantry Divisions, with the latter having the final responsibility. Major units were to withdraw gradually by side-slipping until only reinforced platoons remained as covering forces holding strong points. Plans called for naval gunfire and air support to be stepped up as the perimeter contracted.

U.S. MARINE OPERATIONS IN KOREA

Maj. Gen. OLIVER P. SMITH
Commanding General, 1st Marine Division
At first X Corps had the idea that because of the 1st Marine Division's amphibious background, it would defend the beachhead and be the last outfit out of Hungnam. Well, someone eventually saw the light of day.

We had taken all of X Corps's casualties. The 7th Division, beside the battalions that were messed up at the Reservoir, had had no casualties. We had 4,000 to 5,000 casualties. Our first orders were to go into assembly areas around Hungnam and defend the port. Those orders were changed and we went aboard ship. It didn't take us long to get out.

The withdrawal was pretty orderly. When the Chinese first hit [27 November], X Corps in Hungnam kind of stampeded and began to burn and destroy equipment. When they found the Marines were holding and coming out slowly, they stopped the burning. Eventu-

ally, 17,500 vehicles, 105,000 troops,* and 91,000 refugees went out
of Hungnam in 109 ships.†

Admiral ARLEIGH BURKE
Deputy Chief of Staff, COMNAVFE
When General [Charles] Willoughby [MacArthur's G-2] chose not to
accept our interpretation of whether the Chinese were going to enter
the war, I wrote a dispatch to Admiral [Forrest] Sherman [Chief of
Naval Operations]. After I explained our position on Chinese intervention, I told him in case anything happened I was going to save
every fifth merchant ship that reached us. I also intended to save all
the heavy-lift ships I could lay hands on. We had in the Pacific Ocean
at that time five ships that had heavy-lift cranes which could raise a
tank. Admiral Sherman did not say no to this plan and I began saving
ships. By the time we needed them in Hungnam, we had sixty or
seventy large empty ships. No other way those ships would have been
ready for the evacuation.‡

13 December 1950
The 5th Marines loaded personnel on the USS *Randall* commencing at 2:30 P.M. on the 12th and continued until 2:00 A.M.

The regimental and battalion aid stations discovered and
evacuated several hundred frostbite cases and some respiratory cases
directly to hospital ships. Most of these cases had refused evacuation until they reached their final objective.

Hot food and showers were available to all hands. About
4,200 passengers were embarked in the *Randall* which had a rated
troop capacity of 2,500.

HISTORICAL DIARY, 5TH MARINE REGIMENT

* Of these, 22,215 were Marines.
† Smith interview, MCHC.
‡ Burke interview, Nav. Inst.

Pfc. JACK WRIGHT
G/5

We received word to saddle up; we were going aboard ship. We marched down to the harbor where landing craft waited. They took us out to the USS *General G. M. Randall,* one of the biggest troop transports. The first person I saw around was an old boot-camp buddy of mine who was a member of the ship's Marine detachment. "Wright!" he said, and grinned. He leaned over and sniffed. "Boy, you need a bath." I didn't argue. I was carrying the clean clothes which had been given to us on shore. He took me down to the Marine detachment berthing area. I must have looked a sight. These other guys wore nice, clean, freshly pressed green uniforms; a few even wore their dress blues. One of these guys went in and checked the hot water. Another gave me a bar of soap. Someone else asked if I needed help. On board ship you usually take saltwater showers. Freshwater, if you're lucky, is turned on to get you wet, then turned off while you scrub and turned back on to wash off. One Marine said, "Don't worry about the water rationing. Enjoy yourself." A freshwater hot shower, as much of it as I wanted. Pure heaven! No one complained later because I had used all their hot water—or tried to, anyway. When I dried off, one of the Marines brought me a hot cup of coffee. I dressed in my new clothes. Someone asked what I wanted done with my old clothes. I said, "Like all dead things, bury them."

Sgt. SHERMAN RICHTER
B/7

On board ship we were filthy dirty, crummy, had scales on our flesh. They cut our boots off. A doctor walked down the line looking at frostbitten toes. "Treatment. Treatment. Amputate. Treatment. Amputate. Treatment. Treatment . . ." Everyone held his breath. If your toes were black, it was too bad for you.

Cpl. FRANK BIFULK
B/7

I've read Hungnam was burning and smoke filled the air. You wanna really know the truth? I don't know this to be true. I climbed aboard the ship, went straight down to the messroom and never looked back.

From: CO 5th Marines

To: CG, 1st Marine Aircraft Wing

Please pass to 1st Marine Aircraft Wing deepest thanks from officers and all enlisted men 5th Marines. But for your superlative support, coupled with indomitable spirit of all, we could be at Yudam-ni instead of the sea.*

---

* Marine losses during the Chosin campaign totaled 4,418 battle casualties—604 KIA, 114 DOW, 192 MIA, 3,508 WIA. In addition, there were 7,313 nonbattle casualties, most of whom were frostbite or indigestion cases and were soon restored to active duty.

Enemy losses were estimated at a total of 37,500—15,000 killed and 7,500 wounded by Marine ground forces, plus 10,000 killed and 5,000 wounded by Marine air.

RETREAT

11

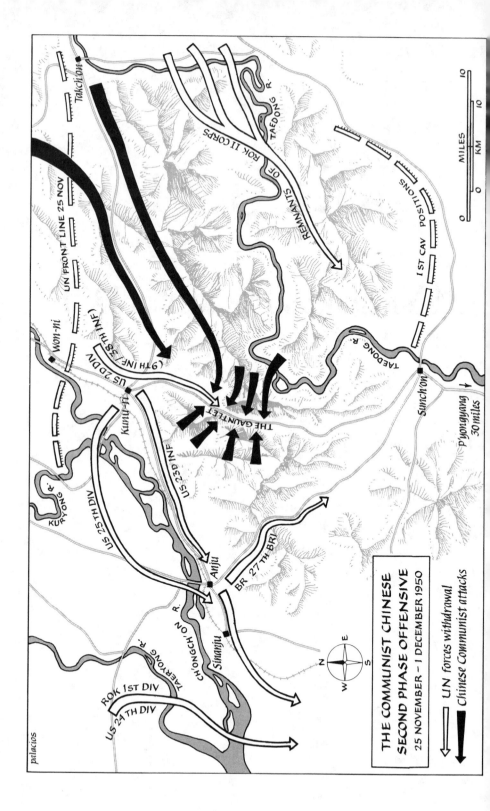

THE COMMUNIST CHINESE
SECOND PHASE OFFENSIVE
25 NOVEMBER – 1 DECEMBER 1950

⇨ UN forces withdrawal
⬛ Chinese Communist attacks

At the same time the 1st Marine Division was fighting its way down the MSR, another equally fierce and important battle was being waged seventy air miles southwest of the Chosin Reservoir. There, beyond the great barrier mountains that divide North Korea, Eighth Army and the Chinese were again locked in battle. The two forces had first clashed in early November, but the enemy had broken off the engagement. The succeeding weeks had done nothing to lessen the differences in their combat personalities. When they met for the second time, they could not have been more dissimilar: one was 6,000 miles from home, the other in its own backyard; one was boisterous and issued daily communiqués to the world, the other was taciturn; one had armor, artillery, and air cover, the other had men—180,000 of them; one had trucks of every size and shape, the other carried only what a man could pack on his back; one competed with itself for road space, the other glided overland from valley to valley, hilltop to hilltop; one left a trail wherever it went, the other left no trail at all; one didn't know where the other was, the other did; one hadn't read the tragedy that would soon be enacted, the other had written it.

After the Chinese launched their first-phase offensive and stunned Eighth Army, they had retired behind a range of harsh, inhospitable mountains and not been seen in force again. The dilemma facing General MacArthur was clear: should he dig in or resume the march to the Yalu? If he advanced, he risked another massive enemy counterattack; if he remained where he was, north of P'yongyang, he sur-

rendered whatever initiative he had to the Chinese, who could then dictate the time and place of their next offensive. True to form, MacArthur chose to attack. With Eighth Army and X Corps ensconced on the Yalu, the war ends, bringing peace and unity to Korea; the curtain comes down, the UN Command takes its bow, and the spear carriers are sent home. It was a scenario MacArthur had seen played out before, and each time it had ended in victory. Why not this time, too?

After a week's delay caused by logistical problems, Eighth Army's advance began on Friday, 24 November, the day after Thanksgiving. Opposition that day was negligible and the advance netted eight miles.

Pfc. KENNETH POSS
Heavy Mortar Company/9th Infantry

On Friday we left the small village where the day before we had eaten the big meal and began to drive north. About a mile out, it was discovered we had left our radio back in the village. One of our lieutenants, a Japanese-American, went back to retrieve it. In the village he was told by the Koreans that as soon as we had pulled out a Chinese patrol had come through. This was the first we knew the Chinese were nearby, let alone behind us.

[Cpl. Don Thomas was from Merced, California, and had joined the Army in 1947 at age fifteen. He served a tour in West Germany and was discharged from the service five days before the Korean War began. Less than two months later, Thomas reenlisted and was sent to Korea in late November. Trained in weapons repair, he figured he would be sent to an ordnance company. Thanksgiving Day Thomas learned he had been assigned instead to an infantry regiment. The next day he set off to find his new unit.]

Cpl. DON THOMAS
K Company/23d Infantry

Twelve of us climbed on top of a truck loaded with rations for the trip to the 23d Infantry Service Company. From there we would be assigned to a rifle company. It was a very cold all-day ride. We arrived after dark at the company and were split up and put in tents with members of the service company. The guys in my tent told me I was lucky to be getting there then. My records would show I had served in a combat zone which would be good to have when promotion time came. They said word was out the war was over and everyone would be home for Christmas. Their unit, they said, was partly packed.

Three of us were selected to go to K Company. We caught a ride in the mail jeep to the company area. We arrived after dark and went at once to report in to the company commander. That night the three of us slept on the floor in the company command post. I heard the company vehicles start up every half hour all night. Someone told me it was to keep them from freezing as the temperature was near zero.

[Saturday, 25 November,* would be Corporal Thomas's first full day with K Company. He was surprised to find only four men in his new squad; he had expected twice as many.

Pfc. Jimmy Marks spent his Saturday driving over the same road Don Thomas had traveled the day before, the one that runs through the Ch'ongch'on River valley. His unit's three firing batteries and H & S Battery had received march orders that morning. The 61st Field Artillery Battalion was going to reinforce the U.S. 2d Division in its drive to the Yalu.]

---

*On this day, in the east, Litzenberg's 7th Marines passed over Toktong Pass and seized Yudam-ni, and Murray's 5th Marines was relieved east of the Chosin Reservoir by Lt. Col. Don Faith's 1st Battalion, 32d Infantry.

Pfc. JIMMY MARKS
A Battery/61st Field Artillery Battalion

The area we were to move to had been selected earlier by a recon party—not by choice, but by what was left. The officers of the 61st were emphatically not pleased with the location, as it squeezed the battalion between the Ch'ongch'on River to the left and a high railroad embankment and the river road to the right. A nearby hill [329] looked down on the site. Because of its shape it soon became known as Chinaman's Hat.

When the battalion occupied the position along the south bank of the Ch'ongch'on, late in the afternoon of the 25th, the men began the routine jobs of laying wire to the guns, digging parapets for the guns, pitching tents, fixing evening chow, and all the little chores that prepare an artillery battalion for delivering fire from its 105-mm howitzers. Around 4:00 P.M. the guns were registered with an air observer and the evening meal served. The U.S. Air Force was making air strikes on targets three or four miles to our north, and many of us watched the show until there was no more light for the bombers to see their targets. When the sun disappeared below the horizon, the 61st settled in for another cold night.

M/Sgt. ALLAN STANBERRY
A Battery/61st Field Artillery Battalion

Supper Saturday night consisted of a half canteen-cup of heated tomato juice and water. Sergeant [Earl] Collette and I usually bedded down together. We had a piece of a bottle of Scotch he'd carried all the way from Naktong. "Kee-reist, it's cold tonight. Let's have an up."

We each took a sip and then very carefully put the bottle back in its hiding place.

Pfc. KENNETH POSS
Heavy Mortar Company/9th Infantry

Because I was sort of a spare part that night, the company CO ordered me and three other guys to take a jeep and make sure the road that led to regimental headquarters was open. We took off down the road, and around a large hill [Chinaman's Hat] we had to fight our way through a small roadblock. When we finally reached the regimental CP, we reported our firefight and got ready to return to the company.

Pfc. JIMMY MARKS
A Battery/61st Field Artillery Battalion

I was on duty in the Fire Direction Center [FDC] pulling the 6:00 to midnight shift with Louis Iglesias of Detroit, Michigan. Around 8:00 P.M. I received the first report from the machine-gun outpost closest to the Ch'ongch'on that they could hear an unusual amount of noise across the river.

Captain [Rex] Gunnell, the battery CO, was not overly emotional (he had earned a Silver Star for his actions in the road battle of November 5). He lit up another pipeload of Mixture 79 and soon the FDC tent was filled with its aromatic smell. The machine-gun outpost again and again reported the strange noises coming from across the Ch'ongch'on. It sounded to them as if troops were on the move. Captain Gunnell decided to check with "Sinew" (61st FA Battalion HQ). Iglesias rang HQ and the captain reported what the other batteries had reported—noise on the other side of the river. Colonel Knott at regiment answered the call by saying he did not know anything more except that across the Ch'ongch'on there were supposed to be friendly troops.

At 8:30 the men in the outpost along the bank of the river were becoming annoyed that no one was acting on their information. They were convinced something out of the ordinary was happening. Half an hour later the outpost reported they believed the noise was being made by enemy activity. Contact was made by landline with nearby units of the 9th Infantry (to our north) and 23d Infantry (to our west). Each was asked whether they had information on enemy activity in our area. We were assured that any activity we heard was from friendly patrols returning from west of the river.

By 9:00 P.M. the 61st outpost was so convinced the enemy was on the far riverbank they requested permission to open fire. They were ordered to hold their fire and told that what they heard were friendly patrols. At 11:30 P.M. on Saturday the 25th, A Battery was attacked by a Chinese force, estimated at battalion size, which had waded across the river.

M/Sgt. ALLAN STANBERRY
A Battery/61st Field Artillery Battalion
The next thing I knew Collette and I were busy trying to decide who to shoot at. I drew down once on a silhouette only to find it was one of our South Koreans. Didn't shoot, but it rattled me so that I was afraid to fire.

Pfc. JIMMY MARKS
A Battery/61st Field Artillery Battalion
We immediately began to take incoming machine-gun fire. While the attack was no surprise in a sense, the failure of anyone in command to comprehend the real situation permitted the Chinese to penetrate our perimeter very quickly.

I'd left the FDC tent a moment earlier to go to my pup tent, probably to get cigarettes. It was then the Communists had hit. There was so much machine-gun fire, the entire sky was solid with streaks of tracers. An occasional flare eerily illuminated the landscape. I turned and ran back to the FDC. Men sprinted in every direction. I grabbed our medic (who was killed later that night): "What'n hell's goin' on?" "Get out of here. We're overrun."

I reached the FDC tent. It was deserted. I learned later that when Captain Gunnell had stepped out of the tent to check on the firing, he'd been cut down by a burp gun. The captain was loaded onto a jeep and taken to a MASH down the road, where he died. Lt. Jack Kean, a West Pointer and our executive officer, had then assumed command. He got on the radio and reported A Battery was engaged by a large enemy force and would appreciate support from infantry units in the area. The infantry operations officer to whom he spoke gave him a hard time. "What's the matter? Is it getting too hot for you artillerymen down there?" Kean was in no mood to be ribbed but he kept his cool and was promised: "We'll check it out and get back to you." Nothing was heard again from the infantry.

The Chinese by this time were overrunning the 105-mm gun positions, one by one, despite point-blank fire delivered on them.

Lieutenant Kean bumped into Sgt. Carl Gumina. "Why aren't you with your gun?" "It's captured, sir." "Like hell, Sar'nt. I see men in the gun position." "Them's Chinks, sir." Kean knew now the battery was in trouble. In the road battle of November 5, Gumina had earned a Silver Star and would be the last man to leave a gun position. Kean then ordered Gumina and all the men he could find to assemble behind the railroad track to our rear and await further orders.

I was already there. With a few others I crouched down and watched the red and orange tracers flying helter-skelter. A figure would occasionally run by, but it was impossible to tell if it was a friendly or a Chinese. Once I yelled at a silhouette that I made out in the dim light of a dying flare, "Halt! You Chinese?" "Man, where'n hell you ever see a black Chinese?" It was my buddy Pugh.

All up and down the river valley, all hell had broken loose. Tracers and explosions, left and right. Flares would explode, giving too much light, then flutter down and extinguish themselves in frozen corn stubble. The Chinese blew bugles and whistles and shouted American profanity. I thought their bugles were playing, "Silent Night, Holy Night." Between shots and explosions I could hear the wounded crying for help.

Meanwhile, Lieutenant Kean continued to hold the battery's position. At one point, he came upon a group of men crouched around the FDC tent with their backs to the river. He ordered them to assemble with Gumina. Then he saw they carried burp guns. They were too stunned to react. Kean almost fired his .45 at them, but realized one shot from him could bring them to life and he'd be a goner. It was then Lieutenant Kean realized his entire battery position was in the hands of the enemy. When Kean eventually worked his way to the railroad embankment, Sergeant Gumina already had about half the battery there.

M/Sgt. ALLAN STANBERRY
A Battery/61st Field Artillery Battalion

Eventually backed up to the railroad embankment, where, along with Corporal Dement and about eighteen others, I tried to decide what to do next. Each man decided for himself; most joined a reserve infantry unit which was about 300 yards to our rear. Dement and I decided, however, to move parallel to the river and the Chinese assault and make our way back to one of the Cav units we'd seen just before dark. Along the way we came on a 2d Division artillery battalion headquarters and attempted to alert the men to what was going on. We found them to be well in their cups from the booze ration which had arrived that day. The battalion exec asked, "How many men do you have, Sergeant?" I responded, "Me and a corporal." "All right, we'll form a line," he said. He then proceeded to get his men out into the middle of an open rice paddy. "Where do you want us?" I asked. "Down on the end of the line," he answered. That's where Dement and I went, way down to the end of the line. When we got there we kept going and left these drunks to whatever fate held for them. I still wanted to find a Cav unit. A little while later, while we were climbing across the nose of a short, steep hill, several unknown persons opened fire on me. The ballistic pop of the fire was good and close. Through it, I heard the calm voice of the rotund Corporal Dement: "Hey, Sarge, them 'gators is shootin' at you." Then a second time, only this time with a little more emphasis: "Hey, Sarge, them 'gators is SHOOTIN' at YOU!" I rolled over the crest and yelled down, "Hell, man, I know it." Then I suggested he take the long way around the base of the hill so he wouldn't expose himself as I had. He joined me on the other side and we climbed up and over another hill. In an exposed rice paddy between hills, a .50-cal machine gun opened fire. Dement, who was trailing me, promptly ran back to a nearby draw. I circled the paddy looking for him, running at top speed the whole time. Finally, exhausted, I jumped into a clump of bushes. I lay for a long time catching my breath and trying to decide what to do next. I called to Dement, at first softly, then louder and louder. I received no answer. Convinced he was dead, I decided the best thing to do was get up slowly, sling arms, and walk out casually as if I belonged there. Right then, I remember desperately wanting a drink of water and finding my canteen frozen. My boots were just as they were when I left the battery, unlaced. I slowly came to my feet and slung my carbine over my shoulder. I expected to be blasted any moment. When there was no fire I started to walk slowly to the nearest hill. When I was fifty yards away, I took off and believe I would have beaten Jesse Owens to the cover the hill offered.

A few minutes later I came across an officer from one of the 2d Division's regiments helping his driver who had been wounded slightly. The two of us then half carried the man over several more hills until we stumbled into the perimeter of one of the Cav's units. I felt like I had reached home.

Pfc. JIMMY MARKS
A Battery/61st Field Artillery Battalion
One group behind the embankment made its way down the tracks to battalion headquarters, where Colonel Knott ordered Kean to assemble three or four miles down the road at Kunu-ri. The group I was with was still back behind the battery. Trapped on one side of a trestle, we attracted a lot of machine-gun fire. Whenever a flare died out, we crossed the open space one by one. The group finally reached battalion headquarters as the trucks carrying Lieutenant Kean's group were pulling out. By running at top speed, we managed to jump on the last truck and were driven to our new assembly area.

We stopped at Kujan-dong. I found about half the battery there. A few men tried to sleep, but most just crowded around small fires. The earth began to shake from nearby eight-inch "long toms" that had begun to fire. We waited for the sun to rise.

Pfc. KENNETH POSS
Heavy Mortar Company/9th Infantry
Once the Chinese attacked across the river, the situation became very confused. I had worked my way back up the road to my company's position. When I reached it, it was deserted. There was a tank down by the riverbank that had been knocked out. I wondered what had become of the regiment's rifle companies that were north of the river. (I learned later they'd been overrun earlier in the evening.) I joined a group of about fifteen GIs making its way southward. There was still sporadic firing along the road, but we didn't run into anything heavy. Word was somehow passed that it was now every man for himself.

Pfc. JIMMY MARKS
A Battery/61st Field Artillery Battalion
When the sun finally rose [26 November], Lieutenant Kean received a report that the situation upriver had stabilized, and around 7:00 A.M. twenty of us volunteered to return with him to try and retrieve the howitzers.

When our trucks returned to our position of the night before, we were met by enemy machine-gun and rifle fire. Quickly bailing out of the vehicles, we hooked the howitzers to the trucks. Each trail had to be closed, then lifted so the ring dropped on the hook on the truck. We left the ammo behind. A Chinese machine gun hidden behind the dual wheels of an abandoned supply truck continued to fire at us. Lieutenant Kean asked our supply sergeant what was on the truck. "Nothing but toilet paper, sir." "Leave it." One by one the trucks began pulling the howitzers out of the frozen cornfield.

We were very demoralized. We had lost equipment and our battery commander, Rex Gunnell. Morale hit rock bottom. We had come out second best on the Ch'ongch'on. We felt betrayed. Our outpost had wanted to open fire and, just moments before the Chinese plowed into us, was told to hold its fire. Lieutenant Kean's main job now was to try and get the battery back on its feet. He ordered everyone, including NCOs and men in the other sections, to pitch in and help dig new gun pits. The ploy worked; frustration and rage were taken out on the frozen ground with pickaxes and shovels. Within twenty-four hours Rex Gunnell's A Battery, 61st FA Battalion, was again a fighting unit.

M/Sgt. ALLAN STANBERRY
A Battery/61st Field Artillery Battalion

I well remember the agony of meeting each incoming little group of survivors and learning who wouldn't be coming back. Even now, it is extremely upsetting to me. I recall beating the frozen ground with a stick I'd used to walk with and wanting to cry for Rex Gunnell and not being able to. I remember Rex had only recently been married; he'd told me his wife had never even cooked a meal for them.

Cpl. DON THOMAS
K Company/23d Infantry

The company loaded up on trucks for the trip north. The trucks were open in the back. The wind-chill factor in the moving trucks was well below zero. We sat jammed, knee to knee, and did our best to keep moving our feet and legs to keep up the circulation. I kept rubbing my knees so they would not become numb.

Later in the day we entered a small town called Samin. There was another convoy coming toward us. Both convoys stopped side by side in the town. The bumper marking on the other trucks showed they were from the 9th Infantry Regiment, 2d Division. There was a soldier standing in the rear of one of the trucks. Someone in our truck asked him how the 9th was making out. He didn't answer. He curled his hand into a fist with his thumb pointing out and indicated the answer was behind him. I did not know what he meant. Neither did the other guys in our truck until the other line of trucks began to pull forward. The backs of those trucks were stacked to the top of the bows with litters. There was a dead American soldier on each litter. The bodies were not covered or encased in anything. I felt sick. Tears came to my eyes. A knot rose up in my throat. Prior to this everyone on the truck had been talking and joking. There was silence now. It was many miles before anyone loosened up. I heard later than the 9th Regiment had been at a place called "Chinaman's Hat."

[The enemy's main effort on the 25th, however, had not been directed at the American units astride the Ch'ongch'on River, but against three ROK divisions that held the Eighth Army's right flank. Wave upon wave of Chinese infantry attacked the South Koreans around the central Korean city of Tokch'on, and in one night the ROKs tottered, then collapsed. In the morning the Chinese wheeled westward and rolled toward the sea through the now open American flank.† The six Chinese armies of XIII Army Group, comprising eighteen divisions and nearly 200,000 men, had once again been let loose on Eighth Army. Their idea was to cut off General Walker's command from reinforcements in the south, then pin the trapped divisions against the coast and pick them off one by one. At Tokch'on the plan had gotten off to a flying start.*

Before dawn on Monday, 27 November,‡ the Chinese collided with the two U.S. divisions, the 2d and 25th, that held the line next to the ROKs. Up and down the Ch'ongch'on, wherever Americans tried to cross the river and get back to more defensible positions, they were hammered by the Chinese. In the broken country along the river, on hills and in valleys, the fighting was everywhere savage, at times desperate.]

1st Lt. LUTHER WEAVER
A Company/35th Infantry

We moved with a platoon of tanks and some other vehicles north toward Unsan, and by late afternoon had made several miles. When

---

*Eighth Army's order of battle west to east, from Korea Bay to Tokch'on, was: U.S. I Corps (U.S. 24th Division, British 27th Commonwealth Brigade, ROK 1st Division); U.S. IX Corps (U.S. 25th and 2d Divisions, the Turkish Brigade); ROK II Corps (ROK 6th, 7th, 8th Divisions). The 1st Cavalry Division was south of the front and in Army reserve.

† At Yudam-ni on the 26th, the 5th Marines was preparing to advance westward the next morning in an attempt to close the gap that existed between X Corps and Eighth Army.

‡ The night of the 27th, the Chinese attacked the 5th and 7th Marine Regiments at Yudam-ni and the Army battalions east of the Chosin Reservoir.

the light first began to fade, the company spread out in an area of open rice paddies. Unsan was a few miles beyond a ridge I could see real well. Chow was brought up in a deuce-and-a-half which also pulled a trailer carrying bedrolls and ammunition.

There was still full daylight when we first observed movement to our front on the ridge. About then, Capt. Sidney Barry, the company CO, received word the Chinese were attacking and battalion had orders to move back and consolidate positions. My job then was to reload the vehicles and turn them around as fast as possible. While I was doing this, the deuce-and-a-half got stuck in the rice paddy. On the ridge now there were so many Chinese it looked to me like an army of ants crawling over it. Never had I seen so many enemy soldiers—and they were moving in my direction. Captain Barry pulled the platoons in and got them moving southward. With only a little light left, the troublesome truck was pushed out onto the road and it, too, started for the rear. We rolled through the 2d and 3d Battalions, which were across the road and on some relatively high ground.

Farther south we stopped in the town of Yongsan-dong and set up the company CP a few hundred yards north of the battalion HQ. Captain Barry decided to unload the bedrolls and then to send the kitchen truck back to battalion trains. Next he positioned three rifle platoons on the high ground overlooking the little village. Once they were in position, the platoons sent details down to pick up their sleeping bags. It was now completely dark. Once communications were set up and checked and security posted, the CP settled down. I noticed some men, including Captain Barry, taking their boots off and crawling into their sleeping bags. All I could remember of the day were those Chinks near Unsan flowing over the ridge in our direction. I figured, traveling at a dogtrot, it wouldn't be long before we would be hearing from them.

I walked outside the CP to relieve myself. Off to the right [east], in the area where I understood Task Force Dolvin* to be, I could hear a real good firefight in progress. There was also some firing toward Unsan, in the direction of the regiment's 2d and 3d Battalions.

---

* This task force, named after its commander, Lt. Col. Welborn Dolvin, was advancing east of the 35th Infantry and along the Kuryong River, a major tributary of the Ch'ongch'on.

I went back inside and fought the temptation to get warm by sliding into my sleeping bag. A report arrived stating one of the platoons on a nearby hill had spotted an unidentified column of men moving in the open across a rice paddy. They hadn't fired because they thought it was one of our units moving to a new position. A few minutes later another platoon reported hearing movement to their front. Within the hour the firing I'd heard toward Unsan became more distinct. Finally, a call from our battalion alerted us to the possibility of some action in our area. Within minutes, heavy firing broke out on the ridge above the CP. The Chinese had hit a rifle platoon and, after a brief firefight, the GIs gave ground. Several ran by the CP. Captain Barry and I immediately grabbed what men we could find in the area and led them in a counterattack back up the hill. The Chinese apparently had no intention of engaging us for any length of time on the hill and were more intent on moving along the ridge to a better position overlooking the road. We found out a short time later they had stopped south of the battalion HQ and on a hill above the road established a roadblock.

When our counterattack did not discover any Chinese, Captain Barry ordered me to gather on top of the hill as many sleeping bags as I could find. A full moon was out now and in its light I could see bags scattered from the top of the ridge all the way down to the CP area. With a few men I flagged down, I gathered up a sizable number of bags and loaded them onto a trailer.

Within minutes, orders were received to pull in the platoons and get them ready to move south. So the bugout, that commonly heard phrase of those days, the bugout of Eighth Army would soon begin and A Company, 35th Infantry, would be a part of it. At that time we did not realize the big picture and the critical situation we were in.

Not much time was wasted in preparing the company to move. The road was already choked with trucks, trailers, tanks, artillery, and shuffling men. I was responsible for getting the company's vehicles out. Captain Barry led the rifle platoons off the road and set up security for the column and I was ordered to follow our battalion headquarters' vehicles. While we were preparing to join the vehicles on the road, the Chinese force that had brushed us off the hill above the

CP opened fire on the road. First Battalion headquarters personnel moved onto the road and with some tanks out front moved toward the enemy roadblock. I managed to squeeze my vehicles onto the crowded road. The tanks in front sprayed the hillside where the Chinese were dug in, then clanked on through the block. Captain Barry moved his troops wide of the roadblock. The column of vehicles I was a part of moved a few hundred yards, then stopped abruptly. Everyone waited; nothing happened. I could see ahead where the roadblock was and it appeared the enemy's fire was sporadic and high. As I could not understand why we weren't moving, and growing more impatient by the minute, I told the driver of my vehicle, "When the column moves you move with it. I'll catch up with you later." With that, I walked to the front of the stalled column to see for myself what the problem was. I found the battalion CO's jeep, motor still running, abandoned in the middle of the road. All the other drivers, their trucks all neatly lined up behind it, sat and waited for something to happen. They would have had one long wait.

I surveyed the empty road to the front and the hills on either side. Once I had timed the enemy's short bursts, I decided to drive the jeep through the block myself. When I did so, the column could resume its withdrawal. I took off as fast as the jeep would go. Bullets popped overhead, but I got through without a scratch. Down the road, maybe a mile or so, I caught up with the rest of the convoy. I slipped the clutch into second and crawled up to the last vehicle. Out of the darkness a GI ran over to me: "Sir, you're driving my jeep." I pulled on the brake, then I gave this individual my choicest remarks about what he had done and what would happen to him if I ever again found his jeep holding up a convoy. I returned the jeep to its chastened driver and waited by the side of the road for one of A Company's vehicles to come by and pick me up.

1st Lt. CHARLES PAYNE
3d Battalion/19th Infantry

We had a terrible scrap one night. Actually, it was dusk and the out-fit was atop a big hill. Several rings of men were positioned around the crest. When darkness fell, the commo lines were cut by the Chinese and we found ourselves alone. It began to snow like mad. Most of that night we went back to back and fought like wild people. One gook, stronger than I, grabbed my pack and actually dragged me some way before I rode him down; had both hands in his face tearing at his mouth, nose, and eyes. I made it back to the perimeter with my pack, which had a whole bottle of whiskey in it. We held through the night. The snow was very deep. In the morning the weather broke and a small liaison plane dropped a message that we should fight our way out. When we made our move to leave the hill, our own tanks, which were below on the road, fired a few rounds into our position. I know we lost some men. We moved down the ridge, not in any kind of order, and enemy snipers were in on us. The battalion CO, who was behind, cussed me for wearing my red hunting mittens (which my mom had sent). Told me they made too good a target and I should get rid of them. I told him he could go down another ridge if he didn't want to follow me. He stayed, said I was too lucky to leave. Shortly afterward I lost the left mitten and, I thought, the hand with it, when I was hit.

2d Lt. ROBERT CURTIS
F Company/23d Infantry

I took over a rifle platoon. My battalion commander called on the radio for me to attack the enemy. I said, "Sir, you want me to attack? I can't attack." "You must," he said. "You've got to go." Here we were, fighting for our damn life, and he wanted us to attack. There was no way I could mount an attack. We were barely hanging on as it was. Shortly after that, I began to hear firing behind our position. Battalion said I must be nuts, that there weren't any Chinese behind me. It turned out it was battalion that was nuts.

Cpl. DONALD HOFFMAN
F Company/23d Infantry

After the regimental CP area was overrun, it became real quiet down there. We were told to retake the area and I went out on a patrol to see if we could find where the Chinese had gone. Platoon sergeant told me to take the point. "Bullshit! I'm always getting stuck with the goddamn point. How 'bout a break?" He said, "Take the point!" I took the point.

    There were three shacks west of the CP area. The road ran between the railroad tracks and the river. The shacks were on our left when we approached. It was dark. We never gave them any thought. The Chinese let us reach the last shack, then opened up. Just cut us to pieces. A platoon behind us got into the scrap. For a while it was total chaos—like organized grab-ass. One of the platoon sergeants was hit. He lay in the open and repeated over and over, "Jesus Christ, Almighty God, save me." It was just a mess. He kept moaning and asking God to save him. "What are we gonna do?" I asked the guy lying next to me. "We're gonna go get him." We ran to the road and dragged him back. He was very heavy and we worked hard. Inside our perimeter we flipped his ass into a shell crater. A medic came by later, told us the guy had been shot in the groin. He died later. To the end he moaned, "Oh, my God, oh, my God, am I hurt?"

2d Lt. ROBERT CURTIS
F Company/23d Infantry

There was one time that I was down in the regimental area. It was night. I had a Korean with me whom I called Mr. Too. Fox Company was on a hill to our front. I found a hole next to a boulder and went to sleep. All of a sudden I was awakened by Mr. Too banging on my helmet shouting, "Chinese coming now." All around men were running in different directions. I grabbed an officer and asked what was happening. "We got overrun," he yelled. "We don't have any ammo left and we gotta go." I looked around, men streamed by. They all had bandoliers filled with ammunition.

A couple of Chinese ran through and opened fire. I decided to try to reach Fox Company. The Chinese seemed to be everywhere by now. Mr. Too and I threw away everything that would slow us down and took off running for Fox Company.

When morning broke, the company was still on the hill. Another company passed through our lines. I spoke to one of their officers. "Where'n hell you going?" "We can't hold this," he answered. "We gotta get back. We're leaving." I told him to tell battalion when he got back that F Company was still on the hill. I didn't want them to forget about us. A little while later another goddamn rifle company came through us treading south. Told one of their officers the same thing: "You tell 'em we're here."

The morning became warm. The sun felt good. Suddenly, we began receiving artillery and tank fire from our rear. Jesus Christ, here were American tanks on the road below firing at our hill. No one had told battalion we were on the hill. It was then we decided we better get out.

Lt. Col. LEITH CRUE
Canadian Military Mission/Far East Command
In the evening I returned to a billet in Pusan which I shared with several American Army officers. I had spent most of the day in a jeep facing cold Korean winds and I was happy to get back to my warm billets. We played cribbage that night. A radio on a small mantel played hit tunes. Shortly before 8:00 P.M. the tired voice of an announcer reported that in a few minutes General MacArthur would make an important announcement. Someone muttered, "Guess he's gonna tell us we'll all be home for Christmas for sure." The volume was turned up; none of us wanted to miss a syllable of the good news. Exactly at 8:00 the general's well-known voice told us about the disastrous defeat our forces in North Korea had suffered at the hands of the Chinese. He said, ". . . all United Nations Forces in Korea are facing annihilation."

The cribbage game was forgotten. I'll never forget how those few words caused such a drop in the morale of men who had faced many hardships and always come up smiling. The faces now expressed disgust, concern, and disbelief.

The two engineer officers who lived with us silently crawled into their combat jackets. They were going out into the night to begin laying demolition charges in the port's huge supply depot.

[*Headquarters, Eighth Army, had begun almost immediately to extricate I Corps's two U.S. and one ROK divisions from the west coast. Farther east the 25th Division began to fall back. On their right Maj. Gen. Lawrence Keiser's 2d Division, comprising the 9th, 23d, and 38th Infantry Regiments, was given the dour, thankless task of holding the Chinese long enough for the bulk of Eighth Army to escape. The rearguard situation was summed up by Walter Winchell, who wrote at the time, "If you have a son overseas, write to him. If you have a son in the 2d Division, pray for him."*

Roads leading southward were bumper to bumper with vehicles; the columns extended from village to village and beyond. Gridlock afflicted the road junctions at Pakch'on, Anju, Sinanju, and Kunu-ri. In an attempt to stem the Communist tide, General Walker spent his reserve and the 1st Cavalry Division was rushed forward.

One of the units sent northward was Capt. Norman Allen's Item Company, 5th Cavalry, with orders to investigate and eliminate, if possible, a strong Chinese roadblock preventing the withdrawal of his regiment's 2d Battalion from Sadun. Allen hurried forward a patrol Tuesday afternoon, 28 November, then followed it with the rest of his company, which had been reinforced by a platoon of tanks.]

Sgt. F/C DONALD PATE
I Company/5th Cavalry

My platoon leader, 2d Lt. Wallace Nelson—Nellie to me—advised that he and I and three jeeps plus two M Company [Weapons Company] machine gunners were going on a combat patrol to contact one of our battalions which had been engaged about twenty miles to our northeast by a superior Chinese force. The patrol carried two water-cooled .30s [machine guns] and a .50-cal machine gun. Dick Sorenson from I Company was to drive one of the jeeps.

We traveled northeast, from near Sunch'on to where the road crossed the Taedong. When we drove over the bridge, we sighted what we thought were Chinese troops on a distant hill and the patrol spread out. Lieutenant Nelson stopped his jeep near some trucks with Cav markings and found a couple of dead troopers. Shortly afterward the patrol came under heavy fire and we were forced back over the bridge. We lost a machine gunner at this time and Lieutenant Nelson took a round through the calf of his leg. We stopped south of the bridge and assessed our damage while I dressed Nellie's wound. The jeep I was riding in had had its radiator knocked out by a slug. This was the vehicle with the pedestal-mounted .50-cal. No great loss. I'd found the gun had a faulty driving spring and would jam after firing two rounds. Nellie seemed to be in a state of shock. We put him in one of the jeeps and he was driven to the rear with the vehicle from M Company. Dick Sorenson and I waited at the bridge with the useless jeep and machine gun for the rest of Item Company to show up. A truckload of approximately thirty ROKs joined us at the bridge. The South Koreans stayed only until they saw the Chinese on a ridge overlooking the river, then took off toward Sunch'on at high speed. Late in the afternoon I Company and about six tanks drove up to the bridge.

Capt. NORMAN ALLEN
I Company/5th Cavalry

On the road to the river crossing, I met my returning recon patrol. Lieutenant Nelson and another man had been wounded in what Nellie described as the heaviest hail of fire he'd ever experienced. After questioning him further, I continued along the road until I reached the bridge that crossed the Taedong. There I set up a defensive position and contacted the 2d Battalion. Its commander [Lt. Col. John Clifford] told me over the radio, "Using five companies in the attack. Am moving back." This meant he had even thrown his headquarters company into the battle and I knew it had to really be balls to the wall.

Sgt. F/C DONALD PATE
I Company/5th Cavalry
Captain Allen set up a large perimeter south of the bridge, which was too light to support our tanks, had they tried to cross over it. While it was still light, hundreds of Chinese were seen across the river and they were all wearing U.S. Army winter clothing which hadn't even been issued to us at that time. (Some of the men thought the enemy had more aggressive supply sergeants than we had.) Some Chinese came down the hill to the riverbank. We opened fire. A couple of them were hit, the others cowered in a nearby ravine. One began to run back to his unit. Captain Allen yelled, "Get the bastard!" We all opened fire. Even one of the tanks fired at him with its 75-mm gun. The Chink continued to run, tracers flew around him. Finally he fell, only to immediately get up and run again. The Chink made it back, although he may have dropped dead of fright afterward.

Cpl. JERRY EMER
I Company/5th Cavalry
Around sunset, way up the valley, some people appeared on the skyline of one of the distant hills. Our officers with the aid of binoculars determined they were Chinese soldiers and not Korean civilians. Some of our Sherman tanks fired .50-cal machine guns in their direction. The big .50 tracers, after they'd flown 1,000 or more yards, seemed to float toward the Chinese, but they did the job and ran the enemy off the ridge.

About the time the sun began to dip behind the western hills

and it grew colder, I began to see the vehicles and men of the 2d
Battalion moving toward us. Soon they were passing through our position. Some of their officers stopped to brief Captain Allen, and the
Pfcs and NCOs spoke with guys they knew in our outfit. Everyone
was uptight and the adrenaline really began to pump. Second Battalion people spoke of a large Chink force only hours behind them.

Capt. NORMAN ALLEN
I Company/5th Cavalry
The 2d Battalion came out in pieces; it had lost most of its vehicles
and heavy weapons along with 202 men and 13 officers. I learned
that contact with the regimental I & R Platoon had been lost.* The
last heard from them, they had been taken prisoner in a small village
about four miles to our north. I told Colonel Clifford, 2d Battalion's
CO, that if he could afford to have me divide my company, I was
willing to take two platoons and go to I & R Platoon's rescue. It was
a harebrained idea at best, but I thought I owed that much to Lieutenant Toomey † and the I & R Platoon. Clifford turned down my
request. He needed everything I had to help save the rest of his battalion. He thought the info on the I & R Platoon was too vague to
be treated as reliable, and I could end up chasing ghosts. Most important, he said, there was a whole field army of Chinese to our front,
". . . and what the hell do you think you could do with two platoons?" Maybe I was relieved to have him reject my offer.

Colonel Clifford then tried to bring me under his command. I
didn't like that idea, told him I was acting under division orders and
reported directly to them. I was afraid if I turned I Company and the
two platoons of tanks attached to me over to him, he might sacrifice
the company for his own 2d Battalion if he had been forced to the
choice.

---

*The regiment's Intelligence and Reconnaissance Platoon was ambushed northeast of the Tae-
dong River near Sohang-ni.
† Lieutenant Toomey, who had earlier commanded I Company's 1st Platoon, was given command of the 5th Cavalry's I & R Platoon before the capture of P'yongyang. He was wounded
on the 28th, captured, and died sometime subsequently.

Cpl. JERRY EMER
I Company/5th Cavalry

It was now dark and the cold seemed to bite into my bones. Most of us stood and hopped from foot to foot and tried to keep warm. I wondered what had happened to Lieutenant Toomey. Suddenly we heard the sound of running feet. A patrol sent out by Captain Allen was returning. The guys were wheezing and cussing. I overheard Sergeant Sims tell another sergeant, who'd been on the patrol, "Whole Chink army is comin' straight down the valley." The other guy said, "Yer full of shit!" "OK," Sims said angrily, "come with me then." Both men disappeared in the darkness down the road. Silence. Cold. Fear. I heard the two men returning. They were running. Sims was cussing and hollering, "Goddamn, didn't I tell yuh!" The other sergeant said, "Fuckin' Chinks, aw right."

Capt. NORMAN ALLEN
I Company/5th Cavalry

I moved Item Company down to a bridge to cover the 2d Battalion's withdrawal better and it became really nasty. Men continued to come back in threes and fours, sometimes a dozen—lost, wounded, and confused, officers and men alike. I stripped vehicles and sent the wounded out and kept my men in defensive positions. The enemy moved in. At one point I was standing in the snow by the frozen river, 400 yards from my perimeter, helping guide in 2d Battalion men, when I saw about fifty silhouettes moving toward me along the river. I reported this to Colonel Clifford. He believed they were more of his men. I thought they were Chinese. Nevertheless, I told my machine gunner to hold his fire. Suddenly the shadows opened up and we were forced to return to the company's perimeter hurriedly. A few minutes later one of my listening posts reported another group of Chinese moving in our direction down the road. This force attacked with mortars and machine guns and broke through the platoon guarding the right of the intersection. I counterattacked with the reserve platoon and threw them back. It was now time to get out of the area.

Cpl. JERRY EMER
I Company/5th Cavalry
Captain Allen yelled, "Mount up!" The engines on our trucks and
tanks coughed into life. There was a wild scramble to haul ass out of
there. Tracers cut the air around the trucks. They looked like our
own rounds, probably from machine guns captured earlier in the day
from the I & R Platoon. They were terrifying, some looked like they
were coming right at me. There was a good deal of confusion. Our
tanks returned fire. The trucks rolled down the road. The KATUSAs
did real well and hung in with us. The vehicles picked up speed.
Bugout time again—not the utter panic I've read about, but we weren't
attacking in the opposite direction either.

Capt. NORMAN ALLEN
I Company/5th Cavalry
When I moved my company out, Chinese machine-gun tracers cut
right across my ass. I had the tanks spray the area to our front and
along our flanks. This prevented the enemy from becoming too aggressive. We managed to break out and not one man in the company
was killed. *

Cpl. FRED DUVE
A Company/7th Cavalry
We had marched and been in firefights most of one day. About 6:00
P.M. the platoon climbed a hill and dug in for the night. When we
reached the hill, it had begun to snow. The ground was so hard all
we could do was sit or lie on the ground and shiver. I was the BAR
man, and with my assistant was on a point that jutted out from the
main perimeter. A little before midnight it stopped snowing, fog set

---

* On this same night, at Hagaru-ri, the Marines beat back a determined Chinese attack.

in, and it seemed to grow colder and colder. Around 1:00 A.M. the Chinese attacked. No one could see anything in the fog, but the outfit opened fire toward the sound of bugles and whistles. We heard their screams and hollering all around us. At times it seemed like there were thousands of them.

My buddy threw a white-phosphorus grenade, and for some reason it slipped out of his hand and landed five feet in front of us. With the wind blowing back at us, we moved quickly to another position. I was in such a hurry I grabbed the BAR by its barrel. I dropped it fast; it was red-hot! My buddy thought this was very funny.

Next thing I knew our artillery began to land in front of the position. Came in damn close but, this time at least, none landed on top of us.

The platoon sergeant crawled by and let us know the rest of the battalion was on the hills to our left and right and not to mistake the firing coming from there for the Chinks.

It began to snow again. The miserable weather never once interfered with the killing. The Chinese fired flares, but because of the weather they were of little use to them. The enemy bugles sounded eerie. It might have given some comfort if we could have seen the enemy; then, again, maybe we were better off the way we were.

Near dawn the Chinese broke off the fight and, except for some firing on our flanks, it was quiet enough for us to plainly hear the screaming and moaning of the wounded on both sides of the lines. In another hour the fog began to lift. Down in the valley where the Chinese had made their attack I could now see there was no enemy waiting to resume the battle. Fearing a trap, we did not at first move off the hill. With the sun up full, many of us were detailed to climb down into the valley and either gather up prisoners or care for the wounded. Both sides, it appeared, had been hurt, but this time the enemy had come out on the short end. Their wounded and dead lay all over the place.

My buddy and I found a wounded Chinese. He lay against a bank holding his left side, which was covered in blood. He was in a great deal of pain. He wore a big, bulky, quilted uniform that was filthy. Rice sacks hung around his neck, grenades were tied to his ammo belt. A rifle lay between his legs. I motioned to him to put his hands on top of his head. My buddy then removed the ammo belt and picked up the rifle. I lit a cigarette and put it in the Chink's mouth. He stunk terribly. I took a closer look and saw a big wound in his side. Tears rolled down his cheeks. I thought he might be fifteen or sixteen years old.

[*The main Chinese force was now rushing toward the important road junction at Kunu-ri, where it planned on cutting off Eighth Army's rear guard. The 2d Division had been ordered to fall back to Kunu-ri on Tuesday, the 28th, and shield I Corps and the 25th Division when they crossed the Ch'ongch'on. Eighth Army command believed that once these units were safely south of the river, all 2d Division would have to do to escape the enemy trap was smash through several lightly held Chinese roadblocks. Tragically, this was not to be. Because of the confusing nature of the battle and the broken ground on which it was being fought, no one realized that by Wednesday, the 29th, the Chinese were in fact spread across the rear of the 2d Division's withdrawal route in depth.* Soon the entire weight of the Chinese offensive would fall on one U.S. division; what had been a shield would now become an anvil.*]*

Cpl. DON THOMAS
K Company/23d Infantry
During the night I heard the steady rattle of a heavy machine gun in the distance. Some artillery also. We woke up on the 29th with the sun. George Chamberlain, the platoon sergeant, hollered, "Get up, my dreamy friends, it's coffee time." Most mornings we didn't have coffee and it was true this morning, too. However, someone found a case of cornflakes and each man received one box. Ate them plain and dry like potato chips. An hour or so after daylight, the company formed up a column on each side of the road and began to march north. Supplies and equipment were burning alongside the road. This was the road that led past the Sunch'on road junction to Anju.

Later in the day we encountered a convoy heading south from

---

* In the east on this day, the Chinese attack at Koto-ri was repulsed by units of the 1st Marine Regiment.

the 27th Infantry [25th Division]. They had been shattered earlier, in a battle on the Kuryong River. I didn't feel too good that they were pulling out and we were moving up.

Unknown to us, our 2d Division had been ordered to hold the line in a rearguard action to allow the rest of the Eighth Army to clear. When the 2d Division's turn came, the 23d Infantry Regiment would pull the rear guard for the other two regiments. We did not know this either. That, however, was why we were heading north and everyone else was heading south.

We walked north all day until 11:00 at night, when we arrived a few hundred yards from a river and a small village. Our company moved off the road up a draw to the left. From the draw we turned right and moved up a low ridgeline that ran east and west. The ridge was only 100 or 200 feet high. We set up a roadblock. Part of the company extended onto this ridge. We had so many men on the ridge that to dig our usual size hole, every other hole had to be dug behind the end of the one in front. We were in there right, with plenty of firepower. The ground was frozen deeper than we were able to dig through. We had individual entrenching tools which were like a small shovel. However, the end is rotated and locked in position, which allows it to be used like a hoe. Each stroke tore out a piece of soil about the size of a tennis ball. After about two hours of chopping, my tool began to bounce at impact. It was too dark to see what was wrong. I did not take off my mittens, as my bare hands would have stuck to the shovel. I went down the reverse slope with someone who lit a match to check what was wrong. We found the blade had split down the center. One half of it curled forward and the other half curled to the rear. It bounced just like a spring.

There were 500 or 600 yards of frozen rice paddies to our front. The river was alongside the outer edge. Across the river was a raised railroad embankment. Behind it was a small village. On our extreme right was a concrete bridge that crossed the river. That road then turned and went west through the village. To our extreme left [west] was a large open plain. By the light of the moon, I could see there were 200 or 300 Chinese soldiers on the railroad embankment. They were gathered around large bonfires in three or four groups. There we were, noisily digging in within sight of the enemy. The scene spurred us on in our effort to get a hole dug. We knew it would be a disaster if morning came and we were still above ground. We were sweating, even though the temperature was near zero. We dug, chopped, and sweated until just before dawn. My hole was only a foot deep by then. I gathered rocks and logs and built up the edge so that I had about three feet of protection. Our line became extremely quiet as dawn came. The Chinese had left the embankment earlier and bedded down in the village.

Then I saw them [30 November]. The Chinese were in single file and crossing the bridge. They walked some five feet apart. After the front of the line crossed the bridge, it turned to the west and passed in front of our position. It appeared they did not know we were there. The word was whispered from hole to hole to hold our fire. Finally, our machine gun opened up. The rest of us joined in. Complete surprise. Many Chinese fell to the ground. Some of them tried to run back to the bridge but were cut down. From that distance it was hard to hit them on the run. The river was somehow not frozen yet. The impact of the bullet into the water gave me an idea of how much lead I needed. I only hit one Chinese out of every five or six shots. Many of them got up and ran toward the bridge. Some of them fired back at us. The incoming fire was only moderate. Apparently, they did not have heavy machine guns or mortars, only rifles and submachine guns. It must have been an advance party. The incoming fire snapped over our heads and kicked up chunks of frozen ground around us.

This was my first view of George Chamberlain under fire. He walked casually back and forth on the ridge and assured us everything was under control. He did not crouch low and hurry along the ridge as I would have. He acted like it was just another day on the rifle range. What courage. The members of the platoon would follow George anywhere. Everyone called him George, not Sergeant Chamberlain.

In the middle of the morning, the Air Force arrived to give us a hand. Twin-engine World War II B-26 bombers came in over the village and dropped bombs, napalm, and rockets. They set the village on fire. We had a ringside seat to all of this. Later in the day some fighters came in over the village and added to the destruction.

I could see some Chinese soldiers standing under the bridge on our side of the river. The fighter pilots saw them also and started a rocket and machine-gun run on the bridge. The Chinese scattered like chickens as the rockets slammed in.

George passed the word to hold our firing as we would need all the ammunition we had for the battle that was sure to come that night. The Chinese would regroup and get reinforcements and come at us then. They usually attacked well after dark, often between midnight and 3:00 in the morning.

Unknown to us, the rest of the division had withdrawn from this area. Soon it was our turn. We did not know that the other units in the division were being shattered trying to run a six-mile roadblock south of Kunu-ri. However, due to good luck or a misunderstanding—the history books are not sure which—the 23d Infantry received clearance to retreat southwest toward Anju, rather than run the road-block that was destroying the rest of 2d Division.

[The last act of the tragedy along the Ch'ongch'on was played out when the time came for the 2d Division's three regiments to follow Eighth Army south. One, the 23d, took the river road running west from Kunu-ri and slipped out of the enemy's grasp. The other two, the 9th and 38th Infantry Regiments, turned due south, away from the river, and attempted to reach Sunch'on over the mountain road. There they found the Chinese not only squeezing their rear, but their flanks and front as well. In fact, an entire enemy division lay in wait for them along six miles of the withdrawal route. Caught in this gauntlet, the Americans could not go forward and they could not go back; thousands of abandoned or burning vehicles locked them in a vise of Chinese steel. Small groups did manage to reach friendly lines to the south, but for the 2d Division as a whole, 30 November was a catastrophe. In one afternoon it suffered 3,000 casualties, lost most of its equipment, and all its artillery, and was declared combat-noneffective. One week before, the men of the division had celebrated Thanksgiving.]

Pfc. KENNETH POSS
Heavy Mortar Company/9th Infantry
The Chinese hit us from both sides. The road was clogged with every imaginable type of vehicle—jeeps, trucks of all sizes, tanks, and artillery. I was walking, sometimes I caught a ride. It was mass confu-

sion on the road. The noise of the battle was tremendous. A mortar round landed nearby and the concussion blew out both my eardrums. An old sergeant I knew, we called him Pappy and he was rumored to have made the landing on Omaha Beach at Normandy, had his head blown off. Some guys went over to him and it seemed that the firing on both sides stopped until his body was brought back to the road. A company would go up and try to clear the Chinese off a hill but would be blown away. The Chinese were hitting us with machine guns and mortars. They would let the tanks go by, then close in behind them. They'd knock out the lead vehicle, then beat hell out of us while we tried to push the thing off the road or went around it. In certain areas along the road, there was more discipline than at others. Where there were officers who still had control of their units, the job was being done. At other places it was a mess and you made your way as best you could. At one spot another guy and I pushed a jeep off the road so the vehicles behind could move. At another point the road climbed up a steep grade and doubled back on itself in a U-turn. At the top of the U, the Chinese had a machine gun. I was riding in a truck at the time. The machine gun opened fire and many of the men riding with me were hit. The guy next to me fell across me and took another bullet, the one meant for me. I grabbed my rifle and jumped out of the truck. A shot went between my legs. I ran over and hid in a little depression in the rock wall running along the road. The Chinese had us pinned in there. On the other side of the road, there was a steep gulley. I waited for the Chinese to stop firing—hoped they were reloading—then bounded across the road and fell, tumbled, and rolled down the steep side of the gulley. Lucky I didn't break my neck. When I stopped rolling, I found myself in a dry streambed. There were bodies down there and some wounded GIs. One guy was drunk as a skunk. I looked up toward the road and from where I was I could see the Chinese machine gun. I stopped and thought, I can take that damn thing out. I still had my M1. There were three Chinese operating the gun. I picked each of them off. I then moved along the dry riverbed a mile or so until I reached the lines of the British Brigade, which was holding the line above Sunch'on.

Sgt. ARTHUR MACEDO
Headquarters/38th Infantry

Some of us, on receiving news about "the Gauntlet," grabbed jeeps and vehicles and traveled north to assist the battle-worn troopers. We picked up stragglers and returned them to collecting points. Men don't cry, do they? I know I did. Stories I heard sounded like nightmares and escapes like movie adventures. Men I saw were dazed, their eyes glazed. Some men told of others, too wounded to move from where they fell, ground up like hamburger by escaping tanks. It was terrible, terrible.

[The time had arrived to get out of North Korea. As November turned into December, Eighth Army protected its flanks, stabilized its units, and backed down the peninsula. Within a week of starting its second-phase offensive, the Chinese had pushed General Walker's command fifty miles south. When it became apparent that a solid line could not be established from P'yongyang in the west to Wonsan in the East, the UN forces fell back farther.

The retreat evolved into a series of blocking and turning actions. Unlike the first week of November, the Chinese now had no intention of breaking off contact and allowing Eighth Army time to lick its wounds. Push had come to shove. The enemy would follow General Walker's forces southward like a bad dream. During the early days of December, whenever they looked over their shoulders, they saw the Chinese were still there, maybe miles back, behind the last range of frozen hills, but there, always there. The shivering, hungry, miserable GIs, many of them veterans of the Pusan Perimeter, some even of Tae-jon, turned their backs on the Yalu and trudged southward toward the scenes of the war's earliest battles. North Korea's snowcapped ridges and icy rivers were left behind. The thousands of men now slogging toward the 38th Parallel could not know how many mean, sleepless nights lay ahead before they would stop, turn around, and face the enemy again. If they had, they might have felt even more wretched.]

Cpl. DONALD HOFFMAN
F Company/23d Infantry
The company pulled back. I stood on top of a hill and on the reverse slope saw two GIs lying facedown in the snow. Someone said, "Get down there and take a look at them, make sure they're both dead." The snow was asshole deep and it was cold. I turned one body over and he was definitely out of it. When I went to turn the other one, I got hit. My piece went flying and I was spun around. I still knew where I was but couldn't find the gook that shot me. I yelled, "I'm hit. I'm hit." No one came down for me. I left my piece in the snow and took off. Don't know where in hell I went. Somehow I ended up curled around a tree. Tried to hide behind it. When I came to and tried to stand, I collapsed like a coat falling off a hook. While I lay unconscious I froze one arm, one leg, and half of the other leg. I managed to crawl out onto a road. I reached for the rosary around my neck and began to say the acts of contrition. I heard rumbling next. Now I knew I was done for. The Chinks weren't going to take a wounded man prisoner. Turned out what I heard was an American tank. Some guys picked me up and laid me on the back of it.

2d Lt. ROBERT CURTIS
F Company/23d Infantry
We rode out on tanks. All day long we rolled along the road. We reached one area and stopped, knew we had outdistanced the Chinese. It would be good to take a breather. I no more than took off my harness when the Chinese ran right over the top of us. I lost my harness, lost my pack, lost the whole goddamn works. Managed to just get out of there. I was amazed. The Chinese had been as fast using their feet as we'd been riding on tanks.

Capt. NORMAN ALLEN
I Company/5th Cavalry

2 December—Sunch'on

Mother darling:

We moved about four miles back to a little higher ground and am tied into a tight battalion perimeter, one of these orders to "take care of yourself." We are alerted for another move south, the Chinese thing is getting out of control. Pulling back and pulling back and still don't know the southern extent of the Chinese movement. Several of the outfits have had a hell of a scrap getting out. The Turks and the 2d Division took very heavy casualties the other night trying to run an ambush. It was a *six* mile ambush and a messy one. We are going to have to fight our way out too, I'm afraid. These ambushes are real murder. The Chinks have driven a deep penetration south past us and from there are putting out fingers *west*, which cut our roads. They're sitting there waiting. When we go by they'll pour it into us.

This war has to be settled in a hurry or many more people are going to be hurt and it must be on the tables at the UN (Excuse my scrawl, it's very cold and my fingers are numb.) Give the Reds a seat in the UN, how the hell can things be talked over if everyone isn't there? The biggest gangster of all (Russia) is there already, why draw the line at the little gangsters? We certainly can't beat the Chinese in Korea. We can't bomb China and to fight and *win*, which would take all we've got, we must fight *in* China. The thing is really a tangle, the NKs, the Chinks, the UN all fighting to liberate Korea—a united Korea for the Koreans. We ought to be able to get together somehow—instead of fighting. Trying to fight, with all the strategic angles completely tied up in politics is impossible. The UN ought to withdraw to the 38th [Parallel]. We still haven't made a unified Korea, but we didn't come over for that, not originally. We were originally committed to protect the democratic rights of a small nation from armed Communist aggression. We accomplished this when we hit the 38th Parallel in October. I can see where we had to eliminate the threat of the NKs doing it all over again. But the Chinese intervention has changed the whole picture. It's almost a case of saving what we can unless the politicos can arrive at some compromise, and soon.

Our jets are circling overhead looking us over and also potential enemy targets. Hope they give them hell. I always say that to beat us the enemy better bring their lunch and plan on staying all day. The Chinks I saw the other day brought with them a whole week's worth of lunches.

It's about time to start invoking the infantryman's prayer, "Please God, just a little wound." But a little wound doesn't get you home. Hate to think of being well laid up just to get home, but it seems the only way unless the UN gets on the stick. They ought to bring the UN conferees over here, put them in this cold, give them insufficient food, no smokes, let them get dirty and tired. Tell them then, "Now you all just sit here until you get things settled."

Our tank officer just came up and said some of his men have found and are cooking a couple of chickens. So being hungry, I shall go down now and try to talk them out of something to eat. . . .

Pfc. JAMES CARDINAL
I Company/5th Cavalry

December 2

Dear Folks,
This letter is being written on a rifle butt in a field about ten miles south of Sunch'on. The roads are clogged with troops and vehicles and refugees. It's bitterly cold and my hands as I write this are freezing. They just served us noon chow but such a little amount it wouldn't fill a pigeon. Boy, how I wish I had some of Mom's cooking now.

I guess I told you I've been recommended for the Silver Star for my part in the attack on Armistice Day on that hill. I'd gladly give away all the medals and honors to be home with you. Those things don't seem important now.

We've just received word that there was a major Communist breakthrough to the north and the whole UN Army is pulling back to avoid being trapped. I'm sure you know more about it than I do. I hope and pray to God that I'll get out of here alive so I'll be with you all again. Things look pretty grim now. . . .

Pfc. VICTOR FOX
I Company/5th Cavalry

Everyone realized that something different had happened. To stand and fight meant to stand and die. With that enormous mass of Chinese now in the field, a withdrawal or "retrograde movement" was necessary if we were to fight another day. Where we would stop and set up our lines was known only to God.

At the beginning our morale was still peppy. We didn't know then we would withdraw all the way back to South Korea. Some of our good spirit was due in part to leaving behind the harsh mountains of northern Korea.

Cpl. DON THOMAS
K Company/23d Infantry

Once again, just at dark we pulled off the ridge. There were some tanks waiting for us down on the road. This was the coldest ride I ever experienced. A dozen of us climbed on the tank. I was one of the last ones up and therefore the only spot I found was behind the turret over the grate where air is drawn in by the engine-cooling fan. I was so exhausted, cold, and hungry, I just lay down on the grate and went to sleep. In addition to the wind chill from the tank movement, I had the additional wind from the drawing engine fan. The convoy clanked down the road all night. I was on that grate eight hours. I never knew when the tank stopped. I was carried off and walked up and down between two guys until I "woke up" or came to.

Before I got out of North Korea I also rode on a [Boffers] twin 40-mm full-tracked anti-aircraft vehicle [M19]. It looked like a tank but had an open turret and mounted twin guns. This vehicle developed engine trouble and was pulled off the road and burned. We stood on the road with our thumbs out and hitched a ride on a truck. I recall seeing a group of soldiers riding on a full-track type of personnel carrier. The engine had been throwing oil and everyone in that vehicle was black and oil-soaked.

Farther south we encountered the British units. They were setting up a defense line across the road. These soldiers were clean and neat as pins. We were a dirty and raunchy bunch.

The companies were split up and coming in piecemeal. We finally located K Company in a churchyard. In a day or so, I found out I had badly frostbitten feet and two fingers. My feet swelled and looked like boiled hot dogs. They ached and itched severely.

Capt. NORMAN ALLEN
I Company/5th Cavalry

Mother dearest,
Boy, have things become a *damn* mess!! Everyone is running. There are only a few effectives left. The divisions have lost much equipment in these night withdrawals and especially the ambushes. Sweating out the Chinese crossing the parallel; if they don't we can still save the men and some stuff.

Since we fought the withdrawal action around Sunch'on it's been a series of roadblocks until other units pass through, then withdrawing when they do. If we stay too long, here's the big bad wolf huffing and puffing at the door.

It seems to me a crime to give up Korea after all it has cost us. But there is no holding the place if the Chinese want it. Even with complete air superiority, they can't be stopped. The Chinks are in droves and herds. Jesus, but I never saw so many. Squeeze off a round, watch one fold, suddenly two more appear, take his place and keep coming. . . .

Cpl. FRED DUVE
A Company/7th Cavalry

On the long drive south, the Chinese were behind us and the North Koreans we'd bypassed in the drive to the Yalu were in our front. There was no letup, day or night. We would dig in, fight a holding action, then move out when another company arrived to take our place. We would dig in again and another company would pass through us. I would say at this time we were all feeling pretty sorry for ourselves and just didn't give a damn about anything except getting out of North Korea alive.

Pfc. VICTOR FOX
I Company/5th Cavalry

At times tempers flared for no reason other than the want of nourishment, warm weather, rest, good news, and the knowledge that our new enemy, the Chinese, had a million men poised to throw at us if we paused or stopped.

One icy morning, while saddling up, I slammed my M1 to the frozen ground, splitting the muzzle by the front site and cracking the upper, wooden handguard. I then engaged a sergeant from another platoon in a vicious shouting match. He yelled, "That rifle could save your life and that of others." He was, of course, right.

Capt. NORMAN ALLEN
I Company/5th Cavalry

I was aware tempers were short—mine, too. The retreat shattered the morale of Eighth Army. Men took out their frustrations with fights. Those were dark and dismal days, and very difficult to cope with. No one around had much experience in how to survive a retreat. Two men I knew did—Lt. Col. Harold K. Johnson and our own Sgt. Joe Radovich. Both had been in the Second World War and on Bataan when the Japanese captured the Philippines. Each man carried his own thoughts, his own tribulations, and tried to make out best he could.

1st Lt. LUTHER WEAVER
A Company/35th Infantry
For many days and nights, with temperatures hovering around zero
or below, we pulled back. There were periods as long as four or five
days when we went without sleep and received few rations, if any at
all. There was not only the chaos caused by the enemy, but the confusion caused by the thousands of refugees who moved with us. I still
hear their mournful cries and see their pitiful faces.

Pfc. JAMES CARDINAL
I Company/5th Cavalry

Dear Folks,
It's late in the afternoon and I'm on a roadblock. The Chinese
are only about ten miles away.
I feel terribly sorry for the refugees. They seem so miserable
and all are hungry and cold. Six little girls, none older than seven,
just came down the road. Three are without shoes or socks; they
are all homeless orphans. We are letting them set by the fire and
are feeding them. They'll probably wander along till they freeze
or starve to death. . . .

Capt. NORMAN ALLEN
I Company/5th Cavalry
The refugees—awful moments there, deep memories. So pitiful, so
desperate; they also hampered our movement by day and threatened
our positions at night. Oh, my God, what to do about them? The
problem drove me wild.
Once there were hundreds of them in one valley, maybe 400
yards wide. We were tied in on the road with a company from another battalion. Both companies stretched to the high ground on both
sides of the roads. Cold, bitter cold, and dark. There must have been
a million refugees. They came right up to our lines and we had to
fire tracers over their heads to stop them from overrunning us. They
finally stopped and built fires for the night.
Shortly after, both companies began receiving incoming mortar

fire. The other company reported one of its platoons overrun by the enemy who had mixed with the refugees. I never was able to verify this, but it piled concern on top of my frustration. When our road-block reported that refugees were pressing in on them and the pressure was growing, the men requested permission to fire. I asked who the refugees were—men, women, what? They replied, "Mostly women and children, but there are men dressed in white right behind them, men who look to us to be of military age." I paused. The pause went on. The roadblock came on again—urgent, desperate, requesting permission to fire.

By this time the other company CO had called in artillery, high bursts. It was fired more to discourage than to kill. I instructed the roadblock to fire full tracer along the final protective line, then to fall back onto the high ground. If an enemy unit was in and among those refugees, well, then they just simply would be in our rear in the morning. I could not order firing on those thousands upon thousands of pitiful refugees.

Cpl. FRED DUVE
A Company/7th Cavalry
I remember the bitter cold and the snow and never being warm. I remember always being hungry, never having enough rations or being able to find any food. I remember the chicken my buddy found, killed, and gutted. I remember how small and skinny it was and how I carried that chicken in my field pack for three days before getting a chance to eat it. We got these tankers to give us some oleo. We fried the chicken in my helmet and shared it with four other guys.

I can still see all the fires and hear the explosions from the ammo dumps that were being destroyed so they would not fall into the enemy's hands. Everything, including supplies and vehicles that could not be gotten out, were blown up, set on fire, or destroyed. Rice fields were set on fire. When the rice caught fire, it popped. Guys were always running into the fields and grabbing handfuls of popped rice.

Pfc. VICTOR FOX
I Company/5th Cavalry

Intensifying the piercing coldness was hunger. In actual fact, the company at this time began to starve. No one was spared and each man began to lose weight. The company mess even showed us empty larders. When rations somehow got to the kitchens, they were never enough. It was pitiful to get a tablespoon dab of dried scrambled eggs for breakfast. We were lucky to have individual C rations, but most times they were frozen. It did not help matters to hear that food and cigarette rations were not problems with rear-echelon troops. Many of us even scrounged around other regimental trains looking for biscuits—it was like something out of the Depression.

More demoralizing than short rations was when we passed areas where great amounts of equipment, fuel, ammo—even rations, we heard—had been torched or dynamited. Everything in the long retreat that might aid the enemy was destroyed.

Capt. NORMAN ALLEN
I Company/5th Cavalry

When we withdrew through P'yongyang, the company passed a railroad spur where I counted thirty-two new Pershing tanks. Several men were in the process of thrusting thermite grenades down their muzzles—made me sick! Our supply sergeant, Jim Huber, and Top Mitchell reported to me that they saw a pile of QM [Quartermaster] clothing, mostly winter gear, being put to the torch and they requested permission to go back and rescue what they could of it. The company had a mission to secure another road junction miles to the east, but I told them to go back and in fifteen minutes collect what they could. After that we couldn't delay our movement.

They arrived back at the company before it was time to pull out. Mitchell told me that while they were at the dump, he and Huber had been discovered by the major responsible for burning it. They had had to put a carbine on this officer while they loaded the truck, and were gone before he received reinforcements.

1st Lt. LUTHER WEAVER
A Company/35th Infantry

By the time we reached P'yongyang, I had been without sleep or food for some time and was rather like a walking zombie. A large number of vehicles that had run out of gas were abandoned and left alongside the road. One deuce-and-a-half caught my eye, so a couple of men and I gave it a going-over. I lifted the front seat and hit the jackpot—one can of C-ration vegetable stew. While we waited for the column to resume moving, we scavenged enough cardboard and grass and twigs to start a small fire over which we thawed our can of stew. You have no idea, even divided three ways, how good that C ration tasted.

Cpl. LEONARD KORGIE
Headquarters Company/2d Battalion
21st Infantry

We went through P'yongyang at night and the whole city looked like it was burning.* In one place the engineers burned a rations dump about the size of a football field. God, it was a shame to see in a land of hunger all the food going up in smoke. There was U.S. military equipment everywhere. I don't know how much was destroyed. It looked like we were going to pursue a scorched-earth policy. I believe we set on fire most of the villages we passed through. We weren't going to give the Chinese too many places to shelter in during the rest of the winter.

1st Lt. LUTHER WEAVER
A Company/35th Infantry

After moving through P'yongyang we established a blocking position behind the British brigade "Nottingham," so they could withdraw their

---

*Eighth Army abandoned P'yongyang on 5 December. That same day, at Hagaru-ri, the 5th and 7th Marine Regiments were preparing to fight their way down the MSR to Koto-ri.

three- and six-pound artillery pieces which had been firing in support
of some withdrawing American units. After the British cleared, we
leapfrogged through another unit and hastily established a defense life
north of the Imjin River. This was Defense Line Able. It soon became a joke with the troops. Every order to dig in was always accompanied by the phrase "This is it. We will hold here!" No sooner had
we dug our holes when new orders would arrive and we would move
back farther.

[*Even during the long retreat, matériel and men continued to flow
into Korea. S/Sgt. "Woody" Woodruff, Jr., was one of the replacements
hurriedly sent north to make up the losses Eighth Army had suffered
in the battles along the Ch'ongch'on. He had first shipped overseas in
1944 as an eighteen-year-old private. After some combat in Burma,
he had spent a year in China in various staff assignments. Discharged
in 1946, Woodruff had remained in the enlisted Reserve Corps. Returning to school, he received a law degree at the University of Texas.
In September 1950, Woodruff was recalled to active duty. He arrived
at Inch'on, South Korea, on the afternoon of 5 December and was at
once assigned to L Company, 35th Infantry Regiment. Three days later
he was in North Korea, but unlike the rest of the men in Eighth Army,
Sergeant Woodruff was heading north.*]

S/Sgt. W. B. WOODRUFF, JR.
L Company/35th Infantry

Next morning [8 December]* the trucks rolled again; soon we passed
a cluster of vehicles with 2d Division markings. Rumor had it (the
grapevine was working overtime) that this was all that remained of the
2d; we knew it had been one of the units hardest hit during the last

---

* This same day the Marines fought their battle south of Koto-ri in the swirling snowstorm and
Baker 7's Joe Owen was wounded. The next day the treadway bridge would be laid and the 1st
Marine Division would begin to march down Funchilin Pass.

ten days. Trucks began to peel out of the convoy until only ours was left. It continued north. Somewhere ahead, we were more than vaguely aware, the Chinese Army was moving south down this same road; the gap was steadily closing. Toward midday we at last turned off into the command post of Company L. Scattered among the trees I could see a stretch of canvas, a couple of vehicles, and cooks loading the remains of breakfast into a jeep trailer. The fifteen or so of us—weary, unshaven, mostly strangers to each other, now in the hands of total strangers somewhere near the end of the world—began unloading and dragging off our gear.

From someone we received instructions for putting on all the clothing we had, retaining our necessary gear, and placing everything we could not carry back in the duffel bags, which were to be turned in. Yes, they would be kept safe and eventually returned to us (I never saw mine again). So, shortly I found myself wearing two pairs of wool underwear, two complete wool uniforms, a heavy sweater, two suits of fatigues, and a field jacket complete with hood and pile liner. In this attire one perspired freely during the day—if on the trail or digging in—but froze at night, once in stationary positions, and especially if still wet from perspiration. It would be a month before I got my first shower and clean underwear.

We were next approached by a man whose appearance and bearing marked him as one of those grizzled old Regular Army sergeants. Early in my military career, I had feared them like the devil himself. Quickly I learned a respect for them which never wavered; now I look back on them with a fondness and admiration approaching reverence. This one smiled and addressed us in a reassuringly friendly manner, called off about five names, including mine, and told us to follow him. En route we learned we had been assigned to 1st Platoon and that he was Joe Goggins, the platoon sergeant. I supposed we would go maybe 300 yards. It turned out to be a hard hour's climb, and a distance of maybe a mile, to the platoon CP. Mentally I calculated the company must be "holding" two miles or more of front. The 1st Platoon was located atop high ground from which we could see far to the north; over on our flank in the distance was visible the same road we had traveled to the company. There we met four others: the platoon leader, Lieutenant Fry, Sergeant Lopez, Corporal Hernandez, and Private First Class Fisher. Fisher was seated with a businesslike grip on a light machine gun, over which he maintained a silent lookout to the north. The others were calmly going about routine chores, checking equipment or cleaning weapons. I waited in vain for some kind of briefing on the situation. Finally, Goggins came back to tell us it was time for the first group to go to afternoon chow. He explained half of the platoon went at a time, the other half remaining in position. Since this meant a long climb back down to the company CP and back up the hill again, I elected to wait for the second sitting. While waiting, I got up courage to ask the whereabouts of the rest of the platoon; to me, "platoon" meant 40 or so men and "company" meant nearly 200. My inquiry evoked mild surprise. The five I had met *were* the platoon; with the arrival of the five replacements, its strength had just doubled. The company, I would later learn, had been down to 43 men. I did not feel it proper to ask a lot of questions as to how this had come about, and no explanations were volunteered. I did learn that one unit was still out in front of us, this being the 1st Cavalry Division. It was scheduled to withdraw through our lines the next day, to set up somewhere to our rear; then we would in due course continue this leapfrogging movement rearward.

Nothing further of note occurred until about noon the next day, when Goggins returned with ten new replacements in tow. Two additional truckloads arrived on this day and 1st Platoon grew to twenty men. Lieutenant Fry called together Hernandez, Baker, and me to announce reorganization of the platoon. There were to be three rifle squads of about five men each, and we three were now squad leaders. Lieutenant Fry, Goggins, Lopez, and Fisher would constitute a sort of combined platoon CP and weapons squad. I drew at this time—as best I recall—Lund, Bacon, and Bressard, all younger men whose previous service had been postwar, plus John Skirvin, a war veteran from Iowa who had been wounded on Luzon with this same 25th Division about five years earlier. Skirvin was a corporal, so he automatically became assistant squad leader. That afternoon we watched 1st Cavalry elements being trucked back through our position. In a matter of hours, my new squad would be in the northernmost line of Eighth Army. As I went back to chow that afternoon, responsibility could not have weighed heavier on me if I had been a corps commander.

During all this period, when a unit was in the line, its mess would set up from ten to twenty miles to the rear. Chow would be brought forward twice a day, by truck or more often by jeep, because a jeep could get closer to our strung-out ridgeline positions. During the short daylight hours—about 8:00 A.M. to 5:00 P.M.—two round trips by the mess vehicles was all that time permitted. Two feedings would also use up all the time available to the units to rotate down to chow and back. The first group would leave soon after daylight. By the time the second group had returned from breakfast, it was almost time for the first group to go to supper. Chow seemed in short supply; most of us never felt we had enough to eat. Two meals a day was all the supply line could then produce. I wondered about C rations; they were reported unavailable. Some men got by on one meal per day, on the theory they used more calories getting to chow and back than the meals provided.

On this particular night [9 December] I was late to chow, probably because my relief from the first "sitting" was late returning to the platoon. None of us, after a month on shipboard, were in good mountain-climbing condition. Darkness was falling as I finished eating. To one side the then company commander was talking with the first sergeant. I overheard the captain say something like: "We know we can depend on our old members, but we don't know what we can expect out of all these new men." I was shocked to be thus placed in a "doubtful" category. On reflection, I recognized we were retreads and quasi-civilians, and that we had not been tested as the old-timers had, and the captain was right to consider all aspects of his situation. Still, I resented it. Later, I mentioned this incident to Baker, who said nothing. But I think we both mentally made some appropriate resolutions, and it may have all worked out for the best. Next day Lopez took my brand-new 3d Squad out on its first patrol. It was uneventful, but made me wish I had paid more attention back during training. We had now arrived at the moment of truth; though still feeling somewhat amateurish, our shakedown period was well under way.

The leapfrogging rearward continued a few days. By December 15 we were digging in on the south bank of the Imjin at Munsan-ni, just south of the 38th Parallel. This, it was announced, was not just another phase line for withdrawal. Here we would prepare fortifications in a line extending across the peninsula; here the Chinese drive was to be halted. It didn't happen exactly that way, but we did remain in this position until about noon on New Year's Day.

[*The UN's long retreat ended in mid-December, and above the South Korean capital the regiments turned around and dug in. All armies, even Chinese armies, travel on their stomachs, and Eighth Army's contact with the enemy lessened when he began outrunning his supplies and communications. The Communists, too, had been badly hurt around the Ch'ongch'on.*]

1st Lt. LUTHER WEAVER
A Company/35th Infantry

We gained a breather when we stopped on the south bank of the Imjin. I learned the company still had about 75 percent of the personnel it started the withdrawal with. Our morale soared when we saw the engineers preparing to blow bridges and laying minefields and other obstacles in front of our positions. No question in our minds, this was where we were going to stop the Chinese. Our defenses included a new idea: oil drums filled with gasoline positioned to our front. Thermite grenades were attached and wire run from them to our line. When the Chinese attacked at night, we'd blow the gasoline and illuminate the enemy. A searchlight unit also set up around Munsan-ni, and after sunset covered our front.

While these events occurred, another of equal or greater importance took place: Captain Barry authorized the rifle platoons to establish warm-up houses near each of their sectors. These small houses were in a deserted village near our position and overlooked the Imjin River and a blown bridge. We rotated the men from the front lines to the houses. The Korean heating system of a flue running under the floor from the firebox was really put to good use by the troops.

Seeing our supply sergeant one day for the first time in several weeks was quite an occasion; like an early Santa Claus, he brought with him what each of us wanted most—winter clothing.

From our viewpoint, the next fortune of war to come our way indicated maybe we had outsmarted the Chinese after all, and as a reward were being given an early Christmas present. Or perhaps we looked or smelled so bad to the rear-echelon troops, they couldn't stand us. In any event, one day we were trucked back several miles to a QM portable shower unit for a hot shower and clean clothing.

[About the time advance units of Eighth Army crossed the 38th Parallel and reentered South Korea, General Smith's 1st Marine Division was embarking from the east coast port of Hungnam. The wounded were airlifted to military hospitals in Japan. Many of these medical facilities were established on an ad hoc basis to handle the unexpectedly large number of wounded men. Some of the hospitals were so small a Saturday-night auto accident would have taxed their capabilities.]

S/Sgt. CHESTER BAIR
Task Force Faith

The plane was unloaded in Osaka and we were placed on a bus that drove us to a hospital. A doctor there apologized and told us he would not be able to accept us, but that we would be sent miles away to an annex where we would be admitted.

At the next hospital we assumed the staff had just arrived in Japan, as they were all recovering from being airsick. The beds had not yet been set up nor any other facilities. We were carried into a large room and welcomed by the hospital administrator, who was a bird colonel. He apologized for his staff and for the hospital and promised they would all get to us as soon as possible. A general materialized from somewhere; he wasn't wounded, but he was with us. He said, "Colonel, we understand your problem, but you must understand these men have problems, too. Some were wounded more than a week ago, all are battle casualties. They have received very little treatment; they are dirty, tired, and hungry. Get your staff on the ball now and take care of these people. That is an order!"

In a few minutes our wounds and ills were being treated and hot chow served.

S/Sgt. LEE BERGEE
E/1

There were so many casualties at the naval hospital at Yokosuka, Japan, some of us were placed in the halls. I remember the bright electric light bulbs in the receiving room. I was carried in with a Royal Marine Commando. Everything seemed so bright and clean. (Weeks later my skin still seemed to be embedded with grime.)

I remember how the frostbite cases had their feet propped up over the end of their beds with wash pans placed below. Their skin was black, like charcoal.

It's in the hospital that you really witness the true horrors of war. I remember a blind nineteen-year-old. He carried around the two-inch hunk of shrapnel that had struck him on the forehead. He would never allow any of us to assist him on his trips down the corridor to the head.

Pfc. FRANCIS KILLEEN
A/7

Our clothing was so rotten the first thing they had us do in the hospital was strip and take a shower. A Jap came along and threw my cruddy clothes in an incinerator. Now, I had a couple of spare clips in the pockets of my parka. Boy, did that cause a commotion. Later, they had a couple of big Air Police guys go through the stuff before they burned it. When they were through, they had some pile of ammo. We could have held out for months.

I lay at first on a stretcher in a big hall. I did not realize then that the brass in my side and the earlier wound in my leg from Sudong would keep me hospitalized for almost a year. A young soldier from the 31st lay next to me. He was in bad shape. He talked to a doctor, could only whisper. The doctor leaned over to hear better. The doc began to laugh. "Under the circumstances," he said, "it's quite normal not to have an erection."

Chaplain CORNELIUS GRIFFIN (USN)
7th Marines

While I recuperated in the hospital, Colonel Litzenberg stopped by for a visit and I knew at once what he would say.

When I had discarded my Navy blue and gold and put on my Marine fatigues for the first time, I looked like the Sad Sack. Other Marines looked starched and fresh; I looked like a total and irreversible disaster and smelled like a barrel of mothballs. I was in Camp Lejeune in August 1950, at the railroad loading dock and wearing my ill-fitting uniform, when I first had the privilege, not so regarded at that moment, however, of meeting my new commanding officer, the silver-haired fox, Homer Litzenberg, Colonel, United States Marine Corps. The great Litz said to me, not directly, you understand, but through the senior chaplain at whose side I stood, "Jesus Christ, is this what I'm getting for a Catholic chaplain!" I spoke up: "If the colonel knows, or can, in any way, devise some way to ameliorate this messy situation, it will please the chaplain concerned. By your leave, sir!" He replied, and this time he spoke directly to me, "Get on that train, goddamn it! I'll make a Marine out of you even if it kills you."

Litz sat at the foot of my hospital bed. He grabbed my hand. "Well, damn it to hell. I did exactly what I said I would, almost. I damn near killed you, but I sure as hell made a Marine of you." We laughed. But what a compliment.

2d Lt. JOSEPH OWEN
B/7

I lay next to a kid who'd been with Task Force Faith. He asked me what outfit I was from. I told him 1st Marine Division, 7th Marines.

He said, "Boy, you were lucky. I'll bet they carried you out." I said, "You bet your ass they did." There was a pause. Then he said, "I had to crawl out on my own."

[The ships carrying what was left of the Marine regiments made their way down Korea's east coast and landed the men at Pusan.* From the port the Marines were trucked on 16 December to an assembly area in the vicinity of Masan, South Korea. Men who had served in the Marine brigade during the grim days of August remembered the area well; it was the familiar Bean Patch where they had bivouacked after the first battle of the Naktong. Four months, almost to the day, had passed from that sultry day in August to this frozen one in December. In between had been the second go at Obong-ni Ridge, the Inch'on landings, Seoul, and the frozen Chosin. Somehow, it seemed much longer.]

Pfc. PAUL MARTIN
Reconnaissance Company/1st Marine Division

At Pusan we were greeted by a small Army band that played the Marine hymn. This little band had more impact on me than any Marine band I ever heard. I fantasized I was back home and this was the beginning of a victory parade, the one we thought we'd have after Inch'on and the fall of Seoul. I continued the fantasy during the train ride to Masan, and imagined I was on a cross-country ride that was taking me home for Christmas.

Once I hit the Bean Patch, I did what everyone else did—rushed letters to my worried family.

---

*The U.S. 3d and 7th Divisions held the perimeter at Hungnam after the Marine division was evacuated. It was not until Sunday afternoon, 24 December, that their rear guard units cleared the beaches and sailed south.

Pfc. DEAN WESTBERG
B/7

I went looking for people I knew. My brother-in-law was in the 11th Marines. I first found his unit, then his headquarters section. I found two Marines in a tent sitting back to back on a cot looking at the ground. I asked if they knew anything about my brother-in-law. They told me he was listed as missing in action. Then I went looking for a high school buddy who had joined the Marines and been sent to Korea as part of the first replacement draft. I located his outfit and learned he had been killed in the fighting around Yudam-ni.

Cpl. FRANK BIFULK
B/7

Some little guy came around the Bean Patch asking questions. He asked me, "Who are you fighting for? Why are you fighting?" Well, any time I'm dropped off in a strange country and asked to fight the Chinese, my answer is simple. I told the guy, "I'm fighting for one thing—me!" Truman really slapped us in the face. He called Korea a police action. Here we were in Korea fighting and dying and our president says that. Some thanks. "What are you fighting for, son?" "For my life, buddy. For my life."

Pfc. DOUG MICHAUD
Headquarters & Service Company/1/5

It wasn't until we returned to the Bean Patch that the experience sank in. Before, there had been too much going on and we had no way of knowing whether a buddy had been evacuated, transferred, or killed.

All of a sudden, in Masan, everything stopped moving and the parts came together. Some guy from another company would stop by and you'd compare notes. After a few beers you realized you'd just been through hell. It came as a shock. Jesus Christ, I thought, did I really go through that? The newspapers filled in the big picture. That's when the real shock set in. Up until then it was "I was frozen," or "I was scared." Now we learned we had been outnumbered five or six to one. We learned Eighth Army had been mauled. It wasn't until I was safe that I realized what might have happened to me. I couldn't believe I'd really gotten through it all.

Replacements came in. We pumped up our chests a little. Three months before we'd been the greenhorns, those dumb Reservists who had come right off hometown streets. Now we were the salts and had some sea stories to tell. The new guys looked at us the way we'd looked at the veterans of the brigade—you know, eyes wide open, mouth slightly agape. "Holy cow, that guy's been at Inch'on, been up and back from the Reservoir."

I had changed. I no longer wanted any buddies. Afraid I'd lose them. If I liked someone, I believed he'd get killed. Who needed the additional trauma? I sure as hell didn't. If you get killed, I don't know you and I don't care. You're just another number, another rifle— who cares? New people: "What's your name? How ya doin'?" But nothing more. Don't tell me your hopes and dreams. You're going to get killed and I don't want to know you, think about you, remember you.

I stopped writing home because to write family I had to think about them. I didn't want to; I didn't want to cry. This macho, tough-guy stuff in the middle of the night when you're alone with your thoughts is bullshit. I built a shell around myself. I didn't write my mother. I didn't write my girlfriend. The hell with it. I got into card games, I drank beer. I did all the things a Marine is supposed to do. I wasn't expected to be a baby and write home. What the hell. Once I accomplished this in my mind, life became more tolerable. I didn't let myself worry about another life. I lived for the beer ration, the crap game, pay call, a chance to change skivvies and dungarees. "Hey, ya hear? They're bringing up fresh clothes, and gonna set up shower tents." Shit, that was good stuff, the things I built my world around, things I could reach out and touch. Not something half a world away.

[UN reinforcements poured into South Korea during December and were warmly welcomed by Eighth Army. A Dutch battalion had arrived in November; infantry units from Canada, Greece, and France, and artillerymen from New Zealand, came ashore before Christmas. But even with these additions, the enemy still outnumbered the UN forces two to one.]

Maj. Gen. OLIVER P. SMITH
Commanding General, 1st Marine Division
At this stage of the game the Army was coming backward. They'd had phase lines for that purpose. I read Army orders directing the units to fall back to, for example, Phase Line D, then to Phase Line Umpty-Ump. I didn't know when it was going to stop. Staff people from the Army divisions came looking for CP locations as far south as we were. Then the Army began to lay out defensive setups in our vicinity. It was a defeated outfit.*

[Before Christmas, UN patrols returning from above the Parallel reported the Chinese growing restless and beginning to shift their divisions away from the coast and concentrating them in the center of the peninsula. It was also discovered they were transporting forward large amounts of food and ammunition by every means available: foot, sledge, pony, oxen, and Mongolian camel. Eighth Army dug deeper and braced itself for another long series of icy battles; winter, after all, had just begun. The men looked north and pondered what the Chinese would do next and whether MacArthur carried another ace like Inch'on up his sleeve. They also thought some about returning to the Yalu and asked not would they, but could they? Hunkered down in their vile, frozen holes, they waited for the new year to arrive and answer their questions. The events of 1950 seemed too distant to remember. The old

---

* Smith interview, MCHC.

year, the old war; the new year, the new war. An old enemy had been
defeated, a new one had taken the field. It was as if retreating from
Osan and battling for Taejon, crashing out of the Pusan Perimeter
and pursuing the enemy across the Parallel, capturing P'yongyang and
crossing the Ch'ongch'on, had all taken place in a different war, in
another time. The truth was, they had.]

Cpl. LEONARD KORGIE
Headquarters Company/2d Battalion/21st Infantry
Each day the Chinese were reported moving closer to our lines. For
the week before New Year's, I could hear sounds coming from the
hills to our north—sounded to me like a large animal growling. Our
line companies would send out patrols that often made contact. After
a short flurry they would withdraw. Our artillery worked over the hills
to our front with regularity.

Around Christmas, packages came in by the hundreds. It was
kind of a happy time. Over everything, however, was the ominous
feeling that the Chinese, whenever it suited them, were going to come
down and bust our asses.

S/Sgt. W. B. WOODRUFF, JR.
L Company/35th Infantry
More snow fell, the cold intensified, the ground froze to a depth of
a foot or more, and the Imjin was frozen except in the center, where
the current was strongest. The December full moon came on, briefly
raising our spirits, then waned. By now we knew that the army preponderant in firepower ruled the day, but the one preponderant in
manpower ruled the night. North Korean refugees arrived; whole
families, all heavily laden, passed through our lines four abreast, all
day long, day after day, their column extending to the horizon, winding like a huge snake along the road. At daybreak we would open the
barricade and they, already up and waiting patiently, would begin to
pour through. We watched them closely for enemy infiltrators, but
discovered none. At night, when the barricade was closed, they would
settle down in the snow along the road, their cooking fires visible in
a line as far as the eye could see. There along the frozen road the old

died and babies were born. We learned what people thought of Communism, after living five years under its rule; generally, those who looked favorably on Communism had not made acquaintance with its true face. Each day the foxholes and gun emplacements were dug deeper, the minefields and barbed wire expanded.

Pfc. VICTOR FOX
I Company/5th Cavalry
I remember railroad trains in a marshaling yard. These trains were piled high and crammed with refugees, stoically waiting for whatever fate their God held for them. When I found some English-speaking civilians, I discovered many of them were highly educated and before the war had held prominent positions in their communities. It was very cold in the yards. In one boxcar I saw the bodies of dead GIs piled on top of equipment. Nearly a dozen of them wore spotlessly clean white robes and must have been sent south by a field hospital which had no other way of disposing of its corpses. Amid all this cleanliness I remember one GI; in his chest he had a large, gaping, red hole.

It looked as if the war was lost. Eighth Army appeared to me to be at sixes and sevens, with no other purpose on its agenda than to get south.

[Right before Christmas, Eighth Army's morale worsened when it was learned that the Army's commander, Walton H. Walker, while traveling north of Seoul on 23 December to present citations, was killed in a collision of his jeep with a ROK Army truck. Lt. Gen. Matthew Ridgway, a famous and experienced commander of airborne units in the Second World War, was immediately given command of all UN ground forces in Korea. Most of the younger troops in Eighth Army had never heard of him, but were informed by the veterans of his record with the 82d Airborne Division at Sicily and Normandy and with an airborne corps at the Battle of the Bulge. But never before, the men realized, had he held a position comparable to the one he had just been given. In Korea replacements and veterans alike wondered whether Ridgway would be as successful fighting the Chinese as he'd been fighting the Germans.]

Lt. Gen. MATTHEW B. RIDGWAY
Commanding General, Eighth Army

Before the Eighth Army could return to the offensive, it needed to
have its fighting spirit restored, to have pride in itself, to feel confidence in its leadership, and have faith in its mission. These qualities
could not be assessed at secondhand, and I determined to make an
immediate tour of the battlefront to meet and talk with the field commanders in their forward command posts and to size up the Eighth
Army's spirit with my own eyes and senses.

Every command post I visited gave me the same sense of lost
confidence and lack of spirit.* The leaders, from sergeant on up,
seemed unresponsive, reluctant to answer my questions. Even their
gripes had to be dragged out of them and information was provided
glumly, without the alertness of men whose spirits are high.

What I told the field commanders in essence was that their infantry ancestors would roll over in their graves could they see how
roadbound this army was, how often it forgot to seize the high ground
along its route, how it failed to seek and maintain contact in its front,
how little it knew of the terrain . . . how reluctant it was to get off
its bloody wheels and put shoe leather to earth, to get into the hills
and among the scrub and meet the enemy where he lived.

I repeated to the commanders as forcefully as I could, the ancient army slogan: "Find them! Fix them! Fight them! Finish them!"†

Pfc. VICTOR FOX
I Company/5th Cavalry

It was sometime around Christmas that Colonel Crombez [CO, 5th
Cavalry Regiment] initiated an early-evening snack of bouillon soup
for all 5th Cav troopers. It was said, "If no one got bouillon soup,
everybody goes without it." We did get soup for a while, then later
the program faded away.

---

*It should be noted that X Corps, with its three divisions, the 3d, 7th, and 1st Marine, had
not yet joined Eighth Army.
†Gen. Matthew Ridgway, *The Korean War* (Garden City, N.Y.: Doubleday, 1967), 85, 88–
89.

Capt. NORMAN ALLEN
I Company/5th Cavalry

When I returned to the company,* I learned that Colonel Crombez had been in the kitchen area raising hell with the acting CO [William Hunter] and Colonel Treacy about providing the men with bouillon soup. I heard the complete story a little later. Colonel Crombez had asked the men standing in the area whether they wouldn't prefer bouillon to soup. One man answered, "Yes, sir!" After the regimental CO left, Top Mitchell took that man aside. "You dumb sonovabitch, why did you tell Colonel Crombez you liked bouillon? You don't even know what the shit it is!" The man admitted this was true, but in his defense said, "When I'm asked a question by a high-ranking officer, I was always told to say, 'Yes, sir.' "

I walked down to the kitchen and asked the mess sergeant, "Van [Van Curran], how much of that bouillon are the men taking?" He replied, "None, sir. They don't like it. That Lyster bag [a cloth bag with spigot that holds about thirty gallons of liquid and sits on a tripod] is just as full of bouillon now as it was when I filled it day before yesterday." I kicked the legs out from under the Lyster bag. "That's enough of this bullshit."

About this time I also learned that Colonel Crombez had tried to raise the men's morale by going about kicking the snow and saying loudly enough for men around him to hear, "See here, just kick the snow away and you'll find green grass. I've been in Korea before. Spring is almost here. Just any day now." This to GIs who had been living every day for the last six or seven weeks in foxholes in subzero weather. I walked through the company area and told the men, "Don't believe that bullshit about spring being just around the corner. This is the dead of winter. It's gonna get a lot worse before it gets better."

Cpl. DON THOMAS
K Company/23d Infantry

We arrived by open truck at a pass on the 24th of December. There were four or five Korean huts at the top. My squad took the first watch

---

*Captain Allen had been injured east of P'yongyang on 6 December and evacuated the next day to Pusan.

up on the right-hand ridge. We went up at six o'clock in the evening. Another platoon took up a position on the left ridge. The company now had a fourth platoon. Therefore, two platoons were left on the road in the huts to relieve the two on the ridges. The ridge ran just 300 or 400 feet up. The snow on the forward slope was about two feet deep. We had the honor of digging the holes. The first two feet of snow was easy. Then the next foot was frozen ground. After the foot of frozen ground the rest was easy. In a couple of hours, I had my hole down the regular three feet.

Night came clear and cold. I could see two or three miles down the road. The moon was partly out. The temperature was below zero. I began to get cold to the bone. I had raised a sweat during the digging and was now paying for it. My feet were becoming numb from the ankles down. I stomped around in the hole and was able to get some feeling back. Coffee. I decided to make some coffee right on that ridge. All of us carried extra powdered coffee and sugar from the C rations in our pockets. I had also picked up a can of jelled alcohol (canned heat) at the last encampment. It gave off a lazy blue flame. I scooped up a canteen cup of snow, lit the alcohol, and began to heat it up. It took a number of additional handfuls of snow to get enough water to fill the cup. Finally, after an hour, I had a cup of hot water. I put in three packets of coffee. Normally, one would do, but now I wanted *strong* coffee. It was. I took a swallow. I could actually feel the warmth spread out from my stomach and run down my arms and legs. I felt like I had received a warm blood transfusion. I took this cup up the ridge and shared it with the rest of the squad.

At each hole I wished the guys a Merry Christmas, as it was just after midnight. One hell of a cold Christmas. It was white, though. At 1:00 A.M., the other platoon arrived to relieve us. What a break.

We dropped off the ridge and went inside the warm hut. A Korean family was still in it in the adjoining rooms. I flopped down and slept like a rock.

Christmas morning, 1950. Two of the platoons would hike back from the pass to where a kitchen had been set up for Christmas turkey with all the trimmings. The other two would stay at the pass until relieved. We went first. The kitchen was set up in what looked like a schoolhouse. It was warm inside. The smell was overpowering. What a dinner!

S/Sgt. W . B . WOODRUFF , JR .
L Company/35th Infantry
There was some thought a surprise attack might be planned for Christmas Day. Consequently, our Christmas dinner was served on Christmas Eve. Chow was much improved by now, and that day we had all the trimmings. An officer stood at the head of the chow line, pouring about a tablespoon of bourbon into each man's canteen cup. I gagged a bit, but thought it a nice touch, under the circumstances; I have never seen this done before or since. Sleeping bags had been brought up, which also helped. The standard routine was to maintain 50 percent alert, that is, half the men, or one in each foxhole, awake at all times. We learned to get by on three or four hours' sleep per night; I did not average much more my entire Korean tour. Ammo and grenades were in good supply and distributed to each position. There was still no enemy contact, but about this time the refugee column dried up, which could mean only one thing.

Battalion ordered a patrol; my squad was elected. We reported to battalion headquarters one afternoon for a briefing, remaining there overnight for an early start next morning. In the hut assigned us that evening, I met M/Sgt. Joe V. Alford for the first time. I would later serve under him and find him quite remarkable, one of the three or four finest fighting soldiers I ever knew. On that occasion he was a little down. Formerly platoon sergeant of L Company's 2d Platoon, he had been relieved for some misdeed, and was just hanging around battalion awaiting his fate. He feared this would be a court-martial, and reduction (for the umpteenth time) back to private. What made this problem acute was that he had now completed nineteen years' Army service, and had entertained some hope of keeping his stripes, this time, long enough to retire in what was then the highest enlisted pay grade. Al's problem was related to drinking, though he would not have described it that way and really did not regard it as a problem. Getting promoted, drinking, and getting busted was to him just a way of life, and had been since 1931, in a dozen countries, in peacetime and wartime. It was nothing to get shook up about, only a source of mild regret when he contemplated retirement on a private's pay. He regaled me an hour or more with stories of the "old Army" in Panama and Hawaii. In World War II he had been one of the volunteers sent from Guadalcanal to Burma, to what the press would call Merrill's Marauders. He found out, early on, that I had also been in the CBI [China-Burma-India Theater]; probably this was one reason he was willing to share his military life story with me so openly. When old (or "older") soldiers meet, the conversation immediately and invariably turns to past assignments and acquaintances in a search for common ground, which usually is found. I went to sleep wishing the best for Sergeant Al.

Next morning, before first light, I led 3d Squad across the frozen Imjin near the remnants of a blown bridge. We checked out a village on the other side and found it empty. One of my greenest recruits fired a short burst from his BAR by mistake, providing the only excitement of the day. I made a mental note to find another BAR man. About a mile out, from high ground, we observed to the north all day without result, and returned to the company at dark.

Cpl. DON THOMAS
K Company/23d Infantry
We stayed at the pass until the 29th of December. From there we went on open trucks to a deserted airfield. The company was put in Quonset huts. Ours had a stove made from oil drums.

The only wood around was the flooring. After a while I had to watch where I was stepping. Now it seemed we would finally get warm. Yes? No! The bottom three feet of side metal was missing from the entire building. I could squat down and see out into the snow- and wind-swept base. I was only warm on the side next to the stove; turn around and the other side got cold. Lie down on the floor to get some sleep and everything got cold. I spent the night alternating between the stove and lying down on what was left of the floor. By morning there was not much floor left.

We trucked farther north the next day. The platoon moved out onto a low ridge to bed down for the night. No straw or branches were handy, so I stomped the snow down flat and laid my sleeping bag on it. I took off my shoepacs and crawled into the bag with my clothes on. I warmed up quickly and slept soundly until morning.

"Wake up, you guys," someone hollered. Daylight already. It was still near zero. This was New Year's Eve, December 31, 1950. I crawled out of the bag and sat on it, trying to get my shoepacs on. I had to remove my mittens for a few seconds to handle the rawhide laces. Due to the temperature the laces were stiff like baling wire. I had to push them into each eyelet and at the same time pull them out on the other side. I could only do this a half minute before my fingers became numb. Then on went the mittens for a minute to thaw them out. Then off again to work on the laces. It took me at least ten minutes to get the shoepacs on.

There was a large fire down the hill. Everyone gathered around it. C rations were there. I heated up a can and got some instant coffee going. George [Sergeant Chamberlain] was there telling us to burn any letters we had, as we were going to move up and attack a roadblock. He said to travel light and leave our poncho and sleeping bag behind. Also, we were to take just one can of C rations, as this was to be a long and fast march. I kept a can of cherries.

S/Sgt. W . B . WOODRUFF, JR.
L Company/35th Infantry
By the morning of December 31, all knew the resumption of the Chinese offensive was imminent, if not past due. They had prepared long and carefully. In later years I would become familiar with the old Armor motto: "Plan deliberately, execute violently." I never had to ask for an explanation. From deep foxholes, looking out across our barbed wire and minefields, we waited. We were as ready as the circumstances permitted. We were determined, and a little impatient. We would not have long to wait.

Capt. NORMAN ALLEN
I Company/5th Cavalry

New Year's Eve
35 miles NE of Seoul

Mother darling,

We all rather expect to have the Chinese attempt to give us a
New Year's present so we are on a 50% officers alert. It's my
trick awake and am dressed and sitting next to the radio in the
command post which is in a dirty little farmhouse.

There is a little celebration of sorts going on—the booming is
nothing new on New Year's, except this year it's not pots and
pans making the racket, but artillery. The big guns have been
incessant since 8:00 P.M., just a continual rumble from several
thousand yards away. Not all, but most, is outgoing. It's now
about six hours to dawn, then we'll be OK till tomorrow night.
Not that the days are safe, but at least we can see them and that
makes it not nearly as fearful.

The ROKs have a thin screen in front of us along the 38th,
but it has gaps in it and the enemy can give them trouble. . . .
We're kind of stuck out on a limb here. Mess sergeant told me
he drew some turkeys for New Year's Day dinner. Hope we aren't
still here for Easter eggs. . . .

APPENDIX

Table of Organization and Equipment

United States Army

Korean War

INFANTRY DIVISION

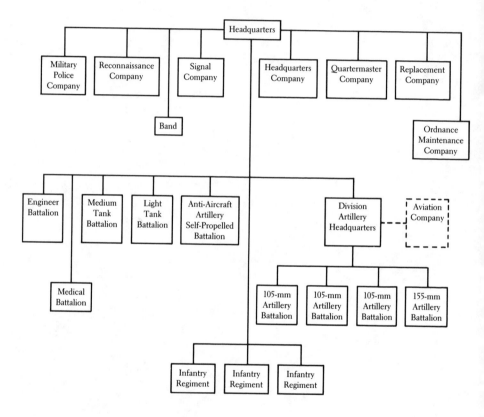

1. Infantry division authorized manpower strength: 15,000–16,000.
2. The 1st Marine Division in Korea had an authorized manpower strength of 22,000–22,500.

INFANTRY REGIMENT

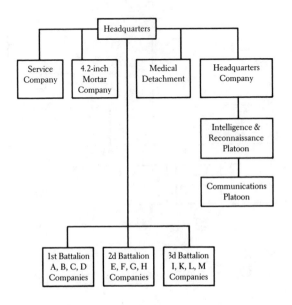

Infantry regiment authorized manpower strength: 3,200–3,500.

INFANTRY BATTALION

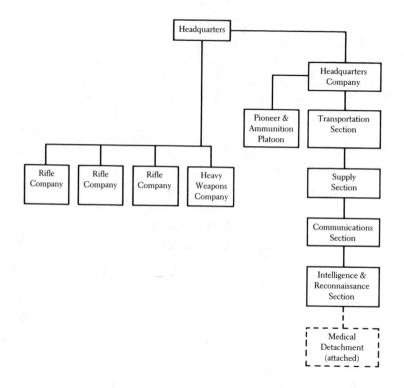

1. Infantry battalion authorized manpower strength: 850–950.
2. The heavy weapons company of an infantry battalion is authorized the largest caliber weapons in battalion, consisting of 81-mm mortars, 75-mm recoilless rifles, .50-caliber machine guns, and .30-caliber water-cooled machine guns. Heavy weapons company authorized manpower strength: 166.
3. Unlike Army battalions, Marine battalions do not use letter designations for their weapons companies. Thus, 1st Battalion comprises A, B, C, and Weapons Company; 2d Battalion—D, E, F, and Weapons Company; 3d Battalion—G, H, I, and Weapons Company.

INFANTRY RIFLE COMPANY

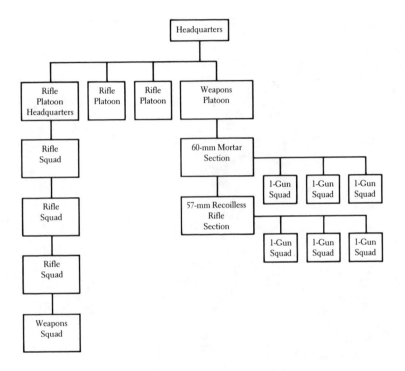

1. Infantry company authorized manpower strength: 203.
2. Infantry company authorized weapons consists of .45-caliber pistols, .30-caliber carbines, M1 rifles, .30-caliber BARs (Browning automatic rifles), .30-caliber light machine guns, (3) 60-mm mortars, (3) 57-mm recoilless rifles, (3) 3.5-inch rocket launchers.
3. An infantry rifle platoon consists of four squads of 9 enlisted men. A weapons platoon consists of six squads of 5 enlisted men.

Index

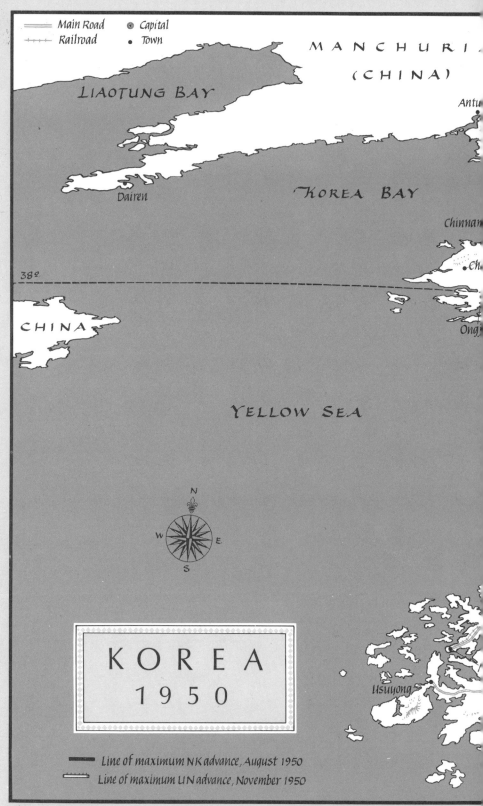